MAKING MIGRATION LAW

The Foreigner, Sovereignty, and the Case of Australia

The emergence of international human rights law and the end of the White Australia immigration policy were events of great historical moment. Yet, they were not harbingers of a new dawn in migration law. This is because migration law in Australia is best understood as part of a longer jurisprudential tradition in which certain political-economic interests have shaped the relationship between the foreigner and the sovereign. Eve Lester explores how this relationship has been wrought by a political-economic desire to regulate race and labour; a desire that has produced the claim that there exists an absolute sovereign right to exclude or condition the entry and stay of foreigners. Lester calls this putative right a discourse of 'absolute sovereignty'. She argues that 'absolute sovereignty' talk continues to be a driver of migration lawmaking, shaping the foreigner-sovereign relation, and making thinkable some of the world's harshest asylum policies.

Eve Lester (Ph.D. (Melb)) is a member of the Institute for International Law and the Humanities at Melbourne Law School and an independent consultant. A public and international lawyer with a background in refugee, migration and human rights law, policy and practice spanning more than twenty-five years, she has worked in Africa, the Americas, Asia, Australia, Europe, and the Pacific in a range of capacities in the non-government sector, with the UN, and as an independent adviser to governments. She has taught at the Australian Catholic University, the Australian National University, the International Institute for Humanitarian Law, Italy, New York University, and the University of New South Wales.

Making Migration Law

THE FOREIGNER, SOVEREIGNTY, AND THE CASE OF AUSTRALIA

EVE LESTER

CAMBRIDGE
UNIVERSITY PRESS

CAMBRIDGE
UNIVERSITY PRESS

University Printing House, Cambridge CB2 8BS, United Kingdom

One Liberty Plaza, 20th Floor, New York, NY 10006, USA

477 Williamstown Road, Port Melbourne, VIC 3207, Australia

314–321, 3rd Floor, Plot 3, Splendor Forum, Jasola District Centre, New Delhi – 110025, India

79 Anson Road, #06–04/06, Singapore 079906

Cambridge University Press is part of the University of Cambridge.

It furthers the University's mission by disseminating knowledge in the pursuit of education, learning, and research at the highest international levels of excellence.

www.cambridge.org
Information on this title: www.cambridge.org/9781107173279
DOI: 10.1017/9781316779910

First published 2018

Printed in the United States of America by Sheridan Books, Inc.

A catalogue record for this publication is available from the British Library.

ISBN 978-1-107-17327-9 Hardback

In honour of those who still bear the burden;
in memory of my father, Bill Lester (1925–2012);
and
for Malcolm and Hal

Contents

Acknowledgements   *page* ix

List of Abbreviations   xii

Prologue: Living Realities   1

1 **Introduction**   6
   1.1   Institutional Responses to Unsolicited Migration   6
   1.2   Understanding Our Juridical Inheritance
         and Its Usages   21
   1.3   Making Migration Law: An Overview   39

PART I   49

2 **Early International Law and the Foreigner**   51
   2.1   Francisco de Vitoria (c 1485–1546)   54
   2.2   Hugo Grotius (1583–1645)   60
   2.3   Samuel Pufendorf (1632–1694)   67
   2.4   Emmerich de Vattel (1714–1767)   73
   2.5   The Foreigner: Always and Already European   77

3 **A Common Law Doctrine of Sovereignty**   81
   3.1   New Migrations, New Communities   83
   3.2   Restrictive Migration Laws: An 'Imperative'   90
   3.3   A Jurisprudence of 'Absolute Sovereignty'   94
   3.4   'Absolute Sovereignty': A Contingent
         Historical Artefact   107

4 **A Constitutionalisation of Sovereignty**   112
   4.1   Constitutionalising 'Absolute Sovereignty'   114
   4.2   Entrenching 'Absolute Sovereignty'   120

4.3 Cementing Difference 136
4.4 'Absolute Sovereignty': A Hallowed Doctrinal Place 155

PART II 159
Introduction to Part II 159

5 Mandatory Detention 163
5.1 Mandatory Detention: The Parliamentary Debates 167
5.2 *Chu Kheng Lim*: The Proceedings 187
5.3 *Chu Kheng Lim*: The Decision 202
5.4 Decision-less Detention: A Thinkable
Institutional Response 227

6 Planned Destitution 231
6.1 Rationalising Destitution 237
6.2 Work: An Obsession with Discretion 258
6.3 Welfare: Governance by Fiat 272
6.4 Planned Destitution: Part of the Order of Things 277

7 Conclusion 281
7.1 Making Migration Law 281
7.2 A Discourse of 'Absolute Sovereignty' 282
7.3 Reflections 286
7.4 Implications 288
7.5 Possibilities 289

Epilogue: A Campaign to 'Stop the Boats' 292
A Military-Led Operation: As if We Were at War 293
Secret Detention on the High Seas 295
Silencing Dissent: A Criminal Offence to Expose
Human Rights Abuses 299
Putting Beyond Doubt the Power to Do Any Thing at Any Cost 302
Manus Island: One Place, Two Constitutions 303
Offshore Detention and Processing: In Search of an Exit Strategy 305
Not Even if You Are a Nobel Prize–Winning Genius 307
Death, Cruelty, and Inhumanity 310
The New Normal? 312

Bibliography 313
Index 356

Acknowledgements

It is both trite and true that a book such as this one is not only the product of much solitude and soul-searching, but also would not have been possible at many levels without the support and generosity of a large and diverse community of scholars, colleagues, friends, and family.

For intellectual support and guidance, my first thanks are to Shaun McVeigh and Sundhya Pahuja at Melbourne Law School, and Pene Mathew, now Dean of Griffith Law School. Their advice has been careful and thought-provoking, and their attention to detail meticulous. Other scholars to whom I am particularly indebted are Jenny Beard, Hilary Charlesworth, and Diane Otto (Melbourne Law School), and Kim Rubenstein (Australian National University). My gratitude also goes to Catherine Dauvergne (University of British Columbia) and Satvinder S Juss (King's College London), and for their kindness and encouragement over the years to Geoff Gilbert (University of Essex), Guy S Goodwin-Gill (University of Oxford), Gregor Noll (University of Lund), and the late Tony Vinson (University of New South Wales). Also from (or through) the University of Melbourne (both past and present), I am grateful to Tony Anghie, Carolyn Evans, Colin Fenwick, Michelle Foster, Ann Genovese, Jim Hathaway, Marilyn Lake, Wendy Larcombe, Pip Nicholson, Andrew Robertson, Peter Rush, and Gerry Simpson. I also thank Meghan Bergamin, Domi de Cordoba, Mas Generis, Madeline Gray, Jenny McFadden, Lucy O'Brien, and Vesna Stefanovski.

One of the greatest pleasures of this project has been sharing the road with a wonderful multidisciplinary community of scholars (both near and far) – new collegial and personal friendships as well as renewed and enduring ones. I have appreciated the kindness, company, and solidarity of many. Three fellow travellers deserve special mention. To them I am more grateful than they can know for intellectual, personal, and gastronomic companionship and nourishment along the road and for enduring friendships since they have moved (back) to Nairobi, London, and Chicago. They are Daniel Wanjau Muriu, Yoriko Otomo, and Jothie Rajah. Jothie, in particular, has been remarkable. Generous and gracious in every way, I have found in her a tremendously supportive friend, my most faithful and attentive reader, and a trusted and meticulous critic. I cannot thank her enough for both her generosity and her belief in this project.

Others who have read parts of earlier drafts of this work and who have been invaluable and faithful friends and colleagues over many years are Mariette Grange, Kerry Murphy, Nick Poynder, and Jo Szwarc. I also thank for their invaluable assistance Maeve Brown, Chanelle Burns, Joyce Chia, Michael Clothier, Mary Anne Kenny, Joanne Kinslor, Anthony Krohn, Paul Macgregor, David Manne, Don Miller, Vicki Parker, Chris Rummery, Kate Temby, and Christopher Weymouth. For editorial assistance, I thank John Berger and his team at Cambridge University Press, as well as Kim Greenwell and Mary Quinn.

Because of the stage in my professional life at which I embarked on this project, for me this book represents so much more than the time it has taken. I have – and therefore this book has – been shaped over the years by many conversations with refugees, asylum seekers, and others in Australia and many other places – people who have left deep impressions on me. Their words, actions, insight, and grace continue to inspire me. For some, I am happy to know that they are now in places where they have a legal status and security that enables them to get on with their lives. For too many, their predicament remains painfully unresolved. They are the true bearers of the burden, as the title of the inspirational artwork of Jade Tomlinson and Kev James that I feel privileged to be able to use on the book's front cover underscores.

I have also been influenced at many levels by countless formative, generous, and often enduring professional encounters and relationships over the years. Many have developed into personal friendships. If long lists were only risky, I would take the risk and list them all despite the possibility that I might have inadvertently left someone off. But my list is longer than even I could have imagined. So, I hope it is enough to say that I could never have dreamed that my life would be filled with such a rich and inspiring mix of colleagues – scholars, practitioners, and policymakers. I am grateful to them all.

At a personal level, I am ever grateful to my family: my late father Bill, whose patience, strength of character, intellect, and personal integrity will always be an inspiration to me; my mother Harriet, a generous thesaurus with zing; my lovely brothers Richard, Tom, and Will, and their families. I am also grateful to my family-in-law, who have been both supportive and understanding along the way. For friendship I value deeply and that has made all the difference during stages of this journey, I thank Alice and Tom; Alice, Alison, Rosemary, and Sam; Ani, Bianca, Hoang, Justin, Nick, Rebecca, Symon, and Zoe; Carolyn and Martin; Christine and David; Chris and Michael; Elisabeth and Udo; Daniel; Gidget; Greta and Franz; Klaus, Lars, and Pia; Jane Louise; Jenny and Michael; Jo and Simon; Joan; Justine and Philip; Kirsten and Scotty; Lauren and Ulf; Lay Lee; Leonie; Loretta and Jonathan and their children, Thea, Gabe, and Seb; Margaret and Mike; Murray and Puthy and their children, Lachie, Rochie, and Fitzie; Nee; Rachael and Rory; Sadikh; Sarah; Susana and Mark; Vanessa and Stephen; and Sue, whose magic hands massaged out the knots in my neck and shoulders.

My final and most heartfelt thanks are to Malcolm and our son Hal. None of this would have been possible without them. Hal, who was born in the midst of it all, has immeasurably enriched our lives, and I am grateful to him beyond his knowing. Malcolm has endured and survived with me, and I am deeply grateful for his unwavering love and support.

Abbreviations

ADJR	*Administrative Decisions (Judicial Review) Act 1977* (Cth)
AIA	*Acts Interpretation Act 1901* (Cth)
ALP	Australian Labor Party
ASAS	Asylum Seekers Assistance Scheme
ASRC	Asylum Seekers Resource Centre
AustLII	Australian Legal Information Institute
CAS	Community Assistance Support Program
CPD	Commonwealth, *Parliamentary Debates*
DIAC	Department of Immigration and Citizenship
DIBP	Department of Immigration and Border Protection
DIMA	Department of Immigration and Multicultural Affairs
DIMIA	Department of Immigration and Indigenous Affairs
HRC	United Nations Human Rights Committee
HREOC	Human Rights and Equal Opportunity Commission (now Australian Human Rights Commission)
ICCPR	International Covenant on Civil and Political Rights
ICESCR	International Covenant on Economic, Social and Cultural Rights
JSCM	Joint Standing Committee on Migration, Parliament of Australia
LIA	*Legislative Instruments Act 2003* (Cth)
MIMA	Minister for Immigration and Multicultural Affairs
NSC	National Security Committee
OED	*Oxford English Dictionary*
PAM3	DIBP, 'Procedures Advice Manual 3: Guidelines for Officers Administering Migration Legislation' (2016)
RACS	Refugee Advice & Casework Service
RDA	*Racial Discrimination Act 1975* (Cth)
RRT	Refugee Review Tribunal

RSD   Refugee Status Determination
SRSS   Status Resolution Support Services Programme
UNHCR   Office of the United Nations High Commissioner for Refugees
VCCL   Victorian Council for Civil Liberties
VOC   *Vereenigde Oostindische Compagnie*
          (Dutch East India Company)

Prologue

Living Realities

It is 5 May 1992. A Tuesday. I am working as a refugee lawyer at the Refugee Advice & Casework Service (RACS), a community legal centre in Melbourne. Our office is a windowless cubbyhole in a Migrant Resource Centre in a back street in the inner-city suburb of Prahran. It is a space we share with another community legal centre, social workers, English language teachers, and countless community groups, their religious gatherings, and their (mostly) delicious cooking smells. On a modest budget, and armed with state-of-the-art equipment including one computer, a typewriter that miraculously memorises the previous line so you can make corrections before it is committed to paper, and a mobile phone the size of a brick, we provide free advice and assistance to as many asylum seekers as we can manage.

As part of this work, we are responsible for the representation of 119 Cambodians among a cohort of 389 so-called 'boat people' who have arrived in Australia over the past few years, since November 1989. Their arrival triggered a public response bordering on hysteria encapsulated in the uncompromising unwelcome they received from then Prime Minister Bob Hawke:

> [W]e're not here with an open-door policy saying anyone who wants to come to Australia can come. These people are not political refugees. . . . What we make of it is that there is obviously a combination of economic refugeeism, if you like. People saying they don't like a particular regime or they don't like their economic circumstances, therefore they're going to up, pull up stumps, get in a boat and lob in Australia. Well that's not on. . . . [W]e have an orderly migration program. We're not going to allow people just to jump that queue by saying we'll jump into a boat, here we are, bugger the people who've been around the world.[1]

---

[1] Jana Wendt, Interview with Bob Hawke, Prime Minister (Nine Network, *A Current Affair*, Parliament House, 6 June 1990).

On another occasion, Hawke said,

> Now I'm simply saying: do not let any people, or any group of people, think
> that because Australia has that proud record, that all they've got to do is break
> the rules, jump the queue, lob here and Bob's your uncle. Bob is not your
> uncle on this issue other than in accordance with the appropriate rules. We
> will continue to be one of the most humanitarian countries in the world. I am
> not ambivalent about this matter. My compassion goes to those people who
> have been waiting for years in refugee camps to come to this country. And I
> am not going to see those with prior rights and prior claims upon our
> compassion overridden by people who take the law into their own hands.[2]

In April, a group of these Cambodians, many of whom were our clients,
received decisions rejecting their applications for refugee status. They applied
to the Federal Court of Australia ('the Federal Court') for judicial review of
these decisions. The Minister for Immigration, Gerry Hand, has been quick to
concede that the decision-making process was flawed; they have been denied
natural justice. Their cases have been remitted by consent for a new decision.

The problem is that our clients are still in detention. They have been there
for more than two years. They are already depressed and anxious, and this is
going to prolong their detention even more. So we have amended their
applications to the Court to seek their release from detention pending the
outcome of their claims. The case, which will be heard by Justice O'Loughlin,
is set down for hearing on Thursday morning, 7 May, the day after tomorrow.

It is the end of the day – a little before 6 PM – and I am sitting in our office
preparing for the case. I get a call from a colleague in Sydney. What he tells me
stuns me. A Bill has been introduced into Parliament around 4 PM and has
already passed the lower House. It provides for the mandatory detention of our
clients and has been specifically designed to stymie their case before Justice
O'Loughlin. It has bipartisan support and is set to pass the Senate this evening.
Following only three hours of debate in the Senate – stretched out by a spirited
but powerless minority (the Australian Democrats and Independent Senator
Brian Harradine) – the Bill becomes law.[3] The next day, despite the best efforts
of my colleague, Anthony Krohn, who crafts a superb letter to the Governor-
General, Bill Hayden, about why he should seriously consider not doing so,
the Act is given Royal Assent.

The Act declares that 'boat people' (referred to as 'designated persons') *must*
be detained and that they have no remedy of release through the Courts: 'A

---

[2] Glenn Milne and Tracey Aubin, 'Bob's Not Your Uncle PM Tells Boat People', *The Weekend
     Australian*, 21–22 July 1990, 3, quoting Bob Hawke, Prime Minister of Australia.
[3] *Migration Amendment Act 1992* (Cth).

court is not to order the release from custody of a designated person', says s 54R. These measures are, the Act declares, in "the national interest". Justice O'Loughlin's hands are tied.

As the enormity of what has happened sinks in, I try to explain the implications to our bewildered clients. A constitutional challenge is our only choice. I take instructions, and we secure the pro bono assistance of a leading law firm and senior counsel. The pyrrhic victory in the High Court of Australia seven months later, which validates mandatory detention but finds detention prior to May 1992 to have been unlawful, is little consolation.[4]

~~~

The day-to-day work of representing asylum seekers is principally focused on conditions in their country of origin. This is the traditional turf of refugee law. Does the harm a client fears amount to persecution or not? Is her fear well-founded? Is her fear of persecution for reasons of race, religion, nationality, membership of a particular social group, or political opinion?

Recognition as a refugee within the definition set out in the *Refugee Convention*[5] is vital for protection against *refoulement* – that is, forcible return of a person to a place where her life or freedom is threatened.[6] This principle of *non-refoulement* is the cornerstone of international refugee law.[7]

Determination of refugee status is a process that considers the past and then determines an asylum seeker's status through a prospective assessment of risk. But what of her present, her here and now? While meeting the challenges of this and similar migration processes, asylum seekers living in the community need a means of subsistence pending determination of their request for protection.

One of my clients at RACS was a young Sri Lankan Tamil man. He arrived with his wife and five-year-old daughter. He lodged his application for refugee status with a substantial amount of detail supporting his claims. I took statements from him, did the necessary country research, wrote

---

4   *Chu Kheng Lim v Minister for Immigration, Local Government and Ethnic Affairs* (1992) 176 CLR 1.

5   *Convention relating to the Status of Refugees*, opened for signature 28 July 1951, 189 UNTS 150 (entered into force 22 April 1954) art 1A(2).

6   Ibid art 33; see also *Migration Act 1958* (Cth) s 36(2)(a). Cf *Migration and Maritime Powers Legislation Amendment (Resolving the Asylum Legacy Caseload) Act 2014* (Cth), inserting s 197C into the *Migration Act 1958* (Cth), which declares that *non-refoulement* obligations are irrelevant to the obligation to remove unlawful non-citizens under s 198.

7   See, eg, United Nations High Commissioner for Refugees, *Declaration of States Parties to the 1951 Convention and or Its 1967 Protocol relating to the Status of Refugees*, UN Doc HCR/ MMSP/2001/09 (16 January 2002) Preamble para 4.

submissions in support of his case, and accompanied him to interviews and hearings. At the end of one of our appointments, I was closing his file. I was under pressure to move onto the next client, to meet another deadline. He stopped me. He needed to tell me something. He had no permission to work. He could not support his family. He could not have put it more simply, powerfully, devastatingly: "Madam, *I* can eat every second day, but I can't ask my daughter to."

In another case, a Kurdish couple we were assisting was homeless. No work. No social assistance. One afternoon they took me outside into the street to show me where they lived. It was the back of an old van, strewn with all they had: a few clothes, a bit of bedding, some vital papers, and an enormous jar full of brine with the last of their pickled cucumbers afloat in it. They showered in public swimming pools. They were at the end of their tether. In utter despair, the husband thumped the back window of their van. As it crumbled beneath his hands, he broke down.

Stories like these are not uncommon. However, the laws and policies that produce them are rarely subject to judicial scrutiny. On one occasion, a case on work rights came before the Federal Court. It settled, but rather than consigning it to the oblivion that is the destiny of cases that settle out of court, Justice Merkel took the unusual step of placing the circumstances that gave rise to it on the public record. He did so because, he said, "[o]ccasionally cases come before the Court that show that the law can be used as an instrument of injustice. The present is such a case."[8]

The case before Justice Merkel was of another Sri Lankan couple, this time with a young son. They were not asylum seekers. That they were unwelcome was nevertheless clear. They were subject to a mandatory 'no work' condition on their temporary processing visa (known as a bridging visa). With access only to limited support from their wider family, they relied on food vouchers from the Red Cross and other charities and begged for free food from convenience stores like McDonald's and Kentucky Fried Chicken. This led to what Justice Merkel described as

> the Kafkaesque situation in which the applicant, evidently under surveil-
> lance, was twice apprehended for working in order to provide for his wife and
> young child. Under the statutory regime that was an offence, and resulted in
> the cancellation of the applicant's bridging visa and his indefinite detention
> away from his wife and child.[9]

---

[8]   *De Silva v Minister for Immigration and Multicultural Affairs* (2001) 113 FCR 350, 350.
[9]   Ibid 351.

Drawing together the vignettes offered in this prologue, each of these living realities reflects law's capacity to legitimise – and to normalise – the Kafkaesque. Thinking about Justice Merkel's explanation for placing on the public record an example of law's capacity to be used as an instrument of injustice, we might ask how migration law has made these dehumanising realities possible. It is this question that animates this book.

1

Introduction

What men, what monsters, what inhuman race,
What laws, what barb'rous customs of the place,
Shut up a desert shore to drowning men,
And drive us to the cruel seas again![1]

1.1 INSTITUTIONAL RESPONSES TO UNSOLICITED MIGRATION

The spectre of vast hordes arriving on Australian shores in little fishing boats has long captured the public imagination. Ever since the exodus from Vietnam that began in 1975, the arrival of so-called 'boat people' has been met with growing hostility and increasingly harsh measures.[2] Since 1992, 'boat people' seeking Australia's protection have been subject to mandatory detention for months and often years without meaningful recourse to the courts. Described at the time as an "interim" measure,[3] the practice of mandatory detention has survived constitutional

---

[1] Virgil, *Aeneis* in John Dryden, *The Poetical Works of John Dryden, with the Life of Virgil* (Milner and Sowerby, 1864) 104.

[2] While numbers of 'boat people' arriving in Australia since this time have increased significantly, they remain modest in global terms: see United Nations High Commissioner for Refugees (UNHCR), *UNHCR Statistical Yearbook 2014* (UNHCR, 14th ed, 2015); Janet Phillips and Harriet Spinks, 'Boat Arrivals in Australia Since 1976' (Research Paper, Parliamentary Library, Parliament of Australia, first published 25 June 2009, statistical appendix updated 23 July 2013). For an overview of Australia's responses to unauthorised arrivals over the last quarter of the twentieth century, see Andreas Schloenhardt, 'Australia and the Boat People: 25 Years of Unauthorised Arrivals' (2000) 23(3) *University of New South Wales Law Journal* 33.

[3] Commonwealth, *Parliamentary Debates*, House of Representatives, 5 May 1992, 2370 (Gerry Hand, Minister for Immigration) (Commonwealth parliamentary debates are hereinafter referred to as 'CPD').

challenge,[4] been exported,[5] and, more than 25 years later, remains a central platform of contemporary migration law and policy both in Australia[6] and as part of Australia's offshore detention and processing policy.[7]

Between 1997 and 2009, many asylum seekers applying to remain in Australia had a 'no work' condition[8] imposed on their stay while they awaited the outcome of lawful immigration procedures. These procedures could take months and sometimes years to run their course. Although some of the harshest consequences of the no-work policies of this 12-year period[9] were mitigated by policy and regulatory changes from 2009,[10] the way in which they were framed and rationalised is of more than historical interest. This is because, notwithstanding the relaxation of the policy for some, work rights are still regarded as a privilege.[11] The regulatory framework for imposing the no-work condition remains in place,[12] and the risk of detention for breach of the no-work condition remains real.[13] In 2014, at least 19,000 asylum seekers

---

[4] See especially *Chu Kheng Lim v Minister for Immigration, Local Government and Ethnic Affairs* (1992) 176 CLR 1 ('*Lim*'); *Al-Kateb v Godwin* (2004) 219 CLR 562 ('*Al-Kateb*'); *Plaintiff M76-2013 v Minister for Immigration, Multicultural Affairs and Citizenship* (2013) 251 CLR 322 ('*Plaintiff M76*'); *Plaintiff S156/2013 v Minister for Immigration and Border Protection* (2014) 254 CLR 28 ('*Manus Island Case*'); *Plaintiff S4/2014 v Minister for Immigration and Border Protection* (2014) 253 CLR 219 ('*Plaintiff S4*'); *Plaintiff M96A/2016 v Commonwealth of Australia* [2017] HCA 16 (3 May 2017) ('*Plaintiff M96A*'); *Plaintiff S195/2016 v Minister for Immigration and Border Protection and Ors* [2017] HCA 31, 17 August 2017. See also Chapter 5.

[5] Although there have been some recent changes to the offshore detention regime established under memoranda of understanding between Australia and Nauru and Papua New Guinea, 'boat people' transferred from Australia to Nauru and Manus Island, Papua New Guinea, have been mandatorily detained for long periods and the validity of the regional processing scheme upheld: see *Manus Island Case* (2014) 254 CLR 28; *Plaintiff M68-2015 v Minister for Immigration and Border Protection* (2016) 257 CLR 42 ('*Nauru Detention Case*'). Cf *Namah v Pato* [2016] PGSC 13; SC1497 (26 April 2016); *Plaintiff M70/2011 v Minister for Immigration and Citizenship* (2011) 244 CLR 144 ('*Malaysian Declaration Case*'). The relaxation of policy notwithstanding, the confinement of a person on an island may nevertheless constitute a deprivation of liberty: *Case of Guzzardi v Italy* (1980) 3 Eur Court HR (ser A, no 39) 533.

[6] See especially *Migration Act 1958* (Cth) divs 6–7 ('*Migration Act*').

[7] See, eg, *Manus Island Case* (2014) 254 CLR 28; *Nauru Detention Case* (2016) 257 CLR 42; *Namah v Pato* [2016] PGSC 13; SC1497 (26 April 2016).

[8] *Migration Regulations 1994* (Cth) reg 2.05(1), sch 8 reg 8101('*Migration Regulations*').

[9] See, eg, Grant Mitchell et al, 'Welfare Issues and Immigration Outcomes: Asylum Seekers Living in Australia on Bridging Visa E' (2003) 25(3) *Migration Action* 20.

[10] *Migration Amendment Regulations 2009* (No 6) (Cth).

[11] Joint Standing Committee on Migration, Parliament of Australia, *Immigration Detention in Australia: Community-Based Alternatives to Detention – Second Report of the Inquiry into Immigration Detention in Australia* (2009) 139 [5.38].

[12] *Migration Regulations* sch 2.

[13] For example, since 14 December 2013, 'boat people' released into the community pending the determination of their status are also required to sign a code of conduct the breach of

lived in the Australian community without work rights,[14] and although (since that time) many of those asylum seekers have now been given work rights, pursuant to a deal brokered between then Immigration Minister Scott Morrison and minor-party senators,[15] the grant of such rights is still discretionary and subject to withdrawal.[16]

As well as the prospect of a no-work condition, many asylum seekers have also been, and indeed continue to be, denied access to any or adequate welfare support.[17] They have been left to depend on charity and forced into homelessness and begging.[18] As a result, many asylum seekers face

which risks reduction or cessation of welfare support or visa cancellation and return to immigration detention. Furthermore, breach of the code may lead to the refusal of further visa applications and, in certain circumstances, permanent exclusion from Australia. The terms of the code of behaviour include an expectation that asylum seekers will comply with all Australian laws including road laws: *Migration Amendment (Bridging Visas – Code of Behaviour) Regulation 2013* (Cth); *Instrument IMMI 13/155: Code of Behaviour for Public Interest Criterion 4022* (Cth), signed on 12 December 2013, made under *Migration Regulations* sch 4 pt 4 cl 4.1. However, even without the Code of Behaviour, breach of the no-work condition can lead to visa cancellation and re-detention on the grounds of being an 'unlawful non-citizen': *Migration Act* ss 13, 14, 116(1)(b), 189. Note also that *Migration Amendment (Employer Sanctions) Act 2007* (Cth) amended the *Migration Act* to include both civil and criminal liability on employers for allowing a person to work in breach of the no-work condition: *Migration Act* ss 245AA–245AP.

14   This was especially the case for a cohort of 'boat people' released from detention pursuant to a ministerial discretion and subject to a 'no advantage' policy recommended by an expert panel on asylum seekers in August 2012: Evidence to Senate Legal and Constitutional Affairs Legislation Committee, Parliament of Australia, *Estimates 2013–2014 (Immigration and Border Protection)*, Canberra, 27 May 2014, 81 (Martin Bowles, Secretary, Department of Immigration and Border Protection (DIBP); Chris Bowen, Minister for Immigration and Citizenship, 'No Advantage Onshore for Boat Arrivals' (Media Release, 21 November 2012); *Instrument IMMI 12/114: Classes of Persons* (Cth), signed on 20 November 2012, made under *Migration Regulations* sch 2 regs 050.613A(1)(b), 051.611A(1)(c); Australian Human Rights Commission, Submission No 8 to Joint Committee on Human Rights, Parliament of Australia, *Examination of the Migration (Regional Processing) Package of Legislation*, January 2013, 47–9; Lisa Hartley and Caroline Fleay, 'Policy as Punishment: Asylum Seekers in the Community without the Right to Work' (Centre for Human Rights Education, Curtin University, 2014) 34; Peter Mares, 'Refuge without Work: "This is a Poison, a Poison for the Life of a Person"' (2014) 45 *Griffith Review* 103, 105. On the expert panel report, see below n 38.

15   Morrison agreed to grant work rights and to exercise his discretion to release children from detention in exchange for the passage of controversial legislation enabling extraterritorial detention on the high seas: Scott Morrison, Minister for Immigration and Border Protection, Press Conference, Migration and Maritime Powers Legislation Amendment (Resolving the Asylum Legacy Caseload) Bill 2014, Coalition Government, Parliament House, Canberra, 5 December 2014.

16   See Chapter 6, Section 6.2, 258–72.   17   Hartley and Fleay, above n 14, 34.

18   Nadine Liddy, Sarah Sanders, and Caz Coleman, 'Australia's Hidden Homeless: Community-Based Options for Asylum Homelessness' (Hotham Mission Asylum Seeker Project, 2010).

destitution[19] or, for those denied work rights, risk detention for trying to mitigate their hardship – an effect that, as we saw in the prologue, has been described by a senior member of the judiciary as Kafkaesque.[20] The relaxation of the work rights policy notwithstanding, for many, the denial or piecemeal grant of work rights[21] and the denial of access to adequate welfare has fostered social and economic exclusion, with far-reaching and damaging effects.[22] This exclusion, coupled with the uncertainty of a precarious legal status that conditions access to protection procedures by 'boat people'[23] on a non-compellable 'public interest' discretion[24] and the imposition of arbitrary and unrealistic 'lodge or leave' deadlines,[25] has put asylum seekers under

[19] See, eg, Hartley and Fleay, above n 14, 34; Asylum Seekers Resource Centre (ASRC), 'Destitute and Uncertain: The Reality of Seeking Asylum in Australia' (October 2010).

[20] *De Silva v Minister for Immigration and Multicultural Affairs* (2001) 113 FCR 350, 351 (Merkel J).

[21] A practice has emerged of granting bridging visas with work rights for three-month periods. This creates an almost insurmountable practical barrier to securing work: Refugee Council of Australia (RCOA), 'State of the Nation: Refugees and People Seeking Asylum in Australia' (RCOA Report No 1/17, February 2017) 10 http://www.refugeecouncil.org.au/publications/re ports/state-nation-2017/.

[22] See, eg, Jesuit Social Services, 'The Living Conditions of People Seeking Asylum in Australia' (Jesuit Social Services, 2015); see also Carolyn Webb and Cameron Houston, 'Springvale Bank Fire: Asylum Seekers' Lives Precarious, Say Advocates', *The Age* (online), 20 November 2016, www.theage.com.au/victoria/springvale-bank-fire-asylum-seekers-lives-precarious-say-advo cates-20161120-gstexl.html.

[23] The cohort affected by these measures comprises some 30,923 'boat people' currently in Australia who are part of what has become known as the 'legacy caseload' – that is, 'boat people' who either arrived before 13 August 2012 and had not had their protection visa application finalised by 18 September 2013, or who arrived on or after 13 August 2012 and who are subject to a fast-track assessment process. The date 13 August 2012 signifies the date on which an expert panel on asylum seekers published a report recommending reinstatement of extraterritorial processing of asylum seekers: see below n 38. 18 September 2013 signifies the commencement date of the military-led campaign to 'Stop the Boats', codenamed Operation Sovereign Borders: Thea Cowie, 'Coalition Launches Operation Sovereign Borders' SBS Radio (online), 18 September 2013 www.sbs.com.au/news/article/2013/09/18/coalition-laun ches-operation-sovereign-borders. For a departmental description of the 'legacy caseload' and statistical data see DIBP, 'IMA Legacy Caseload: Report on Status and Processing Outcomes' (February 2017) <www.border.gov.au/ReportsandPublications/Documents/statis tics/ima-legacy-caseload-feb-17.pdf>.

[24] *Migration Act* ss 46A(1), (2), and (7). Members of the 'legacy caseload' are prohibited from applying for permanent protection. They can only apply for a temporary protection visa if the Minister decides that it is in the 'public interest' to exercise his discretion to lift a legislative bar on making such an application. Even then, they are subject to a fast-track assessment process that makes access to merits review a matter of departmental discretion.

[25] A ministerial announcement in May 2017, setting a lodgment deadline of 1 October 2017, led to an explosion in demand for legal advice and assistance: RCOA, 'Recent Changes in Australian Refugee Policy' (RCOA Media Release, 8 June 2017) <www.refugeecouncil.org .au/publications/recent-changes-australian-refugee-policy/>; see also Amnesty International,

immense strain. Indeed, the administration of policy has heightened rather
than diminished vulnerability to destitution, detention and ultimately the
risk of *refoulement*. These conditions have been described by UNHCR's
most senior protection official, Volker Türk, as a "social time bomb".[26]

Mandatory detention and planned destitution[27] can, as we can see, operate
with dehumanising effects, separately or in combination. They are two of the
most significant developments in Australian migration policy since the 1990s.
Even today, as they seem to be overshadowed by increasingly strident
responses to unsolicited migration – in particular the controversial policies
of interception, boat turnbacks,[28] and extraterritorial detention and processing
of asylum seekers[29] – mandatory detention and planned destitution remain
central planks of current policy and continue to be viewed as both lawful and
legitimate.

It is with this context in mind that this book aims to explain how policies
such as the mandatory detention and planned destitution of certain
foreigners[30] have come to be characterised as both lawful and legitimate
institutional responses to unsolicited migration – policies that are central to,
indeed underpin, Australia's contemporary responses to unsolicited migration. To do this, I unearth the juridical tradition in which migration lawmaking in Australia is embedded in order to show how certain kinds of

'Government Sets Impossible Deadlines for Asylum Applications', 13 March 2017.

[26]   Michael Gordon, '"Social Time Bomb": UNHCR's Warning on the Plight of 30,000 Asylum
       Seekers Already Living in Australia', *The Age* (online), 23 November 2016, quoting Volker
       Türk, UNHCR's Assistant High Commissioner for Refugees (Protection), <www.smh.com
       .au/federal-politics/political-news/social-time-bomb-unhcrs-warning-on-the-plight-of-30000-
       asylum-seekers-already-living-in-australia-20161122-gsuyk5.html>.

[27]   In March 2008, then Minister for Immigration and Citizenship, Senator Chris Evans,
       characterised the policy of denying work rights and restricting access to welfare as planning
       for people to be destitute: CPD, Senate, 18 March 2008, 1090 (Chris Evans). Cholewinski
       describes similar practices in the United Kingdom as 'enforced destitution': Ryszard
       Cholewinski, 'Enforced Destitution of Asylum Seekers in the United Kingdom: The Denial
       of Fundamental Human Rights' (1998) 10(3) *International Journal of Refugee Law* 462.

[28]   There have even been suggestions that effecting turnbacks may entail making government-
       sanctioned payments to people smugglers to do so: Jared Owens, 'Were Asylum Seeker Boats
       Paid to Turn Back?' *The Australian* (online), 14 June 2015 www.theaustralian.com.au/national-
       affairs/immigration/were-asylum-seeker-boats-paid-to-turn-back/news-story/f19bd5b8e14e590
       b31e0579a80b4c535 .

[29]   See Section 1.2.2.1, 'Selection of the Case Studies', in this chapter. See also the epilogue, 'A
       Campaign to "Stop the Boats"', 292.

[30]   In this book, I use the terms 'foreigner' and 'alien' more or less interchangeably, according to
       their usage in the particular texts with which I am working. However, as will become clear, my
       genealogical analysis of the figure of the foreigner in international law suggests the foreigner to
       be a figure with a more complex juridical history.

political-economic interests have shaped the relationship between the foreigner and the sovereign ('the foreigner-sovereign relation'). I argue that a discourse of 'absolute sovereignty'[31] emerged in the nineteenth century as the conceptual frame of that relation and continues to inform migration law-making today. It is this discourse that has helped make current institutional responses to unsolicited migration thinkable and, for some, seemingly inevitable. Yet, as I argue, it is a discourse whose past and present are contingent, undermining the sense that such responses are inevitable and raising the possibility of a different future.

1.1.1 Common Humanity: A Backdrop

In this book, I take the notion of our 'common humanity' as a backdrop.[32] As a notion, it impels us to think from – and to treat as axiomatic – the idea that all people are connected to one another through a common bond of human aspiration, frailty, and experience. It is a notion to which the Australian state gestures through its embrace of immigration and humanitarian obligation,[33]

---

[31] Throughout this book, 'absolute sovereignty' is a term I use in inverted commas as shorthand for the claim that there is an absolute sovereign right to exclude and condition the entry and stay of (even friendly) aliens. In addition, the convention is adopted of using inverted commas to mark the terms the book problematises as social constructs or embodied in discursive techniques. At least in their first use, I wrap such terms in inverted commas. I depart from this style when I see a particular value in doing so. For example, in the case of 'absolute sovereignty', inverted commas provide a way of reminding the reader that it has a particular meaning in this book and that it holds in relation a number of different political and juridical modes and registers. In relation to 'boat people', inverted commas provide a way of reminding my reader (and myself) that the term's ambiguity is part of the work it is doing. In addition, while using quotation marks in the usual way, inverted commas are used where text is quoted from legislation or where previously quoted text is requoted or paraphrased for analytical purposes. See Piet Strydom, *Discourse and Knowledge: The Making of Enlightenment Sociology* (Liverpool University Press, 2000) 10; Jothie Rajah, *Authoritarian Rule of Law: Legislation, Discourse and Legitimacy in Singapore* (Cambridge University Press, 2012) 4. See also Chapter 5, Section 5.1.1.3, 175–6.

[32] Emmerich de Vattel, *The Law of Nations; or, Principles of the Law of Nature, Applied to the Conduct and Affairs of Nations and of Sovereigns* (Joseph Chitty ed and trans, Lawbook Exchange, first published 1854, 2005 ed) bk I ch XIX §229 [trans of: *Le Droit des gens; ou Principes de la loi naturelle, appliqués à la conduite et aux affaires des Nations et des Souverains* (first published 1758)]; see Chapter 2, Section 2.4.2, 74–5.

[33] As Dauvergne has noted, although humanitarian admissions "[do] not fit in with an ideological vision of community or family – admitting people because they are 'us'" – such admissions are "vital" because they "mark the nation as good, prosperous, and generous." Yet, as she saliently observes, "[h]umanitarianism is an impoverished stand-in for justice": Catherine Dauvergne, *Humanitarianism, Identity and Nation: Migration Laws of Australia and Canada* (University of British Columbia Press, 2005) 7.

not least through its accession to international human rights[34] and refugee law instruments.[35] Yet the policies that I introduced through the prologue have effects on asylum seekers that deny or disremember[36] the bond of a common humanity that we share with those who seek Australia's protection.[37] And, discordantly, a common humanity is at the same time a notion the Australian state claims (unabashedly) to uphold in the execution of the same – or similar –

[34]   Australia is a party to: *International Covenant on Civil and Political Rights*, opened for signature 16 December 1966, 999 UNTS 171 (entered into force 23 March 1976); *International Convention on the Elimination of All Forms of Racial Discrimination*, opened for signature 21 December 1965, 660 UNTS 195 (entered into force 4 January 1969); *International Covenant on Economic, Social and Cultural Rights*, opened for signature 16 December 1966, 993 UNTS 3 (entered into force 3 January 1976); *Convention on the Elimination of All Forms of Discrimination against Women*, opened for signature 18 December 1979, 1249 UNTS 13 (entered into force 3 September 1981); *Convention against Torture and Other Cruel, Inhuman or Degrading Treatment or Punishment*, opened for signature 10 December 1984, 1465 UNTS 85 (entered into force 26 June 1987); *Convention on the Rights of the Child*, opened for signature 20 November 1989, 1577 UNTS 3 (entered into force 2 September 1990); *Convention on the Rights of Persons with Disabilities*, opened for signature 30 March 2007, 2515 UNTS 3 (entered into force, 3 May 2008). There are only two core international human rights instruments to which Australia is not a party: *International Convention on the Protection of the Rights of All Migrant Workers and Members of Their Families*, opened for signature 18 December 1990, 2220 UNTS 3 (entered into force 1 July 2003); *International Convention for the Protection of All Persons from Enforced Disappearance*, opened for signature 6 February 2007, UN Doc A/61/488 (entered into force 23 December 2010).

[35]   Australia is a party to: *Convention relating to the Status of Refugees*, opened for signature 28 July 1951, 189 UNTS 137 (entered into force 22 April 1954) ('*Refugee Convention*'); *Convention relating to the Status of Stateless Persons*, opened for signature 28 September 1954, 360 UNTS 117 (entered into force 6 June 1960); *Convention on the Reduction of Statelessness*, opened for signature 30 August 1961, 989 UNTS 175 (entered into force 13 December 1975); *Protocol relating to the Status of Refugees*, opened for signature 31 January 1967, 606 UNTS 267 (entered into force 4 October 1967). Australia reaffirmed its commitment to the *Refugee Convention* in UNHCR, *Declaration of States Parties to the 1951 Convention and or Its 1967 Protocol relating to the Status of Refugees*, UN Doc HCR/MMSP/2001/09 (16 January 2002); see also UNHCR, *Ministerial Communiqué*, UN Doc HCR/MINCOMMS/2011/6 (8 December 2011), marking the 60th anniversary of the *Refugee Convention* and the 50th anniversary of the *Convention on the Reduction of Statelessness*.

[36]   On disremembering as a form of social or institutional forgetting in the context of indigenous Australians, see W E H Stanner, 'The Boyer Lectures: After the Dreaming (1968)' in W E H Stanner, *The Dreaming and Other Essays* (Black Inc, first published 2009, 2010 ed) 172, 189.

[37]   See also a storyboard on people smuggling depicting Afghan asylum seekers engaging people smugglers in an attempt to seek protection and instead having their hopes dashed and finding themselves detained in communal tents on remote islands, covered in malarial mosquito bites and suffering the effects of isolation, dislocation, boredom, anxiety, and uncertainty: Australian Customs and Border Protection Service, *Operation Sovereign Borders: A Storyboard on People Smuggling* (1 November 2013) <http://newsroom.border.gov.au/chan nels/Operation-Sovereign-Borders/photos/a-storyboard-on-people-smuggling>.

policies as those I problematise here.[38] This discordance gives rise to ethical questions about motivation and the ways in which we acknowledge the humanity of unsolicited migrants. However, for the purposes of this book, our common humanity provides a setting for my inquiry into how the policies I have identified can be considered thinkable, even appropriate, and further-more in Australia's 'national interest'.

With this in mind, the book is motivated by the following questions: How could legislation providing for mandatory detention without mean-ingful recourse to the courts pass so effortlessly onto the statute books? How could the High Court of Australia ('the High Court') uphold the constitutional validity of such legislation when it is manifestly oppressive? What makes mandatory detention conceivable within Australian migra-tion law? How is it possible to deny people the right to work and/or access to any or adequate welfare for months and years while they pursue lawful immigration procedures? How is it possible that indefinite deten-tion could be the result of working to try and provide for one's family in such circumstances? What is it about migration lawmaking that leads to work and welfare policies that produce the destitution of unsolicited migrants, including children?

The answer to each of these questions, offered from within the politico-legal frame of reference from which those questions emanate, is that there is an absolute sovereign right to exclude and condition the entry and stay of

---

[38] "I want to stop the boats for Australia's sake and for the sake of common humanity": Leigh Sales, Interview with Tony Abbott, Prime Minister (ABC, 7:30 *Report*, 13 November 2013) 00:12:18 (Tony Abbott), <www.abc.net.au/7.30/content/2013/s3890402.htm>. The context of this claim is the argument that the 'stop the boats' policy and detention and processing of asylum seekers offshore are necessary to save lives at sea. The directive to save lives at sea was central to the terms of reference of an expert panel on asylum seekers established in mid-2012 following a spike in unauthorised boat arrivals. The panel recommended, inter alia, reopen-ing offshore processing facilities in 2012: Angus Houston, Paris Aristotle, and Michael L'Estrange, 'Report of the Expert Panel on Asylum Seekers' (Australian Government, August 2012) 9. David Manne responds to the policy of consciously-harming-people-to-save-lives-at-sea justification from the ethical dimension of law's purpose – of striving to be a just and good society. He frames what he describes as the "ethics of protection", where human dignity is promoted and protected, not abused; where "the ethical rock ... is the conviction that cruelty is an unjustifiable abuse of the human dignity of people we are obliged to protect": David Manne, Address to UNHCR Annual Consultations (Speech delivered at UNHCR Annual Consultations, Canberra, 15 October 2013); see also Andrew Hamilton, 'Asylum Seeker Ethics Is Simple' (2014) 24(5) *Eureka Street* (2014), <https://www .eurekastreet.com.au/article.aspx?aeid=39123#.WW_8hitLdTI>. On the axiom of a 'com-mon humanity', see also CPD, House of Representatives, 14 February 2008, 350 (Scott Morrison, Maiden Speech).

aliens[39] – an answer popularly encapsulated in the Australian public conversation in the statement *"we will decide who comes here and the circumstances in which they come"*[40] and for which I use the shorthand 'absolute
sovereignty' throughout this book.[41] However, behind this answer lies a
multifaceted story of considerable complexity.

1.1.2 *'Absolute Sovereignty': A Backstory*

The claim of 'absolute sovereignty', as I use the term, relies on a
particular idea and practice of sovereignty cast in terms which ostensibly
embody an unfettered right of the state to exclude and condition the
entry and stay of aliens. As the argument goes, the performance of this
sovereign right is consistent with[42] – or at least not "significantly shaken
by"[43] – international human rights or refugee law; so it retains its validity.
In Australia, the doctrinal claim that there is an absolute sovereign right

---

[39]   *Constitution* ss 51(xix), 51(xxvii); *Migration Act* s 4. For recent expressions of sovereignty in
       connection with offshore detention and processing and the related policies of interdiction and
       boat tow-backs, see Leigh Sales, Interview with Tony Abbott, Prime Minister (ABC, 7:30
       Report, 13 November 2013) 00:08:42, 00:09:46, 00:14:04, <www.abc.net.au/7.30/content/2013/
       s3890402.htm> : "This is a humanitarian disaster as well as an affront to our Australian
       sovereignty", "this is a sovereignty issue", "a very serious affront to our national sovereignty
       and is into the bargain a humanitarian disaster" (Tony Abbott); Stephanie Anderson,
       'Refugee, asylum seeker ban won't break international obligations, Peter Dutton says', *ABC
       News* (online), 31 October 2016, <www.abc.net.au/news/2016-10-31/dutton-says-refugee-ban-w
       on't-break-international-obligations/7979242>: "[W]e decide who is coming here. We don't
       outsource that to the people smugglers" (Malcolm Turnbull, Prime Minister).
[40]   See, eg, ABC, 'Liberals Accused of Trying to Rewrite History', *Lateline*, 21 November 2001
       (John Howard, former Prime Minister). Recent restatements of the claim have been made by
       Minister for Immigration and Border Protection, Peter Dutton, and former Prime Minister,
       Tony Abbott: Peter Dutton, *Address to the Australian Strategic Policy Institute*, 20 September
       2016 <www.minister.border.gov.au/peterdutton/2016/Pages/address-australian-strategic-pol
       icy-institute-15092016.aspx>; Tony Abbott, *Address to the Alliance of European Conservatives
       and Reformists*, Lobkowicz Palace, Prague, Czech Republic, 18 September 2016 <http://tony
       abbott.com.au/2016/09/address-alliance-european-conservatives-reformists-lobkowicz-palace-
       prague-czech-republic/>.
[41]   See also Martijn C Stronks, 'The Question of Salah Sheekh: Derrida's Hospitality and
       Migration Law' (2012) 8(1) *International Journal of Law in Context* 73, 75; on the oppositional
       relation between hospitality and hostility, see Giannacopoulos's engagement with Derrida's
       notion of 'hostipitality': Maria Giannacopoulos, 'Offshore Hospitality: Law, Asylum and
       Colonisation' (2013) 17 *Law, Texture, Culture* 163.
[42]   See, eg, CPD, House of Representatives, 5 May 1992, 2370–90; CPD, Senate, 5 May 1992,
       2234–62. See also Chapter 5.
[43]   Brian Opeskin, 'Managing International Migration in Australia: Human Rights and the "Last
       Major Redoubt of Unfettered National Sovereignty"' (2012) 46(3) *International Migration
       Review* 551, 579.

to exclude and condition the entry and stay of aliens holds an authority in migration law that is seldom questioned by the judiciary[44] or the academy,[45] much less the legislature.[46] Indeed, it is on the strength of 'absolute sovereignty' that laws, policies, and practices such as mandatory detention and planned destitution, and more recently offshore detention and processing, have been positioned and validated as thinkable responses to unsolicited migration. And in Australia the claim of 'absolute sovereignty' endures notwithstanding the end of the White Australia policy,[47] which was the provenance of 'absolute sovereignty' as a constitutional claim.[48] Proponents of these policies also assume that the foreigner is an outsider and thus, *a priori*, she[49] has lesser rights than the 'citizen'.

[44]   In Australia, see, eg, *Musgrove v Chun Teeong Toy* [1891] AC 272 ('*Musgrove*'); *Robtelmes v Brenan* (1906) 4 CLR 395; *Lim* (1992) 176 CLR 1; *Ruddock v Vadarlis* (2001) 110 FCR 491 ('*Vadarlis*'); *Al-Kateb* (2004) 219 CLR 562; *Ruhani v Director of Police (No 2)* (2005) 222 CLR 580; *Plaintiff M47-2012 v Director General of Security* (2012) 251 CLR 1 ('*Plaintiff M47*'); *CPCF v Minister for Immigration and Border Protection* (2015) 255 CLR 514 ('*Detention on the High Seas Case*'); *Nauru Detention Case* (2016) 257 CLR 42.

[45]   See, eg, Mirko Bagaric and John R Morss, 'State Sovereignty and Migration Control: The Ultimate Act of Discrimination?' (2005) 1(1) *Journal of Migration and Refugee Issues* 25; Jacqueline Bailey, 'Australia and Asylum Seekers: Is a Policy of Protection in the "National Interest"?' (2002) 8(1) *Australian Journal of Human Rights* 57; Simon Evans, 'The Rule of Law, Constitutionalism and the MV Tampa' (2002) 13(2) *Public Law Review* 94. Cf Catherine Dauvergne, 'Illegal Migration and Sovereignty' in Catherine Dauvergne (ed), *Jurisprudence for an International Globe* (Ashgate, 2003) 187; Catherine Dauvergne, 'Challenges to Sovereignty: Migration Laws for the 21st Century' (New Issues in Refugee Research Working Paper No 92, UNHCR, July 2003); Catherine Dauvergne, 'Sovereignty, Migration and the Rule of Law in Global Times' (2004) 67(4) *Modern Law Review* 588.

[46]   See, eg, parliamentary debates on mandatory detention legislation, in which no questions were raised about the scope of Australia's sovereignty: CPD, House of Representatives, 5 May 1992, 2370–89; CPD, Senate, 5 May 1992, 2234–62. See further Chapter 5, Section 5.1, 167–86. While there is increasing recognition among some commentators that there may be some limits on the sovereign right of states to do so, this analysis tends to relate to ceding a measure of sovereignty in the context of international agreements rather than a rethinking of sovereignty itself: T Alexander Aleinikoff, 'International Legal Norms and Migration: A Report' in T Alexander Aleinikoff and Vincent Chetail (eds), *Migration and International Legal Norms* (TMC Asser Press, 2003) 1; Stephen Legomsky, 'The Last Bastions of State Sovereignty: Immigration and Nationality Go Global' in Andrew C Sobel (ed), *Challenges of Globalization: Immigration, Social Welfare, Global Governance* (Routledge, 2009) 43, 44. For a more far-reaching challenge to the foundations of 'absolute sovereignty' in the context of the United States, see Matthew J Lindsay, 'Immigration, Sovereignty, and the Constitution of Foreignness' (2013) 45(3) *Connecticut Law Review* 743.

[47]   On the end of the White Australia policy, see generally Gwenda Tavan, *The Long Slow Death of White Australia* (Scribe, 2005).

[48]   See Chapter 4.

[49]   Although from time to time I use the male pronoun intentionally, I use the female pronoun generically throughout this book. In making this choice, I am persuaded by Haddad's thinking, which goes beyond the more usual justification that the majority of the world's

In this book, I treat 'absolute sovereignty' as a term of art that works in different ways and on multiple registers rather than as a simple doctrinal statement about authority. In other words, I understand 'absolute sovereignty' as a term whose usages can be disaggregated into political doctrine, judicial formulation, constitutional doctrine, or public rhetoric. So, while we see that mandatory detention (possibly for life)[50] and planned destitution (through denial of work and welfare rights) are policies that are habitually justified – explicitly or implicitly – by reference to the claim of 'absolute sovereignty', we need to understand that claim to hold in relation a number of different political and juridical claims. In this connection, I am interested in 'absolute sovereignty' as an historical claim about institutional practice, as a doctrinal claim about political and juridical authority, and as an analytical claim which enables us to trace how these different claims came together to produce 'absolute sovereignty' as a discourse.

Thus, for example, we will see how, in political doctrine and public rhetoric, the trope of 'absolute sovereignty' – for which I argue the 'national interest' serves as a proxy[51] – has become *the* well-rehearsed response to the unwelcome foreigner,[52] an unanswerable answer. We will also see that this claim is different

---

refugees and migrants are women and children (see, eg, James C Hathaway, *The Law of Refugee Status* (Butterworths, 1991) v). Haddad recognises that the habitual use of the male pronoun can allow the identity of the subject to go unnoticed by the reader. In other words, generic use of the male pronoun can have an anaesthetising effect. On the other hand, I see use of the generic 'she' as an important part of critically engaging with law and history; 'she' is a conscious pronoun with transformative possibilities. 'Her' use can, therefore, be understood as a form of resistance, and as a way of arousing us lest we should lapse into the slumber of convention and tradition: Emma Haddad, *The Refugee in International Society: Between Sovereigns* (Cambridge University Press, 2008) 39–41; see also Wendy Martyna, 'What Does "He" Mean? Use of the Generic Masculine' (1978) 28(1) *Journal of Communication* 131. For a survey of developments, results, and effects of gender in refugee law, see generally Efrat Arbel, Catherine Dauvergne, and Jenni Millbank (eds), *Gender Equality in Refugee Law: From the Margins to the Centre* (Routledge, 2014).

50 *Al-Kateb* (2004) 219 CLR 562; *Behrooz v Secretary, Department of Immigration and Multicultural and Indigenous Affairs* (2004) 219 CLR 486 ('*Behrooz*'); *Minister for Immigration and Multicultural and Indigenous Affairs v Al Khafaji* (2004) 219 CLR 664; *Plaintiff M47* (2012) 251 CLR 1; *Plaintiff M76* (2013) 251 CLR 322; *Plaintiff M96A* [2017] HCA 16 (3 May 2017).

51 See Chapter 5, Section 5.1.1.2–1.3, 174–6.

52 This message was a central platform of the 2001 federal election campaign of the Coalition Government of Prime Minister John Howard. It was again invoked in the Coalition's Abbott-led federal election campaign of 2013 as part of its 'Operation Sovereign Borders' (or 'stop the boats') policy platform: Liberal Party of Australia and National Party of Australia, 'The Coalition's Operation Sovereign Borders Policy' (July 2013) <www.aph.gov.au> (parlinfo). In relation to the 2016 federal election and the prominence of the asylum policy platform, see, eg, Paige Taylor, 'Federal Election 2016: New Boats to Return Asylum-Seekers', *The Australian*

from, but related to, the claim of 'absolute sovereignty' as a juridical concept and as an institutional practice. Finally, we will see how, in its doctrinal form (the detail of which is taken up in Part I) 'absolute sovereignty' in Australia derives its putative authority from international law,[53] the common law,[54] and the Australian *Constitution*.[55] Overall, the common characteristic we see in each claim is acceptance of the idea that 'absolute sovereignty' as doctrine and practice has a value (both politically and juridically) that locates it "beyond all question",[56] a value that treats 'absolute sovereignty' as an impenetrable truth whatever its content.

So, if mandatory detention and planned destitution of asylum seekers are the contemporary context for this book, and 'absolute sovereignty' their backstory, then a further question arises regarding how the claim of 'absolute sovereignty' – the idea that there is an absolute sovereign right to exclude and condition the entry and stay of (even friendly) aliens – has come to assume the authority it is accorded in the domain of migration law- and policy-making in Australia. To this end, this book builds on an existing literature to argue that, as a subject of international law, the 'foreigner' within the foreigner-sovereign relation is an historically mutable figure. In other words, I argue that there is no basis for the assumption that she is necessarily a (juridical) outsider. I argue that the foreigner-sovereign relation was only framed as a claim of 'absolute sovereignty' – which treats the foreigner as an excludable outsider – when certain political-economic events and interests coalesced. In other words, far from being inevitable, 'absolute sovereignty' is historically contingent both as juridical form and state practice. I argue, therefore, that the resilience and power of 'absolute sovereignty' as an idea and practice in Australian migration law relies on a putative inevitability, sustained by a discourse which, in reality, draws on diverse historical contingencies.

To make these arguments, I use two distinct but related methodologies: genealogy (Part I) and discourse analysis (Part II). As I elaborate in Section 1.2 in this chapter, this pairing provides a way to think about how the institutional responses to unsolicited migration I have identified can be viewed as lawful and legitimate, both from the perspective of their juridical history (genealogy) and their present conceptualisations (discourse analysis).

(online), 30 June 2016, <www.theaustralian.com.au/federal-election-2016/federal-election-2016-new-boats-to-return-asylumseekers/news-story/9e57526ab66d4e055aedef3b70cbd2f9>.
[53] See Chapters 2–3. [54] See Chapter 3. [55] See Chapter 4.
[56] Friedrich Nietzsche, *On the Genealogy of Morals: A Polemic* (Douglas Smith trans, Oxford University Press, 1996) 8 [trans of: *Zur Genealogie der Moral: Eine Streitschrift* (first published 1887)].

1.1.3 Not 'Simply' a Human Rights Issue

This project, which started with the contemporary policies of mandatory detention and planned destitution described earlier, has an interest in these issues that differs from the question of whether and how such policies might be in breach of international human rights[57] and refugee law standards.[58] Given my background as a human rights lawyer, looking to the international human rights framework[59] as a way of thinking about these policies might seem a

---

[57] Mandatory detention by Australia has been found to be in breach of international human rights law in numerous individual cases: see, eg, Human Rights Committee (HRC), *Views: Communication No 560/1993*, 59th sess, UN Doc CCPR/C/59/D/560/1993 (30 April 1997) ('A v Australia'); HRC, *Views: Communication No 900/1999*, 76th sess, UN Doc CCPR/C/76/D/ 900/1999 (13 November 2002) ('C v Australia'); HRC, *Views: Communication No 1069/2002*, 79th sess, UN Doc CCPR/C/79/D/1069/2002 (6 November 2003) ('*Bakhtiyari v Australia*'); HRC, *Views: Communication No 2094/2011*, 108th sess, UN Doc CCPR/C/108/D/2094/2011 (20 August 2013) ('F K A G v Australia'); HRC, *Views: Communication No 2136/2011*, 108th sess, UN Doc CCPR/C/108/D/2136/2012 (20 August 2013) ('M M M v Australia'). See also HRC, *Concluding Observations of the Human Rights Committee: Australia*, 95th sess, UN Doc CCPR/C/AUS/CO/5 (7 May 2009).

[58] There is no treaty-monitoring body for the *Refugee Convention*. However, under that Convention states parties undertake to cooperate with the UNHCR in the exercise of its functions, including its role in supervising application of the provisions of the Convention: *Refugee Convention* art 35. The UNHCR has longstanding concerns in relation to Australia's practice of mandatory detention of refugees and asylum seekers, as well as policies and practices that deny refugees and asylum seekers access to work and welfare: see, eg, UNHCR, Submission No 110 to Joint Select Committee on Australia's Immigration Detention Network, Parliament of Australia, Inquiry into Australia's Immigration Detention Network, 19 August 2011; UNHCR, 'Asylum-Seekers on Bridging Visas in Australia: Protection Gaps – UNHCR Consultation, 2013' (UNHCR Regional Representation, 16 December 2013). On the scope and content of art 35, see Walter Kälin, 'Supervising the 1951 Convention relating to the Status of Refugees: Article 35 and Beyond' in Erika Feller, Volker Türk, and Frances Nicholson (eds), *Refugee Protection in International Law: UNHCR's Global Consultations on International Protection* (Cambridge University Press, 2003) 613; Marjoleine Zieck, 'Article 35 1951 Convention/Article II 1967 Protocol' in Andreas Zimmermann (ed), *The 1951 Convention relating to the Status of Refugees and Its 1967 Protocol: A Commentary* (Oxford University Press, 2011) 1459. See generally James C Simeon (ed), *The UNHCR and the Supervision of International Refugee Law* (Cambridge University Press, 2013).

[59] In this analysis, although specific reference will from time to time be made to international refugee law, I use the terms 'international human rights framework' and 'international human rights law' in a broad sense to denote a body of law that has as its focus the protection of the human rights of the individual. This is for two reasons. First, it reflects growing recognition that international refugee law does not stand alone as a discrete body of law unaffected and unconstrained by a larger "mosaic" of international human rights law, which includes a treaty dedicated to the protection of the rights of migrant workers and members of their families. Second, it reflects my intention that this book train a wider lens on the 'migration problematic': Kate Jastram and Marilyn Achiron, *Refugee Protection: A Guide to International Refugee Law* (UNHCR/Inter-Parliamentary Union, 2001) 18.

logical point of departure. However, for two main reasons, this is not 'simply' a human rights issue. First, although the international human rights framework has been a critical development in the protection of the individual against state excess, it is a paradigm that remains a creation of states framing human rights as much as a principle of state aggrandisement as a principle of protection[60] – a paradigm in relation to which states are, simultaneously, both agents of harm and agents of protection. As such, the individual is vulnerable to the "shifting relations of fear, affection and care" by which the paradigm is calibrated.[61] And as Douzinas has observed, human rights lose their protective value against the state when fear – of, say, foreigners, refugees, or latterly people smugglers[62] – becomes their institutional logic.[63] The "fissured"[64] nature of the paradigm is brought into sharp relief when we consider also that key international human rights instruments have, with Australia's insistence, integrated many of the same legitimising assumptions that are embodied in the idea of 'absolute sovereignty'.[65]

Second, the dualist system of law under which Australia operates – whereby international law is treated as a separate body of law that must be explicitly integrated into municipal law[66] – creates a paradox in which the idea of

---

[60]   Costas Douzinas, *The End of Human Rights* (Hart, 2000) 375–6.   [61]   Ibid 376.

[62]   Migration discourse began targeting people smugglers decisively from 1999. This coincided with an increase in refugee recognition rates. In the year ended 30 June 1999, approximately 97% of Iraqis and 92% of Afghans who applied for protection in Australia were found to meet the refugee definition: Refugee Council of Australia, 'Statement on "illegal" boat arrivals' (RCOA, 15 November 1999) <https://www.refugeecouncil.org.au/docs/resources/ppapers/pp-boatarrivals-nov99.pdf>. Prior to this, references to people smuggling in parliamentary debates were rare, migration discourse typically targeting asylum seekers themselves, impugning their bona fides and dismissing them as 'economic refugees' and 'queue jumpers'. A search for 'people smuggling' in the Parliamentary Hansard yielded 2,566 results, only eight of which predate 1999. A search for 'people smugglers' yielded 2,081 results, only one of which predates 1999: searches conducted 16 December 2016 <www.aph.gov.au/Help/Federated_Search_Res ults?q=%22people%20smuggling%22> and <www.aph.gov.au/Help/Federated_Search_Resu lts?q=%22people%20smugglers%22>.

[63]   Douzinas, above n 60, 376.   [64]   Ibid.

[65]   On the influence of Australia's immigration policies and interests on the development of international law in the twentieth century, see Eve Lester, 'Internationalising Constitutional Law: An Inward-Looking Outlook' (2016) 42(2) *Australian Feminist Law Journal* 321. See also Naoko Shimazu, *Japan, Race and Equality* (Routledge, 1998); Aneurin Hughes, *Billy Hughes: Prime Minister and Controversial Founding Father of the Australian Labor Party* (Wiley, 2005) 75–83; Annemarie Devereux, *Australia and the Birth of the International Bill of Human Rights 1946–1966* (Federation Press, 2005) 206–7; John Murphy, *Evatt: A Life* (NewSouth Publishing, 2016) 82–3, 222; Opeskin, above n 43, 558–62.

[66]   Under the dualist system, international law is only enforceable at a national level to the extent that it has been expressly incorporated into municipal law. However, prima facie, Parliament is taken to intend to give effect to Australia's international obligations. To that extent, therefore, a statute should be interpreted, as far as its language permits, so that it is in conformity

sovereignty enables states voluntarily to subscribe to a set of binding obligations knowing that they are unenforceable in the event of divergent state policy or practice. This paradox means that, for reasons of sovereignty, municipal migration law- and policymakers can both gesture (rhetorically) to international legal standards and, at the same time, be juridically and institutionally unresponsive to exhortations to comply with them.[67] In other words, the gestures, exhortations, or unresponsiveness represent an entanglement of politico-legal claims and interests that impedes productive dialogue. Thus, notwithstanding that Australia's international legal obligations raise compelling questions and points of critical engagement[68] – and while more effective enforcement of those standards, such as a Bill of Rights,[69] may well improve the lives of people

---

and not in conflict with established rules of international law: *Polites v Commonwealth* (1945) 70 CLR 60, 68–9, 77, 80–8; *Commonwealth v Tasmania* (1983) 158 CLR 1 (*'Tasmanian Dams Case'*); *Minister of State for Immigration and Ethnic Affairs v Ah Hin Teoh* (1995) 183 CLR 273. The extent to which the *Constitution* can be interpreted in the light of international legal obligations was the subject of a heated judicial exchange between McHugh and Kirby JJ in *Al-Kateb* (2004) 219 CLR 562, in which McHugh J, at 589, described the notion as "heretical".

[67]   This is especially so because, unlike other comparable common law jurisdictions, Australia does not have a Bill of Rights. In Australia, protection of human rights is limited to monitoring and promoting human rights (see *Australian Human Rights Commission Act 1986* (Cth)), scrutiny by a Parliamentary Joint Committee on Human Rights and the requirement for Statements of Compatibility to accompany all new Bills and disallowable legislative instruments (*Human Rights (Parliamentary Scrutiny) Act 2011* (Cth)). On the relationship between international law and the Australian legal system, see generally Hilary Charlesworth et al, *No Country Is an Island: Australia and International Law* (UNSW Press, 2006).

[68]   Some recent examples include: Andreas Schloenhardt and Colin Craig, '"Turning Back the Boats": Australia's Interdiction of Irregular Migrants at Sea' (2015) 27(4) *International Journal of Refugee Law* 536, 567–70; Jane McAdam, 'Australia and Asylum Seekers' (2013) 25(3) *International Journal of Refugee Law* 435; Human Rights Law Centre, Written Statement Submitted by the Human Rights Law Centre, a Non-Governmental Organization in Special Consultative Status, UN GAOR, 24th sess, Agenda Item 4, UN Doc A/HRC/24/NGO/27 (24 August 2013); ABC Radio, 'Greens Ask the Federal Police to Investigate if the Government's Breached Its Own Anti-People Smuggling Laws', PM, 7 May 2014 (Ben Saul) <www.abc.net .au/pm/content/2014/s3999932.htm>.

[69]   See, eg, Jane McAdam and Fiona Chong, *Refugees: Why Seeking Asylum Is Legal and Australia's Policies Are Not* (NewSouth Publishing, 2014); Jane McAdam, 'Leading on Protection' in Bob Douglas and Jo Wodak (eds), *Refugees and Asylum Seekers: Finding a Better Way* (Australia21, 2013) 11, 12; Susan Kneebone, 'The Australian Story: Asylum Seekers outside the Law' in Susan Kneebone (ed), *Refugees, Asylum Seekers and the Rule of Law: Comparative Perspectives* (Cambridge University Press, 2009) 171, 173, 189; Angus Francis, 'The Review of Australia's Asylum Laws and Policies: A Case For Strengthening Parliament's Role in Protecting Rights through Post-Enactment Scrutiny' (2008) 32(1) *Melbourne University Law Review* 83. Under the common law, there is a presumption that the Parliament does not intend to limit fundamental rights. This is commonly how the absence of a Bill of Rights is defended. However, that presumption is negated if an intention to interfere with fundamental rights is clearly manifested by unmistakable and unambiguous language: *Coco v The Queen* (1994) 179 CLR 427, 437.

subject to the policies I problematise – as things stand, not only is the international human rights framework unable to provide all the answers,[70] but also it cannot sufficiently explain *how* the laws and policies I have identified have become thinkable. For these reasons I felt the pull to put the human rights dilemma[71] to one side and take a different approach: to hold my normative inclination lightly in order to think more deeply about what law- and policy-makers are doing by thinking about how and why they feel impelled, able, and entitled to make a claim on sovereignty in absolute terms.

1.2 UNDERSTANDING OUR JURIDICAL INHERITANCE AND ITS USAGES

The central purpose of this book is to explain how policies such as mandatory detention and planned destitution have come to be characterised as lawful and legitimate institutional responses to unsolicited migration. To do this, I engage in a close analysis of original text and archival material in order to deepen the juridical account of 'absolute sovereignty' in the making of migration law, both historically and contemporarily. To this end, I explore how the foreigner-sovereign relation has shaped migration lawmaking in two parts, using two forms of critical engagement: genealogy[72] and discourse analysis.[73] This pairing helps deepen our understanding of how 'absolute sovereignty' has taken shape doctrinally and politically, and how it is used discursively in particular circumstances. By using these two forms of critical engagement, I make visible continuities and discontinuities between legal traditions of the

---

[70] Guy S Goodwin-Gill, 'Foreword' in Satvinder Singh Juss, *International Migration and Global Justice* (Ashgate, 2006) xvi. For a creative and compelling engagement with the generation and avoidance of 'the human rights encounter' between the state (or its agents) and the refugee in the context of maritime migration, see Itamar Mann, *Humanity at Sea: Maritime Migration and the Foundations of International Law* (Cambridge University Press, 2016). For a critical engagement with international law's imperial history and its well-documented intimacy with the powerful, see Sundhya Pahuja, *Decolonising International Law: Development, Economic Growth and the Politics of Universality* (Cambridge University Press, 2011).

[71] For a discussion of the tension between rights claims made by the state and those made by asylum seekers, see Catherine Dauvergne, 'The Dilemma of Rights Discourses for Refugees' (2000) 23(3) *University of New South Wales Law Journal* 56; Savitri Taylor, 'The Importance of Human Rights Talk in Asylum Seeker Advocacy: A Response to Catherine Dauvergne' (2001) 24(1) *University of New South Wales Law Journal* 191.

[72] I use 'genealogy' in a broad Foucaultian sense, in keeping with Foucault's hope that scholars, activists, and writers would find value in his concepts as a 'toolkit' to advance analysis and facilitate advocacy: Ben Golder and Peter Fitzpatrick, *Foucault's Law* (Routledge, 2009) 5.

[73] Michel Foucault, *The Archaeology of Knowledge* (A M Sheridan-Smith trans, Routledge, 1989) [trans of: *L'archéologie du savoir* (first published 1969)]; Nietzsche, *Genealogy of Morals*, above n 56.

past and discourses of the present. I am interested in how legal discourses have given particular shape to our juridical inheritance of the foreigner-sovereign relation (most notably, 'absolute sovereignty') – that is, *how* that inheritance was authorised, executed, or performed (genealogy), not just what authority it purports to carry doctrinally or politically.[74] I am also interested in how we use that inheritance in the contemporary context (discourse analysis).

Reflecting on migration law's founding assumption that there is an absolute sovereign right to exclude and condition the entry and stay of aliens is important because it impels us to think more carefully and consciously about what migration law- and policymakers do and why they do it.[75] In this regard, it is important to make clear that, while I reflect on the *assumption* that there is a foundational account of the making of migration law, this is an intellectual endeavour that does not seek or insist upon there being such an account.[76] Indeed, my inquiry reveals that there *is* no foundational account of the making of migration law. Instead, my argument is that the foreigner-sovereign relation, and 'absolute sovereignty' as a particular form of that relation, are elements of migration lawmaking that are what Owen calls *contingent historical artefacts*, whose authority can be coherently taken as an object of critical reflection.[77]

In critically engaging with the idea of 'absolute sovereignty', I am mindful of the complexity of the broader concept of sovereignty, which has been a dominant feature of international legal discourse since the sixteenth century and migration lawmaking since the nineteenth century. As Mathew has noted, 'sovereignty' remains "an ill-defined term in international law."[78] Likewise, Bartelson argues that sovereignty "has eluded almost every attempt of rigorous definition and conceptual analysis."[79] As he asserts, "the relationship between the very *term* sovereignty, the *concept* of sovereignty and the *reality* of sovereignty is historically open, contingent and unstable".[80] While these observations remind us that we can think about the idea of sovereignty in many

[74]	Shaunnagh Dorsett and Shaun McVeigh, *Jurisdiction* (Routledge, 2012) 54.
[75]	Margaret Davies, *Asking the Law Question* (Law Book Company, 2008) 1.
[76]	David Owen, *Nietzsche's Genealogy of Morality* (McGill-Queen's University Press, 2007) 6.
[77]	This is in keeping with the Nietzschean approach to genealogy: Nietzsche, *Genealogy of Morals*, above n 56, 8; Owen, above n 76, 6.
[78]	Penelope Mathew, 'Sovereignty and the Right to Seek Asylum: The Case of Cambodian Asylum-Seekers in Australia' (1994) 15 *Australian Year Book of International Law* 35, 45; Kim Rubenstein, 'Citizenship, Sovereignty and Migration: Australia's Exclusive Approach to Membership of the Community' (2002) 13(2) *Public Law Review* 102, 104.
[79]	Jens Bartelson, *A Genealogy of Sovereignty* (Cambridge University Press, 1995) 13.
[80]	Ibid 2 (emphases added). In contrast to Bartelson, I consider 'absolute sovereignty' to be historically contingent, though not necessarily unstable.

different ways, it is important to emphasise that my focus here is on a particular form of sovereignty (the power to exclude) and how it has become a practice in a particular context (the making of migration law) in a particular setting (Australia). That is, within this more limited frame of reference, my focus is on the practice of sovereignty – and more specifically 'absolute sovereignty' – as a particular style of legal and political thought rather than treating it as a coherent concept. I do not, therefore, tackle what Bartelson describes as the "essentially essentialist question" of what sovereignty *is*[81] or examine how effective it is.

So, as the description of my methodology elaborates, my approach is to deepen the account of the 'how' of migration lawmaking. That is, I consider how the foreigner-sovereign relation has been given expression in the making of migration law through the emergence of 'absolute sovereignty' as both juridical form and state practice, and how this has produced particular kinds of policies. If we understand sovereignty in this way, we can then see how – in order to think about why – certain ideas, practices, forms of engagement, and techniques[82] have enabled the doctrinal, genealogical, and discursive dimensions of the foreigner-sovereign relation to shape 'absolute sovereignty' as a form of authority and as a practice. Here, I reiterate that I use 'absolute sovereignty' as a term of art rather than treating it as a simple (and impenetrable) doctrinal statement of authority.

1.2.1 *Genealogy: The Foreigner and the Sovereign*

As ideas, both the foreigner and the sovereign have contemporary effects. They are also ideas that have a history and, together, they carry authority drawn from legal tradition and doctrine.[83] But when we speak of the 'foreigner', of and to whom do we speak? What bearing has the identity of the foreigner had on the way in which the power of the sovereign has been conceptualised as an absolute power of exclusion in the context of migration? Adapting an observation of Nietzsche, do we problematise the claim of 'absolute sovereignty', or do we accept it to be a *hallowed doctrinal place* where our jurists can take a rest from consideration of law's effects?[84] In sum, if we are to think carefully,

---

[81] Ibid.
[82] For the purposes of this book, questions of technique consider the formal or practical manner in which 'absolute sovereignty' has emerged, linguistically and technically. Dorsett and McVeigh, above n 74, 55; James E K Parker, *Acoustic Jurisprudence: Listening to the Trial of Simon Bikindi* (Oxford University Press, 2015) 39.
[83] Owen, above n 76, 1.
[84] "It is clear that up to now, morality has been no problem at all but rather that on which, after all mistrust, discord and contradiction, one could agree – the hallowed place of peace where

differently, and even disruptively about what it means for our backstory of 'absolute sovereignty' to have been received uncritically into contemporary migration law, we need to start by thinking about its past.

Part I of this book offers a genealogy of the different ways in which the foreigner-sovereign relation has been juridically constructed and authorised. By 'genealogy', I mean a (re-)descriptive process of how juridical relationships are organised and authorised. The genealogy pays close textual attention to legal arguments of the past in order to make visible how the foreigner and the sovereign have, as ideas and relationally, been used and shaped into a discourse of 'absolute sovereignty'.[85]

The genealogy comprises three phases, which I detail in the next subsection. Together they show how a diverse juridical history has positioned 'absolute sovereignty' at the forefront of migration lawmaking. They provide insight into how elemental legal frameworks and traditions of international law, the common law, and constitutional law have coalesced and been used in the making of migration law to ascribe a centrality to 'absolute sovereignty', enabling us to see how these frameworks and traditions have shaped contemporary migration discourses. Following from this, the discourse analysis of mandatory detention and planned destitution offered in Part II draws out lines of continuity and discontinuity between past and present. This makes visible the ways in which contemporary migration discourse remains captive to its historical antecedents through the use of 'absolute sovereignty'.

1.2.1.1 Three Genealogical Phases

The genealogy of the foreigner-sovereign relation in early international law (Chapter 2) examines particular treatises of four key international jurists – Vitoria, Grotius, Pufendorf, and Vattel – selected on account of their enduring influence through theoretical and canonical texts in both public and international law concerning the movement of people.[86] This part of the genealogy has the discrete and limited purpose of making visible *who* the 'foreigner' was

thinkers took a rest from themselves, took a deep breath, and felt revived": Friedrich Nietzsche, *The Gay Science* (Bernard Williams ed, Josefine Nauckhoff and Adrian Del Caro trans, Cambridge University Press, 2001) 202 [trans of: *Die fröhliche Wissenschaft* (first published 1882)]; Owen, above n 76, 4.

85 Owen, above n 76, 3; Anne Orford, 'In Praise of Description' (2012) 25(3) *Leiden Journal of International Law* 609, 609.

86 See, eg, Richard Plender, *International Migration Law* (Martinus Nijhoff, 2nd ed, 1988) 61–94; Guy S Goodwin-Gill, *International Law and the Movement of Persons between States* (Clarendon Press, 1978) 94–6; James A R Nafziger, 'The General Admission of Aliens under International Law' (1983) 77(4) *American Journal of International Law* 804.

in the work of each of these publicists, concluding that each conceptualised the foreigner not as an outsider, but as a (European) insider. The analysis in this chapter enables us to see that the foreigner is a mutable figure. This is important because, as we will see in Chapter 3, the conceptualisation of the foreigner changed in the nineteenth century, a time when the central preoccupation in an expanding common law world was with regulating the activities of the foreigner as non-European outsider. Recognition of this shift is crucial to understanding how relations of power changed in the making of migration law. It enables us to notice how the foreigner-sovereign relation was reconceptualised in the face of particular historical contingencies and, in this connection, to see the points of emergence of a discourse of 'absolute sovereignty' as a relational frame.

In Chapter 3,[87] I examine nineteenth-century common law jurisprudence of the Privy Council and the US Supreme Court and the international legal authorities on which this jurisprudence relies.[88] I also examine in that chapter the legislative text during the same period in order to chart the emergence of restrictive migration laws designed to exclude non-European outsiders – laws whose legitimacy was endorsed and justified through the nascent common law doctrine of 'absolute sovereignty'. The chapter further elaborates the point that when the foreigner changes from ('civilised') European insider to ('barbarian') non-European outsider, a common law doctrine of 'absolute sovereignty' begins to emerge. It shows how this occurred within a broader context of the political economy of the movement of people – a context in which migration lawmaking was consonant with a political-economic desire to regulate race and labour.

Chapter 4 concludes the genealogy with an examination of the way in which the foreigner and the sovereign were brought into relation through a process of constitutionalisation. This shows how a particular form of 'absolute sovereignty' secured its constitutional place. It also makes visible how 'absolute sovereignty' in its constitutional form was used and consolidated legislatively and jurisprudentially. To this end, Chapter 4 studies key aspects of the political, legislative, and judicial record from the Federation of Australia until mid-century. Drawing on constitutional convention debates, parliamentary

---

[87] Substantial parts of Chapter 3 have been published in Eve Lester, 'Myth-Conceiving Sovereignty: The Legacy of the Nineteenth Century' in Kim Rubenstein, Mark Nolan, and Fiona Jenkins (eds), *Allegiance and Identity in a Globalised World* (Cambridge University Press, 2014) 354.

[88] Although some of this analysis considers the jurisdictions of other white settler societies, the focus of this analysis is on jurisprudence impacting on the development of a common law jurisprudence in Australia.

debates, legislative text, and judicial pronouncements, I show how the foreigner-sovereign relation was shaped in Australia.

1.2.1.2 What Work Does Genealogy Do?

As both history and critique, the work of genealogy has a number of elements.
First, in a Foucaultian sense, it offers an account of the way in which relations
of power between the foreigner and the sovereign are constructed and
authorised.[89] In other words, rather than treating as impenetrable truths the
characterisation of the foreigner as outsider and the sovereign right to exclude
her as absolute, it treats them both as having been (juridically) produced,
inscribed, and shaped by discourse and relations of power. This genealogy
therefore pays close attention to the language, purpose, and shaping of arguments in the texts of key publicists, judicial decisions, legislation, and the
institutional archive. In doing so, it reveals how interpretative assumptions
about sovereignty as absolute and the foreigner as outsider have been made
and authorised – assumptions that, as Part II shows, have produced particular
kinds of contemporary effects.

This account does not claim to chart the 'making of migration law' as a
progress story, exhibiting a teleological structure across the march of history, or
indeed having a developmental or degenerative logic.[90] Rather, it sees its
history as comprising a constellation of responses to and rationalisations for
contingent events, whether inadvertent, improvised, or intentional.[91] So, by
examining the foreigner-sovereign relation in its earlier appearances in legal
discourse, it becomes possible to see how an emergent claim of 'absolute
sovereignty' was framed and, in turn, how 'absolute sovereignty' *as a discourse*
was inscribed, used, and shaped.

Second, genealogy provides a way of accessing the repertoires and patterns of
argument that have produced and shaped conceptualisations of the foreigner as
a juridical figure and sovereignty as a form of independent authority – that is, a
way of seeing how certain styles of argument are used to (re)situate the foreigner
within the foreigner-sovereign relation. And as Part II shows, these repertoires
and patterns of argument are still reproduced and shaped by lawmakers as they
think, write, and speak about them. Genealogy therefore enables us to see and

---

[89]   Michel Foucault, 'Nietzsche, Genealogy, History' in Donald F Bouchard (ed), *Language,
Counter-Memory, Practice: Selected Essays and Interviews by Michel Foucault* (Donald F
Bouchard and Sherry Simon trans, Cornell University Press 1977) 139 [trans of: 'Nietzsche, la
généalogie, l'histoire' (first published 1971)].
[90]   Owen, above n 76, 4–5.   [91]   Ibid 6.

think critically about where and how such arguments have been drawn from earlier texts and how they have been reused and/or reshaped.

Finally, the genealogy enables us to recognise the discourses of the present *as* discourses (rather than universal truths) that are historically produced within and through public and international legal traditions. Genealogy is, in this sense, a *way in* to understanding 'absolute sovereignty' as the product of a complex institutional story of ideas, practices, and forms of engagement that carries across time and space. It is a story that resonates even if no necessary or direct connection can be established between the history of the ideas or concepts underpinning 'absolute sovereignty' and their present discursive purpose, value, or form.[92]

1.2.1.3 The Movement of Meaning: Why Genealogy Is Useful

Methodology is a choice, and each choice has its value and purpose – as well as its limits and critics.[93] A number of methodological approaches to this inquiry might be possible. For example, a sociological inquiry may yield insights into political and institutional culture in the context of (global or parochial) social and political dynamics that other methods may fail to reach. Likewise, a contextualist historian's approach would offer understandings of the meaning of text in its 'proper' time and place.[94] However, while the juridical texts and institutional archive on which I draw are likely to be the same texts and archival material on which a contextualist (legal) historian or sociologist might draw, as a public and international lawyer what I am asking of this material is different.[95]

As Orford observes, legal concepts, arguments, and structures are "constantly being retrieved as a source or rationalisation of a present obligation."[96]

---

[92] Ibid 64.

[93] For critiques of genealogy as a method, see Randall Lesaffer, 'International Law and Its History: The Story of an Unrequited Love' in Matthew Craven, Malgosia Fitzmaurice, and Maria Vogiatzi (eds), *Time, History and International Law* (Martinus Nijhoff, 2007) 27, 34–5; Georg Cavallar, 'Vitoria, Grotius, Pufendorf, Wolff and Vattel: Accomplices of European Colonialism and Exploitation or True Cosmopolitans?' (2008) 10 *Journal of the History of International Law* 181; Ian Hunter, 'Global Justice and Regional Metaphysics: On the Critical History of the Law of Nature and Nations' in Shaunnagh Dorsett and Ian Hunter (eds), *Law and Politics in British Colonial Thought: Transpositions of Empire* (Palgrave Macmillan, 2010) 11.

[94] Anne Orford, 'On International Legal Method' (2013) 1(1) *London Review of International Law* 166, 175. See especially Quentin Skinner, 'Meaning and Understanding in the History of Ideas' (1969) 8 *History and Theory* 3; Quentin Skinner, *Visions of Politics: Volume I – Regarding Method* (Cambridge University Press, 2002) 103 (chapter titled 'Interpretation and the Understanding of Speech Acts').

[95] Orford, 'On International Legal Method', above n 94, 169.   [96] Ibid 175.

In that sense, their proper time and place is constantly being re-ascribed through the (legal) process of retrieval. This is what she means when she says that the study of law requires attention to the "movement of meaning".[97] It is also why the study of legal argument does not sit easily with the methodological framework of the contextualist historian. Law as a discipline is both past and present. It is therefore more volatile than the events and texts of a particular time and place. This is why it lends itself to genealogy, a form of inquiry that is temporally and spatially responsive.

So, although I neither overlook historical context nor underestimate its value, I am reading the materials with a different purpose and emphasis – that is, for the history they reveal of the arguments underpinning the foreigner-sovereign relation and certain conceptualisations of 'absolute sovereignty'. I do so with a view to elucidating how these dimensions in the making of migration law have been used, reused, shaped, and reshaped, and in order to explore their contemporary resonances and effects in migration discourse. This is genealogy. It is also an approach that is emblematic of law as a discipline, the study of past texts and orthodoxies to discern the nature and scope of present obligations.[98] Like law, the purpose of genealogy is to help us understand a context that is, temporally and spatially, different to the historical context(s) from which it draws.[99] It is therefore not surprising that genealogy resonates as a methodology for legal scholars interested in critically engaging with the present effects of the past.[100] Indeed, as Orford has observed, law lends itself to genealogy precisely because it depends on the transmission of concepts, language, and norms across time and space.[101]

As the following section elaborates, Part II of the book shifts into a different but related mode of inquiry. Through two case studies – mandatory detention (Chapter 5) and planned destitution (Chapter 6) – I explore the contemporary resonances and effects of the discourse of 'absolute sovereignty' in migration lawmaking.

1.2.2 *Discourse Analysis: Mandatory Detention and Planned Destitution*

The methodological shift to discourse analysis provides a way of deepening our understanding of the continuities and discontinuities between the legal traditions and orthodoxies of the past and current politico-legal discourses of

---

[97]   Ibid.   [98]   Ibid 171.   [99]   Owen, above n 76, 7.
[100]   See, eg, Antony Anghie, *Imperialism, Sovereignty and the Making of International Law* (Cambridge University Press, 2005); Anne Orford, *International Authority and the Responsibility to Protect* (Cambridge University Press, 2011).
[101]   Orford, 'On International Legal Method', above n 94, 175.

migration. In other words, the analysis makes visible how the meaning of 'absolute sovereignty' in contemporary migration law- and policymaking remains captive to its historical antecedents. At this point it is important to clarify how exactly I engage with discourse in this book.[102]

First, discourse analysis enables me to study the structures and strategies of language use in particular situations, for particular purposes, and by particular users.[103] In other words, I study language use by a variety of actors – such as politicians, jurists, adjudicators, and public administrators – in a range of contexts, whether parliamentary debates and other political discourse, the courtroom, judicial pronouncements, legislation and its extrinsic material, or policy statements and guidance. This includes verbal (and non-verbal)[104] communications and written text, and even the absence of text (law's silences).[105]

Second, discourse analysis provides a way of thinking about the language of migration law- and policymaking as a system of thought and practice, not in a mysterious way but in an ordinary way.[106] In other words, it considers the

---

[102] The plurality of approaches to discourse and discourse theory confirms discourse analysis to be a broad church. For example, van Dijk argues that "Discourse Analysis is not a method of research, but a (cross) discipline": Teun A van Dijk (ed), *Discourse Studies: A Multidisciplinary Introduction* (Sage, 2nd ed, 2011) 6. In a similar vein, Chouliarki and Fairclough describe critical discourse analysis "as contributing to a field of critical research on late modernity [rather than] a particular theory or narrative": Lilie Chouliarki and Norman Fairclough, *Discourse in Late Modernity: Rethinking Critical Discourse Analysis* (Edinburgh University Press, 1999) 3. This plurality is at once liberating and potentially dangerous, for its seemingly endless possibilities mean that it risks being taken for granted: Gary Wickham, 'Foucault and Law' in Reza Banakar and Max Travers (eds), *An Introduction to Law and Social Theory* (Hart, 2002) 249, 256; Rajah, above n 31, 55.

[103] Van Dijk, *Discourse Studies*, above n 102, 2.

[104] As Fairclough observes, talk is interwoven with what he calls "visuals" (gesture, facial expression, movement, posture) "to such an extent that it cannot be properly understood without reference to these 'extras'". They can complement, contradict, or otherwise change meaning: Norman Fairclough, *Language and Power* (Routledge, 2nd ed, 2013) 22–3. Like tone of voice, visuals do not ordinarily appear on the public record. Although this is beginning to change in some jurisdictions, this analysis does not extend its reach to them. On law's capacity to engage with sound, see Parker, *Acoustic Jurisprudence*, above n 82.

[105] Marianne Constable, *Just Silences: The Limits and Possibilities of Modern Law* (Princeton University Press, 2005); Hilary Charlesworth, 'Feminist Methods in International Law' (1999) 93(2) *American Journal of International Law* 379, 381. Indeed, applying Wickham's reading, legal discourses may even extend to the design of the physical arenas in which those discourses take place (or, I would suggest, as a reflection of those discourses) and the comportment of the range of actors. Although it is beyond the scope of this book, this suggests that legal discourses involved in the regulation of unsolicited migration would extend to the design of places of detention, the comportment and conversations of and between detainees and staff, security arrangements and practices, and access to them: Wickham, above n 102, 257.

[106] Wickham, above n 102, 257.

linguistic strategies and attributes of migration law- and policymaking, their effects, and migration law's role in producing and encoding relations of power.[107] Before elaborating further, the following two sections outline my rationale for selecting the case studies and explain the shift from genealogy to discourse analysis.

1.2.2.1 Selection of the Case Studies

The effects of mandatory detention and planned destitution to which the prologue alludes are well documented.[108] They are the centrepieces of this book not only on this account, but also because both their substance and their success (in legal and policy terms) have provided the scaffolding for the development of more recent policy responses.[109] These later responses include

---

[107]   Fairclough, above n 104, 1.

[108]   On mandatory detention see, eg, Human Rights and Equal Opportunity Commission (HREOC), 'Those Who've Come Across the Seas: Detention of Unauthorised Arrivals' (Report, 1998); Aamer Sultan and Kevin O'Sullivan, 'Psychological Disturbances in Asylum Seekers Held in Long Term Detention: A Participant–Observer Account' (2001) 175(11) *Medical Journal of Australia* 593; Zachary Steel and Derrick M Silove, 'The Mental Health Implications of Detaining Asylum Seekers' (2001) 175(11) *Medical Journal of Australia* 596; HREOC, 'A Last Resort? National Inquiry into Children in Immigration Detention' (Report, April 2004); *C v Australia*, UN Doc CCPR/C/76/D/900/1999. On planned destitution see, eg, Anne McNevin, 'Seeking Safety, Not Charity: A Report in Support of Work-Rights for Asylum-Seekers Living in the Community on Bridging Visa E' (Network of Asylum Seeker Agencies Victoria, March 2005) 28; ASRC, 'Destitute and Uncertain', above n 19, 5. See also CPD, Senate, 8 September 2009, 5962–66 (Concetta Fierravanti-Wells), regarding Motion for Disallowance, *Migration Amendment Regulations 2009 (No 6)* (Cth). From November 2012, on account of overcrowding in detention centres, 'boat people' could be released into the community on bridging visas but without permission to work: Bowen, above n 14; ASRC, 'Asylum Seekers and the Right to Work' (Policy Position Paper, March 2013); Hartley and Fleay, above n 14. Since December 2014, the practice has been to issue work rights more widely but still on a discretionary basis: Refugee Advice and Casework Service (RACS), 'Work Rights for People Who Arrived by Boat', *RACS Fact Sheet* (RACS, October 2015) <www.racs.org.au/wp-content/uploads/RACS-F ACT-SHEET-Work-Rights-for-people-who-arrived-by-boat.pdf>; RACS, 'BVEs and Work Rights for People Who Arrived by Boat, *RACS Fact Sheet* (RACS, updated August 2016) <www.racs.org.au/wp-content/uploads/2016/10/RACS-FACT-SHEET-BVEs-and-Work-Ri ghts-for-people-who-arrived-by-boat-aug-2016.pdf>; RACS, 'Briefing Note for Lawyers: Bridging Visas for People Seeking Asylum during Judicial Review', *RACS Fact Sheet* (RACS, updated October 2016) <www.racs.org.au/wp-content/uploads/2016/10/RACS-FA CT-SHEET-Briefing-note-for-lawyers-on-Bridging-Visas-for-asylum-seekers-at-Judicial-Re view.pdf>.

[109]   This point is also made by Kneebone, who describes later policies as a "natural outgrowth of restrictive and deterrent policies to refugees which had developed over the previous decade and which demonstrated the power of the executive to drive a legislative agenda to keep asylum seekers apart from the Australian community": Kneebone, above n 69, 172.

invocation of the prerogative power to exclude or expel aliens;[110] extraterritorial detention and processing of 'boat people' on the Republic of Nauru, Manus Island, Papua New Guinea,[111] and even on the high seas;[112] excision of territory from Australia's 'migration zone',[113] including the Australian mainland (in order to block access by 'boat people' to Australian protection procedures);[114]

[110] The scope of the prerogative power was considered by the Federal Court of Australia in the *Tampa* cases, which followed the 26 August 2001 rescue of 433 'boat people' in international waters near Christmas Island by the Norwegian vessel *MV Tampa*. The 'boat people' were mostly Afghans. The Australian government argued that the 'boat people' were the responsibility of Indonesia and Norway. Attempts to land them in Australia were frustrated by the intervention of SAS troops: *Victorian Council for Civil Liberties Inc v Minister for Immigration and Multicultural Affairs* (2001) 110 FCR 452 ('*VCCL v MIMA*'); *Vadarlis* (2001) 110 FCR 491. See also: *Detention on the High Seas Case* (2015) 255 CLR 514; *Nauru Detention Case* (2016) 257 CLR 42. Note that in Australia, the historical distinction between the terms 'non-citizen' and 'alien', whereby the latter did not include a British subject, no longer applies. With this in mind, this book treats the term 'alien' according to its historical context, recognising that 'non-citizen' and 'alien' are now regarded as synonymous: *Nolan v Minister for Immigration and Ethnic Affairs* (1988) 165 CLR 178, 183–4; *Lim* (1992) 176 CLR 1, 25.

[111] Offshore processing, introduced in 2001 and known as the 'Pacific Solution', was supported by the following legislative framework: *Border Protection (Validation and Enforcement Powers) Act 2001* (Cth), *Migration Amendment (Excision from Migration Zone) Act 2001* (Cth); *Migration Amendment (Excision from Migration Zone) (Consequential Provisions) Act 2001* (Cth). For a description of the Pacific Solution framework see, eg, Penelope Mathew, 'Australian Refugee Protection in the Wake of the *Tampa*' (2002) 96(3) *American Journal of International Law* 661. In 2010, attempts to reinvigorate offshore processing through the establishment of a regional processing scheme in Malaysia were found to be flawed: *Plaintiff M61/2010E v Commonwealth* (2010) 243 CLR 319 ('*Offshore Processing Case*'); *Plaintiff M70/2011 v Minister for Immigration and Citizenship* (2011) 244 CLR 144 ('*Malaysian Declaration Case*'). In response to these cases, further legislation designed to facilitate offshore processing was passed: *Migration Legislation Amendment (Regional Processing and Other Measures) Act 2012* (Cth). In August 2012, a proposal to reopen processing facilities on Nauru and Manus Island was described as a "circuit breaker" to be used in the "short term": Houston, Aristotle, and L'Estrange, above n 38, 47. For a description of conditions on Nauru and Manus Island, see: UNHCR, 'UNHCR Monitoring Visit to Manus Island, Papua New Guinea: 23 to 25 October 2013' (26 November 2013); UNHCR, 'UNHCR Monitoring Visit to the Republic of Nauru: 7 to 9 October 2013' (26 November 2013). For a recent exposition of extraterritorial detention and processing of asylum seekers, see Madeline Gleeson, *Offshore: Behind the Wire on Manus and Nauru* (NewSouth Publishing, 2016).

[112] See *Detention on the High Seas Case* (2015) 255 CLR 514; see also *Maritime Powers Act 2013* (Cth); *Migration and Maritime Powers Legislation Amendment (Resolving the Asylum Legacy Caseload) Act 2014* (Cth).

[113] *Migration Amendment (Excision from Migration Zone) Act 2001* (Cth); *Migration Amendment (Excision from Migration Zone) (Consequential Provisions) Act 2001* (Cth). For the definition of 'migration zone', see *Migration Act* s 5.

[114] *Migration Amendment (Unauthorised Maritime Arrivals and Other Measures) Act 2013* (Cth); see also Houston, Aristotle, and L'Estrange, above n 38, 52 [3.72]–[3.73]. Note that an attempt by a previous government to introduce similar legislation was shelved after it was met with strong opposition: Migration Amendment (Designated Unauthorised Arrivals) Bill 2006 (Cth). For discussion of this, see, eg, Kneebone, above n 69, 196.

the 'no advantage' policy (whereby privations and processing delays imposed on 'boat people' were framed as ensuring that they gain no advantage for arriving by boat over people in other countries seeking humanitarian resettlement to Australia);[115] and, finally, what might be termed the 'no way, never' policy. This last policy took effect from 19 July 2013 and is encapsulated in the following declaration about 'boat people' seeking Australia's protection:[116] *No way. You will not make Australia home.*[117] Attempts have recently been made to shore up this policy by imposing a lifetime visa ban for post–19 July 2013 boat arrivals.[118] As noted earlier, even as mandatory detention and planned

---

[115]   According to the 'no advantage principle' conceived by the expert panel on asylum seekers, asylum seekers should "gain no benefit by choosing not to seek protection through established mechanisms": Houston, Aristotle, and L'Estrange, above n 38, 8, 14, 20. Although the term has fallen out of use due to policy changes in 2013 (see below n 117), 'no advantage' is a policy term that has never had any formal legal meaning, and official explanations offered as to its scope and content have lacked clarity: see, eg, Evidence to Senate Legal and Constitutional Affairs Legislation Committee, Parliament of Australia, *Supplementary Budget Estimates 2012–2013 (Immigration and Citizenship)*, Canberra, 15 October 2012, 31, 145–60 (Martin Bowles, Secretary, Department of Immigration and Citizenship). Central to Bowles' lack of explanation as to its content was that any detail on what it meant in practice would provide a 'how to' guide to people smugglers: at 31 (Bowles). On UNHCR's concerns about the 'no advantage principle', see letter from António Guterres, High Commissioner for Refugees, to the Hon Chris Bowen MP, Minister for Immigration and Citizenship of Australia, 9 October 2012.

[116]   In current political discourse, 'boat people' are, under instruction from the Immigration Minister, officially described as "illegal maritime arrivals": Evidence to Senate Legal and Constitutional Affairs Legislation Committee, Parliament of Australia, *Supplementary Budget Estimates 2013–2014 (Immigration and Border Protection)*, Canberra, 19 November 2013, 31–2 (Martin Bowles, Secretary, DIBP; Vicki Parker, Chief Lawyer, DIBP). On use of the term 'illegalised' refugees and immigrants, see Harald Bauder, 'Why We Should Use the Term "Illegalized" Refugee or Immigrant: A Commentary' (2014) 26(3) *International Journal of Refugee Law* 327.

[117]   See, eg, Australian Customs and Border Protection Service <www.customs.gov.au/>; see also Kevin Rudd, 'Prime Minister Kevin Rudd – Address to the Nation' on *YouTube* (19 July 2013) 00:00:31, 00:00:38 <https://www.youtube.com/watch?v=kIapYIBRZIs>, where Rudd declares that asylum seekers arriving by boat "have no prospect of being resettled in Australia" and, later, that they will "never permanently" live in Australia; AusCustomsNews, 'No Way. You Will Not Make Australia Home – English' on *YouTube* (15 April 2014) <www.youtube.com/watch?v=rT12WH4a92w>.

[118]   Senate Legal and Constitutional Affairs Legislation Committee, Parliament of Australia, *Inquiry into Migration Legislation Amendment (Regional Processing Cohort) Bill 2016 [Provisions]* 5 (Michael Pezzullo, Secretary, DIBP). Migration Legislation Amendment (Regional Processing Cohort) Bill 2016 (Cth) was introduced into Parliament on 8 November 2016 and was passed by the House of Representatives on 10 November 2016. The Bill, yet to be passed by the Senate, would have retroactive effect, applying to all 'boat people' seeking to enter Australia on or after 19 July 2013. In its aforementioned report the Senate Legal and Constitutional Affairs Legislation Committee recommended, by a majority, that the Senate pass the Bill: at 13 [2.35]. Cf Parliamentary Joint Committee on Human Rights, *Human Rights Scrutiny Report* (Report 9, 2016) 15–22.

destitution seem to be overshadowed by the stridency of these responses, they are foundational to current policy, and it is for this reason that they are the focus of this study.

As case studies, mandatory detention and planned destitution also exemplify two different approaches to border and immigration control. On the one hand, mandatory detention is conceptualised as a tool for control of Australia's territorial borders – that is, as a tool of physical exclusion. On the other, the circumscription of work and welfare rights, which can be understood as a technique for creating a 'virtual' or conceptual border,[119] is a tool of social and economic exclusion.[120] To link the case studies back to the genealogy of the foreigner-sovereign relation, each is a contemporary manifestation of the absolute sovereign right to *exclude* (in the case of mandatory detention) and to *condition entry and stay* (in the case of denial of work and welfare). In this connection, discourse analysis can help us understand how we make contemporary use of 'absolute sovereignty' as a discourse.

Mandatory detention and planned destitution are therefore central to an analysis of contemporary migration law, policy, and practice on three grounds. First, they remain core features of Australia's current migration policy. Second, they underpin more recent policy formulations that draw on the discourse of 'absolute sovereignty'. Finally, and arguably most importantly, it is their success (in legal and policy terms) that has provided law- and policymakers with a platform from which to devise and perform newer policies, including extraterritorial processing, excision of territory, 'no advantage', and 'no way, never'.

1.2.2.2 A Methodological Transition: From Genealogy to Discourse Analysis

Genealogy, as I have outlined above, is a (re)descriptive process that enables me to offer an account of how particular juridical relations are authorised and, in the light of that, to re-evaluate the legal traditions we have inherited in the making of migration law. The prologue to this book introduced the contemporary problem whereby certain policies and practices that run counter to the notion of a common humanity are regarded as lawful and legitimate institutional responses to unsolicited migration. This provides context for the genealogical inquiry into the foreigner-sovereign relation undertaken in Part I. In Part II, I return to the contemporary problem through the examination of the

---

[119] On the concept and development of the border as a kinetic structure, see Thomas Nail, *Theory of the Border* (Oxford University Press, 2016).

[120] See also Étienne Balibar, *We, the People of Europe? Reflections on Transnational Citizenship* (James Swenson trans, Princeton University Press, 2004) 23 [trans of: *Nous, citoyens d'Europe: Les Frontières, l'État, le peuple* (first published 2001)].

two case studies. Here, the analysis shifts from a re-description of *what* we have inherited (and how that happened) to an evaluation of *how* we understand, use, and shape that inheritance. In other words, Part II moves back into the context that the genealogy is trying to help us understand. It is this movement that marks the need for a different kind of critical engagement.

As a methodology, discourse analysis complements genealogy. As methods of intellectual inquiry, each is interested in how law and lawmakers produce, use, and sustain meaning. Each pays close attention to how arguments are shaped, how relations of power are encoded, and how language is used as abstraction as well as how it is affected by context and place. But genealogy and discourse analysis are also different. Genealogy provides a way of critically engaging with law's history and the way in which relations of power are authorised. Discourse analysis, on the other hand, is a way of paying attention to and critically engaging with law's present, rhetorically and juridically, and the way in which relations of power are practised. In the context of migration law, the combination of the two allows us to see more clearly the continuing resonances and effects of 'absolute sovereignty'.

1.2.2.3 Reading Law as Discourse

There is no doubt that law, which is created, performed, and executed through the spoken and written word, is a "fertile field for discourse analysts".[121] But why read law as discourse? Does discourse analysis offer something that other methodological approaches do not? As I elaborate further on, discourse analysis is a form of critique that works with law as it is spoken, written, and practised but in a way that is not constrained by doctrinal conventions.

As a method, discourse analysis enables an analytical approach that is external to, and therefore not analytically constrained by, the conventions of black-letter law and lawmaking such as doctrine, statutory interpretation, and doctrinal analysis – conventions which, as we will see, can limit or even close off certain lines of inquiry. To be clear, however, this does not mean that discourse analysis is irrelevant to the doctrinal lawyer; rather, it sharpens her senses and heightens her awareness of the contexts – political, historical, and social – through which law is constituted and in which law operates. Nor does this mean that discourse analysis does not *engage* with these conventional styles of legal analysis and practice; on the contrary, it must, because the power of law still lies in the status

---

[121]   Roger W Shuy, 'Discourse Analysis in the Legal Context' in Deborah Schiffrin, Deborah Tannen, and Heidi E Hamilton (eds), *The Handbook of Discourse Analysis* (Blackwell, 2001) 437, 437.

and authority of doctrine, statute, and jurisprudence as well as the way in which law is practised.

Here, it is important to emphasise that my primary purpose in reading law as discourse is more analytical than normative. With this in mind, discourse analysis as a method enables us to take a step back, observe, and think differently about *how* doctrine is used, statute interpreted, and jurisprudence developed, and to think about whether those uses, interpretations, or developments are inadvertent, improvised, or intentional. In particular, it enables us to give broader consideration to the linguistic choices and purposes of legislators and jurists. The analysis can take place in and between texts, speech, and text; in silence; and within and across legal genres. As such, discourse analysis enables us to look at and think differently about how law is spoken and written and how it remains silent or is silenced, be it through political discourses (of legislators and policymakers), legal discourses (of jurists and adjudicators), or administrative discourses (of public officials). This leads us to ask what work discourse analysis does.

Here, discourse analysis provides a way of showing how the predicament of the unwelcome migrant is constructed by a dominant politico-legal discourse of migration produced under conditions of unequal power.[122] It shows migration discourse to be redolent of the political-economic dynamics that shaped the foreigner-sovereign relation into a claim of 'absolute sovereignty'. It recognises the role of language in establishing (and freezing) the relations of power that are the order of things by creating and ascribing material realities.[123] In other words, the analysis shows how certain representations of the foreigner remain dominant and shape indelibly the way in which her realities continue to be imagined and acted upon in the name of 'absolute sovereignty',[124] whether explicitly or implicitly.

In short, the discourse analysis makes visible contemporary migration law's lineage. It carries into our reading of contemporary texts their historical contingency revealed by the genealogy. In doing so, discourse analysis recognises that there are lines of continuity and discontinuity between contemporary migration discourse and the repertoires and patterns of argument that shaped the foreigner-sovereign relation as a claim of 'absolute sovereignty'. As such, it invites us to name and think differently and critically about the

---

[122] Arturo Escobar, *Encountering Development: The Making and Unmaking of the Third World* (Princeton University Press, 1995) 9.

[123] Michel Foucault, *The Order of Things: An Archaeology of the Human Sciences* (A M Sheridan Smith trans, Routledge, 2002) 45, 132 [trans of: *Les mots et les choses: Une archéologie des sciences humaines* (first published 1966)].

[124] Escobar, above n 122, 5.

contemporary resonances of the complex institutional story of the foreigner-sovereign relation retrieved through the genealogy. It enables us to think more perspicuously about what happens when lawmakers uphold a contestable and contingent historical artefact as a universal, timeless, and irrefutable truth; about what happens when the ideas that underpin institutional policies and practices are co-opted because of the power of prevailing ideologies;[125] and about what happens when they turn out to be so (or too) close, so (or too) immediate, so (or too) much a part of us that we – as a polity – can see them but scarcely notice how deeply they affect our thinking.[126]

The analysis thematises a number of recurring discursive techniques, considered in the next subsection. These enable us to see how the authorisation of 'absolute sovereignty' as a particular doctrinal form of the foreigner-sovereign relation is performed and sustained as a practice. They make clear that this practice is a product of law's inextricable relation with language, that as practice and discourse 'absolute sovereignty' is shaped by particular linguistic styles, conventions, and usages which make visible the depth of historical and discursive meaning that 'absolute sovereignty' carries.

1.2.2.4 Three Discursive Techniques

Through a close reading of text, talk, and their silences, I order thematically three recurring discourses. In the first instance, a discourse of (state) control and restraint gives expression to discourses of 'absolute sovereignty'. Second, a discourse of (asylum seeker) deviance and opportunism gives expression to discourses of migration.[127] Third, a discourse of (institutional) silence gives overarching expression to the non-textual ways in which discourse is structured – whether audibly or inaudibly – to include or exclude (people or action) politically, legislatively, and jurisprudentially. In this way, I show

---

[125] Davies, above n 75, 199.

[126] "Il y a longtemps qu'on sait que le rôle de la philosophie n'est pas de découvrir ce qui est caché, mais de rendre visible ce qui précisément est visible, c'est-à-dire de faire apparaître ce qui est si proche, ce qui est si immédiat, ce qui est si intimement lié à nous-mêmes qu'à cause de cela nous ne le percevons pas": Michel Foucault, 'La philosophie analytique de la politique' in Daniel Defert and François Ewald (eds), with Jacques Lagrange, *Michel Foucault: Dits et écrits – 1954–1988* (Gallimard, 1994) vol 3, 534, 540–1; Orford, 'In Praise of Description', above n 85, 617–18.

[127] See generally Sharon Pickering, 'Common Sense and Original Deviancy: News Discourses and Asylum Seekers in Australia' (2001) 14(2) *Journal of Refugee Studies* 169; Sharon Pickering and Caroline Lambert, 'Deterrence: Australia's Refugee Policy' (2002) 14(1) *Current Issues in Criminal Justice* 65.

how each of these discourses (whether implicitly or explicitly) is used to justify and rationalise mandatory detention and planned destitution.

Discursive techniques may be rhetorical or institutional. In this book, much of the discourse analysis is rhetorical. In other words, it considers how institutional actors draw on political and juridical tradition to make speech persuasive and what rhetorical devices people use, consciously or unconsciously, to persuade – devices such as metaphor, repetition, innuendo, hyperbole, linguistic inversion of the power relation,[128] deflection, 'splitting',[129] and positive self-presentation juxtaposed with negative characterisation of the out-group. This approach is useful for textual analysis of parliamentary debates, political speech, courtroom advocacy, and judicial analysis from the perspective of linguistic meaning and technique for both user and (intended) audience.

In a subject field rich with rhetoric,[130] it is useful to draw on the work of Lakoff and Johnson[131] and others[132] for the insights they offer on the rhetorical power (verbal and non-verbal)[133] of metaphoric language and on understanding metaphor as an ordinary part of – and central to[134] – thinking, talking, and writing about (migration) law.[135] In addition, the scholarship of others, including van Dijk,[136] enables insight into the use of rhetorical

---

[128] That is, characterising the powerful as defenceless.

[129] Splitting is a discursive device that fends off the accusation of racism or other prejudice by conceding that some members of an out-group are good: see Raymond G Nairn and Timothy N McCreanor, 'Race Talk and Common Sense: Patterns in Pakeha Discourse on Maori/ Pakeha Relations in New Zealand' (1991) 10(4) *Journal of Language and Social Psychology* 245, 251; Martha Agoustinos and Danielle Every, 'The Language of "Race" and Prejudice: A Discourse of Denial, Reason, and Liberal-Practical Politics' (2007) 26(2) *Journal of Language and Social Psychology* 123, 132.

[130] See, generally, Keith Cunningham-Parmeter, 'Alien Language: Immigration Metaphors and the Jurisprudence of Otherness' (2011) 79(4) *Fordham Law Review* 1545.

[131] George Lakoff and Mark Johnson, *Metaphors We Live By* (University of Chicago Press 1981); see also Mark Johnson, 'Law Incarnate' (2002) 67 *Brooklyn Law Review* 959, 950; Mark L Johnson, 'Mind, Metaphor, Law' (2007) 58 *Mercer Law Review* 845, 859–60.

[132] See, eg, Paul Ricoeur, 'The Metaphorical Process as Cognition, Imagination and Feeling' in Mark Johnson (ed), *Philosophical Perspectives on Metaphor* (University of Minnesota Press, 1981) 228 (first published in: (1978) 5(1) *Critical Inquiry* 143).

[133] Ibid.   [134] Ibid 240.

[135] Cf Davidson, who argues against the idea that a metaphor has, in addition to its literal sense or meaning, another sense or meaning: Donald Davidson, 'What Metaphors Mean' (1978) 5(1) *Critical Inquiry* 31, 32; Max Black, 'Metaphor' in Mark Johnson (ed), *Philosophical Perspectives on Metaphor* (University of Minnesota Press, 1981) 63 (first published 1955). On the philosophical rebirth of metaphor, see: I A Richards, *The Philosophy of Rhetoric* (Oxford University Press, 1936); Max Black, *Models and Metaphors: Studies in Language and Philosophy* (Cornell University Press, first published 1954, 1962 ed).

[136] Teun A van Dijk, *Elite Discourse and Racism* (Sage, 1993).

devices such as pre-emptive defence strategies in elite discourse. Such strategies include patterns of positive self-presentation followed by negative statements[137] and justificatory 'but' framings that characterise stringency against out-groups as a virtue – for example, strict *but* fair,[138] tough *but* necessary.[139]

Thinking about technique institutionally enables a close examination of the technical ways in which juridical forms are used in legislation, in jurisprudence, and in framing policy. This institutional dimension to technique engages with what lawmakers do and what they think (and, arguably, what they think they do) in a way that deepens our understanding of the inextricable relation between law and language and its effects. This means that we need to consider how doctrinal and other juridical techniques of exclusion in migration law- and policymaking integrate and institutionalise 'absolute sovereignty' – tacitly or otherwise – in a manner that makes certain rules, practices, and patterns of interpretation thinkable.[140]

Through the discourse analysis undertaken in Part II, it is possible to discern the (dominant) discourse of migration as historically produced.[141] That is, the analysis reveals a pattern of law- and policymaking that embodies the same power dynamics and rhetorical and institutional devices that produced 'absolute sovereignty'. It is a pattern that is epitomised by what I describe as 'decision-less detention' (mandatory detention that occurs by operation of law and is not meaningfully subject to judicial review),[142] 'obsession with discretion' (discretionary powers to grant or deny work rights designed to avert the prospect of judicial scrutiny),[143] and unaccountable administration (an approach to welfare distribution that is policy-based and largely unreviewable).[144] This pattern treats particular persons differently because the discourse of 'absolute sovereignty' accepts that the state regards them, as a class, as unwelcome outsiders. That is, it treats them, as a class, as deviants and opportunists so unworthy of law's protection that resulting detention or destitution is regarded as both justifiably created and enforced; indeed, subject to exceptions that are themselves exceptional, such detention and destitution is characterised as self-inflicted.

---

[137] This is the rhetorical device of 'I'm not racist/sexist/etc, but ... ': ibid 72, 78, 93; Agoustinos and Every, above n 129, 129.
[138] Van Dijk, *Elite Discourse*, above n 136, 100–102. See Chapter 5.
[139] CPD, House of Representatives, 5 May 1992, 2370–3 (Gerry Hand). See Chapter 5.
[140] Steven L Winter, *A Clearing in the Forest: Law, Life and Mind* (University of Chicago Press, 2003) 3, citing John Dewey, 'Logic and Legal Method' (1924) 12 *Cornell Law Quarterly* 1.
[141] Escobar, above n 122, 6.   [142] See Chapter 5.   [143] See Chapter 6.   [144] Ibid.

1.3 MAKING MIGRATION LAW: AN OVERVIEW

In this final part of the introduction, I outline the five substantive chapters of the book, noting where it breaks new ground through original archival research. I then offer an overview of commentary on the doctrine of 'absolute sovereignty', in order to provide an entry point to the existing literature. Finally, I offer a brief description of how I see the book opening up the possibility for a radical rethinking of the foreigner-sovereign relation in the making of migration law.

1.3.1 *The Roadmap*

Chapter 2 is the first phase of the genealogy of the foreigner-sovereign relation. I ask who the 'foreigner' was in early international law. Through a close examination of selected treatises of four international legal theorists – Vitoria, Grotius, Pufendorf, and Vattel – from the sixteenth to eighteenth centuries, I show that the foreigner in early international law was not an outsider but rather a European insider in whose interests international law was framed. As I argue, this challenges the assumption that the foreigner is inevitably an outsider, suggesting instead that she is a mutable juridical figure who could be characterised sometimes as an insider and other times as an outsider according to historical contingencies and interests. I argue that these insights help us see that when the foreigner was a European, a discourse of 'absolute sovereignty' was not evident because he was aligned with the sovereign.

Chapter 3 charts the points of emergence of 'absolute sovereignty' as a common law doctrine. In this chapter, I analyse common law jurisprudence of the Privy Council and the US Supreme Court and the international legal authorities on which this jurisprudence relies, as well as legislative text during the same period. I do so in order to see how the 'foreigner' and the 'sovereign' were brought into juridical relation in the nineteenth century. I argue that a coalescence of the foreigner (as non-European outsider) and the sovereign produced an absolute right to exclude and condition the entry and stay of (even friendly) aliens. This suggests that the mutability of the figure of the foreigner was not pure or constant but rather contingent upon the political-economic desire to regulate race and labour. In other words, when the foreigner was a European (say, coloniser, settler, trader, or exile), he was viewed as an insider whose mobility was authorised, a figure of privilege and power aligned with the sovereign and sovereign interests. But when the foreigner was a non-European (say, a free or indentured labourer), she was marked as an outsider – an excludable, exploitable, expendable, and deportable figure unworthy of law's protection.

Chapter 4 covers the period from the lead-up to the Federation of Australia through to the post–World War II era. In this chapter I engage in a close textual analysis of the constitutional convention debates, parliamentary debates, legislation, and jurisprudence of the High Court. I do so in order to make visible how the particular ways in which the nineteenth-century crystallisation of the foreigner-sovereign relation as a common law doctrine was pivotal in the constitutional framing of 'absolute sovereignty'. I argue that 'absolute sovereignty' as a constitutional form held in place the priority of regulating race and labour – a privileging of (racial) purity and (economic) prosperity – buttressed by particular legal traditions and orthodoxies, including the doctrines of precedent and responsible government.

To this point, Part I of the book locates conceptualisations of the sovereign and the foreigner in a broader context in which migration lawmaking was consonant with the political-economic desire to regulate race and labour. The genealogy makes visible how the foreigner-sovereign relation produced 'absolute sovereignty' as a discourse in four key ways. First, it shows how the point of emergence of 'absolute sovereignty' coincided with the appearance of (non-European) outsider foreigners. Second, it shows how migration law and lawmaking has essentialised 'absolute sovereignty'. Third, it shows how any risk of abuse that inheres in the exercise of this absolute power has been cast as (only) theoretical because those who enjoy such power can be relied upon to exercise it responsibly. Finally, it shows how 'absolute sovereignty' as a discourse has been justified by deeming certain people to have lesser rights on account of their characterisation as undesirable or unworthy of law's protection.

In Part II, we return to the contemporary context outlined in the prologue, shifting from genealogy to discourse analysis as my methodological frame. Chapters 5 and 6 explore how 'absolute sovereignty' as a discourse – made visible through the genealogy – plays out in the two contemporary case studies: mandatory detention as a measure of physical exclusion (Chapter 5) and the circumscription of work and welfare as a measure of social and economic exclusion (Chapter 6).

The discourse analysis undertaken in the two case studies delves into a significant body of archival material hitherto largely unexamined. In Chapter 5, I consider the parliamentary debates around *Migration Amendment Act 1992* (Cth), the first legislative framing of mandatory detention. I then examine the transcript, court file, and judgment in the constitutional challenge to the legislation in the 1992 case of *Chu Kheng Lim v*

Minister for Immigration, Local Government and Ethnic Affairs.[145] The focus of this analysis is on the High Court's treatment of the constitutional powers to make laws with respect to aliens and immigration,[146] which stands in sometimes quite striking contrast to its approach to the more jealously and insistently guarded judicial power in migration decision-making.[147]

Much has of course happened since the mandatory detention policy was first adopted. My focus on *Lim* reflects the fact that the introduction and validation of mandatory detention in 1992 marked a turning point that set Australian migration lawmaking onto a trajectory that is still being realised. Decisions of the High Court since *Lim* have not only continued to uphold the constitutional validity of mandatory detention, but they have also extended or clarified *Lim*, making findings, for example, that mandatory detention (a) is permissible, and not punitive, even if it is for life;[148] (b) is lawful, and not punitive, even where conditions include harsh or inhumane treatment;[149] (c) applies to children;[150] and (d) is permissible on the high seas.[151] The courts have also drawn on *Lim* in validating detention for the purposes of exclusion and removal (as in the case of the *MV Tampa*)[152] as well as detention in the context of extraterritorial processing.[153] Although there have been some notable dissenting opinions expressed, the jurisprudence still strongly favours the majority in *Lim*.[154] It is a case whose implications are yet to be fully unpacked

---

[145]   *Lim* (1992) 176 CLR 1. I was the solicitor acting for the plaintiffs in this case, supported by a team of *pro bono* lawyers from Mallesons Stephen Jaques, as it was then known. However, apart from the stories I tell in the prologue, all the materials on which I have drawn in this analysis are sourced from the public record.

[146]   *Constitution* ss 51(xix) (aliens and naturalisation), 51(xxvii) (immigration and emigration).

[147]   Decisions of an officer of the Commonwealth remain subject to the judicial power: ibid s 75 (v). The High Court has strongly resisted legislative attempts to curtail judicial scrutiny of administrative decisions through, for example, the introduction of a privative clause (*Migration Act* s 474) or the construction of 'nonstatutory decision-making processes': see, eg, *Plaintiff S157/2002 v Commonwealth* (2003) 211 CLR 476; *Offshore Processing Case* (2010) 243 CLR 319. For a recent example of these contrasting approaches handed down in the same week, see *Manus Island Case* (2014) 254 CLR 28 (relating to the 'aliens power'); *Plaintiff S297/ 2013 v Minister for Immigration and Border Protection* (2015) 255 CLR 231; *Plaintiff M150/2013 v Minister for Immigration and Border Protection* (2014) 309 ALR 225 (both S297 and M150 deal with the obligation to grant permanent Protection Visas).

[148]   *Al-Kateb* (2004) 219 CLR 562; cf *Minister for Immigration and Multicultural and Indigenous Affairs v Al Masri* (2003) 197 ALR 241, in which the Full Federal Court made a contrary finding.

[149]   *Behrooz* (2004) 219 CLR 486.

[150]   *Re Woolley; Ex parte Applicants M276/2003* (2004) 225 CLR 1.

[151]   *Detention on the High Seas Case* (2015) 255 CLR 514.   [152]   *Vadarlis* (2001) 110 FCR 491.

[153]   *Manus Island Case* (2014) 254 CLR 28; *Nauru Detention Case* (2016) 257 CLR 42.

[154]   See, in particular, the judgment of Black CJ in *Vadarlis* (2001) 110 FCR 491, 494–521 and the judgment of Kirby J in *Al-Kateb* (2004) 219 CLR 562, 614–30.

and that has not lost its currency. It is therefore opportune to revisit the authority of *Lim* from a new perspective.

In Chapter 6, I undertake, in the first instance, a rhetorical analysis of the rationale for the policy of planned destitution. Second, I engage in an institutional analysis of legal, policy, and practice frameworks governing the no-work condition that attaches to certain temporary processing visas (known as bridging visas). Finally, I analyse the legal, policy, and practice context governing the policy-based governance and distribution of welfare to asylum seekers, including a complaint to the Human Rights and Equal Opportunity Commission (HREOC)[155] by the Sydney-based Asylum Seekers Centre. The discourse analysis in Part II shows the (dominant) contemporary usages of 'absolute sovereignty' to be historically produced.[156] 'Absolute sovereignty' is, I argue, a discourse operating in multiple modes and registers that maintains extant links between the (genealogical) past and migration discourses of the present by (re)producing a legal tradition that it neither doubts nor challenges.

Finally, the concluding chapter draws together the strands of my analysis and opens up a space from which to rethink and reimagine the foreigner-sovereign relation. I suggest that the book provides a basis for us to think about the doctrinal, genealogical, and discursive dimensions of what is going on when the claim of 'absolute sovereignty' is made and to think differently, more consciously, and less inevitably about 'absolute sovereignty' as the embodiment of the foreigner-sovereign relation. I also suggest that the book offers a point of departure from which to begin a new conversation that sees the foreigner-sovereign relation as one of mutuality, vitality, and exchange. An epilogue – which looks at 'Operation Sovereign Borders' (a military-led national border control strategy aimed at stopping 'boat people' from reaching Australia) – underscores the need for that conversation to begin.

1.3.2 *An Entry Point to the Existing Literature*

There is a significant branch of scholarly writing that has engaged critically with the doctrine of sovereignty as an absolute right to exclude aliens, sometimes viewing it as a counter-notion to the idea of state interdependence.[157] This scholarship provides an entry point into the existing literature, which is vast and complex. Plender and Goodwin-Gill have considered the scope of the

---

[155] Now the Australian Human Rights Commission.   [156] Escobar, above n 122, 6.
[157] Marcel Sibert, *Traité de Droit International Public: Le Droit de la Paix* (Dalloz, 1951) vol I, 574; Plender, above n 86, 61. On the conflict between the sovereignty theory and the interdependence theory, see Plender, above n 86, 61–94.

doctrine of sovereignty, not least by reference back to early international legal theorists including Vitoria, Grotius, Pufendorf, and Vattel.[158] Nafziger concludes that the absolute sovereign right to exclude aliens as it has been incorporated into the common law is a "discredited proposition".[159] He argues that it relies not only on questionable interpretations and selective use of scholarly writings and political theory, but also on jurisprudence that openly condones racial discrimination.[160] On the strength of this, he makes the case for international law to shape a "qualified duty to admit aliens".[161] Others, as Juss reminds us,[162] uphold the doctrine citing no (or little) authority for it.[163] Martin concedes the doctrine to be "highly permissive"[164] but *contra* Nafziger regards sweeping state authority to control migration to be so deeply rooted in state practice and popular understanding as to provide the "appropriate starting point" for modern legal analysis, even if that authority is based on a misreading of the jurisprudence.[165] In a similar vein, referring to but not engaging with Nafziger's analysis, Opeskin (quoting Martin) has concluded that in Australia, with only modest qualifications, migration policy remains "the last major redoubt of unfettered national sovereignty."[166]

---

[158] Plender, above n 86, 61–94; Goodwin-Gill, *Movement of Persons*, above n 86, 94–6.
[159] Nafziger, above n 86, 846. On this 'old-style' version of sovereignty, which is "out of place in an age of human rights" yet remains "stubbornly ingrained", see also Cathryn Costello, *The Human Rights of Migrants in European Law* (Oxford University Press, 2016) 10.
[160] Ibid 845.
[161] Ibid. See also Rubenstein, 'Citizenship, Sovereignty, and Migration', above n 78; Peter Billings, 'Refugees, The Rule of Law and Executive Power: A(nother) Case of the Conjuror's Rabbit?' (2003) 54(4) *Northern Ireland Legal Quarterly* 412; Satvinder Singh Juss, *International Migration and Global Justice* (Ashgate, 2006) 12–15.
[162] See Juss, above n 161, 12, who aligns himself with Nafziger, above n 86.
[163] See, eg, Rona Aybay, 'The Right to Leave and the Right to Return: The International Aspect of Freedom of Movement' (1978) 1 *Comparative Law Yearbook* 121, 121–2; James Leslie Brierly, *The Law of Nations: An Introduction to the International Law of Peace* (Sir Humphrey Waldock ed, Oxford University Press, 6th ed, 1963) 276; Lassa Oppenheim, *International Law: A Treatise* (Hersch Lauterpacht ed, Longman, 8th ed, 1955) 675–6; S Prakash Sinha, *New Nations and the Law of Nations* (Martinus Nijhoff, 1967) 97, cited in Juss, above n 161, 12; Paul Weis, *Nationality and Statelessness in International Law* (Sijthoff & Noordhoff, 2nd ed, 1979) 45. Those who do cite authority for the proposition refer to the case of *Musgrove* [1891] AC 272, 282, which does not cite authority for it: see Chapter 3, 96–7.
[164] David A Martin, 'The Authority and Responsibility of States' in T Alexander Aleinikoff and Vincent Chetail (eds), *Migration and International Legal Norms* (TMC Asser Press, 2003) 31, 31 n 1.
[165] Ibid.
[166] Opeskin, above n 43, 579, quoting David Martin, 'Effects of International Law on Migration Policy and Practice: The Uses of Hypocrisy' (1989) 23(3) *International Migration Review* 547, 547. For an interesting discussion of the 'open borders' literature and debate, see Penelope Mathew, *Reworking the Relationship between Asylum and Employment* (Routledge, 2012) 61–75.

Rubenstein has considered the Nafziger analysis in the context of jurisprudence of the Federal Court of Australia following the *Tampa* incident.[167] She
notes that the principle of sovereignty as a legitimising basis for the executive
and legislative response to that incident – during which 433 rescued asylum
seekers were interdicted and prevented from entering Australian territory – was
"almost universally accepted by legislators, judges, commentators, policymakers and large sections of the public" to be absolute.[168] Drawing on
Nafziger's analysis, she decries that "there has not been enough opposition
to the rhetoric of absolute sovereign power to exclude aliens."[169] Indeed, even
commentary that is critical of Australian state practice does not necessarily
question the strength of the state's claim of 'absolute sovereignty'.[170]

Using the aforementioned literature as an entry point, this book departs in
two respects from, but also complements, the doctrinal analysis of the absolute
sovereign right to exclude and condition the entry and stay of aliens ('absolute
sovereignty') undertaken most explicitly by Nafziger. First, the book takes as its
focus the idea of 'absolute sovereignty' as it is understood in Australian migration
law, drawing together its international law, common law, and public law
dimensions. It is the first full-length study to do so. Second, in contrast to the
analyses canvassed above, which are in many respects classically doctrinal and
normative in their critique, I have sought to take a step back in my analysis. My
purpose in doing so is to test not only the assumption that 'absolute sovereignty'
is a timeless given,[171] but also the normative assumption implicit in some of the
doctrinal analyses that behind the edifice of 'absolute sovereignty' lies a space in
which a purer, more authentic form of law waits to be reclaimed.[172]

This analysis thus offers a systematic critique of how 'absolute sovereignty'
has been authorised. This entails examining both the conscious use of international legal authority and the unstated juridical assumptions made by lawmakers because of the power of prevailing ideologies.[173] As such, I bring
genealogy and discourse analysis together in the hope of deepening our
understanding of how the story of 'absolute sovereignty' took centre stage
through a process that is critically engaged and yet avoids the constraints of
doctrinal conventions.

---

[167]   See *VCCL v MIMA* (2001) 110 FCR 452; *Vadarlis* (2001) 110 FCR 491. Rubenstein,
        'Citizenship, Sovereignty, and Migration', above n 78; see also Billings, above n 161.
[168]   Rubenstein, 'Citizenship, Sovereignty, and Migration', above n 78, 104–5.   [169]   Ibid 106.
[170]   See, eg, Simon Evans, above n 45, 97: "'Does the Government of Australia (in the sense of all
        of the branches of government operating in their own spheres) have the power to exclude or
        expel aliens and to detain them for the purposes of exclusion or expulsion?' The answer to that
        question must be 'yes'."
[171]   Orford, 'In Praise of Description', above n 85, 624; Bartelson, above n 79, 49.
[172]   Wickham, above n 102, 256.   [173]   Davies, above n 75, 1, 199.

1.3.3 *The Contribution: A Provocation and a Clarion Call*

Before turning to the body of the book, let me offer a final explanatory note on the impetus for and objectives of this project. As I explain here, it is my hope that this book might make a contribution in two ways. In the first instance, I hope it will serve as a provocation for a new consciousness and conversation about Australia's responses to unsolicited migration. In the second, I hope it will serve as a clarion call to other states not to replicate the harsh exceptionalism that has become normalised in the framing and operationalisation of those responses.

Having worked in this field for more than twenty-five years, it would be artificial, if not impossible, for me to conceal the fact that I find repugnant the policies of mandatory detention and planned destitution. I am also troubled by the way in which the assumptions that underpin them – embodied in the discourse of 'absolute sovereignty' – seem to have led inexorably to the range of offshore policy responses to unsolicited (boat) migration, with all their human effects.[174] More broadly, these assumptions appear to portend a (growing) pattern of law- and policymaking that extends its reach into other areas of public policy, including the domain of citizenship and national security.

There is an observable pattern that draws together two techniques of impenetrability that are revealed through the case studies. In the first instance is the technique of decision-lessness that clothes with legislative authority, and absolves public officials of responsibility for, unbridled and unchecked executive action. In the second, we see the technique of purporting or promising to temper the effects of decision-lessness with non-compellable, non-enforceable, and non-reviewable discretionary powers vested in the Minister. Three recent examples of this pattern illustrate the way hostility towards the unwelcome migrant is enacted and how the counterweight of discretionary hospitality seeks to mitigate it:[175] the 'evolved' form of mandatory detention whereby an unlawful non-citizen must be detained by operation of law, but the Minister retains a non-compellable discretionary power to release her;[176]

---

[174] For a compilation of reports relating to conditions of detention on Nauru and Manus Island, see Elibritt Karlsen, 'Australia's Offshore Processing of Asylum Seekers in Nauru and PNG: A Quick Guide to Statistics and Resources' (Research Paper Series, 2016–17, Parliamentary Library, Parliament of Australia, 19 December 2016) 11–12. On the (un)sustainability of Australia's policy see, eg, Claire Higgins, 'The (Un)-Sustainability of Australia's Offshore Processing and Settlement Policy' in Violeta Moreno-Lax and Efthymios Papastavridis (eds), *'Boat Refugees' and Migrants at Sea: A Comprehensive Approach* (Brill, 2016) 303.

[175] Giannacopoulos, above n 41, discussing Derrida.

[176] *Migration Act* s 195A, added by *Migration Amendment (Detention Arrangements) Act* 2005 (Cth).

a legislative framework enacted in 2015 that couples the mandatory issue of a notice effectively stripping citizenship from certain Australian citizens said to have engaged in terrorist activities with a non-compellable discretionary power to rescind the notice;[177] and, finally, the introduction in November 2016 of a Bill coupling a mandatory lifetime visa ban on certain 'boat people' with a non-compellable ministerial discretion to lift it.[178] To me, the most troubling aspect of this pattern is the backstory of 'absolute sovereignty' on which it is grounded, and which has become the unanswerable answer to the unwelcome migrant. It is this backstory that has enabled collective practices and discourses to produce and sustain the authoritarian management of unsolicited migration that we see today.[179] Nevertheless, in critically engaging with both the history of 'absolute sovereignty' and its present, my immediate purpose is not to argue for a normative position on the foreigner-sovereign relation. Rather, it is to excavate the assumptions underpinning our legal frameworks and traditions, and contemporary migration discourse, in order to provoke a new conversation about what we do and how and why we do it.

So, although I am in no doubt that a radical break from current approaches to migration law- and policymaking is urgently needed in Australia, this project is not about what I think could or should happen in the future. Instead, in a Foucaultian sense, while I hope this book will provide a tool for radical action, its purpose is not to stipulate what those changes or actions might or should be.[180] In other words, the book is an effort to *hasten slowly* by deepening our understandings of how policies like mandatory detention and planned destitution can be considered appropriate adaptations of the power to regulate migration. As I see it, if we do not understand how such policies have become thinkable, we stand little prospect of being able to think about how

---

[177] *Australian Citizenship Amendment (Allegiance to Australia) Act 2015* (Cth), inserting s 33AA 'Renunciation by Conduct' into the *Australian Citizenship Act 2007* (Cth). Apart from the pattern of mandatory deprivation of a right coupled with a discretionary power to reinstate it, the most striking effect of the amendments is that it turns citizens into aliens, thereby making them subject to exclusion on the strength of the claim of 'absolute sovereignty'. The constitutional validity of the amendments is yet to be tested. These amendments are discussed in Kim Rubenstein, *Australian Citizenship Law* (Law Book Company, 2nd ed, 2016).

[178] See Migration Legislation Amendment (Regional Processing Cohort) Bill 2016 (Cth), discussed above n 118.

[179] Balibar, above n 120, 33.

[180] Michel Foucault and Gilles Deleuze, 'Intellectuals and Power: A Conversation between Michel Foucault and Gilles Deleuze' in Donald F Bouchard (ed), *Language, Counter-Memory, Practice: Selected Essays and Interviews by Michel Foucault* (Donald F Bouchard and Sherry Simon trans, Cornell University Press 1977) 205 [trans of: 'Les intellectuels et le pouvoir' (first published 1972)].

(and why) we should respond to unsolicited migration in new ways. For me, this research has created a space from which to look forward by looking back and to pause in the present to listen and think carefully, differently, and more consciously about what lawmakers do and why they do it. In doing so, therefore, my conclusions are grounded in law's inextricable relation with history and language as a fundamental condition of its (and our) knowledge and being.[181]

Finally, although its focus is on Australia – home to some of the world's harshest asylum policies – this book has also been written with a broader context and audience in mind. Beyond Australia, the global issue of unsolicited migration is firmly on the political agendas of states in many other parts of the world, and in far greater numbers. As a mass of humanity is cast adrift by conflict, atrocity, and poverty and – most visibly and hauntingly – washed ashore, states grapple with the juridical challenges and political impulses that feed into and off what is often dubbed the 'asylum crisis'.[182] The relationship between the sovereign and the unwelcome foreigner (as refugee) is in constant tension, often at sea. Whether in the Mediterranean, the Bay of Bengal or the Gulf of Aden, tragedy after unspeakable tragedy continues to befall those in flight.

With this global landscape in mind, my hope is that this book will deepen understandings within the wider international community about how and why Australian law- and policymakers pathologise unsolicited migration. This is important because, in the migration domain and largely driven by self-interest, Australia has historically 'punched above its weight' in the development of international law and policies.[183] It continues to seek to peddle its wares, and, as Jacubowicz has noted, some political leaders are listening.[184] Recently, Immigration Minister Peter Dutton went so far as to suggest that Australia is a "migration super power".[185] In my view, it is imperative that law- and policymakers outside Australia, whether at an international level or in other states, understand the unedifying backstory implicit in this claim to superpower status and the discourses that continue to play out in justification of the contemporary

---

[181] Davies, above n 75, 168.
[182] On the complex layers and dimensions of refugee law as crisis, see Catherine Dauvergne, 'Refugee Law as Perpetual Crisis' in Satvinder Singh Juss and Colin Harvey (eds), *Contemporary Issues in Refugee Law* (Edward Elgar, 2013) 13.
[183] See generally Shimazu, above n 65; Devereux, above n 65; Lester, above n 65.
[184] See, eg, Tony Abbott, Second Annual Margaret Thatcher Lecture, London, 27 October 2015 <https://www.thatchercentre.com/events/annual-lecture/ii/>; Andrew Jacubowicz, 'European Leaders Taking Cues from Australia on Asylum Seeker Policies' *The Conversation* (online), 7 November 2016, <http://theconversation.com/european-leaders-taking-cues-from-australia-on-asylum-seeker-policies-66336>; Lester, above n 65.
[185] Dutton, *Address to the Australian Strategic Policy Institute*, above n 40.

legal and policy context. So, to reiterate, my hope is not only that this book might provoke a new conversation in Australia in which our imagination for alternatives is not straitened by the discourse of 'absolute sovereignty', but also that other states will hear it as a clarion call not to emulate the Australian example.[186]

---

[186] For a recent exploration of approaches and responses to 'boat migration' see Violeta Moreno-Lax and Efthymios Papastavridis (eds), *'Boat Refugees' and Migrants at Sea: A Comprehensive Approach* (Brill, 2016).

PART I

2

Early International Law and the Foreigner

From its earliest conceptions (European) international legal theory contemplated the foreigner's mobility in terms of rights: rights to set forth and travel, to sojourn, to hospitality, to trade, and to share in common property.[1] Free movement rights[2] all found voice in the work of early international jurists, including rights of passage, the right to leave one's country,[3] the right of asylum, and (perhaps most striking for the modern international lawyer) the right to enter and reside in the territory of *another* state.[4] Likewise, the right of necessity played a significant and evolving role in shaping how international law framed and conditioned the foreigner's stay.

By any measure, this presents as a dazzlingly impressive array of rights. It contrasts starkly with the widely held (current) assumption that the foreigner has – and has always had – less rights than the citizen vis-à-vis the imperial or

---

[1] For some early reflections, see Eve Lester, 'Imagining the "Promise of Justice" in the Prohibition on Racial Discrimination: Paradoxes and Prospects' [2007] *International and Humanitarian Law Resources* 8 <www.worldlii.org/int/journals/IHLRes/2007/8.html>.

[2] The notion of free movement is used here in a broad sense rather than in the stricter contemporary sense of the right to freedom of movement within the territory of a state.

[3] For a study focusing on the right to emigrate, see Jane McAdam, 'An Intellectual History of Freedom of Movement in International Law: The Right to Leave as a Personal Liberty' (2011) 12(1) *Melbourne Journal of International Law* 27.

[4] See, eg, below, 59, 65. Cf *International Covenant on Civil and Political Rights*, opened for signature 16 December 1966, 999 UNTS 171 (entered into force 23 March 1976) art 12; *Universal Declaration of Human Rights*, GA Res 217A (III), UN GAOR, 3rd sess, 183rd plen mtg, UN Doc A/810 (10 December 1948) art 13. Although in modern international law there is no general right to enter and reside in the territory of another state, a number of regional economic blocs have made provision for entry and residence of citizens of member states in other member states. See, eg, *Council Directive 2004/38/EC of 29 April 2004 on the Right of Citizens of the Union and Their Family Members to Move and Reside Freely within the Territory of the Member States* [2004] OJ L158/77, arts 5–7; Economic Community of West African States, *Protocol relating to Free Movement of Persons, Residence and Establishment*, Doc No A/P.1/5/79 (signed and entered into force provisionally on 29 May 1979) art 2.

sovereign power.[5] So, what do we make of this rights framework? Does it tell an originary story of universal human rights that has somehow gone awry and is now ripe for renewal? Who *was* the 'foreigner' in early conceptions of international law? Why did he[6] enjoy these rights? And is the casting of the foreigner as an outsider (welcome or unwelcome) with lesser rights than the citizen a timeless given? Or is the juridical figure of the foreigner a *contingent historical artefact* on which we need to reflect critically?[7]

This is the first chapter in the genealogy of the foreigner-sovereign relation. Overall, the genealogy helps explain how policies such as mandatory detention and planned destitution have come to be characterised as lawful and legitimate responses to unsolicited migration by locating migration lawmaking within a longer jurisprudential tradition. The purpose of this chapter is to make visible *who* the figure of the foreigner was in early conceptualisations of international law. My central argument in this chapter has three elements: first, that the foreigner is a mutable figure and, therefore, that there is nothing inevitable about her 'outsider-ness'; second, that her mutability was shaped by historical contingencies;[8] and third, that when the foreigner was a privileged European insider there was no discourse of 'absolute sovereignty'. The chapter serves as a kind of prehistory of 'absolute sovereignty', in that it enables us to trace how the claim of 'absolute sovereignty' emerged as a common law doctrine (Chapter 3) and, in turn, became entrenched as a constitutional doctrine (Chapter 4).

In summary, my argument is that the 'foreigner' in early international law was conceptualised as an insider, not an outsider, a 'civilised' European, not a 'barbarian' non-European. In other words, the foreigner was a figure of privilege and power conceptually aligned with, rather than opposed to, the sovereign. As such, being a foreigner was historically an enabling, rather than residual, status, and there is nothing inevitable about the foreigner's outsiderness. Indeed, whether imperialists, aristocrats, men of letters, or merchants, it

---

[5]   This assumption has its origins in the French Revolution, which invented (although not *ex nihilo*) both the nation-state and the modern institution (and ideology) of citizenship: see, eg, William Rogers Brubaker, 'The French Revolution and the Invention of Citizenship' (1989) 7(3) *French Politics and Society* 30, 30.

[6]   On use of the male and female pronouns in this book, see Chapter 1, 15 n 49.

[7]   Friedrich Nietzsche, *On the Genealogy of Morals: A Polemic* (Douglas Smith trans, Oxford University Press, 1996) 8 [trans of: *Zur Genealogie der Moral: Eine Streitschrift* (first published 1887)]; David Owen, *Nietzsche's Genealogy of Morality* (McGill-Queen's University Press, 2007) 6. See Chapter 1, 22.

[8]   As we will see in Chapter 3, an increased mobility of a non-European (free or indentured) labour force in a period of colonial expansion was pivotal in shaping the foreigner as a non-European outsider.

was quite natural for foreigners to cross borders[9] precisely *because* they were European.

In this chapter, the sixteenth century, where the common historical narrative of European public international law begins, is my starting point. This is because it is European international legal theory that has – for better and worse – had global contemporary impact.[10] The chapter is divided into four parts, in which I examine selected treatises of four key international jurists: Vitoria, Grotius, Pufendorf, and Vattel – canonical authorities in public and international law and, more specifically, in the juridical framing of the foreigner-sovereign relation. In each instance, I consider the context in which the jurist was writing, who his foreigner was, and how he framed the foreigner's rights.

That each jurist holds an authoritative place within the canon is well established. Vitoria's contribution as a leader in the Salamanca School included theorisation of relations between (European and non-European) peoples – notably the Spanish and the 'barbarian' Indians – as an international legal problem (*ius gentium*).[11] Treatises of Grotius, whose work was strongly influenced by Vitoria,[12] are studied for the place Grotius is widely regarded to hold in international legal scholarship as the father of international law.[13] Grotius' texts offer important insights into both the juridical framing of relations between European and non-European nations and peoples as well as intra-European relations. Pufendorf's post-Westphalian texts are examined for their integration of the foreigner into sovereign relations between nation-states. Finally, Vattel is examined both for the authority he carries as a leading international jurist and, more specifically, because his authority is still invoked in the assertion of 'absolute sovereignty' in migration law and policymaking in

---

9   Lucien Febvre (1878–1956), 'Frontière: The Word and the Concept' in Peter Burke (ed), *A New Kind of History: From the Writings of Febvre* (K Folca trans, Harper & Row, 1973) 208, 214. Indeed, as Febvre observed at 214, "the *frontière* only existed for soldiers and princes, and only then in time of war".

10 Nevertheless, the first international legal treatise was written by an Islamic jurist, Mohammed ibn al-Hasan (al-Shaybānī), towards the end of the eighth century, with multivolume Islamic international legal treatises emerging over the next two centuries: Christopher Weeramantry, *Justice without Frontiers: Furthering Human Rights* (Martinus Nijhoff, 1997) vol 1, 136; John Kelsay, 'Al-Shaybani and the Islamic Law of War' (2003) 2(1) *Journal of Military Ethics* 63; Muḥammad ibn al-Ḥasan Shaybānī (ca 750–804 or 5), *The Islamic Law of Nations: Shaybānī's Siyar* (Majid Khadduri trans, Johns Hopkins Press, 1966).

11 Francisco de Vitoria (c 1486–1546), *Political Writings* (Anthony Pagden and Jeremy Lawrance eds, Jeremy Lawrance trans, Cambridge University Press, 1991) xiii.

12 See, eg, David Kennedy, 'Primitive Legal Scholarship' (1986) 27(1) *Harvard International Law Journal* 1, 76–7.

13 Ibid 77.

Australia.[14] I turn first to Vitoria, whose work in the sixteenth century marked the emergence of a public international legal discourse in Europe.[15]

2.1 FRANCISCO DE VITORIA (c 1485–1546)

A "scholar of empire",[16] Vitoria offered, after the event, both a justification for the Spanish colonisation of the Indies and an apology for its excesses.[17] On the one hand, an abiding sense of economic entitlement, racial and religious superiority, and duty to pursue a Christianising and civilising mission in the New World meant that Vitoria's international law and legal discourse[18] needed to legitimise Spanish travel, Christianisation, and profiteering in Indian territory in the service of imperial interests.[19] On the other, although it may at first seem counter-intuitive, his construction of the 'barbarian' Indian as a legal subject is best understood as a *raison d'état* – that is, as a gesture of (Spanish) self-interest. This is because the barbarian was made subject to the law yet unworthy of its protection, subjugated rather than outlawed.[20] So, what does the barbarian's status tell us about who the foreigner was? Did Vitoria imagine the foreigner to be an outsider? Was the barbarian a foreigner? Or was the foreigner someone else? To make visible who Vitoria's foreigner was, it is important to consider first the context in which he was writing.

---

[14] See especially *Robtelmes v Brenan* (1906) 4 CLR 395, 400 (Griffith CJ); *Chu Kheng Lim v Minister for Immigration, Local Government and Ethnic Affairs* (1992) 176 CLR 1, 29–30 (Brennan, Deane and Dawson JJ) ('*Lim*'); *Al-Kateb v Godwin* (2004) 219 CLR 562, 632–3 (Hayne J); *Ruhani v Director of Police (No 2)* (2005) 222 CLR 580, 276 n 6; *Plaintiff M47-2012 v Director-General of Security* (2012) 251 CLR 1, 313 n 243; *Plaintiff M76-2013 v Minister for Immigration, Multicultural Affairs and Citizenship* (2013) 251 CLR 322, 177 (Kiefel and Keane JJ). See also *Ruddock v Vadarlis* (2001) 110 FCR 491, 520 (Beaumont J).

[15] James Brown Scott, *The Spanish Origins of International Law: Francisco de Vitoria and his Law of Nations* (Lawbook Exchange, first published 1934, 2000 ed); Arthur Nussbaum, *A Concise History of the Law of Nations* (Macmillan, first published 1947, 1954 ed); Kennedy, above n 12; Antony Anghie, *Imperialism, Sovereignty and the Making of International Law* (Cambridge University Press, 2005) 13.

[16] Martti Koskenniemi, 'International Law in Europe: Between Tradition and Renewal' (2005) 16(1) *European Journal of International Law* 113, 117.

[17] See, eg, James Crawford, 'Foreword' in Antony Anghie, *Imperialism, Sovereignty and the Making of International Law* (Cambridge University Press, 2005) xi.

[18] Williams describes law and legal discourse as "perfect instruments of empire": Robert A Williams Jr, *The American Indian in Western Legal Thought: The Discourses of Conquest* (Oxford University Press, 1990) 8, 37.

[19] Anghie, above n 15, 251.

[20] Ibid 20. Cf *Lim* (1992) 176 CLR 1, 19 (Brennan, Deane and Dawson JJ), discussed in Chapter 5, Section 5.3.1.2, 204–6.

2.1.1 *Context: Imperialism, Conquest, and a Culture of Mobility*

The Iberian Peninsula of the fifteenth and early sixteenth centuries, comprising politically and geographically fragmented kingdoms,[21] was already a society characterised by high levels of mobility. The 'discovery' of the Indies by Columbus in 1492 triggered a massive expansion of the Spanish Empire, including a significant amount of emigration from the metropole.[22] Economic hardship and the promise of wealth in the colonies served as push and pull factors for an estimated 250,000 to 300,000 emigrants from the Iberian Peninsula to the Indies,[23] an unprecedented level of emigration amongst European powers.[24]

At the same time, Spain had a cultural and religious diversity that was greater than anywhere else in Europe.[25] Spanish mobility was characterised by foreign travel to[26] and from[27] Spain for trade within Europe and across the Strait of Gibraltar,[28] as well as migratory movements that included seasonal[29] and urban migration.[30] Many migrant workers were from neighbouring countries.[31] So, the heterogeneity of Spanish society in the sixteenth century reflected often long-standing patterns of both internal and external migration. Indeed, with a prevailing "culture of mobility"[32] it was surely a society accustomed to the presence of foreigners engaged in labour and commerce.

Sixteenth-century Spain already had a long history of internecine struggles[33] and religio-racial persecution.[34] Systemic discrimination reflecting class

---

[21] Teofilo F Ruiz, *Spanish Society: 1400–1600* (Longman, 2001) 11, 17.

[22] David E Vassberg, *The Village and the Outside World in Golden Age Castile: Mobility and Migration in Everyday Rural Life* (Cambridge University Press, 1996) 83–4. According to Cholewinski, just under half a million people migrated from Spain to the Caribbean and to Central and South America and Mexico between 1506 and 1650: Ryszard Cholewinski, *Migrant Workers in International Law: Their Protection in Countries of Employment* (Clarendon Press, 1997) 15.

[23] Vassberg suggests that the official lists of legal emigrants were incomplete but that the best estimates are that about 250,000 to 300,000 emigrated from the Iberian Peninsula to the Americas during the sixteenth century. By contrast, the population of Castile at the time was in the order of seven million: Vassberg, above n 22, 83–4. Vicens Vives estimates that 500,000 emigrated to the Americas: Jaime Vicens Vives with the collaboration of Jorge Nadal Oller, *An Economic History of Spain* (Frances M López-Morillas trans, Princeton University Press, 1969) 291 [trans of: *Manuel de historia económica de España* (first published 1955 as *Apuntes del curso de historia económica de España*)].

[24] Ruiz, above n 21, 26.   [25] Ibid 93.   [26] Ibid 48, 53; Vicens Vives, above n 23, 355–7.

[27] See, eg, Ruiz, above n 21, 104; Vicens Vives, above n 23, 364.

[28] See, eg, Vicens Vives, above n 23, 301.   [29] Ruiz, above n 21, 56, 60–1.   [30] Ibid 41, 65.

[31] Vassberg, above n 22, 151–2.

[32] David Sven Reher, *Town and Country in Pre-Industrial Spain: Cuenca, 1550–1870* (Cambridge University Press, 1990) 299–304; Vassberg, above n 22, 175.

[33] Ruiz, above n 21, 18.   [34] For example, the fourteenth-century Jewish pogroms: ibid 98–9.

distinctions defined by blood and race were commonplace.[35] The push for
religious homogeneity prompted decrees of expulsion as well as the Spanish
Inquisition, primarily affecting the Jews and Moors, including *conversos*
(Jewish converts to Christianity) and *moriscos* (Muslim converts), as well as
other 'heretics' and marginalised groups such as the Roma.[36] This context is
indicative of a sociopolitical dynamic in which conversos, moriscos, and other
heretics were marked as outsiders subject to expulsion. Vitoria was himself *de
sangre semita* – that is, of Jewish ancestry descended from conversos[37] – so for
this context to permeate his conscious thought would have been almost
unavoidable. However, as the following subsection shows, even though this
was the context *in* which he was writing, it was not the context *for* which he was
writing. This is so notwithstanding that certain features of Vitoria's arguments
may have been influenced by his personal circumstances as well as the broader
exigencies of the Iberian context.[38]

2.1.2 *The Foreigner: Insider or Outsider?*

As we know, part of Vitoria's brief was to justify the Spanish colonisation of the
Indies. In this connection, even his defenders such as Cavallar acknowledge
that this meant that Vitoria's treatises needed to maintain imperial power
interests.[39] It is no surprise, then, that notwithstanding reports of gross brutality
by the conquistadors and his own outrage,[40] he generated juridical authority
for the perception that the 'barbarian' Indian was racially, culturally, and
religiously inferior. Thus, for example, Vitoria acknowledged in the Indians

---

[35] Ibid 69, 103–5; John H Elliott, *Imperial Spain: 1479–1716* (Pelican, 1963) 212–48.

[36] The Roma, believed to have first come to Europe as early as the tenth century, had a
significant presence in Spain, living on the margins of society and thus the targets of social
and official discrimination: Peter Bakker and Khristo Kiuchukov (eds), *What Is the Romani
Language?* (University of Hertfordshire Press, 2000) 13.

[37] Berta Ares Queija, Jésus Bustamante, and Francisco Castilla (eds), *Humanismo y visión del
otro en la España moderna: cuatro estudios* (Biblioteca de Historia de América, CSIC,
1993) 24.

[38] Georg Cavallar, *The Rights of Strangers: Theories of International Hospitality, the Global
Community, and Political Justice since Vitoria* (Ashgate, 2002) 115. At n 143, Cavallar notes that
Vitoria was on the government payroll and his Dominican prior had received threatening
correspondence from Charles V following Vitoria's second 'unjust titles' lecture on the
American Indians, in which Vitoria articulated limits on the conduct of the Spanish in
bringing the 'barbarians' under their rule.

[39] Although Cavallar acknowledges that he presents a "rather benign" interpretation of Vitoria's
thinking, he cannot be seen entirely as an apologist, offering as he does some more unfavour-
able interpretations of his work with regard to the problem of humanitarian intervention and
the right to hospitality: ibid 98–112.

[40] See, eg, Vitoria, above n 11, 332, regarding the conquest of Peru; Cavallar, above n 38, 117.

attributes of method, order, and reason[41] but simultaneously cast them as "insensate and slow-witted" on account of "their evil and barbarous education".[42] He regarded them as "born in sin" but not having "the use of reason to prompt them to seek baptism or the things necessary for salvation".[43] They were described as "peasants" who could be regarded as "little different from brute animals".[44] Thus, although credited by some with crafting a legal framework that championed the rights of the barbarians,[45] Vitoria conceptualised Indians as outsiders (though not outlaws) within the imperial frame. In so doing, Vitoria maintained the power interests of the Spanish.[46] Indeed, by recognising true dominion in the barbarians,[47] jurisdiction over them could serve as an effective justification for social, political, and economic control – a control that Vitoria would later (re)claim,[48] articulating the bases on which the barbarians had passed under Spanish rule. Whether inadvertent, improvised, or intentional, the effect of this was to neutralise or negate any idea that power or control may have been wrested from the Spanish through the ideas he had earlier expressed.[49]

Vitoria's 'just titles' constructed the foreigner as a figure of privilege and power, as a rights-bearing subject who was a Spaniard, not an Indian. In doing so, it is clear that Vitoria was not encoding a broader framework of general application to outsider-ness. Had he done so, he might have formulated a framework that served and protected the interests of a different group of 'outsiders' – that is, those in Spain who were instead the targets of domestic policies and priorities of religious homogeneity that resulted in decrees of expulsion and the Spanish Inquisition. But that was not his purpose. Instead, Vitoria situated his legal framework in the New World physically, while his point of analytical and ideological departure remained always and already the 'our world' of Spanish interests. There, he privileged the foreigner (an insider), subjugated the barbarian (an outsider), and sustained empire. As the following subsection shows, this privileging is also reflected in the framework of rights accorded the foreigner.

---

[41] Vitoria, above n 11, 250.   [42] Ibid.   [43] Ibid.   [44] Ibid.
[45] See, eg, Cavallar, above n 38, 75–121; cf Anghie, above n 15, 28.
[46] This was also a criticism of the *Leyes de Burgos* of 1512, which codified the conduct of the Spanish in the Americas: Ruiz, above n 21, 84.
[47] Vitoria, above n 11, 250–1.
[48] "The just titles by which the barbarians of the New World passed under the rule of the Spaniards": ibid 277–92.
[49] On the seeming incompatibility of the second and third lectures on the American Indians, cf Cavallar, above n 38, 188.

2.1.3 On Rights: A Foreigner's Framework

A key attribute of Vitoria's foreigner was the right to travel and dwell in other countries (*ius peregrinandi*). Indeed, his theories asserted that, as long as he did no harm, his foreigner could not be barred by the barbarian from entry to the barbarian's homeland.[50] To support this, Vitoria's reasons may be grouped into three broad propositions: first, that the foreigner has a right to hospitality;[51] second, that he has a right to travel or residence; and third, that he should enjoy rights relating to entry, exile, and expulsion. This section looks briefly at each, showing that Vitoria did not conceptualise these rights as universal or cosmopolitan rights, but as reflecting contingent (European) interests in the specific context of legitimising Spanish imperialism.

2.1.3.1 The Right to Hospitality

In relation to hospitality, Vitoria reasoned that it is inhuman to treat strangers and travellers badly unless they are hostile,[52] and that borders were never intended to inhibit free movement.[53] He described expulsion or prohibition on entry as acts of war,[54] concluding that those who do no harm cannot lawfully be barred from entry.[55] Indeed, he asserted that it would be a monstrous and inhumane act to do otherwise.[56] Although qualified by the possibility of having a "special cause" (for example, "if travellers were doing something evil by visiting foreign nations"), the "humane and dutiful" obligation to extend hospitality to strangers was his starting point.[57] Drawing on the universalising edicts of divine law, which informed his natural law, Vitoria prohibited the barbarians from turning their backs on the harmless and exhorted them to welcome the stranger. Indeed, he declared that "to refuse to welcome strangers and foreigners is inherently evil."[58] Finally, he asserted that it would be

---

50 Vitoria, above n 11, 278.
51 Gaurier argues that the right to hospitality developed by Grotius, Pufendorf, and Vattel was in essence a right of conquest foundational to the law of nations: Dominique Gaurier, 'Cosmopolis and Utopia' in Bardo Fassbender and Anne Peters (eds), *The Oxford Handbook of the History of International Law* (Oxford University Press, 2013) 250, 264. The Vitorian conception of the right to hospitality may be similarly characterised.
52 Vitoria, above n 11, 278.
53 Ibid; see also James A R Nafziger, 'The General Admission of Aliens under International Law' (1983) 77(4) *American Journal of International Law* 804, 811; Étienne Balibar, *We, the People of Europe? Reflections on Transnational Citizenship* (James Swenson trans, Princeton University Press, 2004) 139–41 [trans of: *Nous, citoyens d'Europe: Les Frontières, l'État, le peuple* (first published 2001)].
54 Vitoria, above n 11, 278.   55 Ibid 279.   56 Ibid 278–9.   57 Ibid 278.   58 Ibid 281.

contrary to the maxim "love thy neighbour" to bar the Spanish from entry into the territory of the barbarian Indians.[59]

2.1.3.2 Right to Travel and Reside

In recognising the right to travel and reside in the territory of another state, Vitoria recognised implicitly that an irrepressible peripatetic urge (whether voluntary or involuntary) predates, and cannot be contained by, the construction of nations or borders. Furthermore, he considered that their construction was never intended to inhibit free movement[60] and that to do otherwise would have been thought "inhuman in the time of Noah".[61] Although he tempered the right to travel with an obligation to do no harm or detriment to others,[62] rather than reflecting high principle, framing the obligation in this way ensured that the travel and residence of the Spanish coloniser could not be construed as causing harm. This is because Vitoria saw fit simply to *assume* the travel of the Spaniards to be neither harmful nor detrimental to the Indians and, therefore, lawful.[63]

2.1.3.3 Entry, Exile, and Expulsion

Concerning rights relating to entry, exile, and expulsion, Vitoria made three points which highlight the enormity of the affront to free movement that he perceived in the denial of entry and in acts of expulsion, banishment, or exile. In this vein, he asserted that the prohibition on entry in the first instance and expulsion in the second might be regarded as acts of war, meriting a 'just war' response. Such a response would, he said, be "within the bounds of blameless self-defence"[64] if, on account of the barbarians' cowardice, foolishness, and ignorance, the Spaniards were unable to convince them of their peaceful intentions.[65] Finally, he suggested that banishment or exile of Spanish foreigners was akin to punishing them for a crime they had not committed; indeed, he declared that it is not lawful to banish visitors who are innocent of any crime. The broad premise of each of these points is that those who do no harm cannot lawfully be barred from entry to or otherwise excluded from territory. Indeed, citing Virgil's *Aeneid*, Vitoria regarded expulsion, exile, or denial of entry of foreigners as a monstrous and inhuman act born of "barbarous customs".[66]

---

[59] Ibid 279. [60] Ibid 278. [61] Ibid. [62] Ibid. [63] Ibid. [64] Ibid 282.
[65] Ibid 281–2.
[66] Ibid 282; see also Hugo Grotius, *De jure praedae commentarius* (Gwladys L Williams and Walter H Zeydel trans, Clarendon Press, first published 1604, 1950 ed) ch XII, 219.

As the foregoing makes visible, Vitoria's framework privileged the rights and interests of foreigners because of *who* he understood the foreigner to be. It was an imperialist rights framework that actively diminished the barbarian Indian, even though it ascribed to her legal rights and personality. Furthermore, it did not take into account an immediate social and historical context of medieval migrations to Spain of, in particular, the Jews, Moors, and Roma and their subsequent discrimination, marginalisation, persecution, and expulsion.[67] The Jews, Moors, and Roma were outsiders, but they were not Vitoria's foreigners. Instead, Vitoria's texts reveal a style of argument according to which only a (certain kind of) foreigner could assert rights to mobility and protection – a style of argument that, as we will see, has been (re)produced and (re)shaped across time and place. In other words, we begin to see that who the foreigner is understood to be has a profound influence on the way in which the foreigner-sovereign relation is juridically authorised, shaped, and used.

This outline of Vitoria's foreigner, and his articulation of the foreigner's attendant rights, provides an important starting point for understanding how the foreigner has been conceptualised in early international law. As the following sections show, although the juridical purposes of Grotius, Pufendorf, and Vattel became more variegated through the seventeenth and eighteenth centuries, the foreigner remained a European insider in international law (as imperialist, trader, or exile), with clearly articulated rights and entitlements. In other words, in the foreigner-sovereign relation, the foreigner remained aligned with, rather than oppositional to, the sovereign. I turn now to Grotius, often regarded as the "principal forerunner" of modern international law.[68]

2.2 HUGO GROTIUS (1583–1645)

Grotius' theories drew significantly on the earlier work of Vitoria,[69] and their respective colonial contexts bear many parallels. Whether out of respect for Vitoria's theories, or as a strategy to influence (and undermine) the

---

[67] Vitoria deals only with the question in the context of conversion of unbelievers, concluding that conversion was not by force. See 'Lecture on the Evangelization of Unbelievers', Vitoria, above n 11, 339–51, particularly at 342–3.

[68] Edward Dumbauld, *The Life and Legal Writings of Hugo Grotius* (University of Oklahoma Press, 1969) 58; Anghie, above n 15, 13. However, this attribution has been the subject of considerable debate. See, eg, Nussbaum, above n 15. Cf Scott, above n 15; Cavallar, above n 38, 164; Weeramantry, above n 10, 136–9.

[69] This is particularly clear in *De jure praedae*: Grotius, *De jure praedae*, above n 66; see also Anghie, above n 15, 14; Cavallar, above n 38, 122; Luis Valenzuela-Vermehren, 'Vitoria, Humanism, and the School of Salamanca in Early Sixteenth-Century Spain: A Heuristic Overview' (2013) 16(2) *Logos: A Journal of Catholic Thought and Culture* 99, 118–20.

Spanish-dominated Portuguese political arena in the scramble for trade monopolies in the East,[70] his often emphatic reliance on Vitoria's theories established a cord of continuity in international legal thinking which Grotius developed in significant ways.

2.2.1 *Context: Trade Monopolies and the Thirty Years War*

One of Grotius' earliest projects was to write *De jure praedae commentarius* (*Commentary On the Law of Prize and Booty*),[71] originally titled *De Indis* ('On the [East] Indies'). It was probably commissioned by the Dutch East India Company.[72]

In the midst of court proceedings regarding the capture in the Straits of Singapore of the Portuguese ship the *Santa Catarina*, his task is said to have been to persuade public opinion that it was legitimate for the Dutch to claim as 'prize' the proceeds of such property.[73]

De jure praedae draws most strongly on the rights to travel and trade enunciated by Vitoria.[74] However, in East Asia particular international relations and trade structures, notably with respect to China and India, attracted a more nuanced European response. Cavallar has suggested that these relations and structures demanded adaptations to the colonial project that explicitly acknowledged the rights of non-European communities and individuals.[75] Although this may be arguable – and Grotius certainly described the Indians of the Orient (in contrast to the American Indians) as "neither insane nor irrational, but clever and sagacious"[76] – it is also possible to see that Grotius' primary interest was to undermine Portuguese claims on 'discovered' territories.[77] Coupled with this, he asserted the rights of trade and hospitality,[78] necessity,[79] (unarmed and innocent) passage,[80] and freedom of the high seas,[81]

---

[70] Cavallar, above n 38, 146, 146 n 77.   [71] Grotius, *De jure praedae*, above n 66.

[72] It is commonly assumed that Grotius was on a retainer from the Dutch East India Company ('*Vereenigde Oostindische Compagnie*' or 'VOC'): see, eg, Cavallar, above n 38, 145. Borschberg considers there to be some doubt about this but concludes that *De jure praedae* was probably commissioned by the directors of the VOC: Peter Borschberg, *Hugo Grotius, the Portuguese and Free Trade in the East Indies* (NUS Press, 2011) 110.

[73] Dumbauld, above n 68, 25–6, 41.

[74] Grotius, *De jure praedae*, above n 66, ch XII, 218, 219–20; Cavallar, above n 38, 124.

[75] Cavallar, above n 38, 145–6.   [76] Grotius, *De jure praedae*, above n 66, ch XII, 222.

[77] Ibid 220–22.   [78] Ibid 219.   [79] Ibid ch XI, 178.   [80] Ibid ch XII, 244.

[81] Ibid 216 n 1, where it is clarified that Grotius' celebrated exposition of the freedom of the high seas, *Mare liberum*, first published in 1608, was a revised version of ch XII of the *De jure praedae* manuscript. Following its publication, *Mare liberum* was placed on the Vatican's *Index of Prohibited Books*: Cavallar, above n 38, 161. The predecessor to freedom of the high seas was the right to common property, a right which Vitoria asserted as extending to the "open

and used liberally the notion of 'just war' to justify the claim of 'prize'.[82] This reflected his ultimate objective of conquering the trade monopoly of the Portuguese. Indeed, his treatise bore an anti-Iberian tone suggestive of this political-economic purpose.[83]

In Grotius' later treatise, *De jure belli ac pacis*,[84] his focus shifted, from the project of asserting and mediating trading rights on the high seas and in the East to Europe. This reflected the troubled times in which he was living, marked most significantly by the catastrophic Thirty Years War. This war of religion would take the lives of an estimated four million people, either directly through conflict or indirectly through its disastrous social and economic consequences, including famine and disease.[85]

Embroiled in the religious turmoil that characterised the Thirty Years War, Grotius knew first-hand the life of a foreigner in exile. In 1619, he was sentenced to life imprisonment for an unspecified crime that would later be classed as treason.[86] In prison he was threatened with torture[87] and held incommunicado, denied permission to see his wife, children, or friends.[88] In 1621, he fled to Paris from his native Netherlands after his wife effected his dramatic escape from prison in a book chest.[89] He lived in exile in Paris (1621–31) and then, after attempting to repatriate, returned to a life in exile in Hamburg (1632–34). He later returned to Paris as an ambassador for Sweden (1635–45), until shortly before his death.[90] It was during his first exile in Paris that he wrote *De jure belli ac pacis* (1625),[91] his most celebrated work. With this context in mind, it

---

seas, rivers and ports": Vitoria, above n 11, 279. Grotius qualified his assertion that the seas could not be occupied and therefore constituted common property, concluding that areas such as bays and straits may be occupied. Grotius, *De jure praedae*, above n 66, ch XII, 239; see also Cavallar, above n 38, 149.

[82] Grotius, *De jure praedae*, above n 66; Dumbauld, above n 68, 25–8.

[83] Borschberg, above n 72, 111.

[84] Hugo Grotius, *De jure belli ac pacis libri tres* (Francis W Kelsey trans, Clarendon Press, first published 1646, 1925 ed) vol 2 [*On the Law of War and Peace: Three Books*].

[85] See, eg, John Merriman, *A History of Modern Europe: From the Renaissance to the Present* (W W Norton, 1996) 176.

[86] Dumbauld, above n 68, 13.   [87] Ibid 104.   [88] Ibid 94, 110.

[89] Ibid 9, 11–19; see also Atle Grahl-Madsen, 'The European Tradition of Asylum and the Development of International Refugee Law' (1966) 3(3) *Journal of Peace and Research* 278, 278. Note that the Italian publicist Alberico Gentili (1552–1608) on whom Grotius relied heavily in his work was also a refugee: Cavallar, above n 38, 156.

[90] Peter Haggenmacher, 'Hugo Grotius (1583–1645)' in Bardo Fassbender and Anne Peters (eds), *The Oxford Handbook of the History of International Law* (Oxford University Press, 2012) 1098–101.

[91] Grotius, *De jure belli*, above n 84.

is no surprise that Grotius' work speaks to the movement of foreigners not only with regard to trade and commerce, but also to that of the social and political upheaval of war.

2.2.2 Foreigners: Protecting 'Prize' and Seeking Peace

Grotius regarded mobility as being part of the natural and advantageous order of things, integrating decisively the rights and needs of the foreigner into his later work as part of his quest to craft a "plausible intellectual foundation for a peaceful world".[92] Notably, he declared that "[i]t is not contrary to friendship to admit individual subjects".[93] This suggests that, at least in the European context, Grotius viewed migration as a presumptively benign dynamic – that is, one that overcomes adversity by providing refuge to those in need as well as facilitating trade and commerce in the interests of host communities and states. In constructing rights crucial to the foreigner (to free movement, to necessity, and indeed to non-discrimination), Grotius tempered them with limitations (discussed in Section 2.2.3) that recognised the authority of the host state and community.

However, while the intra-European context is an important dimension to understanding who the Grotian foreigner was, in *De jure praedae* he cast the foreigner in the role of imperialising trader, thus employing an imperialist perspective that, as he made explicit, drew heavily on Vitoria's work.[94] Indeed, it is clear that even the peaceful world he sought in his later treatise *De jure belli ac pacis* remained one between (European) sovereign (more or less) equals, which maintained at least implicitly the same structural diminishment of the (non-European) *un*equals that had underpinned his earlier conceptions of international law in *De jure praedae*. Furthermore, while the intra-European relations and the disruption caused by Europe's religious wars may be taken to be Grotius' immediate context in crafting *De jure belli ac pacis*, it seems clear that this later work drew on *De jure praedae* in significant respects.[95]

In *De jure praedae*, Grotius was primarily focused on the movement of people for the purposes of imperial trade and commerce in the East Indies. But who did he understand the foreigners in the East Indies to be? As noted earlier, East Asia had international relations and trade structures more clearly recognisable to the European.[96] For example, in the early fifteenth century the

---

[92] Anghie, above n 15, 126 n 38. [93] Grotius, *De jure belli*, above n 84, bk III ch XX, 819.

[94] Grotius, *De jure praedae*, above n 66, ch XII, 219, 221–4, 226, 262.

[95] Dumbauld, above n 68, 31.

[96] Grotius, *De jure praedae*, above n 66, ch XII, 255, 260; Cavallar, above n 38, 145.

Chinese admiral Zheng He had led seven voyages of Ming imperial fleets comprising as many as 350 ships and thousands of crew apiece as far as India, Arabia, and East Africa. So, as Manning has noted evocatively, "when the Portuguese mariner Vasco da Gama rounded the Cape of Good Hope and entered the Indian Ocean in 1498, he was joining an existing network of trade and migration rather than creating a new one."[97] Just over a century later, it is clear that Grotius was aware of significant movements of non-European foreigners across many parts of South and East Asia, as well as between South and East Asia and East Africa.[98] Yet, although credited with rejecting the legal pretexts for taking tribal lands by force and resisting the use of international law to assert cultural or religious superiority or domination,[99] was he concerned about the rights and interests of the likes of Admiral Zheng and his cohorts? There is nothing to indicate that he was. Although there is some ambiguous – and contestable – evidence that Grotius was well disposed to protecting the rights and interests of the non-European,[100] there is scant evidence in his texts to indicate that he was seriously concerned about proclaiming or protecting their rights and interests *qua* foreigners.[101] As such, there is nothing to indicate that the Grotian foreigner was other than a European. On the contrary, the unequal power dynamics of the imperialist international law that characterised *De jure praedae*, particularly in the context of the quest for trade monopolies in East Asia, affirms the view that the Grotian foreigner was, like that envisaged by Vitoria, always and anywhere European. And, as the following subsection elaborates, as a European the Grotian foreigner enjoyed a range of enabling rights.

---

97   Patrick Manning, *Migration in World History* (Routledge, 2nd ed, 2013) 114.
98   Grotius, *De jure praedae*, above n 66, ch XII, 242; Manning, above n 97, 108–12; Borschberg, above n 72, 106–46, 267 n 244.
99   See, eg, Rosalyn Higgins, 'Grotius and the Development of International Law in the United Nations Period' in Hedley Bull, Benedict Kingsbury, and Adam Roberts (eds), *Hugo Grotius and International Relations* (Clarendon Press, 1990) 267, 278.
100 On the controversy surrounding Grotius' treatise on the origin of the American peoples, *De Origine Gentium Americanarum Dissertatio* (1642), see Joan-Pau Rubiés, 'Hugo Grotius's Dissertation on the Origin of the American Peoples and the Use of Comparative Methods' (1991) 52(2) *Journal of the History of Ideas* 221; Cavallar, above n 38, 144–5; Jane O Newman, '"Race", Religion and the Law: Rhetorics of Sameness and Difference in the Work of Hugo Grotius' in Victoria Ann Kahn and Lorna Hutson, *Rhetoric and Law in Early Modern Europe* (Yale University Press, 2001) 285.
101 In one instance, following Vitoria, Grotius poses what he describes as a "heretical" hypothetical in which the American Indians are "the first foreigners to come to Spain" and claim dominion over territory on the strength of divergent religious beliefs. However, it seems clear that his purpose is to subvert any Portuguese claim to dominion over the territory of the East Indies: Grotius, *De jure praedae*, above n 66, ch XII, 222.

2.2.3 *On Rights: A Matter of Mobility and Necessity*

Grotius' conception of international society emphasised certain rights (notably property rights) that were common to all human beings.[102] He constructed a legal framework with three elements: natural law (*ius naturae*), the law of nations (*ius gentium*), and volitional divine law (*divinum voluntarium*).[103] Drawing authority from these legal genres, Grotius' framework of rights focused primarily on questions of mobility and necessity. This framework acknowledged and integrated the inherent tension between the autonomies of the sovereign on the one hand and the migration of the foreigner on the other. It did so by conditioning many of the rights articulated. That is, it vested rights in foreigners themselves as well as authority on the part of states to admit migrants and exiles.[104] The rights of passage, temporary sojourn, and necessity are illustrative. However, the right to enter and reside, to which I turn first, weighs more strongly in favour of the foreigner.

2.2.3.1 The Right to Enter and Reside

Grotius recognised foreigners as having the right to enter and reside in the territory of another state, whether temporarily or permanently.[105] In particular, he considered legitimate the right of passage for those desirous of "[carrying] on commerce with a distant people"[106] and the right of temporary sojourn for the purposes of health, shelter, "or for any other good reason".[107] Likewise, he regarded "those who have been driven from their homes" as having the "right to acquire permanent residence in another country".[108] So, although not explicitly asserting the *obligation* to grant asylum, such an obligation seems implicit in his articulation of the individual's right to asylum and his acknowledgment of the futility of exile where there is nowhere for the exiled person to go.[109] This is also true of the right of those expelled from their homes to acquire a permanent residence in another country.[110] Finally, Grotius considered that the rights of *a people* were not extinguished by migration, whether such migration was of the people's own accord or under compulsion.[111]

---

[102] Cavallar, above n 38, 150.
[103] Grotius, *De jure belli*, above n 84, Prolegomena, 24, bk I ch I, 41; Dumbauld, above n 68, 64.
[104] Grotius, *De jure belli*, above n 84, bk III ch XX, 819–20.   [105] Ibid bk II ch II, 192, 201–2.
[106] Ibid 196–7. Grotius first developed this argument in *De jure praedae*, above n 66, ch XII, 216–20: Cavallar, above n 38, 147.
[107] Grotius, *De jure belli*, above n 84, bk II ch II, 201.   [108] Ibid 201–2.
[109] Grotius quotes Livy Perseus: "What is accomplished by sending any one into exile, if there is not going to be a place anywhere for the person exiled?": ibid bk III ch XX, 820.
[110] Ibid bk II ch II, 201.   [111] Ibid bk II ch IX, 314.

2.2.3.2 Rights of Passage and Temporary Sojourn

Grotius articulated the right of passage as a right only to be exercised "for legitimate reasons", amongst which he included forced migration or trade and commerce.[112] From the point of view of the migrant, right of passage must first be demanded; but then if refused it may be made by force, as long as passage is demanded "without evil intent".[113] As such, passage could be both legitimately asserted and (if ill intentioned) resisted. In analytical (and contextual) contrast to Vitoria, benign purpose was not to be assumed. Furthermore, Grotius asserted that the right of temporary sojourn must be for "good reason" and the right to acquire a permanent residence in another country subject to the obligation to "observe any regulations which are necessary to avoid strifes".[114]

In relation to the right of necessity, Grotius concluded that the right to enjoy basic necessities by non-citizens might temper the authority of a state to condition their presence in its territory. For example, Grotius articulated a primitive state of community ownership that may be revived by necessity, or the imperative of survival; the right of necessity, he said, overrode the right to private ownership because the enjoyment of private ownership remained embedded with an obligation to "depart as little as possible from natural equity".[115] By drawing no distinction between the content of its enjoyment for citizens and foreigners (remember that contextually both citizen and foreigner were European), Grotius made clear that the right of necessity must also be understood as extending to foreigners.[116] Its scope included food,[117] clothing,[118] and health.[119] However, in a gesture of reciprocity among sovereign equals and their subjects, Grotius also conditioned such rights. Necessity, he declared, should be "unavoidable", cannot be exercised in case of equal need, and should carry with it an obligation of restitution "whenever this can be done".[120] Again, he made no distinction between the foreigner and the citizen.

---

[112]   Ibid bk II ch II, 196–7.   [113]   Ibid 198.   [114]   Ibid 201–2.   [115]   Ibid 193.
[116]   Ibid 192–5.
[117]   See, eg, ibid 192, where Grotius indicates that foreigners have an equal right, unless forbidden by law, to own the "wild animals, fish and birds" they have caught.
[118]   Cavallar, above n 38, 148.
[119]   Grotius, *De jure belli*, above n 84, bk II ch II, 201; see also Nafziger, above n 53, 810. In other words, (European) foreigners were also entitled to what have been described in the contemporary context as 'survival rights': Matthew Craven, *The International Covenant on Economic, Social and Cultural Rights: A Perspective on Its Development* (Clarendon Press, 1995) 194.
[120]   Grotius, *De jure belli*, above n 84, bk II ch II, 194–5.

2.2.3.3 Right to Non-Discrimination

The final right of immediate import is the right of foreigners to non-discrimination on the basis of nationality. Grotius articulated this right such that any rights to which foreigners are also entitled – as compared to matters of privilege or favour – "cannot be denied to one people alone, except on account of previous wrong-doing".[121] This prohibition on discrimination would seem to be concerned with distinctions between different groups of foreigners rather than between foreigners and the citizenry, as Grotius' starting premise is that he is only dealing with rights to which foreigners as well as citizens are entitled. "Things permitted" other than rights – in other words, things granted as a favour – were not included in Grotius' conception because, he said, they did not fall within the law of nature.[122] A concession that citizens have different rights to foreigners seems implicit here, but the nature of the rights that he asserted in this context – "to hunt, fish, snare birds, or gather pearls, to inherit by will, to sell property, and even to contract marriages"[123] – included significant rights of a social and economic nature and rights of survival or necessity as well as other rights that might be considered important for an individual to lead a dignified life, or, in Grotius' words, "the right to such acts as human life requires".[124] Again, this framing would seem to make clear that the Grotian foreigner was, always and everywhere, a European and, in that sense, an insider.

To conclude, therefore, even with the spatial shift from international law's imperialising reach to the intra-European context, we can see that the foreigner's European 'insider-ness' remains. This is because the point of analytical and ideological departure is that the foreigner (like the citizen) is an insider in (intra-European) sovereign relations with (more or less) equal rights even though he is physically outside his country of citizenship. Again, therefore, we see that there is nothing inevitable about the foreigner's 'outsider-ness' in the foreigner-sovereign relation; on the contrary, Grotius was casting the foreigner in his own image. And as Section 2.3 shows, Pufendorf took a similar approach.

2.3 SAMUEL PUFENDORF (1632–1694)

Over the course of a prolific career, Pufendorf published a number of treatises that dealt directly with the rights of foreigners largely through the prism of toleration, understood as a right to freedom of religion, albeit a right lacking an

---

[121] Ibid 204–5.   [122] Ibid 205.   [123] Ibid.   [124] Ibid 203–4.

abstract, theoretical character.[125] A trilogy of Pufendorf's treatises are of particular interest:[126] *De jure naturae et gentium libri octo* (1672);[127] *De officio
hominis et civis juxta legem naturalem libri duo* (1673);[128] and *De habitu
religionis Christianae ad vitam civilem* (1687),[129] which has been regarded as
an appendix to *De officio hominis*.[130]

Pufendorf's work was informed by the Thirty Years War of religion and the
subsequent effects of the Revocation of the Edict of Nantes.[131] Most importantly for present purposes, Pufendorf's treatises, like those of Grotius, clearly
anticipated, indeed assumed, mobility to be part of the natural order of things
and necessary for the purposes of self-preservation,[132] particularly in the face of
religious intolerance. However, neither his defence of intellectual freedom
and robust toleration of religious, scientific, and philosophical ideas nor the
necessary corollary of free movement would be clear through an examination
of his text without also having an understanding of the context in which he was
writing.[133] The following subsection contextualises the work of Pufendorf
in order to make visible his conceptualisation of the foreigner-sovereign
relation, specifically his emphases on the foreigner's rights to mobility and
self-preservation and his insistence on the sovereign's tolerance of the foreigner.

---

[125]   Detlef Döring, 'Samuel von Pufendorf and Toleration' in John C Laursen and Cary J
        Nederman (eds), *Beyond the Persecuting Society: Religious Toleration before the
        Enlightenment* (University of Pennsylvania Press, 1998) 178, 184–92.

[126]   The selection of Pufendorf's work examined in this genealogy is intended to provide an
        illustration of the work of Pufendorf as it relates to the figure of the foreigner and the rights to
        which the foreigner was entitled.

[127]   Samuel Pufendorf, *De jure naturae et gentium libri octo* (C H and W A Oldfather trans,
        Clarendon Press, first published 1688, 1934 ed) [*On the Law of Nature and Nations [Peoples]
        in Eight Books*].

[128]   Samuel Pufendorf, *On the Duty of Man and Citizen according to Natural Law* (James Tully
        ed, Michael Silverthorne trans, Cambridge University Press, 1991) [trans of: *De officio hominis
        et civis juxta legem naturalem libri duo* (first published 1673)].

[129]   Samuel Pufendorf, *Of the Nature and Qualification of Religion in Reference to Civil Society*
        (printed by D E for A Roper and A Bofvile, 1698) [trans of: *De habitu religionis Christianae
        ad vitam civilem* (first published 1687)], via Early English Books Online <http://eebo.cha
        dwyck.com/home>.

[130]   Ibid.

[131]   The Revocation of the Edict of Nantes targeted Calvinist Protestants (the Huguenots) in
        France, forbidding Protestant baptism, worship, and education, and requiring the conversion
        to Catholicism of Protestant ministers or their departure: *Edict of Fontainebleau*, proclaimed
        18 October 1685.

[132]   Use of the term 'self-preservation' in relation to the individual in this context contrasts
        strikingly with its use as a justification for state action in the construction of an absolute
        sovereign right to exclude (even friendly) aliens. See Chapter 3.

[133]   John C Laursen (ed), *Religious Toleration: 'The Variety of Rites' from Cyrus to Defoe* (St
        Martin's Press, 1999) xv. Laursen makes this point in relation to the intricacies of toleration
        debates, but it applies equally and by extension to attendant rights to free movement.

2.3.1 Context: War and Peace, Prison and Persecution

Like Grotius, Pufendorf and his family had first-hand experience of the terrors of the wars of religion, which were concluded by the Peace of Westphalia in 1648. Pufendorf was born in Saxony in 1632, in the midst of the Thirty Years War. One of eleven children from a poor Lutheran family, he was among the seven who survived.[134] Later, in 1658, while tutor to the family of Sweden's special envoy in Copenhagen, Pufendorf was imprisoned for eight months along with the other members of the ambassador's retinue. This followed the unexpected revival of war against Denmark by the Swedes.[135] He would also bear witness to the expulsion of the Huguenots from France following Louis XIV's Revocation of the Edict of Nantes.[136]

Writing in the wake of the Peace of Westphalia, Pufendorf's work retained many of the natural law underpinnings that characterised that of Vitoria and Grotius. It was in prison in Copenhagen that Pufendorf wrote his first major work, *Elementorum jurisprudentiae universalis libri II*.[137] After his release in 1659, suffering serious illness and almost dying in a shipwreck, he moved to study in Leiden and later to teach in Heidelberg (1661–68) and Lund (1668–77). He then moved to Stockholm (1677–88) as royal historiographer.[138]

In 1688, Pufendorf was called to the court of Friedrich Wilhelm of Brandenburg in Berlin.[139] Friedrich Wilhelm was known for his "toleration politics",[140] which appear to have drawn him to Pufendorf. Friedrich Wilhelm had issued the Brandenburg Tolerance Edict (1664), which gave equal rights

---

[134] Michael Seidler, 'Pufendorf's Moral and Political Philosophy' (19 March 2013) *The Stanford Encyclopedia of Philosophy* <http://plato.stanford.edu/entries/pufendorf-moral/>, citing Detlef Döring, 'Biographisches zu Samuel Pufendorf' in B Geyer and H Goerlich (eds), *Samuel Pufendorf und seine Wirkungen bis auf die heutige Zeit* (Nomos Verlagsgesellschaft, 1996) 23–37.

[135] Seidler, above n 134.

[136] Also known as the Edict of Fontainebleau, issued in October 1684, the Edict of Nantes was issued in April 1598 and granted a measure of freedom of religion, conscience, and worship to French Protestants, the Huguenots, establishing an uneasy truce and era of religious pluralism. For more on the Edict of Nantes, see Ruth Whelan and Carol Baxter, *Toleration and Religious Identity: The Edict of Nantes and Its Implications in France, Britain and Ireland* (Four Courts Press, 2003). It is in the light of these events that Grahl-Madsen treats the modern European tradition of asylum as dating from 1685: Grahl-Madsen, above n 89, 278.

[137] Samuel Pufendorf, *Elementorum jurisprudentiae universalis libri duo* (W A Oldfather trans, Clarendon Press, first published 1672, 1931 ed).

[138] Knud Haakonssen, 'Samuel Pufendorf (1632–1694)' in Bardo Fassbender and Anne Peters (eds), *The Oxford Handbook of the History of International Law* (Oxford University Press, 2013) 1102.

[139] Samuel Pufendorf, *The Political Writings of Samuel Pufendorf* (Craig L Carr ed, Michael J Seidler trans, Oxford University Press, 1994) 4.

[140] Seidler, above n 134.

to Lutherans and Calvinists and which prohibited open criticism of other religions by priests. Later, he issued the Edict of Potsdam (1685) in direct response to the revocation in the same year of the Edict of Nantes[141] by Louis XIV. The Edict of Potsdam provided for the safe passage of French Protestants (Huguenots) to Brandenburg-Prussia and authorised them to hold church services in their native French.[142] The *dragonnades* policy of Louis XIV (1681), designed to harass and intimidate the Huguenot population in France, had already caused the flight of thousands to seek asylum in England, Germany, Holland, Switzerland, and the North American colonies.[143] These numbers would rise to an estimated 200,000 people following the Revocation of the Edict of Nantes.[144] After issuing the Edict of Potsdam, Friedrich Wilhelm's Brandenburg-Prussia received an estimated 20,000 French Huguenots; the edict also triggered migration by the persecuted of Russia, the Netherlands, and Bohemia.[145] With this as his context, Pufendorf clearly anticipated, indeed assumed, mobility to be part of the natural order of things.

2.3.2 *Becoming a Foreigner: An Act of Self-Preservation*

Pufendorf recognised the right of an individual to flee to the protection of another state for the purposes of self-preservation, particularly as an expression of freedom of religion. In the same connection, he gave expression to the right of passage, asserting that "no one can question the barbarity of showing an indiscriminate hostility to those who come on a peaceful mission".[146] In *De habitu religionis Christianae*, Pufendorf offered, among other things, a rationale for the toleration politics that had informed Friedrich Wilhelm's offer of asylum to the Huguenots embodied in the Edict of Potsdam. Indeed, it was this treatise, dedicated to Friedrich Wilhelm, which is said to have prompted his appointment to the Brandenburg court.[147]

---

[141] The revocation of the Edict of Nantes is also known as the declaration of the Edict of Fontainebleau (1685).

[142] John Stoye, *Europe Unfolding: 1648–1688* (Blackwell, 2nd ed, 2000) 272.

[143] Ibid 263–74.   [144] Ibid.

[145] See, eg, Grahl-Madsen, above n 89, 278; Stoye, above n 142, 270.

[146] Pufendorf, *De jure naturae et gentium*, above n 127, bk VIII 365; Nafziger, above n 53, 811.

[147] David Saunders, 'Hegemon History: Pufendorf's Shifting Perspectives on France and French Power' in Olaf Asbach and Peter Schröder (eds), *War, the State and International Law in the Seventeenth Century* (Ashgate, 2010) 211, 215. The Brandenburg-Prussian refuge in the Palatine region to which the doctrine of religious toleration gave rise would, however, be short-lived; in 1689 the Palatinate became a target of Louis XIV's armies, which devastated the region, forcing the refugees further east: Tim Blanning, *The Pursuit of Glory: Europe 1648–1815* (Penguin, 2008) 87.

Reflecting this post-Westphalian context, it would seem that Pufendorf's international legal theories were less about imperial ambition and expansion than navigating post-Westphalian sovereign relations among European equals. This may explain why, as in Grotius' later work, there is less in Pufendorf's work that is indicative of the foreigner as coloniser and more about the status and attributes of legal subjects, whether citizen, resident, sojourner, or alien.[148] His focus appears instead to have been on the rights, statuses, and attributes of the foreigner – still a European – as émigré and exile *in Europe*. Thus, as Section 2.3.3 shows, under threat of injury or hostile intent, he took the view that it is preferable "to emigrate", "to look out for oneself by fleeing", or "to place oneself under the protection of another state".[149] Likewise, he recognised that such departure and entry into the jurisdiction of another state may be compelled by extreme necessity or by hostile force.

2.3.3 On Rights: Mobility as a Consequential Right

In articulating a rights framework for the foreigner, Pufendorf can be understood as treating mobility as a right, but more as a right of self-preservation consequential to other rights than as a right in itself. Specifically, he reaffirmed the rights to engage in trade and commerce and to freedom of conscience and religion.

To Pufendorf, inter-state trade and commerce remained a key feature of social and economic life and, as he acknowledged, did not compel the coalescence into one state of those who engage in trade and commerce between each other.[150] In this sense mobility must be understood as a necessary corollary of the right to engage in trade and commerce. Perhaps more significantly, Pufendorf recognised the right of an individual to flee the state in which she is a citizen. Contextually, the premise of this right to free movement was the right to freedom of conscience and religion and, in the interests of self-preservation, gave rise to a consequential right to claim the protection of another state.[151] He recognised that some states do not permit emigration without their express consent or the surrender of a surety[152] – that is, where exit is controlled or otherwise authorised. However, he regarded it as "preferable that a free man be understood to have reserved for himself a license to emigrate at his discretion".[153] While the price for this appears to have been the loss of citizenship,

---

[148] The colonial world was within his conscious thought, but with less prominence: Pufendorf, *De jure naturae et gentium*, above n 127, bk VIII ch XI § 6 1355–6.
[149] Pufendorf, *Political Writings*, above n 139, 237.   [150] Ibid 205.   [151] Ibid 237.
[152] Ibid 264.   [153] Ibid.

Pufendorf considered such an émigré to be a (Socratic) "citizen of the world" rather than "someone assigned to a certain lump of soil".[154] As a corollary of mobility, Pufendorf constructed legal subjects with a hierarchy of attachment that is more nuanced. In his estimation, the ("native or naturalized") citizen enjoyed full rights,[155] the resident partial rights,[156] the sojourner a less stable form of temporary attachment, and the alien (who, he said, intends to remain a short time) no attachment at all.[157] He was mindful, however, of the "poverty of language" that compels the use of a single word to express both status and attributes.[158] Applying this reasoning, 'alien' may denote the status of an individual, but it may also be considered an attribute because it is conceived as a passive quality.[159] Here, Pufendorf hinted at the attendant risks of assuming attributes to inhere in status, not least because "several statuses can exist concurrently in the case of a single person".[160] So, while he denied that the status of citizen inheres in the resident alien, foreigner, or temporary inhabitant,[161] he nevertheless characterised them as 'citizens of the world'.

In exploring whether a people is bound to endure a prince's indignities and abuses, whether contractual, social, physical, or legal, Pufendorf was clear about the right to flee and seek refuge elsewhere:

> Even when a prince threatens the most dreadful injury with a hostile intent, it is preferable to emigrate, to look out for oneself by fleeing, or to place oneself under the protection of another state.[162]

Here, Pufendorf departed from Grotius, who he regarded as wrongly asserting that there is no right of a people to leave a state as a group. The Grotian logic appeared to gesture to the continued existence of society through the consolidation of sovereignty,[163] but Pufendorf argued that if there is an individual right to emigrate, it would follow that such a right should also apply to groups, even if it serves to weaken the state from which they have come.[164] However, he did not equate this with withdrawal of sovereignty. Rather, he said, it is vital that the individual or group physically leave the territory of the state:

> For otherwise there would be supreme confusion of sovereignties, if whole cities were permitted to withdraw themselves from the sovereignty of their own state at their pleasure and either subject themselves to another sovereignty or establish their own special commonwealth thereafter.[165]

[154] Ibid.   [155] Pufendorf, *On the Duty of Man and Citizen*, above n 128, 138.   [156] Ibid.
[157] Pufendorf, *Elementorum jurisprudentiae universalis*, above n 137, 16.   [158] Ibid.
[159] Ibid.   [160] Ibid.   [161] Pufendorf, *Political Writings*, above n 139, 216.   [162] Ibid 237.
[163] Grotius, *De jure belli*, above n 84, bk II ch V, 254; cited in Pufendorf, *Political Writings*, above n 139, bk VIII ch 11, 265.
[164] Pufendorf, *Political Writings*, above n 139, bk VIII ch 11, 265.   [165] Ibid.

At the same time, Pufendorf recognised that such departures and entry into the jurisdiction of another state may be compelled by "extreme necessity"[166] or by "hostile force".[167] In so doing, he effectively recognised that the right to survival and to asylum is "licit not only for individual citizens – at least those bound by no other bond than the common bond of citizens – but also for whole cities and provinces, where there appears to be no other way of promoting their welfare".[168]

In sum, therefore, to give leverage to the rights to self-preservation, freedom of religion, and conscience, and to engage in trade and commerce, the right to freedom of movement has to be understood as a consequential right implicit in the mobility that inhered in the figure of the foreigner. Like Vitoria and Grotius before him, this was a framework of rights conceptualised by Pufendorf for the European, a 'foreigner' whose 'insider-ness' in international law gave him – as a (Socratic) 'citizen of the world' – mobility as a right consequential to other rights. I now consider the texts of the Swiss jurist Vattel, writing in the eighteenth century.

2.4 EMMERICH DE VATTEL (1714–1767)

Vattel was fundamentally a natural law theorist, even though it has been argued that he "prepared the ground for the era of uninhibited positivism."[169] His most influential treatise, *The Law of Nations*, was first published in 1758.[170] There is no doubt that the invocation of Vattel has had enduring significance in the making of migration law in the common law world,[171] not least in the context of Australian jurisprudence.[172] This is because the theories of Vattel

---

[166] Ibid 264.   [167] Ibid 265.   [168] Ibid.
[169] Leo Gross, 'The Peace of Westphalia, 1648–1948' (1948) 42(1) *American Journal of International Law* 20, 36.
[170] Vattel's purpose of making the theories of Christian Wolff accessible was consciously and discerningly made: Emmerich de Vattel, *The Law of Nations; or, Principles of the Law of Nature, Applied to the Conduct and Affairs of Nations and of Sovereigns* (Joseph Chitty ed and trans, Lawbook Exchange, first published 1854, 2005 ed) x–xv [trans of: *Le Droit des gens; ou Principes de la loi naturelle, appliqués à la conduite et aux affaires des Nations et des Souverains* (first published 1758)]; Stéphane Beaulac, 'Emer de Vattel and the Externalization of Sovereignty' (2003) 5 *Journal of the History of International Law* 237, 267–8; Martti Koskenniemi, '"International Community" from Dante to Vattel' in Vincent Chetail and Peter Haggenmacher (eds), *Vattel's International Law from a XXIst Century Perspective/Le Droit International de Vattel vu du XXIe Siècle* (Martinus Nijhoff, 2011) 51.
[171] In the context of migration lawmaking, interpretations of Vattel's theories of sovereignty are discussed in Chapter 3: see also Nafziger, above n 53; Satvinder S Juss, *International Migration and Global Justice* (Ashgate, 2006) 13.
[172] See Chapters 3–4.

and his construction of law are regarded as highly responsive to notions of state sovereignty, a factor attributable at least in part to the context in which he was writing.

2.4.1 Context: Conflict, Trade, and Religious Antipathy

Vattel was born a subject of the king of Prussia in 1714 in the principality of Neuchâtel. The son of an ennobled Protestant minister and the daughter of Neuchâtel's counsel at the Prussian court, Vattel was of aristocratic background but of limited means and therefore impelled to offer his services for remuneration, which he did as a diplomat. Although it would seem that the positions he held were modest and his functions light, this gave him time to write.[173]

The Law of Nations was written in the gathering storm of the Seven Years War and published at its height. This was a war with multiple intra- and extra-European flashpoints driven by the antagonisms of competing colonial and trade interests among European powers.[174] An examination of Vattel's text also suggests an awareness of the human realities of migration, informed not only by the general recognition of rights to free trade and commerce, but also in large measure by continuing Catholic-Protestant antipathies that had long driven conflict, persecution, and flight.[175] Indeed, it would seem that the Vattelian framework of rights for the foreigner – which Vattel regarded as proceeding from natural law[176] – had a strong nuancing effect on his conceptualisation of the foreigner-sovereign relation. Vattel's foreigner was, like the Vitorian, Grotian, and Pufendorfian foreigners before him, a 'civilised' Christian European. The analysis of Vattel that follows affirms the view that early international law's foreigner was an insider, not an outsider – a figure whose mobility was privileged and enabled by international law, neither diminished by nor residual to it.

2.4.2 Foreigners: Free Movement and a Just Assistance

An important dimension to Vattel's theories is that they were grounded in the view that there is an equality between sovereign states that secures for their people the bond of a common humanity,[177] a bond whereby states will not

---

[173] Beaulac, above n 170, 242–3.
[174] Daniel Marston, *The Seven Years' War* (Routledge, 2012).
[175] Vattel, above n 170, bk I ch XII §§ 125–157.   [176] Ibid xi.
[177] Ibid bk I ch XIX § 229. Cf Chapter 1, Section 1.1.1, 11–14.

"refuse a retreat to the unfortunate" and will do so free from "unnecessary suspicion and jealousy" or "groundless and frivolous fears".[178] We return to the same question: who is Vattel's foreigner? Or, put another way, between whom is this bond of a common humanity shared?

Like Grotius and Pufendorf, but unlike Vitoria, Vattel was principally focused on relations between different populations within Europe. His immediate context was the even more narrowly bounded but culturally and linguistically diverse region of Switzerland, comprising multiple small but independent principalities that were yet to federate. For these principalities, trade and other relations were well understood to give rise to mutual obligation and the social and economic imperatives of a (European) mobility. However, that is not to suggest that Vattel was not concerned with the wider world, for he undoubtedly was.

Vattel recounted a story which demonstrates that he too was influenced by the foreigner-barbarian dichotomy so strongly framed in the influential treatises of Vitoria. It is the story of Captain Bontekoe, a Dutchman, who,

> having lost his vessel at sea, escaped in his boat, with a part of his crew, and landed on an [Indonesian] coast, where the barbarous inhabitants refusing him provisions, the Dutch [justly] obtained them sword in hand.[179]

Vitoria also cited the highly restrictive practices of China and Japan, where "all foreigners are forbid to penetrate without an express permission".[180] In contrast, there is no evidence that he regarded Chinese or Japanese travellers as enjoying, for example, rights as foreigners in Europe. Rather, his reference to China and Japan served simply to contrast those countries' restrictive practices with the more liberal practices in Europe, where "the access is everywhere free to every person who is not an enemy of the state".[181]

The only exception that Vattel cited to the free movement he promoted as a liberal European virtue was that of people he described as "vagabonds and outcasts"[182] – probably a reference to the Roma and other socially or culturally marginalised populations. This suggests that Vattel's foreigner, for whom he outlined a host of significant rights, was still a European in (or from) Europe.

---

[178] Vattel, above n 170, bk I ch XIX § 231.   [179] Ibid bk II ch IX § 120.
[180] Ibid bk II ch VIII § 100.   [181] Ibid.   [182] Ibid.

2.4.3 *On Rights: Sovereignty and the Duties of Humanity*

Although Vattel located considerable power and choice in the hands of the sovereign, there are some critical provisos in his work affecting the sovereign's relation with the foreigner. For example, he described a right to emigrate as arising from several sources, including as a natural right.[183] Moreover, he asserted that the state must "not refuse human assistance to those whom tempest or necessity obliged to approach their frontiers".[184] This proviso is typical of the way in which Vattel qualified sovereign power. For example, he declared that

> Since the lord of the territory may, whenever he thinks proper, forbid its being entered . . . he has, no doubt, a power to annex what conditions he pleases to the permission to enter. This, as we have already said, is a consequence of the right of domain.[185]

Then, immediately following these observations, Vattel added a critical qualifier, which he posed as a rhetorical question:

> Can it be necessary to add, that the owner of the territory ought, in this instance, to respect the duties of humanity?[186]

Anticipating the possibility that the entry of foreigners may be resisted, Vattel later cautioned that "no nation can, without good reasons, refuse even a perpetual residence to a man driven from his country", unless "particular and substantial reasons prevent her from affording him an asylum".[187] In this connection, Vattel declared that such reasons should be "free from unnecessary suspicion and jealousy" and should not refuse a retreat to the unfortunate "for slight reasons, and on groundless and frivolous fears".[188]

Likewise, Vattel stated that there were cases in which the sovereign "cannot refuse an entrance into his territory".[189] This, he said, included a "duty towards all mankind" that might oblige the sovereign "to allow a free passage through, and a residence in his state."[190] Vattel also addressed the right of innocent passage, which was intended to safeguard "the general right of traversing the earth for the purposes of mutual intercourse, of carrying on commerce with each other, and for other just reasons."[191] Thus, subject only to the qualification that passage would be "prejudicial or dangerous", the sovereign was, he

---

[183] Ibid bk I ch XIX §§ 225–6. Here, he endorses the protection accorded to the Huguenots by Friedrich Wilhelm Brandenburg-Prussia, discussed above, 69–70.
[184] Vattel, above n 170, bk II ch VII § 94.   [185] Ibid bk II ch VIII § 100.   [186] Ibid.
[187] Ibid.   [188] Ibid bk I ch XIX § 231.   [189] Ibid bk II ch VIII § 100.   [190] Ibid.
[191] Ibid bk II ch X § 132.

said, "bound to grant a passage for lawful purposes, whenever he can do it without inconvenience to himself".[192] Moreover, he said that the sovereign "cannot lawfully annex burdensome conditions to a permission which he is obliged to grant, and which he cannot refuse if he wishes to discharge his duty, and not abuse his right of property."[193]

Thus, for Vattel, the foreigner-sovereign relation was significantly affected by his view that an important collection of rights necessarily attends the foreigner and that the power to exclude her should only be exercised in extreme circumstances. In this connection, Vattel articulated the right to emigrate and a range of related rights, including the rights to leave and reside elsewhere, to travel and sojourn, to reside in a foreign country (including as a result of exile or banishment), and the right of necessity. He also underscored the concomitant obligation of hospitality.

2.5 THE FOREIGNER: ALWAYS AND ALREADY EUROPEAN

This genealogical reading of Vitoria, Grotius, Pufendorf, and Vattel has noticed *who* the figure of the foreigner was for each jurist. By reading their texts in a way that is attentive to the genre of their writing – and the way in which language, purpose, time, and context shaped their arguments – we have seen how the meaning of 'foreigner' is mutable. The way in which the figure of the foreigner was framed by each jurist was contingent upon his context and purpose, as well as by time and place. For the most part, the foreigner within the foreigner-sovereign relation was one of two types. On the one hand, he was an intra-European foreigner for whom migration was framed as a human necessity and reality (as trader or exile). On the other, he was an imperialist who, carrying a host of self-proclaimed rights in his pocket,[194] could conquer and claim the coastlines of the New World. Thus, by treating the figure of the foreigner as an historical artefact, shaped and rationalised by contingent events that vary temporally and spatially, we see that her juridical history repudiates the inevitability of her outsider-ness.[195]

To frame the figure of the foreigner as a European insider, each jurist has drawn on a range of legal genres and developed a repertoire of rights and topics

[192]   Ibid.   [193]   Ibid; see also at bk II ch VIII § 100.
[194]   I am grateful to Olivia Barr for this evocative image of the imperialist wandering the world with his own law stuffed in his pocket.
[195]   Owen, above n 7, 6. Cf Thomas Nail, *The Figure of the Migrant* (Stanford University Press, 2015), in which Nail develops an interesting political theory of the migrant that characterises the foreigner as a static political figure in contrast to the migrant who lacks both static place and membership.

moulded and shaped to suit the interests of *his* foreigner. So, for example, biblical injunctions and natural law precepts shaped Vitoria's exhortations to welcome strangers and travellers and to offer them hospitality. These were, in turn, framed as rights of the foreigner under the law of nations (or peoples) (*ius gentium*). However, although tempered by an obligation on the foreigner to do no harm to the 'barbarian' Indian, this obligation may be understood as an empty gesture in view of Vitoria's (ex post facto) assumption that the travels of the Spanish foreigners were neither harmful nor detrimental to the 'barbarian' Indians, and their intentions peaceful. Finally, then, if the foreigner's peaceful attempts to assert his rights were not met with barbarian acquiescence, those rights were framed in ways that meant they could be lawfully obtained by force ('just war'). This pattern of argument tells, above all, an imperialist story of (European) dominance and self-interest.

As this chapter has traced, over time and depending on context, the repertoires and patterns of argument that were used to shape the figure of the foreigner and, in turn, outline a rights framework became more complex. Thus, as my examination of Grotius, Pufendorf, and Vattel suggests, their juridical purpose and outlook was (in contrast to Vitoria's) not purely imperial, even though, as we have seen, the styles of argument voiced by Vitoria retained a continuing relevance and resonance. Rather, conceptualisations of the foreigner as a (European) insider also related to governance of intra-European mobility and attendant social, economic, and political relations, including in the context of Catholic-Protestant tensions.[196] This suggests that wherever the work of international law was situated physically, its point of analytical and ideological departure remained Europe and the European.

So, the foreigner was – always and anywhere – a European insider in early international law. In contrast, the non-European remained a 'barbarian' outsider, enclosed in a legal framework within which she was accorded (at best) implied rights but no corresponding power to enforce them. Thus, although from time to time we have seen the non-European vested with a right to share in common property and to trade, such rights were qualified. Furthermore, we have seen no reciprocal right to emigrate – that is, for a non-European to become a foreigner on European soil. This reminds us that early international law did not seriously contemplate the non-European as a foreigner entitled to benefit from legal rights and protections on that account.

---

[196] Ian Hunter, 'Global Justice and Regional Metaphysics: On the Critical History of the Law of Nature and Nations' in Shaunnagh Dorsett and Ian Hunter (eds), *Law and Politics in British Colonial Thought: Transpositions of Empire* (Palgrave Macmillan, 2010) 11, 12.

In the intra-European context, it is evident that the way in which each jurist thought about the relation between the sovereign and the foreigner, as a bearer of individual (and occasionally collective) rights, was more nuanced. While Grotius, Pufendorf, and Vattel each tempered their foreigner's rights framework with sovereign authority, they were (for the most part) framing mobility (including in some instances a perpetual or permanent residence) as a natural *modus vivendi* between nations and peoples. To do this, they expanded their repertoire of rights and topics to emphasise such rights as freedom of religion and the right (of the individual) to self-preservation.[197] In this way, they gave traction to the political-economic imperatives of mobility, upholding the interests of both people and the state. However, as we know, the people, the states, and their respective interests were all European.

In summary, this chapter has made visible the mutability of the foreigner as a juridical figure. It has shown how conceptualisations of the foreigner as a (rights-bearing) European insider in early international law do not square with the current assumption that the foreigner is – and has always been – an excludable outsider with less rights than the citizen. In other words, it has shown that because early conceptualisations of the foreigner – as European imperialist, émigré, or exile – treated foreignness as an enabling rather than residual status, there is nothing inherently or inevitably 'outside' about the juridical figure of the foreigner. Rather, it tells us that the figure of the foreigner is a juridical artefact whose status and rights have been shaped by historical contingencies in furtherance of certain political-economic interests. And importantly, the analysis suggests that the characteristics of the foreigner of early international law – a figure of privilege and power – explain why there was no discourse of 'absolute sovereignty' during that period.

This chapter has provided an entrée into a complex institutional story of the ideas, practices, and forms of engagement that have, over time, shaped the foreigner-sovereign relation. It sheds light on the particular styles of argument that have been used to produce, sustain, and shape how the foreigner within the foreigner-sovereign relation is conceptualised. Together with the remaining two chapters in the genealogy, this will enable us to see in Part II, with greater clarity, how these styles of argument continue to be discursively (re)-produced and (re)shaped by contemporary lawmakers.

---

[197] The way in which self-preservation became reshaped as a right of states is taken up in Chapter 3.

Chapter 3 argues that the foreigner became a more complex figure within the foreigner-sovereign relation as the political-economic context of human mobility changed. It focuses on the nineteenth century, a period in which we see the alignment of the foreigner with the sovereign wane and 'absolute sovereignty' emerge as a common law doctrine – a tool for the exclusion of a new kind of foreigner.

3

A Common Law Doctrine of Sovereignty

By the beginning of the nineteenth century, the British Empire was the ascendant colonial power. This period heralded the abolition of slavery, significant expansion of international travel and industrialisation, and new migrations. In the colonial context, the migratory landscape was undergoing remarkable and dramatic change. Colonial labour requirements were met by white settlers, transported convicts, and an increasingly mobile population of (non-European) free and indentured labourers.

Of course, the foreigner as European insider, empowered to emigrate within and from Europe, did not disappear from the migratory landscape; on the contrary, European migration to white settler societies like Australia was increasing and encouraged. However, new migrations gave rise to tension in the foreigner-sovereign relation because a new kind of foreigner – a non-European ('barbarian') outsider – was now on the move. This tension was complicated by competing imperial interests, namely the political-economic desire for cheap and expendable non-European labour and the desire to establish settler societies that were racially pure. In this context, a common law doctrine of 'absolute sovereignty' emerged that treated as absolute the sovereign power to exclude and condition the entry and stay of aliens.

Chapter 2 considered who the figure of the foreigner was in early international law. This chapter in the genealogy of the foreigner-sovereign relation charts the emergence of a common law doctrine of 'absolute sovereignty'. As we know, the aim of this book is to explain how the contemporary policies of mandatory detention and planned destitution have come to be characterised as lawful and legitimate responses to unsolicited migration. The central purpose of the genealogy is, therefore, to help us, when we return to the case studies in Part II, to think differently and more carefully about how – and with what effects – the claim of 'absolute sovereignty' has become integral to the way we think about contemporary migration law- and policymaking. With this purpose in mind, the aim of this chapter is to deepen our understanding of what we have inherited through the emergence of a common law doctrine of 'absolute sovereignty'. The chapter traces the development of restrictive migration laws and how they were rationalised through an emergent common law jurisprudence of 'absolute sovereignty'. I argue that the appearance of 'absolute sovereignty' coincided with the 'appearance'[1] of (non-European) outsider foreigners on the migratory landscape. Crucially, it was the appearance of the foreigner as a racialised (non-European) figure and the desire to regulate her labour that led directly to the emergence of restrictive migration laws and then a common law doctrine of 'absolute sovereignty'.

Section 3.1 of the chapter begins with an overview of the migratory landscape of the mid nineteenth century, the context in which the mutability of the foreigner became more complex, and in which she was reframed as a right-less outsider. I then explain the role of nationality and naturalisation laws with a view to elucidating how and why restrictive migration laws emerged. I argue that although nationality and naturalisation laws remained useful ways of ordering and authorising the status and allegiance of certain foreigners, restrictive migration legislation became the primary means by which the movement and labour of non-European outsiders was regulated.

Section 3.2 describes how restrictive migration legislation materialised in the Australian colonies and grounded an emergent logic of border control. Taking into account the broader political-economic context in which this took place, I describe the differently calibrated legislative frameworks that were developed in response to non-European mobility.

Section 3.3 considers how the aforementioned restrictive migration legislation was validated by the development of a common law jurisprudence of 'absolute sovereignty' in the Privy Council and the US Supreme Court. In doing so, I offer a genealogical complement to the doctrinal analysis of Nafziger,[2] as well as the analyses of several other, more recent commentators.[3]

---

[1] Of course, in reality non-European migration was not a new phenomenon. However, as I argued in Chapter 2, non-European migration did not feature as part of the foreigner-sovereign relation.

[2] James A R Nafziger, 'The General Admission of Aliens under International Law' (1983) 77(4) *American Journal of International Law* 804. For discussion of the literature, see Chapter 1, Section 1.3.2, 42–4.

[3] Kim Rubenstein, 'Citizenship, Sovereignty and Migration: Australia's Exclusive Approach to Membership of the Community' (2002) 13(2) *Public Law Review* 102; Satvinder S Juss, 'Free Movement and the World Order' (2004) 16(3) *International Journal of Refugee Law* 289; Satvinder S Juss, *International Migration and Global Justice* (Ashgate, 2006) 12–15; Adam M McKeown, *Melancholy Order: Asian Migration and the Globalization of Borders* (Columbia University Press, 2008); Matthew J Lindsay, 'Immigration, Sovereignty, and the Constitution of Foreignness' (2013) 45(3) *Connecticut Law Review* 743.

Focusing on jurisprudence relevant to the Australian context, my analysis seeks to deepen our understanding of how a common law jurisprudence of 'absolute sovereignty' emerged. In particular, I show that the political-economic 'moment' at which the foreigner became conceptualised as a non-European outsider also marked the point of emergence of a discourse of 'absolute sovereignty' through which the foreigner could be excluded, or her entry and stay conditioned, entirely on the sovereign's terms. This convergence was not accidental; indeed, it was both emphatic and resolute. It was precisely because the foreigner was now conceptualised as a non-European outsider that her relation with the sovereign was now framed as a relation in which there was an absolute sovereign right to exclude her. As I argue, the absence of a discourse of 'absolute sovereignty' prior to this time further supports the view that a new attribute of 'outsider-ness' imputed to the foreigner coincided with the emergence of 'absolute sovereignty'. This helps explain how particular (instrumentalist) readings of the early international legal authorities on which the common law jurisprudence relies produced a doctrine that validated the absolute right to exclude the foreigner or to condition her entry and stay. In other words, we are reminded that, at any point in time, *who* the foreigner was affected in crucial ways how her relation with the sovereign was understood and authorised.

3.1 NEW MIGRATIONS, NEW COMMUNITIES

The nineteenth century was a period characterised by social and economic transition on an unprecedented scale. Slavery in Europe and North America was (largely) (formally) abolished,[4] and the demand for cheap (often migrant) labour increased as a result. Feudalism and serfdom were replaced by capitalism and, later, socialism.[5] Social and economic regulation moved increasingly into the hands of the state.[6] There was increased recognition of the freedoms of the (European) insider, and industrial developments revolutionised who worked, how, where, for whom, and on what terms. These interlocking dynamics had a substantial collective impact on the movement of people. The transition was uneven,[7] but its ripple effect had global implications.

In nineteenth-century Europe, and with broader ramifications, the transition from private to state control that paralleled the shift from feudalism and

---

[4] Maria Ontiveros, 'Noncitizen Immigrant Labor and the Thirteenth Amendment: Challenging Guest Worker Programs' (2007) 38(3) *University of Toledo Law Review* 923.

[5] John Torpey, *The Invention of the Passport: Surveillance, Citizenship and the State* (Cambridge University Press, 2000) 8.

[6] Ibid.   [7] Ibid 9.

serfdom to liberal capitalism[8] served as a socio-legal bellwether for heightened control by the nation-state over the transborder movement of people.[9]
As labour markets became nationalised, states took an increasing interest in
the regulation of movement. The nation-state became the dominant governing structure that, through law, 'oversaw' the newfound mobility of an
expanding population of itinerants and emigrants seeking physical, social,
and economic security. As Torpey observes, the completion of this transi-
tional process represented the nation-state's opportunity to usurp a monopoly over the legitimate means of movement.[10] Indeed, it became important
for the nation-state not only to be able clearly to describe its membership, but
also to identify and control it.[11] Immigration and nationality laws emerged as
prime tools for doing so – laws in which the logic of exclusion became
entrenched.

As noted above, while labour mobility was increasing in Europe, the abolition of slavery added to labour demands elsewhere. Although there is no doubt
that slavery continued in both its 'classic' form as well as in newly styled forms,
colonial labour requirements coupled with strong resistance to slavery[12] created a market for a range of new sources of cheap, unskilled labour.[13] The
increased demand for such labour and advancements in the ease of international travel, through such modes as the steamship and the railway, prompted
colonial interest in recruiting labour on a temporary basis.[14]

3.1.1 The Figure of the Foreigner: A Complex Mutability

Although white settler societies of Australasia and the Americas were established first and foremost through the dispossession of aboriginal communities,
indigenous peoples in those regions were regarded as weak, 'evanescent
races'.[15] They were not considered a threat to the colonial project. On the
other hand, those settler societies were also determined that non-European
migrant labourers should not be allowed to settle, much less to naturalise.[16] A

---

[8]   Ibid 8.   [9]   Ibid 7, 9, 19.   [10]   Ibid 1–2.   [11]   Ibid 2, 3, 7.
[12]   Gwenda Tavan, *The Long Slow Death of White Australia* (Scribe, 2005) 18–19.
[13]   Ryszard Cholewinski, *Migrant Workers in International Law: Their Protection in Countries of
       Employment* (Oxford University Press, 1997) 15–16; Marilyn Lake and Henry Reynolds,
       *Drawing the Global Colour Line: White Men's Countries and the Question of Racial
       Equality* (Melbourne University Press, 2008) 23.
[14]   Janet Ewald, 'Crossers of the Sea: Slaves, Freedmen, and Other Migrants in the Northwestern
       Indian Ocean, c 1750–1914' (2000) 105(1) *The American Historical Review* 69, [15].
[15]   Charles H Pearson, *National Life and Character: A Forecast* (Macmillan, 1893) 32.
[16]   Lake and Reynolds, above n 13, 9, 19, 265. Richards has described assumptions about race as
       "the snake that slithered its way through Australia's immigration history": Eric Richards,

complex dynamic emerged in which white settlers saw neither hypocrisy nor contradiction in their resistance to an underclass of slaves or 'coolies'; support for highly exploitative recruitment of cheap, temporary migrant labour; and vehement opposition to permanent non-European immigration.[17] As such, despite the 'great modern migrations' that saw the movement of an estimated 50 million Chinese and 30 million Indians during the (long) nineteenth century,[18] non-European labourers moving to imperial dominions, often at the invitation or instigation of the British,[19] did so with strictly curtailed employment and residency rights. These temporary migrations were as elemental to the colonial project as indigenous dispossession.[20]

Spontaneous (non-European) migration presented a particular problem. For example, Chinese labourers drawn to the Australian goldfields attracted considerable hostility. Their presence was conspicuous and their work effective. Much of the resistance to them was driven by European labourers and their unions, who perceived the Chinese as willing to work for substandard wages in poor conditions and therefore to be unfair competition.[21] Although employers saw the advantages of cheap labour, both capitalist and socialist sentiments drove the emergent debate on immigration restriction. Few, whether employers or workers, would countenance the idea that non-European labourers should be entitled to permanent settlement and equality rights.[22] Indeed, the objective of racial homogeneity was regarded as essential to the construction of a liberal-democratic society founded on ideas of individual freedom and social equality, as well as means for restricting and preventing non-European immigration, as a sine qua non of liberal democracy.[23]

Meanwhile, colonial powers were actively seeking to expand white settler populations. They did so through the use of sponsorship and other incentives. Assisted migration, a phenomenon that began in the nineteenth century, facilitated the population of settler colonies with 'desirable' white persons.[24]

'Migrations: The Career of British White Australia' in Deryck M Schreuder and Stuart Ward (eds), *Australia's Empire* (Oxford University Press, 2008). See also Robert A Huttenback, *Racism and Empire: White Settlers and Coloured Immigrants in the British Self-Governing Colonies 1830–1910* (Cornell University Press, 1976) 279–316.

[17]   Tavan, above n 12, 18.   [18]   Lake and Reynolds, above n 13, 6.   [19]   Ibid 24.

[20]   Ibid. Cf Cholewinski, above n 13, 16.

[21]   Raymond Markey, 'Race and Organized Labor in Australia, 1850–1901' (1996) 58(2) *Historian* 343.

[22]   Tavan, above n 12, 18. See also McKeown, above n 3.

[23]   Tavan, above n 12, 18. This view was also held in other white settler societies: see McKeown, above n 3, 16.

[24]   Tavan, above n 12, 182–3.

In Australia between 1831 and 1901, assisted passage was provided to paupers, the military, and civil servants.[25]

As this overview suggests, situating the foreigner-sovereign relation within the broader context of a political economy of the movement of people enables us to notice how the mutability of the foreigner – hitherto a European insider in whose interests early international law had been framed – became more complex. However, as we can see, it was not a pure mutability, but one contingent upon the political-economic desire to regulate race and labour. This point is critical to understanding how and why the 'free movement' rights that attached to the foreigner of early international law gave way to 'absolute sovereignty'. It is also critical to understanding why nationality and naturalisation laws came to be regarded as insufficient to manage the new non-European foreigner within the foreigner-sovereign relation, prompting the development of restrictive migration laws and an emergent common law doctrine of 'absolute sovereignty'.[26]

Turning first to nationality and naturalisation laws, the following sub-section considers how and why such laws were not seen as sufficient to manage the juridical relationship between this (new) foreigner and the sovereign. As we will see, although nationality and naturalisation laws remained useful ways of ordering and authorising the status and allegiance of certain foreigners, restrictive migration legislation became the principal means by which the movement and labour of non-European outsiders was regulated.

3.1.2 Nationality and Naturalisation Laws: Insufficient

In Australia throughout the nineteenth century, there was no formal legal concept of Australian citizenship.[27] Instead, British nationality and naturalisation laws figured prominently in the juridical framing of the foreigner-sovereign relation in the Australian colonies. These nationality and naturalisation laws were a mixture of common law principles and legislation.

---

[25] Charles Price, 'Immigration and Ethnic Origin' in Wray Vamplew (ed), *Australians: Historical Statistics* (Fairfax, Syme and Weldon, 1987) 2.

[26] See, eg, Clive Parry, *Nationality and Citizenship Laws of the Commonwealth and of the Republic of Ireland* (Stevens, 1957–1960) 530.

[27] There is no formal legal concept of citizenship in the *Constitution*, and the notion of Australian citizenship was first legislated in *Nationality and Citizenship Act* 1948 (Cth): Kim Rubenstein, 'Citizenship and the Centenary – Inclusion and Exclusion in 20th Century Australia' (2000) 24 *Melbourne University Law Review* 576, 583.

3.1.2.1 Rights of Aliens under the Common Law

Under the common law, anyone born outside the king's dominions was regarded as an alien. In his *Commentaries on the Laws of England*, the highly influential jurist Sir William Blackstone 'chalked out' some of the principal rights that applied to aliens at common law.[28] While broad, they were also limited. They included the right of an alien to purchase land, *but not for his own use*;[29] the right to acquire personal property of a transitory and moveable nature, an "indulgence to strangers . . . necessary for the advancement of trade";[30] the right to trade as freely as other people,[31] albeit subject to higher customs duties; and certain work prohibitions contained in some obsolete but unrepealed statutes of Henry VIII whereby alien artificers were prohibited from working for themselves.[32] These rights applied only to "alien friends".[33] Enemy aliens, on the other hand – that is, those regarded as enemies during time of war or those in relation to whom there was considered to be a "perpetual hostility", such as 'infidels'[34] – were regarded as having neither rights nor privileges "unless by the king's special favour".[35]

3.1.2.2 Denization and Naturalisation

Historically, the process of denization, whereby a foreigner acquired citizenship rights, was a matter of executive discretion. Similarly, naturalisation, although an exercise of legislative rather than executive power, accorded a foreigner citizenship rights with the exception of political rights. Nevertheless, so rare was naturalisation in Britain that the grant of nationality was only made by special Acts of Parliament.[36]

Nationality and naturalisation laws of more general application did not appear until the late eighteenth century; in Britain, the first such act was the

---

[28] Sir William Blackstone (1723–1780), *Commentaries on the Laws of England* (Callaghan and Co, 1884, c 1883) bk 1 ch 10, 371.

[29] Ibid.   [30] Ibid.   [31] Ibid; *Magna Carta* 1215 s 41.

[32] Blackstone, above n 28, bk 1 ch 10, 371.   [33] Ibid.

[34] Included amongst "enemy aliens" were those regarded as "perpetual enemies" (*perpetui inimici*), that is "all infidels", in relation to whom "there is perpetual hostility, and can be no peace": *Calvin's Case* (1608) 7 Coke Report 1a; 77 ER 377, 397 (Sir Edward Coke CJ).

[35] Blackstone, above n 28, bk 1 ch 10, 371.

[36] 'Report of the Interdepartmental Committee of July 24, 1901', extract printed in Cit Bd Report (1906), cited in Richard W Flournoy Jr, Manley O Hudson, and F B Rothman (eds), *A Collection of Nationality Laws of Various Countries, as Contained in Constitutions, Statutes and Treaties* (Carnegie Publishing, 1929) 59.

British Nationality Act 1772.[37] During the nineteenth century, British nationality and naturalisation legislation was passed in 1844,[38] 1847,[39] and 1870.[40]
Most relevantly, this legislation made more general provision for the naturalisation of aliens and expanded its reach to apply, in a limited way, to British
dominions and colonies.[41] Thus, for example, in Hong Kong those born after
the key date of 1842 were regarded as British subjects, including persons of
Chinese descent.[42]

3.1.2.3 Nationality and Naturalisation: An Imperial Embrace

In British colonial territories, and as a direct result of British naturalisation laws,
the granting of British subject status meant that imperial populations rose
dramatically. This increased the population of those owing allegiance to the
British Crown, both colonisers and colonised. Although full citizenship rights
did not necessarily attach to British subject status, the working assumption that
inhered in this approach was that British-born subjects nevertheless had a
"natural allegiance" to the British Crown on the basis of a "debt of gratitude" –
one which could not be "forfeited, cancelled or altered, by any change of time,
place, or circumstance, nor by anything but the united concurrence of the
legislature."[43] Thus, loyalty and duty could be procured and claimed and the
imperial embrace expanded.

However, certain self-governing white settler societies did not welcome the
implications of this expansionist imperial embrace, determined as they were
to ensure "self-preservation" and retain exclusive use and control over 'their'
territory for the "higher races".[44] As the experience of the United States
illustrates, nationality and naturalisation laws could provide a highly racialised
means of constructing nation. In the newly independent United States,

---

[37]   *British Nationality Act* 1772, 13 Geo 3, c 21. Nationality and naturalisation legislation prior to
        this time specifically targeted particular individuals or groups of individuals. The first known
        piece of naturalisation legislation in Britain for such persons was in 1705: Elihu Lauterpacht
        and C J Greenwood (eds), *International Law Reports* (Cambridge University Press, 1963) vol
        26, 380–2.
[38]   *British Nationality Act* 1844, 7 & 8 Vict, c 66.
[39]   *Naturalisation of Aliens Act* 1847, 10 & 11 Vict, c 83.
[40]   *Naturalisation Act* 1870, 33 & 34 Vict, c 14. This Act arose from a convention adopted between
        the United States and Great Britain in an attempt to resolve the issue of dual nationality:
        Mannie Brown, 'Expatriation of Infants: Being a Study in the Conflict of Laws between
        Canada and the United States' (1939) 3(1) *University of Toronto Law Journal* 97, 103.
[41]   The idea of 'colonial naturalisation' could render the same individual a British subject in one
        colony but a foreigner in another, as well as in England: Rieko Karatani, *Defining British
        Citizenship: Empire, Commonwealth and Modern Britain* (Frank Cass, 2003) 55.
[42]   Ibid 59.   [43]   Blackstone, above n 28, bk 1 ch 10, 369.   [44]   Pearson, above n 15, 16.

Congress passed its first naturalisation legislation in 1790, which provided, subject to certain conditions, for the naturalisation of 'any alien, being a free white person'.[45] This of course automatically excluded the population of ex-slaves as well as Native Americans. Although it was not until 1870 that 'aliens of African nativity and persons of African descent' became eligible to natura-lise,[46] for those preoccupied with 'self-preservation' in other white settler societies, the experience of the United States made it clear that even control over nationality and naturalisation laws was not sufficient to manage and maintain the political-economic interests and priorities of a white settler society.

The problem that the Australian colonies perceived was that Britain was making nationality and naturalisation laws which applied to the empire as a whole and which served British imperial interests that did not accord with their own. This political dissonance meant that if non-white colonised peoples with British subject status sought to migrate to Australia, there was nothing to stop them. Having neither sought nor welcomed the allegiance of such peoples to the British Crown, the Australian colonies sought new means to regulate their entry.

From the foregoing discussion, we can see that nationality and naturalisa-tion laws provided a means by which relations between foreigners and their host state could be mediated, secured, and strengthened. This included the conferral of common law rights, which were, in significant measure, eco-nomic in nature.[47] However, the common law drew a line between friendly and enemy aliens: 'friendlies' being entitled to enter, reside, and trade within the realm (though not to own or inherit property), and enemies understood to include 'infidels' with whom there was a 'perpetual hostility' because they were regarded as racial and religious outsiders inherently hostile to the sovereign.[48] Imperial expansion and the expansion of nationality and naturalisation laws meant that distinctions between the infidel – hitherto characterised as an enemy of the sovereign – and the British subject of non-European heritage lost precision. For colonial self-governing territories pre-occupied with the regulation of race and labour, the imperialising expansion of the sovereign's reach could only be countered by measures of sovereign constraint. As such, and as Section 3.2 shows, these colonial governments

---

[45] An Act to Establish an Uniform Rule of Naturalization, ch 3, 1 Stat 103 (1790), repealed by Act of January 29, 1795, ch 20, 1 Stat 414 (1795).

[46] An Act to Amend the Naturalization Laws and to Punish Crimes against the Same, and for Other Purposes, ch 254, 16 Stat 254 (1870). It was not until 1924 that Native Americans were granted citizenship: Indian Citizenship Act 1924, ch 233, 43 Stat 253 (1924).

[47] See above 87.   [48] Calvin's Case (1608) 7 Coke Report 1a; 77 ER 377.

needed to stake their own claim to sovereignty to achieve their own ends. It was in this climate that restrictive migration laws emerged and took hold.[49]

3.2 RESTRICTIVE MIGRATION LAWS: AN 'IMPERATIVE'

In the Australian context, governments were clearly unsettled about the increasing presence of Chinese and, to a lesser extent, Indians[50] in their territories.[51] Some Indians had arrived in the Australian colonies as convict labourers in the early part of the century, while the majority arrived as (indentured) labourers recruited by the British government.[52] Others included agricultural labourers, plantation workers, hawkers, and traders, as well as those from South Asia collectively known as 'Afghans' who ran the camel trains in the Australian interior.[53] However, it was the Chinese arrivals that caused greatest alarm. The Chinese – who were indentured or contract labourers or even free immigrants – were more numerous and offered highly competitive cheap labour, especially on the lucrative goldfields.[54] As noted earlier, part of the problem was that many Chinese (and Indians) enjoyed British subject status and could not, therefore, be regarded as outsiders to the British Empire. With no authority over nationality and naturalisation laws, the legislatures of the Australian self-governing colonies nevertheless had the power to make laws with respect to their internal affairs.

---

[49] Karatani, above n 41, 56. For discussions of how this took place in the United States, see, eg, Lindsay, above n 3; McKeown, above n 3; Lucy E Salyer, *Laws Harsh as Tigers: Chinese Immigrations and the Shaping of Modern Immigration Law* (University of North Carolina Press, 1995); Kathryn Cronin, 'A Culture of Control: An Overview of Immigration Policy Making' in James Jupp and Marie Kabala (eds), *The Politics of Australian Immigration* (AGPS, 1993) 83, 84. Although there are some examples of earlier restrictive measures in Britain, they were both occasional and residual: Bernard Porter, *The Refugee Question in Mid-Victorian Politics* (Cambridge University Press, first published 1979, 2008 ed) 3; Alison Bashford and Jane McAdam, 'The Right to Asylum: Britain's 1905 Aliens Act and the Evolution of Refugee Law' (2014) 32(2) *Law and History Review* 309, 327 n 76.

[50] Strong opposition in Australia thwarted attempts to recruit Indian labour on a large scale: Brij V Lal, 'Indians' in James Jupp (ed), *The Australian People: An Encyclopedia of the Nation, Its People and Their Origins* (Cambridge University Press, 2nd ed, 2001) 426, 427–8.

[51] Sing-Wu Wang, 'Chinese Immigration 1840s–1890s' in James Jupp (ed), *The Australian People: An Encyclopedia of the Nation, Its People and Their Origins* (Cambridge University Press, 2001) 197, 202–4.

[52] Edward Duyker, 'Mauritians' in James Jupp (ed), *The Australian People: An Encyclopedia of the Nation, Its People and Their Origins* (Cambridge University Press, 2nd ed, 2001) 592, 593.

[53] Abdul Khaliq Fazal, 'Afghans' in James Jupp (ed), *The Australian People: An Encyclopedia of the Nation, Its People and Their Origins* (Cambridge University Press, 2nd ed, 2001) 164, 164; Lal, above n 50, 427; Duyker, above n 52, 592; Riaz Hassan, 'Pakistanis' in James Jupp (ed), *The Australian People: An Encyclopedia of the Nation, Its People and Their Origins* (Cambridge University Press, 2nd ed, 2001) 615, 615.

[54] Wang, above n 51, 197.

This included immigration. As such, restrictive migration laws became a key mechanism for the Australian colonies to determine the composition of their communities and counter the broader embrace of imperialist British nationality and naturalisation laws. The experience of the colony of Victoria is instructive.

3.2.1 Restrictive Migration: The Colony of Victoria

In Victoria, restrictive migration legislation variously provided for poll taxes, strict limitations on the numbers of Chinese permitted to enter the colony, and the appointment of 'protectors' to 'regulate' Chinese activity. The legislation also provided broad powers to make such rules and regulations as were deemed necessary for the registration of Chinese; for their removal, protection, and management; and for good government.[55] Similar legislation to that in Victoria was passed in South Australia and New South Wales.[56]

Early anti-Chinese legislation in Victoria took no account of the fact that some Chinese had British subject status.[57] Although later legislation reflected this distinction,[58] under the *Chinese Act 1881* (Vic) the burden of proving exemption from its (onerous) provisions lay with the Chinese person asserting British subject status.[59] In 1888, the *Chinese Immigration Restriction Act* (Vic) followed an inter-colonial conference of Australasian governments which resolved that laws for the restriction of Chinese immigration should be uniform.[60] Accordingly, the Act again abolished the 'privilege' accorded to Chinese with British subject status, unless such individuals were naturalised (by the exercise of a Royal Prerogative) in Victoria.[61] Instead, provision was made for (revocable) special exemptions to be made by proclamation.[62] The legislation also created a rebuttable presumption that a person asserted to be

---

55 Joseph Lee, 'Anti-Chinese Legislation in Australasia' (1889) 3(2) *The Quarterly Journal of Economics* 218, 218–19.

56 Similar laws were also beginning to emerge in the United States, Natal, and Canada. See, generally, Marilyn and Reynolds, above n 13; Marjory Harper and Stephen Constantine, *Migration and Empire* (Oxford University Press, 2010).

57 *An Act to Make Provision for Certain Immigrants 1855* (Vic); *An Act to Regulate the Residence of the Chinese Population in Victoria 1857* (Vic).

58 *Chinese Immigrants Statute 1865* (Vic); *Chinese Act 1881* (Vic) s 5.

59 *Chinese Act 1881* (Vic) s 9.

60 John Quick and Robert Randolph Garran, *The Annotated Constitution of the Australian Commonwealth* (Angus & Robertson, 1901) 626; *Chinese Immigration Restriction Act 1888* (Vic) Preamble ('*Chinese Immigration Restriction Act 1888*').

61 *Chinese Immigration Restriction Act 1888* s 4. In New South Wales, legislation in 1861 also provided, inter alia, that no letters of naturalisation should be issued to Chinese. See also Lee, above n 55, 218; Lake and Reynolds, above n 13, 42–3.

62 *Chinese Immigration Restriction Act 1888* s 5.

Chinese was so for the purposes of the Act, the final decision falling to the adjudicating justices 'upon their own view and judgment'.[63]

By legislatively constructing all Chinese as outsiders, these laws diminished (the value of) British subject status for Chinese. For those who were subjects of the Emperor of China, the position was even clearer.

3.2.2 Exclusion: An Instinct of Self-Preservation

These "rather stringent"[64] legislative steps to limit migration, in particular permanent migration, were driven by what colonial governments, including those in Australia, regarded as an "instinct of self-preservation". In his astonishingly influential book[65] *National Life and Character: A Forecast*, Charles Pearson argued that this instinct was driven by an awareness of the white man's inability to live "other than as an exotic" elsewhere than in the temperate zones and what he regarded as the consequential necessity to "[guard] the last part of the world, in which the higher races can live and increase freely, for the higher civilisation."[66] Pearson's book had a powerful impact on lawmakers and commentators in white settler societies. Among those who regarded his forecast as a clarion call were US President Theodore Roosevelt[67] and Australia's first Prime Minister, Edmund Barton;[68] it was the German Kaiser who, after reading Pearson's book, coined the phrase 'yellow peril'.[69] In addition, influential editorial opinion indicated the extent to which the self-confidence and sense of assured superiority of the European coloniser was shaken by Pearson's rousing words:[70]

> The day will come, and perhaps is not far distant when the European observer will look round to see this globe girdled with a continuous zone of the black and yellow races, no longer too weak for aggression or under tutelage, but independent, or practically so, in government, monopolising the trade of their own regions, and circumscribing the industry of the European; when Chinamen and the nations of Hindostan, the States of Central and South America, by that time predominantly Indian, and it may be African nations of the Congo and the Zambesi, under a dominant caste of foreign rulers, are represented by fleets in the European seas invited

---

[63] Ibid s 10.

[64] Pearson, above n 15, 15. This is a reference to legislative measures taken in the United States, but could equally apply to other British colonial territories.

[65] See, eg, Lake and Reynolds, above n 13, 104, 137.   [66] Pearson, above n 15, 16.

[67] Lake and Reynolds, above n 13, 98–100.   [68] Ibid 137–8.   [69] Ibid 289–90.

[70] See, eg, England's *Fortnightly Review* and Sydney's *Daily Telegraph*, cited in Lake and Reynolds, above n 13, 188, 196.

to international conferences, and welcomed as allies in the quarrels of the civilised world. The citizens of these countries will then be taken up into the social relations of the white races, will throng the English turf, or the salons of Paris, and will be admitted to intermarriage. It is idle to say, that if all this should come to pass our pride of place will not be humiliated. We were struggling among ourselves for supremacy in a world which we thought of as destined to belong to the Aryan races and to the Christian faith; to the letters and arts and charm of social manners which we have inherited from the best times of the past. We shall wake to find ourselves elbowed and hustled, and perhaps even thrust aside by peoples whom we looked down upon as servile, and thought of as bound always to minister to our needs.[71]

Thus Pearson captured the imaginations of white powerbrokers and sowed seeds of deep unease about the future power, purity, and prosperity of white settler societies – unease that would subsequently be used as a trigger and ongoing justification for highly restrictive immigration policies and, in Australia's case, a legislative declaration of racial identity.[72] Legislators and policymakers were determined to ensure that *the day would not come*. Short of "extirpation", which Pearson regarded wryly as "against the fashion of modern humanity",[73] nothing but "vigilant opposition", such as that needed to regulate immigration to the Australian colonies, would suffice in safeguarding the temperate zones for the "higher races".[74]

The emergence of restrictive migration laws brought to the fore an inherent tension between the political-economic impulses of migration and the countervailing political-economic impulses of the sovereign as 'overseer' of nation. In this connection, restrictive legislative measures were regarded not only as instruments of exclusion, but also as essential to the promotion and preservation of liberal democratic ideals of equality. To the European coloniser, only a core of racial *in*equality could realise *white* equality.[75] In this regard, the distinction between temporary and permanent migration in these laws was critical, for it enabled colonial administrations to regard non-European migrants as units of

---

[71] Pearson, above n 15, 84–5, quoted in Commonwealth, *Parliamentary Debates*, House of Representatives, 7 August 1901, 5503 (Edmund Barton, Prime Minister) (Second Reading Speech, Immigration Restriction Bill 1901 (Cth)).

[72] Lake and Reynolds, above n 13, 138, quoting Sir Edmund Barton, Untitled speech on Federation, 1900, held in the *Barton Papers* collection at the National Library of Australia (Series 5, No 977) <http://nla.gov.au/nla.ms-ms51-5-977>.

[73] Pearson, above n 15, 31. [74] Ibid 50.

[75] Tavan, above n 12, 18. This is a view that was also held in other white settler societies: see, eg, McKeown, above n 3, 16. On the foundational inequalities that have enabled the emergence of principles of equality and universality, see Peter Fitzpatrick, 'Racism and the Innocence of Law' (1987) 14(1) *Journal of Law and Society* 119.

temporary labour who were exploitable, excludable, expendable, and, above all, deportable. Although their cheap labour was feared,[76] especially by an imperial working class that insisted on privileged access to the labour market,[77] the capitalist appeal of such labour also made it irresistible, and its temporary character meant that inequalities could be overlooked.[78]

From the foregoing analysis, a picture begins to emerge in which we see the legislature constructing 'absolute sovereignty' as the basis on which to exercise complete control over transborder movement. However, the legislative work of constructing and claiming 'absolute sovereignty' would remain vulnerable unless it was judicially endorsed.[79] To achieve this, the judiciary not only had to uphold the validity of legislation, but it was also necessary to ensure that such findings could not be disturbed by counter-arguments based on principles of international law. Section 3.3 shows how the judiciary gave form to the idea of 'absolute sovereignty' and thereby upheld restrictive legislative measures for the exclusion of the non-European foreigner.

3.3 A JURISPRUDENCE OF 'ABSOLUTE SOVEREIGNTY'

As we know, the nineteenth century was a period of remarkable and dramatic transition in the migratory landscape. This transition meant that the foreigner could no longer be understood primarily or exclusively as a European insider. Changing political-economic interests and activity meant that juridical expressions of the foreigner-barbarian dichotomy and nationality and naturalisation laws were no longer adequate. So by the late 1880s and early 1890s, courts were being asked to interpret and apply newly dominant restrictive migration legislation.

3.3.1 A Transnational Judicial Conversation Begins

Buoyed by a transnational judicial conversation between 'white men's benches' in "white men's countries",[80] a highly exclusionist line of authority on sovereignty began to emerge from the US Supreme Court and the Privy

---

[76]   Eric Richards, 'Migrations: The Career of British White Australia' in Deryck M Schreuder and Stuart Ward (eds), *Australia's Empire* (Oxford University Press, 2008) 163, 167.

[77]   Lake and Reynolds, above n 13, 220–1; Jonathon Hyslop, 'The Imperial Working Class Makes Itself White' (1999) 12(4) *Journal of Historical Sociology* 405.

[78]   On the recruitment of Pacific Island labourers for work on the sugar plantations of the north, see Tracey Banivanua-Mar, *Violence and Colonial Dialogue: The Australian-Pacific Indentured Labor Trade* (University of Hawaii Press, 2007).

[79]   On the constitutionalisation of 'absolute sovereignty', see Chapter 4, Section 4.1, 114–19.

[80]   Lake and Reynolds, above n 13, 3.

Council.[81] These decisions included the Privy Council decision of *Musgrove v Chun Teeong Toy*[82] (*'Musgrove'*) and the US Supreme Court decisions in *Chae Chan Ping v United States*[83] (*'Chinese Exclusion Case'*) (1889), *Nishimura Ekiu v United States*[84] (*'Ekiu'*) (1892), and *Fong Yue Ting v United States*[85] (*'Fong'*) (1893). Each validated the object and purpose of restrictive migration legislation. In doing so, the courts asserted with confidence the claim that international law recognises in unqualified terms the sovereign right of a state to exclude (even friendly) aliens. However, a close examination of the jurisprudence suggests that the authority on which this claim was based is historically contingent.[86]

In the analysis that follows, I argue that the way in which the texts of Vattel[87] and other commentators such as Sir Robert Phillimore[88] were read and applied reflected a political-economic desire to regulate race and labour. The analysis highlights how particular approaches to and reliance on key judicial and jurisprudential authority enabled a line of thinking to develop that viewed the foreigner-sovereign relation in a particular way. It also shows how particular jurisprudential readings were repeated, reinforced, and sustained by other legitimating juridical tools, including the doctrine of precedent and a 'positivist' jurisprudence.[89]

---

[81] Jurisprudence on the same subject from the High Court of Australia will be discussed in Chapter 4, including *Robtelmes v Brenan* (1906) 4 CLR 395 (*'Robtelmes'*). See also *Attorney-General for Canada v Cain* [1906] AC 542.

[82] [1891] AC 272 (*'Musgrove'*).   [83]   130 US 581 (1889) (*'Chinese Exclusion Case'*).

[84] 142 US 651 (1892) (*'Ekiu'*).   [85]   149 US 698 (1893) (*'Fong'*).

[86] *Musgrove* [1891] AC 272, 282.

[87] In *Ekiu*, 142 US 651, 658 (1892), the Supreme Court read Vattel selectively and overlooked key aspects of his treatise: Emmerich de Vattel, *The Law of Nations; or, Principles of the Law of Nature, Applied to the Conduct and Affairs of Nations and of Sovereigns* (Joseph Chitty ed and trans, Lawbook Exchange, first published 1854, 2005 ed) bk II ch VIII § 100, bk II ch X § 132 [trans of: *Le Droit des gens; ou Principes de la loi naturelle, appliqués à la conduite et aux affaires des Nations et des Souverains* (first published 1758)]; the Court's approach in *Ekiu* was reaffirmed in *Fong*, 149 US 698, 708 (1893); see also Nafziger, above n 2; Rubenstein, 'Citizenship, Sovereignty, and Migration', above n 3; Juss, 'Free Movement', above n 3; Juss, *International Migration*, above n 3, 12–15; McKeown, above n 3.

[88] In *Ekiu*, for example, the Court overstated Phillimore's position on the right of self-preservation: Sir Robert Phillimore, *Commentaries upon International Law* (Butterworths, 3rd ed, 1879) pt III ch X, 312–21. See below 100–1; see also Nafziger, above n 2, 826; Juss, *International Migration*, above n 3, 15.

[89] A positivist jurisprudence in the style of Jeremy Bentham insists on making law prospective and putting the responsibility for lawmaking on the legislature. However, the flipside of this approach is that it opens up the possibility for the judiciary to offload responsibility for the outcomes of its decisions: Tom Campbell, *The Legal Theory of Ethical Positivism* (Aldershot, 1996).

3.3.2 *The Privy Council and a Sovereign Prerogative to Exclude*

The 1891 Privy Council decision in *Musgrove* came on appeal from the
Supreme Court of Victoria.[90] In that case, the plaintiff, who was a subject of
the Emperor of China, was denied entry to the colony of Victoria under the
Chinese Act 1881 (Vic).[91] The Act prohibited him from landing without permission from the responsible Minister. The decision cited no international legal
authority. Indeed, the case is significant for its unequivocal statement that "[n]o
authority" existed for the proposition that an alien has a legal right, enforceable
by action, to enter British territory.[92] As such, the Court concluded, the contrary
was proved; that is, in the absence of any positive authority providing for such a
right, no such right can be said to exist. This is *contra* the established constitutional principle that everything is permitted except that which is expressly
forbidden.[93] It also runs counter to the longstanding common law view (at
least in relation to merchants) that foreigners are free to come and go from the
realm unless they shall have been publicly prohibited beforehand,[94] an argument of which the Court in *Musgrove* was unquestionably apprised.[95]

Musgrove points to exclusion of an alien as raising nothing more than the
possibility of "diplomatic remonstrance", thereby subscribing to the position
that treatment of aliens, in particular their exclusion, is ultimately a matter
between states. Counsel for the appellant, Musgrove (the Collector of
Customs), relied on a number of international authorities to support the
claimed Crown prerogative to prevent entry of aliens.[96] Although the judgment does not reveal the extent to which the Court was influenced by the

---

[90] *Chun Teong Toy v Musgrove* (1888) 14 VLR 349.   [91] Discussed above 91–2.
[92] *Musgrove* [1891] AC 272, 282.
[93] Cf A V Dicey, *Introduction to the Study of the Law of the Constitution* (Macmillan, 10th ed,
      first published 1959, 1961) 127–8. See also S S *'Lotus' (France v Turkey) (Judgment)* [1927] PCIJ
      (ser A) No 10, 19, which stands for the reverse proposition of state and personal liberty in
      international law, namely *tout ce qui n'est pas interdit, est permis* (that which is not forbidden,
      is permitted); Commission on Human Rights Drafting Committee, *Draft Outline of
      International Bill of Rights (Prepared by the Division of Human Rights)*, UN Doc E/CN.4/
      AC.1/3 (4 June 1947) 10–11 (draft art 25). See also Bas Schotel, *On the Right of Exclusion: Law
      Ethics and Immigration Policy* (Routledge, 2012) 35.
[94] *Magna Carta* 1215 s 41; on the exceptionality of removal or expulsion, see Porter, above n 49, 3.
[95] The issue had been addressed in the Supreme Court of Victoria: *Chun Teong Toy v Musgrove*
      (1888) 14 VLR 349, 425 (Holroyd J); see also Cronin, above n 49, 84.
[96] *Musgrove* [1891] AC 272, 275. These authorities were cited as follows: "[James] Kent's
      Commentaries [on American Law], vol. i. p. 37; [Sir Robert] Phillimore's [Commentaries
      upon] International Law vol. iv., pp. 2, 219; [Sir William] Blackstone's Commentaries [on the
      Laws of England], vol. i, p. 338 *et seq.*; [Joseph] Chitty on Prerogative[*A Treatise on the Law of
      Prerogatives of the Crown; and the Relative Duties and Rights of the Subject* (Butterworths,
      1820)] p. 49".

sources cited by the Crown, it is significant that none of those sources fully supports the proposition that an alien has no enforceable legal right to enter territory.[97] On the contrary, they variously relate to the requirement that the admission, residence, and expulsion of aliens be subject to statutory regulation. Without attempting to draw on the authority of international law, their Lordships nevertheless

> [could not] assent to the proposition that an alien refused permission to enter British territory [could], in an action in a British Court, compel the decision of such matters as [these] involving delicate and difficult constitutional questions affecting the respective rights of Crown and Parliament, and the relations of this country to her self-governing colonies.[98]

Thus, matters of constitutional and (intra-imperial) relational 'delicacy' were permitted to occlude any question of due process that might be owed an alien friend under the common law.

The priority of regulating race and labour underpinning the legislation and the decision of the Privy Council is clear. As its unanimous judgment, delivered by the Lord Chancellor, observed, "the manifest object of the [*Chinese Act*] was to prevent an excessive number of Chinese, or what the Legislature thought to be an excessive number of Chinese, landing in the Colony . . . "[99] The Court distinguished between Chinese who were British subjects and those owing allegiance to the Emperor of China, British subjects being exempt from the poll tax under the *Chinese Act 1881* (Vic).[100] Nevertheless, signalling the utility of discretionary power, the Court read into the powers of the Collector of Customs the authority to refuse to accept or receive payment of the prescribed poll tax. In the Court's view, to do otherwise would have defeated the manifest object of the legislation.

3.3.3 *The US Supreme Court Weighs In*

The leading jurisprudence of the US Supreme Court around the same time, which was later embraced and adopted by the High Court of Australia ('the High Court'),[101] shows how the political-economic desire to regulate race and labour was central to that Court's willingness to assert an unfettered right to exclude even friendly aliens.[102]

---

[97]   Joseph Chitty, *A Treatise on the Law of Prerogatives of the Crown; and the Relative Duties and Rights of the Subject* (Butterworths, 1820) 50.
[98]   *Musgrove* [1891] AC 272, 283.   [99]   Ibid 281.   [100]   Discussed above 91–2.
[101]   *Robtelmes* (1906) 4 CLR 395; see also Chapter 4.   [102]   Nafziger, above n 2, 805.

3.3.3.1 Chinese Exclusion Case

In the *Chinese Exclusion Case*,[103] the Supreme Court's analysis was overtly grounded in racial prejudice. The decision underscores the (perceived) social and economic vulnerability to unassimilable hordes of industrious and frugal Chinese labourers deemed to be a danger to the peace and security of the community and (possibly even) to the preservation of civilisation.[104]

The Court expressed the view that the authority legislatively to exclude aliens was not a proposition that was even "open to controversy".[105] Revealing its implicit assumption that aliens having allegiance to another sovereign are doing that sovereign's (hostile) bidding,[106] the Court declared that "[i]f it could not exclude aliens, it would be to that extent subject to the control of another power."[107] Fuelling the impression that Chinese labourers were enemy aliens, the Court declared that

> To preserve its independence, and give security against foreign aggression and encroachment, is the highest duty of every nation, and to attain these ends nearly all other considerations are to be subordinated. It matters not in what form such aggression and encroachment come, whether from the foreign nation acting in its national character, or from vast hordes of its people crowding in upon us.[108]

Furthermore, the Court regarded its sovereign jurisdiction in this respect to be "necessarily exclusive and absolute".[109] It cited as authority for this last proposition *The Exchange v McFaddon*[110] ('*McFaddon*'), a case relating to the mobility of sovereign authority not of the foreigner. *McFaddon* dealt with the question of jurisdiction where a sovereign, in the form of a public armed ship sailing under a US flag, entered a foreign territory (Napoleonic France) in a friendly manner (en route to Spain) and was seized and disposed of. The Court concluded that in such a case the ship carried US sovereign jurisdiction with it and should therefore have been exempt from the sovereign jurisdiction of France. As such, it should not have been subject to seizure and disposal. However, the question in *McFaddon* was really one of competing sovereignties, so its authority in the

---

[103] *Chinese Exclusion Case*, 130 US 581 (1889); Nafziger, above n 2, 824–6.
[104] *Chinese Exclusion Case*, 130 US 581, 594, 606 (1889).
[105] Ibid 604, affirmed in *Fong*, 149 US 698, 705 (Gray J) (1893). This is also language used in *Musgrove: Musgrove* [1891] AC 272, 280.
[106] Cf the instrumentalist assumption of Vitoria in the sixteenth century, in which he assumes the travel of the Spaniards to be neither harmful nor detrimental to the barbarians and, therefore, lawful: see Chapter 2, Section 2.1.3.2, 59.
[107] *Chinese Exclusion Case*, 130 US 581, 604 (Field J) (1889); *Fong*, 149 US 698, 705 (Gray J) (1893).
[108] *Chinese Exclusion Case*, 130 US 581, 606 (1889); *Fong*, 149 US 698, 706 (Gray J) (1893).
[109] *Chinese Exclusion Case*, 130 US 581, 604 (Field J) (1889).   [110] 11 US 116 (1812).

context of individual migrants is contestable. The Court subsequently handed down two further decisions of direct relevance: *Ekiu*[111] and *Fong*.[112]

3.3.3.2 Ekiu v United States

In *Ekiu*, a female subject of the Emperor of Japan arrived in California and was refused permission to land. Despite stating that she had come to join her husband, who had been in California for two years, the ship's master concluded that she was likely to become a 'public charge' and should be excluded under the *Immigration Act 1891* (US).[113] Citing Vattel and Phillimore, the Court asserted that

> It is an accepted maxim of international law, that every sovereign nation has the power, as inherent in sovereignty, and essential to self-preservation, to forbid the entrance of foreigners within its dominions, or to admit them only in such cases and upon such conditions as it may see fit to prescribe.[114]

However, an examination of the Vattel text on which the Court relied reveals a more nuanced position. Vattel clearly considered the sovereign entitled to "forbid the entrance of his territory either to foreigners in general or in particular cases, or to certain persons or for certain particular purposes, according as he may think it advantageous to the state".[115] However, he provided important qualifications, namely that it is necessary to make known any such prohibition and resultant penalties, and to ensure that those seeking entry are so informed. Indeed, Vattel suggested that it may not be inconsistent with justice, as had once been the case in imperial China, to forbid all people from entering the empire or, "in case of competition, to prefer ourselves to others", "*provided* they did not refuse human assistance to those whom tempest or necessity obliged to approach their frontiers."[116]

As authority for the same proposition, the Court also considered other text from Vattel which outlined a basis for conditioning the entry and stay of foreigners. It appears to have relied on the following extract:

> Since the lord of the territory may, whenever he thinks proper, forbid its being entered,[117] he has, no doubt, a power to annex what conditions he pleases to the permission to enter. This, as we have already said, is a consequence of the right of domain.[118]

---

[111]   *Ekiu*, 142 US 651 (1892).   [112]   *Fong*, 149 US 698 (1893).
[113]   *Immigration Act 1891* ch 551, § 2, 26 Stat 1084, 1084 (1891).
[114]   *Ekiu*, 142 US 651, 659 (1892), citing Vattel, above n 87, bk II ch VII § 94, bk II ch VIII § 100; Phillimore, above n 88, pt III ch X, 320.
[115]   Vattel, above n 87, bk II ch VII § 94.   [116]   Ibid (emphasis added).   [117]   Ibid.
[118]   Ibid bk II ch VIII § 100.

However, in doing so, the Court overlooked weighty qualifications that Vattel attached to the same paragraph's starting premise. As we know from Chapter 2, in a proviso typical of the way in which he qualified the power of the sovereign, Vattel asked rhetorically, "Can it be necessary to add, that the owner of the territory [or sovereign] ought, in this instance, to respect the duties of humanity?"[119] Likewise, the Court overlooked Vattel's declaration that a "duty towards all mankind" may oblige the sovereign "to allow a free passage through, and a residence in his state"[120] – a right of innocent passage intended to safeguard "the general right of traversing the earth", whether for the purposes of commerce or "for other just reasons."[121] Thus, subject only to the qualification that passage would be "prejudicial or dangerous", "the owner of a country" was "bound to grant a passage for lawful purposes, whenever he can do it without inconvenience to himself".[122] Moreover, "he cannot lawfully annex burdensome conditions to a permission which he is obliged to grant, and which he cannot refuse if he wishes to discharge his duty, and not abuse his right of property."[123] Although it is important to recall that Vattel's foreigner was European and that the rights frameworks variously formulated by Vattel and his predecessor publicists are unlikely to have had within their sights the Chinese and Japanese labourers of the Supreme Court litigation, we can see that the Court has hewn the doctrine of 'absolute sovereignty' out of a body of international law in a way that overlooks rights hitherto conferred on the (European) foreigner, including innocent passage and travel and trade.

Also implicit in *Ekiu* is the assumption that excluding a young Japanese woman was a measure "essential to [the nation's] self-preservation".[124] The Court in this instance appears to have relied on the following passage from Phillimore:[125]

> It is a received maxim of International Law, that the Government of a State may prohibit the entrance of strangers into the country, and may therefore regulate the conditions under which they shall be allowed to remain in it, or may require and compel their departure from it.[126]

This extract is from a chapter entitled "Self-Preservation",[127] which describes the right of self-preservation as constituted "by that defence which prevents, as well as that which repels, attack".[128] Read in full, it is clear that the chapter is intended to address situations of hostility where a society is entitled *in self-defence* to "repel

---

[119] Ibid.   [120] Ibid.   [121] Ibid bk II ch X § 132.   [122] Ibid.
[123] Ibid; see also at bk II ch VIII § 100.   [124] *Ekiu*, 142 US 651, 659 (Gray J) (1892).
[125] Phillimore, above n 88, pt III ch X, 320, cited in Juss, 'Free Movement', above n 3, 301; see also Nafziger, above n 2, 816.
[126] Phillimore, above n 88, pt III ch X, 320.   [127] Ibid 312–21.   [128] Ibid 312.

aggression"[129] "for the preservation of her safety"[130] during "periods of revolutionary disturbances".[131] Even then, Phillimore maintained the right of a nation in such times to afford a peaceful asylum to refugees and exiles,[132] implying that asylum is not inconsistent with the right of self-preservation. To this end, Phillimore recognised both individual duties and the Crown's concomitant obligations of protection[133] for the duration of an alien's residence and while she remained in the dominion of the British Empire. In contrast, there was no evidence in *Ekiu* that the exclusion of the petitioner constituted an act of self-defence against an enemy alien. This suggests that the Court's reading of Phillimore had more to do with the political-economic desire to regulate race and labour than Phillimore's actual framing of self-preservation. Indeed, Phillimore's point of departure was the broader premise that "[i]t has been the policy of wise States, . . . especially the policy of Rome, to open wide the door for the reception and naturalisation of foreigners."[134]

3.3.3.3 Fong Yue Ting v United States

The Court's 1893 decision in *Fong* concerned three Chinese labourers arrested and detained for failing to hold certificates of residence as required by the *Act of May 5, 1892*[135] ('*Geary Act*'). The *Geary Act*'s stated purpose was '[a]n act to prohibit the coming of Chinese persons to the United States'.[136] Section 6 of the Act authorised their arrests and detention. The provision obliged Chinese labourers to obtain a certificate of residence within one year after the Act's passage. The Act included deeming provisions that presumed an individual's presence in the United States to be unlawful, rebuttable only by the evidence of 'at least one credible white witness, that he was a resident of the United States at the time of the passage of this act'. In two instances, the petitioners had applied for but not been granted certificates of residence. In the third, the petitioner had applied for and been refused a certificate on the ground that his witnesses were persons of the Chinese race and not credible witnesses. He was unable to produce a white witness as required under the Act. In these circumstances, failure to obtain a certificate of

---

[129] Ibid.   [130] Ibid 313.   [131] Ibid 320; Nafziger, above n 2, 826.
[132] Phillimore, above n 88, pt III ch X, 316–7.
[133] *Calvin's Case* (1608) 7 Coke Report 1a; 77 ER 377.
[134] Phillimore, above n 88, pt III ch XVIII, 446 ('Right of Jurisdiction over Persons'); Nafziger, above n 2, 826; Juss, *International Migration*, above n 3, 15.
[135] *Act of May 5, 1892*, ch 60, 27 Stat 25 (1892) ('*Geary Act*'), extending for ten years the *Chinese Exclusion Act 1882*, ch 126, 22 Stat 58 (1882).
[136] *Fong*, 149 US 698 (1893).

residence resulted in imprisonment with hard labour for up to one year, followed by deportation.[137] An important part of the international law background to this legislation was a bilateral treaty between the United States and China known as the *Burlingame Treaty*, first signed in 1868. This agreement, inter alia, 'cordially recognised':

> the inherent and inalienable right of man to change his home and allegiance, and also the mutual advantage of the free migration and emigration of their citizens and subjects, respectively, from one country to the other, for the purposes of curiosity, of trade, or as permanent residents.[138]

Moreover, the treaty provided that

> Citizens of the United States visiting or residing in China, . . . and reciprocally, Chinese subjects visiting or residing in the United States, shall enjoy the same privileges, immunities and exemptions, in respect to travel and residence, as may there be enjoyed by the citizens or subjects of the most favored nation.[139]

Modifications to the treaty were made in 1880, which became known as the *Angell Treaty*.[140] The revised provisions empowered the United States to 'regulate, limit or suspend' entry or residence of Chinese labourers where their entry or residence would affect, or threaten to affect, the interests of the United States or endanger good order. However, the (amended) treaty stipulated that the United States 'may not absolutely prohibit' such immigration and that any limitation or suspension be 'reasonable' and apply only to Chinese labourers and not other classes of Chinese persons.[141] Finally, the treaty provided that the government would exert all its power to devise measures for the protection of Chinese labourers or Chinese of any other class and secure to them the same rights, privileges, immunities, and exemptions as may be enjoyed by the citizens or subjects of the most favoured nation.[142]

In dismissing the appeal of the petitioners in *Fong*, the majority had no hesitation in disregarding the provisions of the revised treaty,[143] citing and giving effect instead to the decision in *Ekiu* that the sovereign right to exclude

---

[137] *Geary Act*, ch 60, § 4 27, Stat 25, 25 (1892).
[138] *Treaty between China and the United States 1868*, signed 28 July 1868, 16 Stat 739, Treaty Series 48 (entered into force 23 November 1869) art V ('*Burlingame Treaty*').
[139] Ibid art VI.
[140] *Treaty between the United States and China, concerning Immigration*, signed 17 November 1880, 22 Stat 828, Treaty Series 50 (entered into force 19 July 1881) ('*Angell Treaty*').
[141] *Angell Treaty* art I.   [142] Ibid art III.
[143] See, eg, *Chinese Exclusion Case*, 130 US 581, 600–1 (1889).

and condition the entry and stay of aliens was an accepted maxim of international law.[144] It also reaffirmed that the proposition was "not open to controversy",[145] readily reinforcing the message that foreigners of a different race may be excluded even if they are friendly. By denying that the act of deportation could be punitive, the Court obscured the important distinction between friendly and enemy aliens, before seeking further to reinforce the view that the work of Vattel and others stood as authority for the proposition that sovereignty empowered states to do as they please in matters of exclusion and expulsion. In quick succession, the Court cited Vattel's *Law of Nations*; Ortolan's *Diplomatie de la Mer*; Phillimore's *International Law*; Gillespie's translation of Bar's *International Law*;[146] and some earlier jurisprudence, including the Victorian case of *Musgrove*, discussed above.[147] In this way, the Court further obscured the nuanced view of the foreigner-sovereign relation in the work of Vattel and others.

The Court then quoted the Privy Council's assertion in *Musgrove* that there is no authority for the proposition that an alien has an enforceable legal right to enter territory. This reinforced the view that when it comes to aliens, what is not expressly permitted is forbidden.[148] Furthermore, the Court affirmed "the right to exclude or to expel all aliens, or any class of aliens, absolutely or upon certain conditions, in war or in peace," to be "an inherent and inalienable right of every sovereign and independent nation, essential to its safety, its independence and its welfare".[149] Thus, through mutually reinforcing judicial readings, sovereign rights to exclude or expel friendly as well as enemy aliens became absolute, inherent, inalienable, and incontestable.

Moreover, the Court found that shifting the burden of proof onto the Chinese labourer seeking to assert entitlement to a certificate of residence and the requirement of 'at least one credible white witness' to do so was within

---

[144] *Fong*, 149 US 698, 705 (Gray J) (1893).   [145] Ibid.

[146] Vattel, above n 87, bk I ch XIX §§ 230–231; Théodore Ortolan, *Règles internationales et diplomatie de la mer* (Cosse et J Dumaine, 1st ed, 1845) bk 2 ch 14, 318; Phillimore, above n 88, pt III ch X, 320; L Bar, *International Law: Private and Criminal* (G R Gillespie trans', Soule & Bugbee, 1883) 708 n711 [trans of: *Das Internationale Private- und Strafrecht* (first published 1862)].

[147] *Re Adam* (1837) 1 Moo PC 460; 12 ER 889; *Musgrove* [1891] AC 272. Note, however, that the decision in *Re Adam* regarding the banishment from the island of Mauritius of an alien friend was based on what Lord Brougham described as "the peculiar provisions of the French law" that applied on the island at the time. Indeed, according to Holroyd J, had English law applied, a contrary conclusion would have resulted, because "according to English law no resident in the United Kingdom, whether native or foreigner, can be deported at the arbitrary will of the executive for any offence alleged against him": *Chun Teeong Toy v Musgrove* (1888) 14 VLR 349, 424 (Holroyd J).

[148] See above 96.   [149] *Fong*, 149 US 698, 711 (1893).

the acknowledged power of the legislature. This position was further justified by speculation that "the suspicious nature ... of the testimony offered to establish the residence of the parties" arose from "the loose notions entertained by the witnesses of the obligation of an oath".[150] In this way, certain aberrant characteristics and behaviours were assumed by the majority to inhere in the non-European foreigner and were regarded as establishing sufficient grounds to deny due process rights to foreigners; they were 'barbarian' outsiders subject to the law yet unworthy of its protection.

While much of the restrictive migration jurisprudence was without dissent, the decision in *Fong* is a notable exception. Three justices delivered dissenting judgments. Fuller J found that a legislative sentence of banishment contained the germs of the assertion of an unlimited and arbitrary power that was incompatible with the immutable principles of justice.[151] Brewer J found s 6 of the Act to be unconstitutional on account of its denial of due process rights – rights that were specifically articulated in the (revised) *Burlingame Treaty*.[152] Similarly, Field J, who had been in the majority in the *Chinese Exclusion Case*, recorded a strong dissent in which he drew a distinction between resident and entering aliens, and objected to the elision of friendly and enemy aliens.

Of relevance to Brewer J was the fact that the petitioners were aliens who had been resident for long periods, since 1879, 1877, and 1874, respectively. To Brewer J, the petitioners were domiciled in the United States and should therefore have been entitled to "a more distinct and larger measure of protection than those who are simply passing through, or temporarily in it."[153] In support of this view, he referred to Vattel, Grotius, and Phillimore.[154]

Brewer J expressed grave reservations about absolutist claims of sovereignty. He stated:

It is said that the power here asserted is inherent in sovereignty. This doctrine of powers inherent in sovereignty is one both indefinite and dangerous. Where are the limits to such powers to be found, and by whom are they to be pronounced? Is it within legislative capacity to declare the limits? If so, then the mere assertion of an inherent power creates it, and despotism exists. May the courts establish the boundaries? Whence do they obtain the authority for this? Shall they look to the practices of other nations to ascertain the limits? The governments of other nations have elastic powers – ours is fixed and bounded by a written constitution. The expulsion of a race may be within the inherent powers of a despotism. History, before the adoption of this

---

[150]   Ibid 730 (Gray J), quoting *Chinese Exclusion Case*, 130 US 581, 598 (Field J) (1889).
[151]   *Fong*, 149 US 698, 764 (1893).   [152]   *Angell Treaty* arts II, V.
[153]   *Fong*, 149 US 698, 734 (1893).   [154]   Ibid 734–5; see above 101.

Constitution, was not destitute of examples of the exercise of such a power; and its framers were familiar with history, and wisely as it seems to me, they gave to this government no general power to banish. Banishment may be resorted to as punishment for a crime; but among the powers reserved to the people and not delegated to the government is that of determining whether whole classes in our midst shall, for no crime but that of their race and birthplace, be driven from our territory.[155]

Brewer J could not countenance the idea that deportation of a resident alien did not constitute punishment and could therefore operate without due process guarantees. Citing President Madison, he said:

If the banishment of an alien from a country into which he has been invited as the asylum most auspicious to his happiness – a country where he may have formed the most tender connections; where he may have invested his entire property, and acquired property of the real and permanent, as well as the movable and temporary kind; where he enjoys, under the laws, a greater share of the blessings of personal security and personal liberty than he can elsewhere hope for; ... if, moreover, in the execution of the sentence against him he is to be exposed, not only to the ordinary dangers of the sea, but to the peculiar casualties incident to a crisis of war and of unusual licentiousness on that element, and possibly to vindictive purposes, which his immigration itself may have provoked – if a banishment of this sort be not a punishment, and among the severest of punishments, it will be difficult to imagine a doom to which the name can be applied.[156]

Although describing the Chinese as "obnoxious" and Chinese labourers as a "distasteful class",[157] Brewer J asked, "if the power exists, who shall say it will not be exercised to-morrow against other classes and other people? ... [W]hat security have others that a like disregard of its provisions may not be resorted to?"[158] Noting that "[i]llegitimate and unconstitutional practices get their first footing ... by silent approaches and slight deviations from legal modes of procedure", he recalled that "[i]t is the duty of the courts to be watchful for the constitutional rights of the citizen, and against any stealthy encroachments thereon. Their motto should be *obsta principiis*."[159]

---

155 *Fong*, 149 US 698, 737–8 (1893).
156 Jonathan Elliot (ed), *The Debates in the Several State Conventions on the Adoption of the Federal Constitution* (J B Lippincott, 2nd ed, 1836) vol 4, 555, cited in *Fong*, 149 US 698, 740 (1893).
157 *Fong*, 149 US 698, 743 (1893).
158 Ibid 743–4, citing *Boyd v United States*, 116 US 616, 635 (Bradley J) (1886) ('*Boyd*').
159 That is, 'resist the first advances': *Fong*, 149 US 698, 744 (Brewer J) (1893), citing *Boyd*, 116 US 616, 635 (Bradley J) (1886).

Like Brewer J, Field J's dissenting opinion also distinguished between legislation for the exclusion of entering aliens[160] on the one hand, and for the deportation of alien residents on the other – persons he appears to have regarded as 'insiders' and, as his judgment reveals, whose treatment had ramifications for European foreigners. Field J's central preoccupation was the elision of enemy and friendly aliens embodied in the assertion of 'absolute sovereignty'. To this end, he cited the *Alien Act of 1798*,[161] which, in terms denounced by its critics as unconstitutional and barbarous, and defended by its advocates as a war measure, empowered the President to order all aliens adjudged to be "dangerous to the peace and safety of the United States" or in relation to whom there were reasonable grounds for suspecting them of "treasonable or secret machinations" to depart the country or be subject to a period of imprisonment not exceeding three years.[162] Field J further underscored that "in no other instance has the deportation of friendly aliens been advocated as a lawful measure by any department of our government", decrying the power to do so as "dangerous and despotic", a power that, he surmised, may also apply to the Irish, German, French, and English.[163] Reaffirming the right of *resident* aliens to due process, he declared that "[a]rbitrary and despotic power can no more be exercised over them with reference to their persons and property, than over the persons and property of native-born citizens."[164] To omit or discard any rule in the administration of justice would, he said, be "to establish a pure, simple, undisguised despotism and tyranny with respect to foreigners resident in the country by its consent."[165] "Arbitrary and tyrannical power has no place in our system", he declared; the exercise of such powers as the majority endorsed would, he said, be brutal, oppressive, inhumane, and cruel.[166]

Field J also cast doubt on the international citations claimed to support the absolute nature of sovereignty, particularly the majority's conclusion that these pronouncements apply equally to the exclusion of foreigners entering territory as they do to alien residents. Indeed, he noted that there is a great deal of confusion in the use of the term 'sovereignty' by law writers.[167] Doubting the strength of the assertions made by the majority in relation to English law, Field J stated, "deportation from the realm has not been exercised in England since *Magna Carta*, except in punishment for crime, or as a measure in view of existing or anticipated hostilities."[168] He noted also that European state

---

[160]   This was the basis of his judgment in the *Chinese Exclusion Case*, 130 US 581 (1889).
[161]   *An Act concerning Aliens*, ch 58, 1 Stat 570 (1798) ('*Alien Act of 1798*').
[162]   *Fong*, 149 US 698, 746 (1893).   [163]   Ibid 750.   [164]   Ibid 754.   [165]   Ibid 755.
[166]   Ibid 755–6.   [167]   Ibid 757–8.   [168]   Ibid 757.

practice – including the expulsion of the Moors from Spain, the banishment of 15,000 Jews from Edward I's England, the revocation of the Edict of Nantes and the expulsion of the Huguenots from France, and the banishment of Jews from Russia – had been condemned for its barbarity and cruelty, abrogating all possibility of implying from the nature of government the power to perpetrate such acts.[169]

3.3.4 A *Transnational Judicial Conversation Takes Root*

As these cases show, through a transnational judicial conversation, a narrative of both vulnerability and entitlement, driven by the political-economic desire to regulate race and labour, was given expression. This enabled the idea of 'absolute sovereignty' to become entrenched as an unassailable doctrine and to take hold across much of the Anglo-American common law world through mutually reinforcing jurisdictions.[170] The resulting jurisprudence occurred not only through instrumentalist use of leading publicists and commentators, but also through heavy reliance on the doctrine of precedent. As an approach, it had a powerful influence over how 'absolute sovereignty' was conceived and constructed as a marker of national independence, security, and protection. Furthermore, given that this corpus of jurisprudence related to non-European foreign labourers, the strategic handling of the work of Vattel and others suggests a political-economic desire to interpret away rights and obligations in international law capable of favouring non-European foreigners. Moreover, as we will see in Part II of this book, the doctrine of precedent and a 'positivist' jurisprudential style of argument have enabled the political-economic context in which the 'received maxim'[171] took hold to be obscured in its contemporary usage.

3.4 'ABSOLUTE SOVEREIGNTY': A CONTINGENT HISTORICAL ARTEFACT

We can see from the foregoing how the foreigner-sovereign relation was shaped to produce the claim of 'absolute sovereignty' as a common law doctrine. We can see how this took place in the context of a changing migratory landscape marked by British imperial expansion, the abolition of slavery, industrialisation, and a growing demand for cheap labour. It was in

---

[169] Ibid.   [170] See, generally, Lake and Reynolds, above n 13; McKeown, above n 3.
[171] Phillimore, above n 88, pt III ch X, 320; Juss, *International Migration*, above n 3, 14–15; Nafziger, above n 2, 826.

this context that 'absolute sovereignty' emerged as a common law doctrine in order to enable the regulation of non-European labour migration in white settler societies.

As we know from Chapter 2, in early international law there was no discourse of 'absolute sovereignty'. As such, we can see how the 'appearance' of non-European foreigners on the migratory landscape of the nineteenth century marked the point of emergence of 'absolute sovereignty' as doctrine and discourse – a convergence that was not accidental. Considered together, Chapters 2 and 3 make clear that when the foreigner was a European insider – whether coloniser, trader, or exile – there was no perceived need for a discourse of 'absolute sovereignty' because he, the foreigner, was a figure of privilege and power aligned with the sovereign and sovereign interests. On the other hand, when the foreigner was a non-European, she was marked as a 'barbarian' outsider, an excludable, exploitable, expendable, and deportable figure (instrumentally) subject to the law but unworthy of its protection. This makes clear that it was the desire to exclude and condition non-European labour migration that provided the impetus for restrictive migration legislation and gave 'absolute sovereignty' its doctrinal purpose and shape.

In contrast to the privileged figure of the foreigner who populated the treatises of Vitoria, Grotius, Pufendorf, and Vattel, we have encountered in Chapter 3 a different kind of juridical figure. However, while the 'appearance' of the non-European foreigner marked a change in the relation between the foreigner and the sovereign, it reflected the same kind of political-economic interests that underpinned the construction of the (European) foreigner as rights-bearing. As we saw in Chapter 2, an ideology of colonial legitimisation was a critical dimension implicit in early international law's framing of the foreigner as an insider. This chapter has in turn shown how, in the nineteenth century, a variation on the ideology of colonial legitimisation – which under-pinned the regulation of race and labour in the political-economic interests of white settler societies – was also critical to the way in which the figure of the foreigner was (re)framed as an outsider.

This genealogy of the development of a common law doctrine of 'absolute sovereignty' has made visible how restrictive migration legislation was vali-dated and fortified by an emergent common law jurisprudence of 'absolute sovereignty' – a jurisprudence that ascribed authority to 'absolute sovereignty' through a complex of international law and judicial interpretation, precedent and 'positivism'.[172] Particular repertoires and patterns of argument have been drawn from (and generated in) authoritative text – both contextually and

---

[172]   See above n 89.

acontextually – and have been reused and/or reshaped. We can thus see that the way in which the foreigner-sovereign relation is conceptualised is a product of historical contingencies rather than universal truths.[173] In other words, we can recognise that, as ideas, the elements of the foreigner-sovereign relation are historically produced even though we may see no necessary or direct connection between their history and their present purpose or value.[174] We can recognise that the authority ascribed to 'absolute sovereignty' is an innovation whose juridical history is contingent. Indeed, in the context of nineteenth-century migration, we can see how the putative authority of 'absolute sovereignty' represents a response to and rationalisation for the political-economic desire of certain white settler societies to arrogate to themselves complete power in the regulation of race and labour.

Throughout this chapter, I have paid close attention to underlying political-economic purposes and linguistic choices, as well as to how arguments are shaped. For example, we have seen how particular language gave succour to a line of thinking that has viewed 'absolute sovereignty' as a necessity and that has viewed the practice of sovereignty as an instrument of (complete) control rather than treating the sovereign as a fallible source of authority.[175] Thus, we see 'absolute sovereignty' described as 'essential' to 'self-preservation'. And 'self-preservation' is used to connote the (perceptual) imperative of race and labour regulation rather than as an imperative of self-protection (of the individual, as conceptualised by Pufendorf)[176] or of self-defence (of the state in times of war, as conceptualised by Phillimore).[177] Linguistic choices conjure images of 'vast hordes' of 'elbowing', 'hustling', 'thronging' crowds of non-Europeans, portrayed as hostile and aggressive threats to peace, safety, security, and civilisation. These choices depict the elision of enemy and friendly aliens as essential and logical, and the construction and authorisation of the practice of sovereignty as absolute. Meanwhile, pejorative descriptions of foreigners as 'servile' and 'suspicious' reinforce their unworthiness. Yet the imputed threats to peace, safety, security, and civilisation are asserted but not substantiated. Instead, we see that the logical necessity of sovereignty's absolute character is constructed – a contingent historical artefact.

As this part of the genealogy suggests, discourses of vulnerability and entitlement also helped secure the idea of 'absolute sovereignty' as an unassailable doctrine. Nevertheless, as we have seen, dissenting voices in the US

---

[173] David Owen, *Nietzsche's Genealogy of Morality* (McGill-Queen's University Press, 2007) 6.
[174] Ibid 64.
[175] Stephen D Krasner, *Sovereignty: Organized Hypocrisy* (Princeton University Press, 1999) 13–14; Torpey, above n 5, 4–5.
[176] See Chapter 2, Section 2.3.2, 70–71.   [177] Phillimore, above n 88, 187–93.

Supreme Court recognised the risk of abuse that inheres in the exercise of absolute power, warning of the dangers of 'arbitrary', 'tyrannical', and 'despotic' power; 'encroachments' on rights; and 'deviations' from legal modes of procedure. As we will see in Chapter 4, in the context of juridical developments in Australia, the risk of abuse of power would later be cast as (only) theoretical, because those enjoying such power can be relied upon to exercise it responsibly – a view still used to justify its use in contemporary responses to unsolicited migration.[178]

Finally, we have seen in this chapter how the common law doctrine of 'absolute sovereignty' has been sustained by certain legal genres – in particular, the doctrine of precedent and a 'positivist' jurisprudence. These legal genres underwrite modern law's account of itself as authoritative,[179] a theme that reappears in Chapter 4. As forms of juridical engagement, these legal genres have enabled 'absolute sovereignty' as an idea to be juridically tamed by (selective) repetition and reinforcement in a transnational judicial conversation that spans time and place. Thus, we see how 'absolute sovereignty' acquired resonance – remarkably quickly – as a 'received maxim' that was 'not open to controversy'.[180] This resonance is the product of a judiciary that was in lockstep with legislative and societal expectations in white settler societies about how the non-European migrant labourer should be positioned within the foreigner-sovereign relation – expectations imbued with the racism of their time and attuned to the economic advantages of selective gatekeeping. As such, we see that behind the common law doctrine of 'absolute sovereignty' lies a constellation of political-economic ideas, legislative and administrative practices, and juridical forms of engagement which are best understood as contingent historical artefacts informing the nature of the foreigner-sovereign relation.

Thus far, the genealogy has made visible that *who* the foreigner is understood to be in international law (whether European insider or non-European outsider) is crucial to the way in which her relationship with the sovereign is understood. I have argued that the common law doctrine of 'absolute sovereignty', which emerged contemporaneously with the 'appearance' of (non-European) outsider foreigners on the imperial landscape, represents a particular form of the foreigner-sovereign relation. So even though 'absolute sovereignty' in migration lawmaking has been framed as necessary and, to that end, a common law

---

[178] See especially the parliamentary debates in relation to the mandatory detention legislation, discussed in Chapter 5 Section 5.1, 167–86.

[179] Owen, above n 173, 5.

[180] The doctrine of 'absolute sovereignty' would later be described as "settled law" by the High Court of Australia: *Ah Yin v Christie* (1907) 4 CLR 1428, 1431 (Griffith CJ). See Chapter 4.

doctrine has emerged, like the foreigner's putative 'outsider-ness', it is not inevitable.

Having shown how 'absolute sovereignty' was crystallised in the nineteenth century as a common law doctrine, Chapter 4 examines how the claim of 'absolute sovereignty' secured its place as a constitutional doctrine in the Australian context. Covering the period from the Federation of Australia to mid-century, and drawing together the analyses in Chapters 2 and 3, Chapter 4 describes how the authority of international law, the common law, and constitutional law have coalesced to produce a political and juridical discourse of 'absolute sovereignty' of stunning resilience – a resilience that is still held in place in contemporary migration lawmaking, its contingencies notwithstanding.

4

A Constitutionalisation of Sovereignty

The story of migration, both forced and voluntary, in the first half of the twentieth century is vast and complex, spanning every region and continent and combining an often highly charged mix of influences: political, economic, social, racial and cultural. While much of Australia's story of migration since white settlement has been a regulatory project designed to achieve racial purity and economic prosperity, the first half of the twentieth century is significant as a formative 'moment' in the making of migration law, shaped as it was by the 'imperatives' of the White Australia policy. These imperatives were pivotal to the decision to federate Australia and to the way in which constitutional powers were framed.

However, the political-economic resolve that Australia should 'remain' racially pure stood in constant tension with trading interests and demands for cheap labour embodied in the equally strong resolve to ensure economic prosperity. This tension in the regulation of race and labour became a running sore in the domain of diplomatic and trade relations and would endure in significant measure notwithstanding the White Australia policy's "long, slow death".[1]

Chapter 4 is the final chapter in our genealogy of the foreigner-sovereign relation, the principal aim of which is to explain how the policies of mandatory detention and planned destitution have come to be considered lawful and legitimate responses to unsolicited migration. The overall work of the genealogy to date has been to consider how this relation was framed in early international law and the common law, charting changes in conceptualisations of the figure of the foreigner and how the foreigner-sovereign relation was shaped into a common law doctrine of 'absolute sovereignty'. Following on from this, the work of this chapter is to describe how the foreigner-sovereign

---

[1] Gwenda Tavan, *The Long, Slow Death of White Australia* (Scribe, 2005).

relation was given constitutional form through, inter alia, the aliens and immigration powers,[2] a process that, as we will see, resolutely resisted due process and other safeguards and through which the common law doctrine of 'absolute sovereignty' became entrenched. In this chapter I describe how entrenching 'absolute sovereignty' as a constitutional doctrine created space for abundant use of discretionary power and 'remedial' or 'curative' legislation. In this connection, I argue that the constitutional framing of 'absolute sovereignty' was buttressed by particular legal traditions and orthodoxies, including the doctrines of precedent and responsible government. The central argument of this chapter is that 'absolute sovereignty' has emerged as a multifaceted discourse – encompassing political doctrine, judicial formulation, constitutional doctrine, and public rhetoric – which has, as a practice, become ingrained in the fabric of Australian migration law. The analysis emphasises the enduring presence but increasingly unutterable work of race in shaping constructions and perceptions of the foreigner – work that, as Part II of the book will show, has continuing effects.

The first section of this chapter considers the manner in which the foreigner-sovereign relation was constitutionalised in the framing of the aliens and immigration powers in the *Constitution*.[3] The second considers how the constitutional form of this relationship was used in 1901 to pass the *Pacific Island Labourers Act 1901* (Cth)[4] and the *Immigration Restriction Act 1901* (Cth),[5] and how the High Court of Australia's ('the High Court') interpretation of selected aspects of these Acts gave expression to the foreigner-sovereign relation. The third section extends the analysis to consider the Court's interpretation of a selection of subsequent legislative developments relating to the exclusion of industrial and political activist foreigners (who were European) and those wartime refugees who were non-European. A discussion then follows of the introduction of Migration Bill 1958 (Cth),[6] legislation pitched as a comprehensive overhaul of Australia's immigration laws, promising safeguards against the excesses of 'absolute sovereignty'. In addition to the archive and jurisprudence on which it draws, the genealogy contributes to existing scholarship of jurists,[7]

---

2   *Constitution* ss 51(xix), 51(xxvii).   3   Ibid.
4   *Pacific Island Labourers Act 1901* (Cth) ('*Pacific Island Labourers Act 1901*').
5   *Immigration Restriction Act 1901* (Cth) ('*Immigration Restriction Act 1901*').
6   Migration Bill 1958 (Cth).
7   See especially John M Williams, 'Race, Citizenship and the Formation of the Australian Constitution: Andrew Inglis Clark and the "14th Amendment"' (1996) 42(1) *Australian Journal of Politics and History* 10; Kim Rubenstein, 'Citizenship and the Constitutional Convention Debates: A Mere Legal Inference' (1997) 25(2) *Federal Law Review* 295; Kim Rubenstein, 'Citizenship and the Centenary – Inclusion and Exclusion in 20th Century Australia' (2000)

historians,[8] and legal historians.[9] Its purpose is to offer an analysis focusing on the foreigner-sovereign relation to help us see not only that the history of 'absolute sovereignty' was not accidental, but also, as we move into Part II, that this history is integral to the way the Australian state responds to unsolicited migration today.

Recalling that the context for this project is the present, in which the policies of mandatory detention and planned destitution are seen as thinkable institutional responses to unsolicited migration, it is already possible to detect a contemporary resonance in the styles of argument made visible in Chapters 2 and 3. Extending the genealogical inquiry into how the priority of regulating race and labour gave the foreigner-sovereign relation its constitutional form adds a crucial dimension to the genealogy. It enables us to think more perspicuously about the legal traditions and orthodoxies we have inherited. Exploring how 'absolute sovereignty' became entrenched as a discourse during this period – both politically and juridically – is, therefore, critical in identifying the lines of continuity and discontinuity between juridical responses and rationalisations of the past and contemporary discourses of mandatory detention and planned destitution considered in Part II.

4.1 CONSTITUTIONALISING 'ABSOLUTE SOVEREIGNTY'

As Chapter 3 demonstrated, by the late nineteenth century a common law doctrine of 'absolute sovereignty', which claimed its authority from early international law, was already firmly entrenched in the Australian legal

---

24(3) *Melbourne University Law Review* 576; Hilary Charlesworth, *Writing in Rights: Australia and the Protection of Human Rights* (UNSW Press, 2002); Antony Anghie, *Imperialism, Sovereignty, and the Making of International Law* (Cambridge University Press, 2004). In the United States, see Kevin Pimentel, 'To Yick Wo, Thanks for Nothing! Citizenship for Filipino Veterans' (1999) 4(2) *Michigan Journal of Race Law* 459; Stephen H Legomsky, 'Immigration Law and the Principle of Plenary Congressional Power' (1984) 84 *Supreme Court Review* 255.

8   James Jupp (ed), *The Australian People: An Encyclopedia of the Nation, Its People and Their Origins* (Cambridge University Press, 2001); Tavan, above n 1; Ann Curthoys and Marilyn Lake (eds), *Connected Worlds: History in Transnational Perspective* (ANU E Press, 2005); Glenn Nicholls, *Deported: A History of Forced Departures from Australia* (UNSW Press, 2007); Marilyn Lake and Henry Reynolds, *Drawing the Global Colour Line: White Men's Countries and the Question of Racial Equality* (Melbourne University Press, 2008); Klaus Neumann and Gwenda Tavan (eds), *Does History Matter? Making and Debating Citizenship, Immigration and Refugee Policy in Australia and New Zealand* (ANU E Press, 2009); Klaus Neumann, *Across the Seas: Australia's Response to Refugees* (Black Inc, 2015).

9   Anthony C Palfreeman, *The Administration of the White Australia Policy* (Melbourne University Press, 1967); Adam M McKeown, *Melancholy Order: Asian Migration and the Globalization of Borders* (Columbia University Press, 2008).

imagination and reflected in highly restrictive migration lawmaking.[10] The colonies of pre-federation Australia had introduced restrictive legislation on the strength of it, principally with legislation that targeted the Chinese;[11] and, in lockstep with legislative and societal expectations in these white settler societies, the courts had declared a common law doctrine of 'absolute sovereignty' to be not open to controversy.[12] This section explores how the common law doctrine of 'absolute sovereignty' was constitutionalised. In doing so, it considers not only how 'absolute sovereignty' was given constitutional shape in the aliens and immigration powers, but also how it took its shape from the parallel debate during the constitutional conventions on due process rights and the race power.[13]

4.1.1 Australasian Federal Convention Debates

The Australian *Constitution* is an Act of the Imperial Parliament passed in 1900 following a series of constitutional conventions held between 1891 and 1898.[14] So uncontroversial was the notion of an absolute right to exclude and condition the entry and stay of aliens (which I term 'absolute sovereignty') that there was no debate during the constitutional conventions on the text or implications of the draft plenary powers to legislate with respect to 'naturalization and aliens' and 'immigration and emigration'. As such, the texts of both provisions[15] reflect the absolute and unqualified terms in which they had first appeared in the 1891 draft constitution.[16]

In support of the absolute power of exclusion, the only authority to which the uniquely and magisterially authoritative text of Quick and Garran[17] referred was *Musgrove v Chun Teeong Toy*[18] ('*Musgrove*'), considered in

---

[10] This was, of course, a transnational phenomenon, spawned in the United States and the British colonial territories of Australia, Canada, New Zealand, and South Africa, but rapidly globalising: McKeown, above n 9.

[11] See Chapter 3 Section 3.2.1, 91–2.

[12] *Chae Chan Ping v United States*, 130 US 581, 604 (1889) ('*Chinese Exclusion Case*'); affirmed in *Fong Yue Ting v United States*, 149 US 698, 705 (Gray J) (1893) ('*Fong*'). This is also language used in *Musgrove*: *Musgrove v Chun Teeong Toy* [1891] AC 272, 280 ('*Musgrove*'). See also Chapter 3, 98.

[13] *Constitution* s 51(xxvi).

[14] *Commonwealth of Australia Constitution Act 1900* (Imp) 63 & 64 Vict, c 12, s 9.

[15] *Constitution* ss 51(xix), 51(xxvii).

[16] John Quick and Robert Randolph Garran, *The Annotated Constitution of the Australian Commonwealth* (Angus & Robertson, 1901) 599, 623.

[17] Ibid; on the influence of Quick and Garran, see, eg, John Hirst, *The Sentimental Nation: The Making of the Australian Commonwealth* (Oxford University Press, 2000) 248.

[18] [1891] AC 272.

Chapter 3.[19] In doing so, they intimated that *Musgrove* alone was sufficient to establish authority for such power. Because there had been no debate on the aliens and immigration powers during the constitutional conventions, there is little else to go on other than, ex post facto, Quick and Garran's passing reference to *Musgrove*[20] and the self-assured reference to the case by Prime Minister Edmund Barton, who described it as firmly establishing a power to exclude 'undesirables'.[21] Thus, in a single meta-legal moment and without debate, the idea of 'absolute sovereignty' slid seamlessly into the constitutional framework on the strength of the solitary – and, as we know, contestable – case of *Musgrove*.[22]

4.1.1.1 Responsible Government: The 'Ultimate Guarantee'

As Chapter 3 describes, a (slightly) more nuanced jurisprudential history of the sovereign right of exclusion had emerged in the United States towards the end of the nineteenth century,[23] a jurisprudence that drew heavily on the due process and equal protection rights provided for in the Fourteenth Amendment[24] and included the strong dissents in the case of *Fong Yue Ting v United States*[25] ('*Fong*'). During the constitutional conventions, a Fourteenth Amendment–style proposal was put forward by the Tasmanian Attorney-General Andrew Inglis Clark. In contrast to the undebated aliens and immigration powers, it attracted vigorous debate and was defeated. Even a weaker proposal from Richard O'Connor to insert the words 'deprive any person of life, liberty or property, without due process of law' was rejected.[26]

When O'Connor suggested that such a safeguard would be necessary in the event that "some wave of popular feeling may lead a … Parliament … to commit an injustice by passing a law that would deprive citizens of life, liberty, or property without due process of law",[27] one delegate considered that in such circumstances the appropriate response would be for Royal Assent to be

---

[19] See Chapter 3 Section 3.3.2, 96–7.   [20] Quick and Garran, above n 16, 600.
[21] Commonwealth, *Parliamentary Debates*, House of Representatives, 7 August 1901, 3500 (Commonwealth parliamentary debates are hereinafter referred to as 'CPD').
[22] See Chapter 3 Section 3.3.2, 96–7.   [23] See ibid Section 3.3.3, 97–107.
[24] *United States Constitution* amend XIV
[25] 149 US 698 (1893); see also *Yick Wo v Hopkins*, 118 US 356 (1886) ('*Yick Wo*'). Cf dissenting opinions in *Fong*, discussed in Chapter 3, 104–7.
[26] *Official Record of the Debates of the Australasian Federal Convention*, Melbourne, 8 February 1898, 688 (The Debates of the Australasian Federal Convention are hereinafter referred to as '*Constitutional Convention Debates*').
[27] Ibid 688 (Richard O'Connor).

withheld.[28] Another response came from John Cockburn, a former Premier from South Australia:

> Why should these words be inserted? They would be a reflection on our civilisation. Have any of the colonies of Australia ever attempted to deprive any person of life, liberty or property without due process of law? I repeat that the insertion of these words would be a reflection of our civilisation. People would say – 'Pretty things these states of Australia; they have to be prevented by a provision in the Constitution from doing the grossest injustices.'[29]

In this passage, Cockburn privileges reputation ('people would say') and dismisses even the possibility of breaches of due process through the deployment of a grandiose rhetorical question. In doing so, the doctrine of responsible government is preferred over constitutional guarantees of due process and depicted as not only sufficient to protect individuals against the 'grossest injustices', but as, furthermore, the most 'civilised' means of doing so. Reliance on this doctrine has been described as reflecting one of the most powerful and enduring tenets of Australian constitutional law.[30] Indeed, together, the doctrine of responsible government and the institution of representative government were regarded as indubitable models of propriety that would provide what would later be described as the "ultimate guarantee" of justice and individual rights.[31] As this chapter shows, reassurance that the absolute power embodied in the constitutional doctrine of 'absolute sovereignty' would be used responsibly would be a recurring theme[32] – above all, an effective way of ensuring that due process and equal protection rights were not accorded constitutional space except in the most limited way.[33]

---

[28] Ibid 688 (Sir John Forrest). On an attempt to persuade the Governor-General to withhold Royal Assent to *Migration Amendment Act 1992* (Cth) (the mandatory detention legislation), see Prologue, 3.

[29] *Constitutional Convention Debates*, Melbourne, 8 February 1898, 688 (John Cockburn); Williams, above n 7, 15.

[30] Williams, above n 7, 18; Charlesworth, above n 7, 25.

[31] Robert Menzies, *Central Power in the Australian Commonwealth* (Caswell, 1967) 54; Williams, above n 7, 18.

[32] See also: John Latham MP, discussed below at 138–9; *Re Yates; Ex parte Walsh and Johnson* (1925) 37 CLR 36, 133 (Starke J) ('*Walsh and Johnson*'), discussed below at 142. As the case studies in Chapters 5 and 6 show, the doctrine of responsible governance is given expression through discourses of restraint.

[33] The *Constitution* prohibits disability or discrimination on account of residence in another state: *Constitution* s 117.

4.1.1.2 Due Process, Equal Protection: 'Special Inhibitions'

The rejection of Clark's proposal to insert a US-style Fourteenth Amendment provision has been characterised as a resistance to the 'republican' notion of 'citizenship', as opposed to the imperial notion of 'subject'.[34] However, as Williams has suggested, its rejection might be more critically understood as having "more to do with issues of race and discrimination than with any other".[35] Although the rights of the citizenry were clearly within their contemplation, as he argues, the debate and its rejection centred on the desire to retain the power to discriminate against people of "any undesirable race or of undesirable antecedents".[36]

In their commentary on the *Constitution*, Quick and Garran distinguished jurisprudential patterns in the United States on the grounds that they arose from the "special inhibitions" of the Fourteenth Amendment.[37] Reassuring their Australian readership, they added:

> There is no section in the Constitution of the Commonwealth containing similar inhibitions. On the contrary it would seem that by sub-sec. xxvi. the Federal Parliament will have power to pass special and discriminating laws relating to 'the people of any race,' and that such laws could not be challenged on the ground of unconstitutionality . . .[38]

As such, not only was the Parliament conferred the widest possible powers to legislate for the admission or exclusion of aliens, but even if an alien or non-European British subject were admitted, two other provisions in the *Constitution* would further seal her fate.

First, as Quick and Garran observed, the race power was understood to confer power to discriminate in respect of

> people of any alien race after they have entered the Commonwealth; to localize them within defined areas, to restrict their [internal] migration, to confine them to certain occupations, or to give them special protection and secure their return after a certain period to the country whence they came.[39]

---

[34] Williams, above n 7, 19, citing *Australian Capital Television Pty Ltd v Commonwealth* (1992) 177 CLR 106, 182 (Dawson J), 228–9 (McHugh J).

[35] Williams, above n 7, 18 19.

[36] *Constitutional Convention Debates*, Melbourne, 2 March 1898, 1752 (John Quick); Williams, above n 7, 19. Australia's rejection of the US system of rights guarantees was based above all on a concern to preserve the autonomy of States; a position which drew on apparently contradictory arguments relating to the sovereignty of individual States and their right to discriminate on racial grounds: Charlesworth, above n 7, 25.

[37] Quick and Garran, above n 16, 623.   [38] Ibid.   [39] Ibid 622.

As this passage suggests, the concern was not only to be able to deal with people of 'any alien race' through the exclusionary aliens and immigration powers, but also to secure absolute power to condition the stay of those admitted. This appears to have been particularly so in the context of circumscribing 'coloured labour'.[40]

Second, like the race power, the rejection of a Fourteenth Amendment–style due process right[41] was also intended to ensure that the Commonwealth could discriminate on account of race and colour.[42] This purpose was articulated by a number of delegates during the constitutional conventions, including Sir John Forrest and (most doggedly) Isaac Isaacs.[43] Other delegates made clear their concerns that, above all, the provision should not *prevent* discrimination against non-Europeans.[44]

In summary, therefore, the foreigner-sovereign relation took its constitutional shape primarily from the emergent common law doctrine of 'absolute sovereignty' considered in Chapter 3. This process of constitutionalisation was sealed by the adoption, without any debate, of the aliens and immigration powers. In addition, the inclusion of the race power coupled with the rejection of a due process right ensured that even after entry, aliens and immigrants could be discriminated against on any basis, including race and colour. Thus 'absolute sovereignty' was constitutionalised at a number of levels and the Parliament had been given the "freest Constitution in the world".[45] The following section considers how it gave legislative expression to 'absolute sovereignty' in its constitutional form within its first sitting year.

---

[40] Ibid. As Rubenstein has noted, however, there were differing views regarding the proper treatment of immigrants following admission. As she notes, in contrast to Quick, who during the constitutional convention debates was "anxious to equip the Commonwealth with every power necessary for dealing with the invasion of outside coloured races", Kingston saw differential treatment (in access to the rights and privileges of citizenship) as a potential "source of embarrassment": Rubenstein, 'Citizenship and the Constitutional Convention Debates', above n 7, 306, citing *Constitutional Convention Debates*, Melbourne, 28 January 1898, 246 (John Quick), 247 (Charles Kingston).

[41] On limitations of the Fourteenth Amendment with regard to non-citizens, see Pimentel, above n 7; on due process rights and judicial deference, see also Legomsky, above n 7.

[42] See, eg, *Constitutional Convention Debates*, Melbourne, 8 February 1898, 687 (Isaac Isaacs); Williams, above n 7, 15.

[43] Williams, above n 7, 13–14; Charlesworth, above n 7, 22–4.

[44] See, eg, *Constitutional Convention Debates*, Melbourne, 8 February 1898, 666 (Sir John Forrest, Joseph Carruthers); see Williams, above n 7, 13.

[45] CPD, House of Representatives, 12 September 1901, 4826 (William Morris Hughes).

4.2 ENTRENCHING 'ABSOLUTE SOVEREIGNTY'

As we know, the *Constitution* enshrined little in the way of freedoms for its subjects or those subject to its laws. It incorporated neither rights to due process nor equal protection of the law, and offered little else in the way of explicit safeguards against abuse of power, even with respect to people regarded as citizens.[46] Furthermore, on the subject of aliens and immigration, it conferred plenary powers in relation to which there were no discernible limitations. With the foreigner-sovereign relation so authorised, and emboldened by an almost perfect unanimity,[47] the first Parliament of Australia gave expression to the imperatives of economic prosperity and racial purity that underpinned the White Australia policy, passing two keystone pieces of legislation: the *Immigration Restriction Act 1901* and its sister Act, the *Pacific Island Labourers Act 1901*. Significantly, these were the first substantive Acts to be passed by the new Parliament.[48] Together they were described by the Prime Minister as "not merely the realization of a policy, but a handsome new year's gift for a new nation."[49]

4.2.1 *Legislating for a White Australia: A Perfect Right*

While the *Pacific Island Labourers Act 1901* was focused on the management and phasing out of indentured labour in the sugar plantations of the north, the *Immigration Restriction Act 1901* was focused on the exclusion of Chinese and other 'Asiatics'. As the debates on the Bills make clear, the political-economic imperatives of White Australia that were behind the constitutionalisation of 'absolute sovereignty' were regarded as so uncontroversial that the deliberations turned not on *whether* to give them legislative expression but *how*. That

---

[46] The only individual rights explicitly enshrined in the *Constitution* are the right to vote (s 41), a prohibition on the acquisition of property on other than just terms (s 51(xxxi)), the right to trial by jury (s 80), freedom of religion (s 116), and the right not to be discriminated against on the basis of state of residency (s 117). Note further that s 117 is "all that remains of the attempt to insert into the . . . *Constitution* a federal citizenship" and associated Fourteenth Amendment–style due process and equal protection rights: Williams, above n 7, 16. Note also that the *Constitution* does not engage with the notion of citizenship, referring only to a 'subject of the Queen': Rubenstein, 'Citizenship and the Centenary', above n 7, 580.

[47] Speakers against the racial consequences of the Immigration Restriction Bill 1901 (Cth) in the course of the parliamentary debates were rare: CPD, House of Representatives, 12 September 1901, 4837–40 (Norman Cameron).

[48] Earlier Bills were regarded as establishing government machinery rather than substantively enacting tools for the implementation of government policy: CPD, House of Representatives, 7 August 1901, 3497 (Edmund Barton, Prime Minister).

[49] CPD, House of Representatives, 2 October 1901, 5505 (Edmund Barton).

is, the question was whether exclusion should be effected through a process that was explicitly race-based or whether a discretionary technique whereby prejudicial dictation or education tests – often known as the 'Natal formula'[50] – should be used. Records of the debate elucidate the confidence with which the legislature embraced the (absolute) scope of the powers it had been given. Questions about the nature of absolute power, rights and risks, and the right to self-preservation are illustrative of the fulsome way in which the Parliament embarked on the process of giving legislative expression to 'absolute sovereignty' in its constitutional form.

4.2.1.1 On Despotic Power: 'I Am Not Complaining'

During the debate on the Immigration Restriction Bill, Isaac Isaacs (later Attorney-General, Chief Justice of the High Court, and Governor-General) proposed incorporating an "instant power in any emergency to exclude any person whom this country thinks is undesirable."[51] This proposal was in addition to the dictation test. Receiving an admonition of despotism on that account,[52] the un-defensive response of the future Chief Justice of the High Court characterised his 'instant exclusion' proposal as no more despotic than the proposal for a dictation test that was already on the table:

> Still, I am not complaining. I think we ought to go to that length if it were necessary. But if we are going to offer a reproach to a measure because it is

[50] See, eg, McKeown, above n 9, 196; Lake and Reynolds, above n 8, 129, 145. As Evans and Lake have noted, the test had an earlier historical application, wherein the state of Mississippi (six other states later following suit) originated a dictation test designed to prevent African Americans from voting: Raymond Evans, 'The White Australia Policy' in James Jupp (ed), *The Australian People: An Encyclopedia of the Nation, Its People and Their Origins* (Cambridge University Press, 2001) 46; Marilyn Lake, 'From Mississippi to Melbourne via Natal: The Invention of the Literacy Test as a Technology of Racial Exclusion' in Ann Curthoys and Marilyn Lake (eds), *Connected Worlds: History in Transnational Perspective* (ANU E Press, 2005).

[51] CPD, House of Representatives, 12 September 1901, 4846 (Isaac Isaacs). The breadth of this proposal is not unlike the prerogative power invoked by the Commonwealth in the case *MV Tampa: Ruddock v Vadarlis* (2001) 110 FCR 491. See also the subsequent legislative framework for the so-called 'Pacific Solution': *Border Protection (Validation and Enforcement Powers) Act 2001* (Cth); *Migration Amendment (Excision from Migration Zone) Act 2001* (Cth); *Migration Amendment (Excision from Migration Zone) (Consequential Provisions) Act 2001* (Cth). Cf *International Covenant on Civil and Political Rights*, opened for signature 16 December 1966, 999 UNTS 171 (entered into force 23 March 1976) art 4; Human Rights Committee (HRC), *General Comment No 29: Article 4: Derogations during a State of Emergency*, 72nd sess, UN Doc CCPR/C/21/Rev.1/Add.11 (31 August 2001) para 2; HRC, *General Comment No 5: Article 4 (Derogation of Rights)*, 13th sess, UN Doc HRI/GEN/1/Rev. 1 (31 July 1981) para 3.

[52] CPD, House of Representatives, 12 September 1901, 4846 (Hugh Mahon).

despotic, we must not forget that without a despotic provision we cannot do what we want at all.[53]

With Isaacs simultaneously conceding and excusing the despotic character of the power, critique was defused, if not neutralised.[54]

4.2.1.2 On Perfect Rights and Peculiar Exigencies

Consistent with this bold embrace of absolutist powers, the debates in the House of Representatives[55] on the Immigration Restriction Bill and the Pacific Island Labourers Bill were replete with racial prejudice. Parliamentarians spoke effusively and repeatedly of the importance of the power to exclude on account of immediate, pressing or anticipated 'dangers'[56] should 'influxes'[57] of people of 'undesirable'[58] races be permitted to enter and, in turn, 'stain'[59] and 'contaminate'[60] Australia's racial purity.[61] The parliamentarians

---

[53]   Ibid 4846–7 (Isaac Isaacs).

[54]   Cf *Fong*, 149 US 698, 737–8 (Brewer J), 750, 754–6 (Field J) (1893), discussed in Chapter 3, 104–6.

[55]   Although contributions to the debates in the Senate were sometimes more nuanced, they nevertheless bore many of the characteristics outlined here: see, eg, CPD, Senate, 13 November 1901, 7171 (Edward Harney), 7184–5 (James Macfarlane).

[56]   See, eg, CPD, House of Representatives, 7 August 1901, 3502–3 (Edmund Barton, Prime Minister); CPD, House of Representatives, 12 September 1901, 4812 (Alfred Deakin), 4847 (Isaac Isaacs); CPD, House of Representatives, 26 September 1901, 5233 (Edmund Barton), 5270 (Sir John Forrest); CPD, House of Representatives, 27 September 1901, 5317 (Isaac Isaacs), 5320–2 (Edmund Barton); CPD, Senate, 13 November 1901, 7142–3 (Richard O'Connor).

[57]   See, eg, CPD, House of Representatives, 7 August 1901, 3502–3 (Edmund Barton, Prime Minister); CPD, House of Representatives, 12 September 1901, 4817 (Alfred Deakin); CPD, House of Representatives, 26 September 1901, 5225, 5233 (Edmund Barton); CPD, House of Representatives, 27 September 1901, 5320 (Edmund Barton); CPD, House of Representatives, 9 October 1901, 5823 (Alfred Deakin); CPD, Senate, 15 November 1901, 7354 (Richard O'Connor).

[58]   See, eg, CPD, House of Representatives, 7 August 1901, 3500–1, 3505 (Edmund Barton, Prime Minister); CPD, House of Representatives, 12 September 1901, 4824–5 (Billy Hughes), 4846 (Isaac Isaacs); CPD, House of Representatives, 25 September 1901, 5129 (Isaac Isaacs); CPD, 26 September 1901, 5233 (Edmund Barton), 5263 (Sir John Quick); CPD, House of Representatives, 1 October 1901, 5351 (Edmund Barton); CPD, Senate, 14 November 1901, 7257 (Henry Dobson).

[59]   CPD, House of Representatives, 12 September 1901, 4853 (Dugald Thomson); CPD, House of Representatives, 6 November 1901, 6895 (Richard Edwards); CPD, Senate, 29 November 1901, 8021 (Thomas Playford).

[60]   See, eg, CPD, House of Representatives, 12 September 1901, 4804 (Alfred Deakin), 4826 (Billy Hughes), 4845, 4847 (Isaac Isaacs); CPD, Senate, 14 November 1901, 7269 (Robert Best); CPD, Senate, 22 November 1901, 7688–9 (Thomas Glassey), 4 December 1901, 8237 (Sir Josiah Symon), 8249 (William Higgs).

[61]   See, eg, CPD, House of Representatives, 12 September 1901, 4808 (Alfred Deakin), 4819 (Billy Hughes); CPD, House of Representatives, 27 September 1901, 5319 (Isaac Isaacs); CPD, House

were in no doubt that they had a perfect right[62] to such exclusionary powers. One described the objective of securing racial purity as an exceptional measure justifiable on account of "peculiar exigencies" arising "under special local circumstances" and necessitating a reversal of "that great principle of British freedom and British refuge."[63] However, like his parliamentary colleagues, he was in no doubt about the power to do so and the importance of ridding Australia of what he described as the "curse of many other civilized countries."[64]

4.2.1.3 On Self-Preservation: 'The Highest Law'

At the same time, and in addition to its manifest racial underpinnings, a self-assured sense of economic superiority and entitlement that contrasted with a tangible fear of competition was used to justify the Bill's extreme measures. This fear of competition manifested itself, on the one hand, as a fear of being economically upstaged by the educated classes of non-European races (especially the Chinese, Indians, and Japanese) and, on the other, by being economically undercut by their 'servile' labouring classes who were seen as willing to work for lower wages and tolerant of a lower standard of living. At the heart of the debate, therefore, lay a paradoxical fragility, wherein these drivers melded a self-assured perception of superior entitlement to a certain way of life and a niggling self-doubt embodied in what Pearson had once described as the "instinct of self-preservation"[65] – an instinct seen by Barton as "the highest law",[66] rising above international law and imperial relations.[67]

---

of Representatives, 2 October 1901, 5492 (Edmund Barton); CPD, 9 October 1901, 5820, 5822 (Alfred Deakin); CPD, Senate, 15 November 1901, 7348 (Richard O'Connor).

[62] See, eg, CPD, House of Representatives, 6 September 1901, 4627 (Sir William McMillan); CPD, Senate, 15 November 1901, 7348 (Richard O'Connor).

[63] CPD, House of Representatives, 6 September 1901, 4627 (Sir William McMillan).

[64] Ibid.

[65] Charles H Pearson, *National Life and Character: A Forecast* (Macmillan, 1893) 16. On the strength of the sentiment see, eg, CPD, House of Representatives, 7 August 1901, 3503 (Edmund Barton) (quoting Pearson); CPD, House of Representatives, 12 September 1901, 4804 (Alfred Deakin); CPD, House of Representatives, 27 September 1901, 5316 (Isaac Isaacs); CPD, Senate, 14 November 1901, 7239 (Sir John Downer), 7242 (Staniforth Smith); CPD, Senate, 15 November 1901, 7349 (Richard O'Connor); Naoko Shimazu, *Japan, Race and Equality: The Racial Equality Proposal of 1919* (Routledge, 1998) 70. For variations on the meaning and uses of the term 'self-preservation' see: Chapter 2 Section 2.3.2, 70–71; Chapter 3 Sections 3.2.2, 92–4, and 3.3.3.2, 99–101.

[66] CPD, House of Representatives, 7 August 1901, 3506 (Edmund Barton).

[67] CPD, House of Representatives, 12 September 1901, 4828 (William Wilks).

4.2.2 Pacific Island Labour: Exploitable, Excludable, Deportable

Introducing the Pacific Island Labourers Bill, Barton described the Bill as embodying "the policy, not merely of the Government, but of all Australia, for the preservation of the purity of the race and the equality and reasonableness of its standard of living."[68] He described Pacific Islander labour as a "temporary expedient" designed to serve the particular interests of the Queensland sugar industry,[69] an industry whose economic value to the State – and to the Commonwealth more broadly – he was at pains to emphasise.[70] The Bill affected an estimated 8,710 Pacific Island labourers[71] (known pejoratively as 'Kanakas'), whose cheap labour had been imported for about 40 years prior, largely under Queensland legislation.[72]

There was much in the legislative and political history of Pacific Island labour that aimed to regulate it and claimed to be motivated by a desire to avert abuses and unnecessary hardships akin to slavery.[73] Such regulatory measures arose from what one commentator described as "a cruel, unjust, un-Christlike, demoralising traffic in human flesh".[74] However, nothing in the federal legislation reflects these priorities. Indeed, at the (political) heart of the legislation appears to have been the (protectionist) objection to recruiting black people for ('lower' forms of) labour that, it was argued, could be done in 'higher' (more efficient) forms by white people.[75] Furthermore, any concerns to regulate the Pacific Island labour traffic and to avert abuses were eclipsed by a commitment of an economic character. That is, notwithstanding the manifest and continuing risk of abuse, the legislation was designed to ensure that

---

[68] CPD, House of Representatives, 2 October 1901, 5492 (Edmund Barton).
[69] Ibid 5493, 5495, 5499, 5502–3 (Edmund Barton).
[70] Ibid 5493 (Edmund Barton); CPD, House of Representatives, 9 October 1901, 5840 (Sir Malcolm McEacharn); CPD, House of Representatives, 10 October 1901, 5893 (Richard Edwards).
[71] CPD, House of Representatives, 2 October 1901, 5494 (Edmund Barton).   [72] Ibid.
[73] Ibid 5495–6, 5503 (Edmund Barton). For a description of the effects of depopulation on communities in the Pacific Islands, see the testimony of Rev J D Paton, cited in CPD, House of Representatives, 9 October 1901, 5834 (Joseph Cook). See also Joanne Scott et al, *The Engine Room of Government: The Queensland Premier's Department 1859–2001* (University of Queensland Press, 2001) 38–9.
[74] CPD, House of Representatives, 9 October 1901, 5835 (Joseph Cook), quoting Rev William Gray, described as an old missionary in the Pacific Islands.
[75] See, eg, CPD, House of Representatives, 2 October 1901, 5501–2 (Edmund Barton), quoting Dr Walter Maxwell, an agricultural scientist and author of a number of reports on the sugarcane industry; cf CPD, House of Representatives, 9 October 1901, 5840–8 (Sir Malcolm McEacharn), who argued that work in the sugar industry could not be done by white labourers. On Maxwell, see John D Kerr, 'Maxwell, Walter (1854–1931)' in Bede Nairn and Geoffrey Serle (eds), *Australian Dictionary of Biography* (Melbourne University Press, 1986) vol 10 <http://adb.anu.edu.au/biography/maxwell-walter-7535>.

the use of Pacific Island indentured labour would not be ended so abruptly that it would cause "ruinous loss" to the sugar industry.[76] Instead, therefore, the effect of the legislation was that their labour could continue to be used until they were ultimately subject to complete exclusion.[77] Finally, and notwithstanding concerns expressed about the traffic and exploitation of Pacific Islanders, the resolve to 'preserve' racial purity remained firm; as such, the Bill provided for deportation of Pacific Island labourers not subject to a labour licence or agreement,[78] a power that led to their mass deportation in 1907.[79]

4.2.2.1 "Have We the Power?" "I Will Take the Risk"

On the question of deportation, the Prime Minister was asked, "Have we the power to do that?"[80] He replied, "I think we have the power, and . . . I will take the risk."[81] The Prime Minister would not have known at the time, but judicial scrutiny of the risk would later fall to him. In 1903, Sir Edmund Barton was appointed to the High Court. Together with the first Chief Justice, Sir Samuel Griffith, and Justice Richard O'Connor, Justice Barton would be called upon to pronounce on the constitutional validity of deportation powers that had been legislated under his leadership. Griffith had, as Premier of Queensland, been a leading figure in the legislative history of Pacific Island labour prior to Federation. Likewise, O'Connor was a founding father who, although he had unsuccessfully proposed an amendment to the Clark proposal, subsequently served as Leader in the Senate from 1901 to 1903, at the time the two immigration Acts were passed. Their Honours affirmed the powers.[82]

In the result, the *Pacific Island Labourers Act 1901* provided for the regulation, restriction, prohibition, and deportation of Pacific Island labourers. It also provided for complete exclusion from entry of Pacific Island labourers after 31 March 1904.[83] In addition, like the Chinese exclusion legislation of the

---

[76] CPD, House of Representatives, 2 October 1901, 5497–8 (Edmund Barton), quoting Sir Samuel Griffith.

[77] *Pacific Island Labourers Act 1901* ss 3, 7; cf *Pacific Island Labourers Act 1906* (Cth) s 8A. There appears also to have been another (underlying) purpose motivated by a concern that recruitment practices would so reduce the population of the Pacific Islands from which the labour was drawn that the supply of labour would eventually dry up: CPD, House of Representatives, 2 October 1901, 5500 (Edmund Barton).

[78] *Pacific Island Labourers Act 1901* s 8.   [79] Nicholls, *Deported*, above n 8, 38.

[80] CPD, House of Representatives, 2 October 1901, 5505 (Vaiben Louis Solomon).

[81] Ibid 5505 (Edmund Barton).

[82] *Robtelmes v Brenan* (1906) 4 CLR 395 ('*Robtelmes*'); Nicholls, *Deported*, above n 8, 35–6.

[83] *Pacific Island Labourers Act 1901* s 3.

mid nineteenth century,[84] it incorporated a reverse onus of proof, according to which an allegation that a person was a Pacific Island labourer was sufficient to deem her to be so until the contrary was shown.[85]

4.2.2.2 The High Court in Transnational Judicial Conversation

In October 1906, the case of *Robtelmes v Brenan*[86] ('*Robtelmes*') came before the High Court. It examined the constitutional validity of the power to deport Pacific Island labourers.[87]

In its decision, which found unanimously against the appellant Pacific Islander, Robtelmes, the Court drew heavily on the corpus of jurisprudence that had produced a common law doctrine of 'absolute sovereignty' in the nineteenth century.[88] Citing *Fong*, the Court gave weight to the US Supreme Court's finding that a state has an absolute, inherent, and inalienable sovereign right to exclude or expel aliens, in war or in peace.[89] Although Griffith CJ gestured to the fact that *Fong* was not unanimous, the doctrine of precedent did not oblige him to address substantively the dissents, which included reproaches of oppressive, despotic, and arbitrary use of the claim of 'absolute sovereignty'. Instead, and notwithstanding that many parallels may be drawn between the factual circumstances of the alien resident Chinese labourers in *Fong* and alien resident Pacific Island labourers in Australia, he intimated that the difference of opinion on the US Supreme Court related to the applicability of the doctrine of sovereignty to the (impliedly different) facts of the particular case. However, a more significant difference lay in the process of constitutionalisation. That is, the dissenting opinions in *Fong* had relied on what Quick and Garran had described as the 'special inhibitions' of the Fourteenth Amendment, which had been erased from Australia's constitutional landscape and were therefore seen as no longer jurisprudentially relevant.[90]

---

[84] See Chapter 3 Section 3.2.1, 91–2.   [85] *Pacific Island Labourers Act* 1901 s 10.
[86] (1906) 4 CLR 395.
[87] *Pacific Island Labourers Act* 1901 s 8. Note that, notwithstanding the facts of the case, the constitutionally conferred power to pass special and discriminating laws relating to 'the people of any race' was not firmly in issue: *Constitution* s 51(xxvi); *Robtelmes* (1906) 4 CLR 395, 415 (Barton J); Quick and Garran, above n 16, 623. Later, Higgins J would describe the race power as extending to measures to deport people of a particular race: *Walsh and Johnson* (1925) 37 CLR 36, 117.
[88] See especially *Chinese Exclusion Case*, 130 US 581 (1889); *Fong*, 149 US 698 (1893); *Nishimura Ekiu v United States*, 142 US 651 (1892) ('*Ekiu*'); *Musgrove* [1891] AC 272. See Chapter 3 Section 3.3.3, 97–107.
[89] *Robtelmes* (1906) 4 CLR 395, 403 (Griffith CJ), 413–15 (Barton J).
[90] Although not referred to in the early Australian jurisprudence discussed here, in *Yick Wo*, 118 US 356 (1886), the US Supreme Court held that the due process and equal protection

In addition, Barton J elided enemy and friendly aliens.[91] He did so notwithstanding that no evidence in the case had been adduced that Robtelmes, or any other Pacific Island labourer, was other than a friendly alien, much less someone dangerous to the peace and security of Australia.

4.2.2.3 The Doctrine of Precedent: Settling Law

Robtelmes was quickly characterised as "settled law".[92] Indeed, it remains the leading High Court authority for the proposition that, as constitutional and common law doctrine, 'absolute sovereignty' includes power to expel or deport.[93] The Court underwrote its decision by reliance not only on the earlier jurisprudence of the Privy Council and the US Supreme Court, but also the Privy Council decision in *Attorney-General for Canada v Cain*[94] ('*Cain*'), handed down a few months earlier.

---

guarantees in the Fourteenth Amendment applied to 'persons' without regard to race, colour, or nationality. This and similar jurisprudence appears to have been behind the rejection of a Fourteenth Amendment–style provision in the Australian *Constitution*. See Quick and Garran, above n 16, 623; see above 118.

[91] In doing so, he referred to controversial legislation in the United States: *An Act concerning Aliens*, ch 58, §1, 1 Stat 570, 570–1 (1798); *Robtelmes* (1906) 4 CLR 395, 414 (Barton J); *Fong*, 149 US 698, 746–7 (Field J) (1893). For further discussion of *An Act concerning Aliens*, see Chapter 3, 106.

[92] *Ah Yin v Christie* (1907) 4 CLR 1428, 1431 (Griffith CJ) ('*Ah Yin*').

[93] *Robtelmes* (1906) 4 CLR 395, 415 (Barton J); *Ferrando v Pearce* (1918) 25 CLR 241, 270 (Powers J) ('*Ferrando*'); *R v MacFarlane; Ex parte O'Flanagan* (1923) 32 CLR 518, 533 (Knox CJ) ('*Irish Envoys Case*'); *Walsh and Johnson* (1925) 37 CLR 36, 83 (Isaacs J); *O'Keefe v Calwell* (1949) 77 CLR 261, 277 (Latham CJ) ('*O'Keefe*'); *Koon Wing Lau v Calwell* (1949) 80 CLR 533, 555–6 (Latham CJ) ('*Koon Wing Lau*'); *Pochi v Macphee* (1982) 151 CLR 101, 106 (Gibbs CJ) ('*Pochi*'); *Chu Kheng Lim v Minister for Immigration, Local Government and Ethnic Affairs* (1992) 176 CLR 1, 25–6, 30–1 (Brennan, Deane, and Dawson JJ), 56–7 (Gaudron J), 65 (McHugh J) ('*Lim*'); *A v Minister for Immigration and Ethnic Affairs* (1997) 190 CLR 225, 274 n177 (Gummow J); *Minister for Immigration v Haji Ibrahim* (2000) 204 CLR 1, 45 (Gummow J, Gleeson CJ and Hayne J agreeing); *Re Minister for Immigration and Multicultural Affairs; Ex parte Meng Kok Te* (2002) 212 CLR 162, 170 (Gleeson CJ), 192–3 (Gummow J); *Behrooz v Secretary, Department of Immigration and Multicultural and Indigenous Affairs* (2004) 219 CLR 486, 556–7 (Callinan J); *Al-Kateb v Godwin* (2004) 219 CLR 562, 639 (Hayne J) ('*Al-Kateb*'); *Ruhani v Director of Police (No 2)* (2005) 222 CLR 580, 276 (Gleeson CJ, Gummow, Hayne and Heydon JJ) ('*Ruhani No 2*'); *NAGV and NAGW of 2002 v Minister for Immigration and Multicultural and Indigenous Affairs* (2005) 222 CLR 161, 169–71; *Plaintiff M47-2012 v Director General of Security* (2012) 251 CLR 1, 313 (Heydon J) ('*Plaintiff M47*'); *FTZK v Minister for Immigration and Border Protection* [2014] HCA 26 (27 June 2014). See also *Minister for Immigration and Multicultural Affairs v Khawar* (2002) 210 CLR 1, 15–17; *R (European Roma Rights Centre) v Immigration Officer at Prague Airport (United Nations High Commissioner for Refugees intervening)* [2005] 2 AC 1, 29.

[94] [1906] AC 542 ('*Cain*').

Cain considered the terms of the Canadian *Alien Labour Act 1867*, which prohibited the importation or immigration of certain alien labour. The crux of *Cain* was whether the power to exclude aliens also gave rise to a power to expel them. Lord Atkinson, delivering the joint judgment, upheld 'absolute sovereignty' by reference to *Musgrove* and (selectively) Vattel, holding that

> The power of expulsion is, in truth, but the complement of the power of exclusion. If entry be prohibited, it would seem to follow that the government which has the power to exclude should have the power to expel the alien who enters in opposition to its laws.[95]

As Chapter 2 has shown, a more textured perspective on powers of exclusion and expulsion is discernible from a close reading of Vattel. In contrast, we see that 'absolute sovereignty' *as a discourse* drove the selective way in which his texts were used and interpreted in the jurisprudence, including this extract from *Cain*. As we know, Vattel's position was that "no nation can, without good reasons, refuse even a perpetual residence to a man driven from his country."[96] However, while he qualified this by limiting the nation's obligations,[97] Vattel was equally clear that such reasons should be "free from unnecessary suspicion and jealousy; [and] . . . should not be carried so far as to refuse a retreat to the unfortunate, for slight reasons, and on groundless and frivolous fears."[98]

Of course, as Chapter 2 made visible, in the foreigner-sovereign relation, Vattel's foreigner was a European.[99] However, with the majority of the High Court in *Robtelmes* specifically and assuredly using Vattel,[100] it seems clear that this factor was not noticed. With 'absolute sovereignty' as a common law and constitutional doctrine having secured the place of the foreigner as an

---

[95] Ibid 547 (Lord Atkinson); see also *Robtelmes* (1906) 4 CLR 395, 415 (Barton J), cited with approval in *Walsh and Johnson* (1925) 37 CLR 36, 83 (Isaacs J); *Irish Envoys Case* (1923) 32 CLR 518, 533 (Knox CJ).

[96] Emmerich de Vattel, *The Law of Nations; or, Principles of the Law of Nature, Applied to the Conduct and Affairs of Nations and of Sovereigns* (Joseph Chitty ed and trans, Lawbook Exchange, first published 1854, 2005 ed) bk I ch XIX §231 [trans of: *Le Droit des gens; ou Principes de la loi naturelle, appliqués à la conduite et aux affaires des Nations et des Souverains* (first published 1758)]; see also at bk II ch VIII §100; see Chapter 2, 76.

[97] Obligations could, he said, be limited where a nation's lands are "scarcely sufficient to supply the wants of the citizens", to protect against contagious disease, and if the people will "corrupt the manners of the citizens", "create religious disturbance", or "occasion any other disorder, contrary to the public safety": Vattel, above n 96, bk I ch XIX §231.

[98] Ibid bk I ch XIX §231; see also at bk II ch IX §125. See discussion Chapter 2 Section 2.4.2, 74–5.

[99] See Chapter 2 Section 2.4.3, 76–7.

[100] *Robtelmes* (1906) 4 CLR 395, 400 (Griffith CJ), 409, 414 (Barton J).

excludable and deportable outsider, the doctrine of precedent enabled the Court to rely on and thereby reinforce particular readings of international law in the Privy Council's decision in *Cain*[101] and to treat *Cain* as affirming that the power to deport is beyond controversy.[102] Indeed, so broad were the powers on which the Court regarded the legislature to be entitled to draw that O'Connor J made the following observation:

> [W]here any power or control is expressly granted, there is included in the grant, to the full extent of the capacity of the grantor, and without special mention, every power and every control the denial of which would render the grant itself ineffective.[103]

With 'absolute sovereignty' treated as a settled common law doctrine, and due process and equal protection rights erased during the constitutional convention debates, the only remaining constraint upon any gross injustice or abuse arising from its exercise was, therefore, the assumption that the grantee would not misuse it – that is, the (presumptive and non-constitutional) doctrine, or convention, of responsible government.[104]

4.2.2.4 Judicial Deference: A 'Positivist' Jurisprudence

Robtelmes set a highly deferential tone that has characterised the Court's interpretation of the aliens and immigration powers since.[105] In this regard, Griffith CJ considered the Parliament to have the power to make "any laws" – "wise or unwise" – in relation to aliens and immigrants that "it may think fit" for peace, order, and good government. These included deportation laws, and it was not the place of the courts further to interfere.[106] Likewise, Barton J regarded it as beyond the judicial function to inquire into the *effects* of legislation, as long as the legislation itself was clear and within power.[107] As

---

[101] Ibid 404 (Griffith CJ), 410–1 (Barton J), 418 (O'Connor J).
[102] Ibid 401 (Griffith CJ), 419 (O'Connor J). [103] Ibid 420 (O'Connor J).
[104] Cf *Pochi* (1982) 151 CLR 101, 114 (Murphy J).
[105] *Robtelmes* (1906) 4 CLR 395, 404 (Griffith CJ); *Ah Yin* (1907) 4 CLR 1428, 1432 (Griffith CJ), 1435 (Barton J); *Ferrando* (1918) 25 CLR 241, 270 (Powers J); *Irish Envoys Case* (1923) 32 CLR 518, 577 (Higgins J); *Walsh and Johnson* (1925) 37 CLR 36, 113 (Higgins J), 132–3 (Starke J); *Williamson v Ah On* (1926) 39 CLR 95, 102 (Knox CJ, Gavan Duffy J) ('*Williamson*'); *O'Keefe* (1949) 77 CLR 261, 282 (Latham CJ); *Koon Wing Lau* (1949) 80 CLR 533, 561 (Latham CJ); *Pochi* (1982) 151 CLR 101, 106 (Gibbs CJ); *Lim* (1992) 176 CLR 1, 25–6 (Brennan, Deane, and Dawson JJ, Gaudron J concurring), 64 (McHugh J); *Al-Kateb* (2004) 219 CLR 562, 595 (McHugh J), 632–3 (Hayne J, Heydon J concurring); *Plaintiff S156/2014 v Minister for Immigration and Border Protection* (2014) 309 ALR 29; *CPCF v Minister for Immigration and Border Protection* (2015) 255 CLR 514 ('*Detention on the High Seas Case*').
[106] *Robtelmes* (1906) 4 CLR 395, 404. [107] Ibid 415.

Prime Minister, Barton had admitted that legislating the power to deport was a risk, but one he was prepared to take.[108] As a member of the judiciary, it was a power in relation to which he exercised no doubt. Although this may, in part, be (juridically) explained by the precedent of *Cain*, Barton J gave no hint that he had ever entertained such doubt. Finally, O'Connor J regarded the power to determine the mode and place of deportation as a matter entirely within the discretion of the Parliament.[109]

At some levels, such judicial deference reflects broader principles of constitutional law and the investiture of legislative power that is central to the doctrine of separation of powers.[110] However, the Court's 'hands-off' approach to migration law- and policymaking treats the aliens and immigration powers with a deference that privileges them as 'conversation stoppers',[111] as occupying a hallowed doctrinal place that is structurally indifferent to migration law's effects.[112] This approach suggests a striking unwillingness to engage with the controversial history of 'absolute sovereignty' or bear responsibility for the juridical consequences of plenary omnipotence.[113]

4.2.3 Immigration Restriction: A Matter of Discretion

As we know, the first Parliament passed both the *Pacific Island Labourers Act 1901* and the *Immigration Restriction Act 1901* cognisant of, and content with, the scope and breadth of its absolute power to do so. As noted earlier, the focus of the debate was not on whether such power should be used to achieve the objectives of the White Australia policy, but how it ought to do so. In this regard, the Parliament was particularly exercised about whether a legislative approach to exclusion should be explicitly exclusionist or less overt, reflecting what might be described as a 'gentleman's racism' urged upon it by the British Colonial Office. As such, the debate on the Immigration Restriction Bill turned on whether the Natal formula was the most effective means of achieving the desired outcome. The perceptual advantage of this formula was that even

---

[108]   CPD, House of Representatives, 2 October 1901, 5505 (Edmund Barton), discussed above 125.
[109]   *Robtelmes* (1906) 4 CLR 395, 422.
[110]   See generally Tom Campbell, *The Legal Theory of Ethical Positivism* (Aldershot, 1996).
[111]   Michael Taggart, '"Australian Exceptionalism" in Judicial Review' (Speech delivered at the 10th Annual Geoffrey Sawer Lecture, National Museum of Australia, 9 November 2007) 10.
[112]   Friedrich Nietzsche, *The Gay Science* (Bernard Williams ed, Josefine Nauckhoff and Adrian Del Caro trans, Cambridge University Press, 2001) 202 [trans of: *Die fröhliche Wissenschaft* (first published 1882)]; David Owen, *Nietzsche's Genealogy of Morality* (McGill-Queen's University Press, 2007); see Chapter 1, Section 1.2.1, 23–4.
[113]   See above n 105.

though race was its impetus, it did not have to say so. Thus, it could provide a means for achieving both racial purity and economic advantage while avoiding unnecessarily offending the sensibilities of foreign governments and thereby compromising diplomatic and trade relations.[114]

4.2.3.1 Honesty or a Gentleman's Racism?

The debate on the Immigration Restriction Bill began in August 1901, concluding in December 1901. However, the lengthy debate is not indicative of significant and difficult-to-resolve differences of opinion. Certainly, neither the objective of, nor the right to effect, absolute and complete exclusion was ever in doubt; rather, the debate turned on what would be the best way of achieving that objective. In essence, the Parliament debated whether it was more 'honest' and 'straightforward' to have a Bill that either explicitly and absolutely excluded 'undesirable' aliens and British subjects from 'coloured races' or one embodying the gentleman's racism of the Natal formula.[115] As the debates reveal, this was only partly inspired by a widely claimed desire that the Bill express its legislative purpose (absolute exclusion of coloured immigrants) in clear and unequivocal terms. In significant measure, it was driven by a desire for the Commonwealth to assert its independence by not submitting to the urgings of the imperial power. Where doubt remained in the minds of parliamentarians as to the efficacy of the Natal formula, they were reassured that this legislation was the "first word" not the "last word" in regard to immigration legislation, suggesting that any deficiencies could be 'remedied' or 'cured' by further legislative measures as required.[116] This, we will see, would become a recurring theme for the legislature in migration lawmaking.[117]

For present purposes, there were three key aspects of the *Immigration Restriction Act 1901* that illustrate how the unwelcome foreigner was to be treated. First, it conferred on an administrative officer absolute discretion to subject would-be migrants to a dictation test in a European language of the officer's

---

[114] See, eg, CPD, House of Representatives, 7 August 1901, 3503 (Edmund Barton, Prime Minister); CPD, Senate, 15 November 1901, 7347 (Richard O'Connor).

[115] See, eg, CPD, House of Representatives, 6 September 1901, 4626 (Sir William McMillan), 4647 (James Wilkinson), Wilkinson describing himself as "supremely indifferent" to the prospect of causing offence. See also the noted irony of racial disqualification under the *Pacific Island Labourers Act 1901* and the unwillingness to exclude specifically on the grounds of race or colour in the *Immigration Restriction Act 1901*: CPD, House of Representatives, 9 October 1901, 5830–1 (George Reid).

[116] CPD, House of Representatives, 12 September 1901, 4814 (Alfred Deakin, Attorney-General).

[117] See, eg, CPD, House of Representatives, 1 May 1958, 1396–1400 (Alexander Downer) (Second Reading Speech, Migration Bill 1958 (Cth)): see below n 272. See also Chapters 5 and 6.

choice.[118] Second, it created the offence of being a 'prohibited immigrant', applicable to anyone failing the dictation test[119] or otherwise belonging to a class of undesirable persons.[120] A conviction carried a sentence of imprisonment of up to six months, which could be waived on provision of a surety and/or deportation.[121] Finally, it created one of the earliest examples of what are now widely known as 'carrier sanctions',[122] whereby a ship's master, owner, or charterer could be held liable for carrying a prohibited immigrant entering the Commonwealth.[123] As Evans has observed, it was the threat of fines that would, for decades, serve as White Australia's "first line of defence" in the project of exclusion.[124] However, the notorious dictation test, which effectively operated as a 'reserve power', and to which I now turn, was the most prominent in the early (legal and political) life of the *Immigration Restriction Act 1901*.

4.2.3.2 Dictating Exclusion: A Jurisprudence of Discretion

The dictation test was used to exclude 'undesirable' aliens and coloured British subjects.[125] It was a test designed to ensure failure. As Evans reports, in its first two years (1902–1903) 759 people failed the test, with only 46 passing

---

[118] *Immigration Restriction Act 1901* s 3(a).   [119]   Ibid.

[120] Ibid ss 3(b)–(g), being a public charge, an 'idiot or insane person', a person suffering 'an infectious or contagious disease of a loathsome or dangerous character', certain criminals, prostitutes or those living on the prostitution of others, or indentured labourers. For exemptions, see ss 3(h)–(n).

[121] Ibid s 7. Under this provision, the period of imprisonment could be waived upon the provision of two approved sureties each in the sum of £50, which guaranteed departure from the Commonwealth within one month. £100 is about $10,000 in current terms: Dennis Trewin, 'Year Book Australia' (Year Book No 83, Catalogue No 1301.0, Australian Bureau of Statistics, 2001) 951.

[122] Cf poll taxes, which were imposed as a tax on entry rather than as a penalty for unauthorised arrival or entry: see, eg, Sing-Wu Wang, 'Chinese in Australian Society' in James Jupp (ed), *The Australian People: An Encyclopedia of the Nation, Its People and Their Origins* (Cambridge University Press, 2001) 202–4; cf Cronin, above n 49, 85. On the tension between carrier sanctions and international law, see Erika Feller, 'Carrier Sanctions and International Law' 1989 1(1) *International Journal of Refugee Law* 48; Angus J Francis, 'Removing Barriers to Protection at the Exported Border: Visas, Carrier Sanctions, and International Obligation' in Jeremy Farrall and Kim Rubenstein (eds), *Sanctions, Accountability and Governance in a Globalised World* (Cambridge University Press, 2009) 378.

[123] *Immigration Restriction Act 1901* s 9. The penalty of £100 equates to $10,000 today: Trewin, above n 121, 951.

[124] Evans, above n 50, 48; see also CPD, House of Representatives, 26 September 1901, 5270 (Sir John Forrest).

[125] Certainly there were some exceptions. For example, in 1905 a clause was inserted into the *Immigration Restriction Act 1901* to formalise the possibility of making friendly arrangements whereby tourists, merchants, and others visiting Australia from certain countries would not be subjected to the dictation test. Two such agreements were concluded with the governments of

it. The 46 'successes' were seen as administrative failures and triggered a tightening of procedures. In the following six years (1904–1909), just six people passed the test.[126] In its early years of operation, a number of cases came before the High Court challenging the constitutionality and implementation of key provisions in the *Immigration Restriction Act 1901*, particularly the dictation test.[127] These cases brought to the fore the way in which the foreigner-sovereign relation had been enshrined in the *Constitution* and the view that 'absolute sovereignty' in its constitutional form was "beyond history and beyond inquiry".[128] In the first such case to come before the Court on a constitutional point,[129] *Chia Gee v Martin*,[130] the Court held unanimously that the contention that the constitutionality of the *Immigration Restriction Act 1901* could be challenged on the basis that it was inconsistent with the *Magna Carta* was "not one for serious refutation".[131] The Court explored the question of constitutionality no further. In addition, cementing the absolute power of the sovereign within the foreigner-sovereign relation, the Court had no difficulty concluding that selection of the European language for any given dictation test was a matter only for the officer administering the test, not the alien/immigrant applicant.[132] Several other High Court decisions related to the implementation of the Act in its early years[133] (as from time to time amended),[134] some of which are said to have bedevilled its effective use.[135] However, until its repeal in 1958, the dictation test as a tool of exclusion would not be circumvented

India and Japan: CPD, House of Representatives, 10 November 1905, 4946 (Alfred Deakin, Prime Minister).

[126] Evans, above n 50, 46–7.   [127] Palfreeman, above n 9, 82.   [128] Anghie, above n 7, 50.

[129] Palfreeman, above n 9, 82 n3; at least two earlier cases were considered in state Supreme Courts: *Christie v Ah Foo* (1904) VLR 533 ('*Christie*'); *Mann v Ah On* (1905) 7 WALR 182 ('*Mann*').

[130] (1905) 3 CLR 649 ('*Chia Gee*').

[131] Ibid 653 (Griffith CJ; Barton and O'Connor JJ concurring). Cf *Pochi* (1982) 151 CLR 101, 114 (Murphy J).

[132] *Chia Gee* (1905) 3 CLR 649, 653 (Griffith CJ).

[133] See, eg, *Preston v Donohue* (1906) 3 CLR 1089; *Li Wan Quai v Christie* (1906) 3 CLR 1125; *Ah Yin* (1907) 4 CLR 1428; *Muller v Dalgety & Co Ltd* (1909) 9 CLR 693; *Gabriel v Ah Mook* (1924) 34 CLR 591; *Williamson* (1926) 39 CLR 95; *Wall v The King*; *Ex parte King Won* (No 1) (1927) 39 CLR 245; *Ah You v Gleeson* (1930) 43 CLR 589 ('*Ah You*'); *Ali Abdul v Maher* (1931) 46 CLR 580 ('*Abdul*').

[134] The *Immigration Restriction Act 1901* was amended 14 times: No 17 of 1905 by the following Acts: No 25 of 1908; No 10 of 1910; No 38 of 1912; No 51 of 1920; No 47 of 1924; No 7 of 1925; No 56 of 1930; No 26 of 1932; No 37 of 1933; No 13 of 1935; No 36 of 1940; No 86 of 1948; No 31 of 1949.

[135] Palfreeman, above n 9, 82.

again,[136] except following the High Court challenge in the celebrated *Kisch* case.[137]

In 1934, the power of exclusion was raised to a new level of controversy.[138] Egon Kisch was a Czechoslovakian national. Although European, he was marked as an outsider racially and politically because he was of Jewish extraction and Communist political sympathies.[139] Kisch's attempts to enter Australia in 1934 were repeatedly frustrated. The first attempt to exclude him under s 3(gh) of the *Immigration Act 1901–1925* (Cth) failed on procedural grounds. This provision empowered the Minister to declare a person to be, in his opinion, a 'prohibited immigrant' based on information received through official or diplomatic channels that the person in question would be an undesirable inhabitant or visitor to Australia. A second attempt to exclude him deployed the dictation test.

Two key cases concerning Kisch came before the High Court. The first related to his detention, purportedly as a s 3(gh) 'prohibited immigrant' on the ship on which he had arrived,[140] the second relating to use of the dictation test.[141] For present purposes, the significance of these cases lies in the Court's readiness to scrutinise procedural aspects of attempts to exclude, in contrast to its reticence to scrutinise the scope of the power to exclude.

In the first case, Evatt J found Kisch's detention (by a private individual)[142] to be unlawful[143] and ordered his release. However, he held the challenge to the provision empowering the Minister to declare someone 'undesirable' to be untenable because "the only question is whether it is within the constitutional domain or subject of immigration."[144] Although conceding the power to be "drastic",[145] Evatt J described it as no wider and "no more drastic" than the power to exclude those who fail the dictation test,[146] a power which, as we

---

[136]   Evans, above n 50, 46–7.   [137]   *R v Wilson; Ex parte Kisch* (1934) 52 CLR 234.

[138]   *R v Carter; Ex parte Kisch* (1934) 52 CLR 221. Two prior cases had been resolved by the High Court in favour of the alleged 'prohibited immigrant', but were quashed on other grounds: *Ah You* (1930) 43 CLR 589; *Abdul* (1931) 46 CLR 580. See also *Christie* (1904) 29 VLR 533; *Mann* (1905) 7 WALR 182.

[139]   Carolyn Rasmussen, 'Kisch, Egon Erwin (1885–1948)' in John Ritchie and Diane Langmore (eds), *Australian Dictionary of Biography* (Melbourne University Press, 2000) vol 15 <http://adb.anu.edu.au/biography/kisch-egon-erwin-10755>.

[140]   *R v Carter; Ex parte Kisch* (1934) 52 CLR 221.

[141]   *R v Wilson; Ex parte Kisch* (1934) 52 CLR 234.

[142]   In his reasons, Evatt J distinguished the case of *Musgrove* as having no application, but only on the grounds that Kisch's detention was by a *private* individual (being the Captain of the boat on which he had arrived): *R v Carter; Ex parte Kisch* (1934) 52 CLR 221, 223 (Evatt J), stating "If it were otherwise, an alien slave detained on board a vessel lying at a wharf in Australia could not obtain his liberty."

[143]   *R v Carter; Ex parte Kisch* (1934) 52 CLR 221.   [144]   Ibid 231 (Evatt J).   [145]   Ibid 230.

[146]   Ibid.

know, had already been found to be constitutional[147] and whose constitution-ality he did not see fit to revisit. In other words, 'absolute sovereignty' in its constitutional form was firmly in place.

Although not clear from the judicial record, the attempt to declare Kisch to be a 'prohibited immigrant' under s 3(gh) was probably intended to circum-vent the problem that Kisch spoke multiple European languages – by some accounts up to ten[148] – and would have been difficult to exclude under the dictation test. However, his exclusion under s 3(gh) having failed, Kisch was then convicted of being a 'prohibited immigrant' on the basis that he had failed the dictation test under s 3(a).[149] As we know, the choice of language was a matter for the officer, not for the putative immigrant.[150] In this case, the officer submitted Kisch to a dictation test in Scottish Gaelic. Kisch challenged the conviction, arguing that Scottish Gaelic was not, within the fair meaning of the Act, a European language. The Court upheld Kisch's argument, and his conviction was quashed. Thus, he was able to embark on the lecture tour for which he had come to Australia, at least for a time.[151] As with the first case, the Court considered it unnecessary to address the constitutional questions argued in the case.[152]

In early 1935, a third case relating to Kisch came before the High Court. In *R v Fletcher; Ex parte Kisch*,[153] the Court (again, Evatt J sitting alone) considered an application to punish the editor and proprietor of the *Sydney Morning Herald* for contempt of court for publishing articles and letters critical of the Court's judgment in *R v Wilson; Ex parte Kisch* (the dictation test case), on the grounds that they had exceeded the limits of fair criticism. Although critical of the newspaper's summary of the case,[154] the Court declined to make a punitive order.[155] In the context of the present discussion, the contempt case is sig-nificant as a record of the strong public reaction to the Court's decision that

---

[147] *Chia Gee* (1905) 3 CLR 649, 653.

[148] David J Clark and Gerard McCoy, *Habeas Corpus: Australia, New Zealand, the South Pacific* (Federation Press, 2000) 12.

[149] *Immigration Restriction Act 1901* s 7. The Act was amended in 1905 to substitute 'any prescribed language' for 'European language', largely to appease the Japanese. However, as Palfreeman has noted, to ensure that an 'unscrupulous' administration did not test Japanese immigrants in Japanese, the amending Act also included a clause providing that the pre-scription of a language had to be approved by both Houses of Parliament and stipulating in effect that a European language would be used until further languages were prescribed by Parliament. No other languages were ever prescribed: Palfreeman, above n 9, 82–3.

[150] *Chia Gee* (1905) 3 CLR 649, 653; see also *R v Davey; Ex parte Freer* (1936) 56 CLR 381.

[151] See generally Harold B Segel, *Egon Erwin Kisch, the Raging Reporter: A Bio-Anthology* (Purdue University Press, 1997) 313–44.

[152] *R v Wilson; Ex parte Kisch* (1934) 52 CLR 234, 242 (Rich J), 246 (Dixon J), 247 (Evatt J).

[153] (1935) 52 CLR 248.   [154] Ibid 254.   [155] Ibid 255.

Scottish Gaelic was not a European language under the Act and the societal expectation that, as a matter of practice, the Court should always defer to the *Constitution*, legislature, and executive in matters relating to 'absolute sovereignty'.

To summarise, Section 4.1 has outlined how the plenary omnipotence that characterises the foreigner-sovereign relation in its constitutional form enabled the immigration and aliens powers, without debate, to stake their juridical claim. Illustrating the prodigious expectations of racial purity and economic prosperity that 'absolute sovereignty' was being called upon to deliver, Section 4.2 has made visible the nature and scope of the legislative techniques used to achieve those ends and how they were, for the most part, oxygenated by the judiciary. As the *Kisch* case suggests, any immigration perceived to be racially or politically disruptive to the project of purity and prosperity was strongly resisted not only by the legislature, but also by some members of the judiciary; and above all, such immigration was regarded as constitutionally insuperable. Section 4.3 shows how juridical uses of 'absolute sovereignty' as framed in the *Constitution* and the common law continued to be shaped, adjusted, and refined to meet changing societal needs and expectations through a combination of legislative and jurisprudential responses and rationalisations.

4.3 CEMENTING DIFFERENCE

The *Immigration Restriction Act 1901*, as from time to time amended, remained in force for 57 years.[156] Introduced for the purposes of fine-tuning the legislation's clear intent, none of the 14 amending Acts altered the priority of securing a prosperous and white Australia that underpinned the constitutional framing of the foreigner-sovereign relation. Likewise, other legislation passed during the period maintained this priority, in particular (although not exclusively) in ways designed to prevent entry and residence by non-Europeans (or other 'undesirables') or to effect their removal.[157] Legislative change usually arose in response to weaknesses revealed by or anticipated from the High Court. Legislative measures and amendments in 1925 and 1948 are illustrative of the objective of fine-tuning the corpus of migration legislation rather than changing the central policy and purpose underpinning it, much less curbing the powers conferred on or by the legislature.[158]

---

[156] See above n 134; repealed by *Migration Act 1958* (Cth) s 4(1) ('*Migration Act*').
[157] See, eg, *Contract Immigrants Act 1905* (Cth); *Aliens Deportation Act 1946* (Cth); *Aliens Deportation Act 1948* (Cth); *War-Time Refugees Removal Act 1949* (Cth).
[158] See above 131.

4.3.1 Immigration Act 1901–1925: *Quotas and Industrial and Political Disturbance*

The Immigration Bill 1925 (Cth) amended the *Immigration Restriction Act 1901*. It had two principal purposes. First, the Parliament sought to introduce a flexible quota system.[159] Second, it sought to introduce measures designed to safeguard Australia from industrial and political unrest.[160] These amendments illustrate how 'absolute sovereignty' in the registers of political doctrine and public rhetoric reinforced the place and vulnerability of the undesirable non-European outsider within the foreigner-sovereign relation, using not only the aliens and immigration powers but also the doctrines of precedent and responsible government. At the same time, however, a clear legislative purpose was also the power to exclude some (undesirable) Europeans.

4.3.1.1 Patriotism, Purity, and Politesse

The quota measure was designed to forearm the Australian government and enable it to stem the anticipated arrival of (lower class) Southern European (but legislatively any) aliens perceived to be difficult to assimilate: people described as "a great undigested mass of alien thought, alien sympathy, and alien purpose" and as a "menace to the social, political, and economic life of the country."[161] Expressing and enlisting a patriotic certainty that "every true Australian would desire the Government to have that power", and at the same time reassuring the Australian people that there was no current threat to their "racial purity", Prime Minister Bruce justified the legislation for reasons that were social, economic, and racial in character.[162] Although the provisions of the Bill were not on their face racialised – the Parliament now being well accustomed to gesturing to the "susceptibilities" of other nations[163] – the debates nevertheless show the extent to which the regulation of race and labour remained central. Thus, for example, John Latham (later Chief Justice of the High Court for almost two decades) had no hesitation in stating

---

[159] *Immigration Act 1901–1925* (Cth) s 3K; CPD, House of Representatives, 25 June 1925, 459 (Stanley Bruce, Prime Minister). However, at 456–8, Bruce rejected the quota model adopted by the US.

[160] *Immigration Act 1901–1925* (Cth) ss 8AA–8AB; CPD, House of Representatives, 25 June 1925, 460 (Stanley Bruce).

[161] 65 *Congressional Record* 5698 (1924, House of Representatives); CPD, House of Representatives, 25 June 1925, 457 (Stanley Bruce).

[162] CPD, House of Representatives, 25 June 1925, 457–60 (Stanley Bruce).

[163] CPD, House of Representatives, 1 July 1925, 582 (John Latham).

that "[t]hese provisions are directed towards the maintenance of the racial, social, industrial, and economic standards of Australia."[164]

4.3.1.2 The Most Arbitrary and Uncontrolled Discretion Anyone Could Imagine

The measures designed to safeguard Australia from industrial and political unrest initiated *by* immigrants were described by Bruce as intended to "free this country from the poisonous propaganda of men who are not Australians, and have no Australian ideals or sympathies".[165] To do so, a legislative device empowered the Governor-General to make a proclamation in the event of 'a serious industrial disturbance prejudicing or threatening the peace, order or good government of the Commonwealth'.[166] While the proclamation remained in force, the Minister was empowered to issue a summons to a person believed to be engaged in prejudicial or obstructive acts of a similar character. Such a person was thereupon invited to appear before a Board appointed for the purposes and to show good cause why she should not be deported.[167] In defending the discretion vested in the Minister under the proposed legislation, Latham observed that the die of arbitrary and uncontrolled power had already been cast:

> It is important that honorable members should realize that the most arbitrary and the most uncontrolled discretion any one could imagine exists under the present law. Already the law of Australia is such that the Minister administering it may exclude any one who does not know all the languages of Europe. Accordingly, the criticism based upon administrative discretion ought to have been raised in 1901, and if it had been effective, the Immigration Restriction Act of that year, on which the White Australia policy rests, would not have been passed. The objection, therefore, is now somewhat late in the day.[168]

In addition to indicating that arbitrary and uncontrolled discretionary power was what had facilitated implementation of the White Australia policy, Latham maintained that such power would nevertheless be undertaken with a "full sense of grave responsibility".[169] He noted:

> It is true that a power such as the bill confers on the Minister is open to abuse, and it appears to me that all the arguments of members of the Opposition have been directed to the possibility of its abuse. But I have already pointed

---

[164] Ibid 581 (John Latham).
[165] CPD, House of Representatives, 25 June 1925, 460 (Stanley Bruce).
[166] *Immigration Act 1901–1925* (Cth) s 8AA(1). [167] Ibid s 8AA(2).
[168] CPD, House of Representatives, 1 July 1925, 582 (John Latham). [169] Ibid.

out that powers that might be abused have existed since 1901, and as far as is known they never have been abused, and I see no reason for supposing that these powers in their turn will be abused.[170]

Again, he sought to reassure the Australian people that 'the most arbitrary and uncontrolled discretion anyone could imagine' was in safe hands. Accordingly, he intimated that the doctrine of responsible government provided an adequate safeguard against gross injustices arising from misuses and abuses of power. Furthermore, the House was informed, there was no history to which those concerned about abuse of arbitrary and uncontrolled powers could point.

Shortly after the legislation was passed, two Irish-born trade unionists, Messrs Tom Walsh and Jacob Johnson, were detained in custody pending their deportation. Each applied to the Supreme Court of New South Wales and obtained a rule nisi calling on the respondent (Yates), in whose custody they were detained, to show cause why a writ of habeas corpus should not issue.

4.3.1.3 Deporting Industrial and Political Activists: Walsh and Johnson[171]

Walsh and Johnson successfully sought a writ of habeas corpus in the High Court[172] on the ground that they could no longer be characterised as 'immigrants' and therefore could not properly be said to be subject to, detained, and deported under the immigration power. Although a majority of the Court found in their favour, the Court entertained no doubt that it was within the sovereign power of the Commonwealth to legislate for the exclusion of (socially, racially, industrially, or politically) 'undesirable' immigrants. Isaacs J, who in a former capacity had been a proponent of the freedom that despotic power accords to legislators,[173] recorded an impassioned (partial) dissent encapsulated by the following extract:

The subject matter of the power is 'immigration and emigration.' It is true, and I have expressed my own view emphatically in the *O'Flanagan Case*,[174] that once a person immigrates into Australia he is always subject to the power of the Parliament under construction. I endeavoured to crystallize my view into the maxim 'Once an immigrant always an immigrant.' A person arriving as an immigrant into the Commonwealth comes *subject to all the constitutional*

---

[170]   Ibid 583 (John Latham).   [171]   *Walsh and Johnson* (1925) 37 CLR 36.
[172]   As the cases gave rise to constitutional questions, they were removed to the High Court: *Judiciary Act 1903* (Cth) s 40.
[173]   See above 121–2.   [174]   *Irish Envoys Case* (1923) 32 CLR 518.

powers of the Parliament of Australia. Its permission to him to enter may be either conditional or unconditional. He has no right to enter Australia against the will of its people. He can enter only in pursuance of their will, and subject to their constitutional right to qualify or withdraw that permission at any time or under any circumstances they think proper. No Parliament – for Parliament is only the legislative instrument of the people – can either by action or inaction surrender or weaken or forfeit that national power. Immigration, as I have explained in the *O'Flanagan Case*, is not obliterated for ever by the mere passage across the frontier, nor by the momentary leap over a barrier which magically and instantaneously transforms a Hindoo or a Kanaka, for example, into an Australian. If such were its meaning, the cherished national policy of Australia would indeed be in peril. And it would only nominally lessen the peril if the Hindoo or the Kanaka by immediately adopting Australia as his 'home,' as it is said, could, so to speak, dig himself into this Commonwealth, so as to be irrevocably, so far as the Commonwealth power is concerned, a member of the people of the Commonwealth – a true Australian – and thereby escape the immigration power for ever. He could afterwards, as it is said, irrespective of nationality, of sentiment, of customs, of everything except his resolve to stay in Australia indefinitely as his 'home,' remain here or travel back and forwards, leave when he pleased, enter as he chose, and claim all the rights of a native-born Australian who had never abandoned his country. For this Court to so hold would, in my opinion, be a tragedy. The immigration power would practically be a dead letter once the frontier was passed, whatever shred of theory remained.[175]

This passage is characteristic of much of Isaacs J's judgment and highlights the political and juridical complexity and influence of 'absolute sovereignty' as both doctrine and discourse.[176] As we can see, he frames the foreigner in the foreigner-sovereign relation as immutably an outsider whose status was a matter within the "absolute discretion" of the Parliament.[177] Indeed, on no less than four occasions he deployed the aphorism 'Once an immigrant always an immigrant', first used by him in *R v MacFarlane; Ex parte O'Flanagan*[178] ('*Irish Envoys Case*'). At the same time, his reference to the fidelity and allegiance of 'native-born Australians' was clearly a reference to the descendants of people early international jurists would have characterised as

---

[175] *Walsh and Johnson* (1925) 37 CLR 36, 81–2 (emphasis in original).
[176] This arises, at least in part, on account of British subjects not being regarded as aliens. Therefore, such legislation could not look for its constitutional authority to the aliens power in s 51(xix) of the *Constitution*. See, eg, Rayner Thwaites, *The Liberty of Non-Citizens: Indefinite Detention in Commonwealth Countries* (Hart, 2014) 41; Mary Crock, *Immigration and Refugee Law in Australia* (Federation Press, 1998) 20–3.
[177] *Walsh and Johnson* (1925) 37 CLR 36, 83.   [178] (1923) 32 CLR 518, 555.

foreigners themselves – colonising European *insiders*. That is, it was not a reference to Australia's indigenous population, whose citizenship, voting rights, and status were still years away from recognition.[179]

Nevertheless, apparently for technical reasons, Isaacs J was prepared to draw a line under those who had migrated to Australia prior to Federation. In his view, "[n]o person can be properly styled an immigrant or an emigrant for the purposes of that power unless his immigration or his emigration takes place after the Commonwealth comes into being."[180] This led him to conclude that Walsh, a British subject who had migrated to New South Wales in 1893, could not be regarded as an immigrant to the Commonwealth. In relation to Johnson, also a British subject, who had migrated to Australia after Federation, Isaacs J found that the legislation applied to him but that he had not been properly notified of the proscribed acts in which he was alleged to have been engaged.[181] Indeed, in a condemnation of the deportation mechanism in the instant case, he concluded "arbitrariness and despotism could no farther go"[182] than to enable deportation on the strength of undefended criminal charges.[183] So Isaacs J appears to have been concerned to protect Walsh and Johnson against arbitrary and despotic treatment – specifically deportation – in connection with their political and industrial activism. However, he was also adamant that no jurisprudential space be created (inadvertently or intentionally) through an interpretation of the *Constitution* that could be filled by people of non-European races.

Although finding in favour of Walsh and Johnson, Starke J held that the aliens power permitted the Parliament to legislate that "any alien who in the opinion of the Minister was an undesirable resident of Australia might be deported".[184] Such a law, he said, "would be valid because the Parliament has full power over the subject of aliens."[185] Starke J acknowledged that such legislation would be regarded by some as "obnoxious to the principles of British liberty".[186] However, in upholding its constitutionality, he expressed unqualified trust in the doctrine of responsible governance:

---

[179] *Nationality and Citizenship Act 1948* (Cth); *Commonwealth Electoral Act 1949* (Cth); *Constitution Alteration (Aboriginal People) 1967* (Cth).

[180] *Walsh and Johnson* (1925) 37 CLR 36, 83.

[181] *Immigration Restriction Act 1901 – 1925* (Cth) s 8AA(2) proscribed certain acts that may trigger deportation and in relation to which the alleged perpetrator was invited to show cause why he should not be deported from the Commonwealth.

[182] *Walsh and Johnson* (1925) 37 CLR 36, 105. Cf the contribution of Isaacs to the parliamentary debates on the Immigration Restriction Bill 1901 (Cth): above at 121–2.

[183] Nicholls, *Deported*, above n 8, 60.   [184] *Walsh and Johnson* (1925) 37 CLR 36, 133.

[185] Ibid.   [186] Ibid.

The chance of 'abuse', however, is, as Lord *Dunedin* said in *R v Halliday*,[187] always 'theoretically present' when absolute powers in general terms are delegated to an executive body, but 'practically, as things exist,' he adds, the danger of abuse 'is absent.'[188]

As this discussion suggests, *Walsh and Johnson* illustrates how the Court understood the scope and purpose of the aliens and immigration powers. What we see from this case is that the use of restrictive legislative measures for the expulsion of (white) British subjects (that is, for political and industrial purposes) did not dispense with the race-based dimensions of migration law and policy; rather, it shows how high levels of discretion integrated into these measures could be diverted to respond to and rationalise other contingencies, as required. As the judgments of Isaacs and Higgins JJ suggest, their Honours, in their interpretation of the scope of the constitutional power to expel, were acutely conscious of the implications their judgments would have for the social, racial, and economic future of White Australia.[189]

4.3.2 War-Time Refugees Removal Act 1949: *Restoring Control*

The case of *O'Keefe v Calwell*[190] (*'O'Keefe'*), decided in March 1949, was one of the few cases in which the High Court found against the Commonwealth on a deportation case.[191] Annie O'Keefe, an Ambonese woman who had come to Australia as a wartime refugee in 1942,[192] successfully challenged attempts to remove her from Australia on the basis that she was a British subject by marriage;[193] that is, juridically she was now an insider, but politically she remained an outsider. Although the Court found in her favour, members of the Court who considered the question had no difficulty finding the relevant provisions of the Act to be within the constitutional ambit of the immigration power. Indeed, McTiernan J gave a clear signal to the Parliament that the

---

[187] [1917] AC 260, 271.   [188] *Walsh and Johnson* (1925) 37 CLR 36, 133.

[189] Ibid 81–2 (Isaacs J), 117 (Higgins J). See also *Irish Envoys Case* (1923) 32 CLR 518, 558 (Isaacs J).

[190] (1949) 77 CLR 261.

[191] Glenn Nicholls, 'Gone with Hardly a Trace: Deportees in Immigration Policy' in Klaus Neumann and Gwenda Tavan (eds), *Does History Matter? Making and Debating Citizenship, Immigration and Refugee Policy in Australia and New Zealand* (ANU E Press, 2009) 9, 12.

[192] O'Keefe had remained in Australia on the strength of a series of certificates of exemption, releasing her from certain obligations under the *Immigration Act 1901–1940* (Cth) s 4.

[193] Ibid ss 3(gf), 4(1), 4(4)–(5), 7, 18. While in Australia she was widowed and then subsequently married John William O'Keefe, a British subject. Under s 18 of the Act, she thereby became a British subject herself.

immigration power extended to making laws to expel such persons as the plaintiff from Australia.[194] Immigration Minister, Arthur Calwell, wasted no time in taking his cue.

On 9 June 1949, Calwell introduced concurrently the Immigration Bill 1949 (Cth) and the War-Time Refugees Removal Bill 1949 (Cth). The object of the two Bills was to "remedy defects" revealed by the High Court in *O'Keefe*.[195]

4.3.2.1 Reasserting 'Absolute Sovereignty': A Question of Flexibility

The legislation was introduced to "restore control"[196] over the policy of restricted immigration, prescribed by the *Immigration Restriction Act 1901* (as amended). In this context, the legislative purpose behind the restoration of control was to deport non-Europeans like Annie O'Keefe who (it was said) had been received "purely on compassionate grounds"[197] as wartime refugees because (it was said) they "normally would have been refused admission".[198] Indeed, they were described as having "flagrantly abused our hospitality".[199] Reiterating the doctrine of 'absolute sovereignty', Calwell declared in now familiar terms:

> It would be tantamount to abdicating our sovereign right if we failed to take action that would show conclusively that it is solely for the Government of Australia to say who shall enter our shores and under what conditions they shall be permitted to remain.[200]

He then issued a warning to his detractors:

> I am determined that no matter who criticizes or who complains; no matter what un-Australian activities the haters of this Government and of this Government's maintenance of our immigration restriction laws and practices may resort to, those laws and practices will remain unchanged and unchangeable. They are rooted in the hearts and minds [of] the Australian people, and any political party that would tamper with them would do so at its peril.[201]

---

[194]　*O'Keefe* (1949) 77 CLR 261, 290.
[195]　CPD, House of Representatives, 9 June 1949, 810 (Arthur Calwell, Minister for Information and Minister for Immigration).
[196]　Ibid 807 (Arthur Calwell).
[197]　Ibid 811 (Arthur Calwell). Cf *Koon Wing Lau* (1949) 80 CLR 533, 552, where Latham CJ outlines the political imperative of protecting wartime refugees.
[198]　CPD, House of Representatives, 9 June 1949, 810 (Arthur Calwell).
[199]　Ibid 814 (Arthur Calwell). Cf the right to hospitality of foreigners in early international law: Chapter 2, 58–59 (Section 2.1.3.1), 61, 77.
[200]　CPD, House of Representatives, 9 June 1949, 814 (Arthur Calwell).　　[201]　Ibid.

Hence, 'absolute sovereignty' was positioned not only as an unassailable legal doctrine, but also as being so ingrained in the 'hearts and minds' of 'the people' that it was popularly and politically unshakeable; to doubt it would be dangerous and destructive,[202] indeed 'un-Australian'.[203] In other words, we see 'absolute sovereignty' working at the level of both political doctrine and public rhetoric.

To the Bills' eclectic mix of critics – slated as "the Communists, the seekers after cheap labour and the sentimentalists"[204] – Calwell was emphatic:

> Any person who opposes the bill must, by so doing, label himself a disbeliever in any effective restriction where immigration is concerned, and one who wishes to destroy the living standards and way of life that have been built up in this nation in little more than a century and a half.[205]

To safeguard the sacrosanct 'living standards' and 'way of life' embedded in the ideologies of economic prosperity and racial purity, Calwell outlined how the discretionary administration of the dictation tests and certificates of exemption from deportation had enabled "full control" to be maintained over both the policy itself and the persons admitted under it, as well as a degree of flexibility.[206] This flexibility, he said, had facilitated development of trade and the maintenance of friendly relations with non-European nations.[207] In addition, it had permitted wartime refugees who were "technically prohibited immigrants" (because they were 'undesirable' non-European outsiders) to be admitted on humanitarian grounds.[208] This account of the judicial and political process enables us to see how the foreigner remained a mutable figure whose 'outsider-ness' was shaped by the political will to extend hospitality through a flexible use of 'absolute sovereignty' as political doctrine.

4.3.2.2 Racial Discrimination: "Inevitable"

Introducing the legislation, Calwell rejected the idea of "token" quotas of non-Europeans apparently proposed by some as a means of getting around the inherent injustices in expelling people like Annie O'Keefe.[209] He did so on two grounds. First, he dismissed as "fallacious" the idea that quotas would

---

[202] Ibid 806 (Arthur Calwell).
[203] Similar discourses emerge in the parliamentary debates on the mandatory detention legislation: see Chapter 5, 172.
[204] CPD, House of Representatives, 9 June 1949, 806 (Arthur Calwell); see also at 809, 811 (Arthur Calwell).
[205] Ibid 806 (Arthur Calwell). [206] Ibid. [207] Ibid. [208] Ibid.
[209] Ibid 807 (Arthur Calwell).

satisfy the aspirations and allay the resentment of those perceiving discrimination on racial grounds, suggesting also that a quota system that only applied to
non-Europeans would be "most hurtful to non-European susceptibilities."[210]
Second, and in any event, he conceded as "inevitable" discrimination on
racial grounds in the administration of an immigration policy "based on the
concept that the homogeneous character of the population . . . shall be maintained."[211] However, in doing so he denied the imputation that the policy was
totally to exclude persons regarded as racially inferior:

> Let me make it perfectly clear that our policy is not, and never has been,
> directed at the total exclusion of non-Europeans; nor is it based on any
> assumption of racial superiority. The ideal which underlies our policy is
> the preservation of the homogenous character of our population and the
> avoidance of the friction which inevitably follows an influx of peoples having
> different standards of living, traditions, culture and national characteristics.
> The wide use of the very misleading term 'the White Australia policy' by
> newspapers and others has been largely responsible for the misconception
> that has arisen in regard to the policy. I emphasize that the term has no
> official basis and wherever possible I have avoided its use, not only because it
> describes our immigration policy inaccurately, but because it can be
> regarded as offensive to non-Europeans. It does not appear in any of our
> legislation or regulations or in any laws of any State parliament. One of my
> first actions as Minister for Immigration was to stress on my new department
> that the language used in official correspondence must make no reference to
> this term or to any other expression concerning the pigmentation of other
> people's skins or anything else that could give offence. I would earnestly urge
> that this lead be followed by others. The term 'the White Australia policy'
> might be described as journalese.[212]

The denials in this passage speak as much to the continuing operation of a
policy that excluded or restrictively conditioned entry and stay on the basis of
race as they do to a growing unease with making explicit the 'ideal' underlying
it. As we know, from its inception the policy objective was to regulate race and
labour through a gentleman's racism – that is, to be attentive to the susceptibilities of non-European nations through textual silence but to maintain the
foreigner-sovereign relation within the doctrinal and discursive frame of
'absolute sovereignty'. As such, since Federation, the legislature had concert-
edly not made the objectives of (racial) purity and (economic) prosperity
textually explicit. It had been able to do so through the conferral of broad

[210] Ibid 808 (Arthur Calwell). See also the discussion on quotas, above at 137.
[211] CPD, House of Representatives, 9 June 1949, 807 (Arthur Calwell).
[212] Ibid 808 (Arthur Calwell).

discretionary powers on administrative officers who understood what was required of them. Viewed in this way, we can see how Calwell's instructions to his department to use different language implemented a similar kind of textual silence, while leaving the policy itself unchanged.

Calwell's speech leaves us in no doubt that he was, through remedial legislative measures, upholding the foremost priority of the policy, which was – whatever its name – racial homogeneity.[213] Indeed, at the outset of his speech, Calwell had declared:

> I should like it to be clearly understood that the purpose of this bill is to maintain what every Australian has understood to have been the law of the land for the past 48 years. The bill is designed to continue the administration of the Immigration Act according to the interpretation of it that was thought to be correct by governments of differing political complexions throughout the whole of those 48 years, until a recent High Court judgment revealed that the act had certain weaknesses never before disclosed.[214]

Similarly, in the remainder of his speech, Calwell devoted considerable time to Australia's policy of encouraging European migration "with the utmost vigour" and "to the fullest possible extent", in order to assure Australia's "economic stability" and "future welfare",[215] and further because "[t]hey [Europeans] are not likely to create problems of miscegenation and the like."[216] So, there was a 'full' and 'vigorous' embrace of the European foreigner alongside a continuing resistance to an 'influx' of those foreigners 'having different standards of living, traditions, culture and national characteristics'. Indeed, because of these priorities, Calwell stated that it was "unthinkable" that a quota system that also applied to European migration should be adopted.[217]

4.3.2.3 People of Goodwill, High Principles, and Patriotism

Above all, Calwell's speech reveals a deeply held fear that anything less than total control and total exclusion was insufficient to protect Australia and Australians from the unsavoury realities that pertain to the mass of (non-European) humanity. In further justification, he declared that Australia could only ever offer an "insignificant contribution" to the relief of the "many millions who, unfortunately, are compelled ... to lead miserable and undernourished lives in overcrowded Asia".[218] He thereby implied that there was little to be served by Australia making any contribution at all. Moreover,

---

[213] Ibid 807–8, 810, 812 (Arthur Calwell).   [214] Ibid 806 (Arthur Calwell).
[215] Ibid 808 (Arthur Calwell).   [216] Ibid.   [217] Ibid.   [218] Ibid 809 (Arthur Calwell).

he suggested, racial homogeneity was the only means of living in peace and mutual prosperity:

> There is no evidence anywhere on the face of the earth that great aggregations of peoples of widely differing standards of living, culture and ideals, can live together in the one community in peace and mutual prosperity. When such association is attempted, at worst it leads to hatred, bloodshed and continual outbursts of ferocious civil war. At the very best, it produces furtive fear and dislike, with one race or the other in a hopelessly subordinate position, doing the menial work of the nation and living mean and ambitionless lives on a level somewhere between that of domestic animals and that of free human beings. That 'very best' is not good enough for Australia.[219]

In defending his position, Calwell insisted on the paramount importance of protecting the Australian people from what he saw as the mutual degradations evident in societies comprised of the exploiter and the exploited, in which "[t]he young people of the race which considers itself superior are brought up in daily contact with 'man's inhumanity to man' on a level that would shock and horrify most Australians."[220] Denying the existence of segregation and discrimination of any kind in Australia, he insisted that people of other races "of goodwill and high principles" held Australians in high esteem,[221] implicitly disparaging a contrary view as hostile and unprincipled. Finally, he outlined what might be described as a (paternalistic) development agenda. He proclaimed that the task of the Asian of "goodwill and patriotism" was to stay in his own country, ably assisted, one supposes, by neighbourly Australians who would provide training, technological knowledge, guidance in social organisation, and trade, all of which would assist in raising the standard of living in their own countries.[222] At its heart, however, it is the following statement that encapsulates the unbridled self-interest underpinning this anti-Asian migration agenda: "This land is our land, to own and to develop. . . . We can only preserve our heritage for our descendants by preserving the homogeneity of our race, and that we must and will do."[223]

4.3.2.4 Removing Wartime Refugees: A Sovereign Discretion

The main clauses of the War-Time Refugees Removal Bill sought to ensure that, subject to certain specified exceptions,[224] both alien and non-European British subject wartime refugees were covered by the Act[225] and could be

---

[219] Ibid 808 (Arthur Calwell).   [220] Ibid 809 (Arthur Calwell).
[221] Ibid 810 (Arthur Calwell).   [222] Ibid.   [223] Ibid.
[224] *War-Time Refugees Removal Act 1949* (Cth) ss 4(1)(d)–(g).   [225] Ibid s 4.

deported.[226] They provided for deportation pursuant to ministerial discretion and included what were described as "machinery measures"[227] that provided for detention or release on a surety pending deportation.[228]

The companion amendments in Immigration Bill 1949 (Cth) provided (effectively) for the non-expiry of the (discretionary) power to submit a person to a dictation test, declare her to be a prohibited immigrant, and effect her deportation immediately upon the expiration or cancellation of a certificate of exemption.[229] Although broad in their scope, as Nicholls notes, this was a milder version of the Bill. The original draft had given the Minister power to deport anyone who had entered Australia after 1901, an ambit claim that was pared back on the advice of counsel that its breadth could be its very undoing.[230]

The validity of the 1949 Acts was challenged in the High Court case of *Koon Wing Lau v Calwell*[231] ('*Koon Wing Lau*'), brought by a group of Chinese, most of whom were British subjects from Hong Kong and all of whom the Immigration Minister had sought to deport. The powers on which the Minister sought to rely were the defence power (s 51(vi)) and the aliens and immigration powers. Although divided on the relevance of the defence power, the Court held unanimously that the legislation was a valid exercise of the aliens and immigration powers. Indeed, Latham CJ underscored the doctrine of 'absolute sovereignty' in its constitutional form as follows:

> The Commonwealth Parliament could in my opinion validly provide for the deportation at any time of persons who at any time have come into Australia as immigrants by applying any discrimen which it thought proper, based, for example, on age, sex, race, nationality, personal character, occupation, time of arrival or on the order of a Minister or of an official, in exactly the same way as it could impose any conditions whatever upon immigrants seeking to enter Australia.[232]

Thus, not only did he emphasise that the Parliament had been given carte blanche to discriminate under the *Constitution*, but he also articulated a broad range of bases on which such discrimination could validly take place.

---

[226] Ibid s 5.   [227] CPD, House of Representatives, 9 June 1949, 811 (Arthur Calwell).

[228] *War-Time Refugees Removal Act 1949* (Cth) s 7.

[229] *Immigration Act 1949* (Cth) s 3, amending *Immigration Act 1901–1940* (Cth) s 4.

[230] Nicholls, 'Gone with Hardly a Trace', above n 191, 12 n 14, citing J B Tait, 'Memorandum of Counsel' (Series No A432, Item 1949/472, National Archives of Australia, 25 May 1949).

[231] (1949) 80 CLR 533.

[232] Ibid 561–2. See also Nicholls, 'Gone with Hardly a Trace', above n 191, 13.

4.3.2.5 Shifting the Onus of Proof

The *War-Time Refugees Removal Act 1949* (Cth) also provided for the Minister to certify that an individual was a person to whom the Act applied. Certification constituted prima facie evidence that the person was subject to deportation. The onus of rebuttal fell to the individual in question,[233] a practice that, as we saw in Chapter 3, had long characterised restrictive migration legislation.

4.3.2.6 Unlimited or Indefinite Imprisonment

The Act made provision for custody of wartime refugees pending deportation (s 7). This provision mirrored s 8C of the *Immigration Act 1901–1940* (Cth) (the validity of which had never been challenged).[234] The plaintiffs contended that the custody provision was invalid because it permitted unlimited imprisonment. In his reasons, Latham CJ did not question the position outlined in *Robtelmes* that the immigration power incorporated the power to deport. He also declined to entertain any suggestion that such imprisonment was (or, it would seem, ever could be) punitive, apparently on the ground that the deportation itself was not punitive (and, it would seem, never could be).[235] On this basis, Latham CJ (McTiernan J concurring) concluded that detention for the purposes of deportation also could not be punitive, because it was only a power to detain *pending* deportation. Dixon J agreed but regarded the power to detain pending deportation as placing a limit on detention entitling discharge on habeas if deportation were not effected within a "reasonable time".[236] Likewise, Williams J (Rich J concurring) regarded detention for a period not fixed by legislation to be valid where custody was only for a purpose which could be described as "pending deportation".[237] Thus, at least some members of the Court were beginning to suggest that powers purportedly exercised in pursuance of the aliens and immigration powers could be qualified by considerations of reasonableness and limited purpose.[238]

4.3.2.7 Conditioning Entry and Stay

However, as to aliens, *Musgrove* and *Cain* continued to be treated as sufficient authority for the proposition that aliens could be excluded and prevented from remaining in the country under either common law or statute.[239] In this

---

[233] *Koon Wing Lau* (1949) 80 CLR 533, 550 (Latham CJ).   [234] Ibid 581 (Dixon J).
[235] Ibid 555–6, citing *Walsh and Johnson* (1925) 37 CLR 36, 60, 96.
[236] *Koon Wing Lau* (1949) 80 CLR 533, 581.   [237] Ibid 586–7.
[238] This issue will be developed further in Chapter 5.
[239] *Koon Wing Lau* (1949) 80 CLR 533, 556 (Latham CJ).

regard, the Court reinforced the view that Parliament had untrammelled power.[240] Likewise, the immigration power was held to extend to the power to facilitate, restrict, or prevent both entry to and 'settlement' or 'absorption' in the community.[241] Williams J (Rich J concurring) qualified the power to impose conditions on entry and stay as limited by a requirement of reasonableness. In doing so, Williams J expanded on the views he had previously expressed in *O'Keefe*,[242] in which he had said that a "reasonable" and implicitly limited "period of probation" could be fixed beyond which an immigrant should no longer be subject to the risk of becoming a 'prohibited immigrant' and thereby subject to deportation.[243] The requirement that a "period of probation" be "reasonable", first articulated in *O'Keefe*, qualifies a particular condition attaching to entry and stay. However, such judicial pronouncements were rare. Indeed, it would not be until 1982 that an analogous view would be expressed, and even then only in dissent.[244]

The final judgment in *Koon Wing Lau* was that of Webb J. Although largely concurring with Latham CJ, Webb J made several observations of note. First, he had no difficulty concluding that the scope of the immigration power extended to making legislation that attached retrospective consequences to past acts of immigration and had effects detrimental to the immigrant.[245] Further, he doubted that the *War-Time Refugees Removal Act* was within the defence power. However, he found it unnecessary to decide. Instead, he speculated that in cases of overpopulation it was conceivable that the defence power could still be invoked to effect the deportation of refugees who had become members of the Australian community. This was, he said, conceivable if their presence could be characterised as "harmful" and their deportation required "in the interests of defence".[246] Finally, he concluded that the presence of wartime refugees who did not qualify for membership in the Australian community could still be the subject of valid legislation under the defence power. In doing so, he likened their presence to collateral damage: as "visible and tangible ... and ... maybe as undesirable as the unrepaired damage done by enemy bombing to an Australian city."[247]

In its result, *Koon Wing Lau* affirmed Calwell's efforts to restore control over Australia's immigration policy and to ensure that there was no residual doubt about the scope of the aliens and immigration powers. However, by the time

---

[240] Ibid 558–9 (Latham CJ).   [241] Ibid 560–1 (Latham CJ).   [242] (1949) 77 CLR 261, 294.
[243] *Koon Wing Lau* (1949) 80 CLR 533, 589; cf *Irish Envoys Case* (1923) 32 CLR 518, 533 (Knox CJ), 575 (Higgins J), neither of whom attached a qualification of reasonableness to the notion of probation.
[244] *Pochi* (1982) 151 CLR 101, 114 (Murphy J).   [245] *Koon Wing Lau* (1949) 80 CLR 533, 594.
[246] Ibid 595.   [247] Ibid 594 (Webb J).

the decision was handed down, it had already become (at least for the moment) academic. A change of government brought a change of approach, and in the ensuing decade neither of the next two Immigration Ministers (Harold Holt and Alexander Downer) resorted to the deportation powers contained in the *War-Time Refugees Removal Act* or the *Aliens Deportation Act 1948* (Cth). Instead, deportation powers were exercised under the *Immigration Restriction Act 1901*, as amended.[248]

4.3.3 Migration Act 1958: *A New Beginning?*

In the ensuing years, it became apparent that the immigration system was in need of major overhaul. Described by Immigration Minister Alexander ('Alick') Downer as "the fruit of long deliberation", the Migration Bill 1958 (Cth) was introduced on 1 May 1958.[249] Materially, it dealt with immigration and deportation.[250] Pitched as a "technical document", it was arranged in four parts containing a total of 67 clauses. At the same time, it repealed 19 existing enactments and omitted no less than 24 sections of the existing Act regarded as "unnecessary or outmoded".[251] It promised, in no small measure, to be a new beginning.[252]

4.3.3.1 A 'Neat, Simple Expedient' Replaces a 'Singularly Ugly Museum Piece'

One of the central developments that the introduction of the Migration Bill marked was the abolition of what Downer described as the "ingenious, but contentious, device"[253] of the dictation test:

> [H]owever subtle and convenient it may have seemed 60 years ago, [it] must surely appear to-day as an archaic, heavyhanded piece of machinery, in the category of those singularly ugly museum pieces of the Victorian age, and quite out of keeping with the ideas of the second half of the 20th century.[254]

---

[248] Nicholls, 'Gone with Hardly a Trace', above n 191, 13.

[249] CPD, House of Representatives, 1 May 1958, 1396 (Alexander Downer). Note that Alexander ('Alick') Downer was the father of Alexander John Gosse Downer (b 1951), a former Australian Foreign Minister who was appointed Australian High Commissioner to the United Kingdom in 2014.

[250] It also dealt with the emigration of both children and members of the Aboriginal population, issues that are beyond the scope of this book.

[251] CPD, House of Representatives, 1 May 1958, 1396 (Alexander Downer).

[252] A similar description was given to the Migration Reform Bill 1992: CPD, House of Representatives, 5 May 1992, 2370–3 (Gerry Hand). See further Chapter 5, 179.

[253] CPD, House of Representatives, 1 May 1958, 1396 (Alexander Downer).   [254] Ibid.

Highlighting the disquiet and offence the dictation test had caused in Australia's international relations, Downer continued:

> [Its] clumsy, creaking operation has evoked much resentment outside Australia, and has tarnished our good name in the eyes of the world. The Government, therefore, proposes to abolish it, and to substitute in its stead the neat, simple expedient of an entry permit.[255]

This 'neat, simple expedient' would work as follows:

> When passengers on a ship or aircraft pass before an immigration officer, and he finds one or more of them not eligible to enter, under policy or instructions approved by the Minister, such passengers will not be humiliated and bedazed by a dictation test, but will quietly be told they are not qualified to land, and that if they go ashore they will become prohibited immigrants, liable to arrest and deportation.[256]

As this passage suggests, the same result as the 'ingenious, but contentious, device' of the dictation test would be achieved, but in a 'quiet' way that would not 'humiliate' or 'bedaze' those subject to exclusion. British subjects would only be refused entry permits on the Minister's express authority, and those aliens travelling with visas issued by overseas posts would be granted a (temporary or permanent) entry permit on arrival. As before, the masters, owners, and agents of ships or aircraft carrying prohibited immigrants would still be subject to carrier sanctions – now revised up[257] and extended to obligations to remove a prohibited immigrant, even where the removee could not enter another country, and to facilitate the deportation of a lawfully admitted immigrant who had become subject to deportation.[258] So, although the ways in which the foreigner's exclusion was practised was recalibrated under the legislation, the absolute power to exclude her remained unchanged.

4.3.3.2 Keeping the "Latent Dangers" of "Naked and Uninhibited Power" in Check

On the question of what he described as "mandatory powers of deportation", Downer outlined a reform agenda. Highlighting the Minister's "solemn responsibility" to "wield" his "arbitrary" powers – powers that he recognised were "capable of the gravest abuse" – in a manner that preserved national security but was also "humane and just to the individuals concerned", he

---

[255] Ibid.   [256] Ibid 1397 (Alexander Downer).   [257] The revised sanction was £500: ibid.
[258] Ibid.

foreshadowed the imposition on the Minister's broad deportation powers of "important checks on his authority".[259] Underscoring that his department deals "first and last" with human beings and their future welfare, he opined, "as human values change, so the law must change".[260] Nevertheless, he was clear that the Minister would retain the power to act "swiftly and successfully whenever, in his judgment, the national interest demands".[261]

As to the arrest and detention of 'suspected prohibited immigrants', Downer stated, inter alia, that

> Section 14a of the present act empowers an officer without warrant to arrest any person reasonably supposed to be a prohibited immigrant offending against this act. A moment's thought will show the latent dangers here. Accordingly, clause 38 of the bill provides for a person so arrested to be brought within 48 hours, or as soon as practicable afterwards, before a prescribed authority, who must inquire into whether there are reasonable grounds for supposing the person to be a prohibited immigrant. If the authority finds such grounds, he will order continued detention for a maximum period of seven days pending the Minister's decision as to deportation.[262]

Downer's observation was discerning: '*A moment's thought will show the latent dangers here.*' In the same speech he would add that "naked and uninhibited" powers of arrest (and detention) provided for in existing legislation had the capacity to "cause great injustice".[263] Having declared a maximum period of seven days' detention pending a decision to deport, he then detailed what he described as "elaborate safeguards" against such injustice for which the Migration Bill provided, including retention of the "overriding power of [the courts to order] a person's release from custody if the court finds that the deportation order is invalid."[264] In addition to the right to apply for a writ of habeas corpus or injunctive relief, he added, the Bill would go further, also providing for reasonable facilities for obtaining legal advice and taking legal proceedings. Perhaps the most striking example of the "humanistic quality"[265] of the reforms that Downer outlined was the establishment of detention centres:

> Whenever it has been thought necessary to keep [deportees] in custody, it has always been the practice to cast them into the most convenient gaol, and to hold them there until arrangements for their embarkation are concluded. Such a procedure is undesirable. Very often the deportee has a blameless record; his only offence is a statutory one against our immigration laws. Once in gaol he must sometimes wait several weeks before he can be shipped from

---

[259] Ibid.   [260] Ibid.   [261] Ibid.   [262] Ibid 1398 (Alexander Downer).   [263] Ibid.
[264] Ibid.   [265] Ibid.

Australia. During this period he intermingles with hardened criminals, and as likely as not becomes contaminated by them. By the time he leaves gaol he may be blemished for the rest of his life, and sent upon a downward path.[266]

Describing as 'undesirable' what is now known as commingling of immigration detainees with convicted criminals, particularly in view of the fact that the deportees 'very often' had a 'blameless record', he declared that there was "a compelling case for reform in the treatment of those whom one might call statutory offenders".[267]

4.3.3.3 Detention Centres: A Welcome 'Innovation'

In making these reforms, Downer described his own experience as a prisoner of war of the Japanese for three years as a "comparable situation".[268] Gaols, he said, were "depressing places, especially when you are not in any true sense an offender."[269] It was on this basis that he hailed the introduction of detention centres as a welcome innovation out of which he was "sure" that "nothing but good will come" – an innovation that, along with other ameliorating effects of the legislation, "will place Australia in advance of any other country in the world."[270]

In closing his Second Reading Speech, Downer described the Bill as a "valuable consolidation and amendment of the existing law":

> It introduces order where there is now confusion; it strengthens the hand of the Government where it is now ineffectual; it imparts justice, tolerance, and humanity in accord with liberal principles in their truest sense; in many respects it gives Australia the finest immigration charter that the world has yet seen.[271]

This suggests that the 'elaborate safeguards' framed in the Bill represented a decisive departure from the way in which 'absolute sovereignty' had been practised since Federation. Yet, notwithstanding the promises of 'justice, tolerance and humanity' and the claim that the Bill was the world's finest

---

[266]　Ibid 1398–9 (Alexander Downer).　　[267]　Ibid 1399 (Alexander Downer).
[268]　Ibid. Cf Amy Nethery, "'A Modern-Day Concentration Camp": Using History to Make Sense of Australian Immigration Detention Centres' in Klaus Neumann and Gwenda Tavan (eds), *Does History Matter? Making and Debating Citizenship, Immigration and Refugee Policy in Australia and New Zealand* (ANU E Press, 2009) 65. On the dehumanising effect of seeing people as concentration camp numbers also came up in the course of the High Court proceeding in *Chu Kheng Lim*: see Chapter 5, Section 5.2.3.3, 200–202.
[269]　CPD, House of Representatives, 1 May 1958, 1399 (Alexander Downer).　　[270]　Ibid.
[271]　Ibid 1400 (Alexander Downer).

immigration charter yet, like the Immigration Restriction Bill, there was no intention that the Migration Bill be the "last word".[272] Moreover, Downer had reassured the Parliament at the outset that the Bill's purpose was one of consolidation and amendment rather than a departure from existing policy; it had, he said, "nothing to do with the Government's current immigration policy; its primary concern [was] with the mechanism by which national policy is implemented."[273]

4.4 'ABSOLUTE SOVEREIGNTY': A HALLOWED DOCTRINAL PLACE

As the foregoing has made visible, 'absolute sovereignty' has, as a constitutional form, been ascribed a hallowed doctrinal place in Australian migration lawmaking,[274] bolstered by the common law doctrine of 'absolute sovereignty' that emerged in the nineteenth century. Through a close reading of constitutional convention debates, parliamentary debates, and legislative and judicial text, this chapter has made visible the repertoires and patterns of argument that have enabled the discourse of 'absolute sovereignty' to hold in relation an historical claim about institutional practice and a doctrinal claim about political and juridical authority. As I have argued, the way in which the doctrine of 'absolute sovereignty' has been underwritten as authoritative reveals it to be historically contingent. In addition to showing how the foreigner-sovereign relation has been shaped doctrinally – both constitutionally and through the common law – we have seen how the doctrine of precedent has been used to proclaim 'absolute sovereignty' as uncontroversial and settled law. Likewise, the chapter has made visible the way in which the doctrine of responsible government has been used to justify and validate unbridled power and to repudiate the risk of abuse.

Building on the analysis in the first two chapters of the genealogy, this chapter enables us to see the multiple ways in which 'absolute sovereignty' as a practice has taken juridical shape as an assemblage of responses and rationalisations that have positioned 'absolute sovereignty' as structurally indifferent to migration law's effects.[275] We have seen examples of the ways in which this has happened, including a preference in the legislature for broad discretionary powers. They have also included a predisposition in the judiciary to be highly

---

[272] Ibid 1396 (Alexander Downer). On the Immigration Restriction Bill 1901 (Cth), a similar point was made by Alfred Deakin: above 131.
[273] CPD, House of Representatives, 1 May 1958, 1396 (Alexander Downer).
[274] Nietzsche, above n 112, Owen, above n 112; see also Chapter 1, Section 1.2.1, 23–4.
[275] Nietzsche, above n 112, Owen, above n 112; see also Chapter 1, Section 1.2.1, 23–4.

deferential in interpreting the scope of the aliens and immigration powers, declining to look behind, beneath, or beyond their historical scope or exercise.[276] In addition, the chapter has highlighted recurring themes, such as the tendency of the legislature to treat adverse judicial findings as prompts for 'remedial' or 'curative' legislative measures to 'restore control' rather than opportunities to reflect on and modify excesses in administrative law and practice.

The analysis has also paid close attention to the political-economic purposes that have informed particular linguistic choices, the way in which political and legal arguments have been shaped and counterarguments erased, and the administrative practices and techniques that have been used in their implementation. It has made clear how the political-economic priority of (racial) purity and (economic) prosperity, encapsulated in the 'cherished national policy'[277] of White Australia, shaped political, juridical, and institutional perspectives on 'absolute sovereignty'. It has also shown how particular linguistic choices were designed to uphold its overarching political-economic purposes, to navigate political and diplomatic sensibilities, and to denigrate or neutralise counter-narratives.

So, for example, in the name of 'self-preservation' – pitched as 'the highest law' – unwelcome migrants were depicted as a threat to racial 'purity' and economic 'prosperity'. They were denigrated as a 'dangerous' 'mass of humanity', unworthy of and ungrateful for 'hospitality', and sure to lower 'living standards'. To argue otherwise was dismissed as unpatriotic and 'un-Australian'. And those Asians who (patriotically) remained in their countries were framed, in contrast to their peripatetic compatriots, as people of 'goodwill' and 'high principles' who had not 'abandoned' their country to 'stain' and 'contaminate' the shores of Australia. These were people implicitly content to remain at arm's length and (therefore) to whom the Australian people would gladly provide training, technological knowledge, and expertise, and, what is more, guidance in social organisation, as long as they (Asians) stayed away.[278]

As we have seen in this chapter, the first half of the twentieth century was a period during which sweeping measures of exclusion were made possible through the conferral of wide discretionary powers that would, at least in

---

[276] See, eg, Williams, above n 7.
[277] *Walsh and Johnson* (1925) 37 CLR 36, 81–2 (Isaacs J), discussed above 139–40.
[278] The notion of 'splitting', whereby condemnation of some members of the out-group (unpatriotic Asians) is legitimated by positive representation of other members (patriotic Asians of 'goodwill' and 'high principles') is taken up in Chapter 5, in the context of 'good' refugees who wait in the 'queue' and 'bad' refugees who come by 'boat': see Chapter 5, 184–6.

their conceptualisation,[279] be consistently judicially endorsed. These powers acquired a special resilience, not least through an unswerving adherence to legal precedent and a 'positivist' jurisprudence that upheld 'absolute sovereignty' as constitutional and common law doctrine; indeed, they remained in place for decades.[280] They withstood fleeting insight into the 'latent dangers' of conferring 'naked and uninhibited power',[281] the policy transition from racial to social homogeneity, and the death of the White Australia policy,[282] as well as an increased codification of migration law intended to mitigate the arbitrariness with which migration law could be implemented.[283] Through all these changes, the certitude that underpinned 'absolute sovereignty' as a constitutional doctrine remained deeply embedded, generating and perpetuating a catalogue of practices enabled by the 'freest Constitution in the world'[284] and the 'handsome gift'[285] of the dictation test – 'the most arbitrary and the most uncontrolled discretion any one could imagine'.[286]

Drawing the elements of this three-part genealogy together, it becomes possible to see how meanings within the foreigner-sovereign relation have moved and the way in which the foreigner and the sovereign have been shaped to produce the claim of 'absolute sovereignty'. Together, the three chapters in the genealogy have made visible the contingencies in the foreigner-sovereign relation, highlighting both the mutability of the figure of the foreigner and the non-inevitability of the claim that the sovereign has an absolute power to exclude her. Nevertheless, as we have seen, 'absolute sovereignty' – as an idea, practice, doctrine, and discourse – has acquired a special resilience in Australian migration lawmaking, both politically and juridically, because of the constitutional form it has taken and the way in which it has since been bolstered by legislative power and judicial interpretation. This suggests that even though the political and juridical force that engendered and sustained the foreigner-sovereign relation in the form of 'absolute sovereignty' persists, it is an idea, practice, doctrine, and discourse that is contingent and therefore not inevitable.

---

[279] In a number of cases, the High Court or State Supreme Courts found in favour of the putative immigrant. However, in none of these cases did the Court doubt the constitutional validity of such laws. See *Christie* (1904) VLR 533; *Mann* (1905) 7 WALR 182; *Potter v Minahan* (1908) 7 CLR 272; *R v Wilson; Ex parte Kisch* (1934) 52 CLR 234. Palfreeman, above n 9, 82 n 3.

[280] The *Immigration Restriction Act 1901*, as from time to time amended, including the dictation test provided for in s 3(a), remained in force until 1958, when the *Migration Act* took its place.

[281] See above 152–4.   [282] Tavan, above n 1, 89–108.

[283] See, eg, *Migration Act; Migration Legislation Amendment Act 1989* (Cth); *Migration Reform Act 1992* (Cth).

[284] See above n 45.   [285] See above n 49.   [286] See above n 168.

What we see from the genealogy, then, is that 'absolute sovereignty' is the product of a complex institutional story about the juridical and political relation between the foreigner and the sovereign rather than being foundational to a teleological story. It makes this story visible as a synthesis of political ideas, administrative practices and techniques, and juridical forms of engagement that have been improvised, whether inadvertently or intentionally, in the construction of an unscaleable doctrinal wall of 'absolute sovereignty' – a story that, as Part II will illustrate, has enduring effects.

The discourse analyses of the legal and policy frameworks of mandatory detention and planned destitution offered in Part II show how discretionary powers (both ministerial and administrative) remain a central feature of the discourse of 'absolute sovereignty' in migration lawmaking. As we will see, in contemporary law- and policymaking, many of the practices that have been spawned by 'absolute sovereignty' in its multiple modes and registers remain jealously guarded, whether politically, juridically, or institutionally.

PART II

INTRODUCTION TO PART II

As outlined in Chapter 1, Part II of this book makes a shift from genealogy to discourse analysis. This introduction revisits the reasons for that methodological change and touches on some of the key aspects of the discourse analysis offered in the following chapters. First, however, let me recap the main arguments in Part I.

In the prologue, I introduced the contemporary policies of mandatory detention and planned destitution. I asked how migration law has made these living realities possible, even thinkable. As a way of resisting the idea that 'absolute sovereignty' provides the unanswerable answer to this and other questions, Part I engaged in a genealogy of the foreigner-sovereign relation. This made visible the historical contingency of 'absolute sovereignty' as an idea, a doctrine, and a discourse – a political and juridical inheritance. Through the genealogy, the foreigner was revealed to be a mutable figure – historically a European insider, latterly a non-European outsider – and the absolute sovereign right to exclude and condition her entry and stay to be a contingent historical artefact, which emerged and was fostered in a particular political-economic context. In this context, we saw how the non-European migrant labourer was perceived as an unwelcome (but economically expedient) outsider, the restriction of whose movement and labour was considered paramount. We also saw how the broader context of the political economy of the movement of people – where European migration was encouraged and non-European labour migration highly restricted – profoundly affected the way in which the foreigner-sovereign relation was conceptualised and understood in international law, the common law, and constitutional and administrative law. The genealogy thus provides insights into how 'absolute sovereignty' has been authorised and how we have inherited it as a discourse.

This enables us to recognise the migration discourses on which I focus in Part II *as* discourses (rather than universal truths) that are historically produced from within public and international legal traditions.

Having looked at how we inherited the discourse of 'absolute sovereignty' through the genealogy of the foreigner-sovereign relation, in Part II I look at how we understand and make contemporary use of that inheritance in relation to refugees who, as Douzinas reminds us, "have replaced foreigners as the main category of otherness in our postmodern and globalised world" – "absolute otherness."[1] I do so by analysing how migration discourses have produced and justified the policies of mandatory detention (Chapter 5) and planned destitution (Chapter 6). In this connection, discourse analysis provides insight into the continuities and discontinuities between the legal traditions and orthodoxies of the past and current politico-legal discourses of migration. It enables us to see the extent to which the execution and performance of contemporary migration law- and policymaking remain captive to the discourse of 'absolute sovereignty' and its historical antecedents.

Although the domain of migration law- and policymaking in Australia is a constantly changing – indeed volatile – landscape, mandatory detention and planned destitution remain core features of current migration policy in Australia. Case studies, therefore, enable us to see how border control measures may be conceptualised in different but complementary ways: as tools of physical exclusion (in the case of mandatory detention) and social and economic exclusion (in the case of planned destitution). Each case study seeks to capture the essential features of the policies at particular moments and to reveal how discourse is used to fortify them. In this connection, it is important to be clear that the case studies need to be understood as illustrative rather than exhaustively descriptive. In essence, therefore, their purpose is to elucidate how the predicament of the unwelcome migrant is produced by a dominant politico-legal discourse of migration underpinned – indeed, underwritten – by the discourse of 'absolute sovereignty'.

Like genealogy, as a method of intellectual inquiry, discourse analysis is interested in how law and lawmakers produce, use, and sustain meaning. Accordingly, Part II pays attention to how discursive techniques are used to justify and rationalise contemporary migration policy, whether rhetorically or institutionally. It makes visible the continuing resonances and effects of 'absolute sovereignty' as a discourse and legal tradition of long standing, but in a way that shows that 'absolute sovereignty' talk is something we do – or concede – without thinking. As an analytical frame, discourse analysis reveals

---

[1] Costas Douzinas, *The End of Human Rights* (Hart, 2000) 142.

how law is spoken, written, and practised in ways that engage with, but are not constrained by, the conventions of black-letter lawmaking such as doctrine, statutory interpretation, and doctrinal analysis. In other words, it critically engages with how doctrine is used, statute interpreted, and jurisprudence developed by looking at the structures and strategies underpinning linguistic choices, purposes, and silences – whether in parliamentary debates and other political discourse, the courtroom, judicial decisions, legislation and its extrinsic material, or policy statements and guidance.

The case studies also reflect two different discursive styles. The linguistic texture of mandatory detention discourse is rich in rhetoric, tailored, and integral to the task of persuading diverse audiences: the voting public, the legislature, and the judiciary. This style gives explicit expression to the discourse of 'absolute sovereignty'. In contrast, rhetoric plays a smaller role in the case of planned destitution, a policy domain in which the discourse of 'absolute sovereignty' works implicitly. Dry and technical, the texture of the discourses I consider in the second case study are laboriously complex and, with occasional exceptions, lack much of the rhetorical colour of the first. As I see it, this is because the task of persuasion that characterises discourses in Parliament and the courtroom has a diminished role in this second case study. That is, it describes and analyses discourses that operate under law's radar, in an un- or under-scrutinised space that, I argue, sits below, but somehow above, the law – a space where discursive techniques create silences rather than performing the task of persuasion. What we see through the case studies, then, are the powerful ways in which a discourse of 'absolute sovereignty' affects contemporary law- and policymaking, explicitly and implicitly, rhetorically and institutionally.

Through the analysis in Part II, we see how mandatory detention and planned destitution have become part of an ingrained system of thought and practice. We see how the discourse of 'absolute sovereignty' remains paradigmatic to the way we think, talk, and write about unsolicited migration to the point that we scarcely notice how – or even that – we reproduce it because it is so (or too) close, so (or too) immediate, so (or too) much a part of us.[2] The analysis shows how parallel and mutually self-validating discursive themes of state control and restraint on the one hand and of the asylum seeker's deviance and opportunism on the other operate within an institutional setting

---

[2] Michel Foucault, 'La philosophie analytique de la politique' in Daniel Defert and François Ewald (eds), with Jacques Lagrange, *Michel Foucault: Dits et écrits – 1954–1988* (Gallimard, 1994) vol 3, 534, 540–1; Anne Orford, 'In Praise of Description' (2012) 25(3) *Leiden Journal of International Law* 609, 617–18. See Chapter 1, 36.

accustomed to absolute power. Coupled with the theme of silence, which gives overarching expression to the way in which discourse is structured and managed politically, legislatively, and jurisprudentially, these three themes reveal the linguistic and technical means by which 'absolute sovereignty' as a discourse is executed, performed, and sustained through text, talk, and silence. I argue that this happens in four key ways.

First, migration lawmakers continue to essentialise 'absolute sovereignty'. Second, where a policy targets or predominantly affects (non-European) foreigners, sensitivity to the racialised undercurrents of 'absolute sovereignty' remains high (whether in the form of pre-emptive denial, angry repudiation, or textual silence). Third, any risk of abuse that inheres in the exercise of 'absolute sovereignty' is discursively consigned to the theoretical on the basis that those enjoying such power can be relied upon to exercise it responsibly.[3] Finally, where the idea of 'absolute sovereignty' raises any residual doubt about the propriety of its use, it is justified by characterising those subject to it as undesirable or unworthy of law's protection and those opposed to it as unpatriotic.

The introduction of each chapter in Part II begins by describing the policy I consider, before locating the chapter within the wider argument of the book and offering an outline. The body of each chapter is then divided into three principal parts, describing and analysing the rhetorical and institutional techniques that have shaped the particular policy under consideration.

---

[3] This is the doctrinal coupling of representative government and responsible government, which assumes that governments that do not use their power responsibly will be voted out: see, eg, John M Williams, 'Race, Citizenship and the Formation of the Australian Constitution: Andrew Inglis Clark and the "14th Amendment"' (1996) 42(1) *Australian Journal of Politics and History* 10, 19; Hilary Charlesworth, *Writing in Rights: Australia and the Protection of Human Rights* (UNSW Press, 2002) 25. See further Chapter 4, 116–17.

5

Mandatory Detention

In November 1989, 26 Indochinese[1] 'boat people' arrived in Australian terri-torial waters.[2] They were the first to arrive since 1981. Over the next nine years, 'boat people' continued to arrive,[3] at a rate of less than one person per day.[4] Yet, this spectre was met with a public hysteria that only increased in volume and pitch over the coming years.[5] The Prime Minister of the day, Bob Hawke, who had spontaneously made sweeping humanitarian concessions to thou-sands of Chinese students in the wake of the Tiananmen Square massacre,[6]

[1] Members of this cohort were predominantly Cambodian, Vietnamese, and later Chinese: Human Rights and Equal Opportunity Commission (HREOC), 'Those Who've Come across the Seas: Detention of Unauthorised Arrivals' (Report, 1998) 246–50. For an historical account of 'boat people', see Claire Higgins, *Asylum by Boat: Origin's of Australia's Refugee Policy* (NewSouth Publishing, 2017); for a socio-political account of the Indochinese in Australia, see Nancy Viviani, *The Indochinese in Australia, 1975–1995: From Burnt Boats to Barbecues* (Oxford University Press, 1996).

[2] See, eg, ibid 246–50; Janet Phillips and Harriet Spinks, 'Boat Arrivals in Australia since 1976' (Research Paper, Parliamentary Library, Parliament of Australia, first published 25 June 2009, statistical appendix updated 23 July 2013); Gwenda Tavan, *The Long Slow Death of White Australia* (Scribe, 2005) 205.

[3] Phillips and Spinks, 'Boat Arrivals', above n 2, Appendix A; Department of Immigration and Border Protection (DIBP), *Fact Sheet 65 – Bridging Visas for Illegal Maritime Arrivals* (13 October 2014) <https://www.immi.gov.au/media/fact-sheets/>. From 1998, the demographic profile of arrivals changed as global hotspots changed. Since that time, numbers have increased significantly. See, eg, DIBP, 'Asylum Trends: Australia 2012–13 – Annual Publication' (2013).

[4] Tony Vinson, Marie Leech, and Eve Lester, 'The Number of Boat People: Fact and Perception' (Brief Research Report No 1, Uniya, 1997).

[5] See, eg, Sharon Pickering and Caroline Lambert, 'Deterrence: Australia's Refugee Policy' (2002) 14(1) *Current Issues in Criminal Justice* 65; David Marr and Marian Wilkinson, *Dark Victory* (Allen & Unwin, 2003) 30, 37; John Menadue, Arja Keski-Nummi, and Kate Gauthier, 'A New Approach: Breaking the Stalemate on Refugees and Asylum Seekers' (Centre for Policy Development, August 2011) 18.

[6] See, eg, Jia Gao, 'Chinese Students in Australia' in James Jupp (ed), *The Australian People: An Encyclopedia of the Nation, Its People and Their Origins* (Cambridge University Press, 2001)

was uncompromising in his unwelcome, deploying the remarkably effective but highly misleading metaphor of the 'queue-jumper'.[7]

At the time, it was ordinary practice for the Immigration Department to detain unauthorised arrivals for a limited period of seven days (or longer by consent), and such detention was subject to review by an independent authority.[8] However, for the 'boat people' in this instance, the Department elected to detain them under a different provision.[9] The provision, designed for stowaways, authorised detention as a short-term measure 'until the departure of the vessel' or 'until such earlier time as an authorized officer directs'.[10] Although its use was doubtful and, the High Court of Australia ('the High Court') would eventually conclude, unlawful, its value to government was that it lacked the inconvenience (and safeguards) of periodic review and independent scrutiny.[11]

Lodgement of applications for refugee status was slow and chaotic, and processing of claims was inordinately delayed as a result.[12] This was so even though the number of people held in detention was small.[13] These delays were variously blamed on departmental disarray or the strategy of legal advisers.[14]

<hr/>

222, 223; Don McMaster, *Asylum Seekers: Australia's Response to Refugees* (Melbourne University Press, 2002) 78.

[7]　Jana Wendt, Interview with Bob Hawke, Prime Minister (Network Nine, *A Current Affair*, Parliament House, 6 June 1990); see also Glenn Milne and Tracey Aubin, 'Bob's Not Your Uncle PM Tells Boat People', *The Weekend Australian*, 21–22 July 1990, 3. The term 'queue-jumper' was first used in Australia in 1978 by Moss Cass, Opposition Spokesman on Immigration and Ethnic Affairs: Moss Cass, 'Stop This Unjust Queue Jumping', *The Australian*, 29 June 1978, 7. It appears to have been first used by a Minister in the Australian Parliament in 1982: Commonwealth, *Parliamentary Debates*, House of Representatives, 16 March 1982, 991 (Ian Macphee, Minister for Immigration and Ethnic Affairs) (Commonwealth parliamentary debates are hereinafter referred to as 'CPD'). However, Macphee used the term more carefully than Cass, likening the acceptance as refugees of people who were not refugees as jumping a migration queue, rather than suggesting there to be a refugee queue. See also Prologue, 1.

[8]　*Migration Act 1958* (Cth) s 38 (as at 19 December 1973; now repealed); s 92 (as at 31 December 1989; now repealed).

[9]　Ibid s 88 (as at 31 December 1989; now repealed).

[10]　Ibid s 88(1) (as at 31 December 1989; now repealed).

[11]　Cf the 'elaborate safeguards' against the 'great injustices' that could be caused by 'naked and uninhibited' powers outlined by Immigration Minister Downer when introducing the Migration Bill 1958: CPD, House of Representatives, 1 May 1958, 1398 (Alexander Downer); see Chapter 4, 153.

[12]　Nick Poynder, 'Marooned in Port Hedland' (1993) 18(6) *Alternative Law Journal* 272, 274.

[13]　At the time, there were less than 500 people in immigration detention in Australia: DIBP, 'Immigration Detention and Community Statistics Summary' (30 June 2014) 5.

[14]　Human Rights Committee (HRC), *Views: Communication No 560/1993*, 59th sess, UN Doc CCPR/C/59/D/560/1993 (30 April 1997) [3.7], [5.1], [7.1], [7.4], [7.12], [7.16], [8.3] ('*A v Australia*'); see also Poynder, 'Marooned in Port Hedland', above n 12, 164.

Whatever the reasons, the Immigration Department's capacity was undoubtedly hampered by the number of Chinese students seeking protection post-Tiananmen.

It was against this background that, more than two years after their arrival, some of the asylum seekers sought an order in the Federal Court of Australia ('the Federal Court') for their release pending finalisation of their cases – a move which, as we know, triggered the passage of the mandatory detention legislation that is the focus of this chapter.[15]

~~~

In Part I of this book, the genealogy of the foreigner-sovereign relation charted how Australia has inherited the discourse of 'absolute sovereignty' in migration lawmaking. The purpose of this chapter is to explain how mandatory detention – a tool of physical exclusion – has come to be regarded as a lawful and legitimate response to unsolicited migration. To do so, it explores how Australia uses this inheritance. Asking how a framework of mandatory detention could pass so effortlessly onto the statute books and how its constitutional validity could be upheld, I analyse political and juridical discourses on mandatory detention at three levels: parliamentary debates (Section 5.1), judicial proceedings (Section 5.2) and jurisprudence of the High Court (Section 5.3). I argue that the discourse of 'absolute sovereignty' revealed by the genealogy underpins, and is reinforced by, a range of discursive techniques which have enabled various institutional actors to persuade diverse audiences – the voting public, the legislature, and the judiciary – of the lawfulness and legitimacy of mandatory detention.

This chapter is divided into three parts. In Section 5.1, I scrutinise particular discursive techniques used by the legislature to legitimise mandatory detention as a responsible and restrained form of state control and, conversely, to represent 'boat people' as deviant and opportunistic (ab)users of the system. I argue that these techniques have been integral to enabling particular aspects of mandatory detention to be framed as achieving an appropriate balance between the control imperative and institutional restraint – in short, as being in the 'national interest'. Furthermore, I argue that a discourse of restraint represented those subject to mandatory detention as still enjoying access to due process and equal treatment, despite the legislation denying them both. Finally, I identify multiple rhetorical devices used to justify and rationalise the legislation, particularly in framing 'boat people' as deviant opportunists. These devices include metaphor, repetition, innuendo, hyperbole,

---

[15] Prologue, 1–3.

linguistic inversion,[16] deflection, and 'splitting'.[17] They also include pre-emptive
defence strategies that commonly feature in elite discourse, such as positive self-
presentation juxtaposed with negative descriptions of the target group,[18] as well
as justificatory 'but' framings that characterise stringency against out-groups as a
virtue – for example, strict *but* fair,[19] tough *but* necessary.[20] These devices shape
and colour perceptions, forestalling allegations of racial and other prejudice,
and denigrating criticisms and counter-narratives.

Section 5.2 analyses the High Court proceeding challenging the constitutionality of mandatory detention,[21] a landmark case whose scope and implications are foundational to many more recent developments in Australian
migration law, including extra-territorial detention and processing. I examine
the court file,[22] comprising hearing transcripts, the court book, and written
submissions. Analysing both rhetorical and institutional techniques, I focus on
three aspects of the proceedings: (1) how the question of race rose and fell, (2)
how the metaphors of 'boat people' and the 'national interest' were invoked
and sustained, and (3) how the claim that detention and asylum seeking were
'voluntary' activities was augmented by rhetorical techniques designed to
deflect the imputation that mandatory detention was punitive. As the analysis
shows, discourses that were evident in the parliamentary debates continued to
be audible in the courtroom, albeit in a different register. While this is not
surprising, what is interesting is *how* the discursive techniques deployed in
Parliament filtered into the proceedings and, as Section 5.3 shows, how they
ultimately affected the Court's decision.

Section 5.3's analysis of the judgment in *Lim* shows how the discourse of
'absolute sovereignty' enabled the Court to validate mandatory detention
through reliance on a jurisprudence of long standing,[23] perpetuating a
(contestable) line of authority that was "frozen in an age of racial

---

[16] For example, characterising the powerful as defenceless. On technique, see Chapter 1, 23 n 82,
      above.

[17] See below Section 5.1.3.2, 183–6.

[18] As noted in Chapter 1, 38 n 137, this is the rhetorical device of 'I'm not racist/sexist/etc,
      but . . .': Teun A van Dijk, *Elite Discourse and Racism* (Sage, 1993) 72, 78, 93; Martha
      Agoustinos and Danielle Every, 'The Language of "Race" and Prejudice: A Discourse of
      Denial, Reason, and Liberal-Practical Politics' (2007) 26(2) *Journal of Language and
      Social Psychology* 123, 129.

[19] Van Dijk, above n 18, 100–2; see below n 111.

[20] CPD, House of Representatives, 5 May 1992, 2370–3 (Gerry Hand).

[21] *Chu Kheng Lim v Minister for Immigration, Local Government and Ethnic Affairs* (1992) 176
      CLR 1 ('*Lim*').

[22] *Chu Kheng Lim v Minister for Immigration, Local Government and Ethnic Affairs* (High Court
      of Australia, Proceeding No M23/1992) ('*Lim*').

[23] See Chapters 3–4.

discrimination".[24] I argue that the effect of the Court's reading of the aliens power – on which, we will see, it heard no argument – was more far reaching than upholding an existing jurisprudence; instead, it elasticised its scope. In making this argument, I analyse three interrelated aspects of the decision. First, I consider the discursive practices and techniques that led the Court to treat mandatory detention as a lawful incident of the aliens power. Second, I consider how the Court interpreted the extent to which the judicial power limits the aliens power.[25] Finally, I explore the discursive practices and techniques that enabled the Court to validate a 'decision-less' form of executive detention by characterising it as non-punitive and voluntary.

5.1 MANDATORY DETENTION: THE PARLIAMENTARY DEBATES

As we know from the prologue, in April 1992, a group of Cambodian 'boat people' detained since their arrival in Australia sought judicial review of decisions rejecting their claims for refugee status.[26] When their cases were remitted by consent, the applicants amended their statement of claim to seek interim release from detention. Already detained for over two years, the remittal of their cases would occasion further delays. The case was set down for hearing on 7 May 1992.

---

[24] *Mabo v Queensland (No 2)* (1992) 175 CLR 1, 42 (Brennan J) ('*Mabo*'). The development of a mandatory detention jurisprudence contrasts with the High Court's approach to the doctrine of *terra nullius* in the area of indigenous land rights. In relation to the latter, the High Court was prepared to unseat the doctrine of *terra nullius*. Although the Court in *Mabo* was considering a common law doctrine, not a constitutional one, Brennan J's characterisation of the doctrine of *terra nullius* as frozen in an age of racial discrimination is equally apt in relation to the aliens power and the common law doctrine of 'absolute sovereignty' that underpins it. This criticism of a legal doctrine contrasts with critiques of *Mabo* that have suggested that its theory of sovereignty locked indigenous land claims into a pre-settlement past. See, generally, Gerry Simpson, '*Mabo*, International Law, *Terra Nullius* and the Stories of Settlement: An Unresolved Jurisprudence' (1993) 19(1) *Melbourne University Law Review* 195; David Ritter, 'The "Rejection of Terra Nullius" in *Mabo*: A Critical Analysis' (1996) 18(1) *Sydney Law Review* 5. Cf *Members of the Yorta Yorta Aboriginal Community v Victoria* (2001) 110 FCR 244, 264–7 (Black CJ), addressing the 'frozen in time' approach adopted by Olney J at first instance. See also Shaunnagh Dorsett and Shaun McVeigh, 'An Essay on Jurisprudence, Jurisdiction and Authority: The High Court of Australia in *Yorta Yorta* (2001)' (2005) 56(1) *Northern Ireland Legal Quarterly* 1.

[25] Here, it is apposite to reiterate that my analysis of the Court's treatment of the aliens and immigration powers contrasts strikingly with the way the Court has approached treatment of the judicial power in migration decisionmaking: see Chapter 1, 41.

[26] Until 1993, decisions under the *Migration Act* were reviewable under the *Administrative Decisions (Judicial Review) Act 1977* (Cth) ('*ADJR Act*'): *Migration Reform Act 1992* (Cth) s 33 ('*Migration Reform Act*').

Less than 48 hours before the hearing, in a surprise move timed to stymie the imminent court proceedings, Immigration Minister Gerry Hand introduced Migration Amendment Bill 1992 (Cth). The Bill, which passed both Houses in a single evening, was described by Hand as "extraordinary"[27] and (somewhat misleadingly as it turned out) "only" an "interim" measure.[28] It amended the *Migration Act*, providing for the mandatory detention of 'boat people', termed 'designated persons'.[29] It declared that such persons *must* be detained and that they would have no remedy of release through the courts.[30] This, it was said, reflected 'the national interest'.[31]

The significance of this legislative framing was that there was to be no administrative decision to detain. Instead, detention would occur by operation of law. Because this legislative technique made detention 'decision-less', it could not be subject to judicial review.[32]

Ostensibly, a designated person's detention was to last for a maximum period of 273 days (about nine months), whereupon detainees would (at least theoretically) be subject either to release or removal.[33] This 273-day period was called 'application custody'. As we will see, however, time would be marked differently by 'application custody'. That is, at any point when the Immigration Department was not in complete control of an application – because, say, the detainee had an opportunity to provide further information or she was exercising appeal rights – the detainee remained in *custody* but her '*application* custody'[34] was interrupted.[35] In other words, the 273-day clock would stop running, which meant that 'custody' could be (and was)[36]

---

27 CPD, House of Representatives, 5 May 1992, 2370 (Gerry Hand, Minister for Immigration, Local Government and Ethnic Affairs) (Second Reading Speech, Migration Amendment Bill 1992 (Cth)).

28 Ibid.

29 *Migration Act* s 54K (as at 6 May 1992 1992; now s 177); Supplementary Explanatory Memorandum, Migration Amendment Bill 1992 (Cth).

30 *Migration Act* s 54R (as at 6 May 1992; now s 183).

31 Ibid s 54J (as at 6 May 1992; now s 176); Supplementary Explanatory Memorandum, Migration Amendment Bill 1992 (Cth).

32 Cf Transcript of Proceedings, *Chu Kheng Lim v Minister for Immigration, Local Government and Ethnic Affairs* (High Court of Australia, M23/1992, Mason CJ, Brennan, Deane, Dawson, Toohey, Gaudron, McHugh JJ, 7 August 1992) 48 (Gavan Griffith QC) ('Transcript').

33 *Migration Act* s 54Q (as at 6 May 1992; now s 182).

34 Later, the term 'custody' was omitted and 'immigration detention' substituted: *Migration Reform Act* s 38.

35 Supplementary Explanatory Memorandum, Migration Amendment Bill 1992 (Cth).

36 See, eg, *Bolkus v Tang Jia Xin* (1994) 69 ALJR 8 ('*Tang Jia Xin*'); Marion Lé, 'Reality: The Release of the *Isabella* Refugees' in Mary Crock (ed), *Protection or Punishment? The Detention of Asylum-Seekers in Australia* (Federation Press, 1993) 151.

considerably more prolonged than the 273 days of 'application custody' that the legislation foreshadowed.[37]

During the debates, parliamentarians offered a smorgasbord of colourful immigration metaphors and other rhetorical flourishes that constructed 'boat people' as an enormous problem confronting the Australian polity. This underscored the centrality of 'absolute sovereignty' as a tool for excluding the unwelcome foreigner. Hyperbole, rhetorical questions, and the ambiguity of metaphor framed the state (and the taxpayer) as the vulnerable victim, and 'boat people' as opportunistic deviants. This fuelled the perception that the proposed measures were urgent and necessary. In parallel, discursive techniques of control and restraint spoke to a combination of governmental necessity and responsibility, techniques used to rationalise and justify – and therefore moderate, at least perceptually – the oppressive effects of the provisions. Use of these techniques is addressed thematically in the sections that follow.

5.1.1 *'Boat People' and the 'National Interest': Ambiguous Metaphors*

Most parliamentarians focused on the idea that absolute control of the border was in the 'national interest'. This position was enhanced by the portrayal of 'boat people' as lawless opportunists,[38] people whose entry into the community, it was said, would erode the "integrity" of the immigration programme.[39] Interventions from both sides of politics liberally deployed the rhetoric of vulnerability[40] and risk.[41] Yet, echoing the cry of national fragility that characterised earlier discourses of self-preservation,[42] these vulnerabilities and risks were (by and large) expressed as needs of the Australian community, not the 'boat people'.[43]

---

[37] The mandatory detention scheme was later expanded to include all 'unlawful non-citizens', removed the 273-day time limit on detention, and set no upper limit for the duration of detention: *Migration Reform Act* s 13.

[38] Sharon Pickering, 'Common Sense and Original Deviancy: News Discourses and Asylum Seekers in Australia' (2001) 14(2) *Journal of Refugee Studies* 169; Pickering and Lambert, above n 5, 75. Richards describes the 'boat people' as being (perceptually) "an anarchic and sinister threat to Australian security": Eric Richards, *Destination Australia: Migration to Australia since 1901* (UNSW Press, 2008) 282.

[39] CPD, House of Representatives, 5 May 1992, 2389 (Andrew Theophanous); Supplementary Explanatory Memorandum, Migration Amendment Bill 1992 (Cth).

[40] Tavan, above n 2, 214.

[41] Even the risk of disease was mentioned: CPD, House of Representatives, 5 May 1992, 2378 (Graeme Campbell); cf at 2383 (Michael MacKellar).

[42] See Chapter 3 Sections 3.2.2, 92–4, and 3.3.3.2, 99–101; Chapter 4 Section 4.2.1.3, 123. Cf Chapter 2 Section 2.3.2, 70–71.

[43] Cf CPD, Senate, 5 May 1992, 2245 (Christabel Chamarette).

Introducing the Bill, Hand made no secret of the fact that 'boat people' were the legislative target. Clearly anticipating a constitutional challenge, he described his speech as "very carefully crafted",[44] and he was at pains to characterise this "crucial" and "vital"[45] Bill as meeting an urgent necessity. He described the release of 'boat people' as undermining "the Government's strategy for determining their refugee status or entry claims".[46] Expressing the Government's determination to send a "clear signal ... that migration to Australia may not be achieved by simply arriving in this country and expecting to be allowed into the community", Hand asserted that Australia "cannot afford" to do otherwise.[47]

Although deterrence was undoubtedly the purpose of the 'clear signal',[48] Hand did not elaborate on the claim that Australia was at risk if 'boat people' were not detained. Nor did he elaborate on the claim that the Government's strategy would be undermined, how or why detention was essential to it, or why release was 'unaffordable'. Even though only a small percentage of asylum seekers were held in immigration detention at the time, he did not need to elaborate; the claims already had the irrefutable status of truth. Yet it is clear that any order for release would have been conditional. In other words, there was no legal or factual basis for suggesting that release of those who 'simply' arrive would have 'achieved' migration to Australia. Instead, through hyperbole and innuendo, the complexity of their predicament was obscured by building on the perception that 'boat people' believed they were entitled to protection. This discursively positioned 'boat people' as unwelcome outsiders whose liberty was unworthy of law's protection[49] and whose exclusion was rational and necessary. As we will see, this also provided a way of deflecting debate about the adequacy of safeguards under the proposed scheme.[50]

---

[44]   CPD, House of Representatives, 5 May 1992, 2389 (Gerry Hand). The Second Reading Speech and Explanatory Memorandum to a Bill as well as parliamentary debates relating thereto were regarded as extrinsic material that may be used in the interpretation of a provision in an Act: *Acts Interpretation Act 1901* (Cth) ss 15AB(2)(e), 15AB(2)(f), 15AB(2)(h).

[45]   CPD, House of Representatives, 5 May 1992, 2370–3 (Gerry Hand).   [46]   Ibid.   [47]   Ibid.

[48]   Although 'deterrence' was not a term used during the course of the debates, the Solicitor-General affirmed it as the legislative purpose in the course of his submissions in *Lim*: see below 193.

[49]   In Cabinet, Hand reportedly described the latest boatload as "not a pretty mob, mostly gangsters and madams" and offered "vivid anecdotes of the wickedness of the boat people and their sinister manipulators (Chinese tongs this time)": Neal Blewett, *A Cabinet Diary: A Personal Record of the First Keating Government* (Wakefield Press, 1999) 43, 106; Richards, above n 38, 306.

[50]   See also below 179–81.

In an invidious inversion of the power relation, Hand cast 'boat people' as threats and aggressors, with the Australian government – the repository of absolute power – in the role of defenceless victim.[51] The (innocent) victims in this border drama were, he said, the departmental officers (who "cannot defend themselves")[52] and even Hand himself, who claimed to have been subject to "pressure", "deceit" and "manipulation".[53] On the other hand, the (iniquitous) wrongdoers were constructed through what Pickering and Lambert have since described as "an incessant background hum of discourses of deviance",[54] discourses that cast 'boat people' as 'queue-jumpers'[55] who implicitly lacked bona fides because their entry was 'illegal'.

Nurturing the theme of deviance and opportunism, rhetorical sleights actively denigrated and dismissed criticism. For example, seeking to vitiate their moral identity, the 'boat people's' lawyers[56] were described as "slick" and "sleazy",[57] and other supporters as (misguided) 'do-gooders'[58] or, worse,

---

51 It was not until August 2001, when SAS troops were deployed to intercept 433 asylum seekers rescued at sea by a Norwegian freighter, the *MV Tampa*, that national security discourses (re) claimed a prominent place in the debate on 'absolute sovereignty'. As Chapters 3 and 4 remind us, discourses of security were anything but new. Devetak attributes this revival to the fact that, after the end of the Cold War, 'asylum seekers' replaced 'Communists' as the leading existential threat to Australia: Richard Devetak, 'In Fear of Refugees: The Politics of Border Protection in Australia' (2004) 8(1) *International Journal of Human Rights* 101, 102. See also Don McMaster, 'Asylum-Seekers and the Insecurity of a Nation' (2002) 56(2) *Australian Journal of International Affairs* 279.

52 CPD, House of Representatives, 5 May 1992, 2389 (Gerry Hand).

53 Ibid. For a more recent example, see Paul Karp, 'Peter Dutton "demonised" by Labor over refugee remarks, says Malcolm Turnbull', *The Guardian* (online), 19 May 2016 <https://www.theguardian.com/australia-news/2016/may/19/peter-dutton-demonised-by-labor-over-refugee-remarks-says-malcolm-turnbull>.

54 Pickering and Lambert, above n 5, 75.

55 CPD, House of Representatives, 5 May 1992, 2385 (Andrew Theophanous); see also at 2358 (Philip Ruddock, Shadow Minister for Immigration). Note that the idea of queue jumping also found favour during the Senate debate on the Bill: CPD, Senate, 5 May 1992, 2251 (Michael Baume), 2255 (Nick Bolkus, Brian Harradine). Cf Christobel Chamarette, at 2260, who was the only Senator who took issue with the term 'queue-jumper'. The metaphor of the 'queue-jumper' has both descriptive and normative effect. Not only does it create a (non-existent) queue, but it also creates a normative expectation that people should wait in it. The denial that such a queue exists is met with popular incredulity that is difficult to dislodge: Keith Cunningham-Parmeter, 'Alien Language: Immigration Metaphors and the Jurisprudence of Otherness' (2011) 79(4) *Fordham Law Review* 1545, 1551.

56 In Cabinet, Hand reportedly described immigration lawyers as the "worst kind of human beings" he had ever encountered: Blewett, above n 49, 162; Richards, above n 38, 306.

57 CPD, House of Representatives, 5 May 1992, 2389 (Gerry Hand) ("slick"), 2378 (Graeme Campbell) ("sleazy").

58 Ibid 2361 (Gerry Hand); Richards, above n 38, 306; Blewett, above n 49, 106.

"parasites" feeding off the plight of "these people"[59] and liars.[60] The motives of other 'humanitarians' were disparaged and maligned by use of the qualifying term 'so-called'.[61] And any media outlets casting 'boat people', their representatives, or supporters as anything other than deviant opportunists were scornfully dismissed as 'bleeding hearts'.[62]

5.1.1.1 A System in Crisis: Restoring Control

The debate in both Houses was wide ranging and often strayed from the immediate subject matter of the Bill, but even when the text was off point, it was still on message, maintaining the impression of a system in "crisis".[63] According to this message, it was incumbent on the legislature to restore the control that had been wrested from it by people unconcerned about or uncommitted to Australia's 'national interest', whether 'boat people' or unpatriotic Australians.[64] Concerns were expressed not only about the numbers of 'boat people' currently detained (389 at the time),[65] but also the untold (and invisible) numbers who "may arrive"[66] in Australian territorial waters. It was suggested that there had been "a very significant increase in asylum claims over the last decade",[67] from 500 per year to 23,000. As we know, the bulk of this increase was attributable to humanitarian concessions to Chinese students,[68] not all of whom were asylum seekers and none of whom were 'boat people'. It was therefore neither germane to the issue of detention[69] nor

---

[59] CPD, Senate, 5 May 1992, 2255 (Nick Bolkus). Use of the term 'these people' serves to create both diminishment and distance between the speaker and the category of persons to which it refers: see, eg, Jennifer L Beard, *The Political Economy of Desire* (Routledge-Cavendish, 2007).

[60] A senior member of the Church hierarchy (a bishop) was described by Hand as a liar. However, by declining to name him, or indeed to elaborate on the accusation, Hand ensured that no response was possible: CPD, House of Representatives, 5 May 1992, 2389 (Gerry Hand).

[61] Ibid 2378 (Graeme Campbell).

[62] Ibid. Although the language used by Campbell was undoubtedly more colourful and less restrained than that of his colleagues, he was neither sanctioned nor corrected. At 2389, the Minister thanked him for his participation in the debate.

[63] Ibid 2373 (Philip Ruddock).

[64] Here, reference was made to migration agents who, it was said, were the "scum of the earth" and "do not give a damn about this country or its best interests": ibid 2378 (Graeme Campbell). This call to patriotism is reminiscent of earlier debates: see, eg, CPD, House of Representatives, 9 June 1949, 814 (Arthur Calwell, Minister for Information and Minister for Immigration), discussed in Chapter 4 Section 4.3.2.1, 143–4.

[65] See, eg, CPD, House of Representatives, 5 May 1992, 2373 (Philip Ruddock).   [66] Ibid.

[67] Ibid; CPD, Senate, 5 May 1992, 2251 (Michael Baume).   [68] See above 163.

[69] Except in the context of departmental workload: see above 164–5; see also *Lim* (1992) 176 CLR 1, 71–2 (McHugh J), discussed below 224.

necessarily even to the issue of asylum. Nonetheless, the figures were left hanging, fuelling the impression of a system – and a nation – overwhelmed and in crisis because of the 'boat people'.[70] What we see, then, is that the perception of 'boat people' as deviant opportunists was cultivated through the rhetorical devices of metaphor, innuendo, hyperbole, and linguistic inversion. This enabled a sense of urgency and necessity about mandatory detention to be fostered and enhanced.[71] Simultaneously, these techniques deflected attention from the inadequacy of safeguards.

The absence of land borders was recognised to have diminished the "pressures" of unauthorised arrivals. Nevertheless, in another inversion of the power relation, Australia was described as "particularly vulnerable"[72] to boat arrivals – an observation juxtaposed with the suggestion that the "asylum route is being increasingly abused".[73] Despite asserting (accurately, but extraneously)[74] that the legislation left the refugee status determination procedure "untouched",[75] this assertion characterised 'boat people' as the cause of Australia's particular vulnerability – from which it needed to be protected – and as abusers of the system. Thus, reflection on the vulnerability and protection needs of 'boat people' themselves was silenced – squeezed out by dominant discourses of control,

---

[70] Certainly, an escalation in the number of armed conflicts following the end of the Cold War accounted for significant increases in refugee movements and asylum applications globally. However, while Australia was resettling refugees under its humanitarian resettlement program at the time at an average of 11,255 per annum (1985–1993), it made no 'spontaneous' grants of asylum between 1985 and 1988, and an average of 1,200 per annum between 1989 and 1993: United Nations High Commissioner for Refugees (UNHCR), 'Populations of Concern to UNHCR: A Statistical Overview' (1994) Tables 14–15.

[71] Boletsi sees this as the cultivation of a myth of the 'barbarian' threat: Maria Boletsi, 'Barbaric Encounters: Rethinking Barbarism in C P Cavafy's and J M Coetzee's *Waiting for the Barbarians*' (2007) 44(1/2) *Comparative Literature Studies* 67, 67.

[72] CPD, House of Representatives, 5 May 1992, 2373 (Philip Ruddock); CPD, Senate, 5 May 1992, 2251 (Nick Bolkus, Michael Baume).

[73] CPD, Senate, 5 May 1992, 2251 (Nick Bolkus).

[74] The refugee status determination procedures would later be the subject of considerable change, including establishment of the Refugee Review Tribunal, circumscription of judicial review grounds, and statutory redefinitions of and constraints on eligibility criteria: *Migration Reform Act*.

[75] CPD, Senate, 5 May 1992, 2251 (Nick Bolkus); see also CPD, House of Representatives, 5 May 1992, 2373 (Philip Ruddock). See also Supplementary Explanatory Memorandum, Migration Amendment Bill 1992 (Cth); cf CPD, Senate, 5 May 1992, 2235 (Sid Spindler, Brian Harradine), who raised concerns about the legislation's compliance with international law: *Convention relating to the Status of Refugees*, opened for signature 28 July 1951, 189 UNTS 150 (entered into force 22 April 1954) art 31 ('*Refugee Convention*'); *International Covenant on Civil and Political Rights*, opened for signature 16 December 1966, 999 UNTS 171 (entered into force 23 March 1976) (*ICCPR*) art 9. In 1997, mandatory detention of one of the 'boat people' was found to be arbitrary and unlawful, in breach of *ICCPR* art 9: *A v Australia*, UN Doc CCPR/C/59/D/560/1993.

necessity, and national vulnerability. Instead, the 'national interest', which served an ascendant collectivity while at the same time concealing which – or whose – collective interests were being served,[76] provided the primary justification for the Bill.[77]

5.1.1.2 The 'National Interest': 'Our' Metaphor

The 'national interest' conceptualises the nation as person. It stakes its claim to self-interest and independence (which it calls sovereignty) in order to preserve its integrity.[78] However, what we do not see in the 'national interest' as a claim (what Lakoff calls the State-as-Person metaphor) is how social, racial, religious, and political interests and ideologies[79] have shaped it – here, the political-economic interests and ideologies that historically framed the foreigner-sovereign relation as a claim of 'absolute sovereignty'. As this analysis argues, in contemporary migration lawmaking, 'national interest' is an idea within which this history can reside but remain (usefully) undefined and unclear. The 'national interest' as a claim is, therefore, a perfect proxy for 'absolute sovereignty'.

The debate in both Houses deployed liberally, loosely, and interchangeably the terms 'national interest' and 'best interests' to reference essentially the same (unelaborated) thing.[80] For example, Senator Baume declared, "Let this chamber and this Parliament concentrate on what is in Australia's best interests. ... I believe that it is in our best interests to get on with dealing with this legislation on its merits, now."[81] On the strength of this, he claimed Australia's right to "our own integrity as a nation" and even a "right to ... self-determination".[82] Thus, through repeated (but unelaborated) assertion, the (political) claim that the

---

[76] George Lakoff, 'Metaphor and War: The Metaphor System Used to Justify War in the Gulf' (Pt 1) (1991) 3(3) *Viet Nam Generation: A Journal of Recent History and Contemporary Issues* <www2.iath.virginia.edu/sixties/HTML_docs/Texts/Scholarly/Lakoff_Gulf_Metaphor_1.html>.

[77] *Migration Act* s 54J (as at 6 May 1992; now s 176); see also *Migration Act* s 4.

[78] Lakoff, above n 76.   [79] Ibid.

[80] Decisions as to the meaning of 'national interest' are, according to Barwick CJ, "not hedged, nor can [they] be hedged, around with principles of the kind that the judiciary are wont to consider: nor is it necessary, or convenient, or indeed desirable, that reasons be assigned for the determination of those questions": *Salemi v Mackellar (No 2)* (1977) 137 CLR 396, 402 ('*Salemi*'). The 'national interest' in the context of immigration works at a number of levels. In addition to the 'national interest' providing the justification for mandatory detention, it operates as a general claim (*Migration Act* s 4(1)) and as a justification for non-disclosure of information on the grounds of prejudice to security, defence, international relations, or Cabinet processes (*Migration Act* s 5(1)). More recently, it has operated as a basis for denying access to merits review (*Migration Act* ss 339, 411) and as a non-specified justification for refusal or cancellation on character grounds (*Migration Act* ss 501, 501A, 501B).

[81] CPD, Senate, 5 May 1992, 2239 (Michael Baume).   [82] Ibid.

legislation was in Australia's national and best interests acquired force and momentum. This was so, notwithstanding a (contestable) claim by Hand to be "acting in the best interests of this nation *and the applicants*"[83] and a contrary attempt by a dissenting voice suggesting that Australia's 'best interests' would be better served by "justice, fairness and not changing the rules midstream".[84]

Significantly, as these repeated invocations of 'nation', 'self-determination', and 'best interests' reveal, the metaphor of 'national interest' operated as a proxy for the doctrine of 'absolute sovereignty' and has parallels with the discourses of self-preservation that characterised the 'absolute sovereignty' jurisprudence of the nineteenth century.[85] As the next two subsections show, use of the metaphors 'boat people' and 'national interest' set up a rhetorical interplay between unwelcome foreigners and the sovereign in which the battle lines against the 'barbarians at the border' were dramatically drawn.[86]

5.1.1.3 'Boat People': Visible Invisibility

The legal tradition of 'absolute sovereignty' provides a means by which distinctions that justify differential treatment are carved out. Discursively, techniques such as the use of metaphor encode in a debate multiple and ambiguous meaning. For example, 'boat people' as a term bears no explicit markers of social, economic, and moral value, yet it carries social, economic, and moral meaning. It is a trope that uses 'boat' as an adjective to describe certain 'people' and thereby imputes to them – as if an homogenous whole – certain behaviours and characteristics.

The term's meaning to both user and audience will vary; in some it will evoke compassion, in others resentment. This flexibility (and ambiguity) of meaning is what gives it its discursive value.[87] As a political metaphor, 'boat people' has come to signify undesirability, un-welcomeness, and 'queue-jumpers' unworthy of or abusing the "privilege"[88] of

---

[83] CPD, House of Representatives, 5 May 1992, 2389 (Gerry Hand) (emphasis added).

[84] CPD, Senate, 5 May 1992, 2240 (John Coulter). Senator Coulter (Australian Democrats) voted against the legislation but indicated during debate that he supported the Bill in principle and that his main objection was to its timing and its objective of stymieing an existing legal proceeding.

[85] Chapter 3 Sections 3.2.2, 92–4, and 3.3.2, 96–7; see also Chapter 4 Section 4.2.1.3, 123.

[86] As Lakoff and Johnson point out, it is people in power who get to choose, use, and impose metaphors: George Lakoff and Mark Johnson, *Metaphors We Live By* (University of Chicago Press, 1981) 157; see also Cunningham-Parmeter, above n 55, 1550.

[87] See generally Agoustinos and Every, above n 18.

[88] CPD, Senate, 5 May 1992, 2249 (Jim McKiernan).

Australia's generosity.[89] Accompanied by a moralising discourse of deviance that effectively criminalises 'boat people' and delegitimises their motives, harsh treatment can be characterised as a 'tough' but 'necessary' virtue.

Mindful of this ambiguity, my use of the term 'boat people' is intended to remind my reader (and me) of the work it is doing, evoking an image of huddled masses of foreignness arriving on overcrowded fishing boats.[90] So, I use it to underscore the 'visible invisibility' that the term evokes in the public imagination. This positions 'boat people' very publicly (and visibly) as transgressors but obscures the individual within that same imagination. This is what makes it possible to foster the myth that 'boat people' are a threat from which 'we' need to be protected.[91]

5.1.1.4 'National Interest': An Insuperable Truth

Beneath the colourful rhetoric and at the core of this dramatisation lies a deeply embedded, immovable (and bipartisan) assurance requiring no elaboration: that Parliament is *"entitled to form a view* that people who enter Australia without adequate documentation are to be held in custody"[92] and that simply forming this view provides a sufficient basis for making laws – any laws – with respect to aliens.[93]

As I have argued, because there is no requirement to give meaning and content to the 'national interest', it operates as a proxy for the doctrine of 'absolute sovereignty', a proxy through which 'absolute sovereignty' has been sustained and indeed reinvigorated. Such is its force that no matter what it reveals or conceals, the mere declaration of the 'national interest' suffices,[94] as

---

[89] The Australian Government's claims regarding its generosity towards refugees is a continuing theme: Philip Ruddock, 'The Broad Implications for Administrative Law under the Coalition Government with Particular Reference to Migration Matters' (1997) 48 *Administrative Review* 4, 7; CPD, House of Representatives, 22 November 1999, 12305 (De-Anne Kelly); Chris Bowen, Minister for Immigration and Citizenship, 'Supporting Refugees on World Refugee Day' (Media Release, 20 June 2011). For commentary, see, eg, Pickering and Lambert, above n 5, 75–7; Catherine Dauvergne, *Humanitarianism, Identity and Nation: Migration Laws of Australia and Canada* (University of British Columbia Press, 2005) 7.

[90] Marr and Wilkinson, above n 5, 1–3; see generally Peter Mares, *Borderline: Australia's Treatment of Refugees and Asylum Seekers* (UNSW Press, 2nd ed, 2002).

[91] Boletsi, above n 71, 67.

[92] CPD, House of Representatives, 5 May 1992, 2373 (Philip Ruddock) (emphasis added).

[93] See, eg, *Polites v Commonwealth* (1945) 70 CLR 60, 69 (Latham CJ) ('*Polites*'); *Pochi v Macphee* (1982) 151 CLR 101, 106 (Gibbs CJ) ('*Pochi*').

[94] Campbell described national sovereignty in militaristic terms as something to be defended with Fiiis: CPD, House of Representatives, 5 May 1992, 2378 (Graeme Campbell).

insuperable a truth as 'absolute sovereignty' itself. Thus, the claim that mandatory detention was in the 'national interest' met a bipartisan satisfaction that embedded the policy of mandatory detention in Australian law. In other words, it was the availability of an absolute power that did not need to be explained that made the idea of decision-less detention thinkable and realisable. As the following subsection explores, one of the ways of achieving this was by representing the executive and legislature as rational and restrained.

5.1.2 *Mandatory Detention: Rational and Restrained*

In a gesture apparently designed to encourage members of the House to see Hand as personally epitomising moral restraint and his Government and his Department as models of responsible governance – and, no doubt, with an eye to the judiciary – Hand claimed "no wish" on the part of the Government "to keep people in custody indefinitely".[95] Indeed, he "could not expect Parliament to support such a suggestion".[96] Accordingly, he asserted that custody would be for a "limited period" only – specifically, the 273 days discussed earlier.[97]

5.1.2.1 The 273-Day Rule: A 'Calculated Tactic'

Although Hand explained that the 273-day clock could stop, he did not labour the point.[98] Instead, maintaining the impression that detention would be of limited duration, he described processing times under "optimum conditions"[99] as being about two months – that is, well short of both the nine months for which the legislative scheme provided and the more than two years the plaintiffs had already been detained. This way, he coupled representations of the scheme as rational and restrained with departmental diligence and fairness.

The Minister positioned himself as entitled to – and capable of – policing and adjudging the motives and behaviours of the 'boat people' (and their lawyers).[100] Deflecting departmental responsibility for processing delays, he insinuated that any delays were 'calculated tactics'. The clock-stopping formula was, he said, designed as an "incentive for the parties involved in the process not to embark on tactics calculated to delay the final processing of

---

[95] Ibid 2370 (Gerry Hand).   [96] Ibid.   [97] See above 168.
[98] CPD, House of Representatives, 5 May 1992, 2370 (Gerry Hand); see also at 2373 (Philip Ruddock).
[99] Ibid 2370 (Gerry Hand).   [100] Agoustinos and Every, above n 18, 126.

claims".[101] Thus, responsibility for the duration of detention could be imputed to the 'boat people' (and, by implication, their lawyers), not the executive and the legislature.

5.1.2.2 A Reluctant Jailer: "No Desire" to Detain

Working up his moral identity as a reluctant jailer,[102] Hand re-emphasised that the Government had "no desire to keep these people in custody longer than necessary", thereby amplifying his repeated insistence that he was only doing what was "necessary" and that the detainees had only themselves to blame for their continuing detention.[103] This discursive interplay juxtaposes institutional restraint with representations of 'boat people' as responsible for their own detention. This technique strategically inverted the power relation by presenting detention as within the control of those subject to it. This discursive strategy would prove central to the judgment of the High Court in *Lim*.[104]

5.1.2.3 Targeting 'Boat People': Tough but Temporary

Having established the moral parameters of the legislative scheme and underscored the Government's reluctance to detain people longer than necessary, Hand then referred to the most controversial element of the Bill: the prohibition on any court to order the release of 'boat people'.[105] This prohibition he described as "the most important aspect of this legislation".[106] While this provision ensured that detention was entirely a matter for the executive, he sought to minimise its significance by emphasising that the scheme was time limited and temporary. First, he revisited the 273-day rule. However, in doing so, he overlooked the crucial distinction between 'application custody' (which was time limited) and 'custody' (which was not).[107] Second, in another gesture overplaying the transience of the provisions, he insisted that the scheme was "only" "intended" as an "interim measure".[108]

Hand acknowledged that the legislation targeted a "specific class of persons" (it was "aimed at boat people").[109] It was, he said, intended to address only the "pressing requirements" of the current situation – a euphemism for the imminent court hearing. Then, while conceding that the legislation was

---

[101]   CPD, House of Representatives, 5 May 1992, 2370 (Gerry Hand).
[102]   Agoustinos and Every, above n 18, 126.
[103]   CPD, House of Representatives, 5 May 1992, 2370–3 (Gerry Hand).
[104]   See below Section 5.3.4.3, 223–7.   [105]   *Migration Act* s 54R (as at 6 May 1992; now s 183).
[106]   CPD, House of Representatives, 5 May 1992, 2370 (Gerry Hand).   [107]   See above 168.
[108]   CPD, House of Representatives, 5 May 1992, 2370 (Gerry Hand).   [109]   Ibid.

"tough", he foreshadowed a "revised scheme", which he said would be of "significant benefit" not only to "those responsible for administering our migration law" but also, he suggested, "to those subject to it" in terms of "simplicity, clarity and fairness."[110] So, should the legislation be considered unnecessarily harsh, through the (implicit) use of a justificatory 'but' framing, Hand invited his audience into an acquiescent expectation that the scheme would address the 'pressing requirements of the current situation' and would thereafter be revised as part of a broader vision to accord 'simplicity, clarity and fairness'. This technique of framing the measures as 'tough but temporary' implies virtuous restraint; in other words, although the measures might be 'extraordinary' and 'tough', they are only 'intended' to be short term. So, the future is bright – simple, clear, and fair.

To underscore these assurances, Hand placed his ministerial integrity on the line. Presenting himself as the epitome of responsible governance, he pledged to be "scrupulously fair and firm" and to "leave the job" before engaging in "a manipulation or sleight of hand".[111] In other words, in lieu of procedural safeguards and judicial scrutiny, he offered the personal authority of a Minister of the Crown as a form of moral guarantee of fairness and integrity. As the next subsection shows, assurances of due process would also be an important technique for deflecting criticism of executive excess.

5.1.2.4 Due Process: 'Totally and Utterly Equal'

In defending the Government's treatment of 'boat people', the Minister cast himself as a victim of the vices and voices of a misguided counter-narrative. Notwithstanding the injustice of the 'bagging' he claimed to have received from 'do-gooders',[112] he professed the backbone and determination to adhere to his principles – that is, to ensure "totally and utterly" equal treatment and the implementation of fair processing procedures.[113] Yet as this section shows, the declaration that 'boat people' would be treated 'totally and utterly equally' was a rhetorical device that diverted attention away from consideration of the adequacy of procedural safeguards relating to detention.

---

[110] Ibid 2370–3 (Gerry Hand). In fact, the 'simplified' scheme expanded mandatory detention to include all 'unlawful non-citizens' and incorporated no time limit: *Migration Reform Act* s 13.

[111] CPD, House of Representatives, 5 May 1992, 2389 (Gerry Hand). For a discussion of the analogous term 'strict but fair', see van Dijk, above n 18, 100–102.

[112] CPD, House of Representatives, 5 May 1992, 2364 (Gerry Hand).   [113] Ibid.

5.1.2.5 Ousting the Courts: Securing Fairness

Although most parliamentarians in both Houses insisted that due process (on refugee applications) would be observed,[114] and notwithstanding assurances of 'total and utter equality', with the exception of the Australian Democrats and Independent Senator Brian Harradine,[115] the complete absence of procedural safeguards received no attention. To some, such safeguards were not even a consideration in the face of the (all too familiar) claim of 'absolute sovereignty':

> Australia, and Australia alone, controls its shorelines and who comes in – and who goes out in certain cases, too. What is more, we should make no apology to anyone in the rest of the world for controlling our own shorelines.[116]

The Democrats and Harradine focused on the timing[117] and arbitrary character[118] of the legislation, which they regarded as affronts to principles of due process. In this connection, Harradine, who described the Bill as "draconian",[119] noted that his departmental briefing on the Bill had been silent about the legislation's timing (to stymie an existing legal proceeding)[120] – a silence that suggested the Immigration Department's anticipation that he would regard the Bill's purpose and timing as odious. As the Minister responsible in the Senate, it fell to Senator Bolkus to respond.

Bolkus deflected debate on the timing of the legislation as if it were happenstance, stating that "no time is a good time"[121] and asserting that the legislation (simply) embodied "the old, long held principle – ... a pivotal part of immigration policy – that anyone who enters Australia in an unauthorised way is held in custody until their case is determined."[122] This claim restates the idea of 'absolute sovereignty',[123] but with the additional and (suddenly) 'pivotal' component of mandatory detention woven into its fabric as if mandatory detention too were integral to the 'principle'. Employing the rhetorical force of repetition and

---

[114] Cf ibid 2378 (Graeme Campbell), suggesting that due process standards (that is, merits and judicial tiers of review) "clearly [do] not serve the best interests of the great majority of people of Australia." For the Opposition, Philip Ruddock also expressed the view that the *ADJR Act* should be amended to exclude judicial review of migration decisions: at 2373.

[115] See above n 75.

[116] CPD, Senate, 5 May 1992, 2243 (John Panizza). Even the Australian Democrats reinforced this view: at 2244 (Sid Spindler), 2246 (John Coulter).

[117] This was conceded by the Minister for Immigration in a letter addressed to the Senate Standing Committee for the Scrutiny of Bills: *A v Australia*, UN Doc CCPR/C/59/D/560/1993, [3.5]. However, it was also clear that the Australian Democrats were ultimately likely to have supported the Bill: CPD, Senate, 5 May 1992, 2240 (John Coulter).

[118] See, eg, CPD, Senate, 5 May 1992, 2235 (Sid Spindler, Brian Harradine), 2240 (John Coulter).

[119] Ibid 2235 (Brian Harradine).   [120] Ibid.   [121] Ibid 2237 (Nick Bolkus).   [122] Ibid.

[123] For other references to sovereignty during the debates, see, eg, ibid 2358 (Philip Ruddock), 2365 (Paul Filing), 2378 (Graeme Campbell); CPD, Senate, 5 May 1992, 2243 (John Panizza).

invoking the authority associated with already-established practices, Bolkus asserted, "It is not a new principle; it is an old one."[124] Yet there was no historical precedent in Australia for attaching this kind of exceptionalism to the deprivation of liberty, and on this scale. There was nothing old or long held about the mandatory element of detention, which had hitherto been reviewable under the *ADJR Act*[125] and the prerogative writs. Even the exceptionalism that had histori-cally justified the internment of enemy aliens under wartime and emergency powers incorporated greater safeguards than these measures against a class of persons who no one suggested were other than friendly aliens.[126]

By claiming the new to be old, mandatory detention was inscribed with the authoritative stamp of well-established principle. This had the effect of normal-ising the legislation's exceptionalism as a rational and justifiable institutional response to the unwelcome foreigner. Offering a content-deficient description of the legislation – as "imperative in order to have a process which can work"[127] – Bolkus reframed the idea of sovereignty as one that necessarily and appropriately incorporates a detention framework that is beyond the scrutiny of the courts. Thus, he sought again to deflect attention from the timing of the Bill and the fact that the plaintiffs' detention had already exceeded two years. Even as parliamentary processes actively and substantively undermined any meaningful opportunity for judicial scrutiny, Bolkus (echoing Hand and Ruddock before him) framed the legislation as securing fairness in the refugee status determina-tion (RSD) process[128] rather than subverting judicial scrutiny.

5.1.3 *Denying Prejudice, Denigrating Criticism*

In a society that no longer condones or tolerates the open expression of racist sentiment, discussions of race and racism are likely to cause offence and to elicit visceral responses. Yet notwithstanding Australia's increasing – and often cele-brated – racial diversity, there is no denying that there is still a racial dimension to the immigration debate.[129] In this section, I analyse how the issue of race affected linguistic choices and discursive repertoires and patterns during the parliamen-tary debates. My purpose is not, however, to assess whether the politicians whose

---

[124] CPD, Senate, 5 May 1992, 2237 (Nick Bolkus).   [125] See above n 26.
[126] There was no response to Harradine when he raised the issue: CPD, Senate, 5 May 1992, 2235 (Brian Harradine). On the blurring of the distinction between friendly and enemy aliens see Chapter 3, 103; cf Chapter 3, 104.
[127] CPD, Senate, 5 May 1992, 2239 (Nick Bolkus).
[128] Ibid 2237–8 (Nick Bolkus). On Hand, see above Sections 5.1.2.3–5.1.2.4. On Ruddock, see above 173.
[129] See, generally, James Jupp, *From White Australia to Woomera: The Story of Australian Immigration* (Cambridge University Press, 2nd ed, 2007).

speech choices I analyse were racist, but instead to show how management of (the perception of) prejudice in contemporary migration discourse remains affected by – and arguably captive to – a highly racialised history. This makes visible how minority out-groups continue to be negatively positioned, and their marginalisation or exclusion rationalised, by certain discourses.[130]

The self-presentation of parliamentarians supporting the mandatory detention legislation either expressly or impliedly denied the influence of race or other prejudice. However, a close reading of the *Hansard* reveals the extent to which positive self-presentation was juxtaposed with negative descriptions of 'boat people' (or their supporters and representatives).[131] When we pay attention to such juxtapositions and other recognised discursive techniques such as 'splitting',[132] it becomes clear that the speakers recognised (at least implicitly) that race and other prejudice are part of the discourse of 'absolute sovereignty' we have inherited. They constitute a part of that discourse, however, that is discernible yet unutterable and thus impels the use of strategies of dissociation. Speakers deploy classic discursive strategies to inoculate themselves against the charge of racism or other prejudice with striking regularity.[133] And while their techniques are flexible, ambivalent, and at times even contradictory, they reflect common and recurring discursive patterns that justify and rationalise reliance on a discourse of 'absolute sovereignty' that is inextricable from and inscribed with a racialised history that it cannot erase.[134] Thus, we can see that speakers feel the intractable presence of race even though they deny its influence. This tells us that race (and other forms of prejudice) have nothing and yet somehow everything to do with this legislation.[135]

In the upshot, these discursive techniques enable a 'qualitative difference' between the welcome and unwelcome foreigner to be constructed and justified. This enables claims that uphold the liberal equation of fairness, evenhandedness, decency, and legitimacy[136] but also legislatively locate 'boat

---

[130]   Agoustinos and Every, above n 18, 125.   [131]   Ibid 125–6.
[132]   For an explanation and elaboration of 'splitting', see below 185–6.
[133]   Agoustinos and Every, above n 18, 126; Étienne Balibar, 'Is there a 'Neo-Racism'? in Étienne Balibar and Immanuel Wallerstein, *Race, Nation, Class: Ambiguous Identities* (Chris Turner trans, Verso, 1991) 20 [trans of: *Race, nation, classe* (first published 1988)].
[134]   Ibid 124. See also Balibar, 'Is there a 'Neo-Racism'?, above n 133, 17.
[135]   Cf Robert Manne, who argues that Australia's asylum policy is underpinned by an absolutist ambition rather than a racialised one: Robert Manne, 'How we came to be so cruel to asylum seekers', *The Conversation* (online), 26 October 2016 <https://theconversation.com/robert-m anne-how-we-came-to-be-so-cruel-to-asylum-seekers-67542>.
[136]   Peter Fitzpatrick, 'Racism and the Innocence of Law' (1987) 14(1) *Journal of Law and Society* 119, 120.

'people' beyond that equation in key respects. Speeches by Graeme Campbell and Nick Bolkus are instructive.

5.1.3.1 Campbell: Fending Off Scurrilous Attacks

The most colourful speech in the House of Representatives debate came from Graeme Campbell, a controversial backbencher. Campbell delivered an address in highly inflammatory terms.[137] With unapologetic vitriol, he articulated his intolerance for 'boat people', their lawyers, and others with their "snouts" in the "public trough". He derided those who belonged to what he described as the "immigration industry"; they included humanitarian groups, the media, the elite, "professional multiculturalists" and "professional ethnics", and even "infestations" of academics and bureaucrats.[138] Campbell's speech also expressed anxiety about the threat of imported diseases, the problem of Asianisation, and the threat to the country and culture of the Australian people posed by 'boat people'. Pre-emptively fending off critique of his diatribe as racist, he sought to outmanoeuvre his opponents, implying that any allegation against him would be "a scurrilous attack".[139] Moreover, he condemned alleged governmental inaction concerning the threat of disease as being rooted in "fear of being branded racist".[140]

During the debate, Campbell attracted no serious censure.[141] He clearly served a political purpose beyond his constituency, not least adding popular/ist value to the attack on the counter-narrative. The discursive value of and the historical resonances in his speech suggest that he cannot be dismissed merely as an eccentric aberration.[142]

5.1.3.2 Bolkus: Smacking Down Racism

The leader of the Democrats, Senator Coulter, whose concerns related primarily to the Bill's timing,[143] raised the issue of race head on. He observed: "It smacks of racism that it is being targeted at a particular group."[144] Suggesting that it was

---

[137] CPD, House of Representatives, 5 May 1992, 2378–83 (Graeme Campbell).   [138] Ibid.

[139] Ibid. On pre-emptive defence strategies, see van Dijk, above n 18, 72.

[140] CPD, House of Representatives, 5 May 1992, 2378–83 (Graeme Campbell).

[141] Hand thanked him for his contribution: CPD, House of Representatives, 5 May 1992, 2389 (Gerry Hand). While there was criticism of some of his assertions at 2383 (Michael MacKellar), the critique could not be characterised as censure.

[142] Although Campbell had long been regarded as a maverick politician, he was not disendorsed by the Labor Party until 1998: Scott Bennett, 'The Decline in Support for Australian Major Parties and the Prospect of Minority Government' (Research Paper No 10, Parliamentary Library, Parliament of Australia, 1998–1999) Table 6.

[143] CPD, Senate, 5 May 1992, 2240 (John Coulter).   [144] Ibid 2254 (John Coulter).

possible to redraw the Bill, albeit apparently with the same effect,[145] Coulter's intervention nevertheless touched a raw nerve. Bolkus' response activated – consciously or otherwise – a rich array of rhetorical techniques that reflect the themes of control and restraint and of deviance and opportunism, and are highly sensitive to issues of race and other forms of prejudice.

Bolkus' response was sanctimonious and (strategically) outraged. He used the deflective tactic of accusation to reject out of hand the imputation of racism. In an angry retort, coupling positive self-presentation and hyperbolic prejudice against 'boat people', he clouded the issue in a discourse of deviance and opportunism. With heavy-handed and repetitive use of rhetorical questions, he cast 'boat people' as undeserving 'illegal refugees', while at the same time laying claim to law's fairness and even-handedness – a claim he suggested to be the 'benchmark' of the legislation:

> What right do illegal refugees arriving in Australia as unauthorised entrants have over refugees from other parts of the world, those who cannot come here by boat? What right do they have over refugees from the Middle East, central South America or other parts of the world? What right do they have over other people who want to come to Australia and who are also in difficult circumstances? Under our law, fairly and even-handedly, a person will be classified as to whether he or she is a refugee. That is precisely the benchmark of the Migration Amendment Bill.[146]

Furthermore, Bolkus characterised Coulter as defending the indefensible (illegal arrival): "the only immigrants he will ever defend are those who come into Australia in an unauthorised and illegal way."[147] This pre-emptively averted any counter-criticism (of an oppressive law) in the same terms.

Disparaging Coulter as a "bleeding heart" (and therefore implicitly lacking balance and judgment) who will only defend "illegals" (that is, people implicitly unworthy of being defended), Bolkus actively sought to besmirch Coulter's integrity and thereby denigrate counter-arguments.[148] This technique also 'split' refugees[149] into those who will engage with 'us' on 'our' terms, and those who will not, an approach reminiscent of

---

[145] "Why does the Government not take the opportunity now to withdraw this amendment and draw it up properly so that it does not have this overtone of racial discrimination?": Ibid 2254 (John Coulter).

[146] Ibid 2255 (Nick Bolkus).   [147] Ibid.   [148] Ibid.

[149] My use of the term 'refugee' here is loosely to connote those who are, or who seek protection as, refugees. It is not my intention to confine this discussion only to those who meet the definition of a refugee in *Refugee Convention* art 1A(2).

distinctions drawn by Arthur Calwell between patriotic Asians of 'good-will' and 'high principles' (who stay in Asia) and unpatriotic Asians (wartime refugees loath to leave Australia).[150] According to this approach, condemnation of the out-group is legitimised, while others who are notionally members of the out-group are represented positively. Bolkus sought to impugn the bona fides of the claims of 'boat people' by describing those who have not come by boat (that is, "those who are prepared to wait in the queue") as having "legitimate", "strong" claims that *can be* and *have been* tested".[151] In contrast, he implied, the legitimacy and strength of the claims of "these people"[152] could not even be tested. Then, to counter what he described as Coulter's "gross populism", Bolkus called (twice) for "decent concern" for people prepared to stand in "the queue", for those who are "legitimate refugees" (good refugees)[153] and, at the same time, for "disdain" for those "parasites in this community who are feeding off the plight of these people" (bad people exploiting bad refugees).[154]

'Splitting' is a recognised rhetorical device that fends off the accusation of racism or other prejudice by constructing distinctions within the minority group[155] – in this case, good refugees ('from the Middle East, central South America or other parts of the world', 'who cannot come here by boat')[156] and bad refugees (those coming "in an unauthorised and illegal way" who "just happen to get here by boat").[157] The primary function of this divisive pattern is, through a discursive process of 'illegalisation',[158] to legitimate the condemnation of the target group.[159] It also

---

[150] See Chapter 4, 147.

[151] CPD, Senate, 5 May 1992, 2255 (Nick Bolkus) (emphasis added).

[152] Ibid; Beard, above n 59, 63, 166, 175.

[153] CPD, Senate, 5 May 1992, 2255 (Nick Bolkus). On the politics of humanitarian admissions see Dauvergne, *Humanitarianism, Identity and Nation*, above n 89, 7.

[154] CPD, Senate, 5 May 1992, 2255 (Nick Bolkus).

[155] Raymond G Nairn and Timothy N McCreanor, 'Race Talk and Common Sense: Patterns in Pakeha Discourse on Maori/Pakeha Relations in New Zealand' (1991) 10(4) *Journal of Language and Social Psychology* 245, 251; Agoustinos and Every, above n 18, 132.

[156] As Nairn and McCreanor note, the flexibility that is retained in the device of 'splitting' enables groups and individuals to be moved in and out of categories according to the dictates of the communication goals. Nairn and McCreanor, above n 155, 251. Refugees from the Middle East would begin coming to Australia by boat from 1995: Department of Immigration and Multicultural and Indigenous Affairs (DIMIA), *Fact Sheet 74a: Boat Arrival Details (on Australian Mainland)* (6 October 2004).

[157] CPD, Senate, 5 May 1992, 2255 (Nick Bolkus); Agoustinos and Every, above n 18, 132.

[158] Harald Bauder, 'Why We Should Use the Term "Illegalized" Refugee or Immigrant: A Commentary' (2014) 26(3) *International Journal of Refugee Law* 327.

[159] Agoustinos and Every, above n 18, 132.

sidelines examination of the dominant group's history and practices.[160] Furthermore, if we think about splitting in the context of the foreigner-sovereign relation, we can see that the members of the out-group who are characterised as 'good' are good only because they are not 'here' – that is, because no relation between them as foreigners and Australia as sovereign has been established.

5.1.3.3 Sensing an Uncomfortable Truth

As the rawness of these responses to the issue of racism attest, while Australian political and legal discourse no longer sanctions explicitly racist or racialised language, migration discourse is responsive to the discomfort attached to its racialised history. As such, discursive strategies habitually present harsh treatment of 'boat people' as reasonable and justified and simultaneously protect the messenger from the charge of racism or other prejudice. This encodes an (almost) silent space in which there is an awkward awareness that the political-economic context from which the discourse of 'absolute sovereignty' was produced has residual effects. No longer so crudely hewn, we are nevertheless left with a sense that race remains an undercurrent in contemporary migration discourse even when speakers self-present as race-neutral[161] – an unutterable under-current that surfaces indignantly when prodded or provoked. Even absent a prod or provocation, however, these discursive strategies enable mean-ing to be silently transferred without the social sanction that would accompany more overt language.[162] In other words, this silent transfer neither avoids nor dismantles the underlying political-economic interests and ideologies. It reproduces them.[163] In the following section, I analyse the court file and transcript in *Lim* to see how the discourse of 'absolute sovereignty' affected proceedings.[164]

---

[160] Ibid.
[161] Cf Chapter 4 Section 4.2, 120–36. See Cunningham-Parmeter, above n 55, 1579; see also Phyllis Pease Chock, 'Ambiguity in Policy Discourse: Congressional Talk about Immigration' (1995) 28(2) *Policy Sciences* 165, 167–72, examining the racial codes of immigration rhetoric in the United States, such as words as seemingly innocuous as 'population'.
[162] Cunningham-Parmeter, above n 55, 1579; Gerald V O'Brien, 'Indigestible Food, Conquering Hordes, and Waste Materials: Metaphors of Immigrants and the Early Immigration Restriction Debate in the United States' (2003) 18(1) *Metaphor & Symbol* 33, 44–5, explaining how inhumane social policies often follow dehumanising rhetoric.
[163] Chock, above n 161, 166.   [164] *Lim* (High Court of Australia, M23/1992).

5.2 *CHU KHENG LIM*: THE PROCEEDINGS

The plaintiffs' case centred on three arguments: that the legislation interfered with the judicial power,[165] that it was invalid as an exercise of the 'external affairs power',[166] and that it was in breach of the *Racial Discrimination Act 1975* (Cth)[167] (*RDA*). Although central to the Court's decision, whether the mandatory detention legislation was a valid exercise of the aliens power was not put in issue by the parties. This is striking, yet unsurprising given that the Court has never found legislation in respect of aliens to be beyond the aliens power.

The plaintiffs' claims were distilled into a series of agreed questions, a process that offers institutional efficiency. As a process, it highlights the power of established doctrine and how scope for mounting (or revisiting) novel arguments is limited. In tune with the Chief Justice, who was emphatically unwilling to refer certain questions to the Full Court,[168] the Solicitor-General professed concern that the Court should be "protected" from questions that are "just not tenable".[169] With the weight of precedent against him, Counsel for the plaintiffs was impelled to concede that he had a "hard road to hoe".[170]

In the result, the racial discrimination argument was abandoned and just two questions were referred to the Full Court. The first went to whether s 54L (mandatory detention of designated persons), s 54N (power to detain even where release has been ordered by a court), and s 54R (general prohibition on a court from ordering release of a designated person) constituted a usurpation of the judicial power.[171] The second, consideration of which was contingent upon the invalidity of the aforementioned provisions, asked whether the

---

[165] *Constitution* ch III; Lim & Ors, 'Statement of Claim' in *Chu Kheng Lim and others v Minister for Immigration, Local Government and Ethnic Affairs*, M23/1992, undated, [26]–[28] ('Statement of Claim'). There were two limbs to this argument: first, that the legislation sought to interfere with the power of the courts to make orders for release in an existing proceeding (*ADJR Act* ss 16(1)(d), 23); second, that it purported to prohibit a court from ordering the release of a 'designated person' in any other circumstances (*Migration Act* ss 54L, 54N, 54R (as at 6 May 1992, now ss 178, 180, 183)).

[166] *Constitution* s 51(xxix); Statement of Claim, *Lim*, [4(D)], [10]–[19], [29]–[35]. The plaintiffs alleged that the legislation put Australia in breach of certain international obligations, namely *Refugee Convention* art 31(2) and *ICCPR* arts 9(1), 9(4) – obligations that were assumed pursuant to the external affairs power and were enforceable to the extent that they had been incorporated into the *Human Rights and Equal Opportunity Commission Act 1986* (Cth), the *Migration Act*, and the *Migration Regulations 1994*.

[167] *Racial Discrimination Act 1975* (Cth) (*RDA*) ss 9–10; 'Statement of Claim', *Lim*, [36]–[43].

[168] Transcript, *Lim* (24 June 1992) 6, 7. Nevertheless, he recognised that it remained open to Counsel to apply to have matters raised before the Full Court that had not been referred by him: at 5.

[169] Ibid 3 (Gavan Griffith QC).   [170] Ibid 5 (Peter Rose).

[171] Now *Migration Act* ss 178, 180, 183; *Lim* (1992) 176 CLR 1, 4.

external affairs power required the Commonwealth to have regard to obligations under the *Convention relating to the Status of Refugees*[172] ('*Refugee Convention*') and the *International Covenant on Civil and Political Rights*[173] (*ICCPR*) in deciding applications for release from custody.[174] The sections that follow show how the discursive themes of control and restraint and of deviance and opportunism played out in the courtroom. I consider how these techniques perpetuated 'absolute sovereignty' as a discourse by examining three key issues: race and other prejudice; the opposing metaphors of 'boat people' and the 'national interest'; and, finally, whether detention was voluntary or punitive.

5.2.1 *On Race and Prejudice*

As noted above, contemporary political discourse no longer sanctions (explicit) racism or racial discrimination. This can have the effect of concealing, at least partially, the work of race. Indeed, as the speeches of Campbell and Bolkus illustrate,[175] in a society in which the self-presentation of participants in public discourse is, in general,[176] vigorously to deny the influence and significance of race, evaluating the extent to which law- and policymaking is affected by race discourses becomes more difficult.[177] With this in mind, this section considers the silent transfer[178] of unarticulated – indeed, unutterable – racialised meaning embodied in ambiguous immigration metaphors such as 'illegal entrants', 'designated persons', or 'boat people'. It argues that these metaphors play a part in the structural perpetuation of a complex institutional story that, as we know, emerged in a particular political-economic context; an institutional story in which the historical priority of regulating race and labour leaves race deeply embedded.

5.2.1.1 'Designated Persons': A Discretionary Allocation

During the proceedings, the Court appeared troubled by the category 'designated person'. The Court perceived, for example, that a New Zealander on a boat in Australian territorial waters[179] – say, "fishing for flounder outside

---

[172]　See above n 75.　　[173]　Ibid.　　[174]　*Lim* (1992) 176 CLR 1, 4; see above n 166.
[175]　See above 183–6.
[176]　Cf the statement of Australia's current Attorney-General, in the context of a (now shelved) proposal to amend the *RDA*, that "people do have a right to be bigots" and "to say things that other people find offensive, insulting or bigoted": CPD, Senate, 24 March 2014, 1798 (George Brandis).
[177]　Fitzpatrick, above n 136, 120.
[178]　Cunningham-Parmeter, above n 55, 1579; O'Brien, above n 162, 44–5.
[179]　*Migration Act* s 54K(a) (as at 6 May 1992; now s 177(a)).

Sydney Heads"[180] – who is in the migration zone[181] and has not presented[182] or been granted[183] a visa might be caught by the provision and therefore subject to mandatory detention.[184] The safeguard against this eventuality was to include a discretionary power to give a person otherwise meeting the criteria an identifier – that is, a unique numerical denotation.[185] In other words, the category of 'designated person' relied on the discretionary and potentially arbitrary[186] allocation of an identifier "by departmental fiat".[187] Indeed, as Deane J surmised, definitions of 'designated person' were

> intended to be as wide and handsome as they can be, leaving everything to the good faith of someone in the Department to carry out government policy and only apply it to people within the category of people that the government had in mind.[188]

In response, the Solicitor-General resisted the suggestion that the definition extended to New Zealanders. Rather, he said, it should be understood as targeting a particular group[189] and, he submitted, it would not be "appropriate to read it as having a larger potential application than that which is intended."[190] Then, apparently gesturing to the doctrine of responsible governance, he sought to reassure the Court that the ('wide and handsome') discretionary power would be used appropriately. In other words, the identifier would not be (mis)applied to New Zealanders or other 'exempt non-citizens'[191] not because it was not *authorised*, but because they were classes of person that the Government regarded as welcome foreigners and had no *intention* of detaining. In other words, 'designated person' was nothing more than a statutory trope for 'boat people' cast in terms wide enough to avert any evidentiary problems.[192]

---

[180] Transcript, *Lim* (7 August 1992) 43 (Brian Shaw QC).
[181] *Migration Act* s 54K(c) (as at 6 May 1992; now s 177(c)).
[182] Ibid s 54K(b) (as at 6 May 1992; now s 177(b)).
[183] Ibid s 54K(d) (as at 6 May 1992; now s 177(d)).
[184] Transcript, *Lim* (6 August 1992) 5 (Deane J).
[185] *Migration Act* s 54K(e) (as at 6 May 1992; now s 177(e)). So, for example, those 26 people arriving on the boat codenamed 'Pender Bay' had the identifiers PB1–PB26, and those 119 arriving on the boat codenamed 'Beagle', B1–B119: Transcript, *Lim* (6 August 1992) 5 (Brian Shaw QC); see also DIMIA, *Fact Sheet 74a*, above n 156.
[186] *Lim* (1992) 176 CLR 1, 46 (Toohey J). Nevertheless, Toohey J found that "the discretion thereby vested in the department [did not exceed] that which the Parliament may lawfully entrust to the department as part of a law with respect to aliens".
[187] Transcript, *Lim* (7 August 1992) 49 (McHugh J).   [188] Ibid 45.
[189] The Solicitor-General described it as being "directed to a particular area": ibid 46.
[190] Ibid.
[191] For definition of 'exempt non-citizen' see *Migration Legislation Amendment Act 1989* (Cth) s 4; subsequently omitted by *Migration Reform Act* s 4.
[192] *Lim* (1992) 176 CLR 1, 23 (Brennan, Deane, and Dawson JJ).

As Deane J observed, and as the Solicitor-General confirmed, the discretionary power carried an expectation that departmental officers would understand its intended scope. In other words, the Act entrusted to them the responsibility of simply knowing that the mandatory detention provisions were not for, say, *boating people* or *people on boats* – who may be New Zealanders, flounder fishermen, or a lone yachtsman rescued at sea[193] – but for '*boat people*'. On the strength of this understanding, officers were meant to give 'boat people' a number and then to detain them; further, they were empowered to do so without judicial scrutiny.[194] Of course, both the breadth of the power and the assurance that it would not be abused drew on a long history of administrative discretion, which maintained both 'full control' over unwelcome foreigners and sufficient flexibility to ensure that welcome foreigners were not inadvertently affected.[195]

5.2.1.2 On the Niggling Question of Race: A Polish Blessing

As noted earlier, the plaintiffs dropped their argument that the mandatory detention legislation was racially discriminatory and compromised the right to equality before the law. Why did they do so? While it is clear that Cambodian nationals were not the only 'boat people' to whom the legislation applied,[196] all arrivals up to 5 May 1992 belonged to a racial minority. The argument was not, therefore, bound to fail on the grounds that the Act was *not* racially discriminatory. The key problem was s 54T, which stated that in the event of any inconsistency with any other law in Australia, whether written or unwritten (apart from the *Constitution*), the mandatory detention provisions applied.[197] So, both this provision and the absence of constitutional safeguards prevented even the possibility of making such an argument.[198] And, as we know, due process

---

[193] Tony Bullimore's yacht, *Exide Challenger*, capsized in the Southern Ocean as he attempted to sail around the world single-handedly in the 1996 Vendée Globe. He was rescued at sea by the Australian Navy. When he was brought to Perth, he was not mandatorily detained. On the contrary, more than 40 dignitaries, including federal and state politicians, turned up to welcome him: Tony Bullimore, *Saved: The Extraordinary Tale of Survival and Rescue in the Southern Ocean* (Time Warner, 1997) 228.

[194] A statement by an officer that the department has given a person a designation is conclusive evidence of the same: *Migration Act* s 54U (as at 6 May 1992; now s 187).

[195] CPD, House of Representatives, 9 June 1949, 806 (Arthur Calwell); see Chapter 4, 144. On the discretionary power 'handsomely gifted' to the nation in 1901 in the form of a dictation test, see: CPD, House of Representatives, 2 October 1901, 5505 (Edmund Barton); see Chapter 4, 120.

[196] The cohort also included Vietnamese and Chinese: see, eg, DIMIA, *Fact Sheet 74a*, above n 156.

[197] *Migration Act* s 54T (as at 6 May 1992; now s186); *Lim* (1992) 176 CLR 1, 37–8 (Brennan, Deane, and Dawson JJ), 52 (Toohey J).

[198] *Koowarta v Bjelke-Petersen* (1982) 153 CLR 168, 209, 211 (Stephen J) ('*Koowarta*').

safeguards were intentionally excluded from the *Constitution* in order to *enable* racial discrimination.[199]

Notwithstanding the statutory occlusion of the racial discrimination argument through s 54T, even an allegation of racial discrimination that cannot be tested in court is neither politically welcome nor straightforward to deal with. As discussed above, the Court's questions about New Zealanders and the potential breadth of the definition of designated person intimated disquiet about the narrowness of the legislation's target and purpose. These factors appear to have prompted the Solicitor-General to address the Court on issues of race.

The Solicitor-General argued that the definition of designated person had wider application than the plaintiffs. In particular, he drew attention to the arrival of 12 Polish nationals after the passage of the legislation, an event which appears to have come as a welcome surprise to the Commonwealth. The Solicitor-General, seemingly aware that the exception was aberrant and insufficient to disprove the rule – "perhaps unexpected as [their arrival] might have been"[200] – nevertheless capitalised on the presence of a handful of European faces by weaving into his submissions reference to the Poles in asserting the broad and general application of the legislation to 'boat people'.[201] Thus, he offered the arrival of the Poles to evidence the Act's racial 'innocence', a characterisation that he reinforced through the well-recognised technique of positive self-presentation (of the Government) and negative characterisation of the target group, explored in the following subsections.[202]

5.2.2 *Criminalising 'Boat People' and Rationalising the 'National Interest'*

During the hearing, the discourses of control and restraint, and of deviance and opportunism that typified the parliamentary debates were audible. Mandatory detention was described as necessary but tempered by gestures of institutional reluctance to deprive people of their liberty. At the same time, 'boat people' were connoted as lawless and unworthy deviants.

5.2.2.1 Criminalising 'Boat People': No Offence

In argument, the Solicitor-General used immigration metaphors such as 'boat people' with considerable regularity.[203] Members of the Bench showed a greater tendency to use the (arguably) more anodyne statutory terminology

---

[199] See Chapter 4 Section 4.1.1.2, 118–19. [200] Transcript, *Lim* (7 August 1992) 61.
[201] Ibid 62. [202] See generally Agoustinos and Every, above n 18.
[203] Transcript, *Lim* (7 August 1992) 66, 67, 81.

of 'illegal entrant'[204] or 'designated person' (unavoidably, because they had been statutorily prescribed). However, the discursive effect of such terms has equivalence with the more evocative term 'boat people', because in each case they are (legislatively imposed) tropes. Indeed, their effect is to maintain a 'visible invisibility' that makes visible the transgression but obscures the human beings enveloped by it, characterising them (and the asylum they seek) as illegal.[205]

Although the Solicitor-General reassured the Court at one point that the unauthorised arrival of 'boat people' did not constitute an offence,[206] he worked the theme of deviance and opportunism to considerable effect. On the issue of travel documents, he made sweeping generalisations about 'boat people' and ascribed certain motives to them:

> [I]n the case of dealing with this entry of non-scheduled arrival of boats in Australia of persons who intend to come here for the purpose of, in effect, imposing their presence on Australia without a requisite visa or without ... being granted an entry permit, [i]t is the case that those persons may well and often do choose not to produce any documents of identity; they just arrive and obviously, in some cases, they regard it as appropriate to come without passports or identifying documents. Their intention is to come here and to stay in Australia, in one way or another, possibly by applying for refugee status; possibly by just clandestine arrival.[207]

Here, the Solicitor-General maintained the themes of lawlessness and choice, which he attributed to the target group as a whole. As such, he implied that 'boat people' 'intentionally' travel without required documentation and 'impose' their presence on Australia. Although his broad assertions employed qualifications such as 'may well' and 'in some cases', these are better understood as discursive decoration rather than meaningful modifications to an

---

[204]   Cf a letter from Immigration Minister, Scott Morrison, to the Secretary of the Immigration Department instructing the Department to describe 'boat people' as 'illegal maritime arrivals': Evidence to Senate Legal and Constitutional Affairs Legislation Committee, Parliament of Australia, *Supplementary Budget Estimates 2013–2014 (Immigration and Border Protection)*, Canberra, 19 November 2013, 31–2 (Martin Bowles, Secretary, DIBP; Vicki Parker, Chief Lawyer, DIBP). See Chapter 1, 32 n 116.

[205]   Catherine Dauvergne, *Making People Illegal: What Globalization Means for Migration and Law* (Cambridge University Press, 2008) 8, 50–68. See also Transcript, *Lim* (7 August 1992) 53 (Deane J): "we were approaching this on the basis that these people were all properly in custody. I had assumed that that meant that they were illegal entrants and, I must confess, I had also assumed that they had committed some offence in coming in." See discussion above, 175–6.

[206]   Transcript, *Lim* (7 August 1992) 64 (Gavan Griffith QC); cf below 214–16.

[207]   Transcript, *Lim* (7 August 1992) 46–7 (Gavan Griffith QC).

empirical claim. Thus, making a statement as if it were fact ('it is the case'), he declared (speculatively) that such people 'may well', and then more sure-footedly (but without substantiation) 'often' do, 'choose' not to produce – or indeed "destroy"[208] – identity documents. Persisting with this ascription of deviance, he portrayed 'boat people' as opportunistic and lawless, as 'just arriving' and 'regarding' arrival without documents as 'appropriate'. By ascribing deviance, the act of spontaneously seeking asylum was treated as a 'choice' made by opportunists not willing to engage with 'us' on 'our' terms – a lawless 'choice' depicted as calculated and real, 'possibly' even extending to 'clandestine arrival'.

5.2.2.2 The 'National Interest': Reason Enough

Counsel for the plaintiffs raised the issue of the 'national interest'[209] in argument, questioning how it could be in the national interest that the target group could be singled out for mandatory detention.[210] The Commonwealth explained the 'national interest' as follows:

> There are rational reasons why Parliament might have seen fit to distinguish between certain non-citizens arriving by boat and those arriving by air. Because of the controls at Australian airports, and the controls which airlines are required to carry out at the point of departure, it is much more difficult for an airline passenger surreptitiously to enter Australia undetected than it is for a person arriving by boat. There is therefore a need to provide stronger deterrents for unauthorized arrivals.[211]

In this way, the Commonwealth sought, ex post facto, to attribute to Parliament what 'might' have been its rationale for the 'national interest' claim. As reinforcement for this position, innuendo was used to impute to 'boat people' a deviance *contra* the national interest: 'surreptitious' behaviour

---

[208] Ibid 47 (Gavan Griffith QC). On destruction of documents, see: UNHCR, *Detention of Refugees and Asylum-Seekers* (Conclusion No 44 (XXXVII), 13 October 1986) para (b); UNHCR, 'Guidelines on the Applicable Criteria and Standards relating to the Detention of Asylum-Seekers and Alternatives to Detention' (2012) Guideline 4.1 ('*Detention Guidelines*').

[209] *Migration Act* s 54J (as at 6 May 1992; now s 176); Transcript, *Lim* (6 August 1992) 3 (Brian Shaw QC).

[210] Transcript, *Lim* (6 August 1992) 6 (Brian Shaw QC).

[211] Minister for Immigration, Local Government and Ethnic Affairs and the Commonwealth of Australia, 'Defendants' Supplementary Submissions – 2: Arbitrary Detention – International Human Rights Law', Submission in *Chu Kheng Lim v Minister for Immigration, Local Government and Ethnic Affairs*, HCA No M23/1992, undated, [12] ('Defendants' Supplementary Submissions – 2').

meriting 'stronger deterrents'. This coupling strengthened the claim on the national interest. Yet neither the Commonwealth's oral or written submissions nor the parliamentary debates provided evidence substantiating these assertions. Instead, they utilised a rhetorical technique whereby assertions made and repeated often enough have a tendency to acquire the quality or condition of fact.[212]

Later, the Solicitor-General asserted that although the *Hansard* detailed "ample factual reasons" for the legislation,[213] as a matter of law "Parliament need state no reason" for the national interest claim.[214] In other words, even if an examination of *Hansard* yielded factual reasons of less than the claimed amplitude, merely stating that the legislation was in the national interest provided reason enough. Indeed, claiming an implicit authority in the "unanimity" of views within the Parliament as to the "appropriateness" of the legislation,[215] he suggested that Parliament's reasons for passing the legislation were "beside the point".[216] Hence, as a metaphor, the 'national interest' worked at a level of abstraction able to accord maximum power with minimum accountability. It was, in short, a flexible trope that worked as a proxy for 'absolute sovereignty'.[217]

Repeating aspects of Hand's 'carefully crafted'[218] Second Reading Speech, the Solicitor-General underscored that the measures were both 'extraordinary' and 'interim'.[219] Although inherently illogical, he also described mandatory detention as "merely" enacted to facilitate the processing of refugee claims.[220] We know, however, that processing refugee claims does not necessitate detention. Indeed, at the time, the vast majority of asylum seekers were not detained.[221] Seemingly attuned to the incongruity of the Solicitor-General's assertion,[222] the Court nevertheless declined to receive affidavits on the point when the Solicitor-General – probably trying to avert the possibility – intimated that they might be "contentious" (and therefore time-consuming).[223] More telling still is that the majority did not take this incongruity into account, concluding that detention was "reasonably capable of

---

[212] Agoustinos and Every, above n 18, 128.   [213] Transcript, *Lim* (7 August 1992) 60.
[214] Ibid 59; *Salemi* (1977) 137 CLR 396, 403 (Barwick CJ).
[215] Transcript, *Lim* (7 August 1992) 60.   [216] Ibid 60.
[217] The meaning of the 'national interest' was not addressed in the Court's judgment.
[218] See above 170.
[219] Transcript, *Lim* (7 August 1992) 59–60; see above 171 for discussion on Hand.
[220] Transcript, *Lim* (7 August 1992) 60.
[221] 'Statement of Claim', *Lim*, [39]; Transcript, *Lim* (6 August 1992) 11 (Brian Shaw QC). As noted at above n 13, of the estimated 23,000 applicants for refugee status at the time, less than 500 were in detention.
[222] Transcript, *Lim* (7 August 1992) 60 (McHugh J).   [223] Ibid.

being seen as necessary . . . to enable an application for an entry permit to be made and considered."[224]

5.2.2.3 Tempting the Imagination: Fear of the Floodgates

One of the main premises of the legislation was the perception that, in the absence of strong deterrents, large numbers of 'boat people' would arrive on Australian shores. This premise gained traction notwithstanding that numbers arriving by boat were, at the time, small.[225] To address the disparity between the small number of 'boat people' and asylum seekers in the community, the Solicitor-General argued, "it matters not that there is a ratio of 360 or whatever [mandatorily detained] to many thousands [not detained]".[226] Instead, recognising that the speculative rhetoric of fear is more tantalising to the imagination than fact,[227] he overworked the idea that there were many more who "may arrive".[228] To do so, he highlighted the arrival of two boats carrying Chinese and Polish nationals within days of the legislation being passed.[229] Although, as noted earlier, he did mention that there were 12 Polish nationals on one boat, he was silent on the number of Chinese (there were 10)[230] who had arrived.[231] Instead, numbers rhetoric enabled him speculatively to foreshadow a loss of control:[232] "there might be 10,000 who arrive between now and 1 December".[233] According to this projection, 87 people per day 'might arrive' over that period, an increase of 8,700 per cent on previous arrivals.[234]

---

[224] *Lim* (1992) 176 CLR 1, 33 (Brennan, Deane, and Dawson JJ). Gaudron and McHugh JJ took a similar view, but each used using the term "reasonably necessary" rather than "reasonably capable of being seen as necessary": at 58 (Gaudron J), 65, 71 (McHugh J). See also below 208–11.

[225] In recent years, researchers have gained increasing confidence in asserting that there is no empirical evidence that the use of immigration detention is an effective deterrent: see, eg, Alice Edwards, *Back to Basics: The Right to Liberty and Security of Person and 'Alternatives to Detention' of Refugees, Asylum-Seekers, Stateless Persons and Other Migrants*, UNHCR Doc PPLA/2011/01.Rev.1 (2011). Even one of Australia's most senior public servants has asked if immigration detention is a deterrent: Evidence to Joint Select Committee on Australia's Immigration Detention Network, Parliament of Australia, Inquiry into Australia's Immigration Detention Network, Canberra, 16 August 2011, 3 (Andrew Metcalfe, Secretary, Department of Immigration and Citizenship (DIAC)).

[226] Transcript, *Lim* (7 August 1992) 61.   [227] Boletsi, above n 71, 67.

[228] CPD, House of Representatives, 5 May 1992, 2373 (Philip Ruddock); Boletsi, above n 71, 67.

[229] Transcript, *Lim* (7 August 1992) 61.   [230] DIMIA, *Fact Sheet 74a*, above n 156.

[231] Transcript, *Lim* (7 August 1992) 61.   [232] Van Dijk, above n 18, 107–9.

[233] Transcript, *Lim* (7 August 1992) 62.

[234] In fact, a total of 194 people arrived by boat during that period, being at an average rate of 1.7 people per day: HREOC, 'Those Who've Come across the Seas', above n 1, 252. Even using statistical data on more recent boat arrivals, which are markedly higher than they were in 1992, the Solicitor-General's speculation represents an increase of approximately 87 per cent.

5.2.3 Questions of Power, Exclusion and the Voluntariness of Detention

The object and purpose of the mandatory detention legislation was plain. Although the language of deterrence was not explicitly used during the parliamentary debates, the deterrent purpose was evident from Hand's emphatic insistence that the legislation send a 'clear signal'.[235] This view was confirmed by the Commonwealth's written submissions.[236] Nevertheless, the Commonwealth argued that mandatory detention was not punitive. Central to this argument were two assertions: first, that 'boat people' had no right to .enter and, second, that their presence and custody in Australia was voluntary.

5.2.3.1 Aliens Power: No Right to Enter

The Solicitor-General relied on precedent[237] to suggest that the aliens power has always contemplated detention as an incident of expulsion.[238] He also submitted that

> the aliens power and, if need be, but not here, the immigration power, extends to making of the law which says if an alien comes to Australia without permission that person is free to depart at any time, but otherwise must stay in detention pending a decision as to whether that person is to be permitted to enter. Such a provision does not make that person guilty of an offence or inflict any punishment. It is merely a means of giving effect to the rule that an alien cannot enter Australia without permission.[239]

While insisting that 'boat people' are 'free to depart at any time', the Solicitor-General wove into the scope of the aliens power authority to detain *mandatorily* pending a decision on an entry permit. To sustain this argument, the Solicitor-General then submitted that

> [a]n alien ... cannot assert a right to enter the community ... pending a decision whether permission to enter will be granted or refused, particularly if the statutory regime dealing with that consideration excludes the possibility of entry.[240]

For example, Phillips and Spinks record that a total of 17,202 'boat people' arrived in Australia in 2012: Phillips and Spinks, 'Boat Arrivals', above n 2.

[235] CPD, House of Representatives, 5 May 1992, 2370–3 (Gerry Hand).
[236] Defendants' Supplementary Submissions – 2, *Lim* [12].
[237] *Robtelmes v Brenan* (1906) 4 CLR 395, 404 (Griffith CJ) ('*Robtelmes*'); *Koon Wing Lau v Calwell* (1949) 80 CLR 533, 552 (Latham CJ) ('*Koon Wing Lau*').
[238] Transcript, *Lim* (7 August 1992) 68.   [239] Ibid 68–9.   [240] Ibid 69.

Here, the Solicitor-General made two claims that invite analysis. First, echoing the decision in *Musgrove v Chun Teeong Toy*[241] (*'Musgrove'*), he stated that an alien who comes to Australia cannot assert a 'right to enter the community'. The contrast with the historical right of early international law's foreigner (who was, of course, a European insider) to enter and reside in the territory of another state is notable.[242] However, the plaintiffs' claim was more modest. Their applications for asylum clearly pointed to their hope of being recognised as refugees and thereby granted entry and residence in Australia. In contrast, however, the application to the Federal Court (now before the High Court in a different form) asserted only the right not to be detained indefinitely and without judicial oversight. As such, the temporary entry they sought, which the Commonwealth had the power to grant, was simply a corollary of the right not to be arbitrarily detained. This is not the same as entry being claimed as a right in itself, but the entanglement of detention into the right to enter certainly served the Commonwealth's case.

The second claim in this passage was that the power of the state (mandatorily) to detain was permissible 'pending a decision whether permission to enter will be granted or refused'. Prior to *Lim*, there was no authority for this proposition.[243] Instead, this submission (which the Court ultimately accepted) represents a slippage in interpretation of the scope of an already broad power to detain *for the purposes of deportation*, a (limited) power that the courts have historically recognised as a permissible incident of the exercise of the aliens power.[244] One of the reasons for this is that, historically, detention *for the purposes of deportation* was typically of short duration. Yet as we know from Chapter 4, even in the context of the limited purpose of deportation, it was the

---

[241] [1891] AC 272. See Chapter 3 Section 3.3.2, 96–7.   [242] See Chapter 2.

[243] In the European context, cf *Convention for the Protection of Human Rights and Fundamental Freedoms*, opened for signature 4 November 1950, 213 UNTS 222 (entered into force 3 September 1953), as amended by *Protocol No 14bis to the Convention for the Protection of Human Rights and Fundamental Freedoms*, opened for signature 27 May 2009, CETS No 204 (entered into force 1 September 2009) art 5(1)(f), which permits arrest or detention to prevent an unauthorised entry. However, such detention relies on the (contestable) assumption that states have an "undeniable sovereign right to control aliens' entry into and residence in their country": *Amuur v France* [1996] Eur Court HR 25 [41]; *Chahal v United Kingdom* [1996] V Eur Court HR 54 [73]; *Abdulaziz, Cabales and Blakandali v United Kingdom* [1985] Eur Court HR 7 [67]–[68]. In addition, it must be implemented in a manner "compatible with the overall purpose of Article 5, which is to safeguard the right to liberty and ensure that no one should be dispossessed of his or her right to liberty in an arbitrary fashion": *Saadi v United Kingdom* [2008] Eur Court HR 80 [66].

[244] Historically, the judicial practice of exculpating any punitive element from the act of deportation has contributed to this slippage: see, eg, *Fong Yue Ting v United States*, 149 US 698, 709, 728 (Gray J) (1893) (*'Fong'*), discussed in Chapter 3 Section 3.3.3.3, 101–7.

capacity for "naked and uninhibited" powers of arrest (and detention) to "cause great injustice" that was behind the "elaborate safeguards" introduced in the Migration Bill 1958 (Cth).[245] The second limb of the argument that mandatory detention was not punitive was the assertion that detention was a voluntary activity.

5.2.3.2 Custody: A Voluntary Activity

Deploying the rhetorical device of repetition, the Solicitor-General argued that the plaintiffs were in 'voluntary custody' and that the act of seeking asylum by boat was a 'voluntary activity':

> Dealing with this issue of custody, we do remind the Court that the plaintiffs' custody, *however long it has been* and *however long it continues* under this provision, is *voluntary* custody on their part. They came *voluntarily* to Australia and they are free *voluntarily* to depart at any time.

> Whilst they are now here, having come here *voluntarily*, not being entitled to do so, they *choose* to take advantage of the laws of Australia, including the mechanisms to apply for entry and to review in our courts the operation of the decision-making process in relation to those applications. That is what the plaintiffs do and, of course, there is no complaint about that but it is the case that throughout this process this is a *voluntary* activity [on] behalf of each of the plaintiffs.[246]

As this extract shows, the Solicitor-General's submissions were heavily larded with references to 'voluntariness' and 'choice'.[247] He characterised the custody ('however long it has been and however long it continues') as voluntary and the decision to come to Australia as voluntary. He insisted that the plaintiffs were 'choosing' to 'take advantage of the laws of Australia' (although he maintained that there was no complaint about that) and that they were 'free' to depart voluntarily 'at any time'.[248] In this way, he represented detention as a meaningful choice, projecting responsibility on the part of 'boat people' for their detention and predicament. Yet, a moment's thought tells us that it is counter-intuitive that mandatorily detained asylum seekers making bona fide

---

[245]   CPD, House of Representatives, 1 May 1958, 1398 (Alexander Downer).
[246]   Transcript, *Lim* (7 August 1992) 58 (emphases added).
[247]   See also ibid 52, 63, 65, 66, 69. Cover describes as "grotesque" the suggestion that a person who walks into the hands of her custodians upon conviction is doing so voluntarily, considering it to represent instead an "autonomous recognition of the overwhelming array of violence ranged against [her], and of the hopelessness of resistance or outcry": Robert M Cover, 'Violence and the Word' (1986) 95 *Yale Law Journal* 1601, 1607.
[248]   See also Transcript, *Lim* (7 August 1992) 52.

claims have the "power"[249] to depart voluntarily. It obscures not only their entitlement (under international and municipal law) to see the application process through but also the serious harm they apprehend would befall them on return to their country of origin.[250] Or, in the words of Simon Brown LJ in an analogous context, such a proposition would "[impale them] on the horns of [an] intolerable ... dilemma: the need either to abandon their claims to refugee status"[251] or remain in custody for however long it takes.

McHugh J appeared to be unimpressed by this rhetorical device: "If they are genuine refugees,[252] it is an inappropriate use of the term 'voluntary', is it not?"[253] The Solicitor-General persisted:

> Let us look at that, Your Honour. We submit that the position is that Australia is discharging its obligations in respect of the refugee convention. There has been a consideration of their position and after the setting aside by ... the Federal Court there is further consideration and I am instructed that recently, and certainly in the near future ... some of these people ... will be admitted to refugee status. That is the ordinary process of the law. But we say, Your Honour, there is no entitlement on anyone claiming refugee status to say they should be permitted to enter the country with the possibility of assimilating into the community to the point that they cannot be found in the face of a legislative regime which clearly expressed the fact that they are not to do that.[254]

---

[249] Ibid 64 (Gavan Griffith QC).

[250] *Refugee Convention* arts 1A(2), 33. Note in this regard that refugee status is declaratory not constitutive and therefore that the principle of *non-refoulement* applies also to asylum seekers: UNHCR, *Handbook and Guidelines on Procedures and Criteria for Determining Refugee Status*, UN Doc HCR/1P/4/ENG/REV.3 (December 2011) para 28 ('*Handbook and Guidelines*'); James C Hathaway, *The Rights of Refugees under International Law* (Cambridge University Press, 2005) 11.

[251] *R v Secretary of State for Social Security; Ex parte Joint Council for the Welfare of Immigrants* [1996] 4 All ER 385, 401–2 (Simon Brown LJ). This case related to planned destitution, discussed in Chapter 6. The prohibition on return 'in any manner whatsoever' (*Refugee Convention* art 33) encompasses the use of onerous measures and privations, including immigration detention, that have the effect (directly or indirectly) of forcing a person to 'choose' to return to a place where s/he would face persecution, a practice that has become known as 'constructive *refoulement*': UNHCR, 'Representations to the Social Security Advisory Committee on the "Social Security (Persons from Abroad) Miscellaneous Amendment Regulations 1995"' (10 November 1995).

[252] On the term 'genuine refugees' see, eg, Pickering, above n 38, 172, 175–6.

[253] Transcript, *Lim* (7 August 1992) 58; see also at 64 (Brennan J).

[254] Ibid 58. According to one report, the Immigration Department argued that mandatory detention was necessary given the number of unauthorised boat arrivals who had absconded from unfenced migrant accommodation hostels in the past – a total of 57 between 1991 and

Although the Solicitor-General knew that some of the plaintiffs would be 'admitted to'[255] refugee status and therefore effectively conceded that their claims had been made in good faith, he nevertheless characterised their arrival and stay as 'voluntary'. In other words, the Solicitor-General's submissions sought to draw the Court into the same projection of deviance evident in the parliamentary debates. In doing so, he elided multiple postulations about motives and claims of the asylum seekers – namely, 'entitlement' to be permitted to enter and 'assimilate' into the community 'to the point that they cannot be found'.[256] This communicated an (unsubstantiated) predilection for dishonesty and criminality, tapping into and giving succour to public discourses of fear and threat.[257] He continued:

> Perhaps I have sufficiently made the point that the Act, we submit, is not at all one in respect of punishment. It is not at all in respect of involuntary detention. It is dealing with what is to be done with people who choose to stay here rather than remain [*sic*], while their unsolicited applications for entry here are considered. And Parliament has made it clear, whatever the choice is, that in respect of those persons who are designated persons, they are to be treated in a particular way.[258]

In this passage, the Solicitor-General again insisted that detention was (entirely) voluntary and that the 'choice' to stay was real. At the same time, he characterised asylum applications as 'unsolicited', thereby inverting the involuntariness of the process (and therefore implicitly the involuntariness of the detention). In this way, in the matters of detention – which he insisted was 'not at all' punitive – and of processing of asylum applications, it was presented as if it were the Government that had no choice. Whatever the case, however, Parliament had made clear how 'boat people' were to be treated.

5.2.3.3 Don't Get Too Close: The Basic Issue

At the hearing, Counsel for the plaintiffs argued that the practice of giving 'boat people' an identifier meant they "ceased to be people and [became]

1993, of whom 18 remained at large as at January 1994: Janet Phillips and Harriet Spinks, 'Immigration Detention in Australia' (Background Note, Parliamentary Library, Parliament of Australia, 20 March 2013), referring to Joint Standing Committee on Migration, Parliament of Australia, *Asylum, Border Control and Detention* (1994) 110–11.

[255] Cf above n 250, recalling that refugee status is a declaratory status.

[256] See also Transcript, *Lim* (7 August 1992) 60. See also CPD, House of Representatives, 5 May 1992, 2373 (Philip Ruddock).

[257] See, eg, CPD, House of Representatives, 5 May 1992, 2373 (Philip Ruddock).

[258] Transcript, *Lim* (7 August 1992) 59.

concentration camp numbers".[259] This allusion to the Nazi practice of assigning serial numbers to prisoners did not attract objection or criticism.[260] However, the Solicitor-General later sought to obviate any risk that the practice of using numerical identifiers might have aroused the concern of the Court. In an audacious gesture, he warned the Court against being tempted to look behind the facelessness of the legislative scheme at the people affected *as people*:

> The problem is, Your Honour, when one gets close enough to these people as people who have committed no offence, who have a sincere desire to enter Australia, who have been detained for lengthy periods, one can obscure the basic issue of, we say, legislative power in respect of aliens that we are dealing with here.[261]

In this submission, the Solicitor-General illustrates the effects of the aliens power. Anyone who gets 'close enough' to see those affected 'as people', who recognises that they have 'committed no offence',[262] who acknowledges the sincerity of their desire to enter Australia, and who sees that they have already been detained for lengthy periods, is exhorted to put these considerations aside. Why? Because those realities 'can obscure the basic issue'. That 'basic issue' is power – specifically, the power of the legislature to make laws, any laws, with respect to aliens.[263] So, although this passage apparently represents a gesture to the common humanity of 'boat people', the Solicitor-General's submissions were instead a caution that it would be inappropriate to get 'too close' to the human effects of the legislation.

The Solicitor-General's persistence would yield the desired result. Despite their disquiet on some aspects of the legislation, their Honours

---

[259]   Transcript, *Lim* (6 August 1992) 6 (Brian Shaw QC). The practice of identifying 'boat people' by a number is ongoing: see, eg, Max Chalmers, 'Detention on Nauru: Children Now Identify More with Boat Number than Names, Says Former Worker' *New Matilda* (online), 29 June 2015 <https://newmatilda.com/2015/06/29/detention-nauru-children-now-identify-m ore-boat-number-names-says-former-worker/>.

[260]   Here, it is apposite to recall Alexander Downer describing his own experience as a Japanese prisoner of war as "comparable" to imprisoning people he described as "statutory offenders": CPD, House of Representatives, 1 May 1958, 1399 (Alexander Downer). Of course, Downer addressed the problem he perceived by creating immigration detention centres, an innovation out of which he was "sure" that "nothing but good [would] come". See Chapter 4, 154.

[261]   Transcript, *Lim* (7 August 1992) 76 (Gavan Griffith QC).

[262]   Cf *Migration Act* s 77 (repealed), discussed below at 214–16.

[263]   See, eg, *Lim* (1992) 176 CLR 1, 64–5 (McHugh J), citing *Australian Communist Party v Commonwealth* (1951) 83 CLR 1, 188–9 (Dixon J) ('*Communist Party Case*'); see also *Polites* (1945) 70 CLR 60, 69 (Latham CJ); *Pochi* (1982) 151 CLR 101, 106 (Gibbs CJ).

did not get 'too close'. Indeed, as elaborated in Section 5.3, the Court was ultimately persuaded that the detention was voluntary and non-punitive.

5.3 *CHU KHENG LIM*: THE DECISION

Compared to the rich rhetoric of the parliamentary debates and judicial proceedings, the Court's judgment in *Lim* is anodyne, measured, and dispassionate. Yet, as this analysis shows, by paying close attention to the discursive style of the judgments, we can discern the continuing effects of the legal traditions and orthodoxies that frame the foreigner-sovereign relation. By reading judicial reasoning *as discourse*, this section elicits the ways in which the movement of meaning that typifies doctrinal legal processes shapes 'absolute sovereignty' as a discourse. It educes discursive slippages, assumptions, and silences that classic doctrinal analysis may scarcely notice because they are so (or too) close, so (or too) immediate, so (or too) much a part of who we are and how we think about migration law's purpose and possibilities.[264] The analysis enables us to see more clearly the role the judiciary has played in upholding the mandatory detention scheme as a thinkable institutional response to unsolicited migration. It does so by making visible how judicial discourses move – often imperceptibly – and continue to shape and perpetuate assumptions about the foreigner as a (right-less or rights-limited) outsider and 'absolute sovereignty' as a routine response to her every move. These discursive techniques and practices lock in place a (dominant) discourse that is historically produced and structurally impervious to law's effects.[265]

This analysis of the judgments in *Lim* shows how the judicial arm of government validates discursive techniques of (state) control and restraint doctrinally, including through the use of precedent and a 'positivist' style of judicial deference. The judiciary is less forthright in its engagement of techniques under the theme of deviance and opportunism that we saw so clearly in the parliamentary debates and hearing. However, in my argument, the *effects* of those techniques remain evident in the way the judiciary characterises the conduct and motives of 'boat people'. The

---

[264] Michel Foucault, 'La philosophie analytique de la politique' in Daniel Defert and François Ewald (eds), with Jacques Lagrange, *Michel Foucault: Dits et écrits – 1954–1988* (Gallimard, 1994) vol 3, 534, 540–1; Anne Orford, 'In Praise of Description' (2012) 25(3) *Leiden Journal of International Law* 609, 617–18. See Chapter 1, 36.

[265] Arturo Escobar, *Encountering Development: The Making and Unmaking of the Third World* (Princeton University Press, 1995) 6.

analysis shows how judicial silences are as integral to grasping how *Lim* validated the mandatory detention scheme as the text of the judgment itself.

Following an overview of the decision, my analysis in this section focuses on three aspects of the judgment.[266] First, I consider how the Court read the scope of the aliens power and, more particularly, limits to the incidental power to detain. Second, I explore how it interpreted the scope of the judicial power. Finally, I consider the Court's assessment of administrative detention as non-punitive and its conclusion that detention was voluntary. I show how certain linguistic choices produced a combination of judicial silence, assumption, and slippage. This enabled the validation of a power to detain whose expansiveness – whether intentionally or inadvertently – was unprecedented.

5.3.1 *Overview of the Decision: A Pyrrhic Victory*

The Court concluded (unanimously) that the mandatory detention scheme was a lawful incident of the aliens power.[267] A majority also found the prohibition on courts to order the release of a 'designated person' to be invalid as a usurpation of the judicial power.[268] However, the same majority found the provision to be severable.[269] So, it was a pyrrhic victory for the plaintiffs: mandatory detention could continue perforce.

The Court accepted the premise that there could be no (meaningful or effective) power vested in the courts to scrutinise the custody of 'boat people'. In doing so, it effectively conceded to the Executive "an essentially unexaminable power to imprison".[270] As such, because 'boat people' were (unwelcome) aliens (with no constitutional right to enter), they could be detained pursuant to an unexaminable power; they were subject to the law yet unworthy of its protection.[271] This is so notwithstanding the majority's conclusion that detention prior to the passage of the mandatory

---

[266] The external affairs question did not arise.

[267] *Lim* (1992) 176 CLR 1, particularly 10 (Mason CJ), 32–35 (Brennan, Deane, and Dawson JJ).

[268] Ibid 35–7 (Brennan, Deane, and Dawson JJ), 53 (Gaudron J); cf at 10–12 (Mason CJ), 50–51 (Toohey J), 69 (McHugh J), who concluded that s 54R could be read down. The joint judgment also speculated that s 54U may be unconstitutional and severable: at 35, 37.

[269] Ibid 37 (Brennan, Deane, and Dawson JJ).

[270] Ibid 29 (Brennan, Deane, and Dawson JJ).

[271] Only once has the High Court been asked to consider the constitutionality of the purported use of the aliens power for the 'protection' of aliens (from incompetent or exploitative lawyers): *Cunliffe v Commonwealth* (1994) 182 CLR 272 (*'Migration Agents Case'*). See further Section 5.3.1.2, 204–6 below.

detention legislation had been unlawful and that the detainees had standing.

5.3.1.1 Unlawful Detention: A Morsel of Peripheral Justice

A majority (including Toohey and McHugh JJ, otherwise dissenting) held that the plaintiffs' detention for more than two years was unlawful.[272] This was because s 88 only authorised detention pending the departure of the boat(s) on which they had arrived, and it became clear during the hearing that those boats had been burned or would never leave. It was a morsel of peripheral justice that would, in any event, soon be legislatively scuppered by measures to foreclose or limit the cause of action for unlawful imprisonment.[273]

5.3.1.2 No Rights, No Review, No Remedies: But Still Standing

One of the first substantive points made in the joint judgment of Brennan, Deane, and Dawson JJ ('the joint judgment') was that

> [u]nder the common law of Australia and subject to the qualification in the case of an enemy alien in time of war, an alien who is within this country, whether lawfully or unlawfully, is not an outlaw.[274]

---

[272]   *Lim* (1992) 176 CLR 1, 19–22 (Brennan, Deane, and Dawson JJ) (with whom Gaudron J, at 53, was in general agreement), 42–44 (Toohey J), 64 (McHugh J). Note that McHugh J conceded only that the detention "may have been" unlawful. For other analyses of this case, see Nick Poynder, 'An Opportunity for Justice Goes Begging: *Chu Kheng Lim v Minister for Immigration, Local Government and Ethnic Affairs*' (1994) 1(1) *Australian Journal of Human Rights* 414; Mary E Crock, 'Climbing Jacob's Ladder: The High Court and the Administrative Detention of Asylum Seekers in Australia' (1993) 15(3) *Sydney Law Review* 338; Mary Crock, *Immigration and Refugee Law in Australia* (Federation Press, 1998) 23–5; Justice A M North and Peace Decle, 'Courts and Immigration Detention: The Australian Experience' (2002) 10(1) *Australian Journal of Administrative Law* 5, 12–17.

[273]   The Parliament responded hastily: *Migration Amendment Act (No 4) 1992* (Cth) s 6, inserted s 54RA into the *Migration Act*, which sought to remove any cause of action for unlawful detention and to limit damages for false imprisonment to one dollar per day. Later, *Georgiadis v Australian and Overseas Telecommunications Corporation* (1994) 179 CLR 297 suggested that s 54RA breached s 51(xxxi) of the *Constitution*. In response to *Georgiadis*, the Migration Legislation Amendment Bill (No 3) 1994 (Cth) was introduced and defeated in the Senate (9 November 1994), then reintroduced and passed by both Houses in 1995: see *Migration Legislation Amendment Act (No 6) 1995* (Cth), which rendered s 88 detention retrospectively lawful and repealed s 54RA of the *Migration Act*. For a more recent example of legislative measures designed retrospectively to make lawful otherwise unlawful actions, see *Migration Amendment (Regional Processing Arrangements) Act 2015* (Cth) inserting s 198AHA into the *Migration Act*. The validity of this legislation was upheld by a majority in *Plaintiff M68/2015 v Minister for Immigration and Border Protection* (2016) 257 CLR 42 ('*Nauru Detention Case*').

[274]   *Lim* (1992) 176 CLR 1, 19.

An outlaw is "a person put *outside the law* and deprived of its *benefits* and *protection*".[275] Under the common law, a (friendly) alien is *subject* to (or 'put inside') the law. This might suggest that she is entitled to law's (benefits and) protection. However, *Lim* had a contrary effect: while aliens are not outlaws, under Australian constitutional law the Parliament can validly make laws that deny the common law right to liberty to a particular class of aliens and, in doing so, preclude recourse to substantive review or effective remedy.[276] As such, arbitrary arrest or detention of aliens without judicial mandate is lawful if authorised by constitutionally permissible statutory provision.[277] Furthermore, their Honours implied, it is open to the Parliament, through legislative provision, to deny an alien standing or capacity to invoke the intervention of a court even if she is unlawfully detained.[278]

Here, the Court's analytical approach positions the (absolute) scope of the aliens power as the sole determinant of validity. In other words, it had the effect of rendering the power to detain aliens *essentially unexaminable*,[279] subject only to the (equally unexaminable) doctrine of responsible governance – that 'ultimate guarantee'[280] against the 'grossest injustices'.[281] This stripped the law of any function or pretence as a check against abuse of power, framing instead a power that could be used to clothe with legislative authority unbridled and oppressive executive action.[282] As we know from the genealogy, it is clear that 'absolute sovereignty' in its common law and constitutional forms is the (contestable) product of a particular reading of the foreigner-sovereign relation.[283] With this

---

[275] Oxford English Dictionary <www.oed.com> (emphases added).
[276] This is a technique that was also used by Vitoria: see Chapter 2, 54.
[277] *Lim* (1992) 176 CLR 1, 19 (Brennan, Deane, and Dawson JJ).
[278] "Nor, in the absence of legislative provision to the contrary, does an alien within the country lack standing or capacity to invoke the intervention of a domestic court of competent jurisdiction if he or she is unlawfully detained": *Lim* (1992) 176 CLR 1, 19 (Brennan, Deane, and Dawson JJ), citing *Somerset v Stewart* (1772) Lofft 1; 98 ER 499; *Johnstone v Pedlar* [1921] 2 AC 262, 273, 276, 284–5, 296; *R v Home Secretary, Ex parte Khawaja* [1984] AC 74, 110–12.
[279] *Lim* (1992) 176 CLR 1, 29 (Brennan, Deane, and Dawson JJ).
[280] Robert Menzies, *Central Power in the Australian Commonwealth* (Caswell, 1967) 54; see Chapter 4, 117.
[281] *Constitutional Convention Debates*, Melbourne, 8 February 1898, 688 (John Cockburn). See Chapter 4, 117.
[282] Brian Z Tamanaha, *On the Rule of Law: History, Politics, Theory* (Cambridge University Press, 2004) 3, quoting Li Shuguang.
[283] *Lim* (1992) 176 CLR 1, 25–6 (Brennan, Deane, and Dawson JJ), citing *Robtelmes* (1906) 4 CLR 395, 400–4, 415, 420–2; *Re Yates; Ex parte Walsh and Johnson* (1925) 37 CLR 36, 83, 94, 108, 117, 132–3 ('*Walsh and Johnson*'); *O'Keefe v Calwell* (1949) 77 CLR 261, 277–8, 288 ('*O'Keefe*'); *Koon Wing Lau* (1949) 80 CLR 533, 555–6, 558–9; *Pochi* (1982) 151 CLR 101, 106. See Chapter 4 Sections 4.2.2.2–2.4, 126–30, 4.3.1.3, 139–42, and 4.3.2, 142–51.

in mind, the analysis that follows explores how the linguistic choices of the Court gave effect to the multiple forms and threads of the discourse of 'absolute sovereignty'.

5.3.2 The Legislative Power and the Foreigner

The Court unanimously endorsed mandatory detention of designated persons[284] and the executive power to (re-)detain them if their release was ordered by a court.[285] It held the power to detain to be a lawful incident of the aliens power.[286] However, despite being initially circumspect about whether the scope of the aliens power extended to mandatory detention,[287] the Court did not put it to any meaningful test. The only question was whether there was any limitation on the exercise of the (incidental) power to detain. And the Court held that as long as mandatory detention was "limited" to what was "reasonably capable of being seen as necessary for the purposes of deportation or necessary to enable an application for an entry permit to be made and considered", it was within the executive power to "exclude, admit and deport" an alien.[288]

This finding raises several questions. How did the Court read the scope of the aliens power? On what authority? How did it reach the conclusion that the power to detain is a lawful incident of the aliens power? How did it conclude that the power to detain for the purposes of expulsion and deportation extended to a power to detain for the purposes of admission? How did it frame limitations on the exercise of the incidental power to detain? Viewed through the lens of discourse analysis, this discussion thinks about the doctrinal aspects of these questions in the context of law's inextricable relation with language – about how classic doctrinal practices execute and perform migration law in a particular way, as a rational ordering that reinforces itself through re-use and retelling. I turn first to the scope of the aliens power.

5.3.2.1 The Aliens Power: Scope

The Court unanimously accepted the relevance of the aliens power and found the mandatory detention scheme to fall within its scope.[289] In the joint judgment

---

[284] *Migration Act* s 54L (as at 6 May 1992; now s 178).
[285] Ibid s 54N (as at 6 May 1992; now s 180). [286] *Constitution* s 51(xix).
[287] "If the person was thereafter to be lawfully held in custody in Australia, the justification, *if there was one*, had to be found in some other statutory provision" (emphasis added): *Lim* (1992) 176 CLR 1, 22 (Brennan, Deane, and Dawson, JJ).
[288] *Lim* (1992) 176 CLR 1, 32 (Brennan, Deane, and Dawson JJ).
[289] Ibid 10 (Mason CJ), 25–6 (Brennan, Deane, and Dawson JJ), 44–6 (Toohey J), 54–7 (Gaudron J), 64–6 (McHugh J).

(with which Gaudron J was in general agreement),[290] their Honours concluded that the scheme was, as a matter of "bare characterisation", a law with respect to aliens and therefore prima facie within the scope of the aliens power.[291] Drawing precedential authority from common law readings of international law, their Honours accepted the power of exclusion and expulsion to be an incident of sovereignty.[292] In particular, they quoted from the oft-cited case of *Attorney-General for Canada v Cain*[293] ('*Cain*'), which (selectively) quotes Vattel:[294]

> One of the rights possessed by the supreme power in every State is the right to refuse to permit an alien to enter the State, to annex what conditions it pleases to the permission to enter it, and to expel or deport from the State, at pleasure, even a friendly alien, especially if it considers his presence in the State opposed to its peace, order and good government, or to its social or material interests.[295]

Their Honours also accepted the precedents of *Musgrove*[296] and *Robtelmes v Brenan*[297] ('*Robtelmes*'). Furthermore, they acceded to the "unqualified terms"[298] of the aliens power, concluding that a law to exclude or condition the entry and stay of aliens, and to make provision for their expulsion or deportation, could be enacted "without trespassing beyond the reach of . . . s 51(xix)."[299]

In her reasons, Gaudron J observed that the Court had elsewhere found the race power[300] to authorise the making of laws that "may be benevolent or repressive".[301] She suggested that the same may be said to apply – "by analogy" – to the aliens power.[302] In other words, she intimated that it is within the power of the legislature to use the aliens power in a manner that is "offensive to ordinary notions of what is involved in a just society."[303] McHugh J took a similarly broad view:

---

[290] Ibid 53.   [291] Ibid 26.
[292] "The power to exclude or expel even a friendly alien is recognised by international law as an incident of sovereignty over territory": ibid 29.
[293] [1906] AC 542 ('*Cain*').
[294] See Chapter 2 Section 2.4, 73–7; Chapter 3, 99–101, 103; Chapter 4, 127–9.
[295] *Lim* (1992) 176 CLR 1, 30 (Brennan, Deane, and Dawson JJ), citing *Cain* [1906] AC 542. See Emmerich de Vattel, *The Law of Nations; or, Principles of the Law of Nature, Applied to the Conduct and Affairs of Nations and of Sovereigns* (Joseph Chitty ed and trans, Lawbook Exchange, first published 1854, 2005 ed) bk I ch XIX §231, bk II ch XIX §125 [trans of: *Le Droit des gens; ou Principes de la loi naturelle, appliqués à la conduite et aux affaires des Nations et des Souverains* (first published 1758)].
[296] [1891] AC 272.
[297] (1906) 4 CLR 395; *Robtelmes*, of course, draws on the line of authority from the US Supreme Court. See Chapter 3 Section 3.3.3, 97–107.
[298] *Lim* (1992) 176 CLR 1, 25.   [299] Ibid 25–6.   [300] *Constitution* s 51(xxvi).
[301] *Koowarta* (1982) 153 CLR 168, 209 (Stephen J).   [302] *Lim* (1992) 176 CLR 1, 55.
[303] Ibid. This picks up on the theme of a common humanity discussed in Chapter 1, 11–14.

Subject to the Constitution, [the aliens] power is limited only by the description of the subject-matter. If a law of the Parliament can be characterised as a
law with respect to aliens, it is valid whatever its terms, provided that the law
does not infringe any express or implied prohibition in the Constitution.[304]

In some respects, these extracts implicitly echo early jurisprudence in which
arbitrary powers of deportation considered 'obnoxious to the principles of
British liberty' were validated and the doctrine of responsible government
was said to operate as a restraint. This early jurisprudence suggested the risk of
abuse of such powers to be only theoretically present.[305] In a similar vein, the
majority in *Lim* read the authority to detain as an incident of the aliens power
as a "limited authority",[306] notwithstanding the broad interpretation it gave to
the aliens power. As the following section argues, the Court interpreted the
'limited authority' to detain in a way that merely rendered it a gesture of
restraint, which – inadvertently or otherwise – in effect left so much room to
move that it shaped the power to detain into an 'unlimited limitation'.

5.3.2.2 Mandatory Detention: An Unlimited Limitation

A key question for the Court was whether the power to detain pursuant to the
aliens power was subject to an express or implied restriction or limitation in
the *Constitution* as a whole.[307] In essence the question was this: How far could
the legislature go before the incidental power to detain became a trespass
on the judicial power?

A majority agreed that constitutionally enshrined legislative powers (implicitly) conferred a "limited"[308] and incidental authority upon the executive to
detain aliens "for the purposes of expulsion or deportation".[309] They added,
"by analogy"[310], that the authority to detain extended to detention for the
purposes of executive powers "to *receive, investigate and determine* an application . . . for an entry permit" and then "to *admit* or deport".[311] In doing so, they
invoked the (incongruous) idea that detention is necessary to enable refugee
applications to be processed – an 'abductive leap' which the Solicitor-General

---

[304]   *Lim* (1992) 176 CLR 1, 64–6, citing authorities as above n 263.
[305]   *Walsh and Johnson* (1925) 37 CLR 36, 133 (Starke J). See Chapter 4, 142.
[306]   *Lim* (1992) 176 CLR 1, 10 (Mason CJ), 32 (Brennan, Deane, Dawson JJ).
[307]   Ibid 26 (Brennan, Deane, Dawson JJ).
[308]   Ibid 10 (Mason CJ), 32–33 (Brennan, Deane, Dawson JJ).
[309]   Ibid 10 (Mason CJ), 32 (Brennan, Deane, and Dawson JJ).
[310]   Ibid 32 (Brennan, Deane, and Dawson JJ).
[311]   *Lim* (1992) 176 CLR 1, 10 (Mason CJ), 32 (Brennan, Deane, and Dawson JJ) (emphases
        added).

had invited them to make.[312] With no present intention or power to expel or deport, detention to 'receive, investigate and determine' is one step removed from expulsion or deportation. It is therefore more akin to detention *antici-pating* or *assuming* that eventuality rather than detention *for* that purpose.[313] Yet their Honours concluded that this (expanded) authority to detain could be vested in the Executive without contravening the judicial power.[314] An examination of how the Court reached this conclusion reveals a striking dissonance between jurisprudential intention and effect.

On the one hand, the Court showed a strong inclination to defer to the 'positivist' style of jurisprudence whereby Parliament bears the responsibility for the laws it makes.[315] On the other, although perceiving the need to draw limits on the power to detain, there were nonetheless interpretative slippages in the way the Court analysed and analogised the scope and purpose of that power. These slippages resulted in an elasticising form of deferential legal instrumentalism. In other words, not only did the Court accede to the "unqualified terms"[316] of the aliens power, but it also extended – by analogy and abductive leap – the reach of the (limited) (incidental) power to detain beyond anything that had previously been contemplated by the courts, or indeed Parliament. This happened in two ways.

First, the 'limitation' on the incidental exercise of the power to detain was discursively stretched from permitting detention that was "reasonably necessary"[317] for the purposes of "expulsion or deportation" to what was (a more capacious) "reasonably *capable*" of "*being seen*"[318] as "necessary" for the

---

[312] See above Section 5.2.3.1. On the notion of abductive reasoning, see: Douglas Walton, *Argumentation Methods for Artificial Intelligence in Law* (Springer, 2005) 159–61; Barbara Johnstone, 'Linguistic Strategies and Cultural Styles for Persuasive Discourse' in Stella Ting-Toomey and Felipe Korzenny (eds), *Language, Communication, and Culture: Current Directions* (Sage, 1989) 139, 149.

[313] On the question of whether detention of transitory persons transferred to Australia from an offshore processing facility for the purposes of medical treatment is detention for the purposes of medical treatment or for the purposes of removal, see *Plaintiff M96A/2016 v Commonwealth of Australia* [2017] HCA 16 (3 May 2017), where challenges to the kinds of discursive slippages identified in this chapter were resisted by the Court.

[314] *Lim* (1992) 176 CLR 1, 10 (Mason CJ), 32 (Brennan, Deane, and Dawson JJ).

[315] See, eg, Tom Campbell, *The Legal Theory of Ethical Positivism* (Aldershot, 1996). See also Chapter 3, 95 n 89.

[316] *Lim* (1992) 176 CLR 1, 25 (Brennan, Deane, and Dawson JJ).

[317] See, eg, *Communist Party Case* (1951) 83 CLR 1, 223 (Williams J). Cf *Migration Agents Case* (1994) 182 CLR 272, 297 (Mason CJ), who regarded as material the question of whether a law goes beyond what is reasonably necessary for achieving the legitimate aim sought.

[318] As relevant to the analysis of the scope of constitutional powers, the approach "reasonably capable of being seen" first came into use in the High Court in the 1980s: *Commonwealth v*

purposes of expulsion or deportation *"or"*, in addition, *"to enable an applica-tion for an entry permit to be made and considered"*.[319] Second, the Court did not critically engage with the language of the (now) expanded 'limitation'. So, for example, no insight was offered into the meaning of 'capable of being seen' (by whom?) as 'necessary' (according to a generic or an individualised stan-dard?)[320] even though this formulation almost certainly has a different mean-ing to 'reasonably necessary'. Nor is light shed on how detention was 'necessary' to 'enable' an application to be made and considered.

Similarly, McHugh J said that if a law authorising detention of an alien went "beyond what was reasonably necessary" to effect a deportation, the law "might" be invalid as a trespass on the judicial power.[321] Making the same abductive leap as the majority, he also concluded that if a law authorising detention of an alien "while that person's application for entry was being considered" went "beyond what was necessary" to effect "that purpose", it "might" be invalid as a trespass on the judicial power.[322] Again, rather than engaging with its meaning, his Honour assumed the reasonable necessity of detention for the purposes of deportation to include the (different) purpose of making an application for entry.

As we can see, the notion of 'reasonable necessity' was expanded rather than circumscribed. Discursive slippages, assumptions, and silences led to the

---

Tasmania (1983) 158 CLR 1 (*'Tasmanian Dam Case'*); see also *Polyukhovich v Commonwealth* (1991) 172 CLR 501 (*'War Crimes Act Case'*). It is generally followed by the associated requirement of assessing whether the law is reasonably capable of being seen as *appropriate and adapted* to the juridical purpose.

[319] *Lim* (1992) 176 CLR 1, 33 (Brennan, Deane, and Dawson JJ) (emphases added). Gaudron J expressed the view, at 57, that a law with respect to aliens will be valid if it is "appropriate and adapted to regulating entry or facilitating departure". This slippage is also evident in the *Nauru Detention Case*, where a majority of the Court held that Australia's participation in an offshore detention regime could be characterised as "reasonably necessary" to achieve the purpose of processing even though it did not elaborate on *how* such detention was reasonably necessary for processing: *Nauru Detention Case* (2016) 257 CLR 42, 71–2 [46] (French CJ, Kiefel and Nettle JJ).

[320] In international human rights and refugee law, assessment of the necessity of detention is individualised: see, eg, HRC, *Views: Communications No 305/1988*, 39th sess, UN Doc CCPR/C/39/D/305/1988 (23 July 1990) [5.8] (*'van Alphen v Netherlands'*); *A v Australia*, UN Doc CCPR/C/59/D/560/1993, [9.2], [9.4]. See also *Refugee Convention* art 31(2); Gregor Noll, 'Article 31' in Andreas Zimmermann (ed), *The 1951 Convention relating to the Status of Refugees and Its 1967 Protocol: A Commentary* (Oxford University Press, 2011) 1243, 1268–72; Guy S Goodwin-Gill, 'Article 31 of the 1951 Convention relating to the Status of Refugees: Non-Penalization, Detention, and Protection' in Erika Feller, Volker Türk, and Frances Nicholson (eds), *Refugee Protection in International Law: UNHCR's Global Consultations on International Protection* (Cambridge University Press, 2003) 185; Hathaway, above n 250, 413–39.

[321] *Lim* (1992) 176 CLR 1, 65–6. On the requirement of reasonable necessity see more recently *Nauru Detention Case* (2016) 257 CLR 42, 67 [31] (French CJ, Kiefel and Nettle JJ).

[322] Ibid.

Kafkaesque result that, subject only to the 'limitation' that detention have a non-punitive object,[323] an *unlimited limitation* had effectively been inscribed into the incidental power to detain pursuant to the aliens power. In view of the Court's findings, therefore, the aliens power remained unassailable as long as it was a law with respect to aliens,[324] and the 'limited' power to detain pursuant to it was effectively unconstrained.[325]

5.3.3 *The Judicial Power and the Foreigner*

The Court in *Lim* was unwilling to recognise any substantive function for the judicial power in scrutinising the exercise of executive powers of detention incidental to the aliens power. How did this happen? What did they understand to be the scope of the judicial power? And why did it not extend to the mandatory detention scheme as a whole? Again, discourse analysis provides the lens through which we can consider these doctrinal questions. It enables us to see the continuing effects of the discourse of 'absolute sovereignty': how certain values and histories affected the way in which the Court read the scope of the judicial power and how others were overlooked; how the special vulnerability of aliens (as unwelcome outsiders) excused the use of an essentially unexaminable power to detain.

5.3.3.1 Discerning the Scope of the Judicial Power

The doctrine of separation of powers is the cornerstone of modern liberal democratic governance. It is, in essence, a form of mutual accountability, a safeguard against excesses or misuses of power.[326] However, the demarcation

---

[323] See below Section 5.3.4.2, 221–3.
[324] In the *Nauru Detention Case*, the Court held that a law authorising the Commonwealth to do anything in relation to the arrangement or regional processing functions of a country – take action, make payments, or anything related to such actions or payments – was, for the purposes of s 51(xix) of the *Constitution*, a "law with respect to aliens" with a connection that could be described as "more than insubstantial, tenuous or distant": see *Nauru Detention Case* (2016) 257 CLR 42, 70 [42] (French CJ, Kiefel and Nettle JJ), citing *Cunliffe v Commonwealth* (1994) 182 CLR 272, 314 and *New South Wales v Commonwealth* ('*Work Choices Case*') (2006) 229 CLR 1, 143 [275]; and [77] (Bell J), finding a "sufficient connection".
[325] In *Al-Kateb v Godwin* (2004) 219 CLR 562, 582–3 ('*Al-Kateb*'), McHugh J held that the power to detain aliens dealt with the very subject matter of s 51(xix) and was not, therefore, incidental to the aliens power. See also *Plaintiff S156/2013 v Minister for Immigration and Border Protection* (2014) 254 CLR 28 ('*Manus Island Case*') 42 [24].
[326] M J C Vile, *Constitutionalism and the Separation of Powers* (Liberty Fund, 2nd ed, 1998) 63–4.

of these powers lacks clarity.[327] In *Lim*, the majority did not doubt the clarity of the delineation of the executive, legislative, and judicial powers.[328] Only McHugh J acknowledged imprecision, in particular the "very blurred" line between judicial and executive power.[329] This section analyses the approaches taken by the Court in differentiating between judicial and executive power. I begin with the judgment of McHugh J.

In his reasons, McHugh J suggested that classification of powers could not always be correctly determined through the application of analytical tests and descriptions. Instead, he said, classification frequently depended upon a "value judgment" and reference to "historical practice", the latter playing "an important, sometimes decisive, part" in determining the character of a particular power.[330] This positioned classification of the nature of power beyond the reach of analytical inquiry. In the result, McHugh J classified the mandatory detention scheme "in its ordinary operation" as not in the nature of the judicial power.[331] He was guided in doing so by 'values' and 'history'. Its provisions, he said, "simply" prescribed "a new regime of rights for the future".[332] Yet, it was a regime that, in essence, prescribed no rights at all. There was, he effectively concluded, no interference *with* the judicial process, because there *was* no judicial process.

We cannot be sure what the particular 'value judgments' and 'historical practices' informing McHugh J were. However, their effects are clear enough: they un-blurred the line between judicial and executive power, ascribing 'ordinariness' and 'simplicity' to an administrative detention scheme that foreclosed meaningful judicial scrutiny. Why? For no other reason than because those subject to it were (unwelcome) aliens, not citizens. This suggests that his Honour saw cordoning off the aliens power from the judicial power as validated by 'value judgments' and 'historical practices' (and thus requiring no more) – values and historical practices that, as we have seen through the genealogy of the foreigner-sovereign relation, are contingent historical artefacts that have become embedded in the discourse of 'absolute sovereignty'.

Turning to the joint judgment, their Honours made observations of a similar character. To them, the "adjudgment and punishment of criminal

---

[327] *Lim* (1992) 176 CLR 1, 66–7 (McHugh J): *Huddart, Parker and Co Pty Ltd v Moorehead* (1909) 8 CLR 330, 357 (Griffith CJ); *R v Trade Practices Tribunal; Ex parte Tasmanian Breweries Pty Ltd* (1970) 123 CLR 361, 374–5 (Kitto J), 394 (Windeyer J); *War Crimes Act Case* (1991) 172 CLR 501, 703–4.

[328] *Lim* (1992) 176 CLR 1, 26–7 (Brennan, Deane, and Dawson JJ): *War Crimes Act Case* (1991) 172 CLR 501, 607, 689, 703–4.

[329] *Lim* (1992) 176 CLR 1, 67.   [330] Ibid.   [331] Ibid.   [332] Ibid.

guilt" – of its "nature" and because of "historical considerations" – fell necessarily (indeed, exclusively) under the judicial power.[333] Nevertheless, their Honours described their concern as being with "substance and not mere form".[334] In other words, involuntary detention *by another name* would – subject to certain "exceptional cases" – still fall under the judicial power because it would still be punitive in character.[335] However, their argument was confined to citizens, which prompts us to ask whether the nature and history of safeguards against arbitrary imprisonment were always confined to citizens. The Court would appear to have made this assumption, and in doing so relied on the texts of Sir William Blackstone.

In the only chapter in Blackstone's *Commentaries* dealing substantively with the issue of imprisonment and the personal liberty of individuals, Blackstone said "[t]he confinement of the person, in any wise, is an imprisonment."[336] Although he mentions 'citizens' and 'Englishmen' in this context, an examination of his texts suggests that Blackstone's primary focus was on 'persons', not citizens. This suggests that he was preoccupied more with *how* people were detained rather than with *who* was detained. In particular, he pointed to the need for imprisonment to arise from a reviewable decision, whether by judicial process or executive warrant. Only then could it be (meaningfully) amenable to examination upon a habeas corpus.[337]

The paragraph in Blackstone's text immediately preceding the one cited by the Court is also instructive, because he does not confine his objection to arbitrary imprisonment to citizens:

> Of great importance to the public is the preservation of this personal liberty; for if once it were left in the power of any, the highest, magistrate to imprison arbitrarily whomever he or his officers thought proper . . . there would soon be an end of all other rights and immunities.[338]

Significantly, Blackstone refers in the same paragraph to the "great importance" of the "preservation of liberty", describing "confinement of the person, by secretly hurrying him to gaol" as a "dangerous engine of arbitrary

---

333 Ibid 27 (Brennan, Deane, and Dawson JJ).

334 Ibid. Cf *Decision of the Social Security Commissioner*, Case No CIS 4439/98 (25 November 1999) [16]: Penelope Mathew, 'Australian Refugee Protection in the Wake of the *Tampa*' (2002) 96 *American Journal of International Law* 661, 674 n 128.

335 *Lim* (1992) 176 CLR 1, 27 (Brennan, Deane, and Dawson JJ), quoting A V Dicey, *Introduction to the Study of the Law of the Constitution* (Macmillan, 10th ed, first published 1959, 1961) 202.

336 Sir William Blackstone (1723–1780), *Commentaries on the Laws of England* (Callaghan and Co, 1884, c 1883) bk I ch I, 136–7 (cited in *Lim* as: "*Commentaries*, 17th ed (1830), bk1, paras 136–7": *Lim* (1992) 176 CLR 1, 28).

337 Ibid bk I ch I, 137.   338 Ibid bk I ch I, 135.

government".[339] This was, he said, because the "sufferings" of those arbitrarily
deprived of their liberty is "less known", "less striking", "unknown or forgot-
ten".[340] Furthermore, Blackstone argued that imprisoning "suspected persons"[341] without giving reasons should be restricted to "extreme emergency"
and then only for a "short and limited" time.[342] While normative arguments
might be elicited from this discussion about how the Court could or should
have read Blackstone, the Court's treatment of his texts enables us to see how
assumptions can affect classic doctrinal approaches to migration law. So,
although Blackstone did not draw a distinction between foreigners and citizens
in outlining his position on deprivation of liberty, in drawing on his authority
the Court has clearly assumed otherwise, even though his *Commentaries* predate the emergence of the doctrine of 'absolute sovereignty'.[343]

In the joint judgment, there was no elaboration of which functions have by
their 'nature' or due to 'historical considerations' become established as
essentially and exclusively judicial in character apart from the adjudgment
and punishment of criminal guilt. However, it is pertinent to dwell for a
moment on the implications of that silence.

Historically, unlawful entry to Australia was characterised as a criminal
offence. From Federation, it was an offence punishable by imprisonment
for not more than six months.[344] Following the passage of the *Migration
Act* in 1958, it remained an offence, still punishable by imprisonment for
up to six months.[345] In 1989, amendments to that Act retained the offence

---

[339]   Ibid bk I ch I, 136. Here, one need not accede to Blackstone's views that executive imprison-
        ment was a more dangerous engine of arbitrary government than, for example, arbitrary
        deprivation of life or confiscation of property without accusation or trial to be able to see the
        vulnerabilities of those made invisible by the arbitrary deprivation of liberty – vulnerabilities
        to which Alexander Downer was certainly attuned when introducing the Migration Bill in
        1958: see Chapter 4 Section 4.3.3.2, 152–4.
[340]   Blackstone, above n 336, bk I ch I, 136.
[341]   Ibid. Although normally associated with criminal activity, the language of 'suspicion' is
        deployed in the wider detention powers conferred by *Migration Act* div 7.
[342]   Blackstone, above n 336, bk I ch I, 136. This is the rationale of *ICCPR* art 4; see also HRC,
        General Comment No 29: Article 4: Derogations during a State of Emergency, 72nd sess, UN
        Doc CCPR/C/21/Rev.1/Add.11 (31 August 2001) para 2; HRC, *General Comment No 5: Article
        4 (Derogation of Rights)*, 13th sess, UN Doc HRI/GEN/1/Rev.1 (31 July 1981) para 3. Cf
        Chapter 4, 121, n 51.
[343]   Of course, in all likelihood Blackstone's 'foreigner' was, like that of his international law
        counterparts, a European. In contrast, as we saw in Chapter 3, 87, he regarded 'infidels' to be
        those against whom there was a perpetual hostility and 'persons calling themselves Egyptians,
        or gypsies' as 'outlandish persons': see Blackstone, above n 336, bk IV ch XIII, 124.
        Nevertheless, here this would seem to be beside the point.
[344]   *Immigration Restriction Act 1901* (Cth) s 7.
[345]   *Migration Act* s 27 (later s 77, as amended, now repealed).

and upped the maximum period of imprisonment to two years.[346] It was not until 1992, when the mandatory detention legislation was already in force, that the offence of unlawful entry was repealed.[347] The repealing Act received Royal Assent on 7 December 1992, the day before the High Court delivered its decision in *Lim*.[348] Although the offence of unlawful entry had not been invoked in relation to the plaintiffs – and despite there being good reasons why unlawful entry, particularly of refugees and asylum seekers, should not be seen as criminal activity[349] – the criminal offence of unlawful arrival or entry was of long standing and imprisonment for the offence had been a punishment since 1901. Given that the *Constitution*'s concern is with 'substance and not mere form', and given that unlawful entry was historically a criminal offence, the conclusion that imprisonment for unlawful entry was not penal or punitive in character – because it was purportedly for another purpose ('to exclude, admit, or deport') – is striking.

For better and worse, the nature and history of unlawful entry as a criminal activity is clear. In contradistinction, and for the same activity, the Court accepted an administrative form of detention prescribing a ('maximum') period of (non-criminal) ('application') custody of 273 days (plus) – on top of detention for more than two years already – as non-judicial and, we can extrapolate, therefore 'essentially unexaminable'.[350] Indeed, the subsequent removal of the offence from the statute books points to an attempt to erase this fundamental contradiction.[351]

This analysis also leads irresistibly to the conclusion that the legislature was co-opting a power to detain that was (of its nature and by reason of historical considerations) essentially and exclusively judicial in character. The legislature had vested in the executive a power to detain for periods well capable of enduring beyond those the Parliament had hitherto adjudged appropriate to

---

[346] *Migration Legislation Amendment Act 1989* (Cth) s 14; under s 35, all provisions in the *Migration Act* were renumbered. As a result, s 27 became s 77.

[347] *Migration Reform Act* s 17 (which replaced s 77 of the *Migration Act* with a new s 77 and s 77A).

[348] There is no suggestion that its repeal informed the decision of the Court. However, it is quite a different question to think about whether the High Court proceeding may have prompted the provision's repeal.

[349] See especially *Refugee Convention* art 31 prohibiting the imposition of penalties on account of a refugee's unlawful entry or presence. For related literature, see above n 320.

[350] Cf *Tang Jia Xin* (1994) 69 ALJR 8, which addressed the situation where 'application custody' exceeded 273 days.

[351] Ironically, it also suggests that the seemingly benign decision not to prosecute the plaintiffs may have put them in a weaker position.

the offence of unlawful entry. In other words, it had co-opted a power that was effectively, extra-judicially, and collectively adjudging and 'punishing' 'criminal' 'guilt'.[352]

5.3.3.2 Aliens: Validating Their Vulnerability to an Unexaminable Power

In the joint judgment, their Honours opined that if the definition of designated persons were to apply to *citizens* rather than *non-citizens*,[353] the mandatory detention legislation "would be plainly beyond the legislative competence of the Parliament and invalid."[354] Their Honours provided two reasons for this. First, the *Constitution* provided no relevant head of legislative power in respect of citizens. Second, it would purport to authorise involuntary imprisonment *of citizens* by executive designation and deprive the courts of jurisdiction to order release if the detention were unlawful. This, they said, would confer 'an essentially unexaminable power' on the Executive.[355]

Their Honours held that "involuntary detention of a citizen . . . is penal or punitive in character."[356] Indeed, because it would be inconsistent with the doctrine of separation of powers and the exclusive function of the courts in adjudging and punishing (criminal) guilt, they said this would be so even if the power to detain was framed in terms 'divorced' from that exclusive function.[357] In other words, we see that because mandatory detention was a scheme applicable only to aliens, the power to imprison – still equally unexaminable – lost its inherently punitive character. As the discussion that follows shows, there were two principal bases for this conclusion outlined in the joint judgment: first, the vulnerability of aliens to exclusion and deportation; second, the suggestion that 'boat people' could choose to leave and thereby bring their detention to an end. Let us look at the first.[358]

---

[352] Perhaps the closest analogy is the statutory prescription of sentences of imprisonment for offences of strict liability. In Australia, the Senate Scrutiny of Bills Committee has indicated that one of the basic principles for Commonwealth policy on strict and absolute liability should be that "strict liability offences should be applied only where the penalty does not include imprisonment": Senate Standing Committee for the Scrutiny of Bills, Parliament of Australia, *The Work of the Committee during the 40th Parliament February 2002 – August 2004* (2008) 93. Cf *Al-Kateb* (2004) 219 CLR 562, 571 (Gleeson CJ).

[353] On use of the terms 'alien' and 'non-citizen', see *Nolan v Minister for Immigration and Ethnic Affairs* (1988) 165 CLR 178.

[354] *Lim* (1992) 176 CLR 1, 29 (Brennan, Deane, and Dawson JJ).   [355] Ibid.

[356] Ibid 27 (Brennan, Deane, and Dawson JJ).   [357] Ibid.

[358] On the voluntariness of detention, see below, Section 5.3.4.3, 223–7.

Their Honours stated that "an alien who is actually within this country enjoys the protection of our law".[359] However, while an alien is subject to the law and enjoys the protection of the law in some respects, mandatory detention is an instance where the legislature has done the opposite; that is, it has conferred an 'essentially unexaminable power' to imprison 'boat people'. So, in a matter as fundamental as personal liberty, 'boat people' could neither claim nor enjoy the protection of the law in any meaningful way.

On the strength of the aliens power, their Honours accepted that the differential treatment of 'boat people' was possible because, they said, an alien's "status, rights and immunities" differ from those of a citizen.[360] This difference, they said, lay in the alien's "vulnerability . . . to exclusion and deportation".[361] So it was on account of this vulnerability that any conflict between the mandatory detention scheme and the judicial power was averted. In other words, it was the diminished 'status, rights and immunities' of aliens that validated the use of an 'essentially unexaminable power' to detain those who were unwelcome.[362] As we know from the genealogy, the foreigner was historically not vulnerable, but rather a figure of privilege and power. Her vulnerability arose only once she was recast as a (non-European) outsider and concurrently with the emergence of the discourse of 'absolute sovereignty'. This reminds us that there is nothing juridically inevitable about the foreigner's vulnerability to exclusion and expulsion; rather, her vulnerability is more a (mutable) question of values and history.

So far, in relation to the Court's reading of the mandatory detention legislation, this section has considered how, in the inextricable relation between language and law, certain discursive patterns and repertoires shaped the Court's findings. It has also considered how the Court read the extent to which the judicial power might be invoked to scrutinise a power to detain that is incidental to the aliens power. We have also seen how the discourse of 'absolute sovereignty' permeated judicial thinking about mandatory detention, not least through discursive slippage, assumption, or silence. The final locus of power in this analysis is the executive power.

5.3.4 *The Executive Power and the Foreigner*

Two distinctions are central to the analysis of the executive power to detain aliens. The first is between the alien and the citizen, which is the primary basis on which the Court validated mandatory detention. The second is between

---

[359] *Lim* (1992) 176 CLR 1, 29 (Brennan, Deane, and Dawson JJ).   [360] Ibid.   [361] Ibid.
[362] Ibid.

detention for the purposes of punishment, on the one hand, or for a 'legitimate non-punitive object', on the other. With this in mind, this section looks at the discursive techniques that enabled the Court to conclude that mandatory detention of a certain class of (unwelcome) aliens was an 'exceptional case' and that it was permissible, non-punitive, and, indeed, voluntary. In doing so, I consider discursive slippages, assumptions, and silences that enabled the Court to read the detention of aliens in this way.

In the joint judgment in *Lim*, their Honours presaged some qualifications to the general proposition that the power to order involuntary custody of a citizen falls under the judicial power.[363] These "exceptional cases"[364] included pre-trial, mental health, and public health detention. In her judgment, Gaudron J described detention outside these "well-accepted categories" to be "offensive to ordinary notions of what is involved in a just society", although she resisted the idea that detention falling outside those categories is "inevitably offensive" to the judicial power.[365] In a similar vein, McHugh J noted that certain categories of executive detention are regarded as 'exceptional cases' because, as a rule,

[e]xecutive imprisonment has been considered oppressive and lawless since John, at Runnymede, pledged that no free man should be imprisoned, dispossessed, outlawed, or exiled, save by the judgment of his peers or by the law of the land.[366]

In its decision, the Court upheld mandatory detention of 'boat people' in a form that positioned it beyond the (meaningful) scrutiny of the courts on the basis that such detention was an exceptional case. This leads us to ask how the Court understood certain forms of detention to be 'exceptional'.

The following section considers the exceptional cases of administrative detention that the Court regarded as 'well-accepted'. In doing so, the analysis focuses not on how the Court concluded that the power to detain aliens was an exceptional case, but on how it concluded that mandatory detention of a certain class of aliens for an unspecified period and subject to no meaningful judicial scrutiny was an exceptional case. It argues that the discursive space created by 'absolute sovereignty' meant that the Court did not need to look for (or notice) differences between the mandatory detention scheme and other exceptional powers to detain cited by the Court. As the analysis shows, in contrast to mandatory detention, pre-trial, mental health, or public health

---

[363] Ibid 28 (Brennan, Deane, Dawson JJ), 55 (Gaudron J).
[364] Ibid 27 (Brennan, Deane, Dawson JJ).   [365] Ibid 55.
[366] Ibid 63, citing *Shaughnessy v United States ex rel Mezei*, 345 US 206, 218 (Jackson J) (1953) ('*Mezei*').

detention are not exclusively or necessarily non-judicial in character. Indeed, in each case, there are critical points at which the judiciary is engaged, precisely as a safeguard against excesses and abuses of power.

5.3.4.1 Exceptional Cases: Pre-trial, Mental Health, and Public Health Detention

According to the joint judgment, "[t]he most important" qualification to the general proposition that involuntary detention of a citizen is part of the judicial power is

> the arrest and detention in custody, pursuant to executive warrant, of a person accused of crime to ensure that he or she is available to be dealt with by the courts. Such committal to custody awaiting trial is not seen by the law as punitive or as appertaining exclusively to judicial power.[367]

This example of pre-trial detention gives rise to several points that distinguish it from decision-less detention. First, an executive warrant is a decision and thus remains judicially accountable. Indeed, a person arrested and detained pursuant to an executive warrant must be brought before a court within a prescribed time or released. If a bail application is made, the accused must be brought before a magistrate, who determines whether pre-trial detention is necessary to ensure that she is available to be dealt with by the courts. Second, bail decisions (which are, of course, judicial decisions) relate to the nature of the alleged offence and make an individualised assessment of flight risk. A necessary corollary is that where pre-trial detention of an individual is found to be unnecessary, bail will be granted.[368] Third, while such detention is not ipso facto regarded as punitive in character, there is an element of window dressing to this position, given that any period of pre-trial detention that has been 'served' is usually subtracted from any custodial sentence imposed following conviction. In other words, in the event of an acquittal, its punitive element is excused rather than absent.

Like pre-trial detention, involuntary detention in cases of mental illness or infectious disease can, their Honours observed, "legitimately be seen as non-punitive in character" and, they suggested, does not *necessarily* involve the exercise of judicial power.[369] As the situation in Victoria illustrates, both

---

[367] *Lim* (1992) 176 CLR 1, 28 (Brennan, Deane, and Dawson JJ); see also at 71 (McHugh J).

[368] In Victoria, the only offences for which there is a presumption against bail are treason or murder. Even then, if 'exceptional circumstances exist which justify the making of such an order', bail may be granted: *Bail Act 1977* (Vic) s 13(2).

[369] *Lim* (1992) 176 CLR 1, 28 (Brennan, Deane, and Dawson JJ).

mental health and public health detention can be seen as having a protective purpose.

In the case of mental health detention, such protection is from serious harm to the individual or individuals detained or, in certain cases, the protection of others.[370] Furthermore, such detention is highly individualised, subject to close medical and judicial review and scrutiny,[371] and its duration strictly scrutinised.[372]

In the case of public health detention, orders can be issued to detain non-compliant individuals. However, this is as a last resort,[373] not an initial step. Furthermore, public health detention is rarely used.[374] In Victoria, warrants for arrest and detention on public health grounds are by order of a magistrate unless a state of emergency has been declared.[375] Strict time limits, both to public health detention more generally[376] and to public health detention in the context of a state of emergency, still pertain.[377]

The safeguards built into all these forms of involuntary detention are attentive to both the risks and consequences of excesses or abuses of the power to detain. Indeed, there are merits review procedures available for decisions to detain,[378] and these procedures are subject to judicial review.[379]

As this analysis shows, unlike mandatory detention of 'boat people', none of these exceptional cases confers an 'essentially unexaminable power' to detain, and none is decision-less. So even if, as a general proposition, the detention of aliens may be characterised as exceptional, the scope of the powers conferred by the mandatory detention scheme extends far beyond anything contemplated by other forms of administrative detention, including detention for the purposes of deportation, which

---

[370] *Mental Health Act 2014* (Vic) s 351 ('*Mental Health Act*').
[371] In Victoria, this review is by the Mental Health Tribunal, a body whose decisions are subject to judicial review: *Mental Health Act* pt 8; *Administrative Law Act 1978* (Vic) s 3.
[372] *Mental Health Act* ss 34, 51, 57, 93, 94C.
[373] *Public Health and Wellbeing Act 2008* (Vic) s 113(3)(c). On detention as a last resort, see also: *Convention on the Rights of the Child*, opened for signature 20 November 1989, 1577 UNTS 3 (entered into force 2 September 1990) art 37; UNHCR, *Detention Guidelines*, above n 208, Guideline 2; see also *Migration Act* s 4AA, inserted by *Migration Amendment (Detention Arrangements) Act 2005* (Cth) sch 1 pt 1 cl 1
[374] Sanjaya N Senanayake and Mark J Ferson, 'Detention for Tuberculosis: Public Health and the Law' (2004) 180(11) *Medical Journal of Australia* 573.
[375] *Public Health and Wellbeing Act 2008* (Vic) s 198.
[376] Ibid s 113(3)(c) (limits detention to 72 hours and only for specific purposes).
[377] Ibid s 200 (requires review of continued detention at least every 24 hours).
[378] *Mental Health Act* div 8; ibid ss 121–2.   [379] *Administrative Law Act 1978* (Vic) s 3.

have long been subject to judicial review.[380] This suggests that it was the expansive influence of the discourse of 'absolute sovereignty' that enabled the Court to give unthought credence[381] to the 'exceptional cases' argument.

5.3.4.2 Discerning a 'Legitimate Non-punitive Object'

As noted earlier, central to the decision in *Lim* was whether, or the extent to which, the mandatory detention scheme was subject to the judicial power. This turned principally on whether the detention to which 'boat people' were subject under the legislation was for a punitive or non-punitive purpose. In this and the following section, I explore in greater depth the discourse that has led to the legitimising conclusion that mandatory detention bears a non-punitive character. In particular, I consider the significance of the distinction between legislative purpose and legislative effect in the 'characterisation' and 'legitimisation' processes.

As we know, the Court drew its authority from the suite of jurisprudence from which the common law doctrine of 'absolute sovereignty' emerged and specifically accepted Vattel (as instrumentally interpreted) as international legal authority.[382] Likewise, the joint judgment accepted *Cain*[383] as authority for the proposition that the power to expel and deport imports a concomitant power to detain "to the extent necessary to make expulsion or deportation effective".[384] This, they said, was a position that has been "consistently recognised" as falling within the scope of the aliens power.[385] By underscoring the consistency with which this position had been recognised, their Honours elevated consistency to a virtue. They made no further inquiry into, for example, what 'to the extent necessary' might mean.

So, in its relation to the aliens power, how did they see the purpose of detention? The joint judgment described *Koon Wing Lau v Calwell*[386] ('*Koon*

---

[380] In asserting that there is no inherent power in a court to interfere with the detention of an alien through the grant of bail or habeas corpus in a non-criminal proceeding, McHugh J cited *R v Alamazoff* [1919] 3 WWR 281, 282; 30 Man R 143: *Lim* (1992) 176 CLR 1, 68–9. However, the Court in that case was considering whether there were additional bail rights over and above those already provided by statute. It was not, therefore, endorsing an 'essentially unexaminable power'. On judicial review of decisions to detain, see above 164; see also Chapter 4 Section 4.3.3.2, 152–4.
[381] Jens Bartelson, *A Genealogy of Sovereignty* (Cambridge University Press, 1995) 49.
[382] See Chapter 3, 99–101, 103; Chapter 4 Section 4.2.2.3, 127–9.   [383] [1906] AC 542.
[384] *Lim* (1992) 176 CLR 1, 30 (Brennan, Deane, Dawson JJ); followed in *Nauru Detention Case* (2016) 257 CLR 42, 69–70 [40] (French CJ, Kiefel and Nettle JJ).
[385] Ibid.   [386] (1949) 80 CLR 533.

Wing Lau') as "the clearest example" of detention for the purposes of making a deportation effective.[387] As we know, the case considered the validity of powers in the (post-war) *War-Time Refugees Removal Act* 1949 (Cth) ('*War-Time Refugees Removal Act*') to detain wartime refugees pending deportation.[388] The relevant provision only authorised custody *pending* deportation.[389] Where detention was not necessary, s 7(2) authorised release upon a surety. As such, *Koon Wing Lau* speaks only to detention *pending* deportation, and then only to the extent 'necessary' to make an expulsion or deportation effective.[390] In other words, if expulsion or deportation were not imminent or could be effected in another way, there was no basis under the *War-Time Refugees Removal Act* for detention.

So, how did the joint judgment treat the decision in *Koon Wing Lau*? Their Honours confined their reliance on it to the validation of detention for the (limited) purposes of the executive power of expulsion and deportation. This was, they said, because "to that limited extent, authority to detain in custody is neither punitive in nature[391] nor part of the judicial power of the Commonwealth."[392] In doing so, and notwithstanding that the idea that deportation is inherently non-punitive is contestable,[393] they relied only on *Koon Wing Lau*. This implied that *mandatory* detention was 'required' for the ('non-punitive') purpose of expulsion and deportation because it was "reasonably capable of being seen as necessary for the purposes of deportation."[394]

However, their Honours went further. In a discursive slippage that would have far-reaching effect,[395] they extended their interpretation of the (incidental and limited) authority to detain for the purposes of expulsion or deportation to include what they described as 'executive powers' to *receive, investigate, and determine* an application for entry. As discussed earlier, they paradoxically

---

[387] *Lim* (1992) 176 CLR 1, 31 (Brennan, Deane, and Dawson JJ).
[388] See Chapter 4 Section 4.3.2, 142–51.
[389] *War-Time Refugees Removal Act* 1949 (Cth) s 7.
[390] *Koon Wing Lau* (1949) 80 CLR 533, 551. Cf Toohey J's reading of *Koon Wing Lau*: *Lim* (1992) 176 CLR 1, 46–7.
[391] Citing *Walsh and Johnson* (1925) 37 CLR 36, 60–61, 96; *O'Keefe* (1949) 77 CLR 261, 278; *Koon Wing Lau* (1949) 80 CLR 533, 555; *Chu Shao Hung v The Queen* (1953) 87 CLR 575, 589. See also *Lim* (1992) 176 CLR 1, 71 (McHugh J).
[392] *Lim* (1992) 176 CLR 1, 32 (Brennan, Deane, and Dawson JJ).
[393] See, eg, *Fong*, 149 US 698, 740 (Brewer J) (quoting President Madison), 764 (Fuller J) (1893). See Chapter 3, 105.
[394] *Lim* (1992) 176 CLR 1, 33–4 (Brennan, Deane, and Dawson JJ).
[395] See, eg, *Al-Kateb* (2004) 219 CLR 562, 571 (Gleeson CJ), 582 (McHugh J), 613 (Gummow J); *Behrooz v Secretary, Department of Immigration and Multicultural and Indigenous Affairs* (2004) 219 CLR 486, 498–9 (Gleeson CJ); *Re Woolley; Ex parte Applicants M276/2003* (2004) 225 CLR 1, 13–14 (Gleeson CJ), 20 (McHugh J).

expanded the 'limited' authority to detain (for expulsion or deportation) into an unlimited limitation on the exercise of the aliens power. In other words, their Honours elided power with process, thereby (con)fusing the inherently illogical assertions that detention of a class of persons *as a class* is substantively 'necessary' "in order to ensure"[396] the deportation or removal of each member of that class. That is, they removed the individualised risk assessment that formed part of the 'legitimate non-punitive object' of the (other) 'exceptional cases'. They also accepted the characterisation of detention as (somehow) procedurally 'necessary' to the administrative decision to grant an entry permit.

It is true that the consequences of expulsion and deportation, on the one hand, and entry or admission, on the other, may arise from the same decision and are, in that sense, two sides of the same coin. However, detention for the purposes of expulsion and deportation has quite a different character to detention for the purposes of preventing admission pending determination of an application for entry, especially of the complexity of RSD procedures. This is particularly so given that the power to expel or deport is suspended while an application for entry is pending.[397] It cannot, therefore, be characterised as detention for the purposes of deportation. It is 'just-in-case' detention – that is, detention just in case a person's application to remain fails and she becomes subject to deportation or removal. However, the Court did not critically engage with the question of whether such detention went beyond what was 'reasonably capable of being seen as necessary' for the purpose of deportation, and therefore whether it trespassed on the judicial power. Instead, the Court declared that it was satisfied with the safeguards in place, including the 273-day rule.

5.3.4.3 Executive Detention: On Safeguards, Necessity, and Volition

In considering safeguards against prolonged or indefinite detention, while McHugh J conceded that the 273-day (plus) period seemed to be "inordinately long",[398] he concluded that it did not go 'beyond what was reasonably

---

[396] *Lim* (1992) 176 CLR 1, 47 (Toohey J).

[397] *Migration Act* s 54P (as at 6 May 1992; now s 181) negatively delimits removal/deportation powers by outlining the only circumstances in which removal 'must' take place. In the case of asylum seekers, the obligation not to remove pending determination of a claim derives (in part) from *Refugee Convention* art 33, which prohibits *refoulement*. In this regard, it is important to emphasise that refugee status is declaratory not constitutive: UNHCR, *Handbook and Guidelines*, UN Doc HCR/1P/4/ENG/REV.3, para 28; Hathaway, above n 250, 11.

[398] *Lim* (1992) 176 CLR 1, 71–2.

necessary'. That is, in a similar gesture of deferential legal instrumentalism to his judicial colleagues, he treated mandatory detention as having "the non-punitive object of ensuring that aliens who have no entry permit are kept under supervision and control until their claims for refugee status are determined".[399] In this way, he gave voice to the discourse of control and then erased the possibility that the scheme had gone too far, concluding that the prescribed period of detention was 'appropriately' restrained in view of the "vast number of applications" then before the Immigration Department.[400] His reasons do not reveal that roughly 98 per cent of the 23,000 applicants to whom he made reference were not in detention.[401] Instead, he deemed the administrative burden on the Immigration Department an appropriate justification for prolonged imprisonment. Furthermore, he implied that the "very considerable period of time" the plaintiffs had already spent in pre-mandatory detention custody and the nature of the right to liberty itself were of no consequence in the sense that, he said, the duration of detention did not convert the scheme into a usurpation of the judicial power or destroy the scheme's non-punitive character.[402]

In considering whether the mandatory detention scheme included adequate safeguards against indefinite or prolonged detention, the joint judgment addressed a number of issues, including the 273-day rule. First, while gesturing to the clock-stopping dimensions to the formula, their Honours described the 273-day rule as "effectively" limiting the total period of detention to a "maximum . . . of 273 days".[403] In conjunction with the 273-day rule, they described the statutory obligation of removal 'as soon as practicable' where an application has been finally refused[404] or no application has been made[405] as going "a long way" towards ensuring that detention was "limited to" what was reasonably capable of being seen as necessary for the purposes of deportation or enabling an entry application to be made.[406] However, in the case of the

---

[399] Ibid 71.   [400] Ibid 72.

[401] DIBP, 'Immigration Detention and Community Statistics Summary', above n 13.

[402] *Lim* (1992) 176 CLR 1, 73.

[403] Ibid 33 (Brennan, Deane, and Dawson JJ); see also at 74 (McHugh J). Although they acknowledged that time would not run while events were beyond the control of the Immigration Department, the judgment does not engage substantively with the implications of this. Cf *Tang Jia Xin* (1994) 69 ALJR 8.

[404] *Migration Act* s 54P(3) (as at 6 May 1992; now s 181(3)).

[405] Ibid s 54P(2) (as at 6 May 1992; now s 181(2)). On use of this provision to hold people in incommunicado-like detention see, eg, Nick Poynder, 'The Incommunicado Detention of Boat People' (1997) 3(2) *Australian Journal of Human Rights* 53, 72–6; see also Savitri Taylor, 'Should Unauthorised Arrivals in Australia Have Free Access to Advice and Assistance?' (2000) 6(1) *Australian Journal of Human Rights* 34, 36, 41–4.

[406] *Lim* (1992) 176 CLR 1, 33 (Brennan, Deane, Dawson JJ).

plaintiffs, their Honours did not regard such limitations as of themselves sufficient. This was, they said, because the plaintiffs had been unlawfully detained "for years" prior to the commencement of Division 4B.[407] In that connection, their Honours turned to s 54P(1).[408]

Section 54P(1) created a statutory obligation of removal where a designated person asks the Minister, in writing, to be removed. On the strength of this provision, their Honours held that "it always lies within the power of a designated person to bring his or her detention in custody to an end by requesting to be removed from Australia".[409] By concluding that any continued detention arises only if a designated person "*elects* ... to remain in the country",[410] they accepted the Solicitor-General's 'choice' rhetoric that attributed responsibility to 'boat people' for their (continued) detention and predicament. Indeed, their Honours suggested that the plaintiffs' custody arose from their 'failure'[411] to make a request under s 54P(1) to leave the country, a suggestion which disregards not only the principle of *non-refoulement* under international law,[412] but also that applications for refugee status lapse upon departure.[413]

Likewise, and concurring with their Honours, McHugh J held that s 54P(1) meant that a designated person "may release himself or herself from the custody imposed or enforced" by the legislation. This provision, he said, "makes it *impossible* to regard [mandatory detention] in its ordinary operation as punishment."[414] He reached this conclusion notwithstanding his acknowledgment that a designated person "might regard the choice between detention and leaving the country as not a real choice."[415] Indeed, he described the detention as being "with the *concurrence* or *acquiescence* of the 'detainee'" and considered this "vital" in concluding that detention was not punitive and therefore did not engage the judicial power.[416] Presumably, he placed the word 'detainee' in inverted commas to signify that he did not really regard her as being detained at all:

A person is not being punished if, after entering Australia without permission, he or she *chooses* to be detained in custody pending the determination of an application for entry rather than to leave the country during the period of determination.[417]

[407] *Migration Act* div 4B (now div 6); *Lim* (1992) 176 CLR 1, 33 (Brennan, Deane, Dawson JJ).
[408] *Migration Act* s 54P(1) (as at 6 May 1992; now s 181(1)).
[409] *Lim* (1992) 176 CLR 1, 34 (Brennan, Deane, Dawson JJ).   [410] Ibid (emphasis added).
[411] Ibid.   [412] See above n 397.
[413] A non-citizen is not eligible for a protection visa (that is, the visa granted to a person recognised as a refugee) unless she is in Australia: *Migration Act* s 36(2).
[414] *Lim* (1992) 176 CLR 1, 72 (emphasis added).   [415] Ibid.   [416] Ibid (emphases added).
[417] Ibid (emphasis added).

It is not clear whether McHugh J regarded it (incorrectly) as possible for an application to remain pending even following departure.[418] However, there are two key points in this passage. First, he bought into the discourses of deviance and opportunism by implicitly criticising arrival without permission. Second, he characterised the concomitant 'choice' to be detained as providing a sufficient basis for concluding that such detention is non-punitive,[419] thereby placing responsibility for detention in the hands of 'boat people' themselves, politically and juridically.

As we can see from the joint judgment, while their Honours arrived at their decision in a different way to McHugh J, the result was the same. Most significantly, their Honours were prepared to conclude that a designated person who remains in detention while her application for an entry permit is decided is electing to do so.[420] This inversion of voluntariness effectively absolved the state of responsibility for the nature and duration of mandatory detention without exploring and testing the vagaries of the argument. The incongruity of this conclusion is further highlighted by the following brief analysis – an analysis which draws on jurisprudence, with links that can be traced to the judgment of McHugh J.

In his reasons, McHugh J referred to the decision of the US Supreme Court in *Shaughnessy v United States ex rel Mezei*[421] ('*Mezei*'). He did so for purposes other than those discussed here.[422] Notably, the question of the voluntariness of detention in *Mezei* apparently failed to capture his attention.

In *Mezei*, an alien resident of the United States returning from travel abroad was excluded on undisclosed security grounds. No other country would accept him, so he was detained on Ellis Island in New York harbour for 21 months. Government counsel argued that his detention was a 'refuge' and that he was free to leave at any time, *except* to enter US territory. While the majority relied on the doctrine of sovereignty and limitations on due process outlined in the now-familiar nineteenth-century line of authority of the US Supreme Court, a dissenting opinion of Jackson J resisted the "impeccable legal logic" that Mezei was "free to take leave" as "overworking legal fiction", "artificial", "unreal" and lacking the "commonest of common sense", suggesting sardonically that it "might mean freedom, if only he were an amphibian!"[423]

Whether or not one accepts that there is an (enforceable) right to seek and enjoy asylum, a person who leaves her country and seeks to enter another for

---

[418] See above n 413.   [419] *Lim* (1992) 176 CLR 1, 73.
[420] Ibid 34 (Brennan, Deane, Dawson JJ); see also Crock, 'Climbing Jacob's Ladder', above n 272, 347–8.
[421] 345 US 206 (1953).   [422] See above n 241.
[423] *Mezei*, 345 US 206, 220 (Jackson and Frankfurter JJ) (1953).

reasons of survival and for whom exit from the putative place of refuge would be dangerous has, historically, and for good reason, been regarded as deserving "a just assistance".[424] Recalling the genealogy of the foreigner-sovereign relation in Part I, if a foreigner's rights of necessity and to hospitality are occluded by the deprivation of liberty, it is overworking a legal fiction to say that she can choose to do something else. The availability of that choice does not render the deprivation of liberty lawful, especially if the choice is neither meaningful nor real because of the (obvious)[425] dangers that inhere in the consequences. In addition, as we know, the lawful pursuit of a refugee or other application, including the exercise of any appeal rights, could not be progressed other than by 'choosing' to remain in detention.[426] Yet, there is no doubt that the 'impeccable logic' of volition that the Solicitor-General brought emphatically to the bar table through the rhetorical device of repetition had the desired effect.

5.4 DECISION-LESS DETENTION: A THINKABLE INSTITUTIONAL RESPONSE

This case study has, through an analysis of rhetorical and institutional discourses in Parliament, the courtroom, and on the judicial record, traced how mandatory detention became a thinkable institutional response to unsolicited migration – politically, legislatively, and jurisprudentially. It has drawn out how lines of continuity and discontinuity embodied in the conceptualisation of the figure of the foreigner as (unwelcome) outsider and of the sovereign right to exclude her as absolute are performed and sustained in contemporary migration discourse. It has also shown how discourses across a spectrum of registers move, shape, and influence juridical thinking and argument. As the analysis illustrates, although the discursive techniques at work may differ in each forum, they remain audible and their historical antecedents discernible.

The analysis exposes common and recurring discursive patterns and techniques that influence how law is used, shaped, and understood. It has also shown how classic doctrinal techniques – particularly the doctrines of precedent and responsible government and the related concept of judicial deference – are used to secure acceptance of and acquiescence in the use of harsh measures.

In each place, and in different registers, speakers deployed for their persuasive value a rich array of linguistic choices. For example, metaphor captured complex meaning with simplicity and brevity, but at the expense of precision.

---

[424]   Vattel, above n 295, bk II ch IX §120; See also Chapter 2, 75, earlier, where Vattel recounts the story of Captain Bontekoe.
[425]   See McHugh and Brennan JJ, above n 253.   [426]   See above n 413.

Ambiguous and flexible, metaphor was easy to communicate and hindered counter-argument. Terms such as 'queue-jumper', 'national interest', and 'boat people' could lodge in the imagination, encoding and distorting the debate. And heavy-handed use of repetition and rhetorical questions, popular/ist pejoratives, and hyperbolic prejudice cemented the power relation by denigrating the target group (and anyone who supported them) as deviant opportunists.

Likewise, 'extraordinary' measures were explained using a dominant discourse of control (pitched as imperative) tempered with discursive gestures of restraint that framed state action as appropriate, balanced, necessary, and fair. In case anyone was in any doubt, a rhetoric of restraint signalled ministerial reticence ('no wish to keep people in custody indefinitely') and parliamentary reasonableness ('could not expect Parliament to support such a suggestion'). These discourses carried over into the courtroom and were given expression on the judicial record through a combination of judicial deference and pragmatism: the Parliament must ultimately bear the responsibility for the laws it makes, detention for processing is 'reasonably capable of being seen as necessary', and inordinately long detention is reasonably necessary if the Immigration Department has a heavy workload.

At the same time, oppressive state action was justified through moralising discourses of deviance and opportunism that represented 'boat people' as lawless and unworthy and not 'genuine' refugees, a cohort of unwelcome foreigners supported by an equally deviant, divisive, and manipulative network of 'slick and sleazy' lawyers, 'parasites', 'do-gooders', and 'bleeding hearts'. In the courtroom, the arrival of 'boat people' was described as surreptitious and clandestine, while the 'boat people' themselves were referred to as 'these people' who would not engage with 'us' on 'our' terms and would disappear into the community given half the chance.

These discourses were supplemented by other discursive techniques. For example, we saw the use of over- and understatement to talk up fairness and restraint and, conversely, downplay injustice and repression. Likewise, the technique of temporariness promised (or 'intended') that oppressive measures would be 'interim'[427] and that the future would assuredly be one of simplicity,

---

[427]   In a more recent example of this, an expert panel on asylum seekers holding that extraterritorial detention and processing on Nauru and Manus Island be reinstated as a 'circuit breaker': Angus Houston, Paris Aristotle, and Michael L'Estrange, 'Report of the Expert Panel on Asylum Seekers' (Australian Government, August 2012) 47 <http://expertpanelona sylumseekers.dpmc.gov.au/>. Then, in September 2016, Minister for Immigration, Peter Dutton, told the Australian Strategic Policy Institute that the refugee processing relationship with Nauru "will continue for decades": Peter Dutton, *Address to the Australian Strategic Policy Institute*, 20 September 2016 <http://www.minister.border.gov.au/peterdutton/2016/P ages/address-australian-strategic-policy-institute-15092016.aspx>.

clarity, and fairness. Invidious inversions of the power relation framed the state (and the taxpayer) as the vulnerable[428] and defenceless victim of 'boat people' and the mandatory detention scheme as a restoration of control over a system in crisis.

In addition, we have seen how prejudice, in particular racial prejudice, was managed juridically and politically. In political discourse, techniques that coupled positive self-presentation with denigration of the target group sought to inoculate the speaker against the charge of racism or other prejudice. Other techniques denigrated critics, averted debate, and deflected criticism. The technique of 'splitting' created divisions between good refugees ('real' refugees who stay in the 'queue') and bad ones ('economic' opportunists who jump in boats). This enabled condemnation of 'boat people' and absolution from the charge of prejudice. In the courtroom, we saw the Solicitor-General playing with the race issue (exploiting the 'Polish blessing') in staking a claim to law's innocence.[429] And on the judicial record, with the exception of a tangential issue raised by Gaudron J, we saw the race issue erased by an override provision. Why? Because no argument could be made out in the absence of constitutional safeguards – safeguards that, as we saw in Chapter 4, were omitted from the *Constitution* precisely to *enable* racial discrimination. Understood in this way, we are reminded that race has nothing – yet every-thing – to do with mandatory detention.

We also saw techniques of silence permeating discourses in Parliament, the courtroom, and the jurisprudence. A departmental briefing to Senator Harradine was silent as to the major reason for the timing of the mandatory detention legislation – that is, to stymie an existing legal proceeding. We saw how the 'national interest' metaphor embodied the silent supposition that whatever 'we' *think* or *say* is in the 'national interest' *is* in the 'national interest', whatever unarticulated or unutterable meaning may lie behind it. And through it all we saw the silence of decision-less detention, a product of value judgments and historical practices that is underwritten by the discourse of 'absolute sovereignty'.

Finally, by reading judicial text *as discourse*, we saw how multiple assump-tions, slippages, and silences permeated and expanded an already highly permissive jurisprudence. We saw that the juridical space that the discourse of 'absolute sovereignty' accords is so wide that a limitation on the power to

---

[428] The Australian state is not alone in scripting itself as vulnerable. On the Singapore state's narrative of national vulnerability, see Jothie Rajah, *Authoritarian Rule of Law: Legislation, Discourse and Legitimacy in Singapore* (Cambridge University Press, 2012) 21–4.

[429] Fitzpatrick, above n 136.

detain has effectively become an unlimited limitation. At the same time, together with the obligation to remove 'as soon as practicable' in certain prescribed circumstances, 'application custody' was described as 'going a long way' towards ensuring that detention was limited (even though 'custody' was not). These findings reinforced, and arguably expanded, the special resilience of the aliens power. But the ultimate *coup de grâce* was the Court's conclusion that detention was voluntary. In other words, forced migration is voluntary and any consequence that flows from it – including deprivation of liberty for 'however long it takes' – is also voluntary.

To conclude, this chapter has made visible how rhetorical and institutional techniques work in a complex contemporary migration discourse and how they draw on the threads of a discourse of 'absolute sovereignty' that can be traced to legal traditions and orthodoxies of long standing. It has enabled us to see more clearly what happens when a contestable and contingent historical artefact ('absolute sovereignty') – a synthesis of political-economic purposes, administrative techniques, and juridical forms of engagement – is cradled discursively into a universal, timeless, and irrefutable truth. It highlights how easily the power to exclude and condition the entry and stay of certain classes of (unwelcome) outsider can be used when there is an institutional environment that is so accustomed to "naked and uninhibited power"[430] that lawmakers can remain structurally indifferent to migration law's effects,[431] no matter how oppressive and far-reaching.

In Chapter 6, examination of the policy of planned destitution shows that it, too, is part of an ingrained system of thought and practice, in which the discourse of 'absolute sovereignty' remains paradigmatic to the way we think, talk, and write about policy responses to unsolicited migration. Even though 'absolute sovereignty' is not explicitly articulated, we see that it does not need to be, because it is already integral to how lawmakers think about unsolicited migration.[432] As with mandatory detention, we see how parallel and mutually self-validating themes of control and restraint, and of deviance and opportunism, reflect the discourse of 'absolute sovereignty'. Likewise, we see the discursive power of silence in the framing and shaping of responses to unsolicited migration.

---

[430] CPD, House of Representatives, 1 May 1958, 1398 (Alexander Downer). See Chapter 4, 153.
[431] Friedrich Nietzsche, *The Gay Science* (Bernard Williams ed, Josefine Nauckhoff and Adrian Del Caro trans, Cambridge University Press, 2001) 202 [trans of: *Die fröhliche Wissenschaft* (first published 1882)]; David Owen, *Nietzsche's Genealogy of Morality* (McGill-Queen's University Press, 2007) 4. See Chapter 1, Section 1.2.1, 23–4.
[432] Foucault, above n 264, 534, 540–1; Orford, above n 264, 617–18. See Chapter 1, 23–4.

6

Planned Destitution

In 1997, an amendment to the *Migration Regulations 1994* (Cth) ('*Migration Regulations*') was tabled in Parliament.[1] It became widely known as the '45-day rule'. Under this rule, work rights were automatically denied to any asylum seeker who had been in Australia for 45 days or more in the year prior to the date of her application for refugee status (known as a 'protection visa application').[2] Between 1997 and 2009, this resulted in well-documented, widespread, and long-term destitution, homelessness, and despair.[3] The 'no work' condition[4] that attached to an asylum seeker's temporary processing visa (called a 'bridging visa')[5] applied for the duration of the refugee status determination (RSD) process, including all reviews and appeals. Limited exceptions to the

---

[1] *Migration Regulations (Amendment) 1997* No 185 (Cth).

[2] The first iteration of these changes envisaged a timeframe of 14 days: Explanatory Statement, *Migration Regulations (Amendment) 1997* No 109 (Cth). It was soon revised up to 45 days: Explanatory Statement, *Migration Regulations (Amendment) 1997* No 185 (Cth). *Migration Regulations 1994* (Cth) sch 2 reg 051.611A(1)(b) ('*Migration Regulations*'); *Migration Regulations (Amendment) 1997* No 185 (Cth) regs 10–14. On protection visas, see *Migration Act 1958* (Cth) s 36 ('*Migration Act*').

[3] See, eg, Asylum Seekers Centre, Submission to Department of Immigration and Multicultural Affairs (DIMA), *Review of Bridging Visas*, May 2006; Hotham Mission, Submission to DIMA, *Review of Bridging Visas*, May 2006; Law Council of Australia, Submission to DIMA, *Review of Bridging Visas*, 7 August 2006; Marc Purcell, 'Knife Edge: Surviving Asylum in the Australian Community' (Occasional Paper No 15, Melbourne Catholic Commission for Justice, Development and Peace, 2004); cf Adrienne Millbank, 'Asylum Seekers on Bridging Visa E' (Research Brief No 13, Parliamentary Library, Parliament of Australia, 2007).

[4] There are 16 possible conditions relating to work rights: *Migration Regulations* sch 8 regs 8101–8116.

[5] The bridging visa regime has been described as "very complex", incorporating seven classes of visa, nine subclasses, and more than 30 discrete bases on which a bridging visa may be granted: Law Council of Australia, above n 3, 3. Which bridging visa and subclass a given individual is granted will be determined by her mode of arrival, her current legal status, her eligibility for release from detention, and her travel and residency intentions: *Migration Regulations* sch 1.

no-work condition were if departmental delays in making the primary decision exceeded six months[6] or if the asylum seeker was a member of a class of persons for whom the government had made an exception.[7] In contrast, a person applying for refugee status *within* the 45-day time limit was granted work rights automatically. These rights had effect until her application was 'finally determined',[8] a term which, as this chapter shows, has a particular meaning.[9]

The effects of the 45-day rule were human, institutional, and political. At a human level, an asylum seeker could be left destitute for months and possibly years because she had not, for whatever reason, lodged her application within 45 days of arrival. Indeed, this rule even applied where an applicant still held a valid visa at the time of lodging her application. At an institutional level, because the government chose to regard an application at the end of the merits review process as 'finally determined', but before judicial review processes had been exhausted, an (unsuccessful) applicant was denied work rights and could be described as a 'failed asylum seeker'. As we will see, the no-work condition was reactivated for failed asylum seekers even if they had proceedings on foot, rendering them destitute. Institutional techniques such as these ensured that individuals engaging lawful procedures were rendered statistically invisible because they were no longer regarded as asylum seekers.[10] Politically, the 45-day rule was pitched as a virtuous disincentive to abuse.[11] With the amendment entirely focused on the timing of applications, delay was treated (negatively) as a determinant of merit.

In 2009, following a change of government, the 45-day rule was abolished for 'certain' but not all bridging visa holders.[12] In its place, an asylum seeker holding a valid substantive visa (say, a tourist or student visa) was entitled to work rights if her lawful status remained unbroken – that is, if she lodged her application before her visa expired and maintained lawful status thereafter. However, if at any time she did not have lawful status and she was in Australia for more than 45 days

---

[6] *Migration Regulations (Amendment)* 1997 No 216 (Cth) regs 7–8, sch 2 pts 010 (Bridging Visa A), 020 (Bridging Visa B).

[7] *Migration Regulations (Amendment)* 1997 No 185 (Cth) regs 10–14; see *Migration Regulations* sch 2. Such exceptions include, for example, changed country of origin conditions justifying a late application for protection.

[8] *Migration Act* s 5(9).   [9] See below Section 6.2.1, 259–61.   [10] See below 260–61.

[11] Philip Ruddock, 'The Broad Implications for Administrative Law under the Coalition Government with Particular Reference to Migration Matters' (1997) 48 *Administrative Review* 4, 8.

[12] Explanatory Statement, *Migration Amendment Regulations 2009 (No 6)* No 143 (Cth).

before making her application, the no-work condition was mandatory the first time her bridging visa was issued.[13] Thereafter, subject to a complex of stringent requirements, she could apply to have the no-work condition lifted. In this situation, to be eligible for work rights, she had to establish a 'compelling need to work'[14] on the grounds of 'financial hardship', and her reasons for delaying her application beyond 45 days had to be 'acceptable'.[15]

Individual vulnerability and systemic barriers to social and economic inclusion through the denial of work rights are, of course, heightened when viewed in conjunction with policies that limit access to welfare. Those policies strictly circumscribe access to welfare for asylum seekers. It is this combination of policies that prompted Simon Brown LJ a year earlier to describe asylum seekers in an analogous situation in the UK as faced with a "bleak choice: whether to remain ... destitute and homeless until their claims are finally determined or whether instead to abandon their claims and return to face the very persecution they have fled."[16]

In Australia, subject to limited exceptions, asylum seekers holding bridging visas are not eligible for social security.[17] This means they do not qualify for a healthcare card, the issue of which triggers access to a range of governmental and non-governmental services, concessions, and benefits that help alleviate poverty.[18] Unless otherwise satisfying residency requirements, since 1991, asylum seekers have been ineligible for the Special

---

13 Department of Immigration and Border Protection (DIBP), 'Procedures Advice Manual 3: Guidelines for Officers Administering Migration Legislation' (2016), Bridging E Visas, Compelling Need to Work (PAM3), accessed through LEGENDcom, an online database of Australian migration and citizenship legislation and policy documents. The database is produced and maintained by the Department of Immigration and Border Protection, <www.bord er.gov.au/Trav/Visa/LEGE>.

14 *Migration Regulations* reg 1.08; *Migration Amendment Regulations 2009 (No 6) No 143* (Cth); DIBP, PAM3, above n 13, Bridging E Visas, Compelling Need to Work.

15 See below Section 6.2.2.3, 265–8.

16 *R v Secretary of State for Social Security, Ex parte Joint Council for the Welfare of Immigrants* [1996] 4 All ER 385, 393 ('*Ex parte JCWI*'). On the idea of 'constructive *refoulement*' see Chapter 5, 199 n 251.

17 *Health Insurance Act 1973* (Cth) s 3(1)(v)(B); *Social Security Act 1991* (Cth) ss 7(2), 7(7), 1061ZO, div 3 ('*Social Security Act*'). One exception is for holders of what is known as the (relatively rare) Removal Pending Bridging Visa: *Migration Regulations* sch 1, pt 3, cl 1307(3) (Bridging Visa R (BVR), Subclass 070). The BVR is issued to people who have been detained and have requested to depart Australia but who cannot be returned. Persons on BVR are eligible for social security and have full work rights: *Migration Regulations* sch 2 cl 070.6. The BVR was introduced following the decision of the High Court in *Al-Kateb v Godwin* (2004) 219 CLR 562, in which a narrow majority upheld the constitutionality of indefinite detention of an unlawful non-citizen, even for life: *Migration Amendment Regulations (No 6) 2004* (Cth) sch 1.

18 *Social Security Act* ss 7(2), 7(7), 1061ZO, div 3. A healthcare card is means tested (see s 1071A) and triggers for the holder access to a range of concessions and benefits, including subsidised

Benefit,[19] a discretionary welfare benefit available to Australian residents who cannot get any other income support.[20]

Instead, since 1992,[21] a parallel system that provides limited financial assistance, healthcare, and other services has been in operation. The principal part of this system of welfare distribution, and the focus of this analysis, has been the Asylum Seekers Assistance Scheme (ASAS).[22] Although now known as band 6 in a multi-banded Status Resolution Support Services (SRSS) Programme and administered slightly differently, little has changed substantively.[23] The scheme is policy-based and therefore not governed by legislation or regulation.[24] It is subject to strict eligibility criteria.[25] For those meeting the criteria *and* able to access the program,[26] assistance is calculated

---

healthcare, medicines, and transport, as well as support from charitable institutions: Evidence to Joint Standing Committee on Migration, Parliament of Australia, *Inquiry into Immigration Detention in Australia*, Melbourne, 11 September 2008, M36 (Stephanie Mendis, Hotham Mission Asylum Seeker Project). Since 1991, following amendments to the *Social Security Act*, onshore asylum seekers in Australia have been ineligible for the Special Benefit: Savitri Taylor, 'Do On-Shore Asylum Seekers Have Economic and Social Rights? Dealing with the Moral Contradiction of Liberal Democracy' (2000) 1 *Melbourne Journal of International Law* 70, 76.

[19] See Explanatory Memorandum, Social Security Bill 1990 (Cth) 556; Supplementary Explanatory Memorandum: Amendments and New Clauses to Be Moved on Behalf of the Government, Social Security Legislation (Amendment) Bill 1990 (Cth).

[20] *Social Security Act* s 729; Taylor, above n 18, 76.

[21] Human Rights and Equal Opportunity Commission ('HREOC'), 'Report of an Inquiry into a Complaint by the Asylum Seekers Centre concerning Changes to the Asylum Seekers Assistance Scheme' (Report No 17, 2002) pt 2.2 ('ASAS Report').

[22] ASAS was previously described in DIBP, *Fact Sheet 62 – Assistance for Asylum Seekers in Australia* (27 August 2014).

[23] For a description of the SRSS Programme, see DIBP, 'SRSS Policy Advice Manual' (21 October 2014), <https://www.border.gov.au/AccessandAccountability/Documents/20161006_FA160700108_documents_released.pdf>. Much of the analysis here could equally apply to a parallel program known as the Community Assistance Support Program (CAS): DIBP, *Fact Sheet 64 – Community Assistance Support Program* (27 August 2014). CAS is now band 5 of the SRSS Programme.

[24] Letter from Helen Williams, Secretary, DIMA, to Chris Sidoti, Human Rights Commissioner, 6 August 1997: *Complaint by Mr Frank Elvey of the Asylum Seekers Centre regarding the Asylum Seekers Assistance Scheme* (HREOC File No 13747H); see also below n 34.

[25] Eligibility criteria are, in broad terms, that the individual is "assessed as experiencing financial hardship": see DIBP, 'SRSS Policy Advice Manual', above n 23, 18. For a past statement of eligibility criteria, see DIBP, *Fact Sheet 62*, above n 22; cf Department of Human Services, below n 90.

[26] Because of limited resources, not all people meeting eligibility criteria are able to access ASAS, despite meeting financial hardship criteria: see, eg, Asylum Seekers Resource Centre (ASRC), 'Destitute and Uncertain: The Reality of Seeking Asylum in Australia' (October 2010) 15. The same is also true of SRSS.

at a rate of 89 per cent[27] of the social security Special Benefit.[28] Even with maximum rent assistance,[29] the Special Benefit positions recipients below the poverty line.[30] Based on an income of 89 per cent of that benefit, recipients are positioned even further below that line.

Like the 45-day rule, the effects of policy-based welfare are human, institutional, and political. In terms of human implications, the risk of destitution for both recipients and those who are ineligible is heightened. Institutionally, this policy-based scheme operates in a space that is juridically unaccountable. Politically, even though eligibility criteria do not take account of merit in the substantive application for protection, the scheme is justified as a means of curbing abuse and as fiscally responsible.

~~~

To help explain how the policy of planned destitution of certain foreigners – a tool of social and economic exclusion – has become characterised as a lawful and legitimate institutional response to unsolicited migration, this chapter analyses contemporary migration discourses at a number of levels. It argues that, even though the policy of planned destitution is silent on the question of 'absolute sovereignty', the policy gives expression to the discourse of 'absolute sovereignty' through the use of particular discursive techniques. As with Chapter 5, I group these techniques thematically into discourses of (state) control and restraint, (asylum seeker) deviance and opportunism, and (institutional) silence.

---

[27] Sandi Logan, National Communications Manager, DIAC, 'Refugees Not Better Off', Letter to the Editor, *Adelaide Advertiser* (online), 21 May 2009 <www.immi.gov.au/media/letters/let ters09/le090507.htm>; Luke Buckmaster, 'Australian Government Assistance to Refugees: Fact v Fiction' (Background Note, Parliamentary Library, Parliament of Australia, 2012); DIAC, Supplementary Submission No 32 to Joint Select Committee on Australia's Immigration Detention Network, Parliament of Australia, Inquiry into Australia's Immigration Detention Network, September 2011, 50.

[28] The Special Benefit is a discretionary benefit and is available only to a person who is not able to get any other income support payment: *Social Security Act* s 729. The Special Benefit is currently paid at a rate of $538.80 per fortnight for a single person with no children. This means that, subject to the eligibility criteria, a single asylum seeker with no children would be eligible for a maximum payment of $479.53 per fortnight: Centrelink, *Special Benefit Payment Rates* (20 September 2017) Department of Human Services <www.humanservices.gov.au/cu stomer/services/centrelink/special-benefit>.

[29] Maximum rent assistance for a single person with no children is $133.00 per fortnight: Centrelink, *Payment Rates for Rent Assistance* (20 September 2017) Department of Human Services <www.humanservices.gov.au/customer/enablers/centrelink/rent-assistance/pay ment-rates>.

[30] For a single person not in the workforce, the poverty line is calculated as $832.14 per fortnight (including housing): Melbourne Institute of Applied Economic and Social Research, 'Poverty Lines: Australia' (June Quarter 2017).

Structurally, Section 6.1 of this chapter offers an analysis of the rationales for the denial of work and welfare rights at certain points during the past two decades. Beginning with the 45-day rule, I show how it was justified through the use of a number of rhetorical devices already identified in Chapter 5.[31] In addition, I introduce other rhetorical techniques, including the use of soundbites, slogans, and stock phrases – "short fixed expressions that become well known to an audience and evoke certain reactions [or] emotions usually as a result of association" and "each of which has its own currency."[32] This section then analyses how the 'abolition' of the 45-day rule in 2009 was rationalised, before piecing together the rationale for certain iterations of ASAS. Through this analysis, I make visible the ways in which rhetorical techniques are engaged to validate a pattern of policymaking that treats stringent measures as necessary but restrained and frames the target group as (deviantly and opportunistically) 'gaming the system' and already getting more than they deserve.

Section 6.2 offers an analysis of the institutional techniques used to shape the framework through which work rights are granted or denied. I do this in two ways. First, across two sections, I explore how the regulatory framework is articulated and implemented as a laboriously complex (and colourless) web of terminologies that gives the appearance of balance and restraint while securing maximum power and control. Second, I describe how an institutional 'obsession with discretion' that has emerged as a distinguishing characteristic of migration law- and policymaking in Australia has affected how work rights decisions are made. I argue that certain terminologies and technicalities create both institutional and juridical silences that reflect the absolute power embodied in the discourse of 'absolute sovereignty'.

Section 6.3 explores the institutional techniques that have shaped the denial of any or adequate welfare rights to asylum seekers. First, I consider how law and language come together to create stringent eligibility criteria and other obstacles to accessing welfare support for asylum seekers. Second, I consider the techniques that enable welfare decisions

---

[31] These include 'splitting', patterns of positive self-presentation juxtaposed with negative characterisation of the out-group, deflection, linguistic inversion of the power relation, repetition, and innuendo: see Raymond G Nairn and Timothy N McCreanor, 'Race Talk and Common Sense: Patterns in Pakeha Discourse on Maori/Pakeha Relations in New Zealand' (1991) 10(4) *Journal of Language and Social Psychology* 245, 251; Martha Agoustinos and Danielle Every, 'The Language of "Race" and Prejudice: A Discourse of Denial, Reason, and Liberal-Practical Politics' (2007) 26(2) *Journal of Language and Social Psychology* 123, 132; Teun A van Dijk, *Elite Discourses and Racism* (Sage, 1993) 72–6, 84–93.

[32] Meriel Bloor and Thomas Bloor, *The Practice of Critical Discourse Analysis: An Introduction* (Routledge, 2nd ed, 2013) 72.

to be positioned in an unregulated space, under law's radar. As part of this analysis, I consider the complaint file of an inquiry by the Human Rights and Equal Opportunity Commission (HREOC)[33] into ASAS,[34] commenced in 1996. Although the substance of the complaint – that changes to ASAS were human rights violations – is both interesting and compelling,[35] the focus of this analysis is on the insights the complaint file offers into the policy's rationale. Indeed, more than 20 years later, the HREOC complaint file has an enduring relevance, being the only quasi-judicial record of the workings of ASAS. This archive therefore provides a unique insight into how a combination of rhetorical and institutional techniques converged in the development and justification of the policy and framework underpinning ASAS (and now SRSS). It also enables us to see how a department accounts for policies enclosed in a juridical space that is dominated by the discourse of 'absolute sovereignty'.

6.1 RATIONALISING DESTITUTION

As foreshadowed, Section 6.1 of this chapter engages in an analysis of the rationale for the 45-day rule, its abolition, and certain changes to the policy-based ASAS framework. It provides insight into the rhetorical devices and discursive silences that are used to rationalise and legitimise a policy of planned destitution. This analysis enables us to see more clearly the institutional techniques that are at work in Sections 6.2 and 6.3, below. I turn first to the rationale for the 45-day rule.

6.1.1 Work: The 45-Day Rule and Its Rationale

Tabling Commonwealth Regulations is a formal process of laying a legislative instrument before both Houses of Parliament.[36] Regulations are accompanied by Explanatory Statements, issued by the authority of the relevant Minister. Like

---

[33] Now the Australian Human Rights Commission.
[34] Complaint by Mr Frank Elvey of the Asylum Seekers Centre regarding the Asylum Seekers Assistance Scheme (HREOC File No 13747H, 1996) ('HREOC Complaint File').
[35] Broadly, the alleged human rights violations were that the October 1996 changes were in breach of the obligation to accord equal and effective protection against discrimination, were not in the best interests of the child, and breached the child's right to enjoy the highest attainable standard of health: *International Covenant on Civil and Political Rights*, opened for signature 16 December 1966, 999 UNTS 171 (entered into force 23 March 1976) art 26 (*ICCPR*); *Convention on the Rights of the Child*, opened for signature 20 November 1989, 1577 UNTS 3 (entered into force 2 September 1990) arts 3, 24.
[36] *Legislative Instruments Act 2003* (Cth) s 38(3) (*LIA*). Until 2005, the governing framework was the *Acts Interpretation Act 1901* (Cth) (*AIA*). Since then, as regards delegated legislation, the *AIA* has been replaced by the *LIA*.

Explanatory Memoranda for Bills,[37] they explain the purpose and operation of the instrument,[38] which suggests them to be a logical place to look for a policy rationale for the 45-day rule. However, relevant Explanatory Statements seem blithely uninformative, describing the purpose of the regulations as "to give effect to Government decisions relating to ... work entitlements for certain bridging visa holders"[39] and "to reflect the Government's objective of further reforming the Migration program to accord with the needs of the Australian community".[40] The institutional reserve that we see in these oblique statements contrasts with the bold rhetorical style of a parallel public and political discourse that emotes purposively.[41]

Politically, the rationale for the 45-day rule has been described as being to "deter" or "discourage" people from making "bogus claims".[42] A 1997 speech from then Immigration Minister Philip Ruddock is the most commonly cited, if not the only, source of this rationale.[43] In that speech, which foreshadowed changes to work rights provisions that would later be embodied in the 45-day rule, Ruddock made the following statement:

[37] Patrick O'Neill, "'Was there an EM?'": Explanatory Memoranda and Explanatory Statements in the Commonwealth Parliament' (Research Brief No 15, Parliamentary Library, Parliament of Australia, 2004–05) (first published 2004–05, September 2006 ed) <www.aph.gov.au/Abou t_Parliament/Parliamentary_Departments/Parliamentary_Library/Browse_by_Topic/law/ex planmem/wasthereanEM>.

[38] *LIA* s 26(1A)(b).

[39] Explanatory Statement, *Migration Regulations (Amendment) 1997 No 185* (Cth).

[40] Explanatory Statement, *Migration Regulations (Amendment) 1997 No 109* (Cth).

[41] Public statements external to parliamentary processes are not regarded as extrinsic material for interpretative purposes: *AIA* s 15AB.

[42] See, eg, Commonwealth, *Parliamentary Debates*, Senate, 8 September 2009, 5962 (Concetta Fierravanti-Wells), regarding Motion for Disallowance, *Migration Amendment Regulations 2009 (No 6)* (Cth) (Commonwealth parliamentary debates are hereinafter referred to as 'CPD'); Evidence to Senate Legal and Constitutional Legislation Committee, Parliament of Australia, *Inquiry into the Migration Amendment (Employer Sanctions) Bill 2006*, Sydney, 26 April 2006, 43 (Neil Mann, First Assistant Secretary, Compliance Policy and Case Coordination Division, DIMA).

[43] Ruddock, 'Broad Implications', above n 11, 8, cited by Millbank, 'Asylum Seekers on Bridging Visa E', above n 3, 10; Peter Mares, 'A Routine Removal' (2007) 18 *Griffith Review* 205, 209; CPD, Senate, 8 September 2009, 5962 (Concetta Fierravanti-Wells). See also CPD, House of Representatives, 19 March 1997, 2431 (Philip Ruddock); CPD, House of Representatives, 19 June 1997, 5857 (Philip Ruddock). The rationale appears broadly to reflect the policy rationale for a 1996 UK policy on which the original policy appears to have been modelled, namely "[t]o ensure that the UK remains a haven for those genuinely fleeing from persecution, whilst discouraging unfounded applications from those who are actually economic migrants. The growing number of these unfounded applications prevents speedy processing of applications from those who genuinely merit asylum and imposes an unjustifiable cost on the British taxpayer": see *Ex parte JCWI* [1996] 4 All ER 385, 389.

I am particularly concerned about abuse of the onshore refugee/asylum application process. At the same time, let me make it very clear that I expect any officer of my Department and any member of the Refugee Review Tribunal[44] to grant refugee status to a person who has met the accepted definition of 'refugee' under the Refugees Convention.

We are determined to address problems of abuse, but such determination is not a code for denying protection to genuine refugees. Unfortunately, there are people who seek to abuse our generosity. I have particular concerns in relation to those who travel to Australia on a visitor visa, with the necessary documents issued by their own government to travel here, and who seek to claim refugee status in Australia.

I am gravely concerned by reports I have received that people are using the onshore protection system to obtain work rights and access to Medicare.[45] There are people who apply to my Department asking for the $30 work visa [$30 being the cost, at the time, of lodging a Protection Visa application] who appear not to be bona fide asylum seekers. These applicants seek to delay their departure as long as possible knowing full well they are not refugees. This abuse costs taxpayers millions of dollars, undermines public confidence in the system and causes processing delays, which disadvantages genuine applicants.[46]

In this speech, Ruddock engaged in a discursive interplay between the themes of state control and restraint and asylum seeker deviance and opportunism. By expressing concern about 'abuse' of the asylum process, he could present himself as defender of the system, guardian of the taxpayer dollar, and restorer of public confidence. In his positive self-presentation as protector of (real) refugees – recognised as a general pattern in elite discourse, particularly among politicians[47] – we also see him drawing implicitly on international refugee law standards[48] to validate 'splitting' the out-group into 'genuine refugees' who meet the refugee definition and those 'abusing our generosity' who do not. This technique, as we know, seeks to inoculate the speaker against the charge of prejudice.[49] Ruddock also made purposeful use of language

---

44 On 1 July 2015, the Refugee Review Tribunal merged with the Administrative Appeals Tribunal: *Tribunals Amalgamation Act 2015* (Cth).
45 Medicare is the publicly funded health system.
46 Ruddock, 'Broad Implications', above n 11, 8, 13.
47 Van Dijk, above n 31, 72–6, 84–93; Agoustinos and Every, above n 31, 129.
48 *Convention relating to the Status of Refugees*, opened for signature 28 July 1951, 189 UNTS 150 (entered into force 22 April 1954) art 1A(2) ('*Refugee Convention*').
49 Raymond G Nairn and Timothy N McCreanor, 'Race Talk and Common Sense: Patterns in Pakeha Discourse on Maori/Pakeha Relations in New Zealand' (1991) 10(4) *Journal of Language and Social Psychology* 245, 251; Agoustinos and Every, above n 31, 132; Chapter 5, 185–6.

suggesting that he was a safe, restrained, and principled pair of hands in control of a system in which he claimed to have uncompromisingly high expectations. At the same time, he positioned himself and his Department as privy to substantial evidence of abuse, actively insinuating asylum seeker impropriety, bad faith, and a flagrant disregard for those in need – people he represented as 'knowing full well' that they were not refugees.

By insisting that this was not 'code' for denying protection to 'genuine refugees', Ruddock pre-emptively deflected counter-critique in the same terms. Of course, his rationale could very well have been characterised as code for denying protection in both the immediate and long term to bona fide asylum seekers, people he knew full well might be refugees.[50] One has only to reflect for a moment on a policy that denies access to the labour market for long periods of time on the basis of an application's timing, and regardless of merit or bona fides, to see that the policy was arbitrary and undiscerning as well as socially and economically crippling. Thus, as if a 'willingness' to endure destitution were a marker of their bona fides, it knowingly exposed asylum seekers to homelessness and begging, dependence on charity, and the risk of unlawful exploitative work[51] and (re-)detention.[52] It also inhibited access to determination procedures, including procedural safeguards, by starving people out of the system.[53]

Likewise, by declaring his 'determination' to address problems of 'abuse', Ruddock simultaneously constructed the asylum seekers' conduct as abusive and deflected any charge that the exercise of power might itself be abusive.[54] Ruddock was careful to claim only that there were people applying for protection who 'appeared' not to be bona fide asylum seekers. However, this qualification is best understood as an example of discursive decoration given that he immediately negated it with a sweeping assertion that their motivations were to use the system to obtain work rights and to access Medicare.[55]

---

[50]   Here, it is apposite to recall that refugee status is a declaratory rather than constitutive status: Chapter 5, 199 n 250.

[51]   See, eg, United Nations High Commissioner for Refugees (UNHCR), Representations to the Social Security Advisory Committee on the 'Social Security (Persons from Abroad) Miscellaneous Amendment Regulations 1995' (10 November 1995).

[52]   Prologue, 4; Chapter 1, 9.

[53]   For treatment of these issues in the UK, see *Ex parte JCWI* [1996] 4 All ER 385; *R v Secretary of State for the Home Department, Ex parte Limbuela* [2005] 1 AC 396. On the issue of 'constructive *refoulement*', see also: UNHCR, *Representations*, above n 51.

[54]   On the claim that the risk of abuse of absolute power is only theoretical, see *Re Yates; Ex parte Walsh and Johnson* (1925) 37 CLR 36 (1925) 37 CLR 36, 133 (Starke J), discussed in Chapter 4, 141–2.

[55]   See above n 45. On discursive decoration, see Chapter 5, 192–3.

Moreover, he deployed language that ascribed to asylum seekers an ability to second-guess the outcomes of a complex RSD process, proclaiming that their interest was to delay their departure 'knowing full well' that they were not refugees.

Ruddock also described the target of his concerns as those arriving 'with the necessary documents'. This cast doubt on the bona fides of a protection claim by any person able to obtain and travel on documents issued by her own government.[56] Yet, as we saw in Chapter 5, for 'boat people' the reverse imputation was used; that is, the bona fides of *their* protection claims were impugned on the grounds that they did *not* have the necessary documents.[57] Again, therefore, we can conclude through this discursive inconsistency that the primary objective here was rhetorically to ascribe deviance and opportunism rather than to make a substantive claim. In drawing this conclusion, I am mindful of the fact that the speakers in each instance were different. However, in my argument the conclusion still holds given the broad compatibility of the policy positions and the consistency with which such discursive strategies fit a pattern of ascribing deviance and opportunism.

Above all, and notwithstanding lofty statements of principle and expectation, Ruddock's speech shows how protection priorities and the sober and restrained duties of responsible governance can become secondary to the priority of power and control and the popular/ist appeal and political advantage of ascribing deviance and opportunism to asylum seekers. Thus, the central message from this extract is that people unworthy of Australia's generosity were systematically abusing legal procedures. What is more, it implies, the government was not to blame for processing delays.[58] Instead, responsibility was diverted to 'these applicants' who 'knew' they were not refugees and who were clogging the system and causing the delays that disadvantaged ('genuine') refugees.[59]

These were serious allegations to make. They implied that Ruddock was privy to substantial evidence attesting to both the motives and conduct of (non–bona fide) asylum seekers. However, he put forward no evidence substantiating the 'reports' on which he based these allegations. As a claim, 'reports' can mean anything from carefully documented research to anecdote or even gossip, rumour, or hearsay. In this instance, Ruddock used 'reports' to assert that an untold number of people were engaging in

---

[56] Cf UNHCR, Handbook and Guidelines on Procedures and Criteria for Determining Refugee Status, UN Doc HCR/1P/4/ENG/REV.3 (December 2011) paras 121, 196 ('Handbook and Guidelines').

[57] See Chapter 5, Section 5.2.2.1 191–3.   [58] See also Chapter 5, Section 5.1.2.1, 177–8.

[59] See also insinuations that the target group was not in 'genuine need': below 252.

'abuse'[60] by lodging applications for a '$30 work visa'. How did he know? It is both possible and plausible that he had at his disposal some information to this effect. However, there was no evidence in the public domain of the scope of the (claimed) problem. Instead, the '$30 work visa' was a stock phrase – a soundbite – that *became* the evidence[61] and could be ascribed to any asylum seeker. And it worked. It reverberated across the airwaves, creating a perception that this was a problem that was indeed widespread. Thus, it acquired an authority that far exceeded its anecdotal origins.[62]

In this instance, as a soundbite, the '$30 work visa' captured the fear and disdain embodied in the discourse of deviance and opportunism that former Prime Minister Hawke once called 'economic refugeeism'.[63] Combined with the weight of institutional and political authority – the voice of the Minister and 'reports' from his Department – what would otherwise have been regarded as anecdote and conjecture[64] acquired authority and discursive currency.[65] In particular, its use by a Minister of the Crown invited its audience to trust that beneath the soundbite lay a real and substantial truth. Still, there was no reference to a study or to other documentary or statistical evidence of the (claimed) problem or its scope.[66] Yet he was prepared to assert that this 'abuse' of 'our' 'generosity' by 'these applicants' was costing taxpayers 'millions of

---

60   In parliamentary debates on the same topic, Ruddock sought to neutralise his critics by claiming (accurately but extraneously) that members of civil society regarded abuse as a matter of concern: CPD, House of Representatives, 19 March 1997, 2430–1; CPD, House of Representatives, 19 June 1997, 5857–8.

61   Bloor and Bloor, above n 32, 72.

62   For references to the '$30 work visa', see Mares, 'A Routine Removal', above n 43, 209; Peter Mares, *Borderline: Australia's Response to Refugees and Asylum Seekers in the Wake of the Tampa* (UNSW Press, 2nd ed, 2002) 143; Laura Tingle, 'Vow to Tackle Refugee Visa Abuses', *The Age* (Melbourne), 20 March 1997, A6; Millbank, 'Asylum Seekers on Bridging Visa E', above n 3, 11; Ruddock, 'Broad Implications', above n 11; CPD, House of Representatives, 19 March 1997, 2430–1 (Philip Ruddock); CPD, House of Representatives, 19 June 1997, 5857–8 (Philip Ruddock); CPD, Senate, 8 September 2009, 5962 (Concetta Fierravanti-Wells); Patricia Cruise, 'They Can Turn Back the Boats, but It's Still Plane Sailing', *Sydney Morning Herald*, 11 August 2010, 15. Note that not all these authors/speakers accept the assertion, indeed some actively discredit it, but the position taken by the author appears to be inconsequential in terms of its overall effect.

63   Jana Wendt, Interview with Bob Hawke, Prime Minister (Network Nine, A *Current Affair*, Parliament House, 6 June 1990). See Prologue, 1.

64   See also below 255.   65   Bloor and Bloor, above n 32, 72.

66   The absence of any study or other documentary or statistical evidence raises the further question of whether existing statistics would contradict assertions he made or whether the entire policy foundation and rationale was based only on anecdote and conjecture. Whatever the case, it is reasonable to assume that if there were statistical (or indeed other substantial or empirical) evidence on which to base the assertions being made, they would have been central to any policy announcement.

dollars', thereby making rhetorical use of a quasi-objective but nevertheless undisclosed and unspecified cost claim.[67]

As noted above, Ruddock claimed that the alleged abuse undermined public confidence in the system – a public whose generosity was being exploited and taxpayer dollars leeched. So, while part of the rhetorical work that the speech was doing was to reassure the public that the system was in safe hands, it simultaneously engaged a parallel rhetoric to undermine public confidence in the bona fides of asylum seekers, ascribing to them a deviant opportunism.

This analysis of the 45-day rule suggests that the rationale for the legal and policy framework was driven by a desire to maximise its rhetorical value and impact in public and political discourse rather than to explain a substantive juridical purpose. In terms of its effects, it was a policy whose severity prompted an Immigration Department–initiated review into the bridging visa regime in 2004.[68] The Bridging Visa Review's stated aim was to achieve a simpler, clearer, and more consistent regime that was flexible enough to be responsive to individual circumstances.[69] Concerns of civil society organisations involved in advocacy and support work have been described as a "major impetus" for the review.[70] Given the opacity of the bridging visa scheme, in particular in relation to conferral and denial of work rights, this review might have provided for the public record greater clarity about not only the effects of the policy but also its rationale. The Bridging Visa Review reportedly included recommendations by the Department that strict visa conditions that forced asylum seekers into destitution should be relaxed. It also reportedly accepted that there were valid reasons why people might apply for protection outside the 45-day time limit.[71] However,

[67] Van Dijk, above n 31, 107–9.
[68] Millbank, 'Asylum Seekers on Bridging Visa E', above n 3, 11.
[69] DIMA, 'Bridging Visas and Bridging Visa Es' (2006) 14(2) *People and Place* 39, 41. See also Hand's claims of reforms that would bring 'simplicity, clarity and fairness': Chapter 5, 179, above.
[70] Millbank, 'Asylum Seekers on Bridging Visa E', above n 3, 11. As part of this review, a large number of civil society organisations participated in the consultation process and/or made written submissions. Eighteen submissions were received from civil society organisations, and dozens of organisations participated in the consultations: Senate Legal and Constitutional Affairs Committee, Parliament of Australia, *Supplementary Budget Estimates 2006–2007 (Immigration and Multicultural Affairs)*, Questions on Notice, October 2006, QoN 194. These submissions documented the many deleterious effects of the existing bridging visa scheme, including in particular the introduction and application of the 45-day rule: see, eg, Asylum Seekers Centre, above n 3; Hotham Mission, above n 3; Law Council of Australia, above n 3.
[71] Jewel Topsfield, 'Call to Ease Bridging Visa Rules', *The Age* (online), 18 March 2008 <www.theage.com.au/articles/2008/03/17/1205602291249.html>.

the review was not in the nature of a judicial or quasi-judicial inquiry; it had no enforcement powers and it was not independent.[72] Thus, its publication and the nature of any institutional response to it remained "a matter for the Minister".[73] As it transpired, although the final report of the Bridging Visa Review was sent to then Immigration Minister Amanda Vanstone for her consideration,[74] it was never published.[75] Whatever the rationale for the decision not to publish, the effect of the resultant institutional silence was to defuse, if not neutralise, the effects of a credible counter-narrative.[76]

The Australian Labor Party (ALP) policy platform taken to the November 2007 Federal Election, which it won, included the following statement:

> Labor recognises that the arbitrary 45-day-rule results in legitimate asylum seekers on bridging visas being unnecessarily denied the right to work while their claim is being processed. It also prevents immigration officers from denying work rights to frivolous claims lodged within the 45-day-period.

[72]   Two recent reviews that have been criticised for similar reasons are those of former Secretary of the Attorney-General's Department, Robert Cornall AO, into sexual and other violent incidents on Manus Island, including the alleged murder of Iranian asylum seeker Reza Berati: Robert Cornall, 'Review into Allegations of Sexual and Other Serious Assaults at the Manus Regional Processing Centre' (Report to the Secretary, DIBP, September 2013) (marked 'publication version'); Robert Cornall, 'Review into the Events of February 16–18 2014 at the Manus Regional Processing Centre' (Report to the Secretary, DIBP, 23 May 2014) (redacted). For criticism of these reports, see, eg, Marni Cordell, 'Manus Victims "Treated Better Than Australians": Cornall', *New Matilda* (online), 27 February 2014 <https://newmatilda.com/2014/02/27/manus-victims-treated-better-australians-cornall>; Martin McKenzie-Murray, 'Cornall Report into the Death of Reza Barati on Manus Island', *The Saturday Paper* (online), 31 May 2014 <www.thesaturdaypaper.com.au>. For Cornall's account of his inquiry into the February 2014 violence, see: Evidence to Senate Legal and Constitutional Affairs References Committee, Parliament of Australia, *Inquiry into the Incident at the Manus Island Detention Centre from 16 to 18 February 2014*, Canberra, 12 June 2014, 1–19 (Robert Cornall).

[73]   Evidence to Senate Standing Committee on Legal and Constitutional Affairs, Parliament of Australia, *Supplementary Budget Estimates 2006–07 (Immigration and Multicultural Affairs)*, Canberra, 30 October 2006, 134 (Andrew Metcalfe, Secretary, DIMA).

[74]   Senate Legal and Constitutional Affairs Committee, Parliament of Australia, *Additional Budget Estimates 2006–2007 (Immigration and Citizenship)*, Canberra, 12 February 2007, 34 (Andrew Metcalfe). Some time after 12 February 2007, the review recommendations were then referred to the new Minister for Immigration, Kevin Andrews, for his consideration: Evidence to Standing Committee on Legal and Constitutional Affairs, Senate, *Budget Estimates 2007–2008 (Immigration and Citizenship)*, Canberra, 21 May 2007, 11 (Andrew Metcalfe).

[75]   A copy of the report was, however, leaked in 2008 after a change of government: Topsfield, above n 71.

[76]   See Chapter 4, 122, 156. One commentator went so far as to suggest that the delays in publication of the report were attributable to unreasonable demands being made by advocates: Millbank, 'Asylum Seekers on Bridging Visa E', above n 3, abstract; see also Adrienne Millbank, 'No Compromise, No Quarter, No Controls – No International Asylum System' (2006) 14(2) *People and Place* 42, 45.

Labor will work to develop guidelines based on merit so that frivolous or vexatious visa applications will be denied those rights, instead of applying an arbitrary 45-day-time limit.[77]

This policy platform highlighted ALP concerns about the arbitrariness of the 45-day rule and also identified the possibility that it may in fact have been according work rights to the very applicants that the Ruddock rationale claimed to be targeting. It also committed an ALP government to developing guidelines 'based on merit'. However, as the following section shows, even when some of the harshest effects of the 45-day rule were removed in 2009 and notwithstanding the mobilisation of a milder rhetoric, the rationale remained substantially undisturbed.

6.1.2 Work: The 'Abolition' of the 45-Day Rule

In February 2008, the newly elected ALP Government's Immigration Minister, Senator Chris Evans, effectively endorsed the rationale (but not the effects) of the 45-day rule. He told the Senate Standing Committee on Legal and Constitutional Affairs:

> All I can say about [overturning the 45-day rule] is that I realise how damn complex it is and how difficult it is going to be to resolve. I have a clear appreciation of the difficulty of it and I am open to solutions. But again that is one of the issues I have asked for advice on and it is on the agenda. I think there is a real potential in that area to have unintended consequences. It is on the agenda as well, but no decisions have been taken.[78]

Although using language that differs markedly from the language of the Ruddock rationale, and clearly expressing concern about the effects of the 45-day rule, Evans nevertheless described the policy as having 'real *potential*' for consequences he described as 'unintended'. Although Evans made it clear that he was looking for solutions, this language positioned the policy's adverse effects as prospective and unplanned rather than present and purposeful. At the same time, and without substantiation, his approach to work rights for asylum seekers continued to assume the problem of 'frivolous', 'vexatious', or 'abusive' claims to be of sufficient gravity and magnitude to justify a strong policy response, albeit one that was softened at the edges.

---

[77] Australian Labor Party, 'National Platform and Constitution' (2007) 222–3 [155].
[78] Evidence to Senate Standing Committee on Legal and Constitutional Affairs, Parliament of Australia, *Additional Budget Estimates 2007–2008 (Immigration and Citizenship)*, Canberra, 19 February 2008, 33 (Chris Evans).

As he observed, in finding a solution, he was reliant on the advice of the Immigration Department. In March 2008, Evans told the Senate:

[The 45-day rule] is one of the issues that I am grappling with. I do think it is an unsatisfactory state of affairs. I am trying to find a solution to this issue. It is not that easy. The changes introduced in terms of the 45-day rule were justified to try and prevent some gaming of the system that was alleged at the time. I understand the rationale that was advanced for that, but it is the case that there are large numbers of people who are out in the community on bridging visas while their applications to be treated as asylum seekers are being processed and it is a very unsatisfactory state of affairs. I am committed to trying to fix this. We are working very hard on the options and I hope to be able to do something fairly soon.[79]

This response to a Question Without Notice from Greens Senator Kerry Nettle clearly indicates that resolving the problems with the 45-day rule was on Evans' agenda. However, in his response, Evans indicated that he 'understood' the rationale that was advanced for it. Thus, although clearly preoccupied with 'trying to fix' the 'unsatisfactory' effects of the policy and describing the justifications for the 45-day rule as addressing 'some' 'alleged' 'gaming of the system', the evidentiary basis for the policy was not called into serious question. Indeed, he implicitly accepted it. In Sections 6.2.1 and 6.2.2 below, we will see this reflected in the institutional terminologies and techniques that enabled the 45-day rule to continue perforce.[80]

6.1.3 Welfare: In Search of a Rationale

As we know, subject to stringent criteria, asylum seekers may be eligible for welfare assistance through the policy-based ASAS scheme (band 6 of the SRSS Programme since 1 March 2015).[81] As noted above, the change reflects a restructuring of service delivery rather than a substantive policy change. The language of eligibility criteria varies from time to time, but the stringency of the criteria is a constant theme. Prior to the introduction of the SRSS Programme, eligibility required an asylum seeker to have been waiting for a decision from the Department for more than six months or be "vulnerable", "suffering hardship", *and* "unable to meet their basic needs because they lack adequate support within the

---

79 CPD, Senate, 18 March 2008, 1089 (Chris Evans).   80   See below, 259–62.
81 Victorian Health Refugee Network, 'Casework Support for Asylum Seekers' (11 March 2015) <http://refugeehealthnetwork.org.au/case-work-support-for-asylum-seekers/>.

community".[82] Under the SRSS Programme, eligibility requires an asylum seeker to be "experiencing financial hardship", which is given a particular meaning.[83] Payment continues to be made at 89 per cent of the Special Benefit.[84] Although this reduction was clearly deliberate, its rationale remains a mystery; when asked, a former Secretary of the Immigration Department could not remember why the figure was chosen.[85]

When ASAS was first introduced in 1992, it followed removal in 1991 of access to the Special Benefit for asylum seekers as part of a major overhaul of the social security system, previously governed by the *Social Security Act 1947* (Cth).[86] However, no attention was given to provisions affecting asylum seekers either in the relevant Minister's Second Reading Speech or the Explanatory Memorandum accompanying the Bill.[87] Since then, ASAS has been described by the Immigration Department as having been "introduced to help asylum seekers with needs including accommodation, counselling and income support".[88] However, this characterisation conceals a history in which asylum seekers had previously been entitled to the Special Benefit and where its subsequent removal had overburdened emergency housing and relief agencies.[89] Only later would asylum seekers become entitled to income support under ASAS. Even then, however, their entitlement was at a lower level (mysteriously calculated at 89 per cent of that benefit) and was on the basis of strict eligibility criteria.

[82] DIBP, *Fact Sheet 62*, above n 22.
[83] DIBP, Application for Status Resolution Support Services (SRSS) – Band 6, Form 1455 (November 2016). The meaning of 'experiencing financial hardship' is elaborated below, Section 6.3.2 274–6.
[84] See above nn 23, 28.
[85] "I cannot remember why 89 per cent was chosen, but it was definitely set at underneath the Newstart allowance": Evidence to Senate Legal and Constitutional Legislation Committee, Parliament of Australia, *Budget Estimates 2009–2010 (Immigration and Citizenship)*, Canberra, 28 May 2009, 103 (Andrew Metcalfe, Secretary, DIAC). Although speculative, one can imagine that the purpose was not to give parity with Australian nationals and residents, and, for the purposes of public consumption, 89 per cent was a more effective marker of inequality than 90 per cent.
[86] See *Social Security Act 1991* (Cth).
[87] CPD, House of Representatives, 6 December 1990, 4641–4; Explanatory Memorandum, Social Security Bill 1990 (Cth).
[88] DIAC, Supplementary Submission No 32, above n 27, 104.
[89] Evidence to Senate Legal and Constitutional Legislation Committee, Parliament of Australia, *Inquiry into Social Security Legislation (Newly Arrived Resident's Waiting Periods and Other Measures) Bill 1996*, Canberra, 6 June 1996, 13 (Merle Mitchell, Board Member, Australian Council of Social Services); Taylor, above n 18, 76 n 36.

There is little on the public record in the way of policy rationale for ASAS, or indeed the SRSS Programme more broadly.[90] The Social Security Bill 1990 (Cth) sheds no light,[91] describing the purpose of certain amendments excluding asylum seekers from access to the Special Benefit as "to remedy a minor drafting error".[92] Otherwise, in defending an unregulated policy-based scheme, the Department has talked up its advantages, rationalising it as "broader and more flexible" than those for mainstream recipients of social security benefits,[93] a perspective strikingly inattentive to the absence of independent oversight. For a (slightly) more detailed rationale, we can also look to particular iterations of the policy. The clearest source is a series of policy changes made between 1996 and 1998. In the following two sections, I consider what those changes were and then their rationale.

6.1.3.1 Changes to ASAS from 1996

In May 1996, shortly after the Coalition Government of Prime Minister John Howard was elected, rumours started circulating about proposed changes and cuts to ASAS. Dismissing as media speculation claims made by Senator Sid Spindler that leaked Cabinet documents were the source of the rumours,[94] the Parliamentary Secretary to the Minister for Health and Family Services responded to Spindler with a categorical denial.[95] It would take only three months for Cabinet-approved plans to cut ASAS to be formally announced.

Until the changes, ASAS benefits were payable to asylum seekers awaiting a decision at the primary or review stage of the RSD process. They became eligible automatically if there was no primary decision within six months of the application being made. That waiting period could be waived subject to

---

90   DIBP, 'SRSS Policy Advice Manual', above n 23 (released under freedom of information). Although SRSS is now administered by Centrelink, a perfunctory statement on eligibility shows DIBP retains control: <www.humanservices.gov.au/individuals/services/centrelink>.
91   CPD, House of Representatives, 6 December 1990, 4641–4 (Brian Howe, Minister for Community Services and Health and Minister Assisting the Prime Minister for Social Justice) (Second Reading Speech, Social Security Bill 1990 (Cth)); Explanatory Memorandum, Social Security Bill 1990 (Cth).
92   Supplementary Explanatory Memorandum: Amendments and New Clauses to Be Moved on Behalf of the Government, Social Security Legislation (Amendment) Bill 1990 (Cth).
93   Letter from J J Bedlington, First Assistant Secretary, Refugee and Humanitarian Division, DIMA to Sev Ozdowski, Human Rights Commissioner, 18 May 2001, 2 (in *HREOC Complaint File*, above n 34).
94   CPD, Senate, 29 May 1996, 1241 (Sid Spindler).
95   Ibid 1242 (Bob Woods, Parliamentary Secretary to the Minister for Health and Family Services). In this intervention, however, while defending the government, he was able to deny knowledge of Cabinet dealings because he was not a Cabinet member.

certain exemptions. These related to 'financial hardship' arising from "an unforeseen change of circumstances" since arriving in Australia and to situations where the asylum seeker could not, or could not reasonably, be expected to continue to avail herself of avenues of support on which she had previously relied. Only in "special cases"[96] was it not regarded as necessary to identify an "unforeseen" event.[97]

In October 1996 eligibility requirements were tightened. There were three key changes made.[98] First, the changes removed eligibility for ASAS for those asylum seekers who had not yet received a primary decision on their refugee application. Second, those receiving ASAS who had cases before the Refugee Review Tribunal (RRT) were no longer eligible for assistance. In other words, those with cases that had not even been 'finally determined'[99] were stripped of eligibility for ASAS. Third, the changes ratcheted up the threshold of eligibility for exemptions from the six-month waiting period to require, in addition, the existence of "exceptional circumstances" that were "beyond the control of the applicant".[100] This eligibility threshold required asylum seekers to demonstrate *severe* financial hardship such that basic needs could not be met. In addition, asylum seekers had to show that such hardship arose from a "change in circumstances" that was "beyond [their] control".[101] However, even those able to demonstrate severe financial hardship were denied assistance if they had received a negative primary decision from the Immigration Department.

It was following the announcement of these changes that the Asylum Seekers Centre ('the Centre'), which provides assistance and support to asylum seekers in Sydney,[102] filed a complaint with the HREOC.[103] The

---

[96] Special cases were defined as including, but not limited to: a dependent child in undue hardship, an individual whose dependency constitutes an unreasonable burden on a permanent resident or a charitable organisation. Letter from John Bloomfield, DIMA, to David Norrie, HREOC, 17 November 1998, Attachment A, 'About the Asylum Seeker Assistance (ASA) Scheme' (in *HREOC Complaint File*, above n 34)

[97] HREOC, 'ASAS Report', above n 21, pt 2.2.

[98] For a discussion of the effects of these changes see Frank Elvey, 'The Budget Fallout for Asylum Seekers' (*Focus No 7*, Uniya, 1996).

[99] On the statutory meaning of 'finally determined', see below Section 6.2.1, 259–61.

[100] Letter from Bloomfield to Norrie, above n 96, Attachment B, 'Asylum Seeker Assistance Scheme (ASAS) Exemption Guidelines'.

[101] HREOC, 'ASAS Report', above n 21, pt 2.3.1.

[102] The Centre describes its mission as follows: "To provide a welcoming environment and practical support for community-based asylum seekers, while building community support and pursuing social justice outcomes for them": Asylum Seekers Centre, *About Us* <www.asylumseekerscentre.org.au/about-us/>.

[103] Letter from Frank Elvey, Co-ordinator, Asylum Seekers Centre, to Chris Sidoti, Human Rights Commissioner, 2 September 1996 (in *HREOC Complaint File*, above n 34).

complaint was made against the Commonwealth, and specifically the Immigration Department, pursuant to legislative functions and responsibilities vested in the Human Rights Commissioner for the protection and promotion of human rights.[104]

As the complaint file details, the effects of denial of ASAS at review stage was to render ineligible half of those receiving assistance under the scheme.[105] Indeed, a statement in support of the complaint made by the Australian Red Cross ('Red Cross'), subcontracted by the Department to administer ASAS, described the changes as "intended to reduce the number of approved exemptions from approximately 25 to 30 per month to approximately 25 to 30 per year"[106] – that is, a reduction of about 90 per cent. The Red Cross's chief concern was that "need is no longer the primary determinant for exemption and access to assistance".[107] The statement described the resultant hardship as "massive",[108] prompting increased demand on welfare agencies and charitable organisations.[109] In support of their submissions, both the Centre[110] and the Red Cross[111] provided follow-up submissions that offered case studies of people affected by the ASAS changes.

Changes in May 1998 ostensibly lowered the hardship threshold from 'severe' to (simply) 'financial hardship' but still defined such hardship as being "unable to meet . . . basic needs of food, accommodation and clothing and [having] no continuing and adequate support within the community".[112] Even so, 'financial hardship' was not in itself sufficient to trigger ASAS income support. To be eligible for assistance, an asylum seeker also had to be in an exemption category, which broadly included people considered unable to

---

[104] *Australian Human Rights Commission Act 1986* (Cth) s 11(1)(f). HREOC, 'ASAS Report', above n 21, app A.

[105] Statement made by Ken Hastie, NSW Manager of the Asylum Seekers Assistance Scheme, Australian Red Cross: 'Statement Concerning a Complaint by Mr Frank Elvey against the Department of Immigration and Multicultural Affairs', 14 October 1997 (in *HREOC Complaint File*, above n 34).

[106] Ibid 2.   [107] Ibid.   [108] Ibid 3.

[109] A subsequent submission by the Red Cross to the inquiry indicated that new criteria for seeking exemptions had been developed, to take effect from May 1998. David Fair, National ASAS Supervisor, Australian Red Cross, Submission to Human Rights and Equal Opportunity Commission with respect to Rights of Asylum Seekers, April 1998 (in *HREOC Complaint File*, above n 34).

[110] Letter from Frank Elvey, Co-ordinator, Asylum Seekers Centre, to David Norrie, HREOC, 11 March 1998 (in *HREOC Complaint File*, above n 34).

[111] Fair, above n 109.

[112] DIMA, 'Asylum Seeker Assistance (ASA) Handbook 1998', 21–2, Topic 8: Exemption – Application for Exemption to the ASA Eligibility Criteria (Schedule 1 of the Agreement) (in *HREOC Complaint File*, above n 34) ('ASA Handbook 1998').

care for themselves.[113] If not within one of the exemption categories, she was not eligible for assistance unless her financial hardship resulted from "a change of circumstances" that was "beyond [her] control" *and* that had arisen "since arrival in Australia".[114] This created an evidentiary burden and appeared immediately to exclude any person who had been in financial hardship ever since arriving in Australia. Later, changes in July 1999 restored eligibility for ASAS for applicants with cases at the RRT.[115] However, the tightening of the criteria meant, in effect, that very few could become or remain eligible for ASAS at the review stage. So, what was the rationale for these changes?

6.1.3.2 Rationalising Planned Destitution

In response to the Centre's complaint, the Department denied any breaches of Australia's international obligations. From the complaint file we can piece together its rationale for the changes. The Department relied on four documents to justify its position: an information paper providing details of the ASAS scheme,[116] a ministerial press release,[117] a departmental Fact Sheet,[118] and a letter to the Secretary-General of the Red Cross.[119] Reference was also made to Cabinet documents withheld to assess whether it was appropriate to seek public interest certification.[120]

---

[113] That is, she had to be: an unaccompanied minor or elderly person, disabled or ill and therefore unable to work, a parent of a minor child or children, a full-time carer for someone living at the same address, or a torture or trauma survivor unable to work: ibid 21–2.

[114] HREOC, 'ASAS Report', above n 21, pt 2.3.2.

[115] ASA Handbook 1998, above n 112, 22–3. Two additional exemption categories were added in July 1999. First, a woman with a high-risk pregnancy (which would have had to be medically identified and assessed at someone's expense) would be exempt; second, a person being the spouse, de facto, or sponsored fiancé of an Australian or New Zealand permanent resident or citizen, where the couple's combined income is less than the ASAS payments that would be available to them – that is, where (but for the exemption) the policy would negatively impact on citizens or residents, ie, insiders or welcome outsiders.

[116] Letter from Williams to Sidoti, above n 24, Attachment A 'About the Asylum Seekers Assistance (ASA) Scheme' (as at 28 July 1997).

[117] Philip Ruddock, Minister for Immigration and Multicultural Affairs, 'Speedier Processing for Asylum Claims' (Media Release, MPS 53/96, 20 August 1996) (in *HREOC Complaint File*, above n 34).

[118] DIMA, 'Fact Sheet: Immigration and Multicultural Affairs Budget '96' (20 August 1996) 3 ('Processing Asylum Claims') (in *HREOC Complaint File*, above n 34).

[119] Letter from J J Bedlington, First Assistant Secretary, Australian Client Services Division, DIMA, to the Hon J J Carlton, Secretary General, Australian Red Cross Society, 30 August 1996 (in *HREOC Complaint File*, above n 34).

[120] *Australian Human Rights Commission Act 1986* (Cth) s 24(1). I have found no evidence on the complaint file to suggest that such an assessment was ever made or communicated.

In terms of rationale, the press release made claims of "spiralling costs" and suggested that people accessing the scheme were not in "genuine need".[121] However, neither the press release nor the response to HREOC substantiated the claims by reference to any study or other documentary or statistical evidence to support the (perceived) need to discourage those who have very little chance of success from lodging claims. While conceding that it was "difficult to ascribe motives", the press release nevertheless alleged that people were "using" the system to "prolong" their stay in Australia.[122] These allegations were based on "circumstantial evidence".[123] Furthermore, the Department alleged, the people who were "creating delays" were causing a "build-up" in numbers that "compromise[d]" the Department's capacity to "quickly and effectively identify and assist" those in "genuine" need.[124] Later, the Human Rights Commissioner found this claim that non–bona fide asylum seekers were clogging the system to have only "superficial appeal", further concluding that both the suggestion and the evidence to support it could not withstand analysis.[125] He stated further that

> [i]n the absence of evidence to suggest that applicants suffering financial hardship are more likely to make unmeritorious claims, a common sense approach would suggest that unmeritorious [refugee] applications are as easily made by impecunious as solvent asylum seekers.[126]

This observation points to an institutional silence – that is, an absence of evidence to support the assumptions being made about people abusing the system. Indeed, while clearly recognising the possibility that unmeritorious applications were being made, the Human Rights Commissioner suggested that the policy's rationale did not accord with a 'common sense approach'.

Consistent with the justificatory 'but' framings that we saw in relation to mandatory detention, which characterise stringency against out-groups as a virtue – strict *but* fair,[127] tough *but* necessary[128] – these measures were pitched as being "in fairness" to those in "genuine need", citing as "imperative" the concentration of resources on those applicants at the beginning of the process.[129] Indeed, the ministerial media release asserted that the Department should not be responsible for assisting people whose claims had been rejected by the Department.[130] To do

---

[121] Ruddock, 'Speedier Processing for Asylum Claims', above n 117.   [122] Ibid.   [123] Ibid.
[124] DIMA, 'Fact Sheet', above n 118.
[125] HREOC, 'ASAS Report', above n 21, pt 10.4.1.1(b).   [126] Ibid.
[127] Van Dijk, above n 31, 100–2. See Chapter 5.
[128] CPD, House of Representatives, 5 May 1992, 2370–3 (Gerry Hand). See Chapter 5.
[129] Ruddock, 'Speedier Processing for Asylum Claims', above n 117.
[130] Ibid. See below 259–61.

otherwise, the Department said, would be to encourage "manifestly unfounded claims".[131] These assertions were made notwithstanding that the ASAS policy was clearly to deny access to income support for the first six months of the process (which, in practical terms, meant the primary stage) unless the exemption criteria applied. Moreover, the policy applied notwithstanding that overturn rates at the RRT, particularly of people in financial hardship, were relatively high.[132]

The effect of the institutional techniques that shaped these changes was to limit access to ASAS to only those in an exemption category. Furthermore, asylum seekers were described as '*failed* asylum seekers' after the first decision and alleged to be making 'abusive' claims that were 'manifestly unfounded'. Thus, their pursuit of appeals was (discursively) invalidated, they could evaporate statistically,[133] their conduct was impugned, and they – not the Department – could be held responsible for any continuing financial hardship. Again, as we saw in relation to mandatory detention, through an invidious inversion of the power relation, the powerless asylum seeker was held responsible for her own predicament.

The Department asserted that its policies and practices reflected a fair and balanced approach to protecting refugees, and safeguarded both the system and the Australian taxpayer against abuse. It claimed that its primary decisionmaking processes, which it said were guided by international standards in the *Refugee Convention*, were "fair, just, quick and economical".[134] The Department then claimed that the RRT prioritised review applications of those previously – yet, as a result of the changes, no longer – in receipt of ASAS and those able to demonstrate financial hardship.[135] In contrast, the Human Rights Commissioner later found that the Department's claims of evidence of abuse were exaggerated. Indeed, he concluded that "very limited evidence touching on this issue was actually provided"[136] and that even information that was provided did not, in fact, constitute evidence of abuse. So, for example, he did not accept that "the low rate of success at the review stage [was] evidence of abuse."[137] Furthermore, he regarded it as "entirely legitimate" for asylum seekers to exercise review rights and he said

---

[131] DIMA, 'Fact Sheet', above n 118. On manifestly unfounded or abusive applications, see, eg, UNHCR, 'UNHCR's Position on Manifestly Unfounded Applications for Asylum' (1 December 1992).
[132] HREOC, 'ASAS Report', above n 21, pt 10.4.1.1(a).
[133] On the statistical invisibility of 'failed asylum seekers', see also above 232.
[134] Letter from Helen Williams, Secretary, DIMA, to Chris Sidoti, Human Rights Commissioner, 6 August 1997 (in *HREOC Complaint File*, above n 34).
[135] See also letter from Immigration Department to Red Cross, above n 119.
[136] HREOC, 'ASAS Report', above n 21, pt 10.4.1.1(a).   [137] Ibid.

that "they should not be penalised for doing so."[138] Moreover, he found such review procedures to be statistically necessary.[139]

The Department also made claims relating to its international obligations. In doing so, it claimed – accurately (perhaps) but extraneously – that it was "fully aware" of "all relevant" international obligations when the changes to ASAS were considered and implemented.[140] Of course, awareness of obligations does not equate with compliance. Here, we can see that the Department chose its words both carefully and evasively, maximising the rhetorical value of international obligation while sidestepping the question of compliance. Indeed, cautiously ambivalent legal advice to the Department dated 11 April 1997 (that is, some six months after the changes) indicated that, while breaches of international obligations might be possible in individual cases, the "availability of discretion to depart from the norm in exceptional circumstances assists in providing adequate flexibility so that breaches may be avoided".[141] In other words, in keeping with the idea that abuse of power is only theoretical,[142] an un-scrutinisable discretionary power was framed as an adequate safeguard against breaches of international obligations.[143]

In February 2000, in its written response to the Commissioner's preliminary findings of law and fact, the Department strongly challenged findings that

---

[138]   Ibid.   [139]   Ibid.

[140]   Letter from Bloomfield to Norrie, above n 96. On international standards in relation to the right to welfare, see especially: *Refugee Convention* arts 20, 23, 24; *ICCPR* arts 2, 6(1), 7; *International Covenant on Economic, Social and Cultural Rights*, opened for signature 16 December 1966, 993 UNTS 3 (entered into force 3 January 1976) art 2 (*ICESCR*). For recent commentary in relation to asylum seekers and refugees, see: James C Hathaway, *The Rights of Refugees under International Law* (Cambridge University Press, 2005) 772–86, 800–13; Eve Lester, 'Article 20' in Andreas Zimmermann (ed), *1951 Convention relating to the Status of Refugees and Its 1967 Protocol: A Commentary* (Oxford University Press, 2011) 993 (on rationing); Eve Lester, 'Article 23' in Andreas Zimmermann (ed), *1951 Convention relating to the Status of Refugees and Its 1967 Protocol: A Commentary* (Oxford University Press, 2011) 1043 (on public relief); Eve Lester, 'Article 24' in Andreas Zimmermann (ed), *1951 Convention relating to the Status of Refugees and Its 1967 Protocol: A Commentary* (Oxford University Press, 2011) 1057 (on labour legislation and social security).

[141]   Advice from the Department's Legal Section, 11 April 1997 (in *HREOC Complaint File*, above n 34), also cited in HREOC, 'ASAS Report', above n 21, pt 7.

[142]   See Chapter 4, 117, 142.

[143]   In 2004, the Senate Select Committee on Ministerial Discretion in Migration Matters questioned the adequacy of such safeguards in meeting Australia's *non-refoulement* obligations under international law: Senate Select Committee on Ministerial Discretion in Migration Matters, Parliament of Australia, *Inquiry into Ministerial Discretion in Migration Matters* (2004) 42 [3.52], 125–48. See also Senate Legal and Constitutional References Committee, Parliament of Australia, *A Sanctuary under Review: An Examination of Australia's Refugee and Humanitarian Determination Processes*, June 2000.

there were violations of human rights standards.[144] In its defence, and in language reminiscent of that which characterised the introduction of the 45-day rule, it cast the changes as part of a comprehensive but restrained attempt to take control of a system that was being abused. The changes were, it said, "driven" by "the most appropriate ways of meeting international obligations".[145] It described the provision of material support as "just one measure of many"[146] in this protection project. Stating an accurate but extraneous truism, it cited "high quality and timely decisions" as "fundamental" to protecting the interests of refugees.[147] As such, the ASAS changes were pitched as "removing incentives" for "widespread misuse" of the system by (deviant and opportunistic) people who were not refugees and whose conduct was "directly and seriously harming the interests of refugees".[148] This 'misuse', it said, prolonged processing times. The changes were made because "abuse" was "damaging the interests of refugees".[149] The Department further claimed that the changes were "designed" to "strengthen and support" a system "under considerable pressure", and denied any suggestion that they were designed to punish a particular group.[150] In other words, through a range of discursive techniques, it maintained themes of departmental control and restraint, and deviant and opportunistic applicants. In doing so, it enlisted the rhetorical techniques of 'splitting' and deflection (by pressing extraneous truths).

In its responses, not only did the Department impugn the conduct of asylum seekers as dishonest and abusive and blame them for the damage being done to 'real' refugees, but it also sought to undermine the weight of any contrary evidence. To do so, it used particular rhetorical and institutional techniques. For example, it characterised allegations made in the Centre's written submissions as containing "errors and distortions".[151] However, it did so without substantiation. It labelled the case studies provided by the Centre and the Red Cross as "at most, anecdotal and circumstantial evidence", even though the Department itself had built policies on less.[152] In this way, the Department sought to deflect responsibility for policy and procedural

---

[144] Letter from W J Farmer, Secretary, DIMA, to Chris Sidoti, Human Rights Commissioner, 18 February 2000 (in *HREOC Complaint File*, above n 34).

[145] DIMA, Response to the Preliminary Findings by the Human Rights and Equal Opportunity Commission regarding the Complaint by Mr Frank Elvey, undated, 2, attached to Letter from Farmer to Sidoti, above n 144 (in *HREOC Complaint File*, above n 34) ('Response to HREOC Preliminary Findings').

[146] Ibid.   [147] Ibid 3.   [148] Ibid.   [149] Ibid.   [150] Ibid.

[151] Letter from Bedlington to Ozdowski, above n 93, 2.

[152] DIMA, Response to HREOC Preliminary Findings, above n 145, 5. See Ruddock, 'Speedier Processing for Asylum Claims', above n 117, which based policy changes on 'circumstantial evidence', discussed above at 252. See also the discussion on the '$30 work visa', above at 241–2.

deficiencies and their effects. Furthermore, and despite taking almost a year to respond to this round of submissions from the Centre, the Department alleged that the Centre had not sought "to usefully contribute [to] the resolution of [the] complaint."[153] By implying that the Centre's perspective on the issue was not to be considered accurate, balanced, or useful, it sought to undermine the counter-narrative and deflect attention from its own prevaricative conduct.[154]

During the inquiry, the Department made other claims and comments of a general and self-serving nature. Amongst others, it stated:

> The high quality of the primary determination process as well as the availability of merits and judicial review (as well as the availability of a wide variety of sources of publicly funded, private and community support for the small number of applicants who find themselves in real need of material support) has provided, and continues to provide, an ample 'safety net'.
>
> The 1 October 1996 changes to the Scheme . . . were considered a necessary response to rapidly increasing, and non-affordable, levels of expense associated with a growing proportion of abusive refugee claims. There was compelling evidence that processing delays and the availability of ASA were powerful attractions for those seeking to abuse Australia's refugee determination system. Many asylum seekers were seeking to utilise the refugee determination system to gain an immigration outcome, as evidence[d] in part by high rates of primary refusal, review take-up and review affirm rates.
>
> As part of the package of changes, and in the interest of refugees among ASA recipients, review applicants were accorded processing priority. In addition, they had access to support from the voluntary and non-profit community sector, which received separate Commonwealth, State or local funding at an appropriate level. Such recourse was accessible to aliens and nationals.[155]

Here, we see a number of rhetorical devices giving voice to the discourses of control and restraint, and of deviance and opportunism. Deploying the technique of positive self-presentation juxtaposed with negative characterisation of the out-group,[156] the Department sought to paint a picture of a process that was

---

[153] Letter from Bedlington to Ozdowski, above n 93, 4.
[154] On departmental delays in the process, see below 276–7. See also Bolkus' attack on Coulter in similar terms during the parliamentary debates on mandatory detention: Chapter 5, Section 5.1.3.2, 183–6.
[155] DIMA, Response to HREOC Preliminary Findings, above n 145, 4.
[156] Van Dijk, above n 31, 72–6, 84–93.

of 'high quality' and properly managed but up against a 'growing proportion of abusive' applicants. It represented the changes as a 'necessary' but restrained response that contained 'ample' safeguards and safety nets – safeguards and safety nets delivered, moreover, by an 'appropriate' level of funding.[157] The changes were, it claimed, a response to 'abuse' and 'non-affordable' cost blowouts. It was claimed that the changes were based on 'compelling evidence' and were, above all, in the interests of the 'small' number of people in 'real' need – that is, the (genuine) refugees. It claimed further that the body of evidence of "substantial abuse" – of deviance and opportunism – was "large", "clear", and "compelling".[158] Thus, it deemed the responses to be "entirely appropriate", "properly balanced", and "proportionate"[159] – that is, controlled and restrained. And, as noted earlier, any contrary evidence was to be regarded as 'anecdotal' and therefore (implicitly) not credible.[160]

As we have seen, like the 45-day rule, the rationale for the ASAS changes was not described by technical policy statement, data, or analysis. Instead, it was depicted through purposively emotive rhetoric. Again, we see that discourses of control and restraint (the need to protect the taxpayer by containing 'spiralling' costs) represent state responses as responsible and measured and grounded in evidence. In juxtaposition, discourses of deviance and opportunism, which use language to maximum rhetorical effect, *become* evidence through repetition, discredit the out-group, and deflect the charge of prejudice by 'splitting' asylum seekers. And any evidence that contradicts this position is dismissed as 'anecdotal' or 'circumstantial'. As this discussion shows, therefore, the rationales for the denial of work and welfare rights lie in a rhetoric that validates the construction and performance of an invisible border as a form of social and economic exclusion, as a locus of control and restraint, and as a safeguard against the deviance and opportunism of unworthy and unwelcome outsiders. As we have seen, these policy rationales are light on evidence and heavily dependent on socio-political perception. Yet, they are remarkably effective, because the rhetorical power of the evidentiary claims lies in their making, not their content. As the following sections show, a key reason for the effectiveness of the policy rationales is the institutional silence created by an accountability vacuum.

---

[157] Cf the Centre's response, which was that this contention was "totally outrageous and untrue". Letter from Sylvia Winton, Coordinator, Asylum Seekers Centre, to John Armstrong, Senior Legal Officer, HREOC, 25 May 2000 (in *HREOC Complaint File*, above n 34).

[158] DIMA, Response to HREOC Preliminary Findings, above n 145, 4, 15.   [159] Ibid 15, 16.

[160] See above 255.

The focus in Sections 6.2 and 6.3 switches to the institutional techniques that enable legislation, regulations, and policy-based schemes to operate without (effective) scrutiny. I argue that these institutional techniques give effect to the discourse of 'absolute sovereignty' that underpins the broad policy of planned destitution. As we will see, echoes of state control and restraint and asylum seeker deviance and opportunism remain audible at the level of institutional technique. At the same time, we see how discourses of institutional silence are crucial to maintaining a system that functions (institutionally) to maintain maximum power with minimum accountability.

6.2 WORK: AN OBSESSION WITH DISCRETION

As we know from the foregoing discussion, between 1997 and 2009, an asylum seeker entering Australia on a visa and lodging her refugee application within 45 days of arrival was granted work rights automatically. These rights had effect until her application was 'finally determined'.[161] After 2009, the 45-day rule was relaxed. From that time, if an asylum seeker did not have lawful status and she was in Australia for more than 45 days before making her application, the 'no work' condition was mandatory the first time her bridging visa was issued.[162] Thereafter, however, she could apply to have the no-work condition lifted subject to a complex of stringent requirements. To be eligible for work rights, she had to establish a 'compelling need to work'[163] on the grounds of 'financial hardship', and her reasons for delaying her application beyond 45 days had to be 'acceptable'.[164]

Prima facie, these terms sound balanced, restrained, and flexible. What did they mean in practice? When is a determination final? When is a need to work compelling? What constitutes financial hardship? And when is delaying an application acceptable? Although these are technical questions about how certain terms are understood, the following analysis focuses on how they reflect and effect institutional techniques of social and economic exclusion without meaningful checks and balances – that is, how they give expression to the discourse of 'absolute sovereignty'.

---

[161] *Migration Act* s 5(9).
[162] DIBP, PAM3, above n 13, Bridging E Visas, Compelling Need to Work.
[163] *Migration Regulations* reg 1.08; *Migration Amendment Regulations 2009 (No 6) No 143* (Cth); DIBP, PAM3, above n 13, Bridging E Visas, Compelling Need to Work.
[164] See below, Section 2.2.2.3, 265–8.

6.2.1 Is 'Finally Determined' Final?

According to the *Oxford English Dictionary* (*OED*) 'finally' means "in the end, lastly, at last, ultimately"; "indicating the last point or conclusion of a discourse, treatise, etc"; "so as to make a complete end; in a manner not to be reversed or altered; once for all, decisively, conclusively."[165] In addition, the *OED* defines 'determine' as: "to bring to an end"; "to end, conclude, terminate".[166]

In contrast to these ordinary meanings, 'finally determined' under the *Migration Act* 1958 (Cth) ('*Migration Act*') has been ascribed a particular meaning. It connotes the point at which an individual receives a decision on her application following the exercise of merits review rights.[167] Where that decision is negative, the description 'finally determined' discursively expunges judicial review rights or requests for ministerial intervention on humanitarian grounds. These remaining avenues for protection then are not treated as stages in the application process, even though they are part of the lawful processes an asylum seeker is entitled to engage.[168] The term 'finally determined' therefore enables those seeking judicial review or ministerial intervention to be labelled '*former* protection visa applicants'[169] or '*failed* asylum seekers',[170] as persons not entitled to work because, these descriptors suggest, they do not need or deserve protection. This legitimises disentitlement to work rights by discursively invalidating an asylum seeker's right to pursue remaining judicial review and humanitarian procedures as well as making the pursuit of such processes unaffordable. Yet, as Simon Brown LJ once noted, "[q]uite apart from the need to keep body and soul together pending the final determination of a claim, expense is likely to be incurred in pursuing it."[171] Destitution is the inevitable result.

In the context of the 45-day rule, the practical effect of this framing was to re-engage the no-work condition after a (negative) merits review decision about halfway through the RSD process. This left a (hitherto unsuccessful) applicant without work rights at a point when the process could still endure for months and possibly years.[172] In other words, there was no correlation between 'finally' in the

---

[165] Oxford English Dictionary <www.oed.com/> (OED). [166] Ibid.

[167] *Migration Act* s 5(9); on behavioural and 'status resolution milestone' requirements for continued eligibility, see also DIBP, 'SRSS Policy Advice Manual', above n 23, 21–2.

[168] Ibid pt 8 (judicial review), s 417 (discretionary power of the Minister to substitute a more favourable decision).

[169] DIAC, Supplementary Submission No 129n to Joint Standing Committee on Migration, Parliament of Australia, *Inquiry into Immigration Detention in Australia*, 29 January 2009.

[170] DIBP, *Fact Sheet 62*, above n 22; Millbank, 'Asylum Seekers on Bridging Visa E', above n 3.

[171] *Ex parte JCWI* [1996] 4 All ER 385, 395.

[172] Although there is some evidence that work rights could be granted for individuals at this stage in the process, the weight of evidence suggests that the grant of work rights in such

phrase 'finally determined' and the final stage of the determination process. Recalling the difference between 'application custody' and 'custody' that we saw in the context of mandatory detention, we can see that the ascription of a particular meaning to a term that conceals both its broader purpose and effect is a discursive pattern in migration discourse.[173] We also see how discursive techniques such as these achieve institutional disengagement from (and political invalidation of) parts of a process over which the executive does not have (a measure of) control.[174]

A further effect of this discursive framing was artificially to reduce the number of people seen to be subject to the no-work condition and therefore to diminish institutional responsibility for the size of the problem. Thus, in April 2006, and in the context of the 45-day rule, a senior departmental official could tell the Senate Legal and Constitutional Affairs Committee that 1,600 people nationally had protection visa applications on hand either with the Immigration Department or the RRT. He told the Committee that, "[o]f these, some two-thirds are on bridging visas with work rights, so we are talking about a minority of people seeking protection visas that are not currently able to reside in the community with work rights."[175] Even according to these statistics, this means that a cohort of roughly 530 asylum seekers and their dependents were denied work rights (as well as adequate welfare). More significant in numerical terms, however, was that, because of the way in which 'finally determined' was defined, this testimony did not (need to) tell the Committee that, in the same year, there were an estimated 3,000 asylum seekers, at any one time, who were living in the community and engaged in lawful procedures but who were prohibited from working or accessing welfare support.[176] Moreover, the Immigration Department knew that almost 20 per

circumstances was rare: Department of Immigration and Multicultural Affairs (DIMIA), Submission No 24 to Senate Select Committee on Ministerial Discretion in Migration Matters, Parliament of Australia, *Inquiry into Ministerial Discretion in Migration Matters*, August 2003, 42 [187]; Hotham Mission, Uniting Justice Australia, 'Welfare Issues and Immigration Outcomes for Asylum Seekers on Bridging Visa E' (Research and Evaluation, April 2003), Supplementary Submission No 19A to Senate Select Committee on Ministerial Discretion in Migration Matters, Parliament of Australia, *Inquiry into Ministerial Discretion in Migration Matters*, August 2003.

[173] See Chapter 5, 168, 178.

[174] Of course, the Refugee Review Tribunal is an independent merits review body. However, the scope of its powers is statutorily prescribed: *Migration Act* pt 7.

[175] Evidence to Senate Legal and Constitutional Legislation Committee, Parliament of Australia, *Inquiry into Migration Amendment (Employer Sanctions) Bill 2006*, Sydney, 26 April 2006, 43 (Neil Mann, First Assistant Secretary, Compliance Policy and Case Coordination Division, DIMA).

[176] Topsfield, above n 71.

cent of this group had been living on bridging visas for more than five years.[177] Therefore, by confining his testimony only to those the Department regarded as 'protection visa applicants', we can see how the technical meaning of the term 'finally determined' enabled this evidence to understate the effects of the policy on the asylum seeker population by more than five times. In other words, the term enabled, and the testimony effected, a partial statistical silence that disclosed information covering less than 20 per cent of those affected. This technique of narrowing the statistical frame is the flipside of the numbers rhetoric used in elite discourse to magnify the size of the 'immigration problem'.[178]

As we know, following the changes in 2009, it became possible to have the no-work condition lifted. This could happen where a person initially denied work rights (after applying outside the 45-day time limit) could establish a 'compelling need to work' on the grounds of 'financial hardship', and that her reasons for 'delay' were 'acceptable'. The complexity and implications of this terminology are discussed next.

6.2.2 *Lifting the 'No Work' Condition*

As noted earlier, if at any time an asylum seeker did not have lawful status and she was in Australia for more than 45 days before making her application, the no-work condition was mandatory the first time her bridging visa was issued.[179] Thereafter, the grant of work rights was a matter of discretion.[180] However, even where work rights were granted, the short-term validity of most bridging visas was an obvious obstacle to finding work.[181]

In addition to the requirements I have outlined, the departmental procedures advice manual (the current version of which is known as PAM3)[182] provides that the grant of work rights is also to be informed by a set of "public policy principles". These incorporate requirements and expectations of the applicant, purportedly to counter the risk of deviant and opportunistic behaviour, including "actively and genuinely" pursuing resolution of a claim, "early and sustained" engagement with the Department, and

---

[177] Ibid.
[178] Van Dijk, above n 31, 107–9. For an example of the use of numbers rhetoric to magnify a problem, see Chapter 5, 195.
[179] DIBP, PAM3, above n 13, Bridging E Visas, Compelling Need to Work.   [180] Ibid.
[181] Joint Standing Committee on Migration (JSCM), Parliament of Australia, Immigration Detention in Australia: Community-Based Alternatives to Detention – Second Report of the Inquiry into Immigration Detention in Australia (2009) 65 [3.28]. Although issues relating to rights at work as opposed to the right to work are beyond the scope of this project, it is noteworthy that persons affected often accept work which is dirty, dangerous, and degrading: at 65 [3.29].
[182] DIBP, PAM3, above n 13.

"cooperating in leaving Australia" where there is no basis to remain.[183] The public policy principles state that "such policies" – as opposed to the *implementation* of such policies – "must reflect any international obligations which Australia may owe to individuals".[184] Incongruously, reference is also made to the importance of "reflecting" – rather than managing – "general community expectations that non-citizens will not receive more generous support or entitlements than those available to Australian citizens".[185] The obvious incongruity of these expectations in the context of work rights – which all citizens enjoy – suggests that the principles reflect a public policy position that plays into community assumptions and prejudice rather than adhering to principle or standards.[186]

For those seeking to have the no-work condition lifted, establishing a 'compelling need to work' is critical. Unpacking definitions of the term and associated terminology is a multilayered inquiry, which unearths the many ways in which certain institutional techniques weigh against the possibility of lifting the no-work condition. The next section explores how this takes place. It examines how 'compelling need to work' is framed, how the requirement to establish 'financial hardship' is understood, and how decisionmakers are guided in assessing whether delays in making a protection visa application are 'acceptable'.

6.2.2.1 Compelling Need to Work

Under the *Migration Regulations*, a person who can establish a 'compelling need to work' is entitled to have the no-work condition on her bridging visa lifted.[187] There are specific ways of doing so. Considered together, they reveal some striking incongruities.

---

[183] Ibid, Bridging E Visas, Compelling Need to Work.   [184] Ibid.   [185] Ibid.

[186] On international standards in relation to work rights, see: *Refugee Convention* arts 17–19; *ICESCR* art 6. For recent commentary, see: Hathaway, *Rights of Refugees*, above n 140, 719–30, 730–72, 788–800; Penelope Mathew, *Reworking the Relationship between Asylum and Employment* (Routledge, 2012); Alice Edwards, 'Article 17' in Andreas Zimmermann (ed), *1951 Convention relating to the Status of Refugees and Its 1967 Protocol: A Commentary* (Oxford University Press, January 2011) 951 (on wage-earning employment); Alice Edwards, 'Article 18' in Andreas Zimmermann (ed), *1951 Convention relating to the Status of Refugees and Its 1967 Protocol: A Commentary* (Oxford University Press, January 2011) 973 (on self-employment); Alice Edwards, 'Article 19' in Andreas Zimmermann (ed), *1951 Convention relating to the Status of Refugees and Its 1967 Protocol: A Commentary* (Oxford University Press, January 2011) 983 (on liberal professions); Alice Edwards, 'Human Rights, Refugees, and the Right "To Enjoy" Asylum' (2005) 17(2) *International Journal of Refugee Law* 293; Eve Lester, 'Work, the Right to Work, and Durable Solutions? A Study on Sierra Leonean Refugees in the Gambia' (2005) 17(2) *International Journal of Refugee Law* 331.

[187] *Migration Regulations* reg 1.08; DIBP, PAM3, above n 13, Bridging E Visas, Compelling Need to Work.

The first ground for a 'compelling need to work' is that the person is 'in financial hardship'.[188] This is, prima facie, unremarkable. It appears consistent with the ordinary meaning of 'compelling need'.[189] That is, financial hardship would seem to evoke a powerfully irresistible requirement to accord work rights because they are considered essential or very important rather than just desirable. However, the remaining ways of establishing 'compelling need to work' bear no relation to the ordinary meaning of 'compelling need'.

Under the *Migration Regulations*, a 'compelling need to work' may also be established if a person 'is an applicant for a Temporary Business Entry (Class UC) visa who seeks to satisfy the criteria for the grant of a Subclass 457 (Temporary Work (Skilled)) visa'[190] and is identified by an approved sponsor ('standard business sponsor')[191] or party to a labour agreement.[192] In these cases, there is no requirement to establish 'financial hardship'. Instead, it is sufficient that the nominated or sponsored applicant 'appear' to satisfy the criteria for the substantive visa for which she has applied.[193] Thus, the provisions *assume* her need to work to be 'compelling' not because of financial hardship but, it would seem, because she is a foreigner who has business or other relevant skills that may be regarded as essential or very important. In other words, it is the state's desire for her skills that makes her welcome and that characterises her 'need' to work as 'compelling'.

In contrast, for the asylum seeker, the task of establishing a 'compelling need to work' on the basis of 'financial hardship' is both onerous and opaque. This is so even if she 'appears' to satisfy the criteria for a protection visa. Above all, it is because, as an asylum seeker, she is unwelcome and her destitution is planned as a form of social and economic exclusion.[194]

---

[188] *Migration Regulations* reg 1.08(a).
[189] 'Compelling' may be taken to mean evoking a "powerfully irresistible" requirement "because it is essential or very important, rather than just desirable": OED <www.oed.com/>.
[190] *Migration Regulations* reg 1.08(d)(i).   [191] Ibid reg 1.03.
[192] Ibid reg 1.08(d)(ii)(A) and (B).
[193] Ibid reg 1.08(d)(iii). See also discussion of the Ruddock rationale for the 45-day rule, in which asylum seekers need only 'appear' to be abusing the system to be condemned as miscreants: above 240.
[194] In the context of a discussion in 2002 about the possibility of white Zimbabweans seeking asylum in Australia, then Immigration Minister, Philip Ruddock, was reported as saying "[i]f people have skills that are transportable, recognised, have English language competency and are relatively young, they're able to do very well under our migration selection": Frank Walker, 'Woman, 78, Seen as Refugee Test Case', *Sydney Morning Herald* (online), 2 September 2002 <www.smh.com.au/articles/2002/09/01/1030508159603.html>. Implicit in Ruddock's observation is the assumption that people would not apply for asylum if they had skills. In this connection, the article also reported that in 2001 "868 Zimbabweans entered Australia as skilled migrants, four times the level of five years ago." See also Eve Lester, 'Imagining the "Promise of Justice" in the Prohibition on Racial Discrimination: Paradoxes

In the following subsection, I consider how the term 'financial hardship' is shaped and understood.

6.2.2.2 Financial Hardship

'Financial hardship' is not defined in either the *Migration Act* or its *Regulations*. Instead, the (non-binding) PAM3 provides a definition. It states that "[g]enerally, a person can be taken to be in financial hardship if the cost of reasonable living expenses exceeds [her] ability to pay for them."[195] To establish financial hardship, the applicant is required to provide information and supporting evidence, including details of savings, income, expenses, and any support she is receiving from others.[196] The decisionmaker is then instructed to proceed as follows:

> An officer may accept the claims made by the person based on the evidence provided. However, if the officer has doubts about any claim or evidence, they may seek additional relevant information, either from the person or from departmental records, such as previous visa applications or 'permission to work' applications.[197]
> The delegate should have regard to the following:
> - whether the person's claimed expenses are reasonable – for example, are they within the range considered acceptable for the person's situation
> - how the person has supported himself or herself until now and whether that support will continue
> - whether there are other possible means of support, for example, their sponsor or nominator, relatives or friends in Australia, relatives overseas
> - whether the person will otherwise become an unreasonable charge on public funds or charitable institutions[198]
> - **when** the application for the substantive visa is likely to be decided – however, the likely **outcome** of the substantive visa application is not a relevant consideration in determining financial hardship for bridging visa purposes.[199]

---

and Prospects' [2007] *International and Humanitarian Law Resources* 8 <www.worldlii.org/int/journals/IHLRes/2007/8.html>.

[195] DIBP, PAM3, above n 13, Assessing a Valid Bridging Visa Application.   [196]   Ibid.
[197]   Ibid.
[198] On 'public charge' as a ground of exclusion, see: *Nishimura Ekiu v United States*, 142 US 651, 662 (1892), discussed in Chapter 3, 99; *Immigration Act 1901* (Cth) s 3(b), noted in Chapter 4, 132 n 120.
[199]   DIBP, PAM3, above n 13, Assessing a Valid Bridging Visa Application (emphases in original).

A close reading and analysis of the language of this instruction shows it to be so vague that it is arbitrary. As the instruction suggests, although the delegate 'may' accept the claims a person makes, if there are 'any' 'doubts', the delegate may seek or draw on additional information either from the applicant or from departmental records. This enables the text to be read as a prompt to entertain doubts about her credibility.

A key determinant of the applicant's hardship is an assessment of her ability to pay against the 'reasonableness' of her (documented) expenses. What constitutes 'reasonable' expenses is posed as a spectrum evaluation 'within the range' that is 'considered' to be 'acceptable' for 'the person's situation'. Absent from this instruction are clear, objective benchmarks of reasonableness. The variables in the proposed spectrum evaluation – 'the range' 'considered' 'acceptable' for 'the person's situation' – converge into an instruction so vague as to be entirely dependent on the (pre)disposition of the decisionmaker.

As an assessment tool it raises a multitude of questions. For example, how is 'other possible means of support' to be read and evaluated? When would it be appropriate to expect a person to rely on such support? Can the decisionmaker require, expect, or assume such support to continue or be made available? According to what standard? What does it mean to become a 'reasonable charge' on public funds or charitable institutions as opposed to an 'unreasonable charge'?

Both the discussion and the questions show how onerous and unpredictable the framework for establishing a 'compelling need to work' on the basis of 'financial hardship' can be in practice. Moreover, even if financial hardship can be established, an asylum seeker's next hurdle is to satisfy the decisionmaker that any reasons for delaying her application beyond 45 days after arrival are 'acceptable'.

6.2.2.3 Acceptable Reasons for Delay

Like the requirement of 'financial hardship', 'acceptable reasons for delay' is not defined in the *Migration Act* or *Regulations*.[200] Once again, (non-binding) guidance may be found in the PAM3. The guidance provided is very detailed, spelling out a non-exhaustive list of possible reasons for delay. While the list includes reasons considered 'acceptable', textual emphasis is given to those considered 'unacceptable'.

So, what reasons are 'acceptable'? Broadly, 'acceptable' reasons include being 'prevented' from making an application due to personal circumstances 'beyond their control' and which arose after arrival in Australia. Those reasons and

---

[200]   *Migration Regulations* sch 2 reg 050.212(8)(c)(i).

circumstances must cover all, or almost all, of the period of delay. This may include accident, illness, or serious medical condition of the applicant or a person for whose care she is responsible. They may also include changes in her country of origin giving rise to *sur place* claims.[201]

As elaborated further later, the standard of attainment for 'acceptability' is high, and the threshold of 'unacceptability' low. Evidentiary requirements are onerous. For example, it is expected that the applicant will supply supporting evidence substantiating her reasons for delay. The period of delay is also subject to a test of 'reasonableness'.[202]

Overall, procedural advice to decisionmakers outlines a process that makes the effort involved in concluding that reasons for delay were 'acceptable' more administratively burdensome. For example, decisionmakers are guided into a negative predisposition: "it is *likely* that *many* applicants who have been *unlawful* non-citizens for a *lengthy* period *will* have difficulty demonstrating acceptable reasons for delay throughout the relevant period".[203]

In contrast, decisionmakers are offered examples of reasons that are considered – indeed, *assumed* – to be 'unacceptable'. These include lack of knowledge about processes, lack of access to or poor advice, delay by someone else responsible for lodging the application, inadequate English language skills, or waiting for supporting documentation or evidence.[204] On the face of the text, and as a question of fact, these same reasons might well be objectively acceptable. Yet the decisionmaker is neither invited nor encouraged to so conclude, much less to think about giving an applicant the benefit of the doubt. Indeed, PAM3 even includes an invitation and form of words that a decisionmaker could adopt in assessing reasons for delay to be unacceptable – a form of words that insinuates deviance and opportunism:

> Although all of the reasons for delay put forward by the applicant must be considered, in these situations officers *may find that the applicant in fact delayed making their [refugee] application not for reasons beyond their control but in order to continue acting in breach of their visa conditions or to live unlawfully in the community for as long as possible.*[205]

---

[201] DIBP, PAM3, above n 13, Bridging E Visas, Compelling Need to Work ('acceptable reasons'). Note that a person who was not a refugee when she left her country but who becomes a refugee at a later date is called a refugee *sur place*: UNHCR, *Handbook and Guidelines*, UN Doc HCR/1P/4/ENG/REV.3, paras 94–6.
[202] DIBP, PAM3, above n 13, Bridging E Visas, Compelling Need to Work ('period of delay').
[203] Ibid (emphases added).   [204] Ibid ('unacceptable reasons').
[205] Ibid (emphasis added).

As noted earlier, the evidentiary standards for establishing 'acceptable reasons for delay' are stringent, whether those delays have arisen for medical reasons or on account of changes in country of origin conditions. In the case of accident or illness, documentary evidence from a registered medical practitioner (which the applicant would have to pay for)[206] is required. This must show that it would have been unreasonable to expect the asylum seeker to have made her application within the 45-day time limit. In the case of country of origin conditions, changes must be "recent and substantial", "corroborated" by the Department's research, *and* must also be regarded by the decisionmaker as "reliable".[207] Furthermore, changes must also "appear" to affect the applicant "directly".[208] In particular, they should not be as a consequence of the applicant's own actions since arriving in Australia, such actions being assumed to be self-serving, improperly motivated, and, therefore, unworthy of recognition regardless of their impact.[209] Procedurally, it is expected that any such claims will be referred internally for specialist assessment of their plausibility.[210]

The PAM3 guidance makes only one concession to the possibility of innocent applicant error or mishap. A minor administrative glitch on the part of the applicant is excused as long as the asylum seeker has made a "sound attempt" to comply with application requirements *and* the problem has been "quickly remedied".[211] Although evidentiary benchmarks of soundness or speed are unclear and unelaborated, this concession marks the process as restrained.

The assessment of 'acceptable reasons for delay' is also underpinned by the behavioural requirements and expectations outlined in the public policy principles, discussed earlier.[212] It is supplemented by an inquiry into whether there is "any" "evidence" that the delay was part of a "deliberate effort" by the asylum seeker to prolong her stay for reasons unrelated to her protection claims.[213] The language of these instructions underscores institutional assumptions of asylum seeker deviance and opportunism. It does not

---

[206] Costs would not be covered by Medicare, given that Medicare is tied to work rights: see, eg, Senate Select Committee on Ministerial Discretion in Migration Matters, above n 143, 79 [5.37].

[207] DIBP, PAM3, above n 13, Bridging E Visas, Compelling Need to Work. [208] Ibid.

[209] This echoes measures which significantly curtailed the possibility of making a *sur place* claim by amendments to the *Migration Act* in 2001: *Migration Act* s 91R(3), inserted by *Migration Legislation Amendment Act (No 6) 2001* (Cth) s 5.

[210] Referrals are made to the Department's Onshore Protection Team: DIBP, PAM3, above n 13, Bridging E Visas, Compelling Need to Work.

[211] Departmental error that has adversely affected the applicant is also excused: ibid.

[212] See above 261–2.

[213] DIBP, PAM3, above n 13, Bridging E Visas, Compelling Need to Work.

encourage discernment about the probative value of the 'any' evidence under consideration. Combined with the behavioural expectations in the public policy principles, the administratively burdensome process for making a favourable assessment of 'financial hardship' and 'acceptable reasons for delay', and the onerous evidentiary expectations of the applicant, provide decisionmakers abundant opportunity to disbelieve.

At this point, it is apposite to recall for comparative purposes the other ways in which 'compelling need to work' can be established (for welcome foreigners). That is, a 'compelling need to work' will be established if a person is sponsored or nominated for a visa on skills grounds and she 'appears' to satisfy the criteria for the substantive visa for which she has applied.[214] She does not have to establish 'financial hardship', and there is no arbitrary timeframe within which she must apply.

As we have seen in this section, the discursive framing of the 'compelling need to work' on the grounds of 'financial hardship', coupled with the requirement that reasons for 'delaying' a protection visa application are 'acceptable', makes satisfying the requirements to lift the no-work condition extremely difficult. However, equally important is the decisionmaking process itself. If an asylum seeker's application to have the no-work condition lifted from her bridging visa is unsuccessful, how will she find out why? What recourse does she have if she is found not to meet the criteria for 'financial hardship' and therefore not to have a 'compelling need to work'? What recourse does she have if her reasons for delaying her application beyond 45 days are found to be 'unacceptable'?

As the following section shows, she is likely to encounter an almost impenetrable wall of jurisprudential silence. This is as much a result of the way in which terms have been discursively developed and shaped as it is attributable to institutional techniques that have produced a highly discretionary decisionmaking process. Indeed, in migration lawmaking, what we see is an 'obsession with discretion' that has structurally entrenched unaccountability, with significant implications for the enjoyment of work rights by some asylum seekers.

6.2.3 Institutional Silence and Discretion

In 1989, the *Migration Act* was radically altered, transforming migration legislation from one conferring broad discretionary powers into a rule-based code.[215] This transformation followed a substantial review of the migration program by the

---

[214] *Migration Regulations* reg 1.08(d)(iii). See discussion above at 263.
[215] Sean Cooney, 'The Codification of Migration Policy: Excess Rules?' (Pt 1) (1994) 1(3) *Australian Journal of Administrative Law* 125, 125.

Committee to Advise on Australia's Immigration Policy.[216] One of the overarching premises of this codification was that it was, as a general rule, no longer regarded as appropriate that migration decisions should be made on the strength of discretionary powers. Rather, migration decisions should be the subject of independent merits review and, like other administrative decisions, judicial review.[217]

However, in some key areas, discretionary powers were retained. Indeed, discretion remains, in many respects, an (arguably growing) obsession in migration law-, policy- and decisionmaking, creating what has been described as "a significant accountability 'black hole' in the administration of immigration policy".[218] It manifests as a preoccupation with quarantining migration decisions from review – in particular judicial review – by conferring unimpeachable discretionary powers. Although bearing a character similar to that of the 'decision-lessness' of the mandatory detention scheme considered in Chapter 5, the grant or denial of work rights still requires a decision to be made. To this end, the conferral of discretionary powers, which are, for the most part, vested in the Minister personally, have increasingly been legislatively framed to be non-compellable, non-enforceable, and non-reviewable.[219] As we know from the genealogy, this pattern of decisionmaking in Australian migration law is a legislative and administrative practice of long standing,[220] a practice with identifiable links to the discourse of 'absolute sovereignty'. As we have seen, repeated resort to such strategies is consonant with a style of governance that is accustomed to absolute power and resistant to scrutiny.[221]

As discussed earlier, critical to the statutory requirement to establish a 'compelling need to work' is the assessment of 'financial hardship'. In issuing

---

[216] Committee to Advise on Australia's Immigration Program, 'Immigration: A Commitment to Australia' (Report, 1988).

[217] In 1992, amendments to the *Migration Act* established the Refugee Review Tribunal for merits review and a migration-specific judicial review scheme: *Migration Reform Act* ss 31, 33. Prior to this, judicial review of migration decisions was available under the *Administrative Decisions (Judicial Review) Act 1977* (Cth).

[218] See, eg, Senate Select Committee on Ministerial Discretion in Migration Matters, above n 143, 4 [1.12]. More recently, see Lauren Bull et al, 'Playing God: The Immigration Minister's Unrestrained Power' (Liberty Victoria, 2017).

[219] For example: 'The Minister does not have a duty to consider . . . ': *Migration Act* ss 72(1)(c), 72(7). On grant of access to procedures, see: *Migration Act* ss 46A, 46B, 48B, 91F, 91L, 91Q, 195A.

[220] See Chapter 4 Section 4.2.3.2, 132–6; see also Cooney, above n 215.

[221] Senate Select Committee on Ministerial Discretion in Migration Matters, above n 143, xii, 8 [1.20].

its procedural advice to departmental officers making this assessment, the Immigration Department instructs itself as follows:

> If the officer is satisfied that the person has a compelling need to work (is in financial hardship) and they hold a BVA, BVC or BVE(050), a Bridging visa of the same class and subclass should be granted without a condition that prevents or restricts work.[222]
>
> If the officer is not satisfied that the person is in financial hardship and they hold a BVA, BVC or BVE(050), a Bridging visa of the same class and subclass should be granted (provided the person still satisfies the criteria) with the same condition preventing or restricting work that was previously imposed.[223]

Within these provisions, the effect of the instruction is unarticulated and concealed by language that appears to be procedurally quite ordinary. However, the instruction ensures that departmental assessments of 'financial hardship' (and now 'acceptable reasons for delay') do not, for the most part, see the light of day.[224] As the instruction suggests, if the decisionmaker is not satisfied that the applicant is in financial hardship, a new bridging visa is still granted with a no-work condition. This is so even if the existing bridging visa is still valid. By not refusing the visa, there is no merits-reviewable decision[225] – an effect that has been described by the Law Council of Australia as a non–bona fide exercise of power.[226] The implications of this approach are that, when refusing to grant work rights, merits review rights are rarely triggered. So, even though work rights decisions are technically amenable to merits and judicial review, there is effectively no juridical space within which a work rights jurisprudence can develop. The effect of this instruction is, therefore, that a person seeking to have the no-work condition lifted remains subject to the predisposition of the individual decisionmaker or the broader undulations of policy change and implementation.[227] An examination of the available jurisprudence supports this conclusion.

A database search[228] for the two phrases 'compelling need to work' and 'financial hardship' reveals a combined total of 23 tribunal-level decisions in

---

[222] DIBP, PAM3, above n 13, Assessing a Valid Bridging Visa Application.   [223] Ibid.

[224] Law Council of Australia, above n 3.   [225] *Migration Act* s 338.

[226] Law Council of Australia, above n 3, 6.

[227] In relation to the *Social Security Act*, interpretations of terms such as 'severe financial hardship' and 'unavoidable or reasonable expenditure' are on the public record: see, eg, *Chidiac v Secretary, Department of Education, Employment and Workplace Relations* [2011] AATA 681 (30 September 2011); *Secretary, Department of Education, Employment and Workplace Relations v Ergin* (2010) 54 AAR 60.

[228] Australasian Legal Information Institute (AustLII) <www.austlii.edu.au>: search conducted 30 November 2016.

the two decades since 1990. The Immigration Review Tribunal (1990–1999) records eight decisions, the Migration Review Tribunal (1999–2015) 15 decisions, and the Administrative Appeals Tribunal (since 2015)[229] none. There were no decisions in the Federal Magistrates Court,[230] the Federal Circuit Court, the Federal Court of Australia ('the Federal Court'), or the High Court of Australia ('the High Court'). Over the same period, a search for 'compelling need to work' in the Federal Magistrates Court, the Federal Circuit Court, the Federal Court, and the High Court revealed a combined total of 10 cases: four in the Federal Magistrates Court and six in the Federal Court. None of these cases sheds new light on the meaning of these terms. By way of contrast, and to put these figures in some context and perspective, the number of bridging visas (of all kinds) granted annually has ranged between 250,000 and 490,000.[231] By June 2017, for 'boat people' alone, some 36,182 bridging visas had been issued.[232] It is not possible to state accurately how many of those bridging visas were issued with work rights attached. This is because the Immigration Department does not provide statistical data that can be disaggregated across types, duration, and conditions attached to bridging visas.[233] However, while numbers fluctuate, we can extrapolate from other figures that many bridging visa holders either do not have work rights or, even if they do, have not been able to find work: in 2015–16 there were 32,080 individuals, most of whom would have held bridging visas, who received SRSS support.[234]

---

[229] Like the RRT, the Migration Review Tribunal was subsumed into the Administrative Appeals Tribunal from 1 July 2015: *Tribunals Amalgamation Act 2015* (Cth).

[230] Now the Federal Circuit Court: *Federal Circuit Court of Australia Legislation Amendment Act 2012* (Cth).

[231] In 2005–06, 257,140 bridging visas were issued, and in 2004–05, the figure was 245,950: DIMA, 'Population Flows: Immigration Aspects' (January 2007) 75. In 2010–11, 489,674 bridging visas were issued: DIAC, 'Population Flows: Immigration Aspects 2010–11' (2012) 70. Note, however, that historically the Immigration Department has indicated that it does not hold statistical data on the number of bridging visas issued carrying work rights: Senate Legal and Constitutional Affairs Committee, Parliament of Australia, *Supplementary Budget Estimates 2004–2005 (Immigration and Multicultural and Indigenous Affairs)*, Questions on Notice 21–30, November 2004, QoN 21–2. An edition of 'Population Flows' has not been issued since 2012.

[232] Australian Border Force, *Illegal Maritime Arrivals on Bridging Visa E* (DIBP, June 2017), <www.border.gov.au/about/reports-publications/research-statistics/statistics/live-in-australia/onshore-processing>.

[233] Ibid. A 2007 report of the JSCM indicated that about 37 per cent of Bridging Visa E holders had work rights: JSCM, *Second Report of the Inquiry into Immigration Detention in Australia*, above n 181, 67 [3.36]. Historically, departmental systems have not provided statistical data of this nature: Senate Legal and Constitutional Affairs Committee, Parliament of Australia, *Supplementary Budget Estimates 2004–2005 (Immigration and Multicultural and Indigenous Affairs)*, Questions on Notice 21–30, November 2004, QoN 21–2.

[234] DIBP, *Annual Report 2015–16* (15 September 2016) 49. For all recent annual reports, see: <www.border.gov.au/about/reports-publications/reports/annual>. Some recipients of SRSS

As this section shows, an institutional silence has been created by a combination of techniques. As I have argued, the chosen terminologies and technicalities reflect an obsession with discretion of long standing. One of the key ways in which this institutional silence has manifested is in ensuring the absence of a work rights jurisprudence. This is achieved by quarantining decisionmaking from systems of accountability and the public record. It is a scheme that can quietly privilege the welcome foreigner whose need to work is seen as 'compelling' because of the skills and economic advantage she is assumed to bring. At the same time, by quarantining work rights decisions from review, the unwelcome asylum seeker either remains subject to the arbitrary denial of work rights and resultant destitution or is rendered systemically and structurally vulnerable to the unpredictable ebb and flow of policy change. This is the work of the discourse of 'absolute sovereignty', which purportedly entitles a state to condition entry and stay howsoever it pleases.

The institutional silence is compounded by the absence of informative statistical data about the conferral or denial of work rights. As discussed earlier, lack of availability of statistical data makes accurately ascertaining the scope and depth of the problem of work rights denial almost impossible. To build a picture, such data needs to be painstakingly pieced together from a range of sources. Although even then it can be difficult confidently to attribute accurate meaning to such a statistical jigsaw puzzle, for present purposes the key point is the un-clarity and uncertainty that is maintained by institutional, jurisprudential, and statistical silence. As the third section of this chapter shows, decisions on welfare rights are located even further from the reach of any form of independent review.

6.3 WELFARE: GOVERNANCE BY FIAT

As already noted, since 1991, asylum seekers have been ineligible for the Special Benefit under the *Social Security Act*. Instead, since 1992, income support for asylum seekers has been delivered under a parallel system subject to its own eligibility criteria and standards. Furthermore, and for reasons the public record does not relate, that support is provided at a rate of 89 per cent of the Special Benefit.[235] The following subsection describes how particular institutional techniques have enabled the development and implementation of a nonstatutory, policy-based welfare scheme.

---

assistance do not fall under what was the ASAS scheme (band 6): see DIBP, 'SRSS Policy Advice Manual', above n 23.

[235]   See above nn 27, 85.

6.3.1 *Policymaking by Fact Sheet*

Previously, eligibility criteria for income support under the Asylum Seekers Assistance Scheme (ASAS) were published in departmental information fact sheets. *Fact Sheet 62 – Assistance for Asylum Seekers in Australia*,[236] which outlined eligibility and exemption criteria, was amended from time to time. Tweaking of the criteria came with no explanation or publicly available guidelines or practice instructions.[237] The ephemeral nature of the Internet means that earlier versions vanish from the Department's website without trace. These factors point to the partial silence created through policymaking by fact sheet.

Until it vanished, ASAS policy outlined three key eligibility criteria: an asylum seeker had been waiting more than six months for a decision on her refugee application; she was exempt from that waiting period because she was "vulnerable", "suffering hardship" and unable to meet her "basic needs";[238] or she had lodged an application with the RRT and she "continue[d] to meet the ASAS exemption criteria".[239] In addition, she had to be living lawfully in the community and be ineligible for other income support in Australia or from an overseas government.[240]

Broadly, the eligibility criteria appeared to be objectively assessable as a question of fact. However, the exemption criteria were pivotal, suggesting that the eligibility criteria may have been better understood as framing *ineligibility*. According to the policy, exemptions to the eligibility criteria "may" have been available to "vulnerable" asylum seekers "suffering hardship" *and* "unable to meet their basic needs" because they "lack[ed] adequate support within the community".[241] People regarded as vulnerable included those experiencing "financial hardship" arising from a "change in circumstances since arriving in Australia".[242]

---

[236] DIBP, *Fact Sheet 62*, above n 22.
[237] Guidelines for their implementation do exist but are not publicly available. There are references in publicly available material to an Asylum Seekers Assistance Handbook, produced annually by the Immigration Department, as well as Asylum Seeker Assistance Scheme (ASAS) Exemption Guidelines: see, eg, HREOC, 'ASAS Report', above n 21, pts 2.3.1–2.3.2; DIAC, Supplementary Submission No 129n, above n 169; Hastie, above n 105, 2. However, neither the Handbook nor the Guidelines are publicly available.
[238] Such persons include: unaccompanied minors, elderly persons, families with children under 18 years old, people who are unable to work due to a disability, illness, care responsibilities, or the effects of torture or trauma: DIBP, *Fact Sheet 62*, above n 22.
[239] Note here that the requirement that the change in circumstances be beyond her control is no longer included in the Fact Sheet.
[240] DIBP, *Fact Sheet 62*, above n 22.   [241] Ibid.   [242] Ibid.

The introduction of the SRSS Programme has seen the depletion of an already sparse supply of information about eligibility criteria. Fact sheets are no longer published, and even the Immigration Department's SRSS Policy Advice Manual was only released following a freedom of information request.[243] The only published criteria for 'experiencing financial hardship' are that an individual must have an income "less than 89% of the Centrelink Special Benefit" (which, as we know, is well below the poverty line), "no disposable assets or funds in Australia or overseas", and "no continuing and adequate support" of any kind from anywhere.[244]

As this discussion shows, changes to eligibility and exemption criteria for welfare assistance, prior to and since the introduction of the SRSS Programme, take place primarily through the (electronic) publication of departmental fact sheets or other statements. There is no passage of legislation, no tabling of regulations, and therefore no formal mechanism for publicly accounting for or documenting either the changes or their rationale. As the next subsection shows, decisionmaking under this scheme is even more opaque.

6.3.2 *Eligibility and Exemption Decisions: Under Law's Radar*

As we know, ASAS (and latterly SRSS) is not provided for in legislation or regulations. Administration of the scheme is subcontracted to the Red Cross and, now, multiple other service providers,[245] which implement the program according to unpublished[246] criteria and guidelines provided by the Immigration Department. Statistical data is not readily available. Instead, any data that is reported is issued piecemeal through, for example, parliamentary processes such as Questions on Notice.[247] The Immigration Department funds *and* oversees the program, retaining tight control over it, including making eligibility determinations in individual cases upon receipt of

---

[243] DIBP, 'SRSS Policy Advice Manual', above n 23.
[244] Ibid; DIBP, Application for Status Resolution Support Services (SRSS) – Band 6, above n 83, 1.
[245] At the time of writing, there is no functioning link to a list of SRSS service providers on the DIBP website. above n 90.
[246] There is evidence that there were guidelines in existence at least prior to October 1996, known as 'Asylum Seeker Assistance (ASA) Scheme – Guidelines'. With effect from October 1996, further guidelines were introduced. The 'ASAS Exemption Guidelines' provided guidance on what constituted 'exceptional circumstances'. However, it is not clear whether these guidelines were ever publicly available: HREOC, 'ASAS Report', above n 21. There are no publicly available guidelines under the SRSS Programme.
[247] See, eg, Senate Legal and Constitutional Affairs Committee, Parliament of Australia, *Supplementary Budget Estimates 2004–2005 (Immigration and Multicultural and Indigenous Affairs)*, Questions on Notice 21–30, November 2004, QoN 22–3, 28–30.

submissions from service providers.[248] The program must be implemented within departmental budgetary constraints.[249] This means that the program operates under the auspices of a government policy that determines eligibility through a decisionmaking process that is unregulated and, in that sense, unaccountable. That is, the development and implementation of policy operates under law's radar – below, but somehow above, the law.

Records of decisions are not available publicly or to an applicant or her adviser and, because they are not provided for in legislation or regulation, are not subject to merits or judicial review. Comprehensive statistical data is not routinely published.[250] Rather, gesturing to the institutional expectation of deviance and opportunism, record systems are maintained to ensure that individuals who may be eligible for welfare assistance do not "double-dip" and that the "appropriate" subsistence payment is made.[251] In other words, record systems exist, but they are framed to ensure accountability of clients of the scheme, not its administrators.

The question of 'financial hardship' is illustrative of the opacity of the process. As we know, one of the criteria that triggers eligibility for income support is that the individual or family concerned is 'experiencing financial hardship'.[252] However, in the present context, 'financial hardship' is defined differently to 'financial hardship' in the assessment of 'compelling need to work'.[253] Until recently, there was nothing on the public record to tell us what it meant or how it should be interpreted. Likewise, there was no clarity as to the meaning of other terms in the exemption criteria, such as 'vulnerable', 'basic needs', and 'adequate support'. Now we know a little more: the experience of 'financial hardship' must position an individual or family well below the poverty line before assistance is provided.[254]

As a policy-based scheme, which is subject neither to legislation nor regulation, a powerful and impenetrable institutional silence has been created by the absence of a clear, transparent, and accountable decisionmaking process. As an institutional technique, this silence represents a familiar style of

---

[248] See, eg, HREOC, 'ASAS Report', above n 21, pt 2.2; see also JSCM, *Second Report of the Inquiry into Immigration Detention in Australia*, above n 181, 36 [2.71]. According to the Red Cross, "The Department of Immigration sets the eligibility criteria for the program and must approve all applications made to the program": Australian Red Cross, 'Asylum seekers and refugees', <www.redcross.org.au/asylum-seekers.aspx>.

[249] See also DIAC, Supplementary Submission No 129n, above n 169.

[250] Only through the HREOC Complaint has some statistical data become available: HREOC, 'ASAS Report', above n 21, Appendix E. See also above n 234.

[251] DIAC, Supplementary Submission No 129n, above n 169.

[252] See discussion of eligibility criteria, above 248–51.   [253] See above 262–5.

[254] DIBP, Application for Status Resolution Support Services (SRSS) – Band 6, above n 83, 1.

governance that maximises power and minimises accountability. The doctrine of responsible governance, on which it implicitly rests, sees the risk of abuse of power as only theoretical. This makes possible rhetorical gestures that frame the lack of accountability of a policy-based scheme as an advantage because discretion provides flexibility and a way of avoiding breaches of international standards.[255]

6.3.3 *Departmental Delay: A Form of Institutional Silence*

The lack of accountability of the ASAS scheme is also underscored by the fact that the HREOC inquiry took almost six years to complete.[256] As we have seen, these delays do not point to the complexity of the evidence. Rather, in significant measure, they point to a departmental antipathy towards the complaint process at nearly every stage. Throughout the inquiry, the Department was extremely slow to reply to communications from HREOC. For example, from the initial letter informing the Department of the complaint (which requested a response within 21 days), it took five months and four follow-up letters for the Immigration Department to reply.[257] Later, the Human Rights Commissioner's report revealed his frustration at the way in which the Department prevaricated by making repeated requests for extensions of time in the final stages of the process:

> By letter dated 5 February 2002, I sent my Notice of findings and recommendations pursuant to section 29(2) of the HREOC Act to the Department. I sought advice from the Department as to any action that has been taken or is being taken by it as a result of those findings and recommendations. I requested that this advice be provided by 5 March 2002. On 25 February 2002, the Department requested an extension of time in which to provide this

---

[255] Advice from the Department's Legal Section, above n 141, cited in HREOC, 'ASAS Report', above n 21, pt 7. See also Letter from Bedlington to Ozdowski, above n 93, 2.

[256] CPD, House of Representatives, 26 June 2002, 4475 (report tabled by Peter Slipper); CPD, Senate, 27 June 2002, 2867 (report tabled by Eric Abetz).

[257] Letter from Chris Sidoti, Human Rights Commissioner, to Helen Williams, Secretary, DIMA, 19 March 1997. Three follow-up letters to the Department yielded no detailed response: Letter from David Norrie, Investigation/Conciliation Officer, HREOC to Helen Williams, Secretary, DIMA, 14 April 1997; Letter from David Norrie, Investigation/Conciliation Officer, HREOC to John Bloomfield, Director, Ombudsman, Privacy and FOI Section, DIMA, 27 May 1997; Letter from David Norrie, Investigation/Conciliation Officer, HREOC to John Bloomfield, Director, Ombudsman, Privacy and FOI Section, DIMA, 18 June 1997. A fourth follow-up letter elicited a response, almost five months after receiving notification of the complaint: Letter from Chris Sidoti, Human Rights Commissioner, to Helen Williams, Secretary, DIMA, 28 July 1997. All letters appear in *HREOC Complaint File*, above n 34.

advice. I granted an extension to 15 April 2002. On 11 April 2002, the Department sought a further three month extension until 15 July 2002. I acceded to an extension only for a further two weeks as I was of the view that three months was sufficient time for the Department to respond to my request for advice.

To date, no response to my request for advice has been received by [*sic*] the Department. I am therefore not aware of any action taken or proposed to be taken as a result of the findings and recommendations in my Notice.[258]

The effect of these lengthy delays was to render the inquiry meaningless – or at least ineffective – for those affected by the policy changes. Together with the rhetoric of control and restraint and of deviance and opportunism that characterised the Department's rationale for its policies, they represented a wordless assertion of power – a claim made by a department accustomed to 'absolute sovereignty' as a source of legitimacy and reticent to submit to scrutiny.

As the report of the inquiry shows, while there is clearly a story that lies behind the (institutional) silences and soundbites that frame the publicly articulated welfare policy for asylum seekers, it is a story that is substantively thin and reluctantly told. Departmental discourses, meanwhile, actively resist and undermine any attempt made by a counter-narrative to fill the silent space left by secrecy and partial silence. In the inquiry, the Department's ultimate expression of power was its silence. In a wordless assertion of the exclusive right to articulate (and implement) its policies, it was the Department that had the last word.[259]

6.4 PLANNED DESTITUTION: PART OF THE ORDER OF THINGS

From a close reading of text and its silences in this and the preceding chapter, we have seen three recurring discursive themes emerge. To reiterate, they can be thematically ordered into discourses of control and restraint, deviance and opportunism, and silence. These discourses establish planned destitution as part of the order of things by creating and constructing new

---

[258] HREOC, 'ASAS Report', above n 21, pt 12.
[259] In fact, the Department did ultimately respond but not until after the final deadline set by the Human Rights Commissioner: Letter from W J Farmer, Secretary, DIMIA, to Dr Sev Ozdowski, Human Rights Commissioner, 13 May 2002 (in HREOC *Complaint File*, above n 34). In broad terms, the response did not accept the findings. Nor did it give rise to significant changes to the Human Rights Commissioner's report.

realities.[260] Such new realities form the unequivocal basis on which state practice is rationalised and the asylum seeker's conduct and motives are named, understood, and acted upon. Discourses that represent the asylum seeker as an abusive and opportunistic deviant and the taxpayer as her victim "become dominant and shape indelibly the way in which [her] reality is imagined and acted upon."[261] Because in this context the state assumes the privileged or exclusive right to speak authoritatively,[262] any counter-narrative or its influence is effectively stifled (the Bridging Visa Review that disappeared), denigrated (the voice of the Centre that was undermined), or treated with contempt (the final report of the Human Rights Commissioner that met with institutional silence).

Underpinning the development of law, policy, and practice in relation to work and welfare rights is the discourse of 'absolute sovereignty'.[263] To neutralise any perception that 'absolute sovereignty' is (or could be) despotic or abusive, discourses of restraint speak to the responsible exercise of power. As we have seen, this is a pattern of argument of long standing and is strongly evident in both case studies.[264] Like the mandatory detention laws before them, this chapter has shown how laws and policies that plan for asylum seeker destitution are framed as measured, balanced, and considered. The targets of the policies are cast as deviant and opportunistic. And subject to exceptional exceptions, any resultant destitution is framed as self-inflicted. Criticisms and counter-narratives are, at the same time, pitched as anecdotal, out-of-touch, exaggerated, and even as hastening the demise of the international system.[265]

Between them, the case studies show how a parallel and prevalent discourse of deviance actively and effectively denigrates the conduct and motives of

---

[260] Michel Foucault, *The Order of Things: An Archaeology of the Human Sciences* (A M Sheridan Smith trans, Routledge, 2002) 45 [trans of: *Les mots et les choses: Une archéologie des sciences humaines* (first published 1966)].

[261] Arturo Escobar, *Encountering Development: The Making and Unmaking of the Third World* (Princeton University Press, 1995) 5.

[262] Michel Foucault, 'The Discourse of Language' in Hazard Adams and Leroy Searle (eds), *Critical Theory since 1965* (Florida State University Press, 1986) 148, 149.

[263] The first of the nine immigration principles that the Minister, Michael MacKellar, announced in Parliament in June 1978 was: "It is fundamental to national sovereignty that the Australian Government alone should determine who will be admitted to Australia. No person other than an Australian citizen, or a constituent member of the Australian community, has a basic right to enter Australia": CPD, House of Representatives, 7 June 1978, 3154; Katharine Betts, 'The Problem of Defining Borders in Western Democracies' (1995) 6(1) *The Social Contract* 28, 31–2.

[264] See especially Chapter 4, 117, 142.

[265] See, eg, Millbank, 'Asylum Seekers on Bridging Visa E', above n 3, 5.

certain asylum seekers, whether the 'boat people' discussed in Chapter 5 or the asylum seekers living in the community who are discussed in this chapter. This discourse reinforces the rightness and responsibility implicitly claimed through the discourses of control and restraint. Whether explicitly or implicitly, it ascribes illegality, lawlessness, and impropriety. And it does so as if asylum seekers were an homogenous whole.[266] It creates distance and distinctions between 'we', the normal 'generous' 'taxpaying' insiders, and 'these people', who are the deviant, opportunistic, and 'abusive' 'non–bona fide' outsiders. Through this process of de-legitimising the actions of the uninvited asylum seeker, she is cemented in the public imagination as an unworthy and unwelcome social deviant, located outside the framework of social values and norms to which 'we' subscribe and by which 'we' are governed.

As this chapter has shown, the way in which law and language have come together – rhetorically and institutionally – to shape an overarching policy of planned destitution echoes the claim that 'absolute sovereignty' entitles the state to condition the foreigner's stay howsoever it pleases. The analysis of legal and policy text – as well as the equally significant absence of text – has drawn out lines of continuity and discontinuity between the genealogical past and contemporary migration law- and policymaking. Through the analysis, I have thematically ordered a range of rhetorical and institutional techniques used to legitimise and justify certain migration policies into discourses of state control and restraint and asylum seeker deviance and opportunism. Coupled with the overarching theme of institutional silence, this thematic ordering has provided a way of deepening our understanding of how the policy of planned destitution gives expression to 'absolute sovereignty'. In the result, the rhetorical and institutional techniques I have identified point to the complex ways in which 'absolute sovereignty' *as a discourse* may be executed or performed through text, talk, and silence.

The case study in this chapter also highlights what Foucault describes as a "silent dominion"[267] that underpins some key aspects of migration law- and policymaking. The powerful influence of the technique of silence reveals the limits of an analytical framework that depends upon the production of language and the concomitant power of a domain that secures its place without words – a discursive technique that presents as a complex mix of elements of silence, soundbite, and secrecy. These elements (separately and together) hint at, avoid,

---

[266] Sharon Pickering, 'Common Sense and Original Deviancy: News Discourses and Asylum Seekers in Australia' (2001) 14(2) *Journal of Refugee Studies* 169, 178, 179; Michel Foucault, *Discipline and Punish: The Birth of the Prison* (Alan Sheridan trans, Penguin, 1977) [trans of: *Surveiller et punir: Naissance de la prison* (first published 1975)] 202.

[267] Foucault, *The Order of Things*, above n 260, 45.

or obscure the full nature, depth, and breadth of both their rationale and their effects. Together, they may be said to form a powerful domain of silence – a silence that, as we have seen, has a disqualifying and stifling influence on an emergent counter-narrative. This domain of (institutional) silence speaks because there is an (untold) story that lies behind and beneath it. It may be untold because it is understood (in the sense that it is taken as read) or because it is unsayable (in the sense that it is impermissible or un-utterable). Either way, the silence persists, replete with unsettling uncertainty.

This pattern of silence is epitomised by the 'obsession with discretion' that makes the administration of work rights discretionary and that of welfare support policy-based; these schemes are unreviewable and, to that extent, unaccountable. As we have seen, silence that is institutional – and, indeed, institutionalised – is not indicative of an underlying discursive void. Instead, it produces institutional modes of being and thinking that wordlessly become dominant and indelible.[268] So, an analysis of the domain of silence becomes a search for the (underlying) story that produced the silence, a story that is concealed by techniques of (decision-less) silence. Where did the 45-day rule really come from? What is the story behind the '$30 work visa' claim? Where did the Bridging Visa Review go? How vulnerable is tolerable? How hard must financial hardship be? The silence persists. This is because behind it there is a story that is afraid of what it might say (to us or about us). Instead, these discursive techniques ensure that the elements of the story are only revealed in "enigmatic, murmured"[269] fragments of policy and procedure. Only by painstakingly piecing together these fragments does it become possible to try and articulate what the (underlying) story might be; it is a story of the claim of 'absolute sovereignty' that need not speak its name and that needs no evidence, because it is claim enough.

In summary, what we see from this chapter is that 'absolute sovereignty' is so deeply embedded in the way migration law- and policymakers think, write, and implement policy that planning for the destitution of a particular class of (unwelcome) foreigners is not just seen as possible and thinkable, but as inevitable. We have seen how particular terminologies and techniques crowd the un- or under-scrutinised space created by 'absolute sovereignty'. This is because they are underwritten by the idea that the doctrine of responsible governance is an adequate safeguard against excesses or abuses of power. In other words, we can see that they are historically produced and reflect discursive patterns and repertoires of long standing.[270]

---

[268] Escobar, above n 261, 5.   [269] Foucault, *The Order of Things*, above n 260, 45.
[270] See, eg, Chapter 4, 120, 138–9, 144.

7

Conclusion

Life is porous, the whole world leaks.
There's no such thing as a perfect seal.
It all gets out, it all gets in;
Everything leaks into every thing
So that every thing can heal.
What a terrible, sad neurosis
Is the fear of this osmosis.[1]

7.1 MAKING MIGRATION LAW

This book has asked how two core features of Australia's current migration policy – mandatory detention and planned destitution – designed to effect physical exclusion of asylum seekers on the one hand and their social and economic exclusion on the other, have become thinkable institutional responses to unsolicited migration. I have approached the question, in the first instance, through a genealogical examination of the foreigner-sovereign relation to make visible how the claim that there is an absolute sovereign right to exclude and condition the entry and stay of (even friendly) aliens – which I have called 'absolute sovereignty' – emerged. In the second instance, I have offered a discourse analysis of the two policies in order to show how each was inspired and enabled by 'absolute sovereignty', a totalising discourse whose authority and impenetrability has, I have argued, been received uncritically into contemporary migration law. In offering a genealogy of the foreigner-sovereign relation, my purpose has been to bring a new visibility to how a discourse of 'absolute sovereignty' has emerged and enabled mandatory detention and planned destitution to become thinkable institutional responses to

[1] Michael Leunig, Untitled Poem, A2, *The Saturday Age* (Melbourne), 19 June 2010, 48.

unsolicited migration. By using discourse analysis, we have been able to see how the state of Australia understands, performs, and sustains the authority of 'absolute sovereignty' today. We have seen how it rationalises, legitimises, and normalises mandatory detention and planned destitution in the name of 'absolute sovereignty' and how it is politically and juridically blind to the historical contingencies that enabled 'absolute sovereignty' to emerge as idea, as doctrine, as discourse, and as practice.

By focusing on two aspects of the political-economic context of the emergence of 'absolute sovereignty' – race and labour – we have seen how the regulation of these categories coalesced around a particular figure of the foreigner and a particular idea of sovereignty. This, in turn, has revealed that framing the foreigner-sovereign relation in terms of the emerging juridical idea of 'absolute sovereignty' was neither accidental nor inevitable. As we have also seen, however, 'absolute sovereignty' has acquired a special resilience through judicial reinforcement that made (sometimes overtly instrumentalist) use of doctrinal conventions – in particular, legal precedent, a highly deferential 'positivist' style of jurisprudence, and the doctrine of responsible governance. This resilience has meant that 'absolute sovereignty' continues to underpin Australian migration law- and policymaking to this day – international human rights standards and the end of the White Australia policy notwithstanding. As we have seen, repertoires and patterns of argument that rationalise particular power relations can be traced through the lines of continuity and discontinuity – of resonance and dissonance – between the (genealogical) past and the (discursive) present. This analytical process has made visible not only how we have internalised the discourse of 'absolute sovereignty' and, with it, the idea that the 'foreigner' is an (unwelcome) outsider, but also the juridical (and political) contingency of the foreigner-sovereign relation.

7.2 A DISCOURSE OF 'ABSOLUTE SOVEREIGNTY'

As we have seen, in Australia a discourse of 'absolute sovereignty' with a complex history has become the overarching justification for institutionally hostile responses to unsolicited migration. Through a genealogy of the foreigner-sovereign relation, Part I of the book gave an account of 'absolute sovereignty' as a contingent historical artefact whose authority can be coherently taken as an object of critical reflection.

Through a detailed analysis of treatises of Vitoria, Grotius, Pufendorf, and Vattel, Chapter 2 made visible who their respective figure of the foreigner was, arguing that for each of these seminal publicists the foreigner was not an outsider. On the contrary, whether imperialist, trader, or exile, he[2] was a figure of privilege and power – a European insider aligned with the sovereign and in whose interests international legal theory was framed. In contradistinction to the enabling status of 'foreignness', the juridical figure of the 'barbarian' was accorded an 'outsider-ness', a residual status that enclosed her in a legal framework in which she had no power of enforcement; she was not an outlaw, yet she was diminished by law and deemed unworthy of its protection. Importantly, this chapter made clear that there is nothing inherently or inevitably 'outside' about the juridical figure of the foreigner. Each of these theorists accepted mobility as a natural *modus vivendi*, that a key purpose of early international law was to protect the rights and interests of the foreigner, and that the discourse of 'absolute sovereignty' was, therefore, not *ever thus*. Indeed, what this chapter enabled us to see was that prior to the emergence of a putative right to exclude and condition the entry and stay of (even friendly) aliens as a common law doctrine, there *was* no international legal discourse of 'absolute sovereignty'; and this was precisely because, in the foreigner-sovereign relation, the foreigner in international law was a European, aligned with the sovereign, and in whose interests international law was framed.

Chapter 3 detailed the points of emergence of a common law doctrine of 'absolute sovereignty' as the product of a particular view of the foreigner-sovereign relation. Through an examination of legislative text and an important corpus of Anglo-American jurisprudence, this chapter made visible how a discourse of 'absolute sovereignty' emerged and was essentialised in the political-economic context of white settler societies such as Australia, a context in which the political-economic imperative to regulate race and labour was considered paramount. We saw how, in the broader context of the political economy of the movement of people, the desire to regulate race and labour by encouraging European migration and restricting non-European labour migration into such societies meant that the figure of the foreigner became marked by a mutability – a mutability which enabled the foreigner to be characterised sometimes as an insider in the foreigner-sovereign relation, other times as an outsider. However, as I have argued, it was not a pure mutability. As the genealogy showed, when the foreigner was a European, he was an insider, a figure of privilege, power, and entitlement. Yet when the foreigner was a non-European, she was marked as an outsider, a subjugated and expendable figure regulated by law but unworthy of law's protection. These insights are important because they help us see and understand the emergence of 'absolute sovereignty' as doctrine and discourse. What they make clear is that for as long

---

[2] On my use of male and female pronouns throughout the book, see Chapter 1, 15 n 49.

as the foreigner was (only) a European, 'absolute sovereignty' was not perceived as an imperative; on the contrary, the exercise of sovereignty was qualified by considerations such as necessity, humanity, hospitality, and tolerance.

Chapter 4 made visible the ways in which the foreigner-sovereign relation, as a claim of 'absolute sovereignty', was given constitutional form. I argued that the 'hallowed doctrinal place' thereby ascribed to 'absolute sovereignty' produced a structural indifference to migration law's effects. To do this, I engaged in a close reading of constitutional convention debates, parliamentary debates, and legislative and judicial text to reveal how 'absolute sovereignty', as the form now being given to the foreigner-sovereign relation, was produced doctrinally and how the political-economic context shaped an unswerving and sometimes instrumentalist adherence to (and faith in) the doctrines of precedent and responsible government. This drew out the ways in which 'absolute sovereignty' as a constitutional doctrine entrenched the power to exclude the unwelcome foreigner as impenetrable: through a preference for legislating broad discretionary powers, high levels of judicial deference, and a revisionist approach to legislative reform. The analysis also made visible the way in which 'absolute sovereignty' as a discourse was given shape through a number of different – but mutually reinforcing – political and juridical modes and registers; and in Part II, this discourse was shown to have an enduring contemporary resonance.

Through the two case studies, Part II has shown how particular discourses have been used to persuade particular audiences that particular laws or policies are valid, legitimate, and reasonable. Ordered thematically into discourses of (state) control and restraint and (asylum seeker) deviance and opportunism, and the overarching discourse of (institutional) silence, we have seen how lawmakers continue to essentialise 'absolute sovereignty' in the way they resist even the possibility that unsolicited migration may be part of the order of things. We have seen how conventional styles of legal analysis and practice – including precedent, a 'positivist' form of judicial deference, and responsible governance – continue to be deployed to justify the breadth and uses of the power as necessary and appropriate. At the same time, a moralising and denigrating discourse of asylum seeker deviance and opportunism – informed by race discourses even as it denies racism – imputes to her criminality, 'economic refugeeism', and above all unworthiness. Finally, the discourse analysis has made visible the different institutional techniques through which juridical and jurisprudential silences are created, quarantining certain executive or administrative activities from judicial scrutiny by making them 'decision-less' or nonstatutory – above, below, or beyond law's reach. Together, these discourses reflect a style of governance that has engendered a resistance to scrutiny. We see that the historical antecedents of these discourses are discernible and, without even having to speak its name, we perceive that they are the work of the discourse of 'absolute sovereignty'.

Chapter 5 engaged in a close textual analysis of the parliamentary debates, judicial proceedings, and jurisprudence of the High Court of Australia relating to the first legislative framework of mandatory detention. Through this analysis, we saw how the aforementioned discourses work in different registers, whether in Parliament, in the courtroom, or on the judicial record. And we saw how these discourses move, shape, and influence thinking and argument in each of these institutional sites. Politically and juridically, mutually reinforcing rhetorical and institutional techniques legitimised the claim that decision-less detention of 'boat people' for 'however long' it takes is in the 'national interest' – reasonable but restrained, tough but necessary, and non-punitive because, the *coup de grâce*, it is voluntary. Notwithstanding that such detention is arbitrary and was once described by Blackstone as a 'dangerous engine of arbitrary government',[3] the doctrine of 'absolute sovereignty' appears to have led us inexorably into an un- or under-scrutinised juridical space. Here, institutional technique capitalises on the limitlessness of the 'freest Constitution in the world', while erasing – or disremembering – the effects of its excesses.

In Chapter 6, a close reading of legislative and policy texts and their silences showed how policies that plan for and produce asylum seeker destitution are discursively represented as measured, balanced, and considered responses to unwelcome asylum seekers and as virtuous disincentives to their (alleged) abuse of 'our' 'generosity'. At the same time, however, we saw how, through a range of discursive techniques and institutional silences, evidentiary claims having only 'superficial appeal', and that would not withstand scrutiny, could be used to diminish asylum seekers and to rationalise policies designed to starve them out of the system. As I have argued, institutional techniques and silences have enabled the implementation of these policies to be located in what may be understood as an un- or under-scrutinised space that sits below, but somehow above, the law. This is a space where there is no meaningful judicial (or other independent) analysis or scrutiny – one where the rhetorical devices that complement the policies have enacted an erasure of the asylum seeker's worthiness.

---

[3]   See Chapter 5, 213–14.

In the result, we find an almost impenetrable wall of silence enclosing laws and policies affecting unwelcome foreigners: mandatory detention is decision-less, work rights are discretionary, and welfare distribution is entirely policy-based. Furthermore, the success of mandatory detention and planned destitution (in legal and policy terms) has created a conceptual platform from which to devise and implement increasingly harsh policies, whether in the migration domain or reaching into the separate but related spheres of citizenship and national security.[4] We see that the boundaries of the un- or under-scrutinised space that has been created (in which 'absolute sovereignty' seems to have provided free rein) have acquired an elasticity that is so expansive that the common humanity of the unwelcome foreigner has been both juridically and politically redacted. And we see that the constitutional framework has engendered in the foreigner-sovereign relationship a power relation in which the possibility of resistance to migration law's hostilities is so negligible that it is, or has become, almost meaningless. In other words, powers have been interpreted as so unconstrained that any counterweight to their excessive use, abuse, or misuse remains always and already statutorily vulnerable. 'Absolute sovereignty' is – because it can be – *the* answer.

7.3 REFLECTIONS

At this point it seems fitting to step away for a moment from the 'how' and to posit some speculative answers to some 'why' questions: Why has the Australian politico-legal landscape produced such intolerance and prejudice? Why is it possible for laws and policies like mandatory detention and planned destitution to be seen as thinkable – even acceptable – institutional responses to unsolicited migration, when they so clearly fracture the bond of our common humanity? Are Australians more intolerant, prejudiced, or fearful than other peoples? Answers to these questions are in some respects addressed by, or at least implicit in, the 'how' inquiry with which this book is primarily concerned. Beyond this, the 'why' inquiry may be seen as a different (political or even psychoanalytical) project.[5] Nevertheless, the research and analysis provided here seems to offer us some important clues.

---

[4]   See, eg, *Australian Citizenship Amendment (Allegiance to Australia) Act 2015* (Cth) inserting s 33AA 'Renunciation by Conduct' into the *Australian Citizenship Act 2007* (Cth); see also Kim Rubenstein, *Australian Citizenship Law* (Law Book Company, 2nd ed, 2016).

[5]   Robert Manne posits a combination of absolutism, opportunistic partisan politics, automaticity, 'groupthink', and the banality of evil: Robert Manne, 'How we came to be so cruel to asylum seekers', *The Conversation* (online), 26 October 2016 <https://theconversation.com/robert-manne-how-we-came-to-be-so-cruel-to-asylum-seekers-67542>.

As we ponder answers to these 'why' questions, it is clear that Australia is not alone in propounding an authoritarian approach to unsolicited migration.[6] Comparable civil and common law polities are grappling with similar issues in many parts of the world, both individually and as collectivities, and none may be said to be immune from intolerance and prejudice.[7] Whether as cause or consequence of the framing of 'absolute sovereignty' as a constitutional power, in migration discourse the seeds of intolerance and prejudice have been long sown. And they have endured and indeed flourished without constitutional rupture, despite the "long, slow death" of White Australia.[8]

Generally, when we think about constitutions and the trappings of constitutionalism, we think about frameworks intended both to enable and constrain governments in the exercise of power. In contrast, as we saw in Chapter 4, the constitutionalisation of 'absolute sovereignty' in Australia was accompanied not only by no safeguards, but also by an active resistance to them. This approach, which may be seen as a reflection of the paradoxical fragility that infuses the Australian polity,[9] was designed to enable rather than temper intolerance and prejudice[10] – a purpose that inhered in the White Australia policy.[11] As we have seen, the 'freest Constitution in the world' accorded both the Australian legislature and the executive a degree of latitude that has been interpreted to be so expansive that there is, in effect, no meaningful constraint upon the state – unless the legislature so chooses. When Sir Alick Downer resolved to place legislative constraints on his own powers, attuned as he was to the 'latent dangers' of 'naked and uninhibited' power, he did so knowing the nature and scope of the powers he was choosing to constrain to be 'arbitrary' and 'capable of the gravest abuse'.[12] Downer was not immune to fear or prejudice, but nor did he allow it to devour him. Instead, his own experience as a prisoner of war appears to have enabled him to feel the common bond of human aspiration,

---

6 See, eg, Étienne Balibar, *We, the People of Europe? Reflections on Transnational Citizenship* (James Swenson trans, Princeton University Press, 2004) 33 [trans of: *Nous, citoyens d'Europe: Les Frontières, l'État, le peuple* (first published 2001)].

7 This is a general point and does not make a comparative law claim that seeks to explain whether and why Australia's treatment of refugees and asylum seekers stands out as particularly harsh in comparison to other states. A comparative legal analysis of this kind would be a project in itself.

8 Gwenda Tavan, *The Long, Slow Death of White Australia* (Scribe, 2005).

9 This paradoxical fragility melds an arrogance that asserts superior entitlement to a certain way of life with a niggling self-doubt: see Chapter 4, above, 123. See also Eve Lester, 'Internationalising Constitutional Law: An Inward-Looking Outlook' (2016) 42(2) *Australian Feminist Law Journal* 321, n 102.

10 The shifting relations of fear, affection and care towards the other, of which Douzinas speaks, seems apt here: Costas Douzinas, *The End of Human Rights* (Hart, 2000) 375–6.

11 See Chapter 4, above, 116–20.   12 See Chapter 4, above, 152–4.

frailty, and experience. With this insight into our common humanity, he could not ignore the foreigner's vulnerability to abuses and misuses of his power. It impelled him to take a different approach.

In the face of a (perceived) crisis or threat, it is perhaps a natural human response to reach to the furthest limits of one's powers to resist it. If there are checks and balances placed on such powers, one may be more inclined to reflect – to think twice – about when and how to exercise them and whether or not the crisis or threat for which they are being harnessed is real. In the present case, by nourishing (as the discourse of 'absolute sovereignty' has come to do) the misconception that anything less than complete sovereign *control* would constitute a capitulation of sovereign *authority*,[13] unsolicited encounters between the unwelcome migrant and the sovereign become, a priori, a crisis or threat. And in Australia, the furthest limits of the powers for which law- and policymakers reach in such circumstances are too often dark and unaccountable – indeed, 'despotic'[14] – spaces that would be resisted in many other jurisdictions.

7.4 IMPLICATIONS

This book illuminates how, notwithstanding its contingencies, 'absolute sovereignty' has emerged *as a discourse* – a discourse that is reproduced in contemporary migration law- and policymaking. Directing attention to these concepts and practices is important because it matters that we notice and re-evaluate how we understand power and law and what is done with and in the name of law.[15] In particular, it is important that we[16] pay attention to what happens where contemporary migration discourse relies on and perpetuates institutional practices in a system that has, through the ostensible neutrality and restraint of law and legal process as a social ordering, grown accustomed to having at its disposal absolute power over the movement and activities of foreigners. We see that this arises from the continuing effects of the way in which the foreigner-sovereign relation has been shaped by the emergence of the claim of 'absolute sovereignty'. This particular form of the foreigner-

---

[13] Note the distinction Krasner draws between sovereignty as authority, and sovereignty as control: Stephen D Krasner, *Sovereignty: Organized Hypocrisy* (Princeton University Press, 1999) 13–14, discussed in Chapter 3, above 109.

[14] Commonwealth, *Parliamentary Debates*, House of Representatives, 12 September 1901, 4846–7 (Isaac Isaacs), discussed in Chapter 4, above 121–2; see also Chapter 3, above 106.

[15] Margaret Davies, *Asking the Law Question* (Law Book Company, 2008) 1.

[16] That is, the 'we' who are all connected to one another through that common bond of human aspiration, frailty, and experience, whether as insider or outsider, jurist, policymaker, reader, or scholar.

sovereign relation has become such a deeply ingrained system of thought and practice that we, as a polity,[17] no longer think or wonder about how or why we look at the world in this particular way. Politically and juridically, we do not need to think about the people whose lives are (knowingly) being shattered by these policies. Or perhaps, and more tellingly, as a polity we do not know how to re-invigorate the notion of a 'common humanity' that the discourse of 'absolute sovereignty' has redacted.

With these implications in mind, I see this book as an invitation – even an exhortation – to rethink 'absolute sovereignty' as an impenetrable claim by thinking about how it has emerged as law's unanswerable answer to unsolicited migration and how it continues to operate and, indeed, to extend its reach into other spheres of public policy.[18] I also see it as an invitation to think about how migration law authorises, upholds, and normalises both the absolute character of sovereignty and its conse-quences. It is also an invitation to think about whether the structural indifference to our 'common humanity' that is embedded in the turn to – or the retreat into – the 'hallowed doctrinal place' of 'absolute sovereignty' can ever be said to extend to the barbarity and cruelty of the policies 'absolute sovereignty' is said to authorise.

7.5 POSSIBILITIES

Endings are really beginnings, and the ending of this book is in that sense a provocation for a new beginning, a new conversation. As the book suggests, the discourse of 'absolute sovereignty' seems to have encouraged us to accept one particular form of the foreigner-sovereign relation.[19] It has shut down avenues of thought and debate that make the possibility of thinking about migration law *without* the discourse of 'absolute sovereignty' unimaginable. Because law by its nature is both past and present, living with the discourse of 'absolute sovereignty' in the present impels us to live with its past. No process of juridical filtration or purification can shed the "singularly ugly museum

---

[17] Of course, in drawing this conclusion I do not overlook that there are members of the Australian polity, not least within the academy, who are exercised by this issue. My point is, rather, that *as a polity* we have not found a way to think outside 'absolute sovereignty' as our frame of reference.

[18] See references to patterns of lawmaking that are mirrored in the spheres of citizenship and national security: Chapter 1, above 46.

[19] Febvre thinks about the concept of *la frontière* in these terms: Lucien Febvre, '*Frontière*: The Word and the Concept' in Peter Burke (ed), *A New Kind of History: From the Writings of Febvre* (K Folca trans, Harper & Row, 1973) 208, 212.

pieces"[20] that are integral to its history, because its history is part of its
present.

What, then, are the possibilities? Can we think and do migration law in
Australia without feeling impelled to make a claim on sovereignty in absolute
terms? Can we turn 'absolute sovereignty' into a question – even a problem –
rather than treating it as a given? Can we rethink the un- or under-regulated
space in which the claim of sovereignty resides as an accountable space that is
open to meaningful scrutiny? If we could do this – even try – would the way in
which we talk and think about both unsolicited migrants and ourselves assume
a different quality?

A first step would be to engage more consciously with the foreigner-
sovereign relation as a dynamic relation which eschews the totalising discourse of 'absolute sovereignty' as the answer to unsolicited migration and
refuses the inevitability of the (institutional and spontaneous) structural
violence of the border, whether territorial or conceptual.[21] Instead, the
foreigner-sovereign relation would be (re)imagined as a relation of vitality
and exchange, a relation that can respond humanely to the movement of
people. Recalling the nature of the foreigner-sovereign relation in early
international law, it is a re-imagining that is not, I think, as radical as it
may seem.

What I hope arises from this project is a changed consciousness, both
in Australia and internationally, of how the discourse of 'absolute sovereignty' has enabled structural violence against the unwelcome migrant to
emerge and to continue to be exacted and rationalised – and even
normalised – in Australia and, as the epilogue which follows reminds
us, with an increasing and chilling intensity. I hope it will prompt
reflection and debate about whether and why 'absolute sovereignty', and
all that it entails, should (continue to) be accorded the hallowed doctrinal place it has assumed – reflection and debate that enables us to
grapple with, and take ownership of, the idea that 'absolute sovereignty' is
not inevitable but a choice. I hope, too, that it has deepened understandings of law's dynamic relation with history and language, a relation
that is such a fundamental condition of its (and our) knowledge and
being that it cannot be ignored or erased,[22] a relation whose elements

---

[20]   Commonwealth, *Parliamentary Debates*, House of Representatives, 1 May 1958, 1396
       (Alexander Downer): see Chapter 4, 151.
[21]   Étienne Balibar, *We, the People of Europe? Reflections on Transnational Citizenship* (James
       Swenson trans, Princeton University Press, 2004) 24 [trans of: *Nous, citoyens d'Europe: Les
       Frontières, l'État, le peuple* (first published 2001)].
[22]   Davies, above n 15, 168.

cannot be brushed aside as "discursive debris of a bygone era" cluttering an otherwise "logically sound" unfettered power of exclusion.[23] I hope that it has enabled us to see the totalising discourse of 'absolute sovereignty' as it is, for all it is, and for all it is not, and that it impels us to ask ourselves: Is there any substance to the notion of our 'common humanity'? Is there any substance to the bold declarations of the compassion, generosity, and welcome of the Australian polity that are made from time to time? If there is, then it is incumbent on us to understand and think about how we use the discourse of 'absolute sovereignty' and to ask why we would continue to do so.

---

[23] Matthew J Lindsay, 'Immigration, Sovereignty, and the Constitution of Foreignness' (2013) 45(3) *Connecticut Law Review* 743, 812.

Epilogue

A Campaign to 'Stop the Boats'

[I]n the *short term*, the establishment of processing facilities in Nauru [and Manus Island] as soon as practical is a necessary *circuit breaker* to the current surge in irregular migration to Australia. It is also an important measure to diminish the prospect of further loss of life at sea.[1]

Expert Panel on Asylum Seekers August 2012

In the face of sustained activist opposition, we have maintained Regional Processing Centres on Manus Island and Nauru. Our relationship in this regard with Nauru *will continue for decades.*[2]

Peter Dutton Minister for Immigration and Border Protection September 2016

The Special Rapporteur observes that regarding human rights issues, the *system cannot be salvaged.* ... [T]erritorial sovereignty and the control of borders cannot justify any and all distinctions between foreigners and citizens.[3]

François Crépeau Special Rapporteur on the Human Rights of Migrants April 2017

---

[1] Angus Houston, Paris Aristotle and Michael L'Estrange, 'Report of the Expert Panel on Asylum Seekers' (Australian Government, August 2012) <http://expertpanelonasylumseekers.dpmc.gov .au/> (emphases added).

[2] Peter Dutton, *Address to the Australian Strategic Policy Institute,* 20 September 2016 <www.mi nister.border.gov.au/peterdutton/2016/Pages/address-australian-strategic-policy-institute-15092016 .aspx> (emphasis added).

[3] François Crépeau, *Report of the Special Rapporteur on the Human Rights of Migrants on His Mission to Australia and the Regional Processing Centres in Nauru,* UN Doc A/HRC/35/25/ Add.3 (24 April 2017) 14 [73], 17 [90] (emphasis added).

A MILITARY-LED OPERATION: AS IF WE WERE AT WAR

On 18 September 2013, Australia's newly elected conservative government commenced its military-led response to 'Stop the Boats'. Code-named Operation Sovereign Borders, it includes interception operations, boat tow-backs, and return of asylum seekers travelling on unseaworthy boats in disposable orange lifeboats[4] or, more recently, replica fishing boats.[5] It also includes extraterritorial detention and processing of asylum seekers on both Nauru and Manus Island, Papua New Guinea – a "circuit breaker" to be used in the "short term".[6]

The architects of Operation Sovereign Borders have described the arrival of 'boat people' in recent years as a "crisis", a "national emergency", and "one of the most serious external situations that we have faced in many a long year".[7] A three-star military general, Lieutenant General Angus Campbell, was appointed commander of the response, reporting directly to the Minister for Immigration and Border Protection. In a video posted on YouTube, and echoing a previous declaration made by former Labor Prime Minister Kevin Rudd that asylum seekers arriving by boat would "have no prospect of being resettled in Australia",[8] Campbell declared impassively to his intended audience, "there is *no way* you will *ever* make Australia home."[9]

Silence and secrecy surrounding the activities of Operation Sovereign Borders have been rationalised as "on-water operations",[10] in the "national interest", and an information strategy designed "so as not to give tactical advantage to people

---

4   Tim Leslie and Mark Corcoran, *Operation Sovereign Borders: The First Six Months* (2014) ABC News (online) <www.abc.net.au/news/interactives/operation-sovereign-borders-the-first-6-months/>; Michael Bachelard, 'Vomitous and Terrifying: The Lifeboats Used to Turn Back Asylum Seekers', *Sydney Morning Herald* (online), 2 March 2014 <www.smh.com.au/nation al/vomitous-and-terrifying-the-lifeboats-used-to-turn-back-asylum-seekers-20140301-33t6s .html>.

5   Andrew Probyn, 'Australia's fake fishing boats trawl for asylum seekers', *The West Australian* (online), 27 November 2016 <https://au.news.yahoo.com/thewest/wa/a/33338441/fake-fishing-boats-used-in-the-war-against-people-smugglers/#page1>.

6   See Houston et al, above n 1, 47; Chapter 1, above, 31 n 111.

7   ABC, 'Coalition Wants Military in Charge of Securing Australia's Borders', *7:30 Report*, 25 July 2013 (Tony Abbott) <www.abc.net.au/7.30/content/2013/s3811236.htm>.

8   Kevin Rudd, 'Prime Minister Kevin Rudd – Address to the Nation' on *YouTube* (19 July 2013) 00:00:31, 00:00:38 <https://www.youtube.com/watch?v=kIapYIBRZIs>.

9   AusCustomsNews, 'No Way. You Will Not Make Australia Home – English' on *YouTube* (15 April 2014) 00:00:58 (Angus Campbell) <www.youtube.com/watch?v=rT12WH4a92w>.

10 Evidence to Senate Legal and Constitutional Affairs Legislation Committee, Parliament of Australia, *Supplementary Budget Estimates 2013–2014 (Immigration and Border Protection)*, Canberra, 19 November 2013, 89–93 (Lieutenant General Angus Campbell DSC, AM, Commander Joint Agency Task Force, Operation Sovereign Borders).

smugglers" and to "protect *our people* in the conduct of their duties".[11] Such activities were not, according to then Prime Minister Tony Abbott, "sport for public discussion".[12] Instead, he said, "we are in a fierce contest with these people smugglers and if we were at war we wouldn't be giving out information that is of use to the enemy just because we might have an idle curiosity about it ourselves."[13]

In May 2015, allegations emerged that Australian officials had paid people smugglers to return asylum seekers to Indonesia, a country they had transited en route to Australia. The allegations emerged following the interception by Australian authorities of a boat from Indonesia carrying 65 asylum seekers. The asylum seekers were transferred to two smaller boats and escorted back to Indonesian waters. The six crew members, who faced charges in Indonesia for people smuggling, stated that they were paid US$5,000 each by an Australian official to return the asylum seekers to Indonesia. This information was corroborated by statements from the asylum seekers themselves, who were subsequently detained in Indonesia.[14] Although Immigration Minister Peter Dutton and Foreign Minister Julie Bishop reportedly denied the claim, then Prime Minister Tony Abbott refused to do so, declining to comment on "operational matters" but insisting that the boats be stopped "by hook or by crook".[15]

In June 2015, an inquiry on the matter was referred to the Senate Legal and Constitutional Affairs References Committee. On 16 June 2015, following a motion by Greens Senator Sarah Hanson-Young, the Senate agreed to the issue of an order to the Australian Customs Service for production of documents.[16] On 17 June 2015, in a letter to the Clerk of the Senate, Immigration Minister Peter Dutton declined to accede to the order on the basis that it was not "in the public interest to release information that may compromise current and future

---

[11]   Leslie and Corcoran, above n 4. On the emergence of references to 'people smugglers' in migration discourse, see Chapter 1, 19 n 62.

[12]   Andrew Moore, Interview with Tony Abbott (2GB Radio, 9 January 2014) (Tony Abbott) <www.pm.gov.au/media/2014-01-09/interview-andrew-moore-radio-2gb-0> (emphasis added).

[13]   Natarsha Belling and James Mathison, Interview with Tony Abbott (Network Ten, *Wake Up*, 9 January 2014) 00:00:35 (Tony Abbott) <https://www.youtube.com/watch?v=B66qqYFU6sk>.

[14]   Hilary Charlesworth, Emma Larking, and Jacinta Mulders, Submission No 6 to Senate Legal and Constitutional Affairs References Committee, *Inquiry into Payment of Cash or Other Inducements by the Commonwealth of Australia in Exchange for the Turn Back of Asylum Seeker Boats*, 24 July 2015.

[15]   Dan Conifer, 'Asylum Seekers: Tony Abbott Refuses to Deny Australia Paid Thousands to People Smugglers' *ABC News* (online), 13 June 2015 <www.abc.net.au/news/2015-06-12/abbott-refuses-to-deny-people-smugglers-paid-to-turn-back/6540866>; for transcript, see Julie Doyle, 'PM Refuses to Deny Boat Payment Claims' *ABC News* (online), 12 June 2015 <www.abc.net .au/news/2015-06-12/pm-refuses-to-deny-boat-payment-claims/6543260> (Tony Abbott).

[16]   Commonwealth, *Parliamentary Debates*, Senate, 16 June 2015, 3556–7 (Australian Customs Service, Order for the Production of Documents, Notice of Motion No 724).

operations under Operation Sovereign Borders".[17] In May 2016, the Committee published an interim report, but the inquiry lapsed on account of the imminent federal election.

SECRET DETENTION ON THE HIGH SEAS

Around 13 June 2014, a boat carrying 157[18] Sri Lankan Tamil asylum seekers, including at least 50 children, left Pondicherry, India. For a time, some were in telephone contact with refugee advocate Ian Rintoul, in Australia. On the evening of 26 June, the boat ran into trouble on the high seas.[19] Rintoul notified Australian authorities. On 28 June, Rintoul had contact with the asylum seekers, who said they were 175 nautical miles from Christmas Island.[20] On 29 June, the boat was intercepted in the contiguous zone by an Australian Customs vessel,[21] the *Ocean Protector*.[22] Rintoul lost contact. The 'boat people' were detained incommunicado in crowded, windowless conditions and allowed outside for just three hours per day.[23] This detention was claimed to be pursuant to powers under the *Maritime Powers Act 2013* (Cth),[24] which authorises detention, inside or outside Australia, of a vessel[25] and persons on board that vessel.[26] The Act also

[17] Senate Legal and Constitutional Affairs References Committee, Parliament of Australia, *Payment of Cash or Other Inducements by the Commonwealth of Australia in Exchange for the Turn Back of Asylum Seeker Boats* (Interim Report, May 2016) App 4 (Letter from Peter Dutton, Minister for Immigration and Border Protection to Dr Rosemary Laing, Clerk of the Senate, 17 June 2015).

[18] Minister for Immigration and Border Protection and the Commonwealth of Australia, 'Defendants' Chronology', in *CPCF v Minister for Immigration and Border Protection*, S169/2014, 30 September 2014, 1 ('Defendants' Chronology, CPCF').

[19] Transcript of Proceedings, *JARK (Representing a Class as Defined in Paragraph 1 of 'Nature of the Claim' in the Writ of Summons) v Minister for Immigration and Border Protection* [2014] HCATrans 148 (7 July 2014) (Ron Merkel QC), quoting Statement of Ian Rintoul.

[20] Ibid.

[21] Defendants' Chronology, CPCF, 1; see also Transcript of Proceedings, *JARK (Representing a Class as Defined in Paragraph 1 of 'Nature of the Claim' in the Writ of Summons) v Minister for Immigration and Border Protection* [2014] HCATrans 149 (8 July 2014) (Justin Gleeson SC, Solicitor-General).

[22] Paul Farrell, Oliver Laughland, and Melissa Davey, 'Asylum Seekers Will Be Handed to Police on Return, Sri Lanka Confirms', *The Guardian* (online), 7 July 2014 <www.theguardian.com/world/2014/jul/07/asylum-seekers-will-be-handed-to-police-on-return-sri-lanka-confirms>; Oliver Laughland, 'Tamil Asylum Seekers Being Held at Sea in Windowless Locked Rooms', *The Guardian* (online), 16 July 2014 <www.theguardian.com/world/2014/jul/16/tamil-asylum-seekers-being-held-at-sea-in-windowless-locked-rooms>.

[23] Farrell, Laughland, and Davey, above n 22; Laughland, 'Tamil Asylum Seekers Being Held', above n 22.

[24] *Maritime Powers Act 2013* (Cth) s 72; see also at ss 75, 95.   [25] Ibid ss 69, 70.

[26] Ibid ss 71, 72.

authorises the taking of such detainees to places inside or outside Australia's migration zone[27] and inside or outside Australia.[28] In addition, it declares any restraint on liberty not to constitute an arrest and to be 'not unlawful'.[29] Furthermore, it ousts the jurisdiction of the courts, except the High Court of Australia ('the High Court') under s 75 of the *Constitution*.[30] The statutory history of these provisions is that they were first incorporated into the *Migration Act 1958* (Cth) ('*Migration Act*') as part of the post-*Tampa* package of legislation.[31] When first introduced, the provisions were designed to provide ex post facto validation of the interdiction of the MV *Tampa*.[32]

On 1 July 2014, several days after the boat was intercepted, Australia's National Security Committee (NSC) decided that those now on board the *Ocean Protector* "should be taken to a particular place, which is a place outside Australia".[33] The NSC is a committee of the Cabinet. Its decisions do not require Cabinet endorsement.[34] The *Ocean Protector* began travelling towards India, and some of the asylum seekers were reportedly given training on the use of disposable and unsinkable orange lifeboats ahead of their intended return to India.[35]

For some time the foregoing detail was not in the public domain. On 7 July 2014,[36] lawyers representing some of the asylum seekers obtained an interim injunction in the High Court restraining the Commonwealth from returning them to Sri Lanka.[37] Only then did the government admit that

---

[27] For the definition of 'migration zone', see *Migration Act 1958* (Cth) ('*Migration Act*') s 5.
[28] *Maritime Powers Act 2013* (Cth) s 72(4).   [29] Ibid s 75(1).   [30] Ibid s 75(2).
[31] See also Chapter 4, above 121 n 51.
[32] *Border Protection (Validation and Enforcement Powers) Act 2001* (Cth), inserting *Migration Act* ss 245F(9), 245F(9A). See Australian Human Rights Commission, 'Proposed Submissions of the Australian Human Rights Commission Seeking Leave to Intervene', Submission in *CPCF v Minister for Immigration and Border Protection*, S169/2014, 11 September 2014, 9–11.
[33] Transcript of Proceedings, *CPCF v Minister for Immigration and Border Protection* [2014] HCATrans 153 (23 July 2014). At the relevant time, the National Security Committee of Cabinet comprised the following people: Prime Minister Tony Abbott, Deputy Prime Minister Warren Truss, Foreign Minister Julie Bishop, Treasurer Joe Hockey, Attorney-General George Brandis, Defence Minister David Johnston, and Immigration Minister Scott Morrison.
[34] Australian Government, *National Security Committee* (18 October 2013) Australian Government: Directory <www.directory.gov.au/>.
[35] Oliver Laughland, 'Tamil Asylum Seekers Were Taught How to "Pilot Lifeboats Back to India"', *The Guardian* (online), 3 August 2014 <www.theguardian.com/world/2014/aug/03/ta mil-asylum-seekers-taught-pilot-lifeboats-back-india>.
[36] Transcript of Proceedings, *JARK (Representing a Class as Defined in Paragraph 1 of 'Nature of the Claim' in the Writ of Summons) v Minister for Immigration and Border Protection* [2014] HCATrans 149 (8 July 2014) (Justin Gleeson SC).
[37] Transcript of Proceedings, *JARK (Representing a Class as Defined in Paragraph 1 of 'Nature of the Claim' in the Writ of Summons) v Minister for Immigration and Border Protection* [2014] HCATrans 148 (7 July 2014) (Crennan J).

the group of asylum seekers existed. Still, it refused to disclose their where-
abouts. Indeed, confirmation of the existence, circumstances, and location,
of the asylum seeker boat and its human cargo was reportedly refused by the
Minister 27 times.[38] It later transpired that the government was trying
(unsuccessfully) to return the people to India.[39]

On 27 July 2014, after a month detained on the high seas, the asylum seekers
were brought to the Cocos (Keeling) Islands and thence to the Australian
mainland. They were detained at the remote Curtin detention centre in
Western Australia.[40] This was to enable interviews by Indian consular officials
with a view to negotiating their return to India.[41]

On 1 August 2014, in a "secret overnight operation", all 157 asylum seekers were
forcibly transferred from Curtin detention centre to Nauru.[42] The decision to
transfer them was taken by the Immigration Minister reportedly because the
asylum seekers had 'chosen' not to talk to the consular officials.[43] They had, he is
reported to have said, "squandered" a "rare opportunity" to go back to India,
where, he insisted, "they were living in safety".[44] This 'choice', he said, appeared
to be on the advice of their lawyers, a suggestion the lawyers strenuously denied.[45]
Indeed, according to one of the lawyers, they had only been able to speak to four
of the asylum seekers.[46] Nevertheless, the Minister insinuated that lawyers were

---

[38] ABC, 'Secrecy on the High Seas', *Media Watch*, 14 July 2014 (Paul Barry) <www.abc.net.au/
mediawatch/transcripts/s4045863.htm>.

[39] Minister for Immigration and Border Protection and the Commonwealth of Australia,
'Defendants' Chronology', in *CPCF v Minister for Immigration and Border Protection*, S169/
2014, 30 September 2014, 2.

[40] Matthew Knott, 'Government's Plan for 157 Captive Asylum Seekers Potentially Illegal:
Lawyers', *Sydney Morning Herald* (online), 26 July 2014 <www.smh.com.au/federal-politics/
political-news/governments-plan-for-157-captive-asylum-seekers-potentially-illegal-lawyers-20
140726-3cluv.html>.

[41] Ibid. On the right of consular access and the right of a person in prison, custody, or detention to
refuse such access, see *Vienna Convention on Consular Relations*, opened for signature 24
April 1963, 596 UNTS 261 (entered into force 19 March 1967) art 36.

[42] Oliver Laughland, 'Tamil Asylum Seekers Moved to Nauru', *The Guardian* (online), 2 August
2014 <www.theguardian.com/world/2014/aug/02/tamil-asylum-seekers-moved-to-nauru>, quoting
Scott Morrison.

[43] Kirsty Needham, 'Lawyer George Newhouse in Dark over Asylum Seeker Move', *The Age*
(online), 2 August 2014 <www.theage.com.au/federal-politics/political-news/lawyer-george-n
ewhouse-in-dark-over-asylum-seeker-move-20140802-zzppo.html>.

[44] Dennis Shanahan, 'Immigration Minister Scott Morrison Takes Hard Line: 157 Sent to
Nauru', *The Australian* (online), 2 August 2014 <www.theaustralian.com.au/national-affairs/
immigration/immigration-minister-scott-morrison-takes-hard-line-157-sent-to-nauru/story-fn9
hm1gu-1227010765629>, quoting Scott Morrison.

[45] Needham, above n 43.

[46] Laughland, 'Tamil Asylum Seekers Moved to Nauru', above n 42, quoting Hugh de Kretser,
Executive Director, Human Rights Law Centre.

seeking to frustrate the initiative in furtherance of their own political agenda and to the detriment of their clients.[47]

Notwithstanding the transfer to Nauru, the High Court proceedings remained on foot and were set down for hearing on 14 and 15 October 2014. In broad terms, the plaintiffs made three claims: first, that their imprisonment on the *Ocean Protector* was unlawful; second, that the decision to return them to India involved a denial of natural justice; third, that there was a requirement that the obligation of *non-refoulement* under international law be taken into account.[48] The defendants' case was that detention under the *Maritime Powers Act* was lawful, that there was no obligation to accord natural justice, and that Australia has no extraterritorial obligation under international law to respect the principle of *non-refoulement*.[49]

On 25 September 2014, before the case went to hearing, the Immigration Minister introduced to Parliament the Migration and Maritime Powers Legislation Amendment (Resolving the Asylum Legacy Caseload) Bill 2014 (Cth), a suite of sweeping changes to both the *Maritime Powers Act* and the *Migration Act*. For present purposes, three provisions are of particular interest. First, the Bill provided that the rules of natural justice do not apply to a range of powers in the *Maritime Powers Act*,[50] including the powers to detain and move vessels and people to a place outside Australia. Second, it provided that the exercise of a range of powers under the *Maritime Powers Act* cannot be invalidated even if a court considers that there has been a failure (properly) to consider or comply with Australia's international obligations or the international obligations or domestic law of any other country.[51] Third, the Bill made provision under the *Maritime Powers Act* for exercising expansive powers in relation to the detention and movement of foreigners and foreign vessels on the high seas. It provided that

---

[47]   Shanahan, above n 44; see also Needham, above n 43.
[48]   CPCF, 'Plaintiff's Submissions', Submission in *CPCF v Minister for Immigration and Border Protection*, S169/2014', 11 September 2014; see also CPCF, 'Plaintiff's Amended Submissions in Reply', Submission in *CPCF v Minister for Immigration and Border Protection*, S169/2014, 10 October 2014.
[49]   Minister for Immigration and Border Protection and the Commonwealth of Australia, 'Submissions of the Defendants', Submission in *CPCF v Minister for Immigration and Border Protection*, S169/2014, 30 September 2014.
[50]   Migration and Maritime Powers Legislation Amendment (Resolving the Asylum Legacy Caseload) Bill 2014 (Cth) sch 1 pt 1 cl 19, inserting s 75B into the *Maritime Powers Act 2013* (Cth); Explanatory Memorandum, Migration and Maritime Powers Legislation Amendment (Resolving the Asylum Legacy Caseload) Bill 2014 (Cth) 3.
[51]   Migration and Maritime Powers Legislation Amendment (Resolving the Asylum Legacy Caseload) Bill 2014 (Cth) sch 1 pt 1 cl 19, insertings 75A into the *Maritime Powers Act 2013* (Cth); Explanatory Memorandum, Migration and Maritime Powers Legislation Amendment (Resolving the Asylum Legacy Caseload) Bill 2014 (Cth) 3.

the exercise of such powers is to be governed by ministerial determination and that the only condition for the exercise of the Minister's power to make or vary such a determination is that the Minister 'thinks' it is 'in the national interest' to do so.[52] The Minister described the Bill as providing "clarity and consistency" within a broader policy framework that seeks not to reward those who, he said, "flagrantly disregard our laws and arrive illegally in Australia".[53]

In the early hours of 5 December 2014, the Bill passed into law with a vote in the Senate of 34:32.[54] This followed intense negotiations with minor-party Senators holding the balance of power: in exchange for the broad powers afforded to the Minister under the Bill, he agreed to grant work rights hitherto denied to many asylum seekers living in the Australian community as well as to exercise a long-held but non-compellable ministerial discretion to release children from mandatory detention.[55]

On 28 January 2015, in a 4:3 decision, a majority[56] of the High Court held that (incommunicado) detention on the high seas for the purposes of (even speculatively) taking the plaintiff to India was authorised by the *Maritime Powers Act* and did not give rise to a claim for false imprisonment. The Court also held that detention under the *Maritime Powers Act* was necessary in order to prevent a breach of the *Migration Act* by the plaintiff and (unanimously) that there was no duty to accord the plaintiff procedural fairness in the exercise of the power to 'detain and take' the plaintiff from Australia's contiguous zone to a place outside Australia.

SILENCING DISSENT: A CRIMINAL OFFENCE TO EXPOSE HUMAN RIGHTS ABUSES

In October 2014, the Minister for Immigration invoked s 70 of the *Crimes Act 1914* (Cth) against 10 staff of Save the Children Australia who had been working on Nauru and were accused of communicating privileged

---

[52] Migration and Maritime Powers Legislation Amendment (Resolving the Asylum Legacy Caseload) Bill 2014 (Cth) sch 1 pt 1 cl 19, inserting *Maritime Powers Act 2013* (Cth) s 75D; Explanatory Memorandum, Migration and Maritime Powers Legislation Amendment (Resolving the Asylum Legacy Caseload) Bill 2014 (Cth) 30.

[53] CPD, House of Representatives, 25 September 2014, 10546 (Scott Morrison).

[54] CPD, Senate, 4 December 2014, 145–6.

[55] Scott Morrison, Minister for Immigration and Border Protection, Press Conference, Migration and Maritime Powers Legislation Amendment (Resolving the Asylum Legacy Caseload) Bill 2014, Coalition Government, Parliament House, Canberra, 5 December 2014 <www.minister.immi.gov.au/media/sm/2014/sm219827.htm>.

[56] French CJ, Crennan, Gageler, and Keane JJ (Hayne, Kiefel, and Bell JJ dissenting): *CPCF v Minister for Immigration and Border Protection* (2015) 255 CLR 514.

information to non-Commonwealth workers.[57] In a report dated 6 February 2015, the workers were exonerated following an independent review by a former integrity commissioner.[58]

On 25 February 2015, the Australian Border Force Bill 2015 (Cth) was introduced into the House of Representatives. Among other things, the Bill imposed a general prohibition on people working in immigration detention facilities, in Australia and offshore, from discussing or otherwise disclosing what they see in those facilities.[59] Under the Bill, 'entrusted persons'[60] – which includes departmental consultants, contractors, and sub-contractors – would face a jail term of up to two years for disclosure of 'protected information', that is, information obtained by a person in her capacity as an entrusted person.[61] The Bill was passed by the Senate on 14 May 2015.[62]

On 1 July 2015, the day the *Australian Border Force Act 2015* (Cth) (*'ABF Act'*) came into force, more than 40 current and former workers at Australia's detention centres on Nauru and Manus Island challenged the Prime Minister and Immigration Minister in an open letter to prosecute them under the new law for speaking out over human rights abuses.[63]

In September 2015, the UN Special Rapporteur on the Human Rights of Migrants, François Crépeau, postponed a scheduled visit to Australia, Nauru, and Papua New Guinea. He did so because the Australian Government was not prepared to provide a written guarantee that no one meeting with him during his visit would be at risk of any intimidation or sanctions under the *Border Force Act*.[64]

---

[57] Sarah Whyte, 'Anti-whistleblowing law being used to pursue Save the Children staff used only twice in five years', *Sydney Morning Herald* (online), 13 October 2014 <www.smh.com.au/fe deral-politics/political-news/antiwhistleblowing-law-being-used-to-pursue-save-the-children-s taff-used-only-twice-in-five-years-20141013-1157jt.html>.

[58] Philip Moss, *Review into Recent Allegations relating to Conditions and Circumstances at the Regional Processing Centre in Nauru* (Final Report, 6 February 2015) <https://www.border .gov.au/ReportsandPublications/Documents/reviews-and-inquiries/review-conditions-circum stances-nauru.pdf>.

[59] *Australian Border Force Act 2015* (Cth) pt 6 (*'ABF Act'*).

[60] *ABF Act* ss 4, 5(1)–(2): under the Act, 'entrusted person' is given a broad meaning. It includes an Immigration and Border Protection worker. An 'Immigration and Border Protection worker' extends to departmental consultants and contractors, contracted service providers, and persons specified to be so by the Secretary or the ABF Commissioner.

[61] *ABF Act* ss 4, 42.   [62] CPD, Senate, 14 May 2015, 3200.

[63] Dr John-Paul Sanggaran et al, 'Open Letter on the Border Force Act – We Challenge the Department to Prosecute', *The Guardian* (online), 1 July 2015 <www.theguardian.com/austra lia-news/2015/jul/01/open-letter-on-the-border-force-act-we-challenge-the-department-to-prosecute>.

[64] In relation to the Special Rapporteur on the Human Rights of Migrants, see: Office of the High Commissioner for Human Rights, 'Migrants/Human rights: Official visit to Australia postponed due to protection concerns' (OHCHR, Media Release, 25 September 2015) <http://

In July 2016, Doctors for Refugees Inc brought a constitutional case in the High Court of Australia challenging the validity of the secrecy provisions in the *ABF Act*. They did so on the basis that the secrecy provisions compromised the ethical duties of medical practitioners, systems of accountability within the health profession, and the quality and integrity of healthcare provided to patients under Australia's control and management.[65] Under the legislation as originally framed, doctors and other healthcare professionals were among people considered to be 'entrusted persons' and prohibited from disclosing 'protected information'. Disclosure of information, including public health information, is subject to the approval of the Secretary of the Department of Immigration and Border Protection, even if such disclosure would be in the 'public interest'.[66]

On 30 September 2016, shortly before the government was due to file its defence in the High Court,[67] the Secretary of the Department of Immigration and Border Protection signed an amendment to a Determination regarding who the Secretary considers to be an 'Immigration and Border Protection worker' for the purposes of the *ABF Act*.[68] The effect of the amendment was that persons performing services for the Department as health practitioners were thereafter exempt from the secrecy provisions under the *ABF Act*.[69] The timing of the amendment also meant that the issues the case raised would not be ventilated in the High Court proceeding. While the exemption did not apply to teachers, lawyers, security staff, social workers, and other staff, amendments to the *ABF Act* to avert further litigation covering the wider cohort appear to have gone some way to addressing its deficiencies.[70]

ohchr.org/EN/NewsEvents/Pages/DisplayNews.aspx?NewsID=16503&LangID=E#sthash.N5 tS2e9n.dpuf>.

[65] Doctors for Refugees and Fitzroy Legal Service, *'Doctors for Refugees Inc v Commonwealth of Australia* – High Court of Australia', *Briefing Paper* (Doctors for Refugees and Fitzroy Legal Service, 29 July 2016 <www.fitzroy-legal.org.au/doctors_for_refugees>.

[66] See in particular *ABF Act* ss 44–46. Note that there is no embedded exemption in the *ABF Act* to allow for recording or disclosure that is in the public interest: ibid.

[67] Bianca Hall, '"A Huge Win for Doctors": Turnbull Government Backs Down on Gag Laws for Doctors on Nauru and Manus', *Sydney Morning Herald* (online), 20 October 2016 <www.s mh.com.au/federal-politics/political-news/a-huge-win-for-doctors-turnbull-government-back s-down-on-gag-laws-for-doctors-on-nauru-and-manus-20161019-gs6ecs.html>.

[68] *ABF Act* ss 4(1), 5.

[69] Michael Pezzullo, Secretary, DIBP, 'Determination of Immigration and Border Protection Workers – Amendment No 1', *Australian Border Force Act 2015*, 30 September 2016 <https:// uploads.guim.co.uk/2016/10/19/Determination_Amendment_(1).pdf>.

[70] Ben Doherty, 'Doctors Freed to Speak about Australia's Detention Regime after U-turn', *The Guardian* (online), 20 October 2016 <www.theguardian.com/australia-news/2016/oct/20/doc tors-freed-to-speak-about-australias-detention-regime-after-u-turn>; *Australian Border Force Amendment (Protected Information) Act 2017* (Cth).

PUTTING BEYOND DOUBT THE POWER TO DO
ANY THING AT ANY COST

On 24 June 2015, the Migration Amendment (Regional Processing Arrangements) Bill 2015 (Cth) was introduced into the House of Representatives and was passed by the Senate on 25 June 2015, when Parliament rose for the midwinter break. A companion Bill to *Migration Legislation Amendment (Regional Processing and Other Measures) Act 2012* (Cth), its stated purpose was to insert into the *Migration Act 1958* (Cth) s 198AHA, which would 'put beyond doubt' – both retrospectively and prospectively – the Commonwealth's power to authorise any actions and expenditure of the Commonwealth in regional processing countries.[71] The terms of the provision were intended to capture the "full gamut" of the Commonwealth's actions in relation to regional processing arrangements.[72] Although unstated in either the Bill's Explanatory Memorandum or the Minister's Second Reading Speech, its purpose was to defeat a proceeding brought against the Commonwealth by the Melbourne-based Human Rights Law Centre in May 2015: *Plaintiff M68-2015 v Minister for Immigration and Border Protection*. The case was brought by a Bangladeshi woman temporarily in Australia for health reasons who was resisting return to Nauru. She alleged that she would be subject to unlawful detention in an offshore centre funded and effectively controlled by the Common-wealth and that such detention was not authorised by Australian law.

On 2 October 2015, five days before the case was set down for hearing, a notice was issued in the Nauru Government Gazette declaring that arrange-ments in the regional processing centre in which the plaintiff was to be detained would now permit asylum seekers freedom of movement 24 hours per day, seven days per week. These measures were effective from 5 October 2015. The Minister for Immigration denied that the move had anything to do with the imminent High Court proceeding, which was set down for hearing two days after the measures took effect.[73] At the hearing on 7 October 2015, the Solicitor-General commenced with an application to amend the special case on the basis that the changed conditions made by "Nauru as a sovereign state"[74] rendered the issues in the case hypothetical.

---

[71]   CPD, House of Representatives, 24 June 2015, 7488 (Peter Dutton, Minister for Immigration and Border Protection) (Migration Amendment (Regional Processing Arrangements) Bill 2015 (Cth), Second Reading Speech).

[72]   CPD, Senate, 25 June 2015, 4662–3 (George Brandis, Attorney-General).

[73]   Emma Alberici, Interview with Peter Dutton (ABC, *Lateline*, 5 October 2015) <www.abc.net .au/lateline/content/2015/s4325585.htm>.

[74]   *Plaintiff M68-2015 v Minister for Immigration and Border Protection* [2015] HCATrans 255, 2–3 (7 October 2015) (Justin Gleeson SC).

On 3 February 2016, the High Court delivered its decision, a 6:1 majority upholding the constitutional validity of the offshore detention scheme,[75] including the retrospective nature of the legislative changes made in June 2015. Section 198AHA of the *Migration Act* could, the majority held, be characterised as a law with respect to aliens. On the scope of the aliens power, Gageler J noted that its reach "is not subject to any territorial or purposive limitation."[76] The Court accepted the Commonwealth's argument that detention and latterly the changed living conditions on Nauru were at the behest of Nauru as an independent sovereign state and under its laws; detention was, therefore, effected by Nauru, not Australia. The Court also upheld the principle in *Chu Kheng Lim v Minister for Immigration, Local Government and Ethnic Affairs* that detention will be lawful if it is 'reasonably capable of being seen as necessary for the purposes of deportation or necessary to enable an application for an entry permit to be made and considered.'[77]

MANUS ISLAND: ONE PLACE, TWO CONSTITUTIONS

In June 2014, in the *Manus Island Case*,[78] the High Court of Australia unanimously upheld as a valid exercise of the aliens power the legislative framework underpinning Australia's offshore processing scheme, which had been revised following the decision of the High Court in August 2011 in the *Malaysian Declaration Case*.[79] Under this revised scheme, the Minister was empowered to declare (in this instance) Papua New Guinea to be a 'regional processing country' on the basis that he 'thought' it was 'in the national interest' to do so.[80] The Court held that there was no statutory requirement that the exercise of the Minister's power to make a declaration be evidence-based.[81] Nor was there any obligation to consult widely with, say, UNHCR. As

---

75   Gordon J dissenting.
76   *Plaintiff M68-2015 v Minister for Immigration and Border Protection* (2016) 257 CLR 42, 110–111 [182].
77   (1992) 176 CLR 1, 33 (Brennan, Deane and Dawson JJ); see discussion in Chapter 5, 195, 206, 222, 223, 224.
78   *Plaintiff S156/2013 v Minister for Immigration and Border Protection* (2014) 254 CLR 28 ('*Manus Island Case*').
79   *Plaintiff M70/2011 v Minister for Immigration and Citizenship* (2011) 244 CLR 18 ('*Malaysian Declaration Case*').
80   *Migration Act* 198AB. For another example of the use of this formulation, see above n 52.
81   *Manus Island Case* (2014) 254 CLR 28, 48 [46].

such, the exercise of the Minister's power was not impugned by his having sought, but not waited for, advice from UNHCR.[82]

In April 2016, a unanimous decision of the Supreme Court of Papua New Guinea found detention of refugees and asylum seekers on Manus Island to be unconstitutional.[83] The basis for the decision was a constitutional provision safeguarding the right to liberty.[84] A 2014 amendment to the *PNG Constitution* inserting an exemption to this safeguard, which authorised detention of a foreign national 'under arrangements ... with another country' and at the 'absolute discretion' of the Minister responsible for immigration,[85] was held to be invalid. In particular, the Court held that the amendment failed to comply with the need, under s 38 of the *PNG Constitution*, to demonstrate that the law was 'reasonably justifiable in a democratic society having a proper respect for the rights and dignity of mankind'.[86] In his judgment, Kandakasi J explained the significance of this provision as follows:

> The reasons for that importance [are] simple. Although all humans are born with all of their rights and freedoms, some suppressive regimes and or governments deny the people of their rights or freedoms over the years, until they got restored as nations evolved from their stone ages to more modern democracies.[87]

Closure of the Manus Island detention centre was ordered by the PNG Prime Minister Peter O'Neill in April 2016 following the Supreme Court decision.[88] Nevertheless, it remained open for almost 18 months.[89]

---

[82] By a letter dated 9 October 2012, the High Commissioner for Refugees expressed concern about the designation of Papua New Guinea as a 'regional processing country' because it lacked the "legal safeguards", "competence", or "capacity" to protect and process asylum seekers in the absence of an effective national legal or regulatory framework to do so. He also expressed concern about the "challenges of caring for people transferred to Manus Island" and the "difficulty of preserving the psychosocial and physical health" of those remaining there "for any prolonged period": Letter from António Guterres, UN High Commissioner for Refugees to Chris Bowen, Minister for Immigration and Citizenship, 9 October 2012.

[83] *Namah v Pato* [2016] PGSC 13; SC1497 (26 April 2016).

[84] *Constitution of the Independent State of Papua New Guinea 1975* (PNG) s 42 ('*PNG Constitution*').

[85] *Constitution Amendment (No 37) (Citizenship) Law 2014* (PNG) s 1, inserting s 42(ga).

[86] *PNG Constitution* s 38.   [87] *Namah v Pato* [2016] PGSC 13, 20 [52].

[88] Stephanie Anderson, 'Manus Island Detention Centre to be Shut, Papua New Guinea Prime Minister Peter O'Neill Says', *The Guardian* (online), updated 28 April 2016 <www.abc.net.au/news/2016-04-27/png-pm-oneill-to-shut-manus-island-detention-centre/7364414>.

[89] On the Australian Government's response to Prime Minister O'Neill's order, see, eg, Louise Yaxley, 'PNG's Supreme Court Ruling Does Not Mean Manus Island Centre Must Shut, Says

On 17 August 2017, the High Court of Australia again upheld the legality under Australian constitutional law of offshore detention and processing in Papua New Guinea. An Iranian asylum seeker, relying on the PNG Supreme Court decision in *Namah v Pato*, advanced what the Australian Court described as the "novel and sweeping proposition" that the Australian *Constitution* constrained the exercise by the Commonwealth of Australia of legislative or executive power to authorise or take part in activity in another country that is unlawful as a matter of domestic law in that country.[90] In doing so, the Court emphasised that neither the legislative nor the executive power of the Commonwealth is constitutionally limited by any need to conform either to international law or to the domestic law of another country.[91] Furthermore, the Court held that the Memorandum of Understanding between Australia and Papua New Guinea could not be invalidated under Australian law for want of legal authority under PNG law to enter into the arrangement. The Court said that this was, at least in part, because the term 'arrangement' was given a broad meaning under the *Migration Act*[92] and would include an arrangement that was unlawful as a matter of PNG law because it would still be an arrangement in fact.[93] The Court further expressed the view that, in any event, the decision of the PNG Supreme Court in *Namah v Pato* did not impugn the validity of the Memorandum of Understanding.[94]

When the centre closed on 31 October 2017 many detainees were afraid to leave. At the time of writing, Australian government staff had been withdrawn from the island, leaving the detainees and PNG authorities in a tense standoff.

OFFSHORE DETENTION AND PROCESSING: IN SEARCH OF AN EXIT STRATEGY

In November 2016, shortly after Donald Trump prevailed in the United States presidential election, Prime Minister Malcolm Turnbull announced a one-off resettlement deal that his government had struck with the outgoing

---

Peter Dutton', *ABC News* (online), updated 11 May 2016 <www.abc.net.au/news/2016-05-11/png's-court-ruling-does-not-mean-centre-must-be-shut:-dutton/740360>. See also Government of Australia, *Report of the Special Rapporteur on the Human Rights of Migrants on his Mission to Australia and the Regional Processing Centres in Nauru: Comments by the State*, UN Doc A/HRC/35/25/Add.4 (17 May 2017) 11 ('*Comments by the State*'); Ben Doherty, 'Australia Should Bring Manus and Nauru Refugees to Immediate Safety, UN Says', *The Guardian* (online), 10 November 2017 <www.theguardian.com/australia-news/2017/nov/10/australia-should-bring-manus-and-nauru-refugees-to-immediate-safety-un-says>.

[90] *Plaintiff S195/2016 v Minister for Immigration and Border Protection and Ors* [2017] HCA 31, 17 August 2017, [19] ('*Plaintiff S195*').

[91] Ibid [20]. [92] *Migration Act* s 198AHA.[93] *Plaintiff S195* [2017] HCA 31, [21].

[94] Ibid [25].

administration of President Barack Obama. The deal applied to recognised refugees currently on Nauru and Manus Island and, he said, would be administered with the Office of the UN High Commissioner for Refugees. In the same press conference, Immigration Minister Peter Dutton announced that those on Nauru who decline an offer to resettle in the United States would be offered a 20-year visa for Nauru – a deal in relation to which he said the Australian Government was in the final stages of negotiation with the Republic of Nauru. Dutton said that the resettlement announcement would "never ever" apply to any prospective arrivals.[95]

Within days of announcing the resettlement deal with the United States, Migration Legislation Amendment (Regional Processing Cohort) Bill 2016 (Cth) was introduced to the House of Representatives. The Bill sought to supplement the 'no way, never'[96] policy by imposing a lifetime visa ban for refugees seeking to enter Australia by boat after a specified date. The proposed lifetime visa ban was part of a suite of measures said to form a "strengthened protective shield" to deter unauthorised boat arrivals from attempting to reach Australia.[97] The Bill, whose introduction had been foreshadowed by Turnbull as part of an "unflinching, unequivocal" message to "the people smugglers" in a press conference two weeks earlier,[98] is, at the time of writing, yet to be passed by the Senate. If it is passed in its current form, it will have retroactive effect. In its terms, it adopts the formula of coupling the mandatory lifetime visa ban with a non-compellable, non-enforceable, and non-reviewable ministerial discretion to lift it.[99]

[95] See, eg, Fergus Hunter and Amy Remeikis, 'Turnbull Government Unveils Manus and Nauru Refugee Resettlement Deal with United States', *Sydney Morning Herald* (online), 13 November 2016 <www.smh.com.au/federal-politics/political-news/united-states-confirms-manus-islandand-nauru-deal-with-turnbull-government-20161112-gso2el.html>. Note that the quoted text is taken from video footage accompanying the article cited.

[96] Australian Customs and Border Protection Service <www.customs.gov.au/>; see also Kevin Rudd, 'Prime Minister Kevin Rudd – Address to the Nation' on *YouTube* (19 July 2013) 00:00:31, 00:00:38 <https://www.youtube.com/watch?v=kIapYIBRZIs>; AusCustomsNews, 'No Way. You Will Not Make Australia Home – English' on *YouTube* (15 April 2014) <www.youtube.com/watch?v=rT12WH4a92w>.

[97] Senate Legal and Constitutional Affairs Legislation Committee, Parliament of Australia, *Inquiry into Migration Legislation Amendment (Regional Processing Cohort) Bill 2016 [Provisions]* 5 (Michael Pezzullo, Secretary, DIBP). Migration Legislation Amendment (Regional Processing Cohort) Bill 2016 (Cth) was introduced into Parliament on 8 November 2016 and was passed by the House of Representatives on 10 November 2016. The Legal and Constitutional Affairs Legislation Committee recommended, by a majority, that the Senate pass the Bill. Cf Parliamentary Joint Committee on Human Rights, *Human Rights Scrutiny Report* (Report 9, 2016) 15–22.

[98] See, eg, Gareth Hutchens, 'Asylum Seekers Face Lifetime Ban from Entering Australia if They Arrive by Boat', *The Guardian* (online), 30 October 2016 <www.theguardian.com/australia-news/2016/oct/30/asylum-seekers-face-lifetime-ban-on-entering-australia-if-they-arrive-by-boat>. Note that the quoted text is taken from video footage accompanying the article cited.

[99] Migration Legislation Amendment (Regional Processing Cohort) Bill 2016 (Cth).

NOT EVEN IF YOU ARE A NOBEL PRIZE-WINNING GENIUS

A conversation between US President Donald Trump and Prime Minister Turnbull took place on 28 January 2017, shortly after the President's inauguration. Reports of the conversation varied.[100] Generally they suggested that while it may have been an awkward leader-to-leader call, Trump ultimately said he would still honour the refugee resettlement deal that was the focus of the conversation. However, Trump wasted no time in tweeting his view that it was a "dumb deal".[101]

In July 2017, the future of the resettlement deal was thrown into doubt after US officials were reported as having abruptly ceased interviewing on Nauru and left the facility.[102] One of the explanations for this appears to be that the US resettlement quota, halved under the Trump administration, had already reached its annual cap.[103]

On 3 August 2017, the *Washington Post* published what was reportedly the full transcript of the Trump–Turnbull conversation from 28 January 2017.[104] As the transcript suggests, Turnbull pressed hard for the deal to be honoured, seeking to impress upon the President that domestically the deal was "really, really important". However, in the face of resistance from Trump, Turnbull sought for the US side of the deal to be honoured in name only: "Every individual is subject to your vetting. You can decide to take them or to not take them after vetting. You can decide to take 1,000 or 100. It is entirely up to you. The obligation is to only go

---

[100] See, eg, Sarah Martin and Simon Benson, 'Trump Refugee Ban: Nauru Resettlement Deal Could Be Saved' *The Australian* (online), 29 January 2017 <www.theaustralian.com.au/national-affairs/immigration/trump-refugee-ban-nauru-resettlement-deal-with-australia-could-be-saved/news-story/9cdbe11ff03582bb782a42953c38183d>; Ben Winsor and Myles Morgan, '"This Is the Worst Deal Ever," President Donald Trump Reportedly Said of the Refugee Deal with Australia, according to the Washington Post' *SBS News* (online), 2 February 2017 <www.sbs.com.au/news/article/2017/02/02/talking-turnbull-worst-call-far-trump-says-washington-post>.

[101] Donald J Trump @realDonaldTrump, 7.55 PM, 1 February 2017: "Do you believe it? The Obama Administration agreed to take thousands of illegal immigrants from Australia. Why? I will study this dumb deal!"

[102] Reuters (Sydney and Washington), 'US Officials Walk Out of Australia-Run Nauru Detention Centre' *The Guardian* (online), 16 July 2017 <www.theguardian.com/world/2017/jul/15/us-officials-walk-out-australia-nauru-detention-centre>.

[103] Stephanie March, 'US hits refugee intake cap as Manus Island, Nauru refugees assessed' *ABC News* (online), 14 July 2017 <www.abc.net.au/news/2017-07-14/manus-nauru-refugees-waiting-as-us-intake-cap-reached/8707340>.

[104] Greg Miller, Julie Vitkovskaya, and Reuben Fischer-Baum, '"This Deal Will Make Me Look Terrible": Full Transcripts of Trump's Calls with Mexico and Australia", *Washington Post* (online) 3 August 2017 <www.washingtonpost.com/graphics/2017/politics/australia-mexico-transcripts/?utm_term=.66adbb74f572>.

through the process." On the other hand, Turnbull promised more on the Australian "end of the bargain" – which was apparently to resettle 31 people that the United States "need[ed] to move on": "We will take more. We will take anyone that you want us to take."

In response to Turnbull's (inaccurate) assertions that the "vast bulk" of the people concerned were "basically economic refugees"[105] who he described as having been "under our supervision for over three years now and we know exactly everything about them",[106] Trump asked, "Why haven't you let them out? Why have you not let them into your society?"[107] Turnbull's defence of the policy was unwavering:

> It is not because they are bad people. It is because in order to stop people smugglers, we had to deprive them of the product. So we said if you try to come to Australia by boat, even if we think you are the best person in the world, even if you are a Noble [sic] Prize winning genius, we will not let you in.[108]

Apparently perplexed, Trump asked, "What is the thing with boats? Why do you discriminate against boats?"[109] Turnbull's response resorted to the claim of 'absolute sovereignty':

> The problem with the boats [is] that you are basically outsourcing your immigration program to people smugglers and also you get thousands of people drowning at sea. So what we say is, we will decide which people get to come to Australia who are refugees, economic migrants, businessmen, whatever. We decide. That is our decision.[110]

And later:

> We know exactly who they are. They have been on Nauru or Manus for over three years and the only reason we cannot let them into Australia is because of our commitment to not allow people to come by boat. Otherwise we would have let them in. If they had arrived by airplane and with a tourist visa then they would be here.[111]

---

[105] As of 31 October 2016, 79% of asylum seekers on Nauru and 82% of asylum seekers on Manus Island had been determined to be refugees: Elibritt Karlsen, 'Australia's Offshore Processing of Asylum Seekers in Nauru and PNG: A Quick Guide to Statistics and Resources' (Research Paper Series, 2016–17, Parliamentary Library, Parliament of Australia, 19 December 2016) 10.

[106] On the question of effective control under international law, see Crépeau, above n 3, 14 [73]. See also Human Rights Committee, *General Comment No 31: Nature of the General Legal Obligation Imposed on States Parties to the Covenant*, UN Doc CCPR/C/21/Rev.1/Add.13 (26 May 2004) para 10.

[107] Ibid.   [108] Ibid.   [109] Ibid.   [110] Ibid.   [111] Ibid.

In April 2017, the Special Rapporteur on the Human Rights of Migrants described the distinction based on mode of arrival as "unjustifiable in international refugee and human rights law" and as amounting to discrimination based on a criterion having no connection with the protection claim.[112]

On 10 August 2017, former US Deputy Secretary of State for Management and Resources Heather Higginbottom, who was the Obama Administration official responsible for negotiating the resettlement agreement with Australia's Department of Foreign Affairs and Trade, said this about 'boat people' detained on Nauru and Manus Island:

> These are people who risked their lives on makeshift boats to flee conflict and the lack of access to basic means of survival but were turned back by an Australian government that refuses asylum seekers who arrive by sea. … While the last Administration strongly pressed the Australian government to change its policy toward asylum seekers, we also sought to immediately relieve the suffering of these refugees and agreed to resettle up to 1,200 after they went through the US government's rigorous refugee screening processes. … We also made clear that while we disagreed with their policy of detention, Australia is a critical ally – particularly in the Pacific – and a leader in humanitarian assistance and refugee resettlement globally.[113]

Before its new intake year began on 1 October 2017, just 54 refugees on Nauru and Manus Island were approved under the US resettlement program.[114] In November 2017, the revival of an offer by New Zealand to resettle 150 refugees, which was once described by an Immigration Minister as "putting sugar on the table for people smugglers", was being viewed by the Australian government as potentially damaging to diplomatic relations with New Zealand.[115]

---

[112] Crépeau, above n 3, 9 [36].

[113] Heather Higginbottom, 'You Probably Missed the Big Story Buried in the Latest Trump Leaks', *Time* (online), 10 August 2017 <http://time.com/4894058/donald-trump-malcolm-turn bull-refugees-famine/>.

[114] Calla Wahlquist, 'First Manus Island-held Refugees Flown to US Under Resettlement Deal', *The Guardian* (online), 26 September 2017 <www.theguardian.com/world/2017/sep/26/first-manus-island-held-refugees-flown-to-us-under-resettlement-deal>.

[115] Brendan Nicholson, 'New Zealand to Take 150 Asylum-Seekers from Australia', *The Australian* (online), 10 February 2013, quoting Scott Morrison, <www.theaustralian.com.au/national-affairs/new-zealand-to-take-asylum-seekers-from-australia/news-story/0c1e8c7d37ef d154b8756ba337b141b2>; Paul Karp and Eleanor Ainge Roy, 'New Zealand Seeks Deal with Australia to Resettle Manus and Nauru Refugees' *The Guardian* (online), 17 November 2017 <www.theguardian.com/australia-news/2017/nov/17/new-zealand-and-png-could-do-deal-on-r efugees-peter-dutton-says>.

DEATH, CRUELTY, AND INHUMANITY

On 10 August 2016, more than 2,000 incident reports from the Nauru detention facility were published by *The Guardian*.[116] De-identified, the reports –
which became known as 'The Nauru Files' – documented incidents that had
taken place in the detention centre in Nauru, categorised in a *Guardian*
database by severity and type. Following their publication, the Department
of Immigration issued a short statement in which it described the files as
"evidence of the rigorous reporting procedures that are in place in the regional
processing centre".[117] It also said that "Many of the incident reports reflect
unconfirmed allegations or uncorroborated statements and claims – they are
not statements of proven fact."[118] In addition, on four occasions within the
same statement, the Department disclaimed direct responsibility by describing the Australian Government as providing "support" to the Nauruan
Government to, for example, "protect children from abuse, neglect or
exploitation".[119]

In her foreword to the report of an inquiry by the Senate Legal and
Constitutional Affairs References Committee convened in the wake of the
publication of the 'Nauru Files', the Chair of that inquiry, Senator Louise
Pratt, described the reports as painting the picture of "a deeply troubled
asylum seeker and refugee population, and an unsafe living environment –
especially for children."[120] She described "clear failures by the department in
administering the current policy in a safe and transparent manner" and "a lack
of accountability" that she characterised as "disturbing".[121] Decrying the
secrecy of offshore operations, she emphasised the "duty of care" that the
Australian Government has towards asylum seekers who are subject to offshore
detention and processing and the need for the Australian Government to
acknowledge the (effective) control that it has (but denies) over the centres,
and for which Australian taxpayers bear all the costs.[122] In contrast, a dissenting

---

[116] 'The Nauru Files', *The Guardian* (online) <www.theguardian.com/news/series/nauru-files>.
[117] DIBP, 'The Nauru Files' (Media Release, 10 August 2016) <http://newsroom.border.gov.au/
releases/the-nauru-files>.
[118] Ibid.   [119] Ibid.
[120] Senate Legal and Constitutional Affairs References Committee, Parliament of Australia,
*Serious Allegations of Abuse, Self-Harm and Neglect of Asylum Seekers in relation to the
Nauru Regional Processing Centre, and Any Like Allegations in relation to the Manus
Regional Processing Centre* (Report, April 2017) v.
[121] Ibid.
[122] Ibid vi. On the question of 'effective control' see also Legal and Constitutional Affairs
References Committee, Parliament of Australia, *Incident at the Manus Island Detention
Centre from 16 February to 18 February 2014* (Report, December 2014) 133–8; Select
Committee on the Recent Allegations relating to Conditions and Circumstances at the

report issued by Government senators described the inquiry itself as, among other things, a "politically-motivated public-relations stunt" seeking to "tarnish" the "success" of the policy "by inference and hearsay".[123] Without citing examples, it alleged that the report was "highly speculative" and relied "consistently" on "anecdotal evidence, second- and third-hand reports, and on unsupported allegations that are presented as fact".[124]

Since declining to visit Australia, Nauru, and Manus Island in the absence of assurances that individuals speaking to him would not suffer intimidation or sanction under the *ABF Act*,[125] the Special Rapporteur on the Human Rights of Migrants has visited Australia and Nauru. Following that visit, he concluded that refugees and asylum seekers are subject to conditions in Australia and on Nauru that are "cruel, inhuman and degrading".[126] The Special Rapporteur's report was considered at the 35th session of the UN Human Rights Council in June 2017. In response, the Australian Government reportedly asserted that the Special Rapporteur's report contained a "considerable number"[127] of errors of fact and law and objected to the Special Rapporteur having produced one report in relation to visits to "two independent sovereign nations".[128]

According to the Special Rapporteur,

[p]rolonged and indefinite detention has a profound effect on migrants' mental well-being, with many cases reported of self-harm, post-traumatic stress disorder, anxiety and depression. It is not the right environment for

---

Regional Processing Centre in Nauru, Parliament of Australia, *Taking Responsibility: Conditions and Circumstances at Australia's Regional Processing Centre in Nauru* (Report, August 2015) 12–15. For a critical appraisal of expenditure and contract management in the context of offshore processing, see Australian National Audit Office (ANAO), *Offshore Processing Centres in Nauru and Papua New Guinea: Procurement of Garrison Support and Welfare Services* (Audit Report No 16 of 2016–2017, September 2016), and ANAO, *Offshore Processing Centres in Nauru and Papua New Guinea – Contract Management of Garrison Support and Welfare Services* (ANAO Report No 32 of 2016–2017, January 2017).

[123] Ibid 183. [124] Ibid. [125] See above n 64.

[126] Crépeau, above n 3, 12 [57], 16 [80]; Tekendra Parmar, 'The UN Special Rapporteur on Migrant Rights Says Australia's Refugee Island Is 'Inhuman'', *Time* (online) 17 November 2016 (François Crépeau) <http://time.com/4575976/australia-nauru-refugees-un-francois-crepeau/>.

[127] Henry Belot, 'Nauru a "Blemish" on Australia's Human Rights Record, UN Official Says', *ABC News* (online), 10 June 2017 <www.abc.net.au/news/2017-06-10/nauru-a-blemish-on-australias-human-rights-record:-un-official/8606960>. This article appears to be reporting on the Australian Government's oral intervention at the UN Human Rights Council. In Australia's written response, above n 89, it is claimed that the response makes suggestions 'to correct errors of fact or law'. However, the response is more in the nature of a declaration of the state party's position.

[128] Government of Australia, *Comments by the State*, above n 89.

often already traumatized people. ... The Special Rapporteur joins the
voices of other United Nations human rights mechanisms in saying that
such conditions amount to cruel, inhuman and degrading treatment.[129]

Since Operation Sovereign Borders commenced in September 2013, there
have been 68 'border deaths' in Australia, including 16 deaths in custody either
onshore or offshore.[130] The causes of death have varied and have included
murder, bacterial infection, suicide (including by self-immolation), drowning, natural causes, and alleged delays in providing medical treatment.

THE NEW NORMAL?

In October 2016, one of the architects of Operation Sovereign Borders,
retired Major General Jim Molan, described the scheme as "the new
normal".[131]

---

[129] Crépeau, above n 3, 12 [57].
[130] See Australian Border Deaths Database, which maintains a record of all known deaths
associated with Australia's borders since 1 January 2000: <http://artsonline.monash.edu.au/
thebordercrossingobservatory/publications/australian-border-deaths-database/>. The database indicates a total of 1,994 border deaths since 1 January 2000, including drownings and
assumed drownings, 40 deaths following interdiction at sea (which the database characterises
as deaths in custody), and 35 further deaths in custody prior to Operation Sovereign Borders.
Note that at the time of writing the database did not include the latest death on Manus Island:
Michael Koziol, 'Asylum Seeker on Manus Island Found Dead' *Sydney Morning Herald*
(online), 7 August 2017 <www.smh.com.au/federal-politics/political-news/refugee-on-manus-
island-found-dead-20170807-gxqq2o.html>. See also Leanne Weber and Sharon Pickering,
Globalization and Borders: Death at the Global Frontier (Palgrave Macmillan, 2011).
[131] ABC, 'A Focus on Australia's Refugee Policy', *Q&A*, 10 October 2016 (Jim Molan) 01:09:41.

Bibliography

A ARTICLES AND WORKING PAPERS

Agoustinos, Martha, and Danielle Every, 'The Language of "Race" and Prejudice: A Discourse of Denial, Reason, and Liberal-Practical Politics' (2007) 26(2) *Journal of Language and Social Psychology* 123

Aybay, Rona, 'The Right to Leave and the Right to Return: The International Aspect of Freedom of Movement' (1978) 1 *Comparative Law Yearbook* 121

Bagaric, Mirko, and John R Morss, 'State Sovereignty and Migration Control: The Ultimate Act of Discrimination?' (2005) 1(1) *Journal of Migration and Refugee Issues* 25

Bailey, Jacqueline, 'Australia and Asylum Seekers: Is a Policy of Protection in the "National Interest"?' (2002) 8(1) *Australian Journal of Human Rights* 57

Bashford, Alison, and Jane McAdam, 'The Right to Asylum: Britain's 1905 Aliens Act and the Evolution of Refugee Law' (2014) 32(2) *Law and History Review* 309, 327

Bauder, Harald, 'Why We Should Use the Term "Illegalized" Refugee or Immigrant: A Commentary' (2014) 26(3) *International Journal of Refugee Law* 327

Beaulac, Stéphane, 'Emer de Vattel and the Externalization of Sovereignty' (2003) 5 *Journal of the History of International Law* 237

Betts, Katharine, 'The Problem of Defining Borders in Western Democracies' (1995) 6(1) *The Social Contract* 28

'Boat People and Public Opinion in Australia' (2001) 9(4) *People and Place* 34

Billings, Peter, 'Refugees, The Rule of Law and Executive Power: A(nother) Case of the Conjuror's Rabbit?' (2003) 54(4) *Northern Ireland Legal Quarterly* 412

Boletsi, Maria, 'Barbaric Encounters: Rethinking Barbarism in C P Cavafy's and J M Coetzee's *Waiting for the Barbarians*' (2007) 44(1/2) *Comparative Literature Studies* 67

Bostock, Chantal Marie-Jeanne, 'The International Legal Obligations Owed to the Asylum Seekers on the MV *Tampa*' (2002) 14 (2/3) *International Journal of Refugee Law* 279

Brown, Mannie, 'Expatriation of Infants: Being a Study in the Conflict of Laws between Canada and the United States' (1939) 3(1) *University of Toronto Law Journal* 97

Brubaker, William Rogers, 'The French Revolution and the Invention of Citizenship' (1989) 7(3) *French Politics and Society* 30

Cavallar, Georg, 'Vitoria, Grotius, Pufendorf, Wolff and Vattel: Accomplices of European Colonialism and Exploitation or True Cosmopolitans?' (2008) 10 *Journal of the History of International Law* 181

Charlesworth, Hilary, 'Feminist Methods in International Law' (1999) 93(2) *American Journal of International Law* 379

Chock, Phyllis Pease, 'Ambiguity in Policy Discourse: Congressional Talk about Immigration' (1995) 28(2) *Policy Sciences* 165

Cholewinski, Ryszard, 'Enforced Destitution of Asylum Seekers in the United Kingdom: The Denial of Fundamental Human Rights' (1998) 10(3) *International Journal of Refugee Law* 462

Cooney, Sean, 'The Codification of Migration Policy: Excess Rules?' (Pt 1) (1994) 1(3) *Australian Journal of Administrative Law* 125

Cover, Robert M, 'Violence and the Word' (1986) 95 *Yale Law Journal* 1601

Crock, Mary E, 'Climbing Jacob's Ladder: The High Court and the Administrative Detention of Asylum Seekers in Australia' (1993) 15(3) *Sydney Law Review* 338

Cunningham-Parmeter, Keith, 'Alien Language: Immigration Metaphors and the Jurisprudence of Otherness' (2011) 79(4) *Fordham Law Review* 1545

Dauvergne, Catherine, 'The Dilemma of Rights Discourses for Refugees' (2000) 23(3) *University of New South Wales Law Journal* 56

'Sovereignty, Migration and the Rule of Law in Global Times' (2004) 67(4) *Modern Law Review* 588

Davidson, Donald, 'What Metaphors Mean' (1978) 5(1) *Critical Inquiry* 31

Department of Immigration and Multicultural Affairs, 'Bridging Visas and Bridging Visa Es' (2006) 14(2) *People and Place* 39

Devetak, Richard, 'In Fear of Refugees: The Politics of Border Protection in Australia' (2004) 8(1) *International Journal of Human Rights* 101

Dorsett, Shaunnagh, and Shaun McVeigh, 'An Essay on Jurisprudence, Jurisdiction and Authority: The High Court of Australia in *Yorta Yorta* (2001)' (2005) 56(1) *Northern Ireland Legal Quarterly* 1

Edwards, Alice, 'Human Rights, Refugees, and the Right "To Enjoy" Asylum' (2005) 17(2) *International Journal of Refugee Law* 293

Evans, Simon, 'The Rule of Law, Constitutionalism and the *MV Tampa*' (2002) 13(2) *Public Law Review* 94

Ewald, Janet, 'Crossers of the Sea: Slaves, Freedmen, and Other Migrants in the Northwestern Indian Ocean, c 1750–1914' (2000) 105(1) *The American Historical Review* 69

Feller, Erika, 'Carrier Sanctions and International Law' (1989) 1(1) *International Journal of Refugee Law* 48

Fitzpatrick, Peter, 'Racism and the Innocence of Law' (1987) 14(1) *Journal of Law and Society* 119

Foster, Michelle, 'An "Alien" by the Barest of Threads': The Legality of the Deportation of Long-Term Residents from Australia' (2009) 33 *Melbourne University Law Review* 483

Francis, Angus, 'The Review of Australia's Asylum Laws and Policies: A Case for Strengthening Parliament's Role in Protecting Rights through Post-Enactment Scrutiny' (2008) 32(1) *Melbourne University Law Review* 83

Giannacopoulos, Maria, 'Offshore Hospitality: Law, Asylum and Colonisation' (2013) 17 *Law, Texture, Culture* 163

Grahl-Madsen, Atle, 'The European Tradition of Asylum and the Development of International Refugee Law' (1966) 3(3) *Journal of Peace and Research* 278

Gross, Leo, 'The Peace of Westphalia, 1648–1948' (1948) 42(1) *American Journal of International Law* 20

Hyslop, Jonathon, 'The Imperial Working Class Makes Itself White' (1999) 12(4) *Journal of Historical Sociology* 398

Johnson, Mark, 'Law Incarnate' (2002) 67 *Brooklyn Law Review* 959
    'Mind, Metaphor, Law' (2007) 58 *Mercer Law Review* 845

Juss, Satvinder S, 'Free Movement and the World Order' (2004) 16(3) *International Journal of Refugee Law* 289

Kelsay, John, 'Al-Shaybani and the Islamic Law of War' (2003) 2(1) *Journal of Military Ethics* 63

Kennedy, David, 'Primitive Legal Scholarship' (1986) 27(1) *Harvard International Law Journal* 1

Koskenniemi, Martti, 'International Law in Europe: Between Tradition and Renewal' (2005) 16(1) *European Journal of International Law* 113

Lakoff, George, 'Metaphor and War: The Metaphor System Used to Justify War in the Gulf' (Pt 1) (1991) 3(3) *Viet Nam Generation: A Journal of Recent History and Contemporary Issues* <www2.iath.virginia.edu/sixties/html_docs/journal.html>

Lee, Everett S, 'A Theory of Migration' (1966) 3(1) *Demography* 47

Lee, Joseph, 'Anti-Chinese Legislation in Australasia' (1889) 3(2) *The Quarterly Journal of Economics* 218

Legomsky, Stephen H, 'Immigration Law and the Principle of Plenary Congressional Power' (1984) 84 *Supreme Court Review* 255

Lester, Eve, 'Work, the Right to Work, and Durable Solutions? A Study on Sierra Leonean Refugees in The Gambia' (2005) 17(2) *International Journal of Refugee Law* 331
    'Imagining the "Promise of Justice" in the Prohibition on Racial Discrimination: Paradoxes and Prospects' [2007] *International and Humanitarian Law Resources* 8 <www.worldlii.org/int/journals/ihlres/2007/8.html>
    'Internationalising Constitutional Law: An Inward-Looking Outlook' (2016) 42(2) *Australian Feminist Law Journal* 321

Lindsay, Matthew J, 'Immigration, Sovereignty, and the Constitution of Foreignness' (2013) 45(3) *Connecticut Law Review* 743

McAdam, Jane, 'An Intellectual History of Freedom of Movement in International Law: The Right to Leave as a Personal Liberty' (2011) 12(1) *Melbourne Journal of International Law* 27
    'Australia and Asylum Seekers' (2013) 25(3) *International Journal of Refugee Law* 435

McMaster, Don, 'Asylum-Seekers and the Insecurity of a Nation' (2002) 56(2) *Australian Journal of International Affairs* 279

Magner, Tara, 'A Less than "Pacific" Solution for Asylum Seekers in Australia' (2004) 16(1) *International Journal of Refugee Law* 53

Mares, Peter, 'A Routine Removal' (2007) 18 *Griffith Review* 205

'Refuge without Work: "This Is a Poison, a Poison for the Life of a Person"' (2014) 45 *Griffith Review* 103

Markey, Raymond, 'Race and Organized Labor in Australia, 1850–1901' (1996) 58(2) *Historian* 343

Martin, David, 'Effects of International Law on Migration Policy and Practice: The Uses of Hypocrisy' (1989) 23(3) *International Migration Review* 547

Martyna, Wendy, 'What Does "He" Mean? Use of the Generic Masculine' (1978) 28(1) *Journal of Communication* 131

Mathew, Penelope, 'Sovereignty and the Right to Seek Asylum: The Case of Cambodian Asylum Seekers in Australia' (1994) 15 *Australian Yearbook of International Law* 35

'Australian Refugee Protection in the Wake of the *Tampa*' (2002) 96(3) *American Journal of International Law* 661

Millbank, Adrienne, 'No Compromise, No Quarter, No Controls – No International Asylum System' (2006) 14(2) *People and Place* 42

Mitchell, Grant, Sara Kisner, Katherine Marshall, and Stancea Vichie, 'Welfare Issues and Immigration Outcomes: Asylum Seekers Living in Australia on Bridging Visa E' (2003) 25(3) *Migration Action* 20

Motomura, Hiroshi, 'Immigration Law after a Century of Plenary Power: Phantom Constitutional Norms and Statutory Interpretation' (1990) 100(3) *Yale Law Journal* 545

Nafziger, James A R, 'The General Admission of Aliens under International Law' (1983) 77(4) *American Journal of International Law* 804

Nairn, Raymond G, and Timothy N McCreanor, 'Race Talk and Common Sense: Patterns in Pakeha Discourse on Maori/Pakeha Relations in New Zealand' (1991) 10(4) *Journal of Language and Social Psychology* 245

North, Justice A M, and Peace Decle, 'Courts and Immigration Detention: The Australian Experience' (2002) 10(1) *Australian Journal of Administrative Law* 5

O'Brien, Gerald V, 'Indigestible Food, Conquering Hordes, and Waste Materials: Metaphors of Immigrants and the Early Immigration Restriction Debate in the United States' (2003) 18(1) *Metaphor & Symbol* 33

Ontiveros, Maria, 'Noncitizen Immigrant Labor and the Thirteenth Amendment: Challenging Guest Worker Programs' (2007) 38(3) *University of Toledo Law Review* 923

Opeskin, Brian, 'Managing International Migration in Australia: Human Rights and the "Last Major Redoubt of Unfettered National Sovereignty"' (2012) 46(3) *International Migration Review* 551

Orford, Anne, 'In Praise of Description' (2012) 25(3) *Leiden Journal of International Law* 609

'On International Legal Method' (2013) 1(1) *London Review of International Law* 166

Pickering, Sharon, 'Common Sense and Original Deviancy: News Discourses and Asylum Seekers in Australia' (2001) 14(2) *Journal of Refugee Studies* 169

and Caroline Lambert, 'Deterrence: Australia's Refugee Policy' (2002) 14(1) *Current Issues in Criminal Justice* 65

Pimentel, Kevin, 'To Yick Wo, Thanks for Nothing! Citizenship for Filipino Veterans' (1999) 4(2) *Michigan Journal of Race Law* 459

Poynder, Nick, 'Marooned in Port Hedland' (1993) 18(6) *Alternative Law Journal* 272

'An Opportunity for Justice Goes Begging: *Chu Kheng Lim v Minister for Immigration, Local Government and Ethnic Affairs*' (1994) 1(1) *Australian Journal of Human Rights* 414

'The Incommunicado Detention of Boat People' (1997) 3(2) *Australian Journal of Human Rights* 53

Ritter, David, 'The "Rejection of Terra Nullius" in *Mabo*: A Critical Analysis' (1996) 18(1) *Sydney Law Review* 5

Rubenstein, Kim, 'Citizenship and the Constitutional Convention Debates: A Mere Legal Inference' (1997) 25(2) *Federal Law Review* 295

'Citizenship and the Centenary – Inclusion and Exclusion in 20th Century Australia' (2000) 24 *Melbourne University Law Review* 576

'Citizenship, Sovereignty and Migration: Australia's Exclusive Approach to Membership of the Community' (2002) 13(2) *Public Law Review* 102

Rubiés, Joan-Pau, 'Hugo Grotius's Dissertation on the Origin of the American Peoples and the Use of Comparative Methods' (1991) 52(2) *Journal of the History of Ideas* 221

Ruddock, Philip, 'The Broad Implications for Administrative Law under the Coalition Government with Particular Reference to Migration Matters' (1997) 48 *Administrative Review* 4

Schloenhardt, Andreas, 'Australia and the Boat People: 25 Years of Unauthorised Arrivals' (2000) 23(3) *University of New South Wales Law Journal* 33

and Colin Craig, '"Turning Back the Boats": Australia's Interdiction of Irregular Migrants at Sea' (2015) 27(4) *International Journal of Refugee Law* 536

Senanayake, Sanjaya N, and Mark J Ferson, 'Detention for Tuberculosis: Public Health and the Law' (2004) 180(11) *Medical Journal of Australia* 573

Simpson, Gerry, '*Mabo*, International Law, *Terra Nullius* and the Stories of Settlement: An Unresolved Jurisprudence' (1993) 19(1) *Melbourne University Law Review* 195

Skinner, Quentin, 'Meaning and Understanding in the History of Ideas' (1969) 8 *History and Theory* 3

Sultan, Aamer, and Kevin O'Sullivan, 'Psychological Disturbances in Asylum Seekers Held in Long Term Detention: A Participant–Observer Account' (2001) 175(11) *Medical Journal of Australia* 593

Steel, Zachary, and Derrick M Silove, 'The Mental Health Implications of Detaining Asylum Seekers' (2001) 175(11) *Medical Journal of Australia* 596

Stronks, Martijn C, 'The Question of Salah Sheekh: Derrida's Hospitality and Migration Law' (2012) 8(1) *International Journal of Law in Context* 73

Taylor, Savitri, 'Do On-Shore Asylum Seekers have Economic and Social Rights? Dealing with the Moral Contradiction of Liberal Democracy' (2000) 1 *Melbourne Journal of International Law* 70

'Should Unauthorised Arrivals in Australia Have Free Access to Advice and Assistance?' (2000) 6(1) *Australian Journal of Human Rights* 34

'The Importance of Human Rights Talk in Asylum Seeker Advocacy: A Response to Catherine Dauvergne' (2001) 24(1) *University of New South Wales Law Journal* 191

Valenzuela-Vermehren, Luis, 'Vitoria, Humanism, and the School of Salamanca in Early Sixteenth-Century Spain: A Heuristic Overview' (2013) 16(2) *Logos: A Journal of Catholic Thought and Culture* 99

Williams, John M, 'Race, Citizenship and the Formation of the Australian Constitution: Andrew Inglis Clark and the "14th Amendment"' (1996) 42(1) *Australian Journal of Politics and History* 10

B BOOKS AND BOOK CHAPTERS

Aleinikoff, T Alexander, 'International Legal Norms and Migration: A Report' in T Alexander Aleinikoff and Vincent Chetail (eds), *Migration and International Legal Norms* (TMC Asser Press, 2003) 1

—— and Vincent Chetail (eds), *Migration and International Legal Norms* (TMC Asser Press, 2003)

Anghie, Antony, *Imperialism, Sovereignty and the Making of International Law* (Cambridge University Press, 2005)

Arbel, Efrat, Catherine Dauvergne, and Jenni Millbank (eds), *Gender Equality in Refugee Law: From the Margins to the Centre* (Routledge, 2014)

Bakker, Peter, and Khristo Kiuchukov (eds), *What Is the Romani Language?* (University of Hertfordshire Press, 2000)

Balibar, Étienne, 'Is There a "Neo-Racism"?' in Étienne Balibar and Immanuel Wallerstein, *Race, Nation, Class: Ambiguous Identities* (Chris Turner trans, Verso, 1991) [trans of: *Race, nation, classe* (first published 1988)]

—— *We, the People of Europe? Reflections on Transnational Citizenship* (James Swenson trans, Princeton University Press, 2004) [trans of: *Nous, citoyens d'Europe: Les Frontières, l'État, le peuple* (first published 2001)]

Banivanua-Mar, Tracey, *Violence and Colonial Dialogue: The Australian-Pacific Indentured Labor Trade* (University of Hawaii Press, 2007)

Bartelson, Jens, *A Genealogy of Sovereignty* (Cambridge University Press, 1995)

Beard, Jennifer L, *The Political Economy of Desire* (Routledge, 2007)

Benhabib, Seyla, *The Rights of Others: Aliens, Residents and Citizens* (Cambridge University Press, 2004)

Black, Max, 'Metaphor' in Mark Johnson (ed), *Philosophical Perspectives on Metaphor* (University of Minnesota Press, 1981) 63 (first published 1955)

—— *Models and Metaphors: Studies in Language and Philosophy* (Cornell University Press, first published 1954, 1962 ed)

Blackstone, Sir William, *Commentaries on the Laws of England* (Callaghan and Co, 1884, c 1883)

Blanning, Tim, *The Pursuit of Glory: Europe 1648–1815* (Penguin, 2008)

Blewett, Neal, *A Cabinet Diary: A Personal Record of the First Keating Government* (Wakefield Press, 1999)

Bloor, Meriel, and Thomas Bloor, *The Practice of Critical Discourse Analysis: An Introduction* (Routledge, 2nd ed, 2013)

Borschberg, Peter, *Hugo Grotius, the Portuguese and Free Trade in the East Indies* (NUS Press, 2011)

Brierly, James Leslie, *The Law of Nations: An Introduction to the International Law of Peace* (Sir Humphrey Waldock ed, Oxford University Press, 6th ed, 1963)

Bullimore, Tony, *Saved: The Extraordinary Tale of Survival and Rescue in the Southern Ocean* (Time Warner, 1997)

Campbell, Tom, *The Legal Theory of Ethical Positivism* (Aldershot, 1996)

Carens, Joseph H, *Culture, Citizenship, and Community: A Contextual Exploration of Justice and Evenhandedness* (Oxford University Press, 2000)

Cavallar, Georg, *The Rights of Strangers: Theories of International Hospitality, the Global Community, and Political Justice since Vitoria* (Ashgate, 2002)

Charlesworth, Hilary, *Writing in Rights: Australia and the Protection of Human Rights* (UNSW Press, 2002)

  Madelaine Chiam, Devika Hovell, and George Williams, *No Country Is an Island: Australia and International Law* (UNSW Press, 2006)

Chitty, Joseph, *A Treatise on the Law of Prerogatives of the Crown; and the relative Duties and Rights of the Subject* (Butterworths, 1820)

Cholewinski, Ryszard, *Migrant Workers in International Law: Their Protection in Countries of Employment* (Clarendon Press, 1997)

Chouliarki, Lilie, and Norman Fairclough, *Discourse in Late Modernity: Rethinking Critical Discourse Analysis* (Edinburgh University Press, 1999)

Clark, David J, and Gerard McCoy, *Habeas Corpus: Australia, New Zealand, the South Pacific* (Federation Press, 2000)

Constable, Marianne, *Just Silences: The Limits and Possibilities of Modern Law* (Princeton University Press, 2005)

Costello, Cathryn, *The Human Rights of Migrants in European Law* (Oxford University Press, 2016)

Craven, Matthew, *The International Covenant on Economic, Social and Cultural Rights: A Perspective on Its Development* (Clarendon Press, 1995)

Crock, Mary (ed), *Protection or Punishment: The Detention of Asylum-Seekers in Australia* (Federation Press, 1993)

  Immigration & Refugee Law in Australia (Federation Press, 1998)

Cronin, Kathryn, 'A Culture of Control: An Overview of Immigration Policy Making' in James Jupp and Marie Kabala (eds), *The Politics of Australian Immigration* (AGPS, 1993) 83

Curthoys, Ann, and Marilyn Lake (eds), *Connected Worlds: History in Transnational Perspective* (ANU E Press, 2005)

Darian-Smith, Eve, *Religion, Race, Rights: Landmarks in the History of Modern Anglo-American Law* (Hart, 2010)

Dauvergne, Catherine, 'Illegal Migration and Sovereignty' in Catherine Dauvergne (ed), *Jurisprudence for an International Globe* (Ashgate, 2003) 187

  Humanitarianism, Identity and Nation: Migration Laws of Australia and Canada (University of British Columbia Press, 2005)

  Making People Illegal: What Globalization Means for Migration and Law (Cambridge University Press, 2008)

  'Refugee Law as Perpetual Crisis' in Satvinder Singh Juss and Colin Harvey (eds), *Contemporary Issues in Refugee Law* (Edward Elgar, 2013) 13

Davies, Margaret, *Asking the Law Question* (Law Book Company, 2008)

Devereux, Annemarie, *Australia and the Birth of the International Bill of Human Rights (1946–1966)* (Federation Press, 2005)

Dicey, A V, *Introduction to the Study of the Law of the Constitution* (Macmillan, 10th ed, first published 1959, 1961)

van Dijk, Teun A, *Elite Discourse and Racism* (Sage, 1993)

—— (ed), *Discourse Studies: A Multidisciplinary Introduction* (Sage, 2nd ed, 2011)

Döring, Detlef, 'Samuel von Pufendorf and Toleration' in John C Laursen and Cary J Nederman (eds), *Beyond the Persecuting Society: Religious Toleration before the Enlightenment* (University of Pennsylvania Press, 1998) 178

Dorsett, Shaunnagh, and Shaun McVeigh, *Jurisdiction* (Routledge, 2012)

Douzinas, Costas, *The End of Human Rights* (Hart, 2000)

Dryden, John, *The Poetical Works of John Dryden, with the Life of Virgil* (Milner and Sowerby, 1864)

Dumbauld, Edward, *The Life and Legal Writings of Hugo Grotius* (University of Oklahoma Press, 1969)

Duyker, Edward, 'Mauritians' in James Jupp (ed), *The Australian People: An Encyclopedia of the Nation, Its People and Their Origins* (Cambridge University Press, 2nd ed, 2001) 592

Edwards, Alice, 'Article 17' in Andreas Zimmermann (ed), *1951 Convention relating to the Status of Refugees and Its 1967 Protocol: A Commentary* (Oxford University Press, 2011) 951

—— 'Article 18' in Andreas Zimmermann (ed), *1951 Convention relating to the Status of Refugees and Its 1967 Protocol: A Commentary* (Oxford University Press, 2011) 973

—— 'Article 19' in Andreas Zimmermann (ed), *1951 Convention relating to the Status of Refugees and Its 1967 Protocol: A Commentary* (Oxford University Press, 2011) 983

Elliott, John H, *Imperial Spain: 1479–1716* (Penguin, 1963)

Escobar, Arturo, *Encountering Development: The Making and Unmaking of the Third World* (Princeton University Press, 1995)

Evans, Raymond, 'The White Australia Policy' in James Jupp (ed), *The Australian People: An Encyclopedia of the Nation, Its People and Their Origins* (Cambridge University Press, 2001) 46

Fairclough, Norman, *Language and Power* (Routledge, 2nd ed, 2013)

Fazal, Abdul Khaliq, 'Afghans' in James Jupp (ed), *The Australian People: An Encyclopedia of the Nation, Its People and Their Origins* (Cambridge University Press, 2nd ed, 2001) 164

Febvre, Lucien, '*Frontière*: The Word and the Concept' in Peter Burke (ed), *A New Kind of History: From the Writings of Febvre* (K Folca trans, Harper & Row, 1973) 208

Flournoy Jr, Richard W, and Manley O Hudson (eds), *A Collection of Nationality Laws of Various Countries, as Contained in Constitutions, Statutes and Treaties* (Oxford University Press, 1929)

Foucault, Michel, and Gilles Deleuze, 'Intellectuals and Power: A Conversation between Michel Foucault and Gilles Deleuze' in Donald F Bouchard (ed), *Language, Counter-Memory, Practice: Selected Essays and Interviews by Michel Foucault* (Donald F Bouchard and Sherry Simon trans, Cornell University Press 1977) 205 [trans of: 'Les intellectuels et le pouvoir' (first published 1972)]

Discipline and Punish: The Birth of the Prison (Alan Sheridan trans, Penguin, 1977) [trans of: *Surveiller et punir: Naissance de la prison* (first published 1975)]

'Nietzsche, Genealogy, History' in Donald F Bouchard (ed), *Language, Counter-Memory, Practice: Selected Essays and Interviews by Michel Foucault* (Donald F Bouchard and Sherry Simon trans, Cornell University Press 1977) 139 [trans of: 'Nietzsche, la généalogie, l'histoire' (first published 1971)]

The Archaeology of Knowledge (A M Sheridan-Smith trans, Routledge, 1989) [trans of: *L'archéologie du savoir* (first published 1969)]

'The Discourse of Language' in Hazard Adams and Leroy Searle (eds), *Critical Theory since 1965* (Florida State University Press, 1986) 148

'La philosophie analytique de la politique' in Daniel Defert and François Ewald (eds), with Jacques Lagrange, *Michel Foucault: Dits et écrits – 1954–1988* (Gallimard, 1994) vol 3, 534

The Order of Things: An Archaeology of the Human Sciences (A M Sheridan Smith trans, Routledge, 2002) 45 [trans of: *Les mots et les choses: Une archéologie des sciences humaines* (first published 1966)]

Francis, Angus J, 'Removing Barriers to Protection at the Exported Border: Visas, Carrier Sanctions, and International Obligation' in Jeremy Farrall and Kim Rubenstein (eds), *Sanctions, Accountability and Governance in a Globalised World* (Cambridge University Press, 2009) 378

Gaita, Raimond, *A Common Humanity: Thinking about Love and Truth and Justice* (Text Publishing, 1999)

Gao, Jia, 'Chinese Students in Australia' in James Jupp (ed), *The Australian People: An Encyclopedia of the Nation, Its People and Their Origins* (Cambridge University Press, 2001) 222

Gaurier, Dominique, 'Cosmopolis and Utopia' in Bardo Fassbender and Anne Peters (eds), *The Oxford Handbook of the History of International Law* (Oxford University Press, 2013) 250

Gleeson, Madeline, *Offshore: Behind the Wire on Manus and Nauru* (NewSouth Publishing, 2016)

Golder, Ben, and Peter Fitzpatrick, *Foucault's Law* (Routledge 2009)

Goodwin-Gill, Guy S, *International Law and the Movement of Persons between States* (Clarendon Press, 1978)

'Article 31 of the 1951 Convention relating to the Status of Refugees: Non-Penalization, Detention, and Protection' in Erika Feller, Volker Türk, and Frances Nicholson (eds), *Refugee Protection in International Law: UNHCR's Global Consultations on International Protection* (Cambridge University Press, 2003) 185

and Jane McAdam, *The Refugee in International Law* (Oxford University Press, 3rd ed, 2007)

Grotius, Hugo, *De jure praedae commentarius* (Gwladys L Williams and Walter H Zeydel trans, Clarendon Press, first published 1604, 1950 ed)

De jure belli ac pacis libri tres (Francis W Kelsey trans, Clarendon Press, first published 1646, 1925 ed) vol 2

Haakonssen, Knud, 'Samuel Pufendorf (1632–1694)' in Bardo Fassbender and Anne Peters (eds), *The Oxford Handbook of the History of International Law* (Oxford University Press, 2013) 1102

Haddad, Emma, *The Refugee in International Society: Between Sovereigns* (Cambridge University Press, 2008)

Haggenmacher, Peter, 'Hugo Grotius (1583–1645)' in Bardo Fassbender and Anne Peters (eds), *The Oxford Handbook of the History of International Law* (Oxford University Press, 2012) 1098

Harper, Marjory, and Stephen Constantine, *Migration and Empire* (Oxford University Press, 2010)

Hassan, Riaz, 'Pakistanis' in James Jupp (ed), *The Australian People: An Encyclopedia of the Nation, Its People and Their Origins* (Cambridge University Press, 2nd ed, 2001) 615

Hathaway, James C, *The Law of Refugee Status* (Butterworths, 1991)

The Rights of Refugees under International Law (Cambridge University Press, 2005)

Higgins, Claire, 'The (Un)-Sustainability of Australia's Offshore Processing and Settlement Policy' in Violeta Moreno-Lax and Efthymios Papastavridis (eds), *'Boat Refugees' and Migrants at Sea: A Comprehensive Approach* (Brill, 2016) 303

Asylum by Boat: Origin's of Australia's Refugee Policy (NewSouth Publishing, 2017)

Higgins, Rosalyn, 'Grotius and the Development of International Law in the United Nations Period' in Hedley Bull, Benedict Kingsbury, and Adam Roberts (eds), *Hugo Grotius and International Relations* (Clarendon Press, 1990) 267

Hirst, John, *The Sentimental Nation: The Making of the Australian Commonwealth* (Oxford University press, 2000)

Hobsbawm, Eric, *The Age of Empire: 1875–1914* (Abacus, 1987)

Honig, Bonnie, *Democracy and the Foreigner* (Princeton University Press, 2001)

Emergency Politics: Paradox, Law, Democracy (Princeton University Press, 2001)

Hughes, Aneurin, *Billy Hughes: Prime Minister and Controversial Founding Father of the Australian Labor Party* (Wiley, 2005)

Hunter, Ian, 'Global Justice and Regional Metaphysics: On the Critical History of the Law of Nature and Nations' in Shaunnagh Dorsett and Ian Hunter (eds), *Law and Politics in British Colonial Thought: Transpositions of Empire* (Palgrave Macmillan, 2010) 11

Huttenback, Robert A, *Racism and Empire: White Settlers and Coloured Immigrants in the British Self-Governing Colonies 1830–1910* (Cornell University Press, 1976)

Johnstone, Barbara, 'Linguistic Strategies and Cultural Styles for Persuasive Discourse' in Stella Ting-Toomey and Felipe Korzenny (eds), *Language, Communication, and Culture: Current Directions* (Sage, 1989) 139

Jupp, James (ed), *The Australian People: An Encyclopedia of the Nation, Its People and Their Origins* (Cambridge University Press, 2nd ed, 2001)

From White Australia to Woomera: The Story of Australian Immigration (Cambridge University Press, 2nd ed, 2007)

Juss, Satvinder S, *International Migration and Global Justice* (Ashgate, 2006)

Kälin, Walter, 'Supervising the 1951 Convention relating to the Status of Refugees: Article 35 and Beyond' in Erika Feller, Volker Türk, and Frances Nicholson (eds), *Refugee Protection in International Law: UNHCR's Global Consultations on International Protection* (Cambridge University Press, 2003) 613

Karatani, Rieko, *Defining British Citizenship: Empire, Commonwealth and Modern Britain* (Frank Cass, 2003)

Kneebone, Susan, 'The Australian Story: Asylum Seekers outside the Law' in Susan Kneebone (ed), *Refugees, Asylum Seekers and the Rule of Law: Comparative Perspectives* (Cambridge University Press, 2009) 171

Koskenniemi, Martti, '"International Community" from Dante to Vattel' in Vincent Chetail and Peter Haggenmacher (eds), *Vattel's International Law from a XXIst Century Perspective/Le Droit International de Vattel vu du XXIe Siècle* (Martinus Nijhoff, 2011) 51

Krasner, Stephen D, *Sovereignty: Organized Hypocrisy* (Princeton University Press, 1999)

Kristeva, Julia, *Strangers to Ourselves* (Leon S Roudiez trans, Columbia University Press, 1991) [trans of: *Etrangers à nous-même* (first published 1988)]

Lake, Marilyn, 'From Mississippi to Melbourne via Natal: The Invention of the Literacy Test as a Technology of Racial Exclusion' in Ann Curthoys and Marilyn Lake (eds), *Connected Worlds: History in Transnational Perspective* (ANU E Press, 2005)

and Henry Reynolds, *Drawing the Global Colour Line: White Men's Countries and the Question of Racial Equality* (Melbourne University Press, 2008)

Lakoff, George, and Mark Johnson, *Metaphors We Live By* (University of Chicago Press 1981)

Lal, Brij V, 'Indians' in James Jupp (ed), *The Australian People: An Encyclopedia of the Nation, Its People and Their Origins* (Cambridge University Press, 2nd ed, 2001) 426

Laursen, John C (ed), *Religious Toleration: 'The Variety of Rites' from Cyrus to Defoe* (St Martin's Press, 1999)

Lauterpacht, Elihu, and C J Greenwood (eds), *International Law Reports* (Cambridge University Press, 1963) vol 26

Lé, Marion, 'Reality: The Release of the *Isabella* Refugees' in Mary Crock (ed), *Protection or Punishment? The Detention of Asylum-Seekers in Australia* (Federation Press, 1993) 151

Legomsky, Stephen, 'The Last Bastions of State Sovereignty: Immigration and Nationality Go Global' in Andrew C Sobel (ed), *Challenges of Globalization: Immigration, Social Welfare, Global Governance* (Routledge, 2009) 43

Lesaffer, Randall, 'International Law and Its History: The Story of an Unrequited Love' in Matthew Craven, Malgosia Fitzmaurice, and Maria Vogiatzi (eds), *Time, History and International Law* (Martinus Nijhoff, 2007) 27

Lester, Eve, 'Article 20' in Andreas Zimmermann (ed), *1951 Convention relating to the Status of Refugees and Its 1967 Protocol: A Commentary* (Oxford University Press, 2011) 993

'Article 23' in Andreas Zimmermann (ed), *1951 Convention relating to the Status of Refugees and Its 1967 Protocol: A Commentary* (Oxford University Press, 2011) 1043

'Article 24' in Andreas Zimmermann (ed), *1951 Convention relating to the Status of Refugees and Its 1967 Protocol: A Commentary* (Oxford University Press, 2011) 1057

'Myth-Conceiving Sovereignty: The Legacy of the Nineteenth Century' in Kim Rubenstein, Mark Nolan, and Fiona Jenkins (eds), *Allegiance and Identity in a Globalised World* (Cambridge University Press, 2014) 354

McAdam, Jane, and Fiona Chong, *Refugees: Why Seeking Asylum Is Legal and Australia's Policies Are Not* (NewSouth Publishing, 2014)

McKeown, Adam M, *Melancholy Order: Asian Migration and the Globalization of Borders* (Columbia University Press, 2008)

McMaster, Don, *Asylum Seekers: Australia's Response to Refugees* (Melbourne University Press, 2002)

Mahon, Michael, *Foucault's Nietzschean Genealogy: Truth, Power and the Subject* (State University of New York Press, 1992)

Mann, Itamar, *Humanity at Sea: Maritime Migration and the Foundations of International Law* (Cambridge University Press, 2016)

Manning, Patrick, *Migration in World History* (Routledge, 2nd ed, 2013)

Mares, Peter, *Borderline: Australia's Response to Refugees and Asylum Seekers in the Wake of the* Tampa (UNSW Press, 2nd ed, 2002)

Marr, David, and Marian Wilkinson, *Dark Victory* (Allen & Unwin, 2003)

Marston, Daniel, *The Seven Years' War* (Routledge, 2012)

Martin, David A, 'The Authority and Responsibility of States' in T Alexander Aleinikoff and Vincent Chetail (eds), *Migration and International Legal Norms* (TMC Asser Press, 2003) 31

Mathew, Penelope, *Reworking the Relationship between Asylum and Employment* (Routledge, 2012)

Menzies, Robert, *Central Power in the Australian Commonwealth* (Caswell, 1967)

Merriman, John, *A History of Modern Europe: From the Renaissance to the Present* (W W Norton, 1996)

Moreno-Lax, Violeta, and Efthymios Papastavridis (eds), *'Boat Refugees' and Migrants at Sea: A Comprehensive Approach* (Brill, 2016)

Nail, Thomas, *The Figure of the Migrant* (Stanford University Press, 2015)

Theory of the Border (Oxford University Press, 2016)

Nethery, Amy, '"A Modern-Day Concentration Camp": Using History to Make Sense of Australian Immigration Detention Centres' in Klaus Neumann and Gwenda Tavan (eds), *Does History Matter? Making and Debating Citizenship, Immigration and Refugee Policy in Australia and New Zealand* (ANU E Press, 2009)

Neumann, Klaus, and Gwenda Tavan (eds), *Does History Matter? Making and Debating Citizenship, Immigration and Refugee Policy in Australia and New Zealand* (ANU E Press, 2009)

Across the Seas: Australia's Response to Refugees (Black Inc, 2015)

Newman, Jane O, '"Race", Religion, and the Law: Rhetorics of Sameness and Difference in the Work of Hugo Grotius' in Victoria Ann Kahn and Lorna Hutson (eds), *Rhetoric and Law in Early Modern Europe* (Yale University Press, 2001) 285

Nicholls, Glenn, *Deported: A History of Forced Departures from Australia* (UNSW Press, 2007)

'Gone with Hardly a Trace: Deportees in Immigration Policy' in Klaus Neumann and Gwenda Tavan (eds), *Does History Matter? Making and Debating Citizenship, Immigration and Refugee Policy in Australia and New Zealand* (ANU E Press, 2009)

Nietzsche, Friedrich, *The Gay Science* (Bernard Williams ed, Josefine Nauckhoff and Adrian Del Caro trans, Cambridge University Press, 2001) [trans of: *Die fröhliche Wissenschaft* (first published 1882)]

On the Genealogy of Morals: A Polemic (Douglas Smith trans, Oxford University Press, 1996) [trans of: *Zur Genealogie der Moral: Eine Streitschrift* (first published 1887)]

Noll, Gregor, 'Article 31' in Andreas Zimmermann (ed), *The 1951 Convention relating to the Status of Refugees and Its 1967 Protocol: A Commentary* (Oxford University Press, 2011) 1243

Nussbaum, Arthur, *A Concise History of the Law of Nations* (Macmillan, first published 1947, 1954 ed)

Oppenheim, Lassa, *International Law: A Treatise* (Hersch Lauterpacht ed, Longman, 8th ed, 1955)

Orford, Anne, *International Authority and the Responsibility to Protect* (Cambridge University Press, 2011)

Owen, David, *Nietzsche's Genealogy of Morality* (McGill-Queen's University Press, 2007)

Pahuja, Sundhya, *Decolonising International Law: Development, Economic Growth and the Politics of Universality* (Cambridge University Press, 2011)

Palfreeman, Anthony C, *The Administration of the White Australia Policy* (Melbourne University Press, 1967)

Parker, James E K, *Acoustic Jurisprudence: Listening to the Trial of Simon Bikindi* (Oxford University Press, 2015)

Parry, Clive, *Nationality and Citizenship Laws of the Commonwealth and of the Republic of Ireland* (Stevens, 1957–1960)

Pearson, Charles H, *National Life and Character: A Forecast* (Macmillan, 1893)

Phillimore, Sir Robert, *Commentaries upon International Law* (Butterworths, 3rd ed, 1879)

Plender, Richard, *International Migration Law* (Martinus Nijhoff, 2nd ed, 1988)

Porter, Bernard, *The Refugee Question in Mid-Victorian Politics* (Cambridge University Press, first published 1979, 2008 ed)

Price, Charles, 'Immigration and Ethnic Origin' in Wray Vamplew (ed), *Australians: Historical Statistics* (Fairfax, Syme and Weldon, 1987) 2

Pufendorf, Samuel, *Of the Nature and Qualification of Religion in Reference to Civil Society* (printed by D E for A Roper and A Bofvile, 1698) [trans of: *De habitu religionis Christianae ad vitam civilem* (first published 1687)], via Early English Books Online <http://eebo.chadwyck.com/home>

Elementorum jurisprudentiae universalis libri duo (W A Oldfather trans, Clarendon Press, first published 1672, 1931 ed)

De jure naturae et gentium libri octo (C H and W A Oldfather trans, Clarendon Press, first published 1688, 1934 ed)

On the Duty of Man and Citizen according to Natural Law (James Tully ed, Michael Silverthorne trans, Cambridge University Press, 1991) [trans of: *De officio hominis et civis juxta legem naturalem libri duo* (first published 1673)]

The Political Writings of Samuel Pufendorf (Craig L Carr ed, Michael J Seidler trans, Oxford University Press, 1994)

Queija, Berta Ares, Jésus Bustamante, and Francisco Castilla (eds), *Humanismo y visión del otro en la España moderna: cuatro estudios* (Biblioteca de Historia de América, CSIC, 1993)

Quick, John, and Robert Randolph Garran, *The Annotated Constitution of the Australian Commonwealth* (Angus & Robertson, 1901)

Rajah, Jothie, *Authoritarian Rule of Law: Legislation, Discourse and Legitimacy in Singapore* (Cambridge University Press, 2012)

Reher, David Sven, *Town and Country in Pre-Industrial Spain: Cuenca, 1550–1870* (Cambridge University Press, 1990)

Richards, Eric, *Destination Australia: Migration to Australia since 1901* (UNSW Press, 2008)

'Migrations: The Career of British White Australia' in Deryck M Schreuder and Stuart Ward (eds), *Australia's Empire* (Oxford University Press, 2008) 163

Ricoeur, Paul, 'The Metaphorical Process as Cognition, Imagination and Feeling' in Mark Johnson (ed), *Philosophical Perspectives on Metaphor* (University of Minnesota Press, 1981) 228 (first published in: (1978) 5(1) *Critical Inquiry* 143)

Rubenstein, Kim, *Australian Citizenship Law* (Law Book Company, 2nd ed, 2016)

Ruiz, Teofilo F, *Spanish Society: 1400–1600* (Longman, 2001)

Said, Edward W, *Orientalism* (Vintage, 1979)

Reflections on Exile: And Other Literary and Cultural Essays (Granta, 2001) (essay titled 'Reflection on Exile' 173)

Salyer, Lucy E, *Laws Harsh as Tigers: Chinese Immigrations and the Shaping of Modern Immigration Law* (University of North Carolina Press, 1995)

Sassen, Saskia, *Guests and Aliens* (The New Press, 1999)

Saunders, David, 'Hegemon History: Pufendorf's Shifting Perspectives on France and French Power' in Olaf Asbach and Peter Schröder (eds), *War, the State and International Law in the Seventeenth Century* (Ashgate, 2010) 211

Schiffrin, Deborah, Deborah Tannen and Heidi E Hamilton, *The Handbook of Discourse Analysis* (Blackwell, 2001)

Schotel, Bas, *On the Right of Exclusion: Law Ethics and Immigration Policy* (Routledge, 2012)

Scott, James Brown, *The Spanish Origin of International Law: Francisco de Vitoria and His Law of Nations* (Lawbook Exchange, first published 1934, 2000 ed)

Scott, Joanne, Ross Laurie, Bronwyn Stevens, and Patrick Weller, *The Engine Room of Government: The Queensland Premier's Department 1859–2001* (University of Queensland Press, 2001)

Segel, Harold B, *Egon Erwin Kisch, the Raging Reporter: A Bio-Anthology* (Purdue University Press, 1997)

Shaybānī, Muḥammad ibn al-Ḥasan (ca 750–804 or 5), *The Islamic Law of Nations: Shaybānī's Siyar* (Majid Khadduri trans, Johns Hopkins Press, 1966)

Shimazu, Naoko, *Japan, Race and Equality: The Racial Equality Proposal of 1919* (Routledge, 1998)

Shuy, Roger W, 'Discourse Analysis in the Legal Context' in Deborah Schiffrin, Deborah Tannen, and Heidi E Hamilton (eds), *The Handbook of Discourse Analysis* (Blackwell, 2001) 437

Sibert, Marcel, *Traité de Droit International Public: Le Droit de la Paix* (Dalloz, 1951) vol I

Simeon, James C (ed), *The UNHCR and the Supervision of International Refugee Law* (Cambridge University Press, 2013)

Skinner, Quentin, *Visions of Politics: Volume I – Regarding Method* (Cambridge University Press, 2002)

Stanner, W E H, 'The Boyer Lectures: After the Dreaming (1968)' in W E H Stanner, *The Dreaming and Other Essays* (Black Inc, first published 2009, 2010 ed) 172

Stoye, John, *Europe Unfolding: 1648–1688* (Oxford, 2nd ed, 2000)

Strydom, Piet, *Discourse and Knowledge: The Making of Enlightenment Sociology* (Liverpool University Press, 2000)

Tamanaha, Brian Z, *On the Rule of Law: History, Politics, Theory* (Cambridge University Press, 2004)

Tavan, Gwenda, *The Long Slow Death of White Australia* (Scribe, 2005)

Thwaites, Rayner, *The Liberty of Non-Citizens: Indefinite Detention in Commonwealth Countries* (Hart, 2014)

Torpey, John, *The Invention of the Passport: Surveillance, Citizenship and the State* (Cambridge University Press, 2000)

Vassberg, David E, *The Village and the Outside World in Golden Age Castile: Mobility and Migration in Everyday Rural Life* (Cambridge University Press, 1996)

Vattel, Emmerich de, *The Law of Nations; or, Principles of the Law of Nature, Applied to the Conduct and Affairs of Nations and Sovereigns* (Joseph Chitty ed and trans, Lawbook Exchange, first published 1854, 2005 ed) [trans of: *Le Droit des gens; ou Principes de la loi naturelle, appliqués à la conduite et aux affaires des Nations et des Souverains* (first published 1758)]

Vicens Vives, Jaime and Jorge Nadal Oller, *An Economic History of Spain* (Frances M López-Morillas trans, Princeton University Press, 1969) [trans of: *Manuel de historia económica de España* (first published 1955 as *Apuntes del curso de historia económica de España*)]

Vile, M J C, *Constitutionalism and the Separation of Powers* (Liberty Fund, 2nd ed, 1998)

Vitoria, Francisco de, *Political Writings* (Anthony Pagden and Jeremy Lawrance eds, Jeremy Lawrance trans, Cambridge University Press, 1991)

Viviani, Nancy, *The Indochinese in Australia, 1975–1995: From Burnt Boats to Barbecues* (Oxford University Press, 1996)

Walton, Douglas, *Argumentation Methods for Artificial Intelligence in Law* (Springer, 2005)

Wang, Sing-Wu, 'Chinese Immigration 1840s–1890s' in James Jupp (ed), *The Australian People: An Encyclopedia of the Nation, Its People and Their Origins* (Cambridge University Press, 2001) 197

Weber, Leanne, and Sharon Pickering, *Globalization and Borders: Death at the Global Frontier* (Palgrave Macmillan, 2011)

Weeramantry, Christopher, *Justice without Frontiers: Furthering Human Rights* (Martinus Nijhoff, 1997) vol 1

Weis, Paul, *Nationality and Statelessness in International Law* (Sijthoff & Noordhoff, 2nd ed, 1979)

Whelan, Ruth, and Carol Baxter, *Toleration and Religious Identity: The Edict of Nantes and Its Implications in France, Britain and Ireland* (Four Courts Press, 2003)

Wickham, Gary, 'Foucault and Law' in Reza Banakar and Max Travers (eds), *An Introduction to Law and Social Theory* (Hart, 2002) 249

Williams Jr, Robert A, *The American Indian in Western Legal Thought: The Discourses of Conquest* (Oxford University Press, 1990)

Winter, Steven L, *A Clearing in the Forest: Law, Life and Mind* (University of Chicago Press, 2003)
Zieck, Marjoleine, 'Article 35 1951 Convention/Article II 1967 Protocol' in Andreas Zimmermann (ed), *The 1951 Convention relating to the Status of Refugees and Its 1967 Protocol: A Commentary* (Oxford University Press, 2011) 1459
Zimmermann, Andreas (ed), *The 1951 Convention relating to the Status of Refugees and Its 1967 Protocol: A Commentary* (Oxford University Press, 2011)

C INSTITUTIONAL AND ORGANISATIONAL REPORTS AND STATEMENTS

Asylum Seekers Resource Centre, 'Destitute and Uncertain: The Reality of Seeking Asylum in Australia' (October 2010) <www.asrc.org.au/pdf/asrc-welfare-paper.pdf>
Australian Border Force, *Illegal Maritime Arrivals on Bridging Visa E* (DIBP, June 2017) <www.border.gov.au/about/reports-publications/research-statistics/statistics/live-in-australia/onshore-processing>
Australian Customs and Border Protection Service, *Operation Sovereign Borders: A Storyboard on People Smuggling* (1 November 2013) <http://newsroom.border .gov.au/channels/operation-sovereign-borders/photos/a-storyboard-on-people-smuggling>
Australian Human Rights Commission, 'Tell Me About: The "Enhanced Screening Process"' (June 2013) <https://www.humanrights.gov.au/publications/tell-me-about-enhanced-screening-process>
Australian Labor Party, 'National Platform and Constitution' (2007)
Australian National Audit Office, 'The Management of Boat People' (Commonwealth of Australia, 1998) <www.anao.gov.au/uploads/documents/1997–98_audit_report_32.pdf>
Buckmaster, Luke, 'Australian Government Assistance to Refugees: Fact v Fiction' (Background Note, Parliamentary Library, Parliament of Australia, 2012) <www.aph.gov.au/About_Parliament/Parliamentary_Departments/Parliamen tary_Library/pubs/BN/2012-2013/AustGovAssistRefugees>
Bull, Lauren, Elizabeth Colliver, Emily Fischer, Shawn Rajanayagam, and Edmund Simpson, 'Playing God: The Immigration Minister's Unrestrained Power' (Liberty Victoria, 2017)
Committee to Advise on Australia's Immigration Program, 'Immigration: A Commitment to Australia' (Report, 1988)
Cornall, Robert, 'Review into Allegations of Sexual and Other Serious Assaults at the Manus Regional Processing Centre' (Report to the Secretary, Department of Immigration and Border Protection, September 2013) (publication version) <https://www.immi.gov.au/about/dept-info/reviews-incidents.htm>
'Review into the Events of 16–18 February 2014 at the Manus Regional Processing Centre' (Report to the Secretary, Department of Immigration and Border Protection, 23 May 2014) (redacted version) <https://www.immi.gov.au/about/dept-info/reviews-incidents.htm>
Department of Immigration and Border Protection, 'Asylum Trends: Australia 2012–13 – Annual Publication' (2013) <https://www.immi.gov.au/media/publications/statistics/>

'Immigration Detention and Community Statistics Summary' (30 June 2014) <www
.immi.gov.au/about/pages/detention/about-immigration-detention.aspx>
Annual Report 2015–16 (15 September 2016) <www.border.gov.au/about/reports-pub
lications/reports/annual>
'IMA Legacy Caseload: Report on Status and Processing Outcomes' (February 2017)
<www.border.gov.au/ReportsandPublications/Documents/statistics/ima-legacy-case
load-feb-17.pdf>
Doctors for Refugees and Fitzroy Legal Service, 'Doctors for Refugees Inc v
Commonwealth of Australia – High Court of Australia', *Briefing Paper* (Doctors
for Refugees and Fitzroy Legal Service, 29 July 2016) <www.fitzroy-legal.org.au/
doctors_for_refugees>
Douglas, Bob, and Jo Wodak (eds), *Refugees and Asylum Seekers: Finding a Better Way*
(*Australia21*, 2013)
Edwards, Alice, *Back to Basics: The Right to Liberty and Security of Person and
'Alternatives to Detention' of Refugees, Asylum-Seekers, Stateless Persons and
Other Migrants*, UNHCR Doc PPLA/2011/01.Rev.1, April 2011 <www.unhcr.org/
refworld/docid/4dc935fd2.html>
Elvey, Frank, 'The Budget Fallout for Asylum Seekers' (Focus No 7, Uniya, 1996)
Hartley, Lisa, and Caroline Fleay, 'Policy as Punishment: Asylum Seekers in the
Community without the Right to Work' (Centre for Human Rights Education,
Curtin University, 2014) <http://apo.org.au/node/38122>
House of Representatives, *Infosheet 7 – Making Laws* (2010) Parliament of Australia
<www.aph.gov.au/about_parliament/house_of_representatives/powers_practi
ce_and_procedure/00_-_infosheets/infosheet_7_-_making_laws>
Houston, Angus, Paris Aristotle, and Michael L'Estrange, 'Report of the Expert Panel
on Asylum Seekers' (Australian Government, August 2012) <http://expertpanelo
nasylumseekers.dpmc.gov.au/>
Human Rights and Equal Opportunity Commission, 'Those Who've Come across the
Seas: Detention of Unauthorised Arrivals' (Report, 1998) <https://www.human
rights.gov.au/publications/asylum-seekers-and-refugees>
'Report of an Inquiry into a Complaint by the Asylum Seekers Centre concerning
Changes to the Asylum Seekers Assistance Scheme' (Report No 17, June 2002)
<https://www.humanrights.gov.au/publications/hreoc-report-no-17>
'A Last Resort? National Inquiry into Children in Immigration Detention' (Report,
April 2004) <https://www.humanrights.gov.au/publications/asylum-seekers-and-
refugees>
'Summary of Observations following the Inspection of Mainland Immigration
Detention Facilities' (2007) <www.hreoc.gov.au/pdf/human_rights/dima_id
c_20070119.pdf>
Jastram, Kate, and Marilyn Achiron, *Refugee Protection: A Guide to International
Refugee Law* (UNHCR/Inter-Parliamentary Union, 2001)
Jesuit Social Services, 'The Living Conditions of People Seeking Asylum in Australia'
(Jesuit Social Services, 2015)
Karlsen, Elibritt, 'Australia's Offshore Processing of Asylum Seekers in Nauru and
PNG: A Quick Guide to Statistics and Resources' (Research Paper Series, 2016–
17, Parliamentary Library, Parliament of Australia, 19 December 2016)

Liddy, Nadine, Sarah Sanders, and Caz Coleman, 'Australia's Hidden Homeless: Community-Based Options for Asylum Homelessness' (Hotham Mission Asylum Seeker Project, 2010)

McNevin, Anne, 'Seeking Safety, Not Charity: A Report in Support of Work-Rights for Asylum-Seekers Living in the Community on Bridging Visa E' (Network of Asylum Seeker Agencies Victoria, 2005)

Melbourne Institute of Applied Economic and Social Research, 'Poverty Lines: Australia' (June Quarter 2016)

Menadue, John, Arja Keski-Nummi, and Kate Gauthier, 'A New Approach. Breaking the Stalemate on Refugees and Asylum Seekers' (Centre for Policy Development, August 2011)

Millbank, Adrienne, 'The Detention of Boat People' (Current Issues Brief No 8 2000–01, Parliamentary Library, Parliament of Australia, 2001)

Moss, Philip, *Review into Recent Allegations relating to Conditions and Circumstances at the Regional Processing Centre in Nauru* (Final Report, 6 February 2015) <https://www.border.gov.au/reportsandpublications/docu ments/reviews-and-inquiries/review-conditions-circumstances-nauru.pdf>

O'Neill, Patrick, '"Was there an EM?" Explanatory Memoranda and Explanatory Statements in the Commonwealth Parliament' (Research Brief No 15, Parliamentary Library, Parliament of Australia, first published 2004–05, September 2006 ed) <www.aph.gov.au/about_parliament/parliamentary_depart ments/parliamentary_library/browse_by_topic/law/explanmem/wasther0eanem>

Purcell, Marc, 'Knife Edge: Surviving Asylum in the Australian Community' (Occasional Paper No 15, Melbourne Catholic Commission for Justice, Development and Peace, 2004)

Refugee Advice and Casework Service, 'Work Rights for People Who Arrived by Boat', RACS Fact Sheet (RACS, October 2015) <www.racs.org.au/wp-content/uploads/ racs-fact-sheet-work-rights-for-people-who-arrived-by-boat.pdf>

'BVEs and Work Rights for People Who Arrived by Boat', RACS Fact Sheet (RACS, updated August 2016) <www.racs.org.au/wp-content/uploads/2016/10/racs-fact-sh eet-bves-and-work-rights-for-people-who-arrived-by-boat-aug-2016.pdf>

'Briefing Note for Lawyers: Bridging Visas for People Seeking Asylum During Judicial Review', RACS Fact Sheet (RACS, updated October 2016) <www.racs .org.au/wp-content/uploads/2016/10/racs-fact-sheet-briefing-note-for-lawyers-on-br idging-visas-for-asylum-seekers-at-judicial-review.pdf>

Refugee Council of Australia, 'Statement on "illegal" boat arrivals' (RCOA, 15 November 1999) <https://www.refugeecouncil.org.au/docs/resources/ppapers/pp-boatarrivals-nov99.pdf>

'State of the Nation: Refugees and People Seeking Asylum in Australia' (RCOA Report No 1/17, February 2017) <www.refugeecouncil.org.au/publications/report s/state-nation-2017/>

'Recent Changes in Australian Refugee Policy' (RCOA Media Release, 8 June 2017) <www.refugeecouncil.org.au/publications/recent-changes-australian-ref ugee-policy/>

Senate Standing Committee for the Scrutiny of Bills, Parliament of Australia, *The Work of the Committee during the 40th Parliament February 2002–August 2004* (2008)

Trewin, Dennis, 'Year Book Australia' (Year Book No 83, Catalogue No 1301.0, Australian Bureau of Statistics, 2001)

UNHCR, 'Asylum-Seekers on Bridging Visas in Australia: Protection Gaps – UNHCR Consultation, 2013' (16 December 2013)

'UNHCR's Position on Manifestly Unfounded Applications for Asylum' (1 December 1992) <www.refworld.org/docid/3ae6b31d83.html>

'Populations of Concern to UNHCR: A Statistical Overview' (1994) <www.un hcr.org/3bfa33154.html>

'Representations to the Social Security Advisory Committee on the "Social Security (Persons from Abroad) Miscellaneous Amendment Regulations 1995"' (10 November 1995) <www.refworld.org/docid/3ae6b31daf.html>

'Displacement: The New 21st Century Challenge' (UNHCR Global Trends 2012, 19 June 2013)

'UNHCR Monitoring Visit to the Republic of Nauru: 7 to 9 October 2013' (26 November 2013)

'UNHCR Monitoring Visit to Manus Island, Papua New Guinea: 23 to 25 October 2013' (UNHCR, Canberra, 26 November 2013)

UNHCR Statistical Yearbook 2014 (UNHCR, 14th ed, 2015)

United Nations, *Yearbook of the United Nations, 1946–47* (United Nations, 1947)

Yearbook of the United Nations, 1948–49 (United Nations, 1949)

Vinson, Tony, Marie Leech, and Eve Lester, 'The Number of Boat People: Fact and Perception' (Brief Research Report No 1, Uniya, 1997)

Other Communications

Department of Immigration and Multicultural Affairs, 'DIMA Response to HREOC Report on Annual Visits to Immigration Detention Centres' (19 January 2007) <https://www.humanrights.gov.au/publications/summary-observations-following-inspection-mainland-immigration-detention-facilities-0>

D CONFERENCE AND OTHER PAPERS AND STATEMENTS

Abbott, Tony, Prime Minister, Statement to the House of Representatives, Closing the Gap, Parliament House, Canberra, 12 February 2014

Abbott, Tony, Second Annual Margaret Thatcher Lecture, London, 27 October 2015 <https://www.thatchercentre.com/events/annual-lecture/ii/>

Address to the Alliance of European Conservatives and Reformists, Lobkowicz Palace, Prague, Czech Republic, 18 September 2016 <http://tonyabbott.com.au/2016/09/address-alliance-european-conservatives-reformists-lobkowicz-palace-prague-czec h-republic/>

Brennan, Sir Gerard, 'The Parliament, the Executive and the Courts: Roles and Immunities' (Speech delivered at the School of Law, Bond University, 21 February 1998)

Dauvergne, Catherine, 'Challenges to Sovereignty: Migration Laws for the 21st Century' (New Issues in Refugee Research, Working Paper No 92 UNHCR, July 2003)

Dutton, Peter, *Address to the Australian Strategic Policy Institute*, 20 September 2016 <www.minister.border.gov.au/peterdutton/2016/pages/address-australian-strate gic-policy-institute-15092016.aspx>

Human Rights Law Centre, *Written Statement Submitted by the Human Rights Law Centre, a Non-Governmental Organization in Special Consultative Status*, UN GAOR, 24th sess, Agenda Item 4, UN Doc/HRC/24/NGO/27 (24 August 2013)

Manne, David, Address to UNHCR Annual Consultations (Speech delivered at UNHCR Annual Consultations, Canberra, 15 October 2013)

Millbank, Adrienne, 'Asylum Seekers on Bridging Visa E' (Research Brief No 13, Parliamentary Library, Parliament of Australia, 2007)

Phillips, Janet, and Harriet Spinks, 'Immigration Detention in Australia' (Background Note, Parliamentary Library, Parliament of Australia, 20 March 2013) <www.aph .gov.au/about_parliament/parliamentary_departments/parliamentary_library/ pubs>

'Boat Arrivals in Australia since 1976' (Research Paper, Parliamentary Library, Parliament of Australia, first published 25 June 2009, statistical appendix updated 23 July 2013) <www.aph.gov.au/about_parliament/parliamentary_depart ments/parliamentary_library/pubs>

Sackville, Justice Ronald, 'Courts in Transition: An Australian View' (Paper presented at New Zealand Court of Appeal/High Court Judges' and Masters' Conference, 20–23 March 2003)

Taggart, Michael, '"Australian Exceptionalism" in Judicial Review' (Speech delivered at the 10th Annual Geoffrey Sawer, Lecture National Museum of Australia, 9 November 2007)

E OTHER RESOURCES

Official Correspondence

Letter from António Guterres, United Nations High Commissioner for Refugees, to the Hon Chris Bowen MP, Minister for Immigration and Citizenship of Australia, 9 October 2012 <http://unhcr.org.au/unhcr/images/121009%20response%20to%20m inister%20on%20png.pdf>

Online Resources

ABC, 'Secrecy on the High Seas', *Media Watch*, 14 July 2014 <www.abc.net.au/media watch/transcripts/s4045863.htm>

'Liberals Accused of Trying to Rewrite History', *Lateline*, 21 November 2001 <www .abc.net.au/lateline/content/2001/s422692.htm>

'A focus on Australia's refugee policy', *Q&A*, 10 October 2016 <www.abc.net.au/tv/ qanda/txt/s4528829.htm>

ABC Radio, 'Greens Ask the Federal Police to Investigate if the Government's Breached Its Own Anti-People Smuggling Laws', *PM*, 7 May 2014 <www.abc.ne t.au/pm/content/2014/s3999932.htm>

'High Court Case: Government Reveals Details of 157 Tamils Kept at Sea', *PM*, 22 July 2014 <www.abc.net.au/pm/content/2014/s4051399.htm>

Alberici, Emma, Interview with Peter Dutton (ABC, *Lateline*, 5 October 2015) <www .abc.net.au/lateline/content/2015/s4325585.htm>

Amnesty International, *Australia: Shamefully Inconsistent When It Comes to Human Rights*, 25 February 2014 <www.amnesty.org.au/news/comments/34001/>

'Government Sets Impossible Deadlines for Asylum Applications', 13 March 2017 <www.amnesty.org.au/unrealistic-deadlines-imposed-on-people-seeking-asy lum/>

Anderson, Stephanie, 'Manus Island Detention Centre to be Shut, Papua New Guinea Prime Minister Peter O'Neill Says', *The Guardian* (online), updated 28 April 2016 <www.abc.net.au/news/2016-04-27/png-pm-oneill-to-shut-manus-island-deten tion-centre/7364414>

'Refugee, Asylum Seeker Ban Won't Break International Obligations, Peter Dutton Says', *ABC News* (online), 31 October 2016 <www.abc.net.au/news/2016-10-31/d utton-says-refugee-ban-won't-break-international-obligations/7979242>

Asylum Seekers Centre <www.asylumseekerscentre.org.au>

AusCustomsNews, 'No Way. You Will Not Make Australia Home – English' on *YouTube* (15 April 2014) <https://m.youtube.com/watch?v=rT12WH4a92w>

Australasian Legal Information Institute <www.austlii.edu.au>

Australian Border Deaths Database <http://artsonline.monash.edu.au/thebordercros singobservatory/publications/australian-border-deaths-database/>

Belling, Natarsha, and James Mathison, Interview with Tony Abbott (Network Ten, *Wake Up*, 9 January 2014) <https://www.youtube.com/watch? v=b66qqyfu6sk>

Belot, Henry, 'Nauru a "Blemish" on Australia's Human Rights Record, UN Official Says', *ABC News* (online), 10 June 2017 <www.abc.net.au/news/2017-06-10/nauru- a-blemish-on-australias-human-rights-record:-un-official/8606960>

Bolton, Geoffrey C, 'Evatt, Herbert Vere (Bert) (1894–1965)' in John Ritchie and Christopher Cunneen (eds), *Australian Dictionary of Biography* (Melbourne University Press, 1996) vol 14 <http://adb.anu.edu.au/>

Chalmers, Max, 'Detention On Nauru: Children Now Identify More with Boat Number than Names, Says Former Worker' *New Matilda* (online), 29 June 2015 <https://newmatilda.com/2015/06/29/detention-nauru-children-now-identify-mor e-boat-number-names-says-former-worker/>

Conifer, Dan, 'Asylum Seekers: Tony Abbott Refuses to Deny Australia Paid Thousands to People Smugglers' *ABC News* (online), 13 June 2015 <www.abc.net.au/news/2015- 06-12/abbott-refuses-to-deny-people-smugglers-paid-to-turn-back/6540866>

Cordell, Marni, 'Manus Victims "Treated Better than Australians": Cornall', *New Matilda* (online), 27 February 2014 <https://newmatilda.com/2014/02/27/manus-v ictims-treated-better-australians-cornall>

Cowie, Thea, 'Coalition Launches Operation Sovereign Borders' *SBS Radio* (online), 18 September 2013 <www.sbs.com.au/news/article/2013/09/18/coalition-launches- operation-sovereign-borders>

Cruise, Patricia, 'They Can Turn Back the Boats, but It's Still Plane Sailing', *Sydney Morning Herald* (online), 11 August 2010 <www.smh.com.au/federal-politics/they-can-turn-back-the-boats-but-its-still-plane-sailing-20100810-11y49.html>

Doherty, Ben, 'Doctors Freed to Speak about Australia's Detention Regime after U-turn', *The Guardian* (online), 20 October 2016 <https://www.theguardian.com/australia-news/2016/oct/20/doctors-freed-to-speak-about-australias-detention-regime-after-u-turn>

'Australia Should Bring Manus and Nauru Refugees to Immediate Safety, UN Says', *The Guardian* (online), 10 November 2017 <www.theguardian.com/australia-news/2017/nov/10/australia-should-bring-manus-and-nauru-refugees-to-immediate-safety-un-says>

Doyle, Julie, 'PM Refuses to Deny Boat Payment Claims' *ABC News* (online), 12 June 2015 <www.abc.net.au/news/2015-06-12/pm-refuses-to-deny-boat-payment-claims/6543260>

Farrell, Paul, Oliver Laughland, and Melissa Davey, 'Asylum Seekers Will Be Handed to Police on Return, Sri Lanka Confirms', *The Guardian* (online), 7 July 2014 <www.theguardian.com/world/2014/jul/07/asylum-seekers-will-be-handed-to-police-on-return-sri-lanka-confirms>

Fraser, Malcolm, 'Asylum Seekers Go from Nothing to Zero under Cruel Policy', *Sydney Morning Herald* (online), 13 June 2011 <www.smh.com.au/federal-politics/political-opinion/asylum-seekers-go-from-nothing-to-zero-under-cruel-policy-2011 0612-1fz8s.html>

Address to Asylum Seekers Resource Centre (Speech delivered at the opening of new premises for the Asylum Seekers Resource Centre, Melbourne, 10 December 2014), published as Malcolm Fraser, 'Immigration Minister "Has the Powers of a Tyrant", Says Malcolm Fraser', *The Age* (online), 11 December 2014 <www.theage.com.au/comment/immigration-minister-has-th e-powers-of-a-tyrant-says-malcolm-fraser-20141210-124b4v.html>

Gordon, Michael, '"Social Time Bomb": UNHCR's Warning on the Plight of 30,000 Asylum Seekers Already Living in Australia', *The Age* (online), 23 November 2016 <www.smh.com.au/federal-politics/political-news/social-time-bomb-unhcrs-warn ing-on-the-plight-of-30000-asylum-seekers-already-living-in-australia-20161122-gsu yk5.html>

The Guardian Australia (online), 'The Nauru Files' <www.theguardian.com/news/se ries/nauru-files>

Hall, Bianca, and Judith Ireland, 'Tony Abbott Evokes John Howard in Slamming Doors on Asylum Seekers', *Sydney Morning Herald* (online), 15 August 2013 <www.smh.com.au/federal-politics/federal-election-2013/tony-abbott-evokes-jo hn-howard-in-slamming-doors-on-asylum-seekers-20130815-2rzzy.html>

'"A Huge Win for Doctors": Turnbull Government Backs Down on Gag Laws for Doctors on Nauru and Manus', *Sydney Morning Herald* (online), 20 October 2016 <www.smh.com.au/federal-politics/political-news/a-huge-win-for-doctors-turn bull-government-backs-down-on-gag-laws-for-doctors-on-nauru-and-manus-20161 019-gs6ecs.html>

Hamilton, Andrew, 'Asylum Seeker Ethics Is Simple' (2014) 24(5) *Eureka Street*, 19 March 2014

Higginbottom, Heather, 'You Probably Missed the Big Story Buried in the Latest Trump Leaks', *Time* (online), 10 August 2017 <http://time.com/4894058/donald-trump-malcolm-turnbull-refugees-famine/>

Hunter, Fergus, and Amy Remeikis, 'Turnbull Government Unveils Manus and Nauru
Refugee Resettlement Deal with United States', *Sydney Morning Herald* (online),
13 November 2016 <www.smh.com.au/federal-politics/political-news/united-state
s-confirms-manus-islandand-nauru-deal-with-turnbull-government-20161112-gs02e
l.html>

Hutchens, Gareth, 'Asylum Seekers Face Lifetime Ban from Entering Australia if They
Arrive by Boat', *The Guardian* (online), 30 October 2016 <www.theguardian.com/
australia-news/2016/oct/30/asylum-seekers-face-lifetime-ban-on-entering-austra
lia-if-they-arrive-by-boat>

Jacubowicz, Andrew, 'European Leaders Taking Cues from Australia on Asylum
Seeker Policies' *The Conversation* (online), 7 November 2016 <http://theconversa
tion.com/european-leaders-taking-cues-from-australia-on-asylum-seeker-policies-
66336>

Andrew & Renata Kaldor Centre for International Refugee Law
Karp, Paul, 'Peter Dutton "Demonised" by Labor over Refugee Remarks, Says
Malcolm Turnbull', *The Guardian* (online), 19 May 2016 <https://www.theguar
dian.com/australia-news/2016/may/19/peter-dutton-demonised-by-labor-over-refu
gee-remarks-says-malcolm-turnbull>

and Eleanor Ainge Roy, 'New Zealand Seeks Deal with Australia to Resettle Manus
and Nauru Refugees', *The Guardian* (online), 26 September 2017 <www.theguar
dian.com/australia-news/2017/nov/17/new-zealand-and-png-could-do-deal-on-refu
gees-peter-dutton-says>

Kerr, John D, 'Maxwell, Walter (1854–1931)' in Bede Nairn and Geoffrey Serle (eds),
Australian Dictionary of Biography (Melbourne University Press, 1986) vol 10
<http://adb.anu.edu.au/>

Knott, Matthew, 'Government's Plan for 157 Captive Asylum Seekers Potentially
Illegal: Lawyers', *Sydney Morning Herald* (online), 26 July 2014 <www.smh
.com.au/federal-politics/political-news/governments-plan-for-157-captive-asy
lum-seekers-potentially-illegal-lawyers-20140726-3cluv.html>

Koziol, Michael, 'Asylum Seeker on Manus Island Found Dead' *Sydney Morning
Herald* (online), 7 August 2017 <www.smh.com.au/federal-politics/political-new
s/refugee-on-manus-island-found-dead-20170807-gxqq2o.html>

Laughland, Oliver, 'Tamil Asylum Seekers Being Held at Sea in Windowless Locked
Rooms', *The Guardian* (online), 16 July 2014 <www.theguardian.com/world/2014/
jul/16/tamil-asylum-seekers-being-held-at-sea-in-windowless-locked-rooms>

'Tamil Asylum Seekers Moved to Nauru', *The Guardian* (online), 2 August 2014 <www
.theguardian.com/world/2014/aug/02/tamil-asylum-seekers-moved-to-nauru>

LEGENDcom <www.border.gov.au/trav/visa/lege>

Logan, Sandi, National Communications Manager, Department of Immigration and
Citizenship, 'Hoax Refugee Email', Letter to the Editor, *Adelaide Advertiser*
(online), 7 May 2009 <www.immi.gov.au/media/letters/letters09/le090507.htm>

McAdam, Jane, *Opinion: Australian Parties in "Race to Bottom" on Asylum Policy*, 4
September 2013, CNN <http://edition.cnn.com/2013/09/03/opinion/australia-asy
lum-seekers-mcadam/?hpt=ias_c2>

McKenzie-Murray, Martin, 'Cornall Report into the Death of Reza Barati on Manus
Island', *The Saturday Paper* (online), 31 May 2014 <www.thesaturdaypaper.com

.au/news/politics/2014/05/31/cornall-report-the-death-reza-barati-manus-island/14 01458400#.u9rmyoh4jfq> (first published in the print edition of *The Saturday Paper*, 31 May 2014, as 'Deadly Oversight')

Manne, Robert, 'How We Came to Be So Cruel to Asylum Seekers', *The Conversation* (online), 26 October 2016 <https://theconversation.com/robert-manne-how-we-came-to-be-so-cruel-to-asylum-seekers-67542>

March, Stephanie, *Sri Lankan Asylum Seekers Facing Criminal Investigation after Being Handed Back by Australian Authorities* (7 July 2014) ABC News <www.ab c.net.au/news/2014–07-07/morrison-confirms-sri-lankans-returned-after-intercep tion/5575924>

'US Hits Refugee Intake Cap as Manus Island, Nauru Refugees Assessed' *ABC News* (online), 14 July 2017 <www.abc.net.au/news/2017-07-14/manus-nauru-refugees-w aiting-as-us-intake-cap-reached/8707340>

Martin, Sarah, and Simon Benson, 'Trump Refugee Ban: Nauru Resettlement Deal Could Be Saved' *The Australian* (online), 29 January 2017 <www.theaustralian .com.au/national-affairs/immigration/trump-refugee-ban-nauru-resettlement-dea l-with-australia-could-be-saved/news-story/9cdbe11ff03582bb782a42953c38183d>

Miller, Greg, Julie Vitkovskaya, and Reuben Fischer-Baum, '"This Deal Will Make Me Look Terrible": Full Transcripts of Trump's Calls with Mexico and Australia', *Washington Post* (online) 3 August 2017 <www.washingtonpost.com/graphics/201 7/politics/australia-mexico-transcripts/?utm_term=.66adbb74f572>

Moore, Andrew, Interview with Tony Abbott (2GB Radio, 9 January 2014) <www.pm .gov.au/media/2014–01-09/interview-andrew-moore-radio-2gb-0>

Needham, Kirsty, 'Lawyer George Newhouse in Dark over Asylum Seeker Move' *The Age* (online), 2 August 2014 <www.theage.com.au/federal-politics/political-news/ lawyer-george-newhouse-in-dark-over-asylum-seeker-move-20140802-zzppo .html>

Nicholson, Brendan, 'New Zealand to Take 150 Asylum-Seekers from Australia', *The Australian* (online), 10 February 2013 <www.theaustralian.com.au/national-affairs/n ew-zealand-to-take-asylum-seekers-from-australia/news-story/0c1e8c7d37 efd154b8756ba337b141b2>

Owens, Jared, 'Were Asylum Seeker Boats Paid to Turn Back?' *The Australian* (online), 14 June 2015 <www.theaustralian.com.au/national-affairs/immigration/were-asy lum-seeker-boats-paid-to-turn-back/news-story/f19bd5b8e14e590b31e0579a 80b4c535>

Parmar, Tekendra, 'The UN Special Rapporteur on Migrant Rights Says Australia's Refugee Island Is 'Inhuman', *Time* (online) 17 November 2016 <http://time.com/ 4575976/australia-nauru-refugees-un-francois-crepeau/>

Playford, John, 'Cockburn, Sir John Alexander (1850–1929)' in Bede Nairn and Geoffrey Serle (eds), *Australian Dictionary of Biography* (Melbourne University Press, 1981) vol 8 <http://adb.anu.edu.au/>

Probyn, Andrew, 'Australia's Fake Fishing Boats Trawl for Asylum Seekers', *The West Australian* (online), 27 November 2016 <https://au.news.yahoo.com/the west/wa/a/33338441/fake-fishing-boats-used-in-the-war-against-people-smug glers/#page1>

Rasmussen, Carolyn, 'Kisch, Egon Erwin (1885–1948)' in John Ritchie and Diane Langmore (eds), *Australian Dictionary of Biography* (Melbourne University Press, 2000) vol 15 <http://adb.anu.edu.au/>

Reuters (Sydney and Washington), 'US Officials Walk Out of Australia-Run Nauru Detention Centre' *The Guardian* (online), 16 July 2017 <www.theguardian.com/world/2017/jul/15/us-officials-walk-out-australia-nauru-detention-centre>

Rudd, Kevin, 'Prime Minister Kevin Rudd – Address to the Nation' on *YouTube* (19 July 2013) <https://www.youtube.com/watch?v=kiapyibrzis>

Rutledge, Martha, 'O'Connor, Richard Edward (Dick) (1851–1912)' in Geoffrey Serle and Christopher Cunneen (eds), *Australian Dictionary of Biography* (Melbourne University Press, 1988) vol 11 <http://adb.anu.edu.au/>

Sales, Leigh, Interview with Tony Abbott, Prime Minister (ABC, *7.30 Report*, 13 November 2013) <www.abc.net.au/7.30/content/2013/s3890402.htm>

Sanggaran, Dr John-Paul, and 40 others, 'Open Letter on the Border Force Act – We Challenge the Department to Prosecute', *The Guardian* (online), 1 July 2015 <www.theguardian.com/australia-news/2015/jul/01/open-letter-on-the-border-force-act-we-challenge-the-department-to-prosecute>

Seidler, Michael, 'Pufendorf's Moral and Political Philosophy' (19 March 2013) *The Stanford Encyclopedia of Philosophy* <http://plato.stanford.edu/archives/spr2013/entries/pufendorf-moral/>

Shanahan, Dennis 'Immigration Minister Scott Morrison Takes Hard Line: 157 Sent to Nauru', *The Australian* (online), 2 August 2014 <www.theaustralian.com.au/national-affairs/policy/immigration-minister-scott-morrison-takes-hard-line-157-sent-to-nauru/story-fn9hm1gu-1227010765629>

Swan, Jonathan, 'Two Journalists Arrive in Australia on Asylum Seeker Boat', *Sydney Morning Herald* (online), 9 September 2013 <www.smh.com.au/federal-politics/federal-election-2013/two-journalists-arrive-in-australia-on-asylum-seeker-boat-20130909-2tfnz.html#ixzz33dvolqca>

Taylor, Paige, 'Federal Election 2016: New Boats to Return Asylum-Seekers', *The Australian* (online), 30 June 2016 <www.theaustralian.com.au/federal-election-2016/federal-election-2016-new-boats-to-return-asylumseekers/news-story/9e57526ab66d4e055aedef3b70cbd2f9>

Topsfield, Jewel, 'Call to Ease Bridging Visa Rules', *The Age* (online), 18 March 2008 <www.theage.com.au/articles/2008/03/17/1205602291249.html>

Uhlmann, Chris, Interview with Scott Morrison, Shadow Minister for Immigration and Citizenship (ABC, *7.30 Report*, 18 July 2013) <www.abc.net.au/7.30/content/2013/s3806305.htm>

Wahlquist, Calla, 'First Manus Island-held Refugees Flown to US Under Resettlement Deal', *The Guardian* (online), 26 September 2017, <www.theguardian.com/world/2017/sep/26/first-manus-island-held-refugees-flown-to-us-under-resettlement-deal>

Walker, Frank, 'Woman, 78, Seen as Refugee Test Case', *Sydney Morning Herald* (online), 2 September 2002 <www.smh.com.au/articles/2002/09/01/1030508159603.html>

Webb, Carolyn, and Cameron Houston, 'Springvale Bank Fire: Asylum Seekers' Lives Precarious, Say Advocates', *The Age* (online), 20 November 2016 <www.theage.com.au/victoria/springvale-bank-fire-asylum-seekers-lives-precarious-say-advocates-20161120-gstexl.html>

Wendt, Jana, Interview with Bob Hawke, Prime Minister (Nine Network, *A Current Affair*, Parliament House, 6 June 1990) <http://pmtranscripts.dpmc.gov.au/tran scripts/00008028.pdf>

Whyte, Sarah, 'Anti-Whistleblowing Law Being Used to Pursue Save the Children Staff Used Only Twice in Five Years', *Sydney Morning Herald* (online), 13 October 2014 <www.smh.com.au/federal-politics/political-news/antiwhistleblowing-law-being-use d-to-pursue-save-the-children-staff-used-only-twice-in-five-years-20141013-1157jt.html>

Winsor, Ben, and Myles Morgan, '"This Is the Worst Deal Ever", President Donald Trump Reportedly Said of the Refugee Deal with Australia, According to the Washington Post' *SBS News* (online), 2 February 2017 <www.sbs.com.au/news/a rticle/2017/02/02/talking-turnbull-worst-call-far-trump-says-washington-post>

Yaxley, Louise, 'PNG's Supreme Court Ruling Does Not Mean Manus Island Centre Must Shut, Says Peter Dutton', *ABC News* (online), updated 11 May 2016 <www .abc.net.au/news/2016–05-11/png's-court-ruling-does-not-mean-centre-must-be-sh ut:-dutton/7403600>

Newspapers (see also Online Resources)

Cass, Moss, 'Stop This Unjust Queue Jumping' *The Australian*, 29 June 1978, 7

Logan, Sandi, National Communications Manager, Department of Immigration and Citizenship, 'Refugees Not Better Off', Letter to the Editor, *Adelaide Advertiser*, 21 May 2009, 17

Milne, Glenn, and Tracey Aubin, 'Bob's Not Your Uncle PM Tells Boat People' *The Weekend Australian*, 21–22 July 1990, 3

Tingle, Laura, 'Vow to Tackle Refugee Visa Abuses', The Age (Melbourne), 20 March 1997, A6

F ARCHIVAL MATERIAL

High Court of Australia

Chu Kheng Lim v Minister for Immigration, Local Government and Ethnic Affairs, Court File, High Court of Australia, M23/1992

Human Rights and Equal Opportunity Commission

Complaint by Mr Frank Elvey of the Asylum Seekers Centre regarding the Asylum Seekers Assistance Scheme (HREOC File No 13747 H, 1996)

Media Releases and Press Conferences

Abbott, Tony, and Scott Morrison, Joint Press Conference, Launch of Operation Sovereign Borders, Brisbane, 25 July 2013 <https://www.nsw.liberal.org.au/tony-a bbott-transcript-joint-press-conference-brisbane>

Abbott, Tony, Prime Minister, Press Conference, Parliament House, Canberra, 26 July 2014 <www.pm.gov.au/media/2014–07-26/press-conference-parliament-house-canberra>

Alexander, Chris, Citizenship and Immigration Minister, Canada, 'Protecting the World's Most Vulnerable: Minister Alexander Marks World Refugee Day 2014' (Statement, 20 June 2014) <http://news.gc.ca/web/article-en.do?nid=859849>

Bowen, Chris, Minister for Immigration and Citizenship, 'Supporting Refugees on World Refugee Day' (Media Release, 20 June 2011) <http://pandora.nla.gov.au/pan/67564/20120320–0000/www.minister.immi.gov.au/media/cb/2011/cb166819.htm> 'No Advantage Onshore for Boat Arrivals' (Media Release, 21 November 2012) <www.aph.gov.au> (parlinfo)

Department of Immigration and Border Protection, 'The Nauru Files' (Media Release, 10 August 2016) <http://newsroom.border.gov.au/releases/the-nauru-files>

Morrison, Scott, Minister for Immigration and Border Protection, Press Conference, Migration and Maritime Powers Legislation Amendment (Resolving the Asylum Legacy Caseload) Bill 2014, Coalition Government, Parliament House, Canberra, 5 December 2014 <www.minister.immi.gov.au/media/sm/2014/sm219827.htm>

Office of the High Commissioner for Human Rights, 'Migrants/Human rights: Official Visit to Australia Postponed due to Protection Concerns' (OHCHR, Media Release, 25 September 2015) <http://ohchr.org/en/newsevents/pages/displaynews.aspx?newsid=16503&langid=e#sthash.n5ts2e9 n.dpuf>

Ruddock, Philip, Minister for Immigration and Multicultural Affairs, 'Speedier Processing for Asylum Claims' (Media Release, MPS 53/96, 20 August 1996) 'Immigration Minister Gives More Autonomy to Tribunals' (Media Release, Budget 99 MPS 73/99, 11 May 1999)

US Department of State, 'World Refugee Day: Highlighting a Global Need and America's Response' (Fact Sheet, Bureau of Public Affairs, 20 June 2014) <www.state.gov/r/pa/pl/228037.htm>

Policy Documents and Determinations

Australian Labor Party, 'National Platform and Constitution' (2007)

Department of Immigration and Border Protection, *Fact Sheet 61 – Seeking Protection within Australia* (27 August 2014)
Fact Sheet 62 – Assistance for Asylum Seekers in Australia (27 August 2014)
Fact Sheet 64 – Community Assistance Support Program (27 August 2014)
Fact Sheet 65 – Bridging Visas for Illegal Maritime Arrivals (13 October 2014)
Fact Sheet 82 – Immigration Detention (27 August 2014)
Fact Sheet 83 – Community Detention (27 August 2014)

Michael Pezzullo, Secretary, DIBP, 'Determination of Immigration and Border Protection Workers – Amendment No 1', *Australian Border Force Act 2015*, 30 September 2016 <https://uploads.guim.co.uk/2016/10/19/determination_amendment_(1).pdf>

Department of Immigration and Citizenship, 'Community Care Pilot and Status Resolution Trial' (March 2009) <http://idcoalition.org/australia-diac-paper-community-care-pilot-status-resolution-trial/>

Department of Immigration and Multicultural Affairs, 'Fact Sheet: Immigration and Multicultural Affairs Budget '96' (August 1996)

Department of Immigration and Multicultural and Indigenous Affairs, *Fact Sheet 74a: Boat Arrival Details (on Australian Mainland)* (6 October 2004) <http://sievx.co m/articles/psdp/dimia74a_boatarrivals.pdf>

Liberal Party of Australia and National Party of Australia, 'The Coalition's Operation Sovereign Borders Policy' (July 2013) <www.aph.gov.au> (parlinfo)

G CASES

National

Australia

A v Minister for Immigration and Ethnic Affairs (1997) 190 CLR 225

Ah Yin v Christie (1907) 4 CLR 1428

Ah You v Gleeson (1930) 43 CLR 589

Ali Abdul v Maher (1931) 46 CLR 580

Al Ferdous v Minister for Immigration & Citizenship [2011] FCA 1070

Al-Kateb v Godwin (2004) 219 CLR 562

Al Masri v Minister for Immigration & Multicultural & Indigenous Affairs (2002) 192 ALR 609

Australian Capital Television Pty Ltd v Commonwealth (1992) 177 CLR 106

Australian Communist Party v Commonwealth (1951) 83 CLR 1 ('*Communist Party Case*')

Behrooz v Secretary, Department of Immigration and Multicultural and Indigenous Affairs (2004) 219 CLR 486

Bolkus v Tang Jia Xin (1994) 69 ALJR 8

Chia Gee v Martin (1905) 3 CLR 649

Chidiac v Secretary, Department of Education, Employment and Workplace Relations [2011] AATA 681 (30 September 2011)

Christie v Ah Foo (1904) VLR 533

Chu Kheng Lim v Minister for Immigration, Local Government and Ethnic Affairs and Another (1992) 176 CLR 1

Chu Shao Hung v The Queen (1953) 87 CLR 575

Chun Teeong Toy v Musgrove (1888) 14 VLR 349

Coco v The Queen (1994) 179 CLR 427

Commonwealth v Tasmania (1983) 158 CLR 1

CPCF v Minister for Immigration and Border Protection & Anor (Case S169/2014) [2014] HCATrans 148 (7 July 2014)

[2014] HCATrans 149 (8 July 2014)

[2014] HCATrans 153 (23 July 2014)

Plaintiff's Submissions, 11 September 2014

Defendants' Chronology, 30 September 2014

Submissions of the Defendants, 30 September 2014

Plaintiff's Amended Submissions in Reply, 10 October 2014

CPCF v Minister for Immigration and Border Protection (2015) 255 CLR 514 (*'Detention on the High Seas Case'*)

Cunliffe v Commonwealth (1994) 182 CLR 272

De Silva v Minister for Immigration & Multicultural Affairs (2001) 113 FCR 350

Ferrando v Pearce (1918) 25 CLR 241

FTZK v Minister for Immigration and Border Protection [2014] HCA 26 (27 June 2014)

Gabriel v Ah Mook (1924) 34 CLR 591

Georgiadis v Australian and Overseas Telecommunications Corporation (1994) 179 CLR 297

Griffin v Wilson (1935) 52 CLR 260

Huddart, Parker and Co Pty Ltd v Moorehead (1909) 8 CLR 330

Koon Wing Lau v Calwell (1949) 80 CLR 533

Koowarta v Bjelke-Petersen (1982) 153 CLR 168

Li Wan Quai v Christie (1906) 3 CLR 1125

Minister for Immigration and Multicultural and Indigenous Affairs v Al Masri (2003) 197 ALR 241

Minister for Immigration and Multicultural Affairs v Khawar (2002) 210 CLR 1

NAGV and NAGW of 2002 v Minister for Immigration and Multicultural and Indigenous Affairs (2005) 222 CLR 161

New South Wales v Commonwealth (2006) 229 CLR 1 (*'Work Choices Case'*)

Plaintiff M47-2012 v Director General of Security (2012) 251 CLR 1

Plaintiff M61/2010E v Commonwealth (2010) 243 CLR 319 (*'Offshore Processing Case'*)

Plaintiff M68-2015 v Minister for Immigration and Border Protection (2016) 257 CLR 42 (*'Nauru Detention Case'*)

Plaintiff M70/2011 v Minister for Immigration and Citizenship (2011) 244 CLR 144 (*'Malaysian Declaration Case'*)

Plaintiff M76-2013 v Minister for Immigration, Multicultural Affairs and Citizenship (2013) 251 CLR 322

Plaintiff M96A/2016 v Commonwealth of Australia [2017] HCA 16 (3 May 2017)

Plaintiff M150/2013 v Minister for Immigration and Border Protection (2014) 309 ALR 225

Mabo v Queensland (No 2) (1992) 175 CLR 1

Mann v Ah On (1905) 7 WALR 182

Minister of State for Immigration and Ethnic Affairs v Ah Hin Teoh (1995) 183 CLR 273

Minister for Immigration v Haji Ibrahim (2000) 204 CLR 1

Re Minister for Immigration and Multicultural Affairs; Ex parte Meng Kok Te (2002) 212 CLR 162

Minister for Immigration and Multicultural and Indigenous Affairs v Al Khafaji (2004) 219 CLR 664

Muller v Dalgety & Co Ltd (1909) 9 CLR 693

Nolan v Minister for Immigration and Ethnic Affairs (1988) 165 CLR 178

O'Keefe v Calwell (1949) 77 CLR 261*Pochi v Macphee* (1982) 151 CLR 101

Polites v Commonwealth (1945) 70 CLR 60

Polyukhovich v Commonwealth (1991) 172 CLR 501 ('*War Crimes Act Case*')

Potter v Minahan (1908) 7 CLR 272

Preston v Donohue (1906) 3 CLR 1089

R v Carter; Ex parte Kisch (1934) 52 CLR 221

R v Davey; Ex parte Freer (1936) 56 CLR 381

R v Fletcher; Ex parte Kisch (1935) 52 CLR 248

R v MacFarlane; Ex parte O'Flanagan (1923) 32 CLR 518 ('*Irish Envoys Case*')

R v Trade Practices Tribunal; Ex parte Tasmanian Breweries Pty Ltd (1970) 123 CLR 361

R v Wilson; Ex parte Kisch (1934) 52 CLR 234

Re Woolley; Ex parte Applicants M276/2003 (2004) 225 CLR 1

Robtelmes v Brenan (1906) 4 CLR 395

Ruddock v Vadarlis (2001) 110 FCR 491

Ruhani v Director of Police (No 2) (2005) 222 CLR 580

Plaintiff S4/2014 v Minister for Immigration and Border Protection (2014) 253 CLR 219

Plaintiff S156/2013 v Minister for Immigration and Border Protection (2014) 254 CLR 28 ('*Manus Island Case*')

Plaintiff S157/2002 v Commonwealth (2003) 211 CLR 476

Plaintiff S195/2016 v Minister for Immigration and Border Protection and Ors [2017] HCA 31, 17 August 2017

Plaintiff S297/2013 v Minister for Immigration and Border Protection (2014) 309 ALR 209

Salemi v Mackellar (No 2) (1977) 137 CLR 396

Secretary, Department of Education, Employment and Workplace Relations v Ergin (2010) 54 AAR 60

Singh v Commonwealth (2004) 222 CLR 322

Victorian Council for Civil Liberties Inc v Minister for Immigration and Multicultural Affairs (2001) 110 FCR 452

Wall v The King; Ex parte King Won (No 1) (1927) 39 CLR 245

Williamson v Ah On (1926) 39 CLR 95

Re Yates; Ex parte Walsh and Johnson (1925) 37 CLR 36Canada

R v Alamazoff [1919] 3 WWR 281; 30 Man R 143

Papua New Guinea

Namah v Pato [2016] PGSC 13; SC1497 (26 April 2016)

United Kingdom

Re Adam (1837) 1 Moo P C 460; 12 ER 889
Attorney-General for Canada v Cain [1906] AC 542
Calvin's Case (1608) 7 Coke Report 1a; 77 ER 377
Johnstone v Pedlar [1921] 2 AC 262
Musgrove v Chun Teeong Toy [1891] AC 272
R v Home Secretary; Ex parte Khawaja [1984] AC 74
R v Secretary of State for Social Security, Ex parte Joint Council for the Welfare of Immigrants [1996] 4 All ER 385
R v Secretary of State for the Home Department, Ex parte Limbuela [2006] 1 AC 396
R (European Roma Rights Centre) v Immigration Officer, Prague Airport [2005] 2 AC 1
Somerset v Stewart (1772) Lofft 1; 98 ER 499

United States

Boyd v United States, 116 US 616 (1886)
Chae Chan Ping v United States, 130 US 581 (1889) ('*Chinese Exclusion Case*')
The Exchange v McFaddon, 11 US 116 (1812)
Fong Yue Ting v United States, 149 US 698 (1893)
Nishimura Ekiu v United States, 142 US 651 (1892)
Shaughnessy v United States ex rel Mezei, 345 US 206 (1953)
Yick Wo v Hopkins, 118 US 356 (1886)

Regional

Abdulaziz, Cabales and Blakandali v United Kingdom (1985) 94 Eur Court HR (Ser A) 7
Amuur v France [1996] Eur Court HR 25
Chahal v United Kingdom [1996] V Eur Court HR 54
Case of Guzzardi v Italy (1980) 3 Eur Court HR (Ser A, no 39) 533
M S S v Belgium and Greece [2011] Eur Court HR 108
Saadi v United Kingdom [2008] Eur Court HR 80

International

S S 'Lotus' (France v Turkey) (Judgment) [1927] PCIJ (ser A) No 10

H LEGISLATION

Australia

Bills (Federal)

Australian Border Force Bill 2015 (Cth)
Border Protection (Validation and Enforcement Powers) Bill 2001(Cth)
Immigration Restriction Bill 1901 (Cth)
Migration Bill 1958 (Cth)
Migration Amendment Bill 1992 (Cth)
Migration Legislation Amendment Bill (No 3) 1994 (Cth)
Migration Amendment (Employer Sanctions) Bill 2006 (Cth)
Migration Amendment (Designated Unauthorised Arrivals) Bill 2006 (Cth)
Migration and Maritime Powers Legislation Amendment (Resolving the Asylum
    Legacy Caseload) Bill 2014 (Cth)
Migration Amendment (Regional Processing Arrangements) Bill 2015 (Cth)
Migration Legislation Amendment (Regional Processing Cohort) Bill 2016 (Cth)
Social Security Bill 1990 (Cth)
Social Security Legislation (Newly Arrived Resident's Waiting Periods and Other
    Measures) Bill 1996 (Cth)

Acts of Parliament (Federal)

Administrative Decisions (Judicial Review) Act 1977 (Cth)
Acts Interpretation Act 1901 (Cth)
Aliens Deportation Act 1946 (Cth)
Aliens Deportation Act 1948 (Cth)
Australian Border Force Act 2015 (Cth)
Australian Border Force (Protected Information) Act 2017 (Cth)
Australian Citizenship Act 2007 (Cth)
Australian Citizenship Amendment (Allegiance to Australia) Act 2015 (Cth)
Australian Human Rights Commission Act 1986 (Cth)
Commonwealth Electoral Act 1949 (Cth)
Constitution Alteration (Aboriginal People) 1967 (Cth)
Contract Immigrants Act 1905 (Cth)
Crimes Act 1914 (Cth)
Federal Circuit Court of Australia Legislation Amendment Act 2012 (Cth)
Health Insurance Act 1973 (Cth)
Human Rights (Parliamentary Scrutiny) Act 2011 (Cth)

Immigration Restriction Act 1901 (Cth)
Immigration Restriction Amendment Act 1905 (Cth)
The Immigration Restriction Act 1908 (Cth)
Immigration Restriction Act 1910 (Cth)
Immigration Act 1912 (Cth)
Immigration Act 1920 (Cth)
Immigration Act 1924 (Cth)
Immigration Act 1925 (Cth)
Immigration Act 1930 (Cth)
Immigration Act 1932 (Cth)
Immigration Act 1933 (Cth)
Immigration Act 1935 (Cth)
Immigration Act 1940 (Cth)
Immigration Act 1948 (Cth)
Immigration Act 1949 (Cth)
Judiciary Act 1903 (Cth)
Legislative Instruments Act 2003 (Cth)
Maritime Powers Act 2013 (Cth)
Mental Health Act 1986 (Vic)
Migration Act 1958 (Cth)
Migration Act 1964 (Cth)
Migration Act 1966 (Cth)
Migration Act 1973 (Cth)
Migration Amendment Act 1979 (Cth)
Migration Amendment Act (No 2) 1979 (Cth)
Migration Amendment Act 1980 (Cth)
Immigration (Unauthorized Arrivals) Act 1980 (Cth)
Migration Amendment Act 1980 (Cth)
Immigration (Unauthorized Arrivals) Act 1980 (Cth)
Migration Amendment Act 1983 (Cth)
Migration Amendment Act 1986 (Cth)
Migration Amendment Act 1987 (Cth)
Migration Amendment Act 1988 (Cth)
Migration Amendment Act (No 2) 1988 (Cth)
Migration Legislation Amendment Act 1989 (Cth)
Migration Amendment Act 1989 (Cth)
Migration Legislation Amendment (Consequential Amendments) Act 1989 (Cth)
Migration Legislation Amendment Act (No 2) 1989 (Cth)
Migration Amendment Act 1991 (Cth)
Migration Amendment Act (No 2) 1991 (Cth)

Migration Amendment Act (No 3) 1991 (Cth)

Migration Amendment Act 1992 (Cth)

Migration Amendment Act (No 2) 1992 (Cth)

Migration Amendment Act (No 3) 1992 (Cth)

Migration Laws Amendment Act 1992 (Cth)

Migration Laws Amendment Act (No 2) 1992 (Cth)

Migration Reform Act 1992 (Cth)

Migration Amendment Act (No 4) 1992 (Cth)

Migration Legislation Amendment Act (No 6) 1995 (Cth)

Border Protection (Validation and Enforcement Powers) Act 2001 (Cth)

Migration Legislation Amendment Act (No 6) 2001 (Cth)

Migration Amendment (Excision from Migration Zone) Act 2001 (Cth)

Migration Amendment (Excision from Migration Zone) (Consequential Provisions) Act 2001 (Cth)

Migration Amendment (Detention Arrangements) Act 2005 (Cth)

Migration Amendment (Employer Sanctions) Act 2007 (Cth)

Migration Legislation Amendment (Regional Processing and Other Measures) Act 2012 (Cth)

Migration Amendment (Unauthorised Maritime Arrivals and Other Measures) Act 2013 (Cth)

Migration and Maritime Powers Legislation Amendment (Resolving the Asylum Legacy Caseload) Act 2014 (Cth)

Migration Amendment (Regional Processing Arrangements) Act 2015 (Cth)

Nationality Act 1920–1946 (Cth)

Nationality and Citizenship Act 1948 (Cth)

Pacific Island Labourers Act 1901 (Cth)

Pacific Island Labourers Act 1906 (Cth)

Post and Telegraph Act 1901 (Cth)

Public Health and Wellbeing Act 2008 (Vic)

Racial Discrimination Act 1975 (Cth)

Social Security Act 1991 (Cth)

Tribunals Amalgamation Act 2015 (Cth)

War-Time Refugees Removal Act 1949 (Cth)

Explanatory Memoranda and Statements (Federal)

Explanatory Memorandum, Migration and Maritime Powers Legislation Amendment (Resolving the Asylum Legacy Caseload) Bill 2014 (Cth)

Explanatory Memorandum, Social Security Bill 1990 (Cth)

Supplementary Explanatory Memorandum, Migration Amendment Bill 1992 (Cth)

Supplementary Explanatory Memorandum: Amendments and New Clauses to Be Moved on Behalf of the Government, Social Security Legislation (Amendment) Bill 1990 (Cth)

Subsidiary Legislation & Explanatory Statements (Federal)

Migration Regulations 1994 (Cth)
Migration Regulations (Amendment) 1997 No 109 (Cth)
Migration Regulations (Amendment) 1997 No 185 (Cth)
Migration Regulations (Amendment) 1997 No 216 (Cth)
Migration Amendment Regulations 2004 (No 6) No 269 (Cth)
Migration Amendment Regulations 2009 (No 6) No 143 (Cth)
Migration Amendment (Bridging Visas – Code of Behaviour) Regulation 2013 (Cth)
Instrument IMMI 12/114: Classes of Persons (Cth), signed 20 November 2012
Instrument IMMI 13/155: Code of Behaviour for Public Interest Criterion 4022 (Cth), signed 12 December 2013
Explanatory Statement, *Migration Regulations (Amendment) 1997 No 109* (Cth)
Explanatory Statement, *Migration Regulations (Amendment) 1997 No 185* (Cth)
Explanatory Statement, *Migration Amendment Regulations 1999 (No 1) 1999 No 8* (Cth)
Explanatory Statement, *Migration Amendment Regulations 1999 (No 2) 1999 No 58* (Cth)
Explanatory Statement, *Migration Amendment Regulations 2009 (No 6) No 143* (Cth)

Departmental Guidance

Department of Immigration and Border Protection, 'Procedures Advice Manual 3: Guidelines for Officers Administering Migration Legislation' (2014)

Victoria

An Act to Make Provision for Certain Immigrants 1855 (Vic)
An Act to Regulate the Residence of the Chinese Population in Victoria 1857 (Vic)
Chinese Immigrants Statute 1865 (Vic)
Chinese Act 1881 (Vic)
Chinese Immigration Restriction Act 1888 (Vic)
Bail Act 1977 (Vic)

United Kingdom

Magna Carta 1215
British Nationality Act 1772, 13 Geo 3, c 21
British Nationality Act 1844, 7 and 8 Vict, c 66
Naturalisation of Aliens Act 1847, 10 & 11 Vict, c 83
Naturalisation Act 1870, 33 & 34 Vict, c 14
Commonwealth of Australia Constitution Act 1900 (Imp), 63 & 64 Vict, c 12

United States

Indian Citizenship Act 1924, ch 233, 43 Stat 253 (1924)
An Act to Establish an Uniform Rule of Naturalization, ch 3, 1 Stat 103 (1790)
Act of January 29, 1795, ch 20, 1 Stat 414 (1795)
*An Act to Amend the Naturalization Laws and to Punish Crimes against the Same,
    and for Other Purposes*, ch 254, 16 Stat 254 (1870)
An Act concerning Aliens, ch 58, 1 Stat 570 (1798)
Chinese Exclusion Act 1882, ch 126, 22 Stat 58 (1882)
Immigration Act 1891, ch 551, 26 Stat 1084 (1891)
Act of May 5, 1892, ch 60, 27 Stat 25 (1892)
United States Constitution

Other Legislation

Immigration Restriction Act 1897 (Natal)
Immigrants and Emigrants Act 1949 (Sri Lanka)
Constitution of the Independent State of Papua New Guinea 1975 (PNG)
Immigrants and Emigrants (Amendment) Act, No 31 of 2006 (Sri Lanka)
Constitution Amendment (No 37) *(Citizenship) Law* 2014 (PNG)

I CONSTITUTIONAL AND PARLIAMENTARY DEBATES

Constitutional Convention Debates

Official Record of the Proceedings and Debates of the Australasian Federation
    Conference, Melbourne, 6–14 February 1890
Official Record of the Proceedings and Debates of the National Australasian
    Convention, Sydney, 2 March 1891–9 April 1891

Proceedings of the Australasian Federal Convention, Adelaide, 22 March 1897–5 May 1897

Official Report of the Debates of the Australasian Federal Convention, Sydney, 2–24 September 1897

Official Report of the Debates of the Australasian Federal Convention, Melbourne, 22 January 1898–17 March 1898

Commonwealth Parliamentary Debates

Commonwealth, Parliamentary Debates, House of Representatives, 1901, 1905, 1925, 1949, 1958, 1978, 1982, 1990, 1992, 1997, 1999, 2002, 2008, 2014, 2015

Commonwealth, Parliamentary Debates, Senate, 1901, 1992, 1996, 2002, 2008, 2009, 2014, 2015

J INQUIRIES, SUBMISSIONS, EVIDENCE AND REPORTS

Australian Human Rights Commission

Australian Human Rights Commission, Submission No 8 to Joint Committee on Human Rights, Parliament of Australia, *Examination of the Migration (Regional Processing) Package of Legislation*, January 2013

Australian National Audit Office

Australian National Audit Office (ANAO), *Offshore Processing Centres in Nauru and Papua New Guinea: Procurement of Garrison Support and Welfare Services* (Audit Report No 16 of 2016–2017, September 2016)

Offshore Processing Centres in Nauru and Papua New Guinea – Contract Management of Garrison Support and Welfare Services (ANAO Report No 32 of 2016–2017, January 2017)

Joint Parliamentary Committees (chronological)

Joint Standing Committee on Migration, Parliament of Australia, *Inquiry into Immigration Detention in Australia*

Evidence of Stephanie Mendis, Hotham Mission Asylum Seeker Project, Public Hearing, Melbourne, 11 September 2008

Department of Immigration and Citizenship, Supplementary Submission No 129 n, 29 January 2009

Bibliography

Immigration Detention in Australia: Community-Based Alternatives to Detention – Second Report of the Inquiry into Immigration Detention in Australia (2009) Joint Select Committee on Australia's Immigration Detention Network, Parliament of Australia, Inquiry into Australia's Immigration Detention Network

Evidence of Andrew Metcalfe, Secretary, Department of Immigration and Citizenship, Public Hearing, Canberra, 16 August 2011

UNHCR, Submission No 110, 19 August 2011

Department of Immigration and Citizenship, Supplementary Submission No 32, September 2011

Parliamentary Joint Committee on Human Rights, Parliament of Australia, *Human Rights Scrutiny Report*, Report 9, 22 November 2016

Senate Committee Inquiries (chronological)

Senate Legal and Constitutional Legislation Committee, Parliament of Australia, *Inquiry into Social Security Legislation (Newly Arrived Resident's Waiting Periods and Other Measures) Bill 1996* (1996)

Evidence of Merle Mitchell, Board Member, Australian Council of Social Services, Public Hearing, Canberra, 6 June 1996

Senate Legal and Constitutional References Committee, Parliament of Australia, *A Sanctuary Under Review: An Examination of Australia's Refugee and Humanitarian Determination Processes* (2000)

Senate Select Committee on Ministerial Discretion in Migration Matters, Parliament of Australia, *Inquiry into Ministerial Discretion in Migration Matters* (2004)

Department of Immigration and Multicultural Affairs, Submission No 24

Hotham Mission, Uniting Justice Australia, 'Welfare Issues and Immigration Outcomes for Asylum Seekers on Bridging Visa E' (Research and Evaluation, April 2003), Supplementary Submission No 19A

Senate Legal and Constitutional Legislation Committee, Parliament of Australia, *Inquiry into the Migration Amendment (Employer Sanctions) Bill 2006* (2006)

Evidence of Neil Mann, First Assistant Secretary, Compliance Policy and Case Coordination Division, Department of Immigration and Multicultural Affairs, Public Hearing, Sydney, 26 April 2006

Department of Immigration and Multicultural Affairs, Submission No 5, 18 April 2006

Senate Legal and Constitutional Affairs Committee, Parliament of Australia, *Inquiry into the Migration Amendment (Detention Reform and Procedural Fairness) Bill 2010* (2011)

Department of Immigration and Citizenship, Submission No 25, July 2011

Senate Legal and Constitutional Affairs References Committee, Parliament of Australia, *Inquiry into the Incident at the Manus Island Detention Centre from 16 to 18 February 2014* (2014)

Evidence of Robert Cornall, Public Hearing, Canberra, 12 June 2014

Senate Select Committee on the Recent Allegations relating to Conditions and Circumstances at the Regional Processing Centre in Nauru, Parliament of Australia, *Taking Responsibility: Conditions and Circumstances at Australia's Regional Processing Centre in Nauru* (2015)

Senate Legal and Constitutional Affairs References Committee, Parliament of Australia, *Serious Allegations of Abuse, Self-Harm and Neglect of Asylum Seekers in relation to the Nauru Regional Processing Centre, and Any Like Allegations in relation to the Manus Regional Processing Centre* (2017)

Senate Estimates (chronological)

Senate Legal and Constitutional Affairs Committee, Parliament of Australia, *Supplementary Budget Estimates 2004–2005 (Immigration and Multicultural and Indigenous Affairs)*

Questions on Notice, November 2004

Senate Standing Committee on Legal and Constitutional Affairs, Parliament of Australia, *Supplementary Budget Estimates 2006–2007 (Immigration and Multicultural Affairs)*

Evidence of Andrew Metcalfe, Secretary, Department of Immigration and Multicultural Affairs, Public Hearing, Canberra, 30 October 2006

Questions Taken on Notice, 30 October 2006, (194) Output 1.3: Enforcement of Immigration Law

Senate Legal and Constitutional Affairs Committee, Parliament of Australia, *Additional Budget Estimates 2006–2007 (Immigration and Citizenship)*

Andrew Metcalfe, Secretary, Department of Immigration and Citizenship, Public Hearing, Canberra, 12 February 2007

Senate Standing Committee on Legal and Constitutional Affairs, Parliament of Australia, *Budget Estimates 2007–2008 (Immigration and Citizenship)*

Evidence of Andrew Metcalfe, Secretary, Department of Immigration and Citizenship, Public Hearing, Canberra, 21 May 2007

Senate Standing Committee on Legal and Constitutional Affairs, Parliament of Australia, *Additional Budget Estimates 2007–2008 (Immigration and Citizenship)*

Evidence of Senator Chris Evans, Minister for Immigration and Citizenship, Public Hearing, Canberra, 19 February 2008

Senate Legal and Constitutional Legislation Committee, Parliament of Australia, *Budget Estimates 2009–2010 (Immigration and Citizenship)*

Evidence of Andrew Metcalfe, Secretary, Department of Immigration and Citizenship, Public Hearing, Canberra, 28 May 2009

Senate Legal and Constitutional Affairs Legislation Committee, Parliament of Australia, *Supplementary Budget Estimates 2012–2013 (Immigration and Citizenship)*

Evidence of Martin Bowles, Secretary, Department of Immigration and Citizenship, Public Hearing, Canberra, 15 October 2012

Senate Legal and Constitutional Affairs Legislation Committee, Parliament of Australia, *Supplementary Budget Estimates 2013–2014 (Immigration and Border Protection*

Evidence of Lieutenant General Angus Campbell DSC, AM, Commander Joint Agency Task Force, Operation Sovereign Borders, Public Hearing, Canberra, 19 November 2013

Evidence of Martin Bowles, Secretary, Department of Immigration and Border Protection, Public Hearing, Canberra, 19 November 2013

Evidence of Vicki Parker, Chief Lawyer, Department of Immigration and Border Protection, Public Hearing, Canberra, 19 November 2013

Senate Legal and Constitutional Affairs References Committee, *Inquiry into Payment of Cash or Other Inducements by the Commonwealth of Australia in Exchange for the Turn Back of Asylum Seeker Boats*

Hilary Charlesworth, Emma Larking, Jacinta Mulders, Submission No 6, 24 July 2015

Payment of Cash or Other Inducements by the Commonwealth of Australia in Exchange for the Turn Back of Asylum Seeker Boats (Interim Report, May 2016)

Senate Legal and Constitutional Affairs Legislation Committee, Parliament of Australia, *Inquiry into Migration Legislation Amendment (Regional Processing Cohort) Bill 2016 [Provisions]*

Evidence of Michael Pezzullo, Secretary, Department of Immigration and Border Protection, Public Hearing, Melbourne, 15 November 2016

Departmental Inquiries

Asylum Seekers Centre, Submission to Department of Immigration and Multicultural Affairs, *Review of Bridging Visas*, May 2006

Hotham Mission, Submission to Department of Immigration and Multicultural Affairs, *Review of Bridging Visas*, May 2006

Law Council of Australia, Submission to Department of Immigration and Multicultural Affairs, *Review of Bridging Visas*, 7 August 2006

K TREATIES, JURISPRUDENCE AND INTERPRETATIVE GUIDANCE

Treaties

Bilateral Instruments

Memorandum of Understanding between the Republic of Nauru and the Commonwealth of Australia, relating to the Transfer to and Assessment of Persons in Nauru, and Related Issues, signed 3 August 2013 <www.dfat.gov.au/issues/peo ple-smuggling-mou.html>

Memorandum of Understanding between the Government of the Independent State of Papua New Guinea and the Government of Australia, relating to the Transfer to, and Assessment and Settlement in, Papua New Guinea of Certain Persons, and Related Issues, signed 6 August 2013 <https://www.dfat.gov.au/geo/png/joint-mou-20130806.html>

Treaty between China and the United States 1868, signed 28 July 1868 (entered into force 23 November 1869) ('*Burlingame Treaty*')

Treaty between the United States and China 1880, concerning Immigration, signed 17 November 1880 (entered into force 5 October 1881) ('*Angell Treaty*')

Multilateral Instruments

Convention against Torture and Other Cruel, Inhuman or Degrading Treatment or Punishment, opened for signature 10 December 1984, 1465 UNTS 85 (entered into force 26 June 1987)

Convention on Maritime Search and Rescue, opened for signature 27 April 1979, 1405 UNTS 118 (entered into force 22 June 1985)

Convention on the Elimination of All Forms of Discrimination against Women, opened for signature 18 December 1979, 1249 UNTS 13 (entered into force 3 September 1981)

Convention on the Law of the Sea, opened for signature 10 December 1982, 1833 UNTS 396 (entered into force 16 November 1994)

Convention on the Rights of Persons with Disabilities, opened for signature 30 March 2007, 2515 UNTS 3 (entered into force, 3 May 2008)

Convention on the Rights of the Child, opened for signature 20 November 1989, 1577 UNTS 3 (entered into force 2 September 1990)

Convention relating to the Status of Refugees, opened for signature 28 July 1951, 189 UNTS 150 (entered into force 22 April 1954)

Convention relating to the Status of Stateless Persons, opened for signature 28 September 1954, 360 UNTS 117 (entered into force 6 June 1960)

International Convention on the Elimination of All Forms of Racial Discrimination, opened for signature 21 December 1965, 660 UNTS 195 (entered into force 4 January 1969)

International Covenant on Civil and Political Rights, opened for signature 16 December 1966, 999 UNTS 171 (entered into force 23 March 1976)

International Covenant on Economic, Social and Cultural Rights, opened for signature 16 December 1966, 993 UNTS 3 (entered into force 3 January 1976)

International Convention for the Protection of All Persons from Enforced Disappearance, opened for signature 6 February 2007, UN Doc A/61/488 (entered into force 23 December 2010)

International Convention on the Protection of the Rights of All Migrant Workers and Members of Their Families, opened for signature 18 December 1990, 2220 UNTS 3 (entered into force 1 July 2003)

Protocol relating to the Status of Refugees, opened for signature 31 January 1967, 606 UNTS 267 (entered into force 4 October 1967)

Vienna Convention on Consular Relations, opened for signature 24 April 1963, 596 UNTS 261 (entered into force 19 March 1967)

Declarations and Communiqués

Declaration of States Parties to the 1951 Convention and or Its 1967 Protocol relating to the Status of Refugees, UN Doc HCR/MMSP/2001/09 (16 January 2002)

UNHCR, *Ministerial Communiqué*, UN Doc HCR/MINCOMMS/2011/6 (8 December 2011)

Universal Declaration of Human Rights, GA Res 217 A(III), UN GAOR, 3rd sess, 183rd plen mtg, UN Doc A/810 (10 December 1948)

Regional Instruments

Convention for the Protection of Human Rights and Fundamental Freedoms, opened for signature 4 November 1950, 213 UNTS 222 (entered into force 3 September 1953), as amended by Protocol No 14bis to the *Convention for the Protection of Human Rights and Fundamental Freedoms*, opened for signature 27 May 2009, CETS No 204 (entered into force 1 September 2009)

Council Directive 2004/38/EC of 29 April 2004 on the Right of Citizens of the Union and Their Family Members to Move and Reside Freely within the Territory of the Member States [2004] OJ L158/77

Economic Community of West African States, *Protocol relating to Free Movement of Persons, Residence and Establishment*, Doc No A/P.1/5/79 (signed and entered into force provisionally 29 May 1979)

Treaty Bodies and Special Procedures

Communications

Human Rights Committee, *Views: Communications No 305/1988*, 39th sess, UN Doc CCPR/C/39/D/305/1988 (23 July 1990) ('*van Alphen v Netherlands*')

Views: Communication No 560/1993, 59th sess, UN Doc CCPR/C/59/D/560/1993 (30 April 1997) ('*A v Australia*')

Views: Communication No 900/1999, 76th sess, UN Doc CCPR/C/76/D/900/1999 (28 October 2002) ('*C v Australia*')

Views: Communication No 1069/2002, 79th sess, UN Doc CCPR/C/79/D/1069/2002 (6 November 2003) ('*Bakhtiyari v Australia*')

Views: Communication No 2094/2011, 108th sess, UN Doc CCPR/C/108/D/2094/2011 (20 August 2013) ('*F K A G v Australia*')

Views: Communication No 2136/2011, 108th sess, UN Doc CCPR/C/108/D/2136/2012 (20 August 2013) ('*M M M v Australia*')

Concluding Observations

Human Rights Committee, *Concluding Observations of the Human Rights Committee: Australia*, 95th sess, UN Doc CCPR/C/AUS/CO/5 (7 May 2009)

Reports of Country Visits

Special Rapporteur on the Human Rights of Migrants, François Crépeau, *Report of the Special Rapporteur on the Human Rights of Migrants on His Mission to Australia and the Regional Processing Centres in Nauru*, UN Doc A/HRC/35/25/Add.3 (24 April 2017)

Government of Australia, *Report of the Special Rapporteur on the Human Rights of Migrants on His Mission to Australia and the Regional Processing Centres in Nauru: Comments by the State*, UN Doc A/HRC/35/25/Add.4 (17 May 2017)

Interpretative Guidance

International Maritime Organization

International Maritime Organization, Maritime Safety Committee, *Resolution MSC.70 (69)*, adopted 18 May 1998 (entered into force 1 January 2000)

Resolution MSC.155 (78), adopted 20 May 2004 (entered into force 1 July 2006)

Resolution MSC.167 (78): Guidelines on the Treatment of Persons Rescued at Sea, UN Doc MSC 78/26/Add.2, adopted 20 May 2004 (entered into force 1 July 2006)

Office of the High Commissioner for Human Rights

Human Rights Committee, *General Comment No 5: Article 4 (Derogation of Rights)*, 13th sess, UN Doc HRI/GEN/1/Rev.1 (31 July 1981)

General Comment No 29: Article 4: Derogations during a State of Emergency, 72nd sess, UN Doc CCPR/C/21/Rev.1/Add.11 (31 August 2001)

General Comment No 31: Nature of the General Legal Obligation Imposed on States Parties to the Covenant, UN Doc CCPR/C/21/Rev.1/Add.13 (26 May 2004)

Office of the United Nations High Commissioner for Refugees (UNHCR)

UNHCR, *Detention of Refugees and Asylum-Seekers* (Conclusion No 44 (XXXVII), 13 October 1986)

Handbook and Guidelines on Procedures and Criteria for Determining Refugee Status, UN Doc HCR/1P/4/ENG/REV.3 (December 2011)

'Guidelines on the Applicable Criteria and Standards relating to the Detention of Asylum-Seekers and Alternatives to Detention' (2012)

Index

Abbott, Tony, 13, 14, 16–17, 47, 294
Absolute sovereignty
  overview, 14–17, 94, 155–158
  assumptions in, 22
  call to action regarding, 45–48
  centrality of doctrine, 155–158
  in common law, 81–83, 283–284
  comparative law regarding, 287
  in *Constitution*, 115–116
  constitutionalisation of, 114–115, 284
  as contingent historical artefact, 107–111
  discourse analysis and, 36, 230, 281–282
  entrenchment of, 120
  evolution of jurisprudence, 16–17, 40, 107
  foreigner-sovereign relation, in context of,
    17, 40, 157, 282
  genealogy and, 281
  Grotius and, 104 (*See also* Grotius, Hugo)
  implications of, 288–289
  international human rights law versus, 14–15,
    18–21
  language, use of, 109, 156, 279
  legal positivism and, 110
  Lim case and, 221
  limitations on, 15
  literature review, 42–44
  mandatory detention and, 161–162
  Migration Act 1958 and, 151
  migration laws and, 108–109
  non-European foreigners and, 108, 110–111
  planned destitution and, 161–162, 235, 278,
    279, 280
  precedent and, 110
  in Privy Council (UK) (*See* Privy
    Council (UK))
  Pufendorf and (*See* Pufendorf, Samuel)

  reasons for, 286–288
  refugee law versus, 14–15, 18–21
  rethinking of, 42, 289–291
  'self-preservation' and, 109
  in Supreme Court (US) (*See* Supreme
    Court (US))
  unassailability of, 109–110
  use of term, 11
  Vattel and, 95, 99–100, 103, 104, 128–129, 221
    (*See also* Vattel, Emmerich de)
  Vitoria and (*See* Vitoria, Francisco de)
  War-Time Refugees Removal Act 1949 and,
    143–144
  White Australia policy and (*See* White
    Australia policy)
Administrative Appeals Tribunal, 270–271
Administrative Decisions (Judicial Review) Act
  1977 (Cth), 167, 180, 181, 187, 269
Aeneid (Virgil), 6, 59
Afghan asylum seekers, 12, 19, 31
'Afghan' cameleers, 90–91
Alamazoff, R v (1919), 221
Aliens. *See* Foreigners
Aliens Deportation Act 1948 (Cth), 151
Aliens power
  constitutional scope of, 115–116, 118–119,
    206–208
  deportation and, 141–142, 196–198
  detention and, 221–223
  legislative power and, 206–208
  Lim case and, 187, 196–198, 203, 206–208
  mandatory detention and, 166–167, 196–198,
    203, 206–208
  right of entry and, 196–198
American Indians, 49, 56, 61, 64
Andrews, Kevin, 244

Angell Treaty, 102
'Application custody,' 168–169, 177–178, 215, 223–225
Aristotle, Paris, 13, 31, 32, 228
Armstrong, John, 257
Arrest. *See* Detention
Asylum seekers
 Afghan asylum seekers, 12, 19, 31
 bona fides of, 19, 171, 185, 198–199, 239–241, 243, 252
 Cambodian asylum seekers, 1–2, 163, 167, 190
 'failed asylum seekers,' 232, 253, 259
 Indochinese asylum seekers, 163
 Kurdish asylum seekers, 4
 Sri Lankan asylum seekers, 3–4, 295–298
 Vietnamese asylum seekers, 6–7, 163, 190
 Zimbabwean asylum seekers, 263–264
Asylum Seekers Assistance Scheme (ASAS)
 overview, 233–235, 246–248
 changes to, 248–251
 complaint regarding, 249–250
 control and restraint as discursive technique and, 256–258, 277
 costs of, 252
 decisions regarding, 274–276
 delay and, 276–277
 deviance and opportunism as discursive technique and, 256–258, 275, 277
 discursive techniques regarding, 256–258
 effect of denial, 250
 eligibility, 249, 273, 274–276
 exemptions, 251, 253, 273, 274–276
 Fact Sheet 62, 273
 fairness of, 252–254
 financial hardship exception, 248–249, 250–251, 275
 Guidelines for exemptions, 273, 274
 Handbook, 273
 Immigration Department and, 249–250, 251–258, 274–275, 276–277
 institutional silence and, 252, 275–277
 institutional techniques, 236–237
 international human rights law and, 251, 254–256, 261–262
 international obligations regarding, 254
 judicial review of decisions, lack of, 275
 merits review, lack of, 254
 rationale for (and for denial of), 246–248, 251–253
 Refugee Convention and, 253–254
Asylum Seekers Centre, 42, 249–251, 255–256

Atkinson, John, 128
Australian Border Force Act 2015 (Cth), 300, 301, 311
Australian Democrats, 2, 180, 183
Australian Human Rights Commission. *See* Human Rights and Equal Opportunity Commission (HREOC)
Australian Labor Party, 244–245
Australian Red Cross, 4, 250, 251, 255–256, 274, 275

'Bad refugees,' 184–186, 229
Bail, 219, 221
Banishment
 of Huguenots, 69, 106–107
 of Jews, 106–107
 of Moors, 106–107
 as punishment, 104–107
 of Spanish foreigners, 59
 Vitoria on, 59
Bar, L., 103
Barbarians
 hospitality and, 58–59
 rights of, 57
 as subjects of international law, 54
 Vitoria on, 54, 56–57
Bartelson, Jens, 22–23
Barton, Edmund, 92, 116, 122, 123, 124, 125, 127, 129–130
Baume, Michael, 174
Bedlington, Jennifer J., 248, 251, 255–256, 276
Bentham, Jeremy, 95
Blackstone, William, 87, 88, 213–214, 285
'Boat people'
 generally, 6
 arrival in Australia, 6–7, 163–165
 from Cambodia, 1–2, 163, 167, 190
 from China, 163, 190
 clandestine arrival of, 192
 control and restraint as discursive technique (*See* Control and restraint)
 criminalisation of, 176, 191–193
 deviance and opportunism as discursive technique (*See* Deviance and opportunism)
 'floodgates,' fear of, 195
 'illegalisation' of, 185–186
 as 'illegal maritime arrivals,' 32, 192
 from Indochina, 163
 Manus Island, detention in, 7, 31, 228, 244, 293

'Boat people' (cont.)
  as metaphor, 169–172, 175–176
  MV Tampa incident, 31, 44, 171, 296
  Nauru, detention in, 7, 31, 228, 244, 293
  Papua New Guinea, detention in, 7, 31, 228, 244, 293
  from Poland, 191, 195
  prohibition on release of, 2–3, 178–179, 203, 206
  as 'queue-jumpers,' 1, 163–164, 171, 175–176, 228
  racialised discourse in parliamentary debate, 181–183, 186, 188, 228, 229
  targeting of, 19, 170, 178–179, 183, 189, 191
  from Vietnam, 6, 163, 190
Boat turnbacks, 10, 293–295
Boletsi, Maria, 173
Bolkus, Nick, 180–181, 183–185, 188
Bontekoe (Dutch Captain), 75
Borschberg, Peter, 61
Bowles, Martin, 8, 32, 192
Brandenburg Tolerance Edict, 69–70
Brennan, Gerard, 167, 204
Brewer, David J., 104–105
Bridging Visa Review, 243–244
Bridging Visas, 231, 233, 243–244, 271
Brown, Simon, 199, 233, 259
Bruce, Stanley, 137, 138
Bullimore, Tony, 190
Burlingame Treaty, 102, 104

Calwell, Arthur, 143–147, 150–151, 184–185
Cambodian asylum seekers, 1–2, 163, 167, 190
Campbell, Angus, 293
Campbell, Graeme, 171, 172, 176, 183, 188
Canada
  Alien Labour Act 1867, 128
  Attorney-General for Canada v Cain (1906), 127–129, 149–150, 207, 221
Capitalism
  effect on migration, 83–85
  shift from feudalism and serfdom, 83–84
Carlton, James Joseph, 251
'Carrier sanctions,' 132, 152
Carter, R v; Ex parte Kisch (1934), 134–135
Case studies, selection of, 30–33
Cass, Moss, 164
Cavallar, Georg, 56, 61
Chamarette, Christobel, 169, 171
Chia Gee v Martin (1905), 133–134

Children, detention of, 8, 41, 295, 299, 310
China
  Angell Treaty, 102
  'boat people' from, 163, 190
  British subjects, Chinese as, 88, 90–92, 97
  Burlingame Treaty, 102, 104
  enemy aliens, Chinese as, 98–99
  exclusion of Chinese, 90–92, 120–121
  labour migration from, 90–91, 123
  migration to Australia from, 85, 90–91, 163, 195
  students, humanitarian concessions to, 163–164, 172
  US, migration to, 101–102
  Victoria, Chinese in, 91–92
  Vitoria on, 75
Chinese Act 1881 (Vic), 91, 96, 97
Chinese Immigration Restriction Act 1888 (Vic), 91–92
Cholewinski, Ryszard, 10, 55
Chouliarki, Lilie, 29
Christmas Island, 31, 295
Chu Kheng Lim v Minister for Immigration (1992). See _Lim v Minister for Immigration_ (1992)
Citizenship
  lack of formal concept of, 86
  loss of, 46
Clandestine arrival
  'boat people' (_See_ 'Boat people')
  deterrence, mandatory detention and, 170
  'illegal maritime arrivals,' 32, 192
Clark, Andrew Inglis, 116, 118
Cockburn, John, 117
Colonialism
  British and, 81, 88
  ideologies of legitimisation, 108
  labour requirements of, 81, 84
  permanent migration in context of, 84–85
  Spanish and, 55–56
  temporary migration in context of, 84–85
Columbus, Christopher, 55
Commentaries on the Laws of England (Blackstone), 87, 213–214
Committee to Advise on Australia's Immigration Policy, 268–269
Common humanity, context of, 11–14, 74–75, 200–202, 287–289
Common law
  absolute sovereignty in, 81–83, 283–284

aliens, common law rights of, 87
 in Privy Council (UK) (*See* Privy
 Council (UK))
 in Supreme Court (US) (*See* Supreme
 Court (US))
Communications about detention, restrictions
 on, 299–300
Community Assistance Support Program, 234
'Compelling need to work' exception to 45-day
 rule, 262–264
Conquest, right of, 55–56, 58
Constitution
 overview, 113
 absolute sovereignty in, 115–116
 aliens and naturalization power in (*See*
 Aliens power)
 Australasian Federal Convention debates,
 115–116
 defence power in, 148, 150
 due process, lack of, 118–119, 190–191
 equal protection, lack of, 118–119
 executive power (*See* Executive power)
 external affairs power, 187–188
 individual rights in, 120
 judicial power (*See* Judicial power)
 legislative power (*See* Legislative power)
 race power in, 118–119
 responsible government doctrine and,
 116–117
 safeguards, lack of, 120, 229, 287
 US compared, 118–119
Constitutionalisation
 overview, 25–26, 40, 112–114
 of absolute sovereignty, 114–115, 284
 of foreigner-sovereign relation, 25–26
Constructive *refoulement*, 199
Contingent historical artefacts, 22, 52, 107–111
Contract labour, 90–91
Control and restraint
 overview, 161–162, 284–285
 ASAS and, 254–258, 277
 as discursive technique, 36, 228
 in *Lim* case, 188, 191, 202–203
 mandatory detention and, 169, 172–174,
 183–184, 228
 metaphor, crisis as, 172–174
 planned destitution and, 230, 235, 239–240,
 277–278, 279
Convention against Torture and Other Cruel,
 Inhuman or Degrading Treatment or
 Punishment, 12

Convention for the Protection of All Persons
 from Enforced Disappearance, 12
Convention on the Elimination of All Forms of
 Discrimination against Women, 12
Convention on the Reduction of
 Statelessness, 12
Convention on the Rights of Persons with
 Disabilities, 12
Convention on the Rights of the Child
 Australia in, 12
 detention under, 220
 planned destitution and, 237
Convention relating to the Status of Refugees
 (Refugee Convention)
 ASAS and, 253–254
 Australia and, 12, 18, 199
 detention under, 210
 Lim case and, 187–188
 mandatory detention and, 173
 non-refoulement under, 223
 recognition under, 3
 UNHCR and, 18
 unlawful entry under, 210, 214–216
 welfare under, 254
Convention relating to the Status of Stateless
 Persons, 12
Convict labour, 90–91
Coulter, John, 183–185
Cover, Robert M., 198
Crépeau, François, 292, 300, 312
Crimes Act 1914 (Cth), 299–300
Criminalisation of 'boat people,' 176, 191–193
Custody versus 'application custody,'
 168–169, 178

Dauvergne, Catherine, 11
Davidson, Donald, 37
Dawson, Daryl, 204
Deane, William, 188–190, 204
Defence power, 148, 150
*De habitu religionis Christianae ad vitam
 civilem* (Pufendorf), 68, 70
De Jure Belli ac Pacis (Grotius), 62–63
De jure naturae et gentium libri octo
 (Pufendorf), 68
De Jure Praedae Commentarius (Grotius),
 61–62, 63–64
Delay
 acceptable reasons for, 232–233, 265–268
 ASAS and, 256, 276–277
 of departure, 239

Delay (cont.)
45-day rule and, 265–268
by lawyers, alleged as calculated tactic, 164,
177–178
in processing, 32, 164, 177, 232, 239, 241, 256
Denization, 87–88
*De officio hominis et civis juxta legem
naturalem libri duo* (Pufendorf), 68
Deportation
aliens power and, 129–130, 141–142, 196–198
defence power and, 150–151
exemption from, 144, 148
of friendly aliens, 106
under *Migration Act 1958*, 152–153
national security and, 152–153
under *Pacific Island Labourers Act 1901*,
125–127
for political and labour unrest, 139–142
as punitive, 103, 105, 149
statutory obligation of removal, 224–225
Derrida, Jacques, 14
'Designated persons,' 168, 188–190, 203
Destitution. *See* Planned destitution
Detention
aliens power and, 221–223
Blackstone on, 213–214
of 'boat people,' 7, 31, 228
of children, 8, 41, 295, 299
communications about detention,
restrictions on, 299–300
under Convention on the Rights of the
Child, 220
deportation, for the purposes of, 197–198,
206–207, 208–210
duration of, 169, 177–178, 223, 224
exceptional cases, 218–221
expulsion, as incident of, 196
extraterritorial detention and processing, 31,
293, 301–304
on high seas, 31, 295–299
immigration detention centres,
establishment of, 153–155
incommunicado detention, 224, 295, 299
judicial power and, 211–216
judicial review of decisions, 168, 220, 269
legitimate non-punitive object of, 221–223
mandatory detention (*See* Mandatory
detention)
for mental health, 219–220
under *Migration Act 1958*, 153–154, 164 (*See
also Migration Amendment Act 1992*)

'no work' condition, for breach of, 7–10
pre-trial detention, 219
for public health, 219–220
as punitive, 41–42, 149, 221–223
as racially discriminatory, 187, 190, 191
as reasonably necessary, 209–211,
223–224, 228
under Refugee Convention, 210
regional processing centres, 301–303
reviewability of, 45–46, 181, 269
safeguards, 220, 223–225
of Sri Lankan asylum seekers, 295–299
273-day rule, 168–169, 177–178, 215, 223–225
unlawful detention, 204
under *War-Time Refugees Removal Act 1949*,
149, 221–222
Detention centres, establishment of, 153–155
Deterrence, mandatory detention and, 170,
193, 196
Devetak, Richard, 171
Deviance and opportunism
overview, 161–162, 284–285
ASAS and, 256–258, 275, 277
as discursive technique, 36
45-day rule and, 266, 267–268
in *Lim* case, 188, 191–192, 202–203, 226
mandatory detention and, 171–172,
183–184, 228
planned destitution and, 230, 235, 239–240,
241, 277–278, 279
Dictation tests
abolition of, 151–152
under *Immigration Act 1949*, 148
under *Immigration Restriction Act 1901*,
131–136
'instant exclusion' compared, 120–121
'Natal formula', 120–121, 130–131
in US, 121
Diplomatie de la Mer (Ortolan), 103
Discourse analysis
overview, 28–30, 160
absolute sovereignty and, 36, 230, 281–282
ASAS and, 256–258 (*See also* Asylum Seekers
Assistance Scheme (ASAS))
case studies, selection of, 30–33
control and restraint (*See* Control and
restraint)
deviance and opportunism (*See* Deviance
and opportunism)
doctrinal lawyers, relevance to, 34–35
exclusion and, 36

45-day rule (*See* 45-day rule)
genealogy, transition from, 33–34
institutional silence (*See* Institutional
  silence)
judicial text as discourse, 229–230
language and, 227–228
mandatory detention (*See* Mandatory
  detention)
migration and, 35–36
planned destitution (*See* Planned
  destitution)
reading law as discourse, 34–36
'splitting,' 37
techniques, 36–38, 160–161
Discretion
overview, 45–46
exclusion and, 156–157
45-day rule and, 268–272
under *Immigration Restriction Act 1901*,
  131–132, 138–139, 144
and institutional silence, 268–272
under *Migration Act 1958*, 152–154, 188–190
non-compellability of, 45–46, 269
non-enforceability of, 45–46, 269
non-reviewability of, 45–46, 269
'no work' condition, lifting of, 232–233, 258,
  261–262, 268
planned destitution and, 280
political and labour unrest and, 138–139
under *War-Time Refugees Removal Act 1949*,
  147–148
Discrimination
on basis of mode of arrival, 309
on basis of nationality, 67, 148
inevitability of, 144–146
on basis of race, 190–191
Racial Discrimination Act 1975 (Cth),
  187, 188
right to non-discrimination, 67
Dixon, Owen, 149
Doctors for Refugees, 301
Documents of identity, 192, 193, 239, 241
Douzinas, Costas, 19, 160
Downer, Alexander ('Alick'), 151–155, 201, 214,
  287–288
Downer, John, 123
Dualist system of law, 19–21
Due process
Constitution, lack in, 118–119, 190–191
mandatory detention and, 179
in US, 118–119, 126–127

Dutch East India Company, 61
Dutton, Peter, 14, 47, 292, 294–295, 305–306

Early international law
foreigners in, 51–54
genealogy and, 24–25, 39
Grotius (*See* Grotius, Hugo)
Pufendorf (*See* Pufendorf, Samuel)
Vattel (*See* Vattel, Emmerich de)
Vitoria (*See* Vitoria, Francisco de)
'Economic refugeeism,' 1–2, 19, 242,
  284–285, 308
Edict of Fontainebleau, 68, 69, 70
Edict of Nantes, 68, 69–70, 106–107
Edict of Potsdam, 69–70
Edward I (England), 106–107
Elementorum jurisprudentiae universalis libri II
  (Pufendorf), 69
Elvey, Frank, 237, 249–250, 255
Enemy aliens, 87, 89–90, 98–99, 102–104, 106,
  181, 204
elision with friendly aliens, 104, 106, 109, 127
Entry, right of
generally, 51
aliens power and, 196–198
Grotius on, 65
unlawful entry, 214–216
Vattel on, 76–77, 207
Vitoria on, 59–60
Equal protection
lack of in Australia, 118–119
in US, 126–127
European Convention for the Protection of
  Human Rights and Fundamental
  Freedoms, 197
Evans, Chris, 10, 245–246
Evans, Raymond, 121, 132–133
Evans, Simon, 14–15, 44
Evatt, H.V., 134–135
Exclusion
of 'Asiatics,' 120
of Chinese, 120–121
of citizens, 46
discourse analysis and, 36
discretion and, 156–157
under *Immigration Restriction Act 1901*,
  120–121
'instant exclusion,' 121–122
under *Pacific Island Labourers Act 1901*,
  124–126
power of, 31, 96–97, 121, 128, 207

Exclusion (cont.)
  in Privy Council (UK), 94–95,
    96–97, 127–129
  racism and, 92–94
  as 'self-preservation,' 92–94, 123
  sovereign power, 44, 76, 81, 139
  in Supreme Court (US), 94–95, 97–107
  under *War-Time Refugees Removal Act 1949*,
    143–147
Executive power
  overview, 217–219
  application custody and, 223–225
  exceptional cases of detention, 218–221
  legitimate non-punitive object of detention,
    221–223
  Lim case and, 203–204, 217–227
  mandatory detention and, 203–204
  unchecked executive power, 45–46
Exile, 59–60, 65, 101
Expert Panel on Asylum Seekers, 292
Explanatory Statements, 237–238
Expulsion
  as act of war, 58–59
  of aliens, 30–31, 44, 96–97
  of British subjects, 142
  exile and, 59–60
  of Huguenots, 69, 106–107
  detention as incident of, 196, 208–210, 221–223
  of Jews, 60, 106–107
  of Moors, 60, 106–107
  power of, 103–105, 128, 207
  of Roma, 60
  Spanish Inquisition and, 55–56, 57
  Vitoria on, 59–60
Extraterritorial detention and processing, 31,
    293, 301–304
  on high seas, 31, 295–299
  international human rights law and, 292
  on Manus Island, Papua New Guinea, 31,
    293, 303–305
  in Nauru, 31, 293, 301–303

'Failed asylum seekers,' 232, 253, 259
Fair, David, 250
Fairclough, Norman, 29
Farmer, William J., 254–255, 277
Febvre, Lucien, 53
Federal Circuit Court, 271
Federal Court of Australia, 2, 4, 31, 44, 165, 197,
    199, 271
Federal Magistrates Court, 271

Field, Stephen J., 104, 106–107
Financial hardship exception
  ASAS, 248–249, 250–251, 252–254, 274, 275
  45-day rule, 263–265, 268, 269–271
Fitzroy Legal Service, 301
Fletcher, R v; Ex parte Kisch (1935), 135–136
Foreigners
  absolute sovereignty in context of foreign-
    sovereign relation, 17, 40, 157, 282
  'barbarians' versus, 78, 81, 104, 108
  common law rights of, 87
  denization, 87–88
  in early international law, 51–54, 77–80,
    282–283
  elision of enemy and friendly aliens, 104,
    106, 109, 127
  as enemy aliens, 87, 89–90, 104
  as 'Europeans,' 52–53, 77–80, 214, 282–283
  as friendly aliens, 87, 89–90, 102–104
  Grotius on, 63–64, 78, 79, 108, 282–283
  as infidels, 87, 89–90
  as insiders, 56–57
  legislative power and, 206–211
  migration and concept of, 84–86
  mutability of concept, 77, 79, 84–86, 144,
    157, 159, 283–284
  naturalisation, 87–88
  non-European foreigners, 108, 110–111
  as outsiders, 56–57
  Pufendorf on, 70–71, 73, 78, 79, 108, 282–283
  as strangers, 58–59, 77–78, 87, 100–101
  use of term, 10
  Vattel on, 74–75, 78, 79, 108, 282–283
  Vitoria on, 56–58, 77–78, 108, 282–283
Foreigner-sovereign relation
  absolute sovereignty in context of, 17, 40,
    157, 282
  constitutionalisation of, 25–26
  genealogy of (*See* Genealogy)
  rethinking of, 42, 289–291
Forrest, John, 119
45-day rule
  overview, 7–8, 231–233, 258
  abolition of, 245–246
  abuse prevention as purpose of, 238–243
  breach of, 7–8
  'compelling need to work' exception,
    262–264
  delay, acceptable reasons for, 265–268
  deviance and opportunism as discursive
    technique and, 266, 267–268

discretion and, 268–272
'finally determined' and, 259–261
financial hardship exception, 264–265
Immigration Department and, 260–261
institutional silence and, 244, 268–272
institutional techniques, 236
lifting of 'no work' condition, 261–262
political purposes of, 243–244
rationale for, 236, 237–245
'$30 work visa' and, 241–242
Foucault, Michel, 21, 36, 279
French Revolution, 52
Friedrich Wilhelm (Brandenburg), 69–70
Friendly aliens, 87, 89–90, 102–104, 106
elision with enemy aliens, 104, 106, 109, 127
status of at common law, 205
Fuller, Melville, 104

Gageler, Stephen, 303
Gama, Vasco da, 64
Garran, Randolph, 115–116, 118–119, 126
Gaudron, Mary, 195, 207, 210, 218, 229
Gaurier, Dominique, 58
Genealogy
overview, 23–24, 159–160
absolute sovereignty and, 281
account of foreigner-sovereign relationship
in, 26
constitutionalisation (*See*
Constitutionalisation)
discourse analysis, transition to, 33–34, 159–161
early international law phase, 24–25, 39
Pacific Island Labourers Act 1901 (*See Pacific
Island Labourers Act 1901* (Cth))
Privy Council (UK) (*See* Privy
Council (UK))
recognition of discourses through, 27,
228, 238
Supreme Court (US) (*See* Supreme
Court (US))
usefulness of, 27–28
Gentili, Alberico, 62
'Gentleman's racism', 130–131, 145–146
'Genuine refugees,' 199, 239–241, 252–257
*Georgiadis v Australian and Overseas
Telecommunications Corporation*
(1994), 204
Giannacopoulos, Maria, 14
Gillespie, G.R., 103
Gleeson, Justin, 295, 296, 302
Gleeson, Madeline, 31

'Good refugees,' 184–186, 229
Goodwin-Gill, Guy S., 42–43
Griffith, Gavan, 168, 187, 191–193, 198–202
Griffith, Samuel, 125, 126, 129
Grotius, Hugo
generally, 24–25, 42–43
overview, 39, 53–54, 60–61
absolute sovereignty jurisprudence
and, 104
context of, 61–63
escape and exile of, 62–63
on foreigners, 63–64, 78, 79, 108, 282–283
on hospitality, 58, 61–62
imprisonment of, 62–63
on 'just war,' 61–62
on mobility, 63, 65
on non-discrimination, 67
on right of entry, 65
on right of passage, 66
on right of residence, 65
on right of sojourn, 66
on right to trade, 60–63, 66

Habeas corpus, 139–142, 149, 153, 213, 221
Haddad, Emma, 15–16
Hand, Gerry
generally, 2, 172, 194
alleged reluctance regarding mandatory
detention, 177, 178
on application custody, 177–178
on 'boat people,' 170–171, 178–179
on due process, 179
on immigration lawyers, 171
Migration Amendment Bill 1992 and, 168
on 'national interest,' 175
rational and restrained, mandatory
detention portrayed as, 177
on supporters of 'boat people', 171–172
as victim, 171
Hanson-Young, Sarah, 294
Harradine, Brian, 2, 173, 180, 181, 229
Hastie, Ken, 250
Hawke, Bob, 1–2, 163–164, 242
Hayden, Bill, 2
Healthcare cards, 233–234
Higginbottom, Heather, 309
Higgins, H.B., 142
High Court of Australia, 271. *See also specific
cases*
contrasting approaches to judicial review
and constitutional cases, 41

High Court of Australia (cont.)
approaches to pre-settlement past, 167
Holt, Harold, 151
Hong Kong, British subjects in, 88
Hospitality
Derrida's 'hostipitality' and, 14
Grotius on, 58, 61–62
hostility and, 14
as right of conquest, 58
Vitoria on, 58–59
Houston, Angus, 13, 31, 32, 228
Howard, John, 16–17, 248
Huguenots, 68, 69–70, 106–107
Humanitarians, metaphors regarding, 172
Human rights. *See also* Rights
abuses, offences for exposing, 299–301
dilemma of rights discourses, 19–21
dualist system of law, effect on, 19–21
limitations of paradigm, 18–19
mandatory detention and, 18
Human Rights and Equal Opportunity
Commission (HREOC), 42, 236–237,
249–250, 252, 276–277
Human Rights Law Centre, 302

ibn al-Hasan, Mohammed, 53
'Illegal maritime arrivals,' 32, 192
Immigration Bill 1925 (Cth), 137
Immigration Bill 1949 (Cth), 143, 148
Immigration Department
generally, 180
application custody and, 168–169
ASAS and, 249–250, 251–258, 274–275, 276–277
Bridging Visas and, 271
45-day rule and, 260–261
institutional silence and, 269–270
mandatory detention and, 164–165, 199–200,
224, 228
Procedures Advice Manual (PAM3), 261,
264, 265, 266–267
Immigration detention centres, establishment
of, 153–155
Immigration Restriction Act 1901 (Cth)
generally, 120, 149, 151
overview, 113, 130–131, 136
'carrier sanctions' under, 132
Chinese, exclusion of, 120–121
constitutionality of, 133–134
detention under, 149
dictation tests under, 131–136
discretion under, 131–132, 138–139, 144

exclusion under, 120–121
political and labour unrest and, 137
'prohibited immigrants' under, 132,
134, 135
quotas and, 137–138
racism in, 122–123
Immigration Review Tribunal, 270–271
Imperialism
of British (*See* Colonialism)
naturalisation and, 88, 89–90
of Spain, 55–56
Vitoria in context of, 55–56, 56–58, 60
Imprisonment. *See* Detention
Incommunicado detention, 224, 295, 299
Indentured labourers, 81, 90, 120, 124–125
as undesirable persons, 132
India, labour migration from, 85, 90–91, 123
Indochinese asylum seekers, 163
Indonesia, return of asylum seekers to, 294
Infidels, 87, 89–90
Insiders, foreigners as, 56–57, 60, 67, 73, 74,
77–79
'Instant exclusion,' 121–122
Institutional silence
overview, 284–285
ASAS and, 252, 275–277
and discretion, 268–272
as discursive technique, 36, 229
45-day rule and, 243–244, 268–272
planned destitution and, 257–258, 279–280
Interception, 10, 171, 293–294
boat turnbacks, 10, 293
on the high seas, 295–299
MV Tampa incident, 31, 44, 171, 296
Ocean Protector incident, 295–299
International Convention on the Elimination
of All Forms of Racial Discrimination, 12
International Convention on the Protection of
the Rights of All Migrant Workers and
Members of Their Families, 12
International Covenant on Civil and Political
Rights (ICCPR)
Australia in, 12
Lim case and, 187–188
mandatory detention and, 173, 187–188
planned destitution and, 237, 254
International Covenant on Economic, Social
and Cultural Rights (ICESCR), 12, 254
International human rights law
absolute sovereignty versus, 14–15, 18–21, 282
ASAS and, 236–237, 254–256

Australia's obligations under, 12, 18–21, 254–255 (*See also* International obligations)
and discrimination against 'boat people', 309
and extraterritorial detention and processing, 292
mandatory detention and, 18
use of term, 18
International Law (Bar), 103
International Law (Phillimore), 103
International obligations, government perspectives on, 187, 251, 254–255, 261–262, 298
International refugee law
  non-refoulement principle, 3, 199, 223, 225, 298
  as part of international human rights law, 18–19
  discretion as safeguard against breaches of, 254
  refugee defined, 184
  rhetorical value of, 11–12, 239, 254–255, 262
Isaacs, Isaac, 119, 121–122, 139–141, 142

Japan
  labour migration from, 99–101, 123
  migration to Australia from, 123, 135
  Vitoria on, 75
Johnson, Jacob, 139–142
Johnson, Mark, 37
Judicial deference, 129–130, 155–156, 202, 209, 224, 227–228, 282
Judicial power
  overview, 211
  application custody and, 215
  detention and, 211–216
  Lim case and, 187, 211–217
  separation of powers and, 211–212
  unexaminability of mandatory detention and, 216–217
  unlawful entry and, 214–216
Judicial review
  under *Administrative Decisions (Judicial Review) Act*, 167, 180, 181, 187, 269
  of ASAS decisions, lack of, 275
  circumscription of grounds for, 173
  of detention decisions, 164, 168, 220
  exceptional cases of administrative detention and, 219–220
  'finally determined' and, 259
  under *Migration Act 1958*, 167, 269

of migration decisions, 41, 180, 269
  prerogative writs, 181
  of refugee decisions, 167
  as safeguard in exceptional cases, 220
  of work rights decisions, 270
Judicial silence, 202–203, 210–211, 214, 218, 229
Juss, Satvinder S., 43
'Just war'
  Grotius on, 61–62
  Vitoria on, 59

Kisch, Egon, 134
Kneebone, Susan, 30
Koon Wing Lau v Calwell (1949), 148, 150–151, 221–222
de Kretser, Hugh, 297
Krohn, Anthony, 2
Kurdish asylum seekers, 4

Labour migration
  access to labour market, 93–94, 240
  by Chinese, 90–91, 123
  contract labour, 90–91
  convict labour, 90–91
  educated classes, migration of compared, 123
  indentured labour, 81, 90, 120, 124–125, 132
  by Indians, 85, 90–91, 123
  by Japanese, 99–101, 123
  non-Europeans, 81, 84–85, 107–108, 159, 283
  by Pacific Islanders, 124–127
  regulation of, 107–108
  slavery, effect of abolition, 83–84
  unrest, 137, 138–142
Lake, Marilyn, 121
Lakoff, George, 37, 174, 175
Lambert, Caroline, 171
Latham, John, 137–139, 148, 149
Laursen, John C., 68
Law Council of Australia, 270
The Law of Nations (Vattel), 73, 74, 103
Lawyers
  criticism of, 171, 183, 203, 297–298
  delay by, alleged as calculated tactic, 177–178
  discourse analysis, relevance of, 34–35
  metaphors regarding, 171–172
'Legacy caseload', 9
Legal and Constitutional Affairs Committee (Senate), 243, 244, 245, 260, 271, 274, 294, 306, 310

Legal positivism, 73, 95, 110, 129–130, 209
Legislative power
    overview, 130, 206
    aliens power and, 201, 206–208
    foreigners and, 206–211
    Lim case and, 206–211
    mandatory detention and, 208–211
'Legitimate refugees,' 185
L'Estrange, Michael, 13, 31, 32, 228, 292
Leunig, Michael, 281
Liberty
    deprivation of, 7, 116–117, 181, 191, 213–214,
        226–227, 295–296
    personal liberty, 96, 170, 213–214, 217
    'principles of British liberty', 141, 208
    right to, 116–117, 205, 213–214, 224, 226–227,
        295–296
Lim v Minister for Immigration (1992)
    generally, 303
    overview, 40–42, 187–188, 202–203
    absolute sovereignty and, 221
    aliens power and, 187, 196–198, 203, 206–208
    application custody and, 215, 223–225
    control and restraint as discursive technique
        in, 188, 191, 202–203
    criminalisation of 'boat people,' 191–193
    dehumanisation and, 200–202
    'designated persons' and, 188–190, 203
    deviance and opportunism as discursive
        technique in, 188, 191, 202–203, 226
    executive power and, 203–204, 217–227 (*See
        also* Executive power)
    external affairs power and, 187–188
    'floodgates,' fear of, 195
    ICCPR and, 187–188
    judicial power and, 187, 211–217 (*See also*
        Judicial power)
    legislative power and, 206–211 (*See also*
        Legislative power)
    legitimate non-punitive object of detention
        and, 221–223
    'national interest' and, 193–195
    non-refoulement and, 225
    outlaws and, 204–205
    plaintiffs' arguments, 187–188
    racial discrimination and, 190–191
    'reasonable necessity,' 209–211
    Refugee Convention and, 187–188
    unexaminability of mandatory detention,
        203–204, 205–206, 216–217
    unlawful detention in, 204

voluntary, mandatory detention portrayed
    as, 198–200, 225–227
Literature review, 42–44
Livy Perseus, 65
Louis XIV (France), 69–70

Mabo v Queensland (1992), 167
MacFarlane, R v; Ex parte O'Flanagan (1923),
    139–140
MacKellar, Michael, 278
Macphee, Ian, 164
Madison, James, 105
Magna Carta, 106–107, 133–134
Mandatory detention
    overview, 6–7, 10–11, 40–42, 160, 165–167,
        227–230, 285
    absolute sovereignty and, 161–162
    aliens power and, 166–167, 196–198, 203,
        206–208
    alleged reluctance regarding, 177, 178
    application custody, 168–169, 177–178, 215,
        223–225
    call to action regarding, 45–48
    case studies, selection of, 30–33
    control and restraint as discursive technique
        and, 169, 172–174, 183–184, 228
    crisis, as response to, 172–174
    dehumanisation and, 200–202
    'designated persons' and, 2–3, 168,
        188–190, 203
    deterrence and, 170, 193, 196
    deviance and opportunism as discursive
        technique and, 171–172, 183–184,
        228
    discursive techniques regarding, 161,
        227–230
    due process and, 179
    duration of, 169, 177–178, 223–224
    exceptionalism and, 180–181
    executive power and, 203–204
    fairness and, 180–181
    ICCPR and, 173
    Immigration Department and, 164–165, 168,
        177–178, 180, 189–190, 199–200, 224, 228
    as interim measure, 9, 168, 178, 194,
        228–229
    international human rights law and, 18
    introduction of, 2, 168 (*See also Migration
        Amendment Act 1992* (Cth))
    judicial review, removal of, 168
    legislative power and, 208–211

Lim case (*See Lim v Minister for Immigration* (1992))
  metaphors regarding, 227–228
  national security and, 171
  outlaws and, 204–205, 218
  parliamentary debate regarding, 167–186
  rational and restrained, portrayed as, 177–181
  'reasonable necessity,' 209–211
  Refugee Convention and, 173
  requests for removal and, 225–227
  safeguards, 180–181, 223–225
  'self-preservation' and, 169
  targeting of 'boat people,' 170, 178–179
  273-day rule, 168–169, 177–178, 215, 223–225
  as tool of physical exclusion, 33, 165
  unexaminability of, 205–206, 216–217, 220–221
  unlawfulness of prior detention, 204
  voluntary, portrayed as, 198–200, 225–227
Mann, Neil, 260
Manne, David, 13
Manne, Robert, 286
Manning, Patrick, 64
Manus Island
  'boat people,' detention of, 7, 31, 228
  communications about detention, restrictions on, 299–301
  deaths on, 312
  extraterritorial detention and processing in, 292–293, 303–309
Mare Liberum (Grotius), 61–62
Maritime Powers Act 2013 (Cth), 295–296, 298–299
Martin, David A., 43
Mathew, Penelope, 22
McCreanor, Timothy N., 185
McHugh, Michael, 195, 199, 204, 207–208, 210–211, 212, 218, 221, 223–224, 225–226
McTiernan, Edward, 142–143, 149
Media, metaphors regarding, 172
Mental health, detention for, 219–220
Merits review
  detention and, 220
  discretionary powers compared, 9, 269
  exceptional cases of administrative detention and, 219–220
  fast-track assessment and, 9
  'national interest' and, 174
  refugee decisions, effect on work rights, 259
  Refugee Review Tribunal, establishment of, 169

work rights decisions, lack in, 232, 259–260, 270
Merkel, Ronald, 4–5
Metaphors
  ambiguity of, 169–172
  'boat people,' 169–172, 175–176
  'control,' restoring, 143, 172–174
  'crisis,' 172–174
  humanitarians, regarding, 172
  lawyers, regarding, 171–172
  mandatory detention, regarding, 227–228
  media, regarding, 172
  migration agents, regarding, 172
  'national interest,' 174–175, 176–177
Metcalfe, Andrew, 195, 244, 247
Methodology
  overview, 21–23, 159–162
  discourse analysis (*See* Discourse analysis)
  genealogy (*See* Genealogy)
  transition from genealogy to discourse analysis, 33–34, 159–161
Middle East, refugees from, 184, 185
Migration
  overview, 82, 83–84
  assisted migration of 'desirable' white people, 85–86
  authoritarian management of, 46, 287
  capitalism, effect of, 83–84
  by Chinese, 85, 90–91, 163, 195
  comparative law regarding, 287
  contemporary discourse of, 181–183, 186
  discourse analysis and, 36
  by Europeans (to white settler societies), 81, 84–85, 88–89
  foreigners, concept of, 84–86
  historical background, 55–56, 61–63, 69–70, 74, 83–84
  by Indians, 85, 90–91, 123
  by Japanese, 135
  labour migration (*See* Labour migration)
  permanent, resistance to, 84–85
  by Poles, 191, 195
  slavery, effect of abolition, 83–84
  temporary, in context of colonial project, 84–85
  unsolicited, responses to, 6–7, 10
  to white settler societies, 81, 84–86, 88–89
  by Zimbabweans, 263–264
Migration Act 1958 (Cth)
  generally, 197–198
  overview, 113, 151

Migration Act 1958 (Cth) (cont.)
  delay, acceptable reasons for, 265
  deportation under, 152–153
  detention centres under, 154–155
  detention under, 153–154 (*See also*
    Mandatory detention and *Migration
    Amendment Act 1992*)
  dictation tests, abolition of, 151–152
  discretion under, 152–154, 188–190, 268–269
  'finally determined' under, 259
  financial hardship exception and, 264
  institutional silence and, 268–269
  judicial review under, 41, 167, 269
  Maritime Powers Act 2013 and, 296, 299
  Refugee Review Tribunal and, 269
  regional processing centres and, 302, 303
  unlawful entry under, 214–216
*Migration agents, metaphors regarding, 172
Migration Amendment Act 1992 (Cth)
  generally, 2
  overview, 40–41
  application custody, 168–169
  introduction of, 168
  parliamentary debate regarding, 167–186
  and request to withhold Royal Assent, 2, 117
Migration Amendment Act (No 4) 1992 (Cth), 204
*Migration Amendment (Regional Processing
    Arrangements) Act 2015* (Cth), 204, 302
*Migration Amendment (Designated
    Unauthorized Arrivals) Bill 2006* (Cth),
    31, 32
*Migration Amendment (Regional Processing
    Arrangements) Bill 2015* (Cth), 302
*Migration and Maritime Powers Legislation
    Amendment (Resolving the Asylum Legacy
    Caseload) Act 2014* (Cth), 3, 8, 298–299
Migration laws
  overview, 82, 83–84
  absolute sovereignty and, 108–109
  discretionary power, use of (*See* Discretion)
  emergence of restrictive migration laws,
    89–90, 90–92
  in New South Wales, 91
  race and labour, regulation of, 25, 39–40,
    86, 95, 97, 101, 107, 108–109, 112,
    137, 145–146, 188, 283
  remedial or curative legislation, 113, 146,
    155–156
  retrospective legislation, use of, 150, 204,
    301–302, 303
  in Victoria, 91–92

*Migration Legislation Amendment (Regional
    Processing and Other Measures) Act 2012*
    (Cth), 31, 302
*Migration Legislation Amendment (Regional
    Processing Cohort) Bill 2016* (Cth),
    32, 306
Migration Regulations 1994 (Cth), 231, 262, 263,
    264, 265
Migration Review Tribunal, 270–271
Migration zone
  excision of territory from, 31–32
  presence in, 189, 295–296
Millbank, Adrienne, 244
Miscegenation, perceived problem of, 146
Mitchell, Merle, 247
Mobility
  Grotius and, 63, 65
  Pufendorf and, 68–69, 70, 71–73
  Vattel and, 74–75, 76–77
  Vitoria and, 55–56, 59
Molan, Jim, 312
Morrison, Scott, 7–8, 13, 192, 297, 299, 309
Movement of people, political economy of, 25,
    86, 159, 283
MV Tampa incident, 31, 44, 171, 296

Nafziger, James A.R., 43–44, 82–83
Nairn, Raymond G., 185
'Natal formula,' 120–121, 130–131
'National interest'
  Lim case and, 193–195
  merits review and, 174
  as metaphor, 174–175, 176–177
National Life and Character: A Forecast
    (Pearson), 92–93
National security
  deportation and, 152–153
  discourses of, 98, 107, 109, 169, 171, 174,
    293–295
National Security Committee, 296
Naturalisation
  of foreigners, 87–88
  imperialism and, 88, 89–90
  in UK, 88, 89–90
  in US, 88–89
Nauru
  'boat people,' detention of, 7, 31,
    228
  communications about detention,
    restrictions on, 299–300
  deaths on, 312

extraterritorial detention and processing, 292, 293, 301–303

Sri Lankan asylum seekers, detention of, 297–298

Nauru Detention Case (2016), 210, 211

'Nauru Files', 309–310

Necessity
   and duties of humanity, 76, 100
   right of, 61, 63, 65, 66, 67

Nettle, Kerry, 246

New South Wales, migration laws in, 91

New Zealanders as 'designated persons,' 188–190

Nicholls, Glenn, 148

Nietzsche, Friedrich, 23

'No advantage' policy, 8, 32

Non-citizens
   exempt, 189
   indefinite detention of, 4, 177, 197, 223–225, 233, 311–312
   unlawful, 3, 7–8, 45–46, 169, 179, 233, 266

Non-discrimination, Grotius on, 67 *See also* Discrimination

Non-refoulement principle, 3, 199, 223, 225, 298
   disregard for, 225, 298

Norrie, David, 249, 250, 254, 276

'No work' condition. *See also* 45-day rule
   asylum seekers and, 7–8
   detention for breach of, 7–9
   discretion to lift, 232–233, 258, 261–262, 268
   effect of, 7–8
   rationale for imposition of, 7–8

Obama, Barack, 305, 309

Ocean Protector, 295–296, 298

O'Connor, Richard, 116–117, 125, 129, 130

Office of the United Nations High Commissioner for Refugees (UNHCR), 18, 305

Offshore detention and processing. *See* Extraterritorial detention and processing

O'Keefe, Annie, 142, 143, 144

O'Keefe v Calwell (1949), 142–143, 150

O'Loughlin, Maurice, 2–3

O'Neill, Peter, 304

Operation Sovereign Borders, 9, 16, 42, 293–295, 311–312

Opeskin, Brian, 43

Opportunism. *See* Deviance and opportunism

Orford, Anne, 27–28

Ortolan, Théodore, 103

'Outcasts,' 75

Outlaws, 54, 57, 204–205, 218, 283

Outsiders, 56–57, 60, 67, 74, 77–79

Owen, David, 22

Ozdowski, Sev, 248, 252, 254, 255–256, 276, 277

Pacific Islanders, labour migration by, 124–127

Pacific Island Labourers Act 1901 (Cth)
   generally, 120
   overview, 113, 124–125
   deportation under, 125–127
   economic purposes of, 124–125
   effects of, 124
   exclusion under, 125–126
   judicial deference and, 129–130
   legal positivism and, 129–130
   precedent and, 127–129
   racism in, 122–123, 124–125
   Robtelmes v Brenan (1906), 126–130

'Pacific Solution,' 31, 121

Papua New Guinea
   'boat people,' detention of, 7, 31, 228
   communications about detention, restrictions on, 299–300
   Constitution, 304
   extraterritorial detention and processing in, 293, 304–305

Passage, right of
   Edict of Potsdam and, 69–70
   Grotius on, 61, 65, 66
   Pufendorf on, 70
   Supreme Court (US) on, 99–100
   Vattel on, 76–77

Peace of Westphalia, 69

Pearson, Charles H., 92–93, 123

People-smuggling, 10, 12, 19, 32, 293–295, 306, 308

Pezzullo, Michael, 32, 301, 306

Phillimore, Robert, 95, 99, 100–101, 103, 104, 109

Phillips, Janet, 195–196, 199–200

Pickering, Sharon, 171

Planned destitution
   generally, 285
   overview, 8–11, 42, 160, 235–237, 277–280
   absolute sovereignty and, 161–162, 235, 278, 279, 280
   ASAS (*See* Asylum Seekers Assistance Scheme (ASAS))
   call to action regarding, 45–48

Planned destitution (cont.)
  case studies, selection of, 30–33
  control and restraint as discursive
    technique and, 230, 235, 239–240,
    277–278, 279
  Convention on the Rights of the Child
    and, 237
  deviance and opportunism as discursive
    technique and, 230, 235, 239–240, 241,
    277–278, 279
  discretion and, 280
  discursive techniques regarding, 161,
    277–280
  45-day rule (See 45-day rule)
  ICCPR and, 237
  institutional silence and, 257–258, 279–280
  'no work' condition (See 'No work'
    condition)
  rationale for policy of, 237–245, 246–258
  as tool of social and economic exclusion, 33,
    160, 235
Plender, Richard, 42–43
Poland, 'boat people' from, 190–191, 195
Political unrest, safeguards against, 137, 138–142
Poll taxes, 91, 132
Positivism. See Legal positivism
Poverty line, 235, 275
Precedent
  absolute sovereignty and doctrine of, 110
  doctrine of, 95, 107, 110, 126, 127–129
  interpretation of Pacific Island Labourers Act
    1901, 127–129
Prerogative writs, 181
Pre-trial detention, 219
Privy Council (UK)
  overview, 25, 39–40, 82–83
  Attorney-General for Canada v Cain (1906),
    127–129, 149–150, 207, 221
  exclusionist jurisprudence in, 94–95, 96–97
  Musgrove v Chun Teeong Toy (1891), 94–95,
    96–97, 103, 115–116, 128, 149–150, 197, 207
Procedures Advice Manual (PAM3), 261, 264,
    265, 266–267
'Prohibited immigrants,' 132, 134, 135, 144, 148,
    149–150, 152, 153
Property, right to, 61–62, 65, 66, 67, 77, 78, 87,
    89, 100
Protection visas, 9, 225, 231, 260–261, 262,
    263, 268
Protocol relating to the Status of Refugees, 12
Public health, detention for, 218, 220

Pufendorf, Samuel
  generally, 24–25, 42–43
  overview, 39, 53–54, 67–68
  context of, 69–70
  on foreigners, 70–71, 78, 79, 108, 282–283
  on mobility, 71–73
  on right of passage, 70
  on right to trade, 71–73
Purcell, Marc, 231

'Queue-jumpers,' 1–2, 163–164, 171, 175–176,
    185, 228, 229
Quick, John, 115–116, 118–119, 126
Quotas, 137–138, 144–145, 146, 307

Race
  'boat people,' questions of race in
    parliamentary debates, 181–183, 186,
    228, 229
  denial of influence of, 182, 188
  exclusion on basis of, 92–94 (See also White
    Australia policy)
  'gentleman's racism', 130–131, 145–146
  and Immigration Restriction Act 1901,
    122–123
  liberalism and racism, 93–94
  in Pacific Island Labourers Act 1901, 122–123,
    124–125
  race power in Constitution, 118–119
  racial homogeneity, 85, 146–147
  racial identity, 93
  racialised history, impact on contemporary
    migration discourse, 181–183, 186
  racial prejudice, 98, 122–123, 229
  restrictive migration laws and, 25, 39–40, 86,
    95, 97, 101, 107, 108–109, 112, 137, 145–146,
    188, 283
  'self-preservation' and, 156
  in War-Time Refugees Removal Act 1949,
    144–147
Racial discrimination
  'inevitability' of, 144–146
  Racial Discrimination Act 1975 (Cth),
    187, 188
Red Cross. See Australian Red Cross
Refoulement. See Non-refoulement principle
  constructive refoulement, 199
Refugee Advice & Casework Service (RACS),
    1, 3, 30
Refugee Convention. See Convention relating
  to the Status of Refugees

Refugee law, absolute sovereignty versus, 14–15, 18–21
Refugee Review Tribunal, 173, 249, 251, 253, 260, 269, 273
Refugees
  'bad refugees,' 184–186, 229
  defined, 184
  'economic refugeeism,' 1–2, 19, 242, 284–285, 308
  'genuine refugees,' 199, 228, 238, 239–241, 252–257
  'good refugees,' 184–186, 229
  judicial review of decisions, 167
  'legitimate refugees,' 185
  from Middle East, 184, 185
  recognition of, 3
  resettlement of, 30–33, 173, 293, 305–309
  from South America, 184, 185
  use of term, 184
Regional processing centres, 292, 302, 309–310
Removal. *See* Deportation
Rent assistance, 235
Residence, right of
  generally, 51
  Grotius on, 65, 66
  Vattel on, 76–77, 100
  Vitoria on, 59
Responsible government doctrine, 116–117, 129, 137, 139, 155, 162, 208, 227, 284
Restraint. *See* Control and restraint
Restrictive migration laws
  emergence of, 89–92
  race and labour, regulation of, 25, 39–40, 86, 95, 97, 101, 107, 108–109, 112, 137, 145–146, 188, 283
Richards, Eric, 169
Rights *See also* Human rights
  to asylum (*See* Asylum seekers)
  of conquest, 55–56, 58
  of entry (*See* Entry, right of)
  to hospitality (*See* Hospitality)
  to liberty, 116–117, 205, 213–214, 224, 226–227, 304
  of necessity, 61, 63, 65, 66, 67
  of passage (*See* Passage, right of)
  to property, 61–62, 65, 67, 77, 78, 87, 89, 100
  of residence (*See* Residence, right of)
  to 'self-preservation' (*See* 'Self-preservation')
  of sojourn, 66, 77
  to trade (*See* Trade, right to)
  to travel (*See* Travel, right of)

  to welfare (*See* Asylum Seekers Assistance Scheme (ASAS))
  to work (*See* Work rights)
Rintoul, Ian, 295
Robtelmes v Brenan (1906), 126–130, 149, 207
Roma people, 55–56, 60, 75
Roosevelt, Theodore, 92
Royal Assent, power to withhold as safeguard, 2, 116–117
Rubenstein, Kim, 44, 119
Rudd, Kevin, 32, 293
Ruddock, Philip, 181, 238–243, 245, 263–264

Salamanca School, 53
Santa Catarina (ship), 61
Save the Children Australia, 299–300
'Self-preservation'
  absolute sovereignty and, 109
  Barton on, 123
  exclusion as, 92–94, 123
  as individual right, 70
  mandatory detention and, 169
  Pearson on, 92–93
  Phillimore on, 100–101
  Pufendorf on, 109
  racialised forms of, 156
  as right of states, 100–101
  US Supreme Court and *(Ekiu)*, 100–101
Separation of powers, 130, 211–212, 216
Seven Years War, 74
Sidoti, Chris, 234, 249, 253, 255, 276
Silence
  institutional silence (*See* Institutional silence)
  judicial silence, 202–203, 210–211, 214, 218, 229
'Silent dominion,' 279
Slavery, effect of abolition on migration, 83–84
Social Security Act 1947 (Cth), 247
Social Security Act 1991 (Cth), 233–234, 235, 247, 270, 272
Social Security Bill 1990 (Cth), 248
Social Security Special Benefit, 234–235, 246–248, 272, 274
Sojourn, right of, 66, 77
South America, refugees from, 184, 185
Sovereignty
  overview, 22–23
  absolute sovereignty (*See* Absolute sovereignty)

Sovereignty (cont.)
  foreigner-sovereign relationship (*See*
    Foreigners)
  of States, 118
Spain
  conversos in, 55–56
  imperialism of, 55–56
  Jews in, 60
  Moors in, 60
  moriscos in, 55–56
  Roma people in, 60
  Vitoria in context of, 55–56
Spanish Inquisition, 55–56, 57
Special Benefit, 234–235, 246–248, 272, 274
Special Rapporteur on the Human Rights of
    Migrants, 292, 300, 309, 311–312
Spindler, Sid, 173, 248
Spinks, Harriet, 195–196, 199–200
'Splitting,' 37, 156, 166, 182, 184–186, 229, 236,
    239–240, 255, 257
Sri Lankan asylum seekers, 3–4, 295–298
Starke, Hayden, 141–142
Status Resolution Support Services
    Programme, 234, 246–248, 274
'Stop the boats' policy, 13, 42, 293–295
Strangers, 58–59, 77–78, 87, 100–101
Strict liability offences, 216
Supreme Court (US)
  overview, 25, 39–40, 82–83, 97
  Chae Chan Ping v United States (1889),
    94–95, 98–99
  'Chinese Exclusion Case', 94–95, 98–99
  dissenting opinions, 104–107, 109–110
  Ekiu v United States (1892), 94–95, 99–101
  The Exchange v McFaddon (1812), 98–99
  exclusionist jurisprudence in, 94–95,
    97–107
  Fong Yue Ting v United States (1893), 94–95,
    101–107, 116, 126
  Shaughnessy v United States ex rel. Mezei
    (1953), 226
  Yick Wo v Hopkins (1886), 126–127
Supreme Court (Vic)
  Musgrove v Chun Teeong Toy (1891), 94–95,
    96–97, 103, 115–116, 128, 149–150, 197, 207
  Chun Teeong Toy v Musgrove (1888), 103

Temporary processing visas. *See* Bridging Visas
Terra nullius, 167
'$30 work visa,' 239, 241–242
Thirty Years War, 62–63, 68, 69
Torpey, John, 84

Trade, right to
  under common law, 89, 100
  Grotius on, 60–63, 66
  Pufendorf on, 71–73
  Vattel on, 74
Travel, right of
  Grotius on, 61–63, 66
  Vattel on, 76–77
  Vitoria on, 58, 59
Trump, Donald, 305, 307
Türk, Volker, 10
Turnbacks of boats, 10, 293
Turnbull, Malcolm, 14, 305–306, 307–308
273-day rule, 168–169, 177–178, 215, 223–225

'Ultimate guarantee' of justice and individual
    rights, responsible government doctrine
    and, 116–117, 162, 205
Unauthorised arrival
  'boat people' (*See* 'Boat people')
  deterrence, mandatory detention and, 170,
    193, 196
  'illegal maritime arrivals,' 32, 192
Unchecked executive power, 45–46
United Kingdom
  arbitrary deportation from, 103
  asylum in, 233, 238
  British Nationality Act 1772, 87–88
  destitution in, 10, 233, 238
  Naturalisation Act 1870, 88
  naturalisation in, 88, 89–90
  Privy Council jurisprudence (*See* Privy
    Council (UK))
United States
  Alien Act of 1798, 106, 127
  An Act concerning Aliens (1798),
    106, 127
  Angell Treaty, 102
  Burlingame Treaty, 102, 104
  China, migration from, 101–102
  dictation tests in, 121
  due process in, 118–119, 126–127
  equal protection in, 118–119, 126–127
  Fourteenth Amendment, 116, 118, 119,
    126–127
  Geary Act, 101–102
  Immigration Act 1891, 99
  naturalisation in, 88–89
  Supreme Court jurisprudence (*See*
    Supreme Court (US))
Unlawful detention
  cause of action for, 204

in *Lim* case, 204
    retrospective lawfulness of, 204
Unlawful entry
    imprisonment for, 214–215
    under Refugee Convention, 214–215
    repeal of offence of, 214–216
Unsolicited migration
    authoritarian management of, 46
    pathologisation of, 47
    responses to, 6–7, 10

'Vagabonds,' 75
van Dijk, Teun A., 29, 37–38
Vanstone, Amanda, 244
Vassberg, David E., 55
Vattel, Emmerich de
    generally, 24–25, 42–43
    overview, 39, 53–54, 73–74
    absolute sovereignty jurisprudence and, 95,
        99–100, 103, 104, 128–129, 221
    context of, 74
    on foreigners, 74–75, 78, 79, 108, 282–283
    on mobility, 74–75, 76–77
    on right of entry, 76–77, 207
    on right of passage, 76–77
    on right to trade, 74
    on Roma people, 75
Victims
    Minister as, 171, 179
    state as, 169, 171, 228–229
    taxpayers as, 169, 228–229, 278
Victoria
    bail in, 219
    Chinese Act 1881, 91, 96, 97
    Chinese Immigration Restriction Act 1888,
        91–92
    Chinese in, 91–92
    Mental Health Tribunal, 220
    restrictive migration laws in, 91–92
Vienna Convention on Consular
        Relations, 297
Vietnam
    'boat people' from, 190
    Vietnamese asylum seekers, 6–7, 163
Virgil, 6, 59
Vitoria, Francisco de
    generally, 24–25, 42–43
    overview, 39, 53–54
    on banishment, 59
    on barbarians, 54, 56–57
    on China, 75
    context of, 55–56
    on expulsion, 59–60

on foreigners, 56–58, 77–78, 108,
        282–283
    hospitality, on, 58–59
    imperialism and, 55–56, 58
    on Japan, 75
    on 'just war,' 59
    and mobility, 55–56, 59
    on right of entry, 59–60
    on right of residence, 59

Walsh, Tom, 139–142
Walsh and Johnson (1925), 126, 139–142
War-Time Refugees Removal Act 1949 (Cth)
    overview, 142–143
    absolute sovereignty and, 143–144
    conditions of entry and stay under, 150
    defence power and, 150
    deportation, exemption from, 144, 148
    detention under, 149,
        221–222
    discretion under, 147–148
    exclusion under, 143–147
    flexibility of, 144
    onus of proof under, 149
    quotas and, 144–145
    racialised purpose of, 144–147
Webb, William, 150
Welfare. *See* Asylum Seekers Assistance
        Scheme (ASAS)
Westphalia, Peace of, 69
White Australia policy, 15, 112, 120–121, 130–132,
        136, 138–139, 142, 145–146, 156–157,
        282, 287
White settler societies, 81, 84–86, 88–89, 92–93,
        107–109, 110, 115, 283
Wickham, Gary, 29
Williams, Dudley, 149, 150
Williams, Helen, 234, 251, 253, 276
Williams, John M., 118
Wilson, R v; Ex parte Kisch (1934), 135
Winton, Sylvia, 257
Woods, Bob, 248
Work rights
    denial of, 9, 233, 243, 269, 272
    45-day rule (*See* 45-day rule)
    judicial review of decisions, barriers to,
        270
    merits reviewable decisions, barriers to, 270

'Yellow peril,' 92

Zheng He, 63–64
Zimbabwean asylum seekers, 263–264